Accounts of the Wreck of the Commerce

Accounts of the Wreck of the Commerce

Two Narratives of Shipwreck, Capture and Slavery by Arabs of American Seamen, 1815

An Authentic Narrative of the Loss of the American Brig "Commerce"

James Riley

A Journal, Comprising an Account of the Loss of the Brig "Commerce", of Hartford, (Con.) James Riley, Master

Archibald Robbins

Accounts of the Wreck of the Commerce
Two Narratives of Shipwreck, Capture and
Slavery by Arabs of American Seamen, 1815
An Authentic Narrative of the Loss of the American Brig "Commerce"
by James Riley
and
A Journal, Comprising an Account of the Loss of the Brig "Commerce", of Hartford, (Con.) James Riley, Master
by Archibald Robbins

First published under the titles
An Authentic Narrative of the Loss of the American Brig Commerce
and
A Journal, Comprising an Account of the Loss of the Brig "Commerce", of Hartford, (Con.) James Riley, Master

Leonaur is an imprint of Oakpast Ltd

Copyright in this form © 2011 Oakpast Ltd

ISBN: 978-0-85706-719-7 (hardcover)
ISBN:978-0-85706-720-3 (softcover)

Http://www.leonaur.com

Publisher's Notes

The opinions of the authors represent a view of events in which he was a participant related from his own perspective, as such the text is relevant as an historical document.

The views expressed in this book are not necessarily those of the publisher.

Contents

An Authentic Narrative of the Loss of the American
Brig "Commerce"   7

A Journal, Comprising an Account of the Loss of the
Brig "Commerce", of Hartford, (Con.) James Riley, Master   385

An Authentic Narrative of the Loss of the American Brig "Commerce"

James Riley

CAPTAIN JAMES RILEY

Contents

To the Reader	11
Certificate	15
A Brief Sketch of the Author's Life up to May, 1815	19
Voyage in the "Commerce"	24
The Shipwreck of the Brig "Commerce" on the Coast of Africa	28
Description of the Natives	32
The Natives Seize the Author	39
Sufferings Nine Days at Sea	46
Seized as Slaves	54
The Crew are Sold and Distributed	67
Two Arabian Merchants Purchase the Author and Four of His Suffering Companions	85
Their Sufferings	95
Hospitably Entertained by Arabs	103
Further Extreme Sufferings	107
They Come Within Sight of the Ocean	114
Travel in the Night for Fear of Robbers	124
Black Mountains Appear in the East	130

Their Masters are Attacked by a Band of Robbers	137
Meet With Robbers on Horseback	141
Sidi Hamet and His Brother Seid Fight	146
The Author Writes a Letter	153
The Letter	161
Lodge in a City	168
Sheick Ali's Plans Miscarry	183
They Set Off in the Night	197
The Kindness of Mr. Willshire	214
His Former Master's Narrative	223
An Account of the Face of the Great African Desert	248
Some Account of Suse	271
The Bashaw of Swearah is Seized and Put in Irons	276
Mr. Willshire is Grossly Insulted by Moors	294
Horsemanship	302
The Present Arabs and Ancient Jews Compared	312
Villainy of His Jew Companion	317
Continuation of the Journey	328
Arrival at Tangier	344
Embarks for America	357
Appendix	368

To the Reader

The following Narrative of my misfortunes and sufferings, and my consequent travels and observations in Africa, is submitted to the perusal of a candid and an enlightened public, with much diffidence, particularly as I write without having had the advantages that may be derived from an academic education, and being quite unskilled in the art of composing for the press. My aim has been merely to record, in plane and unvarnished language, scenes in which I was a principal actor, of real and heart-appalling distresses. The very deep and indelible impression made on my mind by the extraordinary circumstances attending my late shipwreck, and the miserable captivity of myself and my surviving shipmates, and believing that a knowledge of many of these incidents might prove useful and interesting to the world, as well as peculiarly instructive to my seafaring brethren; together with the strong and repeated solicitations of many of my valuable friends, among whom was the honourable James Monroe, Secretary of State, and several distinguished members of Congress, have induced me to write and to publish the work.

The Narrative up to the time of my redemption, was written entirely from memory, unaided by notes or any journal; but I committed the principal facts to writing in Mogadore, when every circumstance was fresh in my memory, (which is naturally a retentive one,) and I then compared my own recollections with those of my ransomed companions: this was done with a view of showing to my friends the unparalleled sufferings I had endured, and not for the particular purpose of making them public by means of the press. It should be remembered by the reader, that the occurrences here recorded, took place out of the common course of a sailor's life; and that each particular event was of a nature calculated to impress itself so powerfully on the mind, as not easily to be effaced. Having previously, in the course of my life, visited and travelled through many foreign countries, my mind was by no means unaccustomed to pay attention to, and make observations on whatever came within the reach of my notice, and for this reason, the strange events of the desert, and the novel objects and scenes which I had an opportunity of witnessing in the country of the Moors, were not suffered to pass without awakening and exercising my curiosity as well as interest, and becoming the subject of careful and habitual reflections.

Respecting my conversations with the Arabs, I have put down what I knew at the time to be their exact meaning, as nearly as I could translate their words and signs combined. I had, previously, learned the French and Spanish languages, both by grammar and practice, and had also been accustomed to hear spoken the Russian and different dialects of the German, as well as the Portuguese, Italian, and several other languages, so that my ear had become familiar with their sounds and pronunciation. Perceiving an affinity between the Arabian and Spanish, I soon began to learn the names of common things, in Arabic, and to compare them in my mind with those I had met with in Turkish and other Oriental history. I had no hope of ever being redeemed, unless I could make myself understood, and I therefore took the utmost care to treasure up every word and sentence I heard spoken by the Arabs, to reflect on their bearing, and to find out their true meaning, by which means, in the course of a very few days, I was enabled to comprehend the general tenor and drift of their ordinary conversation, and to find out the whole meaning of their signs and gestures. My four companions, however, could scarcely comprehend a single word of Arabic, even after they were redeemed.

In regard to the route, and various courses of our travel, I would observe, that after I was purchased by the Arabian merchants, and taken off across the desert, I was suffering under the most excruciating bodily pains, as well as the most cruel privations; it will not, therefore, be a matter of wonder, if on this vast, smooth, and trackless desert, I should have mistaken one eastern course for another, or have erred in computing the distances travelled over; for I was frequently in such agony and so weighed down with weariness and despair, that a day seemed to me of endless duration. A long experience on the ocean had before taught me to ascertain the latitude by the apparent height of the polar star above the horizon, so that in this particular, I could not be much mistaken; and the tending of the coast where our boat was driven on shore, proves it must have been near Cape Barbas. After we approached the seacoast again, I became more attentive to the surrounding objects, as my hopes of being ransomed increased, so that not only the courses, but the distances as I have given them, will agree in all their essential points.

The designs for the engravings were drawn from my own original sketches; (and they were merely rough sketches, for I have no skill in drawing;) they have, however, been executed by artists of considerable repute, and under my own inspection.

In compiling the map, particular care has been taken to consult the best authorities, but I considered, at the same time, that the information I received from my old Arabian master was sufficiently correct, and would warrant me in giving full scope to my consequent geographical impressions, in tracing the River Niger to the Atlantic ocean. Admitting that my idea prove hereafter to be just, and that this river actually discharges its waters with those of the Congo, into the gulf of Guinea, I am of opinion, that not less than one-fourth of the whole distance in a straight line, should be added for its bends and windings, in order to calculate its real length.

While I was at Mogadore, a number of singular and interesting transactions took place, such as do not often occur even in that country; and a person might reside there for many years, without having an opportunity of witnessing a repetition of them; yet their authenticity, as well as that of the other circumstances I have related, can be substantiated by many living witnesses,—men of respectability and unquestionable veracity.

My observations on the currents which have heretofore proved fatal to a vast number of vessels, and their crews on the western coast of Africa, are made with a view to promote the further investigation of this subject, as well as to caution the unwary mariner against their too often disastrous effects.

It gives me sincere pleasure, to acknowledge the services rendered me by my respectable friend, Anthony Bleecker, Esquire, of New-York, who has, at my request, looked over the whole of my manuscript, and suggested some very important explanations. I have been governed, in my corrections, by his advice, which was of a character that can only flow from the most pure and disinterested motives.

With respect to the extraordinary circumstance mentioned in the Narrative, of the sudden subsiding of the surf when we were about committing ourselves to the open sea, in our shattered boat, I am aware that it will be the subject of much comment, and, probably, of some raillery. I was advised by a friend, to suppress this fact, lest those who are not disposed to believe in the particular interposition of Divine Providence, should make use of it as an argument against the correctness of the other parts of my Narrative. This, probably, would have been good policy in me, as a mere author, for I am pretty sure that previous to this signal mercy, I myself would have entertained a suspicion of the veracity of a writer who should have related what to me would have appeared such an improbable occurrence. Sentiments and feelings, however, of a very different kind from any that mere worldly interest can excite, forbid me to suppress or deny what so clearly appeared to me and my companions at the time, as the immediate and merciful act of the Almighty, at the awful moment when dismay, despair, and death, were pressing close upon us with all their accumulated horrors. My heart still glows with holy gratitude for this mercy, and I will never be ashamed nor afraid to acknowledge and make known to the world, the infinite goodness of my divine Creator and Preserver.

> *The waters of the sea had well-nigh covered us: the proud waves had well-nigh gone over our soul. Then cried we unto thee, O Lord, and thou didst deliver us out of our distresses. Thou didst send forth thy commandment; and the windy storm ceased, and turned into a calm.*
>
> James Riley.

Certificate

Captain James Riley has submitted his Narrative to my perusal, and I have read it over with great care and attention. I was his second mate on board the Commerce, and one of his unfortunate companions through, and a sharer, in his dreadful sufferings and captivity, on the inhospitable shores and deserts of Africa, and I am astonished to find with what precision the whole of those incidents are related—it recalls to my memory all those dismal occurrences and distresses, and I do hereby certify, that the Narrative up to the time of our separation in Mogadore, contains nothing more than a plane statement of facts, and that myself, as well as others of the crew, owe our lives, liberties, and restoration to our country, under God, to his uncommon exertions, fortitude, intelligence, and perseverance, and I hereby request him, as my friend, to publish this my certificate.

Aaron R. Savage.

Done at New-York, this 1st day of February, *A. D.* 1817.

Letters

New-York, 29th October, 1817.

Sir,—The Narrative of Capt. James Riley has excited uncommon interest; and as there are some persons, who, ignorant of his excellent character, doubt the general correctness of his story, and others who disbelieve the authenticity of particular parts, I have been urged by several respectable gentlemen, who, together with myself, repose the utmost confidence in your candour and veracity, and who have been a long time acquainted with the respectability of your standing in society, to solicit from you a statement of your sufferings and adventures in a similar situation; and I am persuaded, that, independently of the gratification which it will afford, and the information which it will convey, there will be a sufficient inducement, when you understand that a compliance with this request may render essential service to a deserving fellow-citizen, and greatly promote the cause of truth.

I am, very respectfully, your most obedient servant,
De Witt Clinton.

Captain Judah Paddock.

Hudson, 25th November, 1817.
To De Witt Clinton, Esq. Governor of the State of New-York.
Esteemed Friend,—Thy favour of 29th *ult.* came to my hands a few days since, by a private conveyance. Its contents I notice. It gave me great satisfaction to find Capt. Riley has such friends as the Governor of the State, as also many of its most respectable citizens, to aid and assist him in his great and worthy undertaking, so far as to give currency to it after diligent examination as to its facts. His Narrative of Shipwreck I have carefully perused the third time through, and am ready to say every part of that which came within my knowledge is correct, or substantially so. Were I to have told my story in my own way, we might have differed in some points, which would not have gone to discredit his assertions. I was wrecked on the same coast, and drank of the same bitter cup of affliction.

All our sufferings were nearly of the same kind. Perhaps no one in our blessed land has it in his power to say so much in behalf of this injured man as I have; therefore I should tax myself with ingratitude to be silent, more particularly when solicited by so many respectable personages that have written me to give an opinion of his work. I say, *injured man,* as doubting the authenticity of the work is an injury which he must feel sensibly, being to a great expense, without funds, and not likely to be very well remunerated for all his expenses and trouble. I have but little personal acquaintance with Capt. Riley; from that little, and from what I learn from those who have long known him, I believe him to be a man of strict integrity, and worthy of public confidence. Thee solicits a statement of my sufferings in that inhospitable clime. I would most readily comply with that request, had I confidence in my own ability to do justice to the public in the exhibition of it. It is a long time since the occurrence took place. Having made at the time but few minutes of the important facts, the body of it must be from recollection. As Capt. Riley took his notes at the moment, and being better qualified for the task than myself, I dare not venture to write a book on the same ground; but I would permit him to affix some observations of mine to his work, as an Appendix, could I think it so important for the public good as my friends have generally thought, since Riley's Narrative made its appearance. Should thee wish further information from me, I hold myself ready to reply to any communication thee wishes to make.

  Thy friend,
    Judah Paddock.

      New-York, 11th mo. 18, 1817.
Esteemed Friend,—Recollecting the lively impressions which a verbal narrative of the sufferings and hardships experienced by thyself and crew on the coast of Africa, produced on my feelings during a visit at Hudson last summer, and reflecting also on the information thy story embraced relative to the nature and state of the country, and of the customs and manners of the Arabs, I have wished sincerely that an account of those events, and the general results of observations made in Africa, drawn up by thyself from thy own notes, might be submitted to the public. The civilized world is now looking towards that country with increasing interest, and any genuine information can hardly fail to be favourably received.

I can assure thee that a publication of thy Narrative would exceedingly gratify me, as well as a number of thy other friends in this city. I have been for some time well acquainted with Capt. Riley, and believe him to be a man of strict integrity, and fully deserving the confidence of the public; but as there are some in every community who are more or less incredulous, with respect to circumstances out of the road of common experience, a publication of the occurrences which befell thyself and crew on the same soil, and among the same people, would, from the well known respectability of thy character, add strength to the testimony of Capt. Riley, and tend to the removal of doubts which some have entertained of the credibility of certain parts of his Narrative. I am, with great regard and esteem,

  thy affectionate friend,   Thomas Eddy.

Hudson, 25th November, 1817.

Esteemed Friend Thomas Eddy,—Thy favour of 18th inst. was handed to me on the 22nd, by a gentleman travelling northward: the contents noticed. On the subject of my shipwreck on the coast of Barbary, I do not think myself adequate to the task of writing a Narrative of it, to say, such a one as the public might anticipate after knowing I had commenced it. It is not a gift I am endowed with, taking into view my inability to do justice to the thing, and that Capt. Riley, to whom, in my opinion, implicit confidence can be given relative to his Narrative, as far as has come within my knowledge, (being both wrecked on the same coast, and our sufferings nearly the same,) and from what little opportunity I have had with him personally, and the correspondence with him while writing his first edition, I think the public may rest assured full confidence may be given to his Narrative generally.

Many parts could not be expected to have come within my notice, which of course I must be silent on. While he was writing that Narrative, which interested me very much, I cautioned him to be very circumspect on every point; at the same time giving him to understand, if injustice was done the thing, he might expect some observations on it that might be disagreeable to him. His answers were prompt and gentlemanly. In the mean time, before the Narrative was made public, I took every opportunity to learn his character, and always found what I now believe him to be, a man of veracity and strict integrity.

If thee and others of my friends should think that what I could say more than Capt. Riley has said on the subject would be advantageous to the human race, I think I would endeavour to gratify those friends and the public, in a brief account of our shipwreck and sufferings, &c. to be attached as an Appendix to another edition of Capt. Riley's, should another be printed, which he may have gratuitously, if he will accept it; but if the above will answer as a confirmation (as far as I know) of his Narrative, it will afford me the greater pleasure: otherwise, I will exert myself and tell the tale just as it transpired, according to the best of my ability, as painful as the task will be. Any communication from thee on this or on any other subject, shall be attended to, by   Thy real friend,

                                        Judah Paddock.

CHAPTER 1
A Brief Sketch of the Author's Life up to May, 1815

I was born in the town of Middletown, in the state of Connecticut, on the 27th of October, in the year 1777, during the war between England and America, which terminated in 1783, with the acknowledgment by the mother country of the freedom, sovereignty, and independence of the thirteen United States. My father, Asher Riley, who still lives in the same place, (as at time of first publication), was bred to the farming business, and at an early age married my mother, Rebecca Sage, who is also yet living. I was their fourth child. Owing to an attack of that dangerous disorder, the liver complaint, my father was rendered incapable of attending to his usual employment for several years, during which time, his property, small at first, was entirely expended; but after his recovery, in 1786, he was enabled, by industry and strict economy, to support his increasing family in a decent manner.

It may not be improper here, before I speak of my education, to give a general idea of what was then termed a common education in Connecticut. This state is divided into counties and towns, and the towns into societies; in each of which societies, the inhabitants, by common consent, and at their common expense, erect a school-house, in which to educate their children. If the society is too large for only one school, it is again subdivided into districts, and each district erects a school-house for its own accommodation. This is generally done by a tax levied by themselves, and apportioned according to the property or capacity of each individual. It being for the general good, all cheerfully pay their apportionment. Thus prepared, they hire a teacher to instruct their children in reading and writing, and some of them are taught the fundamental rules of arithmetic.

They, for the most part, hire a male teacher for four months in the year, say from October to March, and his compensation (at the time I am speaking of) was from six to ten dollars a month, with his board. In order to obtain his board, he was under the necessity of going to each of his employers' houses in rotation, making his time in each family as equal as possible, and in proportion to the number of children therein. In this way all the parents became acquainted with the master or mistress. In the summer one of the best informed girls in the neighbourhood was selected to teach the youngest children. To defray, the expense arising from this system, a tax was laid, and every man, whether married or unmarried, with children or without them, was obliged to pay the sum at which he was rated, and in this manner every one contributed for the good of the whole.

In each society, one or more meeting-houses were established, whose congregations were either Presbyterians or Congregationalists, and a minister (as he is called) regularly ordained and located for a yearly stipend or salary, and generally during life. This was an old and *steady habit.* The minister was considered as the head of the school, as well as of the meeting, and his *like* or *dislike* was equivalent to a law. All the children in each district, whether rich or poor, went to this school: all had an equal right to this kind of country education. To one of these district schools I was sent at the age of four years, where I continued, learning to spell and read, until I was eight years old, when my father's family had increased to seven or eight children, with a fair prospect of more, (it afterwards amounted to thirteen in number.)

Finding it difficult to support us all as he wished, and I having become a stout boy of my age, he placed me with a neighbouring farmer to earn my living, by assisting him in his work. From the age of eight to fourteen years I worked on the land with different farmers in our neighbourhood, who having received but a very scanty education themselves, conceited, nevertheless, that they were over-stocked with learning, as is generally the case with the most ignorant, and in this, their fancied wisdom, concluded that much less than they themselves possessed would answer my purpose, as I was but a poor boy!! Finding therefore that they would lose my labour during school hours, (for they had always taken great care to keep me fully employed in hard drudgery every moment I was out of school, scarcely allowing me the usual hours of refreshment and sleep,) they kept me from school, merely because, as they stated, they could not get along with their work without my help.

When my parents remonstrated against such conduct in those who had come under a most solemn agreement to give me a *plenty of schooling,* they were assured "that I was a very forward boy; that I could spell and read as well as any of the boys of my age; that I could repeat whole chapters in the Bible by heart, and knew all the Catechism and Creed, *viz.* the Presbyterian, which then was, and still is considered, all important in that section of the union called New-England: that I could sing psalms in the *separate meetings* full as well as those who had learned to sing by note; though indeed he cannot write, (said they) because he has no turn for writing."

These representations tended in some measure to allay the anxiety of my parents, who wished me above all things to have a good common country education, as they at that time had no prospect of being able to give me anything better. They had taught me, both by precept and practice, that to be honest, industrious, and prudent; to govern my passions, (which were violent,) to feel for and relieve the distresses of others when in my power; to be mild and affable in my manners, and virtuous in all my actions, was to be happy; and they, generally, had instilled into my youthful mind every good principle.

I had now attained my fifteenth year; was tall and stout for my age; and having become tired of hard work on the land, I concluded that the best way to get rid of it, was to go to sea and visit foreign countries. My parents endeavoured to dissuade me from this project, and wished me to learn some mechanical trade; but finding that I could not fix my mind upon any other business, they, with great reluctance, consented to my choice; and I, accordingly, shipped on board a sloop bound to the West-Indies. Having no friend to push me forward, no dependence but on my own good conduct and exertions, and being ambitious to gain some distinction in the profession I had chosen, I contrived to acquire some knowledge in the art of navigation, theoretically as well as practically, and at the age of twenty years had passed through the grades of cabin boy, cook, ordinary seaman, seaman, second mate, and chief mate, on board different vessels.

I was now six feet and one inch in height, and proportionably strong and athletic, when finding the sphere I then moved in to be too limited for my views and wishes, (it extending only from Connecticut River or New-London to the West-Indies, and back again,) I went to New-York, where I was soon appointed to the command of a good vessel, and since that time have continued in similar employment; making voyages in all climates usually visited by American snips; traversing almost every sea, and travelling by land through many of the principal states and empires of the world. For several years I had charge of the cargoes as well as off the vessels I sailed in, and had a fair share of prosperity, until the month of January, 1808, when my ship, the *Two Marys* of New-York, was seized by the French, as I took shelter in Belle Isle, in the Bay of Biscay, from some English men of war, being bound for Nantz; and the ship, with her valuable cargo, was confiscated, under the memorable Milan Decree of the 17th December, 1807, founded on the well known Orders in Council, of the 11th November, of the same year.

I remained in France until the ship and cargo were condemned, and did not return to my native country and family, till the latter part of the year 1809, with the loss, it is true, of nearly all the property I had before acquired, but wiser than I went out; for I had learned to read, write, and speak both the French and Spanish languages; had travelled pretty much all over France, where I had opportunities of witnessing many important operations in the science of war, calculated to attract my attention to the principles upon which they were founded; and I, at the same time, took lessons in the school of adversity, which tended to prepare and discipline my mind for the future hardships I was destined to undergo. I now strove with all my power to stem the tide of misfortune, which began to set in against me with impetuous force. I had become a husband, and the father of four children, who looked up to me for support, and I strained every nerve to retrieve my lost fortune, by trading to sea: but it was of no avail; everything proved adverse, and after an absence of two years to Spain, Portugal, the Brazils. Rio de la Plata, or River of Silver, in South-America, the West-Indies, New-Orleans, &c. I returned home at the commencement of the late war (1812) penniless.

Unarmed commerce on the ocean, my element, was at an end in an honourable way, and I could not obtain a station I wished for in the navy, nor could I obtain the command of a private armed vessel that suited my views, owing to the want of funds; nor would I accept of the command of a vessel and the consignment of a cargo navigated contrary to the laws of war, under foreign licenses: this I considered would derogate from the character I always wished to support, that of a true friend to my country, (whether in prosperity or adversity,) and a firm supporter of its laws and institutions, which I had proved by long experience in the ways of the world to be as good (at least) as those of any country under heaven. Though the offers that were made me were great and tempting, so that my acceptance of them could scarcely have failed of producing me a handsome fortune, and that in a very short period, yet I remained at home during the whole war, making use of all my faculties to gain a decent subsistence for my family.

Soon after the burning of the Capitol and other public and private buildings at the seat of government, by the enemy, in August, 1814, when their commanders loudly threatened to destroy every assailable place on the seaboard, I believed that the time was near when every arm would be required for the general defence, particularly at the exposed seaport towns; and having enrolled myself in a volunteer company of military exempt artillerists, composed chiefly of masters and mates of vessels, and seamen, I had the honour of being chosen their captain. But our services were not needed in the field.

CHAPTER 2

Voyage in the "Commerce"

After the close of the war, in April, 1815, being then in my native state, I was employed as master and supercargo of the brig *Commerce* of Hartford, in Connecticut: a vessel nearly new, and well fitted, of about two hundred and twenty tons burden, belonging to Messrs. Riley and Brown, Josiah Savage and Co. and Luther Savage, of that city. A light cargo was taken on board, and I shipped a crew, consisting of the following persons, namely; George Williams, chief mate, Aaron R. Savage, second mate, William Porter, Archibald Robbins, Thomas Burns, and James Clark, seaman; James Carrington and Francis Bliss, ordinary seaman; Horace Savage, cabin boy, and Richard Deslisle, (a black man) cook.

With this crew I proceeded to sea from the mouth of Connecticut river, on the sixth day of May, 1815, bound for New-Orleans. We continued to steer for the Bahama Islands, as winds and weather permitted, until the twentieth of the same month, when we saw the southernmost part of the island of Abaco, and passing the Hole in the Wall, on the twenty-first, entered on the Grand Bahama Bank to the leeward of the northernmost Berri Islands; from thence, with a fair wind and good breeze, we steered W. S. W. twelve leagues; then S. S. W. about forty leagues, crossing the Bank, in from three to four fathoms water. On the morning of the twenty-second we saw the Orange Key on our starboard beam; altered our course, and ran off the Bank, leaving them on our starboard hand distant one league. The water on this Great Bank, in most places, appears as white as milk, owing to the white sand at the bottom gleaming through it, and is so clear that an object, the size of a dollar, can be easily seen lying on the bottom in four fathom water, in a still time.

Having got on the Bank, we steered W. S. W. for the Double-headed Shot Bank, and at meridian found ourselves, by good observations, in the latitude of 24. 30. being nearly that of the Orange Keys. In the afternoon it became nearly calm, but a good breeze springing up, we continued our course all night W. S. W. I remained on deck myself, on a sharp look out for the Double-headed Shot Bank, or Keys, until four o'clock, a. m. when judging by our distance we must be far past them, and consequently clear of that danger, I ordered the chief mate, who had charge of the watch, to keep a good look out, on all sides, for land, white water, and breakers; and after repeating the same to the people, I went below to take a nap.

At about five (then fair daylight) I was awakened by a shock, and thought I felt the vessel touch bottom. I sprang on deck, put the helm to starboard, had all hands called in an instant, and saw breakers ahead and to southward, close on board; apparently a sound on our right, and land to the northward, at about two leagues distance. The vessel's head was towards the S. W. and she running at the rate of ten miles the hour. I instantly seized the helm, put it hard to port, ordered all sails to be let run, and the anchors cleared away. The vessel touched lightly, three or four times: when I found she was over the reef, let go an anchor, which brought her up in two and a half fathoms, or fifteen feet of water, which was quite smooth. We now handed all the sails, and lowered down the boat. I went in her with four hands, and sounded out a passage; found plenty of water to leeward of the reef, returned and got under way, and at seven o'clock, a. m. was in the open sea again, with a fresh breeze.

This being the first time, in the course of my navigating, that any vessel which I was in had struck the bottom unexpectedly, I own I was so much surprised and shocked, that my whole frame trembled, and I could scarcely believe that what had happened was really true, until by comparing the causes and effects of the currents of the Gulf Stream, I was convinced that during the light winds, the day before, when in the Santarem channel, the vessel had been drifted by the current that runs N. N. W. (and at that time very strong) so far north of the Double-headed Shot Bank; that my course in the night, though the only proper one I could have steered, was such as kept the current on the larboard bow of the vessel, which had horsed her across it sixty miles out of her course in sixteen hours, and would have landed her on the S. W. part of the Carysford Reef in two minutes more, where she must have been totally lost.

As so many vessels of all nations who navigate this stream have perished with their cargoes, and oftentimes their crews, I mention this incident to warn the navigator of the danger he is in when his vessel is acted upon by these currents, where no calculation can be depended upon, and where nothing but very frequent castings of the lead, and a good look out, can secure him from their too often fatal consequences.

Having settled this point in my own mind, I became tranquil am we continued to run along the Florida Keys from W. S. W. to West by South, in from thirty to forty fathoms water, about four leagues distant, seeing from one to two leagues within us many rocks and little sandy islands, just above the water's edge, with a good depth of water all around them, until noon on the 24th, when we doubled the dry Tortugas Islands in ten fathoms, and on the 26th arrived in the Mississippi River, passed Fort St. Philip at Pluquemines the same night, having shown my papers to the commanding officer of that post (as is customary.)

My previous knowledge of the river and the manner of getting up it, enabled me to pass nearly one hundred sail of vessels that were in before me, and by dint of great and continued exertions, to arrive with my vessel before the city of New-Orleans, on the first day of June. Here we discharged our cargo, and took another on board, principally on freight, in which I was assisted by Messrs. Talcott and Bowers, respectable merchants in that city. This cargo consisted of tobacco and flour. The two ordinary seamen, Francis Bliss and James Carrington, now wished for a discharge, and received it. I then shipped in their stead John Hogan and James Barrett, both seamen and natives of the state of Massachusetts.

With this crew and cargo we sailed from New-Orleans on the twenty-fourth of June; left the river on the twenty-sixth, and proceeded for Gibraltar, where we arrived on the ninth of August following, and landed our cargo. About the thirteenth the schooner *Louisa*, Capt. Peter Price, of and from New-York, in a short passage, came into the Bay, and the captain on his landing told me he was bound up to Barcelona, and that if I would go on board his vessel, which was then standing off and on in the Bay, he would give me a late New-York Price Current, and some newspapers. I was in great want of a Price Current for my guide in making purchases, and accordingly went on board. The wind blowing strong in, and the vessel far out, I had to take four men with me, namely, James Clark, James Barrett, William Porter, and John Hogan. Having received the Price Current, &c. I left the schooner about sunset, when they immediately filled her sails and stood on.

As we were busied in stepping the boat's mast to sail back, a toppling sea struck her, and nearly filled her with water; we all jumped instantly overboard, in the hope of preventing her from filling, but she filled immediately. Providentially the captain of the schooner heard me halloo, though at least a mile from us; put his vessel about, came near us, sent his boat, and saved our lives and our boat, which being cleared of water, and it being after dark, we returned safe along side of the brig by ten o'clock at night. When the boat filled, we were more than three miles from the Rock, in the Gut, where the current would have set us into the Mediterranean, and we must have inevitably perished before morning; but we were spared, in order to suffer a severer doom, and miseries worse than death, on the barbarous shores of Africa.

We now took on board part of a cargo of brandies and wines, and some dollars, say about two thousand, and an old man named Antonio Michel, a native of New-Orleans, who had previously been wrecked on the island of Teneriffe, and was recommended to my charity by Mr. Gavino, who at that time exercised the functions of American Consul at Gibraltar.

CHAPTER 3

The Shipwreck of the Brig "Commerce" on the Coast of Africa

We set sail from the bay of Gibraltar on the 23rd of August, 1815, intending to go by way of the Cape de Verd Islands, to complete the lading of the vessel with salt. We passed Cape Spartel on the morning of the 24th, giving it a berth of from ten to twelve leagues, and steered off to the W. S. W. I intended to make the Canary Islands, and pass between Teneriffe and Palma, having a fair wind; but it being very thick and foggy weather, though we got two observations at noon, neither could be much depended upon. On account of the fog, we saw no land, and found, by good meridian altitudes on the twenty-eighth, that we were in the latitude of 27. 30. N. having differed our latitude by the force of current, one hundred and twenty miles; thus passing the Canaries without seeing any of them. I concluded we must have passed through the intended passage without discovering the land on either side, particularly as it was in the night, which was very dark, and black as pitch; nor could I believe otherwise from having had a fair wind all the way, and having steered one course ever since we took our departure from Cape Spartel.

Soon after we got an observation on the 28th, it became as thick as ever, and the darkness seemed (if possible) to increase. Towards evening I got up my reckoning, and examined it all over, to be sure that I had committed no error, and caused the mates to do the same with theirs. Having thus ascertained that I was correct in calculation, I altered our course to S. W. which ought to have carried us nearly on the course I wished to steer, that is, for the easternmost of the Cape de Verds; but finding the weather becoming more foggy towards night, it being so thick that we could scarcely see the end of the jib-boom, I rounded the vessel to, and sounded with one hundred and twenty fathoms of line, but found no bottom, and continued on our course, still reflecting on what should be the cause of our not seeing land, (as I never had passed near the Canaries before without seeing them, even in thick weather or in the night.) I came to a determination to haul off to the N.W. by the wind at ten p.m. as I should then be by the log only thirty miles north of Cape Bajador. I concluded on this at nine, and thought my fears had never before so much prevailed over my judgment and my reckoning. I ordered the light sails to be handed, and the steering sail booms to be rigged in snug, which was done as fast as it could be by one watch, under the immediate direction of Mr. Savage.

We had just got the men stationed at the braces for hauling off, as the man at helm cried "ten o'clock." Our try-sail boom was on the starboard side, but ready for jibing; the helm was put to port, dreaming of no danger near. I had been on deck all the evening myself; the vessel was running at the rate of nine or ten knots with a very strong breeze, and high sea, when the main boom was jibed over, and I at that instant heard a roaring; the yards were braced up—all hands were tailed. I imagined at first it was a squall, and was near ordering the sails to be lowered down; but I then discovered breakers foaming at a most dreadful rate under our lee. Hope for a moment flattered me that we could fetch off still, as there were no breakers in view ahead: the anchors were made ready; but these hopes vanished in an instant as the vessel was carried by a current and a sea directly towards the breakers, and she struck!

We let go the best bower anchor; all sails were taken in as fast as possible: surge after surge came thundering on, and drove her in spite of anchors, partly with her head on shore. She struck with such violence as to start every man from the deck. Knowing there was no possibility of saving her, and that she must very soon bilge and fill with water, I ordered all the provisions we could get at to be brought on deck, in hopes of saving some, and as much water to be drawn from the large casks as possible. We started several quarter casks of wine, and filled them with water. Every man worked as if his life depended upon his present exertions; all were obedient to every order I gave, and seemed perfectly calm. The vessel was stout and high, as she was only in ballast trim: the sea combed over her stern and swept her decks; but we managed to get the small boat in on deck, to sling her and keep her from staving.

We cut away the bulwark on the larboard side so as to prevent the boats from staving when we should get them out; cleared away the longboat and hung her in tackles, the vessel continuing to strike very heavy, and filling fast. We however, had secured five or six barrels of water, and as many of wine,—three barrels of bread, and three or four of salted provisions. I had as yet been so busily employed, that no pains had been taken to ascertain what distance we were from the land, nor had any of us yet seen it; and in the meantime all the clothing, chests, trunks, &c. were got up, and the books, charts, and sea instruments, were stowed in them, in the hope of their being useful to us in future.

The vessel being now nearly full of water, the surf making a fair breach over her, and fearing she would go to pieces, I prepared a rope, and put it in the small boat, having got a glimpse of the shore, at no great distance, and taking Porter with me, we were lowered down on the larboard or lee side of the vessel, where she broke the violence of the sea, and made it comparatively smooth; we shoved off, but on clearing away from the bow of the vessel, the boat was overwhelmed with a surf, and we were plunged into the foaming surges: we were driven along by the current, aided by what seamen call the undertow, (or recoil of the sea) to the distance of three hundred yards to the westward, covered nearly all the time by the billows, which, following each other in quick succession, scarcely gave us time to catch a breath before we were again literally swallowed by them, till at length we were thrown, together with our boat, upon a sandy beach.

After taking breath a little, and ridding our stomachs of the salt water that had forced its way into them, my first care was to turn the water out of the boat, and haul her up out of the reach of the surf. We found the rope that was made fast to her still remaining; this we carried up along the beach, directly to leeward of the wreck, where we fastened it to sticks about the thickness of handspikes, that had drifted on the shore from the vessel, and which we drove into the sand by the help of other pieces of wood. Before leaving the vessel, I had directed that all the chests, trunks, and everything that would float, should be hove overboard: this all hands were busied in doing. The vessel lay about one hundred fathoms from the beach, at high tide. In order to save the crew, a hawser was made fast to the rope we had on shore, one end of which we hauled to us, and made it fast to a number of sticks we had driven into the sand for the purpose. It was then tautened on board the wreck, and made fast.

This being done, the long boat (in order to save the provisions already in her) was lowered down, and two hands steadied her by ropes fastened to the rings in her stem and stern posts over the hawser, so as to slide, keeping her bow to the surf. In this manner they reached the beach, carried on the top of a heavy wave. The boat was stove by the violence of the shock against the beach; but by great exertions we saved the three barrels of bread in her before they were much damaged; and two barrels of salted provisions were also saved. We were now, four of us, on shore, and busied in picking up the clothing and other things which drifted from the vessel, and carrying them up out of the surf. It was by this time daylight, and high water; the vessel careened deep off shore, and I made signs to have the masts cut away, in the hope of easing her, that she might not go to pieces. They were accordingly cut away, and fell on her starboard side, making a better lee for a boat alongside the wreck, as they projected considerably beyond her bows.

The masts and rigging being gone, the sea breaking very high over the wreck, and nothing left to hold on by, the mates and six men still on board, though secured, as well as they could be, on the bowsprit and in the larboard fore-channels, were yet in imminent danger of being washed off by every surge. The long boat was stove, and it being impossible for the small one to live, my great object was now to save the lives of the crew by means of the hawser. I therefore made signs to them to come, one by one, on the hawser, which had been stretched taut for that purpose. John Hogan ventured first, and having pulled off his jacket, took to the hawser, and made for the shore.

When he had got clear of the immediate lee of the wreck, every surf buried him, combing many feet above his head; but he still held fast to the rope with a death-like grasp, and as soon as the surf was passed, proceeded on towards the shore, until another surf, more powerful than the former, unclenched his hands, and threw him within our reach; when we laid hold of him and dragged him to the beach; we then rolled him on the sand, until he discharged the salt water from his stomach, and revived. I kept in the water up to my chin, steadying myself by the hawser, while the surf passed over me, to catch the others as they approached, and thus, with the assistance of those already on shore, was enabled to save all the rest from a watery grave.

Chapter 4

Description of the Natives

All hands being now landed, our first care was to secure the provisions and water which we had so far saved, knowing it was a barren thirsty land; and we carried the provisions up fifty yards from the water's edge, where we placed them, and then formed a kind of a tent by means of our oars and two steering sails. I had fondly hoped we should not be discovered by any human beings on this inhospitable shore, but that we should be able to repair our boats, with the materials we might get from the wreck, and by taking advantage of a smooth time, (if we should be favoured with one,) put to sea, where by the help of a compass and other instruments which we had saved, we might possibly find some friendly vessel to save our lives, or reach some of the European settlements down the coast, or the Cape de Verd Islands.

Being thus employed, we saw a human figure approach our stuff such as clothing, which lay scattered along the beach for a mile westward of us. It was a man! He began plundering our clothing. I went towards him with all the signs of peace and friendship I could make, but he was extremely shy, and made signs to me to keep my distance, while he all the time seemed intent on plunder. He was unarmed, and I continued to approach him until within ten yards.

He appeared to be about five feet seven or eight inches high, and of a complexion between that of an American Indian and negro. He had about him, to cover his nakedness, a piece of coarse woollen cloth, that reached from below his breast nearly to his knees; his hair was long and bushy, resembling a *pitch mop,* sticking out every way six or eight inches from his head; his face resembled that of an ourang-outang more than a human being; his eyes were red and fiery; his mouth, which stretched nearly from ear to ear, was well lined with sound teeth; and a long curling beard, which depended from his upper lip and chin down upon his breast, gave him altogether a most horrid appearance, and I could not but imagine that those well set teeth were sharpened for the purpose of devouring human flesh!! particularly as I conceived I had before seen in different parts of the world, the human face and form in its most hideous and terrific shape.

He appeared to be very old, yet fierce and vigorous; he was soon joined by two old women of similar appearance, whom I took to be his wives. These looked a little less frightful, though their two eye-teeth stuck out like hogs' tusks, and their tanned skins hung in loose plaits on their faces and breasts; but their hair was long and braided. A girl of from eighteen to twenty, who was not ugly, and five or six children of different ages and sexes, from six to sixteen years, were also in company. These were entirely naked. They brought with them a good English hammer, with a rope-laniard through a hole in its handle. It had, no doubt, belonged to some vessel wrecked on that coast. They had also a kind of axe with them, and some long knives slung on their right sides, in a sheath suspended by their necks. They now felt themselves strong, and commenced a bold and indiscriminate plundering of everything they wanted. They broke open trunks, chests, and boxes, and emptied them of their contents, carrying the clothing on their backs upon the sand-hills, where they spread them out to dry. They emptied the beds of their contents, wanting only the cloth, and were much amused with the flying of the feathers before the wind from my bed. It appeared as though they had never before seen such things.

I had an adventure of silk laced veils and silk handkerchiefs, the former of which the man, woman, and children tied round their heads in the form of turbans; the latter round their legs and arms, though only for a short time, when they took them off again, and stowed them away among the other clothing on the sand-hills. They all seemed highly delighted with their good fortune, and even the old man's features began to relax a little, as he met with no resistance. We had no fire or side arms, but we could easily have driven these creatures off with handspikes, had I not considered that we had no possible means of escaping either by land or water, and had no reason to doubt but they would call others to their assistance, and in revenge destroy us.

I used all the arguments in my power to induce my men to endeavour to conciliate the friendship of these natives, but it was with the greatest difficulty I could restrain some of them from rushing on the savages and putting them to death, if they could have come up with them; but I found they could run like the wind, whilst we could with difficulty move in the deep sand. Such an act I conceived would cost us our lives, as soon as we should be overpowered by numbers, and I therefore permitted them to take what pleased them best, without making any resistance; except our bread and provisions, which, as we could not subsist without them, I was determined to defend to the last extremity.

On our first reaching the shore I allowed my mates and people to share among themselves one thousand Spanish dollars, for I had hauled my trunk on shore by a rope, with my money in it, which I was induced to do in the hope of its being useful to them in procuring a release from this country in case we should be separated, and in aiding them to reach their homes. We had rolled up the casks of water and wine which had been thrown overboard and drifted ashore. I was now determined to mend the long boat, as soon and as well as possible, in order to have a retreat in my power, (or at least the hope of one,) in case of the last necessity. The wind lulled a little in the afternoon, at low water, when William Porter succeeded in reaching the wreck, and procured a few nails and a marline spike; with these he got safe back to the shore. I found the timbers of the boat in so crazy a state, and the nails which held them together, so eaten off by the rust, that she would not hold together, nor support her weight in turning her up in order to get at her bottom.

I tacked her timbers together, however, as well as I could, which was very imperfectly, as I had bad tools to work with, and my crew, now unrestrained by my authority, having broached a cask of wine, and taken copious draughts of it, in order to dispel their sorrows, were most of them in such a state, that instead of assisting me, they tended to increase my embarrassment. We, however, at last, got the boat turned up, and found that one whole plank was out on each side, and very much split. I tacked the pieces in, assisted by Mr. Savage, Horace, and one or two more. We chinced a little oakum into the seams and splits with our knives, as well as we could, and worked upon her until it was quite dark. I had kept sentinels walking with handspikes, to guard the tent and provisions during this time, but the Arabs had managed to rob us of one of our sails from the tent, and to carry it off, and not content with this, they tried to get the other in the same way. This I would not permit them to do.

They then showed their hatchets and their arms, but finding it of no effect, they retired for the night, after promising, as near as I could understand them, that they would not molest us further till morning, when they would bring camels down with them. We had previously seen a great many camel tracks in the sand, and I of course believed there were some near. One of the children had furnished us with fire, which enabled us to roast a fowl that had been drowned, and driven on shore from the wreck, on which, with some salt pork, and a little bread and butter, we made a hearty meal, little thinking that this was to be the last of our provisions we should be permitted to enjoy. A watch was set of two men, who were to walk guard at a distance from the tent, to give an alarm in case of the approach of the natives, and keep burning a guard fire. This we were enabled to do by cutting up some spars we found on the beach, and which must have belonged to some vessel wrecked there before us.

Night had now spread her sable mantle over the face of nature, the savages had retired, and all was still, except the restless and unwearied waves, which dashed against the deserted wreck, and tumbled among the broken rocks a little to the eastward of us, where the high perpendicular cliffs, jutting out into the sea, opposed a barrier to their violence, and threatened, at the same time, inevitable and certain destruction to every ill fated vessel and her crew that should, unfortunately, approach too near their immoveable foundations: these we had escaped only by a few rods. From the time the vessel struck to this moment, I had been so entirely engaged by the laborious exertions which our critical situation demanded, that I had no time for reflection, but it now rushed like a torrent over my mind, and banished from my eyes that sleep which my fatigued frame so much required.

I knew I was on a barren and inhospitable coast; a tempestuous ocean lay before me, whose bosom was continually tossed and agitated by wild and furious winds, blowing directly on shore; no vessel or boat sufficient for our escape, as I thought it impossible for our shattered long boat to live at sea, even if we should succeed in urging her through the tremendous surges that broke upon the shore with such violence as to make the whole coast tremble; behind us were savage beings, bearing the human form indeed, but in its most terrific appearance, whose object I knew, from what had already passed, would be to rob us of our last resource, our provisions; and did not doubt, but they would be sufficiently strong in the morning, not only to accomplish what they meditated, but to take our lives also, or to seize upon our persons, and doom us to slavery, till death should rid us of our miseries.

This was the first time I had ever suffered shipwreck. I had left a wife and five young children behind me, on whom I doated, and who depended on me entirely for their subsistence. My children would have no father's, and perhaps no mother's care, to direct them in the paths of virtue, to instruct their ripening years, or to watch over them, and administer the balm of comfort and consolation in time of sickness; no generous friend to relieve their distresses, and save them from indigence, degradation, and ruin. These reflections harrowed up my soul, nor could I cease to shudder at these imaginary evils, added to my real ones, until I was forced mentally to exclaim, "*Thy ways, great Father of the universe, are wise and just, and what am I! an atom of dust, that dares to murmur at thy dispensations.*"

I next considered, that eleven of my fellow sufferers, who had intrusted themselves to my care, were still alive and with me, and all but two of them (who were on the watch) lying on the ground, and wrapped in the most profound and apparently pleasing sleep; and as I surveyed them with tears of compassion, I felt it was a sacred duty assigned me by Providence, to protect and preserve their lives to my very utmost. The night passed slowly and tediously away; when daylight at length began to dawn in the eastern horizon, and chased darkness before it, not to usher to our view the cheering prospect of approaching relief, but to unfold new scenes of suffering, wretchedness, and distress. So soon as it was fairly light, the old man came down, accompanied by his wives and two young men of the same family—he was armed with a spear of iron, having a handle made with two pieces of wood spliced together, and tied with cords: the handle was about twelve feet long.

This he held balanced in his right hand, above his head, making motions as if to throw it at us; he ordered us off to the wreck, pointing, at the same time to a large drove of camels that were descending the heights to the eastward of us, his women running off at the same time whooping and yelling horribly, throwing up sand in the air, and beckoning to those who had charge of the camels to approach. I ran towards the beach, and seized a small spar that lay there, to parry off the old man's lance, as a handspike was not long enough. He in the mean time came to the tent like a fury, where the people still were, and by slightly pricking one or two of them, and pointing at the same time towards the camels, he succeeded in frightening them, which was his object, as he did not wish to call help, lest he should be obliged to divide the spoil. The crew all made the best of their way to the small boat, while I parried off his spear with my spar, and kept him at a distance. He would doubtless have hurled it at me, but for the fear of losing it.

The small boat was dragged to the water, alongside our hawser, but the people huddling into her in a confused manner, she was filled by the first sea, and bilged. I now thought we had no resource, except trying to get eastward or westward. Abandoning, therefore, our boats, provisions, &c. we tried to retreat eastward, but were opposed by this formidable spear, and could not make much progress; for the old man was very active. He would fly from us like the wind, and return with the same speed. The camels were approaching very fast, and he made signs to inform us, that the people who were with them had fire arms, and would put us instantly to death; at the same time opposing us every way with his young men, with all their weapons, insisting on our going towards the wreck, and refusing to receive our submission, while the women and children still kept up their yelling. We then laid hold of the long boat, turned her over, and got her into the water; and as I would suffer only one at a time to get on board, and that too over her stern, we succeeded at length, and all got off safe alongside the wreck, which made a tolerable lee for the boat, though she was by this time half filled with water.

All hands got on board the wreck except myself and another: we kept bailing the boat and were able to keep her from entirely filling, having one bucket and a keg to work with. The moment we were out of the way, all the family ran together where our tent was; here they were joined by the camels and two young men, which we had not before seen, apparently about the ages of twenty and twenty-six. They were armed with scimitars, and came running on foot from the eastward. The old man and woman ran to meet them, hallooing to us, brandishing their naked weapons and bidding us defiance. They loaded the barrels of bread on their camels, which kneeled down to receive them; the beef and all the other provisions, with the sail that the tent was made of &c. &c. and sent them off with the children, who drove them down.

The old man next came to the beach; with his axe stove in all the heads of our water casks and casks of wines, emptying their contents into the sand. They then gathered up all the trunks, chests, sea instruments, books, and charts, and consumed them by fire in one pile. Our provisions and water being gone, we saw no other alternative but to try to get to sea in our leaky boat, or stay and be washed off the wreck the next night, or to perish by the hands of these barbarians, who we expected would appear in great force, and bring fire arms with them, and they would besides soon be enabled to walk to the wreck, on a sand bar that was fast forming inside of the vessel, and now nearly dry at low water. The tide seemed to ebb and flow about six feet. We had now made all the preparations in our power for our departure, which amounted to nothing more than getting from the wreck a few bottles of wine and a few pieces of salt pork. No water could be procured, and the bread was completely spoiled by being soaked in saltwater.

Our oars were all lost except two that were on shore in the power of the natives. We had split a couple of plank for oars, and attempted to shove off, but a surf striking the boat, came over her bow, and nearly filling her with water, drifted her again alongside the wreck. We now made shift to get on board the wreck again, and bail out the boat; which when done, two hands were able to keep her free, while two others held her steady by ropes, so as to prevent her from dashing to pieces against the wreck.

CHAPTER 5

The Natives Seize the Author

The sight of our deplorable situation seemed to excite pity in the breasts of the savages who had driven us from the shore. They came down to the water's edge, bowed themselves to the ground, beckoning us, and particularly me, whom they knew to be the captain, to come on shore; making at the same time all the signs of peace and friendship they could. They carried all their arms up over the sand-hills, and returned without them. Finding I would not come on shore, one of them ran and fetched a small goat or dog skin, which by signs they made me understand was filled with water, and all retiring to a considerable distance from the beach, except the old man who had it; he came into the water with it up to his armpits, beckoning me to come and fetch it and drink. He was nearly naked, and had no weapons about him. Being very thirsty, and finding we could not get at any water, and no hope remaining of our being able to get out through the surf to sea, I let myself down by the hawser, and went by means of it to the beach, where the old man met me and gave me the skin of water, which I carried off to the wreck, and the people hauled it up on board. This done, he made me understand that he wished to go on board, and me to remain on the beach until his return.

Seeing no possible chance of escaping, or of preserving our lives in any other way but by their assistance, and that that was only to be obtained by conciliating them—telling my men my mind, I went again to the shore. The young men, women, and children were now seated unarmed on the beach, near the water—the grown people nearly, and the children entirely naked. They made all the signs of peace they knew of, looking upwards, as if invoking heaven to witness their sincerity. The old man advancing, took me by the hand, and looking up to heaven, said, "*Allah K. Beer.*" I knew that *Allah* was the Arabic name for the Supreme Being, and supposed *K. Beer* meant "our friend or father." I let him pass to the wreck, and went and seated myself on the beach with the others, who seemed very friendly, interlacing their fingers with mine; putting my hat on one another's head, and returning it to me again; stroking down my trowsers, feeling my head and hands, examining my shoes, and feeling into my pockets, &c.

When the people had hauled the old man on board, I endeavoured to make them understand that they must keep him until I was released, but they did not comprehend my meaning, owing to the noise of the surf; and after he had satisfied his curiosity by looking attentively at everything he could see, which was nothing more than the wreck of the contents of the hold floating in her, inquiring for baftas, for firearms, and for money, as I afterwards learnt, and finding none, he came on shore. When he was near the beach, and I about to rise to meet him, I was seized by both arms by the two stoutest of the young men, who had placed themselves on each side of me for the purpose of safe-keeping. They grasped my arms like lions, and at that instant the women and children presented their daggers, knives, and spears to my head and breast. To strive against them was instant death; I was therefore obliged to remain quiet, and determined to show no concern for my life, or any signs of fear.

The countenance of everyone around me now assumed the most horrid and malignant expressions; they gnashed their teeth at me, and struck their daggers within an inch of every part of my head and body. The young men still held me fast, while the old one, seizing a sharp scimitar, laid hold of my hair at the same instant, as if to cut my throat, or my head off. I concluded my last moments had come, and that my body was doomed to be devoured by these beings, whom I now considered to be none other than cannibals, that would soon glut their hungry stomachs with my flesh. I could only say, "*Thy will be done*," mentally, and felt resigned to my fate, for I thought it could not be prevented. But this conduct on their part, it soon appeared, was only for the purpose of frightening me, and as I had not changed countenance, the old man, after drawing his scimitar lightly across the collar of my shirt, which he cut a little, released my head, bidding me by signs to order all the money we had on board to be brought directly on shore.

My mates and people then on the wreck, had witnessed this scene, and had agreed, as they afterwards informed me, that if I was massacred, which they did not doubt from appearances would soon be the case, to rush on shore in the boat, armed in the best manner they were able, and revenge my death by selling their lives as dearly as possible.

When the old man had quit his hold, and I hailed my people, their hopes began to revive, and one of them came on the hawser to know what they should do. I told him all the money which they had on board must be instantly brought on shore. He was in the water at some distance from me, and could not hear, on account of the noise occasioned by the surf, what I added, which was for them not to part with the money until I should be fairly released. He went on board, and all hands hoping to procure my release, put their money which they still had about them, to the amount of about one thousand dollars into a bucket, and slinging it on the hawser, Porter shoved it along before him near the beach, and was about to bring it up to the place where I sat. With considerable difficulty, however, I prevented him, as the surf made such a roaring, that he could not hear me, though he was only a few yards distant; but he at last understood my signs, and staid in the water until one of the young men went and received it from him. The old man had taken his seat alongside of me, and held his scimitar pointed at my breast.

The bucket of dollars was brought and poured into one end of the old man's blanket, when he bid me rise and go along with them, he and the young men urging me along by both arms, with their daggers drawn before, and the women and children behind with the spear, and their knives near my back. In this manner they made me go with them over the sand drifts to the distance of three or four hundred yards, where they seated themselves and me on the ground. The old man then proceeded to count and divide the money. He made three heaps of it, counting into each heap by tens, and so dividing it exactly, gave to the two young men one-third or heap—to his two wives one-third, and kept the other to himself. Each secured his and their own part, by wrapping and tying it up in some of our clothing.

During this process, they had let go of my arms, though they were all around me. I thought my fate was now decided, if I could not by some means effect my escape. I knew they could outrun me, if I should leap from them, and would undoubtedly plunge their weapons to my heart if I attempted, and failed in the attempt. However, I resolved to risk it, and made a slight movement with that view at a moment when I thought all eyes were turned from me; but one of the young men perceiving my manoeuvre, made a lounge at me with his scimitar. I eluded the force of his blow, by falling backwards on the ground; it however pierced my waistcoat. He was about to repeat it, when the old man bade him desist.

The money being now distributed and tied up, they made me rise with them, and were all going together from the beach, holding me by the arms, with naked daggers all around me. There appealed now no possible means of escape, when the thought suddenly occurred to me, to tempt their avarice. I then, by signs, made them understand that there was more money in the possession of the crew. This seemed to please them, and they instantly turned themselves and me about for the beach, sending the money off by one of the young men and a boy. When they approached to within one hundred yards of the beach, they made me seat myself on the sand between two of them, who held me by the arms, bidding me order the money on shore. I knew there was none on board the wreck, or in the boat, but I imagined if I could get Antonio Michel on shore, I should be able to make my escape. I hailed accordingly, and made signs to my people to have one of them come near the shore; but as they saw, by every movement of the natives, that my situation was dreadfully critical, none of them were inclined to venture, and I waited more than an hour, was often threatened with death, and made to halloo with all my might, until I became so hoarse as scarcely to make myself heard by those around me.

The pity of Mr. Savage at last overcame his fears. He ventured on the hawser, and reaching the beach in safety was about to come up to me, where he would have been certainly seized on as I was, when I endeavoured to make him understand, by signs, that he must stay in the water, and keep clear of the natives, if he valued his life; but not being able to hear me, my guards, who supposed I was giving him orders to fetch the money, obliged me to get up and approach him a little, until I made him understand what I wanted: he then returned on board the wreck, and I was taken back to my former station.

Antonio came to the shore, as soon as he knew it was my wish, and made directly towards me. The natives, expecting he would bring more money, flocked about him to receive it, but finding he had none, struck him with their fists, and the handles of their daggers, and stripped off all his clothing: the children at the same time pricking him with their sharp knives, and all seemed determined to torment him with a slow and cruel death. He begged for his life upon his knees, but they paid no regard to his entreaties. In hopes of saving him from the fury of these wretches, I told him to let them know by signs that there were dollars and other things buried in the sand, near where our tent had stood, and to endeavour to find them by digging. A new spy-glass, a hand-saw, and several other things had been buried there, and a bag containing about four hundred dollars at a short distance from them. He soon made them understand that something was buried, and they hurried him to the spot he had pointed out, and he began to dig. I had imagined that if this man would come on shore, I should be enabled to make my escape; yet I knew not how, nor had I formed any plan for effecting it.

I was seated on the sand, facing the sea, between the old man on my left, with his spear uplifted in his left hand, pointing to my breast, and the stoutest young man on my right, with a naked scimitar in his right hand, pointing to my head—both weapons were within six inches of me, and my guards within a foot on each side. I considered at this time, that so soon as anything should be found by those were digging, they would naturally speak and inform those who guarded me of it; (these had let go of my arms sometime before) and as I was pretty certain that both of them would look round as soon as the discovery of any treasure should be announced, I carefully drew up my legs under me, but without exciting suspicion, in order to be ready for a start.

The place where they were digging, was partly behind us on our right, and upon their making a noise, both my guards turned their heads and eyes from me towards them, when I instantly sprang out from beneath their weapons, and flew to the beach. I was running for my life, and soon reached the water's edge. Knowing I was pursued, and nearly overtaken, I plunged into the sea, with all my force, head foremost, and swam under water as long as I could hold my breath; then rising to the surface, I looked round on my pursuers. The old man was within ten feet of me, up to his chin in water, and was in the act of darting his spear through my body, when a surf rolling over me, saved my life, and dashed him and his comrades on the beach. I was some distance westward of the wreck; but swimming as fast as possible towards her, whilst surf after surf broke in towering heights over me, I was enabled, by almost superhuman exertion, to reach the lee of the wreck, when I was taken into the boat over the stern by the mates and people.

I was so far exhausted that I could not immediately witness what passed on shore, but was informed by those who did, that my pursuers stood motionless on the beach, at the edge of the water, until I was safe in the boat: that they then ran towards poor Antonio, and plunging a spear into his body near his left breast downwards, laid him dead at their feet. They then picked up what things remained, and made off all together. I saw them dragging Antonio's lifeless trunk across the sand-hills, and felt an inexpressible pang, that bereft me for a moment of all sensation, occasioned by a suggestion that to me alone his massacre was imputable; but on my recovery, when I reflected there were no other means whereby my own life could have been preserved, and, under Providence, the lives often men, who had been committed to my charge, I concluded I had not done wrong, nor have I since had occasion to reproach myself for being the innocent cause of his destruction; nor did any of my surviving shipmates, though perfectly at liberty so to do, ever accuse me on this point; from which I think I have an undoubted right to infer, that their feelings perfectly coincided with mine on this melancholy occasion.

Wreck of the Brig "Commerce" on the coast of Africa

CHAPTER 6

Sufferings Nine Days at Sea

Hostilities had now commenced, and we could not doubt but these merciless ruffians would soon return in force, and, when able to overpower us, would massacre us all as they had already done Antonio. The wind blowing strong, and the surf breaking outside and on the wreck twenty or thirty feet high, the hope of getting to sea in oar crazy long boat was indeed but faint. She had been thumping alongside the wreck, and on a sand bank all day, and writhed like an old basket, taking in as much water as two men constantly employed with buckets could throw out. The deck and outside of the wreck were fast going to pieces, and the other parts could not hold together long. The tide, (by being low,) together with the sand bar that had been formed by the washing of the sea from the bow of the wreck to the beach, had very much lessened the danger of communicating with the shore during this day; but it was now returning to sweep everything from the wreck, aided by the wind, which blew a gale on shore every night. To remain on the wreck, or go on shore, was almost certain death; the boat could no longer be kept afloat alongside, and being without provisions or water, if we should put to sea, we must soon perish. We had neither oars nor a rudder to the boat; no compass nor a quadrant to direct our course; but as it was our only chance, I resolved to try and get to sea; expecting, nevertheless, we should be swallowed up by the first surf, and launched into eternity all together.

I, in the first place, sent Porter on shore to get the two broken oars that were still lying there, while I made my way through the water into the hold of the wreck, to try once more if any fresh water could be found. I dove in at the hatchway, which was covered with water, and found, after coming up under the deck on the larboard side, as I expected, just room enough to breathe, and to work among the floating casks, planks, and wreck of the hold. After much labour I found a water cask, partly full, and turning it over, discovered that its bung was tight. This gave me new courage, and after upheading it, I came up and communicated the circumstance to my shipmates, and we then made search for some smaller vessel to fill from the cask. After much trouble, a small keg was found in the after hold; it might probably hold four gallons—the head of the water cask was stove in, and with the help of Mr. Savage and Clark, I got the keg full of water, and a good drink for all hands besides, which was very much needed. The others were in the mean time employed in rigging out spars which we had lashed together over the stern of the wreck with a rope made fast to their outer ends, in order to give the boat headway, and clear her from the wreck, when we should finally shove off. Porter had returned with the oars, and also brought the bag of money that had been buried, containing about four hundred dollars: this he did of his own accord.

We had got the small boat's sails, consisting of a jib and mainsail, into the boat, with a spar that would do for a mast, and the brig's foretopmast staysail; the keg of water, a few pieces of salt pork, a live pig, weighing about twenty pounds, which had escaped to the shore when the vessel struck, and which had swam back to us again when we were driven from the shore; almost four pounds of figs, that had been soaking in salt water ever since the brig was wrecked, and had been fished out of her cabin; this was all our stock of provisions.

Everything being now ready, I endeavoured to encourage the crew as well as I could; representing to them that it was better to be swallowed up all together, than to suffer ourselves to be massacred by the ferocious savages; adding, that the Almighty was able to save, even when the last ray of hope was vanishing; that we should never despair, but exert ourselves to the last extremity, and still hope for his merciful protection.

As we surveyed the dangers that surrounded us, wave following wave, breaking with a dreadful crash just outside of us, at every instant, our hearts indeed failed us, and there appeared no possibility of getting safely beyond the breakers, without a particular interference of Providence in our favour. The particular interference of Providence in any case I had always before doubted; but if there is a general, there must be a particular Providence. Every one trembled with dreadful apprehensions, and each imagined that the moment we ventured past the vessel's stem, would be his last. I then said, "Let us pull off our hats, my shipmates and companions in distress." This was done in an instant; when lifting my eyes and my soul towards heaven, I exclaimed, "*Great Creator and preserver of the universe, who now seest our distresses; we pray thee to spare our lives, and permit us to pass through this overwhelming surf to the open sea; but if we are doomed to perish, thy will be done; we commit our souls to the mercy of thee our God, who gave them: and O! universal Father, protect and preserve our widows and our children.*"

The wind, as if by divine command, at this very moment ceased to blow. We hauled the boat out; the dreadful surges that were nearly bursting upon us, suddenly subsided, making a path for our boat, through which we rowed her out as smoothly as if she had been on a river in a calm, whilst on each side of us, and but a few yards distant, the surf continued to break twenty feet high, and with unabated fury. We had to row nearly a mile in this manner: all were fully convinced that we were saved by the interposition of Divine Providence in this particular instance, and all joined in returning thanks to the Supreme Being for this mercy. As soon as we reached the open sea, and had gained some distance from the wreck, we observed the surf rolling behind us with the same force as it had on each side the boat. We next fitted the mast, and set the small boat's mainsail. The wind now veered four points to the eastward, so that we were enabled to fetch past the point of the Cape, though the boat had neither keel nor rudder. It was sunset when we got out, and night coming on, the wind as usual increased to a gale before morning, and we kept the boat to the wind by the help of an oar, expecting every moment to be swallowed up by the waves.

We were eleven in number on board; two constantly bailing were scarcely able to keep her free, changing hands every half hour. The night was very dark and foggy, and we could not be sure of fetching clear of the land, having nothing to guide us but the wind. In the morning we sailed back again for the land, and had approached it almost within reach of the breakers without seeing it, when we put about again. It had been my intention after we had got to sea, to run down the coast in the hope of finding some vessel, or to discover the mouth of some river, in order to obtain a supply of water. But now the dangers and difficulties we should have to encounter in doing this, were taken into consideration. If we tried to navigate along the coast, it was necessary to know our course, or we should be in imminent danger of being dashed to pieces on it every dark day, and every night. The thick foggy weather would prevent our seeing the land in the daytime; whilst the wind, blowing almost directly on the land, would force us towards it, and endanger the safety of both the boat and our lives, at every turn or point. We had no compass to guide us either by day or night; no instrument by which to find our latitude; no rudder to steer our boat with; nor were we in possession of materials wherewith it was possible to make one; she had no keel to steady her, nor was there a steering place in her stern, where an oar could be fixed by any other means thin by lashing to the stern ring, which afforded a very unsteady hold.

On the one hand, we considered that if we escaped the danger of being driven on shore or foundering at sea, and should succeed in reaching the cultivated country south of the desert, we should have to encounter the ferocious inhabitants, who would not fail, in the hope of plunder, to massacre us, or doom us to slavery. On the other hand, we reflected that we had escaped from savages who had already killed one of our shipmates, had gained the open sea through divine mercy, and could stand off to the westward without fear of being driven on shore. In this direction we might meet with some friendly vessel to save us, which was our only hope in that way; and the worst that could happen to us was to sink altogether in the sea, or gradually perish through want of sustenance.

Having considered, and represented to my companions the dangers that beset us on every side, I asked their opinions one by one, and found they were unanimously in favour of committing themselves to the open sea in preference to keeping along the coast. The dangers appeared to be fewer, and all agreed that it was better to perish on the ocean, if it was God's will, than by the hands of the natives. There being a strong breeze, we stood off by the wind and rigged our jib. We now agreed to put ourselves upon allowance of one bottle of water and half a bottle of wine among eleven of us, and a scrap or pork and two soaked and salted figs for each man.

During this day, which was the 30th August, 1815, we fitted waist cloths to go round above the gunwale of the boat, to prevent the sea from dashing over; they were from eight to ten inches broad, made from the brig's fore-staysail, and were kept up by small pieces of a board which we formed in the boat, so that they helped in some measure to keep off the spray. It had been cloudy all day, and the boat leaked faster than she had done before. As night came on the wind blew hard and raised the sea very high, but the boat was kept near the wind by her sails, and drifted broadside before it, smoothing the sea to the windward, and did not ship a great deal of water.

On the 31st it became more moderate, but the weather was very thick and hazy. Our pig being nearly dead for the want of water, we killed it, taking care, however, to save his blood; which we divided amongst us and drank, our thirst having become almost insupportable. We also divided the pig's liver, intestines, &c. between us, and ate some of them, (as they were fresh,) to satisfy, in some degree, our thirst. Thus this day passed away; no vessel was yet seen to relieve us; we had determined to save our urine for drink, which we accordingly did in some empty bottles, and found great relief from the use of it; for being obliged to labour hard by turns to keep the boat above water, our thirst was much more severely felt than if we had remained still.

The night came on very dark and lowering; the sky seemed big with an impending tempest; the wind blew hard from the N. E. and before midnight the sea dashed into the boat in such quantities as several times to fill her more than half full. All hands were employed in throwing out the water with hats and other things, each believing his final hour had at length arrived, and expecting that every approaching surge would bury him forever in a watery grave.

The boat racked like an old basket, letting in water at every seam and split; her timbers working out or breaking off; the nails I had put in while last on shore were kept from entirely drawing out, merely by the pressure of the water acting on the outside of the boat. Sharp flashes of lightning, caused by heat and vapour, shot across the gloom, rendering the scene doubly horrid. In this situation, some of the men thought it was no longer of use to try to keep the boat afloat, as they said she must soon fill in spite of all their exertions. Having prayed to the Almighty, and implored pardon for our transgressions, each one seemed perfectly resigned to his fate: this was a trying moment, however, and my example and advice could scarcely induce them to continue bailing; whilst some of them, by thrusting their heads into the water, endeavoured to ascertain what the pains of death were, by feeling the effects the water would produce on their organs.

Thus passed this night; all my exertions were necessary to encourage the men to assist me in bailing the boat, by reminding them of our miraculous escape from the savages, and through the surf to the open sea, and enforcing on their minds the consideration that we were still in the hands of the same disposing power, and that we ought not to suppose we were aided in escaping from the shore by a miracle, to be abandoned here and swallowed up by the ocean; and that for my own part I still entertained hopes of our preservation; at any rate, that it was a duty we owed to God and ourselves to strive to the latest breath to prevent our own destruction. Day came on amidst these accumulated horrors; it was the first of September: thirst pressed upon us, which we could only allay by wetting our mouths twice a day with a few drops of wine and water, and as many times with our urine.

The wind continued to blow hard all this day, and the succeeding night with great violence, and the boat to work and leak in the same manner as before. Worn down with fatigues and long continued hunger and thirst, scorched by the burning rays of the sun, and no vessel appearing to save us, our water fast diminishing, as well as our strength, every hope of succour by meeting with a vessel entirely failed me, so that in the afternoon of the 2nd of September, I represented to my companions, that as we were still alive, after enduring so many trials, it was my advice to put about, and make towards the coast again; that if we continued at sea we must inevitably perish, and that we could but perish in returning towards the land; that we might still exist four or five days longer, by means of the water and provisions that remained, and that it might be the will of Providence to send us on the coast where our vessel had been wrecked, and where means were perhaps prepared to bring about our deliverance and restoration to our country and our families. All seemed convinced that it was so, and we immediately put about with a kind of cheerfulness I had not observed in any countenance since our first disaster.

From this time all submitted to their fate with tolerable patience, and kept the boat free, though we had continual bad weather, without murmuring. We wetted our lips with wine and water twice every day, and ate the bones and some of the raw flesh of our pig, with its skin; but at length we became so faint as to be unable to take our turns in bailing, whilst the boat laboured so much as to work off nearly all the nails that kept the planks to her timbers above water.

By the 6th of September, at night, we had not made the land, and could not hope to make the boat hold together in any manner above another day. I expected we should have found the land that day, but was disappointed, and some of the people began again to despair. Impelled by thirst, they forgot what they owed to their shipmates, and in the night got at, and drank off one of the two bottles of wine we had remaining. When I mentioned the loss of the wine on the morning of the 7th, all denied having taken or drank it, adding that it was an unpardonable crime, and that those who did it ought to be thrown overboard instantly. From the heat observable in their conversation, I guessed the offenders; but the wine was gone, and no remedy remained but patience, and stricter vigilance for the future.

In a short time we discovered land at a great distance ahead, and to leeward. This gave all hands new spirits; hope again revived for a moment. The land appeared perfectly smooth in the distant horizon; not the smallest rising or hill was to be seen, and I concluded we must be near a desert coast, where our sufferings would find no relief but in death. We continued to approach the land, driving along to the southward. by a swift current, roaring like a strong tide in a narrow rocky passage, until near sunset.

The coast now appeared to be formed of perpendicular and overhanging cliffs, rising to a great height, with no shelving shore to land on, or way by which we might mount to the top of the precipices. My opinion was, that we should endeavour to keep to sea this night also, and steer along down the coast, until by the help of daylight, we might find a better place to land, and where we should not be in such danger of being overwhelmed by the surf; but in this I was opposed by the united voice of the mates and all the people.

The surf was breaking high among the rocks, near the shore: we were now very near the land, and seeing a small spot that bore the appearance of a sand beach, we made fork, and approaching it with the help of our oars, we were carried on the top of a tremendous wave, so as to be high and dry when the surf retired, on a little piece of sand beach, just large enough for the boat to lie on. Without us, and in the track we came, numerous fragments of rocks showed their craggy heads, over which the surf foamed as it retired, with a dreadful roaring, which made us feel we had once more escaped instant destruction, by what appeared a miraculous interference of Providence.

We got out of the boat, and carried up the little remains of our water and pork among the rocks, beyond the reach of the surf: the remains of the pig had been previously consumed. Our boat was now stove in reality; over our heads pended huge masses of broken and shattered rocks, extending both ways as far as the eye could reach: our limbs had become stiff for the want of exercise; our flesh had wasted away for the want of sustenance, and through fatigue our tongues were so stiff in our parched mouths, that we could with great difficulty speak so as to be understood by each other, though we had finished our last bottle of wine between us, for fear of losing it, just before we ventured to the shore through the surf.

Being thus placed on dry land, we had yet to discover how we were to reach the surface above us; so taking Mr. Savage with me, we clambered over the rocks to the westward, (for the coast running here from E. N. E. to W. S. W. induced me to think we were near Cape Blanco, which indeed afterwards proved to be the case,) but we searched in vain, and as there appeared to be no access to the summit in that direction, we returned (it being then dark) to our shipmates, who had been busied in preparing a place on the sand, between the rocks, to sleep on. We now wet our mouths with water, ate a small slice of the fat of salt pork, and after pouring out our souls before the universal Benefactor, in prayers and thanksgiving for his mercy and his long continued goodness, (as had constantly been our custom,) we laid down to rest, and, notwithstanding our dreadful situation, slept soundly till daylight.

CHAPTER 7

Seized as Slaves

On the morning of September the 8th, as soon as it was light, being much refreshed by our undisturbed sleep, we agreed to leave all we had that was cumbrous or heavy, and try to make our way to the eastward, in hopes of finding a place, whilst we had yet strength remaining, to dig for water, or to get to the surface of the land above us, where we hoped to find some herbage or vegetable juice to allay, in some degree, our burning thirst, which was now rendered more grievous than ever, by our eating a few muscles that were found on the rocks, and extremely salt. Having agreed to keep together, and to render each other mutual assistance, we divided amongst us the little water we had, every one receiving his share in a bottle, in order to preserve it as long as possible: then taking a small piece or two of pork, which we slung on our backs, either in a spare shirt or a piece of canvass, leaving all our clothes but those we had on, and our jackets, we bent our way towards the east. I had, before starting, buried the bag of dollars, and induced each man to throw away everyone he had about him, as I was convinced that money had been the cause of our former ill treatment, by tempting the natives to practise treacherous and cruel means, in order to extort it from us.

We proceeded now, as well as we were able, along close to the water side. The land was either nearly perpendicular, or jutting over our heads, rising to the height of from five to six hundred feet, and we were forced to climb over masses of sharp and craggy rocks, from two to three hundred feet in height; then to descend again by letting ourselves down from rock to rock, until we reached the water's edge; now waiting for a surf to retire, while we rushed one by one past a steep point, up to our necks in the water, to the rocks more favourable on the other side, where by clinging fast hold, we kept ourselves from being washed away by the next surf, until, with each other's assistance, we clambered up beyond the reach of the greedy billows. The beating of the ocean, and the force of the currents against this coast, had undermined the precipices in such a manner, that vast masses of rocks, gravel, and sand, had given way and tumbled to the shore. Rocks falling on rocks, had formed chasms, through which we were forced to pass at times, for a long distance; and surmounting one obstacle, seemed only to open to our view another, and a more dangerous one.

At one place, we were obliged to climb along on a narrow ledge of rocks, between forty and fifty feet high, and not more than eighteen inches broad; those at our backs were perpendicular, and a little higher up, huge pieces that had been broken off from near the surface, and stopped on their way down by other fragments, seemed to totter as if on a pivot, directly over our heads; while the least slip must have plunged us into the frightful abyss below, where the foaming surges would instantly have dashed us to pieces against the rocks. Our shoes were nearly all worn off; our feet were lacerated and bleeding; the rays of the sun, beating on our emaciated bodies, heated them, we thought, nearly to dissolution; and under these towering cliffs, there was not a breath of air to fan our almost boiling blood. I had, in crawling through one of the holes between the rocks, broke my bottle, and spilled the little water it contained; and my tongue, cleaving to the roof of my mouth, was as useless as a dry stick, until I was enabled to loosen it by the expedient before mentioned.

Thus passed this day with us, and when night came on, it brought with it new distresses. We had advanced along the coast not more than about four miles this day, with all the exertion we were capable of, without finding any change for the better in our local situation, whilst our strength was continually diminishing, and no circumstance occurred to revive our hopes. We had seen this day, however, on the broken rocks, several locusts, which we took to be grasshoppers, and concluded, if we could once reach the surface, we should find herbage, at least, to feed on. These locusts were dead, and crumbled to dust on the slightest touch.

We now found a good place in the sand, about one hundred feet from the sea, under a high cliff, to sleep on; here we greased our mouths by eating a small piece of salt pork, and wet them, as usual, with a sip of urine. All hands, except myself, had a little fresh water left; my comrades knew I had not one drop, and two of them offered to let me taste of theirs, with which I just moistened my tongue, and after sending up our prayers to heaven, for mercy and relief in our forlorn and desolate condition, we laid ourselves down to sleep.

I had, on setting out from home, received Horace Savage under my particular charge, from his widowed mother: his father, when living, having been my intimate friend, I promised her to take care of him, as if he was my own son, and this promise I had endeavoured to fulfil. He was now in deep distress, and I determined within myself that I would adopt him as my own son, for his mother was poor; that I would watch over his ripening years, in case we both lived, and if fortune should favour me in future, that he should share it in common with my children. I now took him in my arms, and we all slept soundly till morning, though the change was so great in the night, from extreme heat to a damp cold air, that we awoke in the morning (September 9th) with benumbed and trembling limbs. Sleep, however, had refreshed us, and though our feet were torn, and our frames nearly exhausted, yet we chased away despair, and set forward on our journey.

We had soon discovered, at no great distance ahead, a sand beach that appeared large, and from which the shore upward seemed more sloping, as if opening a way to the surface above it; we also thought we should be able, in case we could reach the beach, to get water that would be drinkable, by digging in the sand down to a level with the sea, and letting it filter into the hole; this I had done on the Little Keys of the Bahama bank with success, and expected it would be the same here;—so we made our way slowly along, as we had done the day before, until we got within a short distance of this beach, where we met with a promontory of rocks, which rose in height even with the surface above us; jutting far out into the sea, whose waves had worn in under its base to the distance of fifty or one hundred feet, and now dashed in a wild and frightful manner against the projecting points, which its washings for ages had formed underneath. To climb over this formidable obstruction, was impossible; to get around it through the water, appeared equally so, as there was not sufficient time, by the greatest exertion, to pass before the return of the surf, which would inevitably hurl the adventurer into the cavities under the cliff, among the sharp rocks, where he must immediately perish.

Thus far we had all got safe; to advance by what appeared to be the only possible way, seemed like seeking instant death; to remain in our present situation, was merely to die a lingering one; and to return was still worse, by increasing our pains, without leading to any chance of relief. Before us was a prospect of getting water, and arriving at the summit of the land, if we could only get round the promontory alive; and fortunately, at this moment we observed a rock about half way across this point, that had tumbled down from above, and had been washed full of holes; it was covered by every surf, and its top left bare as the wave receded. I imagined I could reach it before the wave came in; and after making known my intentions to my companions, I followed the surf out, and laid hold of the rock just as the returning swell overwhelmed me. I clung to it for my life, the surf passing over me, and spending its fury among the crags: the instant it retired I hurried on to the steep rocks beyond the point, where I again held on, while another surf swept over me, and then left me to clamber up, as quick as I was able, on the flat surface of the rock, beyond the reach of the waves.

The tide was not yet entirely out, though I had judged it was; and as it continued to fall, my people following the same course and embracing the same means, all got safe to the first rock, and from thence to the place where I lay prostrate to receive and assist them in getting up. Though out limbs and bodies were very much bruised in this severe encounter, yet we felt somewhat encouraged, and made for the sand beach as fast as we were able. We soon reached it, and began digging in the sand for water, at different distances from the sea, but found it to be as salt as the ocean.

After digging several holes farther off, and meeting with dry rock instead of water, I pitched upon a spot for our last effort; and while the others were digging, I told them I would go and see if I could get up the bank, and if I succeeded that I would return in a short time with the news: the bank here rose abruptly, leaving, however, in some places sufficient slope for a man to ascend it by climbing. Through one of these slopes I made my way up, in the hope of finding some green thing that might help to allay our burning thirst, and some tree to shelter us from the scorching blaze of the sun; but what was my surprise when I came to the spot so long desired, and found it to be a barren plane, extending as far as the eye could reach each way, without a tree, shrub, or spear of grass, that might give the smallest relief to expiring nature? I had exerted myself to the utmost to get there; the dreary sight was more than I could bear; my spirits fainted within me, and I fell to the earth deprived of every sensation. When I recovered, it was some time before I could recollect where I was: my intolerable thirst, however, at length convinced me, and I was enabled to administer the same wretched and disgusting relief to which I had so frequently before been compelled to resort.

Despair now seized on me, and I resolved to cast myself into the sea as soon as I could reach it, and put an end to my life and miseries together. But when I the next moment reflected that I had left ten of my fellow creatures on the shore, who looked up to me for an example of courage and fortitude, and for whom I still felt myself bound to continue my exertions, which might yet be blessed with success; and that at the moment when I supposed the hand of relief far from me, it might be very near; and when I next thought of my wife and children, I felt a kind of conviction within me, that we should not all perish after such signal deliverances. I then made for the sea side about a mile eastward of my men, and finding a good place between some rocks, I bathed myself for half an hour in the sea water, which refreshed and revived me very much, and then returned to my men with a heart lighter than I expected. I was very much fatigued, and threw myself down on the sand. They huddled around me to know what success I had met with; but to waive the subject of my sad discovery, I told them we could go along the beach for two miles before meeting again with the perpendicular cliffs, and would find great relief by bathing our bodies in the saltwater; inquiring, at the same time, if they had found any fresh in the last place they had been digging. I thus diverted their minds, in some measure, from the object they wished to inquire after; and as I found they had dug down six or eight feet, and had found no water, having come to a rock which frustrated all their attempts; with heavy hearts and tottering limbs we staggered along the shore together.

It was about mid-day when we got to the end of the sand beach, my people thought it would be impossible for them to climb the craggy steep; so with common consent we laid ourselves, down under the shade formed by a shelving rock, to rest, and to screen ourselves from the rays of the sun, which had heated the air to such a degree, that it was with the greatest difficulty we could fetch our breath. There was no wind or air stirring at this time, except the hot steam rising from the sandy beach, which had been wet by the sea at the last tide.

Having lain down in our exhausted state, neither thirst nor our reflections, had power to keep our eyes open; we sunk into a lethargic sleep, which continued about two hours, during which time a light breeze from the sea had set in, and gently fanned and refreshed our debilitated bodies. We then ascended the steep bank, crawling frequently on our hands and knees. Though I had previously prepared all their minds for a barren' prospect, yet the sight of it, when they reached its level, had such an effect on their senses that they sunk to the earth involuntary; and as they surveyed the dry and dreary waste, stretching out to an immeasurable extent before them, they exclaimed, "'Tis enough; here we must breathe our last; we have no hope before us of finding either water or provisions, or human beings, or even wild beasts; nothing can live here."

The little moisture yet left in us overflowed at our eyes; but as the salt tears rolled down our woe-worn and haggard cheeks, we were fain to catch them with our fingers and carry them to our mouths, that they might not be lost, and serve to moisten our tongues, that were now nearly as dry as parched leather, and so stiff, that with difficulty we could articulate a sentence so as to be understood by each other.

I began now to exhort and press them to go forward; telling them that we still might find relief, and in this effort I was assisted by Hogan, who thought with me that it was time enough to lie down and die, when we could not walk. Mr. Williams and Mr. Savage were also willing, and we moved on slowly, with scarcely a hope, however, of meeting with the least relief. We continued along on the edge of the cliffs, which could not be less than from five to six hundred feet in perpendicular height: the surface of the ground was baked down almost as hard as flint; it was composed of small ragged stones, gravel, and reddish earth. We observed a small dry stalk of a plant, resembling that of a parsnip, though very low; and some dry remains of locusts were also scattered on the surface as we proceeded. Near night we saw some small holes dug on the surface, and on examination found they had been made in order to get at the root of the dry weed we had just before seen: this we conceived had been done by some wild beasts; but finding no tracks of any kind near them, nor on the dirt dug up, I concluded it was done by man, and declared my hopes to my desponding companions of soon meeting with human beings.

We procured, after great labour in digging with sticks we had brought from the boat and the help of stones, a few small pieces of a root as large as a man's finger; it was very dry, but in taste resembled smellage or celery. We could not get enough to be of any material service to us, owing to the scarcity of the plant, and the hardness of the ground; but about sunset we discovered, on a small spot of sand, the imperfect track of a camel, and thought we saw that of a man, which we took to be a very old track.

Believing from our present feelings that we could not possibly survive a day longer without drink, and no signs of finding any appearing, the last ray of hope faded away, and the gloom of despair, which had at length settled on our hearts, now became visible in every countenance. A little after sunset we saw at a considerable distance in advance, perhaps three or four miles, another sand beach, and I urged myself forwards towards it as fast as I could, in hopes of getting some rest by sleeping on the sand for the night, as the ground we were now on was as hard as a rock, and covered with small sharp stones. I was encouraging the men to follow on, when Clark, being near me, begged me to took towards the beach, saying, "I think I see a light!" It was the light of a fire!

Joy thrilled through my veins like the electric spark: hope again revived within me, and while I showed it to my sinking and despairing crew, I found it communicated to them the same feelings. I told them we must approach the natives, who I could not doubt were encamped for the night, with the greatest caution, for fear of alarming them, and tailing a sacrifice to their fury, in the confusion we might occasion by our sudden approach in the dark. New life and spirits were infused into all the crew, and we soon reached a broken place in the bank, through which we descended carefully over the broken rocks, from three to four hundred feet, to a sandy spot near its base, where we laid ourselves down for the night, after imploring the protection of Almighty God, and wetting our mouths with a few drops of water still remaining in the bottles.

The sand on which we lay was heated by the sun's rays sufficiently to have roasted eggs, and as we were on the side of a sand-hill, we scraped off the top of it for a foot or two deep; when finding the heat more supportable, and the cool breeze of the night setting in, all hands being excessively fatigued, soon forgot their sufferings in the arms of sleep, excepting myself; for my mind had become so excited by alternate hopes, and fears, and reflections, that I was kept awake through the whole of this long and dismal night. I had determined, as soon as daylight appeared, to show ourselves to the natives, and submit either to death or life from their hands. I had no doubt of their being Arabs who would take and hold us as slaves, and though I did not expect myself to live but a short time in that condition, I presumed some of my fellow sufferers might, and that it was a decree of Providence which had set this alternative before us.

I no longer felt any fear of death, for that would put a period to my long sufferings: my thirst had become so insupportable, that I could with difficulty breathe, and thought I would be willing to sell my life for one gill of fresh water. My distresses had been so excessive, and my cares and anxieties for my shipmates so great, that all .thoughts of my family had been driven almost entirely from my mind. I could not sleep—why was I denied what all around me were enjoying? I shut my eyes, and prayed to be permitted to sleep, if only for one hour, but all in vain. I imagined that the savages, who were near us, would not take our lives immediately, as it was contrary to the nature of man to slay his fellow creatures, merely from a thirst for blood.

We had now no arms to defend ourselves, nor any property to excite their jealousy, revenge, or avarice; we were as miserable, I conceived, as human beings could be, and I hoped we should excite pity, even in the breasts of the savage Arabs. I could hardly yet think, that we were to fall a sacrifice to these people, after the providential escapes we had already experienced: next, the remembrance of my wife and children flitted across my mind, and I was forced to acknowledge, that however bad their situation might be, their real distress could in no wise equal mine, and that I had no right to repine at the dispensations of Providence, since every mortal has his circle wisely marked out by heaven; and nothing but blindness to the future, occasions us to complain of the ways of our Creator. If it was the will of the Supreme Being that I should again see and embrace my beloved family, it would certainly take place; if not, that power who ordered all things for the general good, would not forsake them.

Thus passed away the night, which had seemed to me an endless one. I was impatient to know my fate, and chid the slowness of the sun; my great anxiety and wakefulness, rendered my thirst doubly gainful, and having expended all the urine I had so carefully saved, I had recourse before morning to robbery, and actually stole a sip of the cook's water, which he had made and saved in a bottle; but the only taste it had for me was a salt one, and it seemed (if possible) to increase my burning thirst. The day at last arrived that was to decide our fate. It was the 10th of September. I awakened my companions, and told them we must now go forward and show ourselves to the natives— that I expected they would seize upon us as slaves, but had strong hopes that some of us would escape with our lives.

I also mentioned to them the name of the American Consul General at Tangier, and that if it ever was in their power, they must write to him, and inform him of the fate of our vessel and her crew: to write, if possible, to any Christian merchant in Mogadore, Gibraltar, or elsewhere, or to the Consul at Algiers, Tunis, or Tripoli, if they should hear those places mentioned, and exhorted all to submit to their fate like men, and be obedient, as policy required, to their future masters. I reminded them again of the former interpositions of Providence in our favour, and said all I could to encourage and persuade them, that mildness and submission might save our lives—that resistance and stubbornness would certainly tend to make them more miserable while alive, and probably prompt the natives to murder them out of resentment.

All agreed to go forward, and on rising the little sand-hills near us, we discovered a very large drove of camels at about half a mile to the eastward of us, with a large company of people, in a kind of valley formed by a ridge of sand-hills on the north next the sea, and by the high land to the south, rising from five to six hundred feet in upright and overhanging cliffs—through which, a little farther on, we saw a deep hollow that appeared to have been formed by some convulsive shock of the earth, which had thus made a sort of passage, through which camels were enabled to pass up and down, but with great difficulty. The Arabs seemed busied in giving water to their camels; they saw us, and in an instant one man and two women ran towards us with great speed. As they came forward, many others of them who saw us, also began to advance: so taking Mr. Williams and Mr. Savage with me, I went forward to meet them, bowed myself to the ground before them, and with signs implored their compassion.

The man was armed with a scimitar, which he held naked in his hand. He ran up to me as if to cut me to the earth: I bowed again in token of submission, and he began without further ceremony to strip off my clothing, while the women were doing the same to Mr. Williams and Mr. Savage. Thirty or forty more were arriving—some running on foot, with muskets or naked scimitars in their hands; others riding on swift camels, came quickly up:—by the time they arrived, however, we were all stripped naked to the skin. Those Arabs near us threw up sand into the air, as the others approached, yelling loudly, which I now learned was a sign of hostility. The one who stript me had also taken the cook, and had put all the clothing he had stript from us into a blanket, which he had taken from off his own back for that purpose, leaving himself entirely naked. This bundle he laid on the negro's shoulders, making me understand that myself and the black man belonged to him, and that we must not let the others take the clothes in the bundle under pain of death.

As soon as those on the camels were near, they made them lie down, and jumping off, ran to us with their scimitars naked and ready for action; those on foot now joined these, and a great noise and scuffle ensued. Six or eight of them were about me, one hauling me one way and one another: poor Dick, the black man, partook of the hauling, and each man seemed to insist most strenuously that we belonged of right to him. The one who stript us, stuck to us as his lawful property, signifying, "you may have the others, these are mine." They cut at each other over my head, and on every side of me, with their bright weapons, which fairly whizzed through the air within an inch of my naked body, and on every side of me, now hacking each other's arms apparently to the bone, then laying their ribs bare with gashes, while their heads, hands, and thighs, received a full share of cuts and wounds. The blood, streaming from every gash, ran down their bodies, colouring and heightening the natural hideousness of their appearance. I had expected to be cut to pieces in this dreadful affray, but was not injured.

Those who were not actually engaged in combat, seized the occasion, and snatched away the clothing in Dick's bundle, so that when the fight was over, he had nothing left but his master's blanket. This battle and contest lasted for nearly an hour—brother cutting brother, friend slashing friend. Happily for them, their scimitars were not very sharp, so that when they rubbed off the dried blood from their bodies afterwards with sand, their wounds were not so great or deep as I expected they would be, and they did not pay the least apparent attention to them. I had no time to see what they were doing with my shipmates; only myself and the cook were near each other.

The battle over, I saw my distressed companions divided among the Arabs, and all going towards the drove of camels, though they were at some distance from me. We two were delivered into the hands of two old women, who urged us on with sticks towards the camels. Naked and barefoot, I could not go very fast, and showed the women my mouth, which was parched white as frost, and without a sign of moisture. When we got near the well, one of the women called for another, who came to us with a wooden bowl, that held, I should guess, about a gallon of water, and setting it on the ground, made myself and Dick kneel down and put our heads into it like camels. I drank I suppose half a gallon, though I had been very particular in cautioning the men against drinking too much at a time, in case they ever came to water.

THE CAPTURE OF THE AUTHOR AND HIS CREW BY WANDERING ARABS

They then led us to the well, the water of which was nearly as black and disgusting as stale bilge water. A large bowl was now filled with it, and a little sour camel's milk poured from a goat skin into it; this tasted to me delicious, and we all drank of it till our stomachs were literally filled. But this intemperance very soon produced a violent diarrhoea; the consequences of which, however, were not very troublesome, and as our situation was similar to that of a beast, being totally divested of clothing, all we cared about was to slake our unabating thirst, and replenish our stomachs by repeated draughts of this washy and unwholesome swill.

We now begged for something to eat, but these Arabs had nothing for themselves, and seemed very sorry it was not in their power to give us some food. There were at and about the well, I should reckon, about one hundred persons, men, women, and children, and from four to five hundred camels, large and small. The sun beat very fiercely upon us, and our skins seemed actually to fry like meat before the fire. These people continued to draw water for then camels, of which the animals drank enormous quantities. It was about ten o'clock a. m. as I judged by the sun, when one company of the Arabs, having finished watering, separated their camels from among the others, took Mr. Williams, Robins, Porter, Hogan, Barrett, and Burns, mounted them on the bare backs of the camels behind the hump, by the hair of which they were obliged to steady themselves and hold on, without knowing whither they were going, or if I should ever see them again. I took an affectionate leave of them. This their Arab masters permitted me to do without interruption, and could not help showing at this scene, that the feelings of humanity were not totally extinguished in their bosoms. They then hurried them off, and ascending through the hollow or crevice towards the face of the desert, they were all soon out of sight.

There remained with the party to which I belonged, Mr. Savage, Clark, Horace, and Dick the cook. Mr. Savage was permitted to retain an old Guernsey frock, and part of a pair of trowsers about his middle, which they had not pulled off: but the rest of us were entirely stripped. Mr. Savage, Clark, and Horace were forced to assist in drawing water for the camels, until all had drank their fill: then having filled with water a considerable number of goatskins, which had been cut round the neck and stripped off these animals over the tail, leaving them otherwise as whole as when on their backs, they slung them by the skin of their legs on each side of the camels, after tying up the neck to prevent the water escaping, by means of a small rope which they fastened to the forelegs of the skin to keep it up.

They next put on their baskets for the women and children to ride in: these were made of camel's skin, and fixed in such a manner, with a wooden brim around them, over which the skin was sewed, that three or four could sit in them with perfect safety and ease, only taking care to preserve their balance. These baskets were fastened under the camels' bellies with a strong rope: I was obliged to assist in putting them on, and was in hopes of being permitted to ride in one of them; but that was not the intention of my master. I, as well as those who were with me, had drank a great deal of water, while we were at the well, which had passed off, as before observed, without doing us any injury. We had been furnished also with a little milk in our water two or three times, which gave some relief to our hunger. The men had saddles just large enough for their seat: the pads are made of flat pieces of wood; a piece of the same rises in front, being about the length, breadth, and thickness of a man's hand; an iron rim, or a strong wooden one, goes round on each side, forming a circle; covered with a piece of skin stretched and sewed tight over it. The saddle is then placed on the camel's back before the hump, and fastened tight by a rope under his belly.

Thus prepared, we began to mount the sand-hills and get up through the gulley. We were forced to walk and to drive the camels and keep them together, whilst the sand was so soft and yielding, that we sunk into it every step nearly to our knees. The blazing heat of the sun's rays darting on our naked bodies, and reflected from the sand we waded through; the sharp pointed craggy rocks and stones that cut our feet and legs to the bone, in addition to our excessive weakness, which the dysentery had increased, rendered our passage up through this chasm or hollow much more severe than anything of the kind we had before undergone, and nearly deprived us of life. For my own part, I thought I must have died before I could reach the summit, and was obliged to stop in the sand, until by the application of a stick to my sore back by our drivers, I was forced up to its level; and there they made the camels lie down and rest.

CHAPTER 8

The Crew are Sold and Distributed

The Arabs had been much amused in observing our difficulty in ascending the height, and kept up a laugh while they were whipping us forward. Their women and children were on foot as well as themselves, and went up without the smallest difficulty or inconvenience, though it was extremely hard for the camels to mount, and before they got to the top they were covered with sweat and froth. Having now selected five camels for the purpose, one for each of us, they put us on behind the humps, to which we were obliged to cling by grasping its long hair with both hands. The backbone of the one I was set on was only covered with skin, and seemed as sharp as the edge of an oar's blade; his belly, distended with water, made him perfectly smooth, leaving no projection of the hips to keep me from sliding off behind; and his back or rump being as steep as the roof of a house, and so broad across as to keep my legs extended to their utmost stretch, I was in this manner slipping down to his tail every moment. I was forced, however, to keep on, while the camel, rendered extremely restive at the sight of his strange rider, was all the time running about among the drove, and making a most woeful bellowing; and as they have neither bridle, halter, or any other thing whereby to guide or govern them, all I had to do was to stick on as well as I could.

The Arabs, both men and women, were very anxious to know where we had been thrown on shore, whether to the eastward or westward; and being satisfied by me on that point, so soon as they had placed us on the camels, and given the women directions how to steer, they mounted each his camel, seated themselves on the small round saddle, and then crossing their legs on the animal's shoulders, set off to the westward at a great trot, leaving us under the care of the women, some of whom were on foot, and urged the camels forward as fast as they could run, to the S. E. The heavy motions of the camel, not unlike that of a small vessel in a heavy head-beat sea, were so violent, aided by the sharp back bone, as soon to excoriate certain parts of my naked body; the inside of my thighs and legs were also dreadfully chafed, so that the blood dripped from my heels, while the intense neat of the sun had scorched and blistered our bodies and the outside of our legs, so that we were covered with sores, and without any thing to administer relief.

Thus bleeding and smarting under the most excruciating pain, we continued to advance in a S. E. direction, on a plane, flat, hard surface of sand, gravel, and rock, covered with small sharp stones. It seemed as if our bones would he dislocated at every step. Hungry and thirsty, the night came on, and no indication of stopping; the cold night wind began to blow, chilling our blood, which ceased to trickle down our lacerated legs; but although it saved our blood, yet acting on our blistered skins, it increased our pains beyond description. We begged to be permitted to get off, but. the women paid no attention to our distress nor intreaties, intent only on getting forward. We designedly slipped off the camels, when going at a full trot, risking to break our necks by the fall, and tried to excite their compassion and get a drink of water, (which they call *sherub*,) but they paid no attention to our prayers, and kept the camels running faster than before.

This was the first time I had attempted to walk barefooted since I was a schoolboy; we were obliged to keep up with the camels, running over the stones, which were nearly as sharp as gun flints, and cutting our feet nearly to the bone at every step. It was here that my fortitude and reason failed to support me; I cursed my fate aloud, and wished I had rushed into the sea before I gave myself up to these merciless beings in human forms—it was now too late. I would have put an immediate end to my existence, but had neither knife nor any other weapon with which to perform the deed. I searched for a stone, intending if I could find a loose one sufficiently large, to knock out my own brains with it; but searched in vain. This paroxysm passed off in a minute or two, when reason returned, and I recollected that my life was in the hand of the power that gave it, and that "*the Judge of all the earth would do right.*" Then running with all my remaining might, I soon came up with the camels, regardless of my feet and of pain, and felt perfectly resigned and willing to submit to the will of Providence, and the fate that awaited me.

From that time forward, through all my succeeding trials and sufferings, I never once murmured in my heart, but at all times kept my spirits up, doing the utmost to obey and please those whom fortune, fate, or an overruling Providence had placed over me, and to persuade, both by precept and practice, my unhappy comrades to do the same. I had, with my companions, cried aloud with pain, and begged our savage drivers for mercy, and when we had ceased to make a noise, fearing, as it were, to lose us in the dark, they stopped the camels, and again placing us on them as before, drove them on at full speed until about midnight, when we entered a small dell or valley, excavated by the hand of nature, a little below the surface of the desert, about from fifteen to twenty feet deep. Here they stopped the camels, and made them lie down, bidding us to do the same. I judge we must have travelled forty miles this day to the S. E.: the place was hard and rocky, not even sand to lie on, nor any covering to shelter us or keep off the cold damp wind that blew strong from the sea.

They soon set about milking, and then gave us each about a pint of pure milk, warm from the camels, taking great care to divide it for us; it warmed our stomachs, quenched our thirst in some measure, and allayed in a small degree the cravings of hunger. Mr. Savage had been separated from us, and I learned from him afterwards that he fared better than we did, having had a larger allowance of milk. Clark, Horace, and Dick the cook were still with me. We lay down on the ground as close to each other as we could, on the sharp stones, without any lee to fend off the wind from us: our bodies all over blistered and mangled, the stones piercing through the sore naked flesh almost to the ribs and other bones. These distresses, and our sad and desponding reflections, rendered this one of the longest and most dismal nights ever passed by any human beings. We kept shifting births, striving to keep off some of the cold during the night, while sleep, that had hitherto relieved our distresses and fatigues, fled from us in spite of all our efforts and solicitude to embrace it; nor were we able to close our eyes.

The morning of the 11th came on at last, and our industrious mistresses, having milked a little from the camels, and allowed the young ones to suck, gave us about half a pint of milk among four of us, being just enough to wet our mouths, and then made us go forward on foot and drive the camels. The situation of our feet was horrible beyond description, and the very recollection of it, even at this moment, makes my nerves thrill and quiver. We proceeded forward, having gained the level desert, for a considerable time, when entering a small valley, we discovered three or four tents made of coarse cloth, near which we were met by our masters, and a number of men whom we had not before seen, all armed with either a double barrelled musket, a scimitar, or dagger. They were all of the same nation and tribe, for they shook hands at meeting, and seemed very friendly to each other, though they stopped and examined us, as if disposed to question the right of property.

It now appeared there was still some difficulty in deciding to whom each one of us belonged; for seizing hold of us, some dragged one way and some another, disputing very loudly, and frequently drawing their weapons. It was, however, decided at last, after making us go different ways for the space of two or three hours with different men, that myself and the cook should remain, for the present, in the hands of our first master. They gave Clark to another, and Horace to a third. We had come near a couple of tents, and were certainly disgusting objects, being naked and almost skinless; this was sometime about noon, when three women came out who had not before seen us, and having satisfied their curiosity by gazing at us, they expressed their disgust and contempt by spitting on us as we went along, making their faces still more horrid by every possible contortion of their frightful features; this we afterwards found to be their constant practice wherever we went, until after we got off the desert.

Towards evening, a great number of them having collected in a little valley, we were made to stop, and as our bodies were blistered and burned to such a degree as to excite pity in the breasts of some of the men, they used means to have a tent cleared out for us to sit under. They then allowed all those of our crew present to sit under it, and, as may well be supposed, we were glad to meet one another again, miserable as we all were. Porter and Burns, who had been separated from me shortly after our capture, were still absent. A council was now held by the natives near the tent; they were about one hundred and fifty men, some very old, some middle aged, and some quite young. I soon found they were Mohammedans, and the proper names by which they frequently called each other were *Mohammed, Hamet, Seid, Sideullah, Ahdallah,* &c. so that by these and the female names *Fatima, Ezimah, Sarah,* &c. I knew them to be Arabs or Moors.

The council were deliberating about us; and having talked the matter over a long time, seated on the ground with their legs crossed under them, in circles of from ten to twenty each, they afterwards arose and came to us. One of the old men then addressed me; he seemed to be very intelligent, and though he spoke a language that I was unacquainted with, yet he explained himself in such a plane and distinct manner, sounding every letter full like the Spaniards, that with the help of signs I was able to understand his meaning. He wanted to know what country we belonged to; I told him we were English; and as I perceived the Spanish language was in sound more like that which they spoke than any other I knew, I used the phrase *Inglesis*; this seemed to please him, and he said "*O Fransah, O Spaniah*;" meaning, "or Frenchmen, or Spaniards;" I repeated we were English. He next wanted to know which point of the horizon we came from, and I pointed to the north.

They had seen our boat, which they called *Zooerga*, and wanted to know if we had come all the way in that boat: I told them no, and making a kind of coast, by heaping up sand, and forming the shape of a vessel, into which I stuck sticks for masts and bowsprit, &c. I gave him to understand that we had been in a large vessel, and wrecked on the coast by a strong wind; then by tearing down the masts and covering the vessel's form with sand, I signified to him that she was totally lost. Thirty or forty of the other Arabs were sitting around us, paying the strictest attention to every one of my words and gestures, and assisting the old man to comprehend me. He wished to know where we were going, and what cargo the vessel (which I now found they called *Sfenah*) had on board. I satisfied them in the best way I could on this point, telling them that I had on board, among other things, dollars: they wanted to know how many, and gave me a bowl to imitate the measure of them: this I did by filling it with stones and emptying it three times. They were much surprised at the quantity, and seemed to be dissatisfied that they had not got a share of them. They then wanted to know which way the vessel lay from us, and if we had seen any of the natives, whom they called *Moslemin*.

This I took to be what we call Mussulmen, or followers of the Mohammedan doctrine, and in this I was not mistaken. I then explained to them in what manner we had been treated by the inhabitants; that they had got all our clothing, except what we had on when they found us; all our money and provisions: massacred one of our number, and drove us out to sea. They then told me that they heard of the shipwreck of a vessel a great way north, and of the money, &c. but that the crew were drowned in *el M Bahar*; this was so near the Spanish (*La Mar*) for the sea, that I could not misunderstand it. Thus having obtained what information they wanted on those points, they next desired to know if I knew anything about *Marocksh*; this sounded something like Morocco: I answered yes; next of the *Sooltaam*, (the *Sultan*,) to which instead of saying yes, I made signs of assent, for I found they did no more themselves, except by a cluck with the tongue.

They wanted me to tell his name, Soo Mook, but I could not understand them until they mentioned Moolay Solimaan; this I remembered to be the name of the present emperor of Morocco, as pronounced in Spanish, nearly. I gave them to understand that I knew him; had seen him with my eyes, and that he was a friend to me and to my nation. They next made me point out the direction towards his dominions, and having satisfied them that I knew which way his dominions lay from us, I tried to intimate to them, that if they would carry me there, I should be able to pay them for my ransom, and that of my crew. They shook their heads; it was a great distance, and nothing for camels to eat or drink on the way. My shipmates, who went with me, could not understand one syllable of what they said, or of their signs, and did not believe that I was able to communicate at all with them.

Having finished their council, and talked the matter over among themselves, they separated, and our masters, taking each his slave, made off, everyone his own way. Although from the conference I derived hopes of our getting ransomed, and imparted the same to my mates and crew, yet they all seemed to think I was deluding them with false expectations; nor could I convince them of the contrary. We took another leave of each other, when we parted for the night, having travelled this day, I should guess, about fifteen miles, S. E.

I had been so fully occupied since noon, that no thoughts of victuals or drink had occurred to my mind. We had none of us ate or drank anything this day, except about half a gill of milk each in the morning at daylight, and about half a pint of black beach water near the middle of the day. I was delivered over to an Arab named Bickri, and went with him near his tent, where he made me lie down on the ground like a camel. Near midnight he brought me a bowl containing about a quart of milk and water; its taste was delicious, and as my stomach had become contracted by long hunger and thirst, I considered it quite a plentiful draught. I had been shivering with cold for a long time, as I had no covering nor screen, and not even one of my shipmates to lie near me to keep one side warm at a time. I was so far exhausted by fatigues, privations, &c. that my misery could no longer keep me awake. I sank into a deep sleep, and during this sleep I was troubled in the first place with the most frightful dreams.

I thought I was naked and a slave, and dreamed over the principal incidents which had already actually passed. I then thought I was driven by Arabs with red hot iron spears pointed at me on every side, through the most dreadful fire I had ever imagined, for near a mile, naked and barefoot; the flames up to my eyes, scorched every part of my skin off, and wasted away my flesh by roasting, burning, and drying it off to the bones; my torments were inconceivable. I now thought I looked up towards heaven, and prayed to the Almighty to receive my spirit, and end my sufferings; I was still in the midst of the flames; a bright spot like an eye with rays around it, appeared above me in the firmament, with a point below it, reaching towards the N. E.—I thought if I went that way I should go right, and turned from the S. to the N. E.; the fire soon subsided, and I went on, still urged by them about me, with their spears pricking me from time to time, over high sand-hills and rocky steeps, my flesh dropping off in pieces as I went; then descending a deep valley, I thought I saw green trees—flowering shrubs in blossom—cows feeding on green grass, with horses, sheep, and asses near me; and as I moved on, I discovered a brook of clear running water: my thirst being excessive, I dragged my mangled limbs to the brook, threw myself down, and drank my fill of the most delicious water. When my thirst was quenched, I rolled in the brook to cool my body which seemed still consuming with heat; then thanked my God in my heart for his mercies.

My masters, in the meantime, kept hurrying me on in the way pointed out by the All-seeing eye, which was still visible in the heavens above my head, through crooked, thorny, and narrow paths—over high mountains and deep valleys—past hosts of armed men on horseback and on foot, and walled cities, until we met a tall young man dressed in the European and American manner, by the side of a brook, riding on a stately horse, who, upon seeing me alighted, and rushing forward, wild with joy, caught me in his arms, and pressed me to his breast, calling me by the endearing name of brother, in my own language—I thought I fainted in his arms from excess of joy and when I revived, found myself in a neat room, with a table set in the best manner before me, covered with the choicest meats, fruits, and wines, and my deliverer pressing me to eat and drink; but finding me too much overcome to partake of this refreshment, he said, "*take courage, my dear friend, God has decreed that you shall again embrace your beloved wife and children.*" At this instant I was called by my master—I awoke, and found it was a dream.

Being daylight, (Sept. 12th) he ordered me to drive forward the camels; this I did for about an hour, but my feet were so much swelled, being lacerated by the cutting of the stones, which seemed as if they would penetrate my heart at every step—I could not help stooping and crouching down nearly to the ground. In this situation, my first master, Hamet, observed me; he was going on the same course, S. E. riding on his camel; he came near my present master, and after talking with him a good while, he took off the blanket from his back and gave it to Bickri—then coming close to me, made signs for me to stop. He next made his camel lie down; then fixing a piece of skin over his back behind the saddle, and making its two ends fast to the girths to keep it from slipping off, he bade me mount on it, while he got on his saddle and steadied me with his hand until the camel rose. He then went on the same course as before, in company with three or four other men, well armed and mounted.

The sun beat dreadfully hot upon my bare head and body, and it appeared to me that my head must soon split to pieces, as it was racking and cracking with excruciating pain. Though in this horrible distress, yet I still thought of my dream of the last night—"*a drowning man will catch at a straw,*" says the proverb, and I can verily add, that the very faintest gleam of hope will keep alive the declining spirits of a man in the deepest distress and misery; for, from the moment I began to reflect on what had passed through my mind when sleeping, I felt convinced that though this was nothing more than a dream, yet still remembering how narrowly and often I had escaped immediate apparent death, and believing it was through the peculiar interposition of Divine Providence, I could not but believe that the All-seeing eye was watching over my steps, and would in due time, conduct me by his unerring wisdom, into paths that would lead to my deliverance, and restoration to my family.

I was never superstitious, nor ever did I believe in dreams or visions, as they are termed, or even remembered them, so as to relate any I may have had; but this dream made such an impression on my mind, that it was not possible for me remove it from my memory-being now as fresh as at the moment I awoke after dreaming it; and I must add, that when I afterwards saw Mr. Willshire, I knew him to be the same man I had seen in my sleep: he had a particular mark on his chin—wore a light coloured frock coat, had on a white hat, and rode the same horse. From that time I thought if I could once get to the empire of Morocco, I should be sure to find a friend to relieve me and my companions, whose heart was already prepared for it by a superior Power.

My mind was thus employed until we came to a little valley where half a dozen tents were pitched; as soon as we saw them, Hamet made his camel kneel down, and me to dismount; he was met by several women and children, who seemed very glad to see him, and I soon found that they were his relations. He beckoned me to come towards his tent, for he lived there, apparently, with his mother, and brothers and sisters, but the woman and girls would no suffer me to approach them, driving me off with sticks, and throwing stones at me; but Hamet brought me a little sour milk and water in a bowl, which refreshed me considerably.

It was about two o'clock in the day, and I was forced to remain broiling in the sun, without either tree, shrub, or any other shade to shield me from its scorching rays, until night, when Dick (the cook) came in with the camels. Hamet had kept Dick from the beginning, and made him drive the camels, but allowed him to sleep in one corner of the tent, and gave him for the few first days, as much milk as he could drink, once a day; and as he was a domestic slave, he managed to steal water, and sometimes sour milk, when he was dry.

In the evening of this day I was joined by Hogan, and now found that he and myself had been purchased by Hamet that day, and that Horace belonged to an ill-looking old man, whose tent was pitched in company. This old villain came near me, and saluted me by the name of *Rais*, asking me the name of his boy, (Horace); I told him it was Horace, which after repeating a few times he learned so perfectly, that at every instant he was yelling out "*Hoh Rais*" for something or other. Hamet was of a much lighter colour than the other Arabs we were with, and I thought he was less cruel, but in this respect I found I was mistaken, for he made myself and Hogan lie on the ground in a place he chose, where the stones were very thick and baked into the ground so tight that we could not pull them out with our fingers, and we were forced to lie on their sharp points, though at a small distance, not more than fifty yards, was a spot of sand. This I made him understand, pointing at the same time to my skinless flesh, but he signified to us, that if we did not remain where he had ordered, we should get no milk when he milked the camels. I calculate we travelled this day about thirty miles.

Here then we staid, but not to sleep, until about the midnight hour, when Hamet came to us with our milk; it was pure and warm from the camels, and about a pint for each. The wind blew as is usual in the night, and on that part of the desert the air was extremely cold and damp; but its moisture on our bodies was as salt as the ocean. Having received our share of milk, when all was still in the tent, we stole to the sandy place, where we got a little sleep during the remaining part of the night. Horace's master would not permit him to come near me, nor me to approach him, making use of a stick, as well to enforce his commands in this particular, as to teach us to understand him in other respects.

At daylight (Sept. 13th) we were called on to proceed. The families struck their tents, and packed them on camels, together with all their stuff. They made us walk and keep up with the camels, though we were so stiff and sore all over that we could scarcely refrain from crying out at every step: such was our agony; still pursuing our route to the S. E. In the course of the morning, I saw Mr. Williams; he was mounted on a camel, as we had all been the first day, and had been riding with the drove about three hours: I hobbled along towards him; his camel stopped, and I was enabled to take him by the hand. He was still entirely naked; his skin had been burned off; his whole body was so excessively inflamed, and swelled, as well as his face, that I only knew him by his voice which was very feeble. He told me he had been obliged to sleep naked in the open air every night: that his life was fast wasting away amidst the most dreadful torments; that he could not live one day more in such misery; that his mistress had taken pity on him, and anointed his body that morning with butter or grease; but, said he, "I cannot live; should you ever get clear from this dreadful place, and be restored to your country, tell my dear wife that my last breath was spent in prayers for her happiness." He could say no more; tears and sobs choked his utterance.

His master arrived at this time, and drove on his camel, and I could only say to him, "God Almighty bless you," as I took a last look at him, and forgot, for a moment, while contemplating his extreme distress, my own misery. His camel was large, and moved forward with very heavy motions; as he went from me, I could see the inside of his legs and thighs—they hung in strings of torn and chafed flesh—the blood was trickling down the sides of the camel, and off his feet. "My God!" I cried, "suffer us not to live longer in such tortures." I had stopped about fifteen minutes, and my master's camels had gained a great distance from me, so that I was obliged to run that I might come up with them. My mind was so shocked with the distresses of Mr. Williams, that I thought it would be impious for me to complain, though the sharp stones continued to enter my sore feet at every step.

My master saw me and stopped the drove for me to come up; when I got near him he threatened me, shaking his stick over my head, to let me know what I had to expect if I dared to commit another fault. He then rode off, ordering me and Hogan to drive the camels on as fast as we could. About an hour afterwards he came near us, and beckoned to me to come to him, which I did. A tall old man, nearly as black as a negro, one of the most ill-looking and disgusting I had yet seen, soon joined my master, with two young men, whom I found afterwards were his sons: they were also joined by a number more on camels and well armed.

After some time bartering about me, I was given to the old man, whose features showed every sign of the deepest rooted malignity in his disposition. And is this my master? thought I; Great God! defend me from his cruelty! He began to go on: he was on foot; so were his two sons; but they walked faster than camels, and the old man kept snarling at me in the most surly manner, to make me keep up. I tried my very best, as I was extremely anxious to please him, if such a thing was possible, knowing the old adage of *"the devil is good when he is pleased,"* was correct, when applied to human beings; but I could not go fast enough for him; so after he had growled and kept on a considerable time, finding I could not keep up with him he came behind me and thrust me forward with hard blows repeatedly applied to my exposed back, with a stout stick he had in his hand.

Smarting and staggering under my wounds, I made the greatest efforts to get on, but one of his still more inhuman sons, (as I then thought him,) gave me a double barrelled gun to carry, with his powder horn and other accoutrements: they felt very heavy, yet after I had taken them, the old man did not again strike me, but went on towards the place where he meant to pitch his tent, leaving me to follow on as well as I could.

The face of the desert now appeared as smooth as the surface of the ocean, when unruffled by winds or tempests. Camels could be seen on every direction, as soon as they came above the horizon, so that there was no difficulty in knowing which way to go, and I took care to keep sight of my new master's drove, until I reached the valley, in which he had pitched his tent. I was broiling under the sun and tugging along, with my load, which weighed me down to the earth, and should have lain down despairing, had I not seen Mr. Williams in a still worse plight than myself.

Having come near the tent about four p. m. they took the load from me, and bid me lie down in the shade of the tent. I then begged for water, but could get none. The time now came on for prayers, and after the old man and his sons had performed this ceremony very devoutly, they went away. I was in so much pain, I could scarcely contain myself, and my thirst was more painful that it had yet been. I tried to soften the hearts of the women to get me a little water, but they only laughed and spit at me; and to increase my distresses as much as they could, drove me away from the shade of the tent, so that I was forced to remain in the scorching sun for the remainder of this long day.

A little after sunset my old and young masters returned; they were joined by all the men that were near, to the number of from twenty to thirty, and went through their religious ceremonies in a very solemn manner, in which the women and little children did not join them. Soon after this was over, Clark came in with the camels and joined me; it would have been pleasant to be together, but his situation was such that it made my heart ache still worse than it did before; he was nearly without a skin; every part of his body exposed; his flesh excessively mangled, burnt, and inflamed. "I am glad to see you once more, sir," said Clark, "for I cannot live through the approaching night, and now beg of you, if you ever get to our country again, to tell my brothers and sisters how I perished."

I comforted him all I could, and assured him he would not die immediately; that the nourishment we now had, though very little, was sufficient to keep us alive for a considerable time, and that though our skins were roasted off and our flesh inflamed, we were yet alive without any signs of putrefaction on our bodies; that I had great hopes we should all be carried in a few days from this desert to where we might get some food to nourish us, and as I had learned a little of the language of these people, (or savages,) I would keep trying to persuade them that if they would carry us up to the Moorish dominions, I should be able to pay them a great ransom for all the crew; for an old man had told me that as soon as it should rain they would journey to the N. E. and sell us.

The night came on; cold damp winds succeeded to the heat of the day, and I begged of my old master to be permitted to go under the corner of his tent, (for it was a large one,) and he seemed willing, pointing out a place for us to lie down in, but the women would not consent, and we remained outside until the men had milked the camels. They then gave us a good drink of milk, near a quart each, and after the women were asleep, one of my young masters, named Omar, (the same that made me carry his gun the preceding day to keep his father from beating me.) took pity on our distresses, and came and made us creep under one corner of the tent, without waking the women, where some soft sand served us for a bed, and the tent kept off the cold air from us; and here we slept soundly until morning. As soon as the women awoke, and found us under the tent, they were for thrusting us out with blows, but I pretended to be asleep, and the old man looking on us, seemed somewhat concerned, fearing (as I thought) he might lose his property. He told his women to let us alone, and as he was absolute, they were forced to obey him, though with every appearance of reluctance.

After they had milked the camels, and taken a drink themselves, they gave us what remained, that is to say, near a pint between us. They did not move forward this day, and suffered us to remain under the corner of the tent in the shade all the while, and the next night, and even gave us a piece of a skin to cover us with in part, and keep off the night wind. They gave us a good drink of milk when they drank themselves on the second night, and Omar had given us about a pint of water each, in the middle of the day; so that the inflammation seemed to have subsided in a great degree from our flesh and feet.

This attention, together with the two good nights' rest, revived us very much—these were the 14th and 15th days of September. I had not seen any of my unfortunate shipmates except Clark, and did not know where they were during the day we remained still. The camels were driven off early in the morning by a negro slave and two of the small boys, and did not return until in the night—they went out to the east to find shrubs for them to feed on. Clark was obliged, near night, to go out and pull up some dry thorn bush shrubs and roots to make a fire with.

At the return of the camels, the negro slave (who was a stout fellow, named Boireck) seated himself by the fire, stretching out his legs on each side of it, and seeing us under the tent, thought to drive us out; but as he was not permitted by our old master, he contented himself by pointing at us and making comparisons: then sneeringly addressing me by the name of *Rais*, or chief, would set up a loud laugh, which, with the waggery he displayed in his remarks on us, kept the whole family and several strangers who had assembled on the occasion, in a constant roar of laughter until midnight, the hour for milking the camels. He would poke our sore flesh with a sharp stick, to make sport, and show the Arabs what miserable beings we were, who could not even bear the rays of the sun (the image of God, as they term it) to shine upon us.

Being tormented in this manner, my companion Clark could scarcely contain his wrath: "It was bad enough, (he said,) to be reduced to slavery by the savage Arabs; to be stripped, and skinned alive, and mangled, without being obliged to bear the scoffs and derision of a d——d negro slave."

I told him I was very glad to find he still had so much spirits left, and could feel as if he wished to revenge an insult—it proved to me that he felt better than he did the preceding night, and as I was so much relieved myself, my hopes of being able to endure our tortures and privations increased, adding, "let the negro laugh if he can take any pleasure in it; I am willing he should do so, even at my expense: he is a poor slave himself, naked and destitute, far from his family and friends, and is only trying to gain the favour of his masters and mistresses, by making sport of us, whom he considers as much inferior to him as he is to them."

Clark, however, could not be reconciled to this mode of mockery and sport; but the negro kept it up as long as we remained with his master, every night, and always had many spectators to admire his wit, and laugh at his tricks and buffoonery. This reminded me of the story of Samson, when the Philistines wished to make sport with him; he was blind, and they supposed him harmless; but he became so indignant, that he was willing to suffer death to be revenged of them; the difference was, he had strength to execute his will,—we had not. From the 15th to the 18th, we journeyed every day to the S. E about thirty miles a day, merely to find a few shrubs in the small scattered valleys for the camels, and consequently for the inhabitants to subsist on.

As we went on in that direction, the valleys became less frequent and very shallow; the few thorn bushes they produced were very dry, and no other shrubs to be found; the camels could not fill their stomachs with the leaves and shrubs, nor with all that they could crop off, though they pulled away the branches as thick as a man's finger. The milk began to fail, and consequently we had to be scanted, so that our allowance was reduced to half a pint a day, and as all the water they had taken from the well was expended, they could give us no more of that precious article. There were belonging to this tribe four mares that were the general property; they were clean limbed, and very lean;

they fed them on milk every day, and every one took his turn in giving them as much water every two days as they would drink.

These mares drank up the last of our water on the 19th, nor would my master allow me to drink what little was left in the bowl, not exceeding half a pint, and it was poured out as a drink offering before the Lord, while they prayed for rain, which indeed they had reason to expect, as the season they knew was approaching, when some rain generally happens. I supposed our distance from the sea, or the well that we had left, to be three hundred miles in a direct line, and feared very much that we should not find water at any other place. The sustenance we received was just sufficient to keep the breath of life in us, but our flesh was less inflamed than in the first days, for we had continued to lie under a part of the tent at night, and also in the daytime when it was pitched, which was generally the case about two o'clock in the afternoon.

We had, however, become so emaciated, that we could scarcely stand, and they did not attempt to make me or Clark do any kind of work, except gather a few dry sticks, towards evening, to light a fire. The swellings had also gone down in some measure from our feet, as there was not substance enough in us to keep up a running sore; all the moisture in them seemed to dry away, and we could support the prickings and cutting of the stones better, as we became lighter and more inured to it. We had endeavoured to find some of the kind of root that was met with near the sea coast, but none could be procured. In every valley we came to, the natives would run about and search under a thorn bush, in hopes to find some herb, for they were nearly as hungry as ourselves. In some places a small plant was found, resembling what we call shepherd's sprout; they were torn up by them and devoured in an instant. I got one or two, but they proved very bitter, and were impregnated, in a considerable degree, with salt: these plants were so rare as to be scarcely of any benefit.

There were also found by the natives, in particular places, a small ground root, whose top showed itself like a single short spear of grass, about three inches above the ground; they dug it up with a stick; it was of the size of a small walnut, and in shape very much like an onion; its taste fresh, without any strong flavour; but it was very difficult to find, and afforded us very little relief, as we could not get more than half a dozen in a whole day's search, and some days none at all.

On the 19th of September, in the morning, the tribe having held a council the night before, at which I could observe my old master was looked up to as a man of superior judgment and influence, they began a route back again towards the sea, and the well near which we were first made slaves;—this convinced me that no fresh water could be procured nearer, and as the camels were almost dry, I much feared that myself and my companions must perish before we could reach it.

I had been in the habit every day since I was on the desert, of relieving my excessive thirst by the disagreeable expedient before mentioned; but that resource now failed me for the want of moisture, nor had anything passed through my body since the day I left the well. We had journeyed for seven and a half days S. E. and I concluded it would require the same time to return; but on the 18th we had steered N. E. and on the 19th we took a N. W. direction, and in the course of the day we entered a very small valley, where we found a few dwarf thorn bushes, not more than two feet high; on these we found some snails, most of which were dead and dry, but I got about a handful that were alive, and when a fire was kindled, roasted and ate them: Clark did the same, and as we did not receive more than a gill of milk each in twenty-four hours, this nourishment was very serviceable.

On the morning of the 20th we started as soon as it was light, and drove very fast all the day. We had no other drink than the camels' urine, which we caught in our hands as they voided it; its taste was bitter, but not salt, and it relieved our fainting spirits. We were forced to keep up with the drove, but in the course of the day found a handful of snails each, which we at night roasted and ate. Our feet, though not much swollen, were extremely sore; our bodies and limbs were nearly deprived of skin and flesh, for we continually wasted away, and the little we had on our bones was dried hard, and stuck fast to them. My head had now become accustomed to the heat of the sun, and though it remained uncovered, it did not pain me. Hunger, that had preyed upon my companions to such a degree as to cause them to bite off the flesh from their arms, had not the same effect on me.

I was forced in one instance to tie the arms of one of my men behind him, in order to prevent his gnawing his own flesh; and in another instance, two of them having caught one of the boys, a lad about four years old, out of sight of the tents, were about dashing his brains out with a stone, for the purpose of devouring his flesh, when luckily at that instant I came up and rescued the child, with some difficulty, from their voracity. They were so frantic with hunger, as to insist upon having one meal of his flesh, and then they said they would be willing to die; for they knew that not only themselves, but all the crew would be instantly massacred as soon as the murder should be discovered. I convinced them that it would be more manly to die with hunger than to become cannibals and eat their own other human flesh, telling them, at the same time, I did not doubt but our masters would give us sufficient nourishment to keep us alive, until they could sell us.

On the 20th we had proceeded with much speed towards the N. W. or sea shore; but on the 21st we did not go forward. This day I met with Mr. Savage, Horace, Hogan, and the cook; their masters' tents were pitched near ours; they were so weak, emaciated, and sore, that they could scarcely stand, and had been carried on the camels for the last few days. I was extremely glad to see them, and spoke to all but Horace, whose master drove me off with a stick one way, and Horace another, yelling most horribly at the same time, and laying it on Horace's back with great fury. I soon returned to our tent, and felt very much dejected; they all thought they could not live another day: there were no snails to be found here, and we had not one drop of milk or water to drink. Horace, Hogan, and the cook were employed in attending their masters' camels, in company with one or two Arabs, who kept flogging them nearly the whole of the time.

My old master did not employ me or Clark in the same way, because he had two negro slaves to do that work; he was a rich man among them, and owned from sixty to seventy camels; he was also a kind of priest, for every evening he was joined, in his devotions, by all the old and most of the young men near his tent. They all first washed themselves with sand, in place of water; then wrapping themselves up with their strip of cloth and turning their faces to the east, my old master stepped out before them, and commenced by bowing twice, repeating at each time "*Allah Houakibar*," then kneeling and bowing his head to the ground twice; then raising himself up on his feet, and repeating, "*Hi el Allah Sheda Mohammed Rahsool Allah*" bowing himself twice; and again prostrating himself on the earth as many times, then "*Allah Houakibar*" was three times repeated.

He was always accompanied in his motions and words by all present who could see him distinctly, as he stood before them. He would then make a long prayer, and they recited all together what I afterwards found to be a chapter in the *Koran*; and then all joined in chanting or singing some hymn or sacred poetry for a considerable time. This ceremony being finished, they again prostrated themselves with their faces to the earth, and the service concluded.

About the middle of this day two strangers arrived, riding two camels loaded with goods: they came in front of my master's tent, and having made the camels lie down, they dismounted, and seated themselves on the ground opposite the tent, with their faces turned the other way. There were in this valley six tents, besides that of my masters.

CHAPTER 9

Two Arabian Merchants Purchase the Author and Four of His Suffering Companions

All the men had gone out a hunting on their camels, carrying their arms with them; that is to say, seeking for plunder as I concluded. My old and young mistresses went to see the strangers: they had no water to carry, as is customary, but took with them a large skin, with a roll of tent cloth, to make them a shelter. The strangers rose as the women drew near, and saluted them by the words " *Labez, Labez-Salem, Labez-Alikom;*" peace, peace be with you, &c. and the women returned these salutations in similar words. They next ran to our tent, and took a couple of sticks, with the help of which, and the skin and tent cloth, they soon made an awning for the strangers. This done, they took the bundles which were on the camels, and placed them in this tent, with the saddles and all the other things the strangers had brought. The two strangers had a couple of skins that contained water, which the women hung up on a frame they carried from our tent.

During the whole time the women were thus employed, the strangers remained seated on the ground beside their guns, for they had each a double barrelled musket, and so bright that they glittered in the sun like silver. The women having finished their attentions, seated themselves near the strangers, and made inquiries, as near as I could comprehend, by saying, "where did you come from? what foods have you got? how long have you been on your journey?" &c.

Having satisfied their curiosity on these points, they next came to me, and the old woman (in whom as yet I had not discovered one spark of pity) told me that Sidi Hamet had come with blankets and blue cloth to sell; that he came from the *Sultan's* dominions, and that he could buy me and carry me there, if he chose, where I might find my friends, and kiss my wife and children.

Before my master returned I went to the tent of Sidi Hamet, with a wooden bowl, and begged for some water; showing my mouth, which was extremely parched and stiff, so much so, that I could with difficulty speak. He looked at me, and asked if I was *el Rais* (the captain.) I nodded assent. He told his brother, who was with him, to give me some water, but this his benevolent brother would not condescend to do; so taking the bowl himself, he poured into it near a quart of clear water, saying, "*Sherub Rais*;" that is, drink, captain, or chief. I drank about half of it, and after thanking him and imploring the blessing of heaven upon him for his humanity, I was going to take the rest of it to our tent, where Clark lay stretched out on his back, a perfect wreck of almost naked bones; his belly and back nearly collapsed, and breathing like a person in the last agonies of death: but Sidi Hamet would not permit me to carry the water away, bidding me drink it myself.

I pointed out to him my distressed companion; this excited his pity, and he suffered me to give Clark the remainder, The water was perfectly fresh, and revived him exceedingly; it was a cordial to his desponding soul, being the first fresh water either of us had tasted since we left the boat: his eyes, that were sunk deep in their sockets, brightened up—"This is good water (said he) and must have come from a better country than this; if we were once there, (added he,) and I could get one good drink of such water, I could die with pleasure, but now I cannot live another day."

Our masters soon returned, and began, with others of the tribe who had received the news of the arrival of strangers, to form circles and chat with them and each other: this continued till night, and I presume there were at least two hundred men present. After dark they began to separate, and by 10 o'clock at night none remained but my old master's family, and three or four of their relations, at our tent. On this occasion we were turned out into the open air, and were obliged to pass the night without any shelter or covering. It was a long and tedious night; but at the time of milking the camels, our old master coming to us, as if afraid of losing his property by our death, and anxious we should live, dealt out about a pint of milk to each: this milk tasted better than any I had yet drank; it was a sweet and seasonable relief, and saved poor Clark from dissolution.

This was the first nourishment of any kind our master had given us in three days, and I concluded from this circumstance that he had hopes of selling us to the strangers. The next morning Sidi Hamet came towards the tent, and beckoned me to come there; he was at a considerable distance, and I made the best of my way to him, where he bade me sit down on the ground. I had by this time learned many words in their language, which is ancient Arabic, and could understand the general current of their conversation, by paying strict attention to it.

He now began to question me about my country, and the manner in which I had come here. I made him understand that I was an Englishman, and that my vessel and crew were of the same nation. I found he had heard of that country, and I stated as well as I could the manner of my shipwreck—told him we were reduced to the lowest depth of misery; that I had a wife and five children in my own country, besides Horace, whom I called my eldest son, mingling with my story sighs and tears, and all the signs of affection and despair which these recollections and my present situation naturally called forth.

I found him to be a very intelligent and feeling man; for although he knew no language but the Arabic, he comprehended so well what I wished to communicate, that he actually shed tears at the recital of my distresses, notwithstanding that, among the Arabs, weeping is regarded as a womanish weakness. He seemed to be ashamed of his own want of fortitude, and said that men who had beards like him ought not to shed tears; and he retired, wiping his eyes.

Finding I had awakened his sympathy, I thought if I could rouse his interest by large offers of money, he might buy me and my companions, and carry us up from the desert—so accordingly the first time I saw him alone, I went to him, and begged him to buy me, and carry me to the *Sultan* of Morocco, or Marocksh, where I could find a friend to redeem me. He said no, but he would carry me to Swearah, describing it as a walled town and seaport. I told him I had seen the *Sultan*, and that he was a friend to my nation. He then asked me many other questions about *Mohammed Rahsool*, or holy prophet. I bowed, and pointed to the east, then towards heaven, as if I thought he ascended there. This seemed to please him, and he asked me how much money I would give him to carry me up; upon which I counted over fifty pieces of stones, signifying I would give as many dollars for myself and each of my men. "I will not buy the others," said he, "but how much more than fifty dollars will you give me for yourself, if I buy you and carry you to your friends?"

I told him one hundred dollars.

"Have you any money in Swearah" asked he by signs and words, "or do you mean to make me wait till you get it from your country?" I replied that my friend in Swearah would give him the money so soon as he brought me there.

"You are deceiving me," said he. I made the most solemn protestations of my sincerity.

"I will buy *you* then," said he, "but remember, if you deceive me, I will cut your throat," (making a motion to that effect.) This I assented to, and begged of him to buy my son Horace also; but he would not hear a word about any of my companions, as it would be impossible, he said, to get them up off the desert, which was a great distance.

"Say nothing about it to your old master," signified he to me, "nor to my brother, or any of the others." He then left me, and I went out to seek for snails to relieve my hunger.

I saw Mr. Savage and Hogan, and brought them with Clark near Sidi Hamet's tent, where we sat down on the ground. He came out to see us, miserable objects as we were, and seemed very much shocked at the sight. I told my companions I had great hopes we should be bought by this man, and carried up to the cultivated country; but they expressed great fears that they would be left behind. Sidi Hamet asked me many questions about my men—wished to know if any of them had died, and if they had wives and children. I tried all I could to interest him in their behalf, as well as my own, and mentioned to him my son, whom he had not yet seen. I found my companions had been very much stinted in milk as well as myself, and that they had no water: they had found a few snails, which kept them alive; but even these now failed.

The 24th, we journeyed on towards the N. W. all day, the whole tribe, or nearly so, in company, and the strangers also kept in company with us. When my mistress pitched her tent near night, she made up one for Sidi Hamet also. I begged of him on my knees, every time I had an opportunity, for him to buy me and my companions, and on the 25th I had the happiness to see him pay my old master for me: he gave him two blankets or coarse *haicks*, one blue cotton covering, and a bundle of ostrich feathers, with which the old man seemed much pleased, as he had now three suits of clothing. They were a long time in making the bargain.

This day Horace came with his master to fetch something to our tent: at his approach, I went to meet him, and embraced him with tears. Sidi Hamet was then fully convinced that he was my son. I had found a few snails this morning, and divided them between Mr. Savage and Horace before Sidi Hamet, who signified to me in the afternoon that he intended to set out with me in two days for Swearah; that he had tried to buy my son, but could not succeed. for his master would not sell him at any price: then said I, "let me stay in his place; I will be a faithful slave to his master as long as I live; carry *him* up to Swearah; my friend will pay you for him, and send him home to his mother, whom I cannot see unless I bring her son with me."

"You shall have your son, by *Allah*," said Sidi Hamet. The whole tribe was gathered in council, and I supposed relative to this business. In the course of the afternoon the debated the matter over, and seemed to turn it every way;—they fought, besides, three or four battles with fists and scimitars, in their warm and loud discussions in settling individual disputes; but in the evening I was told that Horace was bought, as the tribe in council had forced his master to sell him, though at a great price. I now redoubled my entreaties with my new master to buy Mr. Savage and Clark, telling him that I would give him a large sum of money if he got us up safe; but he told me he should be obliged to carry us through bands of robbers, who would kill him for our sakes, and that his company was not strong enough to resist them by force of arms—I fell down on my knees, and implored him to buy Mr. Savage and Clark, at any rate, thinking if he should buy them, he might be induced to purchase the remaining part of the crew.

My mind had been so busily employed in schemes of redemption, as almost to forget my sufferings since Sidi Hamet had bought me. He had given me two or three drinks of water, and had begged milk for me of my former master. On the morning of the 26th, I renewed my entreaties for him to purchase Mr. Savage, Clark, and Hogan—the others I had not seen since the second or third day after we were in the hands of the Arabs. I did not know where they were, and consequently could not designate them to my master Hamet, though I told him all their names. Mr. Savage and Hogan looked much more healthy and likely to live than Clark, and Sidi Hamet insisted that it was impossible that Clark could live more than three days, and that if he bought him, he should lose his money. I told him no, he should not lose his money, for whether he lived or died, I would pay him the same amount.

Clark was afflicted with the scalded head, rendered a raw sore in consequence of his sufferings, and his hair, which was very long, was, of course, in a very filthy condition: this attracted the attention of Sidi Hamet and his brother, the latter of whom was a very surly and cross looking fellow. They pushed the hair open with their sticks, and demanded to know what was the occasion of that filthy appearance. Clark assured them that it was in consequence of his exposure to the sun; and as. that was the reason I had assigned for the horrible sores and blisters that covered our scorched bodies and half-roasted flesh, they said, it might possibly be so, but asked why the heads of the rest of us were not in the same state. They next found fault with my shins, which had been a long time very sore, and they examined every bone to see if all was right in its place, with the same cautious circumspection that a jockey would use, who was about buying a horse; while we, poor trembling wretches, strove with all possible care and anxiety to hide every fault and infirmity in us, occasioned by our dreadful calamities and cruel sufferings, cheered by the hope of redemption.

Sidi Hamet informed me this day, that he had bought Mr. Savage and Clark, and had bargained for Hogan, and that he was going to kill a camel that night for provisions on our journey. Our water had been expended for two days, and all the families around us were also destitute. I did not get more than a gill of milk in twenty-four hours, and a small handful of snails—these served in a little degree to support nature, and I waited with the greatest impatience for the killing of the camel which had been promised, hoping to have a meal of meat once more before I died. Clark and I had been busy all the afternoon in gathering dry sticks to make a fire, and a little after midnight my master came to me and showed me where to carry the wood we had collected; it was in a little gulley that it might not be seen by our neighbours, whilst our former master and two present ones were leading a camel up to the same place. This camel, on its arrival, they made lie down in the usual manner: it was a very old one, and so poor, that he had not been able to keep pace with the drove during the journey, and Sidi Hamet told me he had bought him for one blanket.

The camel being down, they put a rope round his under jaw, with a noose in it; then hauling his head round on the left side, made the rope fast to his tail, close up to his body; his neck was so long, that the under jaw reached within six inches of the tail: they then brought a copper kettle that would contain probably three gallons. Thus prepared, Sidi Hamet cut open a vein on the right side of the camel's neck, close to his breast; the blood streamed out into the kettle, and soon filled it half full; this they set over the fire and boiled, stirring it all the time with a stick, until it became thick, and of the consistence of a beef's liver; then taking it off the fire, they passed it to me, saying, "*coole*, Riley," (eat Riley.) I did not wait for a second bidding, but fell to, together with Clark: our appetites were voracious, and we soon filled our stomachs with this, to us, delicious food.

Notwithstanding the lateness of the hour, and the privacy observed in killing this meagre camel, many of our hungry neighbours had found it out, and came to assist in the dressing and eating of the animal. They insisted on having some of the blood, and would snatch out a handful in spite of all our masters could do to hinder them; they were then very officious in assisting to take off the hide, which was soon done, and the entrails were rolled out; they next proceeded to put all the small entrails into the kettle, without cleaning them of their contents, together with what remained of the liver and lights; but they had no water to boil them in. Then one of them went to the camel's paunch, which was very large, and cutting a slit in the top of it, dipped out some of the filthy water in a bowl: this they poured into the kettle, and set it a boiling, stirring it round, and now and then taking out a piece, and biting off an end, to ascertain whether it was cooked enough.

During this time, half a dozen hungry wretches were at work on the camel, which they would not leave under pretence of friendship for our masters, for they would not suffer strangers to work, when in their company, and it being dark, they managed to steal and convey away, before morning, more than one half or the camel's bones and meat, with half his skin. Our masters were as hungry as any of the Arabs, yet though they had bought the camel, they could scarcely get a bite of the intestines without fighting for it; for what title or argument can prevail against the ravenous appetite of a half-starved man? Though our masters saw the natives in the very act of stealing and carrying off their meat, they could not prevent them, fearing worse consequences than losing it; it being a standing maxim among the Arabs to feed the hungry if in their power, and give them drink, even if the owner of the provisions be obliged to rob himself and his own family to do it.

Notwithstanding the boiled blood we had eaten was perfectly fresh, yet our thirst seemed to increase in consequence of it. As soon as daylight appeared, a boy of from fourteen to sixteen years old came running up to the camel's paunch, and thrusting his head into it up to his shoulders, began to drink of its contents; my master observing him, and seeing that my mouth was very dry, made signs for me to go and pull the boy away, and drink myself; this I soon did, putting my head in like manner into the paunch; the liquid was very thick, but though its taste was exceedingly strong, yet it was not salt, and allayed my thirst: Clark next took a drink of the same fluid.

This morning we were busied in cutting off the little flesh that remained on the bones of our camel, spreading it out to dry, and roasting the bones on the fire for our masters, who cracked them between two stones, and then sucked out the marrow and juices. Near noon, Horace was brought where I was; he was very hungry and thirsty, and said he had not ate anything of consequence for the last three days. Our common master said to me, "this is your son *Rais*," and seemed extremely glad that he had been able to purchase him, giving him some of the entrails and meat he had boiled and saved for the purpose. I in my turn gave him some of our thick camel's water, which he found to be delicious; so true it is, that hunger and thirst give a zest to everything. Burns was brought up soon after, and my master asked me if he was one of my men; I told him he was: "his master wants to sell him," said Sidi Hamet, "but he is old and good for nothing," added he; "yet I can buy him for this blanket," showing me a very poor old one.

I said, "buy him, he is my countryman, I will repay you as much for him as for the others:" so he went out, and bought him from his master, and then gave him something to eat. Poor Burns was much rejoiced to find there was a prospect of recovering his liberty, or at least of getting where he might procure something to eat and drink. During this day, the natives flocked round in great numbers, men, women, and children, and what with begging and stealing reduced our stock of meat to less than fifteen pounds before night.

Sidi Hamet now told me that he had bought Hogan: this was in the afternoon, and he came to us. I congratulated him on our favourable prospects, and our master gave him something to eat; but his former master, Hamet, now demanded one blanket more for him than had been agreed on, as he was a stout fellow: my master would not be imposed upon, nor had he indeed a blanket left. I begged very hard for poor Hogan, but it was to no purpose, and his old master drove him off, laying on his back with a stick most unmercifully Hamet's eyes seemed fairly to flash fire as he went from us. Hogan's hopes had been raised to a high pitch—they were now blasted, and he driven back like a criminal before his brutal owner, to his former miserable abode.

He informed me that he had never as yet, since our captivity, known what it was to sleep under the cover of a tent; that his allowance of milk had been so scant, that he did not doubt but he must have died with hunger in a day or two: he was extremely wasted and sore on every side. My heart bled for him when I saw the blows fall on his emaciated and mangled frame; but I could not assist him, and all I could do was to turn round and hide my face, so as not to witness his further tortures.

This day was employed in preparing for our departure: our masters made me a pair of sandals with two thicknesses of the camel's skin; they also made Horace a pair in the same manner; but Clark and Burns were fitted with single ones. They had in the morning given me a small knife, which I hung to my neck in a case: this they meant as a mark of confidence; and they also gave me charge of their stuff, the camels, and the slaves. I soon perceived, however, that although I had this kind of command, yet I was obliged to do all the work. My men were so far exhausted, that even the hope of soon obtaining their liberty, could scarcely animate them to the least exertion.

In the evening Sidi Hamet told me *Aaron* (Mr. Savage) would be with us by and by:—that we should start in the morning for Swearah,—and that he hoped, through the blessing of God, I should once more embrace my family: he then told me how much he had paid for each one of us—that he had expended all his property, and that if I had not told him the truth, he was a ruined man—that his brother was a bad man, and had done all he could to prevent his buying us, but that he had at last consented to it, and taken a share.

He next made me repeat, before his brother, my promises to him when we should arrive at Swearah, and my agreement to have my throat cut if my words did not prove true. Late in the evening Mr. Savage joined us: he knew before that I was going to set out, and thought he should be left behind: he was very thankful to be undeceived in this particular, and to get at the same time, something to eat; for Sidi Hamet had saved some of the camel's intestines, which he immediately gave him.

After having satisfied his hunger in some measure, he began to express his doubts as to where we were going; declaring, that he did not believe a word these wretches said;—he could not understand them, and said he did not believe I could; and suggested a hundred doubts and difficulties on the subject, that his ill-boding imagination supplied him with. He did not like the price I had agreed to give for our liberty,—it was too much, and I should find nobody willing to advance it for me, as I was poor.

We had started what water remained in the paunch of the camel, thick as it was, into a goat skin, straining it through our fingers to keep out the thickest of the filth. The night of the 27th, as near as we could keep count by marking the day of the month on our legs with a thorn, we passed in the open air, five of us together.

At daylight on the morning of the 28th, we were called up and made to load our camels. I had strong hopes we were going to ride, but it now appeared not to be the case. All the Arabs in the valley set out in the morning with their camels, to drive them to water: they had not been watered since the 10th, having gone without any for eighteen days. They were now at least two days' journey from the well where we had first been seized, towards which they then steered in a N. W. direction. I mention this circumstance, to show the time these wonderful animals can live without drink, and supply their masters with milk, even when nearly destitute of vegetable substances; and with water from their paunches after death.

Soon after sunrise, our masters bade us drive the camels up the bank: at this moment Archibald Robbins came with his master to see us, and I supposed his master had brought him with the view of selling him. I had not before seen him for fourteen days, and he had only arrived soon enough to witness our departure: I now on my knees begged, as I had done before of Sidi Hamet, to purchase him; but he said he could not, and so hurried us on.

I told Robbins what my present hopes were, and that if I should succeed in getting clear, I would use my utmost endeavours to procure his and the rest of the crew's redemption. I begged him to continue as long as he could with his present master, who, for an Arab, appeared to be a very good man; and to encourage Mr. Williams and all the others to bear up with fortitude, and support life as long as it was possible, in the hope, that through my help or some other means, they might obtain their redemption in a short time; and having taken my leave of him in the most affectionate manner, (in which my companions followed the example,) we set out on our journey, but with heavy hearts, occasioned by the bitter regret we felt at leaving our fellow sufferers behind, although I had done all in my power to make them partakers of our better fortune.

Chapter 10

Their Sufferings

From, the time I was sold to Sidi Hamet, my old master and his family shunned me as they would a pestilence; and the old villain actually stole one piece of our meat from me, or rather robbed me of it, just as we were setting out; for he cut it off the string by which it was tied to the camel, in spite of my efforts to prevent him. Our masters were accompanied for a considerable distance by several men and women, who were talking and taking leave, going on very slowly. We were ordered to keep their camels together, which I thought I did; yet when they were finally ready to depart, they found their big camel had marched off a great distance, probably two miles from us, following a drove of camels going to the N. W.; Sidi Hamet bade me fetch him back, pointing him out: notwithstanding my weak and exhausted state, I was obliged to run a great way to come up with him; but my rising spirits supported me, and I succeeded in bringing him back, where the other camels were collected by my shipmates.

Sidi Hamet and Seid had two old camels on which they had rode, and they had bought also a young one that had not been broke for riding. We were joined here by a young Arab named Abdallah; he had been Mr. Savage's master, and owned a camel and a couple of goat skins to carry water in; but these, as well as those of our masters, were entirely empty. Sidi Hamet had a kind of a pack saddle for each of his old camels; but nothing to cover the bones, of his young one. Having fitted them as well as he could, (for he seemed to be humane,) he placed Mr. Savage, Burns, and Horace on the big one, and myself and Clark on the other old one. Seid and Abdallah took their seats on the one which belonged to Abdallah, and Sidi Hamet mounted the young one himself to break him, sitting behind the hump on his bare back; and thus arranged and equipped, we set off on a full and long striding trot. It was about nine a. m. when we had mounted; and this trot had continued for about three hours, when we stopped a few minutes in a little valley to adjust our saddles.

Here Sidi Hamet pulled out a check shirt from one of his bags and gave it me, declaring he had stolen it, and had tried to get another for Horace, but had not been able: "put it on," said he, "your poor back needs a covering;" (it being then one entire sore.) I kissed his hand in gratitude, and thanked him and my Heavenly Father for this mercy. Clark, a day or two before, had got a piece of an old sail, that partly covered him; Burns had an old jacket, and Horace and Mr. Savage, a small goat skin added to their dress—so that we were all, comparatively, comfortably clad. We did not stop here long, but mounted again, and proceeded on our course to the eastward on a full trot, which was continued till night; when coming to a little valley, we found some thorn bushes and halted for the night.

Here we kindled a fire, and our masters gave us a few mouthfuls of the camel's meat, which we roasted and ate. As we had drank no water for the last three days, except a very little of what we had taken from the camel's paunch, and which was now reduced to about four quarts, we, as well as our masters, suffered exceedingly for the want of it, and it was thereupon determined to make an equal distribution of it among the whole party; which was accordingly done with an impartial hand. This we poor sufferers made out to swallow, foul and ropy as it was, and it considerably relieved our parched throats; and then, finding a good shelter under a thorn bush, notwithstanding our unabated pains, we got a tolerable night's sleep. We had travelled this day steady at a long trot, at the rate, I judged, of between seven and eight miles an hour: making a distance of sixty-three miles at the lowest computation.

Before daylight on the morning of the 28th, we were called up and mounted on the camels as before, and we set off on the long trot, on the same course, *i. e.* about east, as on the preceding day. The same smooth hard surface continued, with now and then a little break, occasioned by the naked heads of rocks just rising above the plane, and forming in some places small ledges. Near one of these, we alighted a few minutes about noon, for our masters to perform their devotions; and we allayed our thirst by drinking some of the camels' urine, which we caught in our hands: our masters did the same, and told me it was good for our stomachs. The camels took very long steps, and their motions being heavy, our legs, unsupported by stirrups or anything else, would fly backwards and forwards, chafing across their hard ribs at every step; nor was it possible for us to prevent it, so that the remaining flesh on our posteriors, and inside of our thighs and legs, was so beat, and literally pounded to pieces, that scarcely any remained on our bones; which felt as if they had been thrown out of their sockets, by the continual and sudden jerks they experienced during this longest of days.

It seemed to me as though the sun would never go down, and when at last it did, our masters had not yet found a place to lodge in; for they wished, if possible, to find a spot where a few shrubs were growing, in order that the camels might browse a little during the night. They stopped at last after dark, in a very small valley, for they could find no better place; here they kindled a little fire, and gave us about a pound of meat between us, which we greedily devoured, and then allayed our thirst in a similar manner as before mentioned.

We had started before daylight this morning, and had made but one stop of about fifteen minutes in the course of the whole day until dark night, having travelled at least fifteen hours, and at the rate of seven miles the hour, making one hundred and five miles. Here in our bare-bone and mangled state, we were forced to lie on the naked ground, without the smallest shelter from the wind, which blew a violent gale all night from the north—suffering in addition to the cold, the cravings of hunger and thirst, and the most excruciating pains in our limbs and numerous sores; nor could either of us close our eyes to sleep; and I cannot imagine that the tortures of the rack can exceed those we then experienced. Sidi Hamet and his two companions, who had been accustomed to ride in this manner, thought nothing of it: nor did they even appear to be fatigued; but when I showed him my sores in the morning, and the situation of my shipmates, he was much distressed, and feared we would not live. He told me we should come to good water soon, when we might drink as much as we wanted of it, and after that we would not travel so fast.

We were placed on our camels soon after daylight, (this was the 29th,) having nothing to eat, and drinking a little camel's water, which we preferred to our own: its taste, as I before observed, though bitter, was not salt; and they void it but seldom in this dry and thirsty country. Proceeding on our journey at a long trot, about nine o'clock in the morning, we discovered before us what seemed like high land, as we were seated on the camels; but on our approach, it proved to be the opposite bank of what appeared once to have been a river or arm of the sea, though its bed was now dry. At about 10 o'clock, we came to the bank nearest us; it was very steep, and four or five hundred feet deep, and in most places perpendicular or overhanging. These banks must have been washed, at some former period, either by the sea or a river; which river, if it was one, does not now exist.

After considerable search, our masters found a place where our camels could descend into it, and having first dismounted, and made us do the same, we drove them down. When we had descended the most difficult part of the bank, Seid and Abdallah went forward (with their guns) to search for a spring of fresh water, which Sidi Hamet told me was not very far distant. He now made me walk along with him, and let the others drive on the camels slowly after us; for they, as well as ourselves, were nearly exhausted. He then asked me a great many questions respecting my country, myself, and family; and whether I had any property at home; if I had been at Swearah, and if I told him the truth concerning my having a friend there who would pay money for me? He said also, that both himself and his brother had parted with all their property to purchase us, and wished me to be candid with him, for he was "my friend."

"God (said he) will deal with you, as you deal with me."

I persisted in asserting that I had a friend at Swearah, who would advance any sum of money I needed, and answered his other questions as well as I was able; evading some I did not choose to answer, pretending I did not understand them.

"Will you buy Clark and Burns? (said he,) they are good for nothing."

They certainly did look worse, if possible, than the rest of us. I told him they were my countrymen, and my brothers, and that he might depend upon it I would ransom them, it he would carry us to the empire of Morocco and to the *Sultan*.

"No, (said he,) the *Sultan* will not pay for you, but I will carry you to Swearah to your friend: what is his name?"

"Consul," said I.

It seemed to please him to hear me name my friend so readily; and after teaching me to count in Arabic, and by my fingers up to twenty, (which was *ashreen*,) he told me I must give him two hundred dollars for myself, two hundred dollars for Horace, and for the others I must pay one hundred dollars each—showing me seven dollars he had about him, to be certain that we understood each other perfectly; and he next made me understand that I must pay for our provisions on the road, over and above this sum. He then made me point out the way to Swearah, which I was enabled to do by the sun and trade wind, making it about N. E.

"Now, (said he,) if you will agree before God the most High, to pay what I have stated, in money, and give me a double-barrelled gun, I will take you up to Swearah; if not, I will carry you off that way," pointing to the S. E. "and sell you for as much as I can get, sooner than carry you up across this long desert, where we must risk our lives every day for your sakes; and if you cannot comply with your agreement and we get there safe, we must cut your throat and sell your comrades for what they will bring."

I assured him that I had told him the truth, and called God to witness the sincerity of my intentions, not in the least doubting if I could once arrive there, I should find someone able and willing to pay the sum they demanded. "You shall go to Swearah, (said he, taking me by the hand,) if God please."

He then showed me the broken pieces of my watch, and a plated candlestick, which he said he had bought from some person who had come from the wreck of my vessel. The candlestick had belonged to Mr. Williams. He said he bought the articles before he saw me, and wished to know what they were worth in Swearah; I satisfied him as well as I could on this point. During this conversation we kept walking on about east, as the bed of the river ran near the northern bank, which was very high, and Sidi Hamet looked at me as if his eye would pierce my very soul, to ascertain the secrets of my heart, and discover whether I was deceiving him or not; and he became satisfied that I was sincere. By this time we had arrived nearly opposite the place where he calculated the spring was. and his brother and Abdallah being not far off, he hailed them to know if they had found it; to which they answered in the negative.

After searching about an hour in the bank, he discovered it, and calling to me, for I was below, bade me come up to where he was, at the foot of a perpendicular cliff. I clambered up over the fragments of great rocks that had fallen down from above, as fast as my strength would permit, and having reached the spot, and seeing no signs of water, the tears flowed fast down my cheeks, for I concluded the spring was dried up, and that we must now inevitably perish.

Sidi Hamet looked at me, and saw my tears of despair—"Look down there," said he, (pointing through a fissure in the rock.) I looked and saw water, but the cleft was too narrow to admit of a passage to it: then showing me another place, about ten or fifteen yards distant, where I could get down to another small spring—"Sherub Riley, (said he,) it is sweet."

I soon reached it, and found it sweet indeed; and taking a copious draught, I called my companions, who scrambled along on their way up, exclaiming with great eagerness, "Where is the water? for God's sake! where is it? Oh, is it sweet?" I showed it to them, and they were soon convinced of the joyful fact. This water was as clear and as sweet as any I had ever tasted.

Sidi Hamet now allowed us to drink our fill, while Seid and Abdallah were driving the four camels up the bank by a zigzag kind of d foot way, from which the stones and other impediments had been before removed, apparently with great trouble and labour. This spring, the most singular perhaps in nature, was covered with large rocks, fifteen to twenty feet high, only leaving a narrow crooked passage next the high bank behind it, by which a common sized man might descend to get at it. It might contain, I should calculate, not more than fifty gallons of water; cool, clear, fresh, and sweet, and I presume it communicated with the one that was first shown me between the rocks, which was much smaller. The camels had been driven to within fifty yards below the spring; our masters then took off the large bowl which they carried for the purpose of watering the camels: then bringing a goatskin near the spring, made me fill it with the water, my three shipmates passing it up to me in the bowl. I kept admonishing my companions to drink with moderation, but at the same time I myself continued to take in large draughts of this delicious water, without knowing when to stop; in consequence of which I was seized with violent pains in my bowels, but soon found relief.

It was here that I had an opportunity of ascertaining the quantity of water which a camel could drink at one draught. We filled a large goat skin fifteen times, containing at least four gallons, and every drop of this water was swallowed down by our largest camel, amounting to the enormous quantity of sixty gallons, or two barrels. The men kept crying out, "*Has not that camel done yet? he alone will drink the spring dry*." It was in effect drained very low; but still held out, as the water kept continually running in, though slowly. This camel was a very large and old one, about nine feet high, stout in proportion, and had not drank any water for twenty days, as I was informed by Sidi Hamet: but the other camels did not drink as much in proportion.

Having finished watering them, we filled two goatskins with the water, which had now become thick and whitish; as the rock in which the basin was formed for holding it, appeared to be chalky, soft, and yielding. We descended this bank, and after preparing the camels, we were mounted thereon, and proceeded as before, but along to the eastward, in this arm of the sea. I call it an arm of the sea, because there could be no doubt in the mind of anyone who should view it, that these high banks were worn and washed by water; they were from six to eight or ten miles distant from each other, and the level bottom was incrusted with marine salt.

The bank rises four or five hundred feet, and nearly perpendicular, in most places. The broken fragments of rock, gravel, and sand, that had been undermined by the water, and tumbled down, filled a considerable space near the cliffs, and did not appear to have been washed by the water for a great number of years. I could not account for the incrustation of salt (as we must have been at least three hundred miles from the sea; this bottom or bed running from the east northwardly to the west or S.W.) in any other way, than by supposing the sea water had once overflowed this level; that it had since either retired from that part of the coast, or formed a bar across its mouth, or outlet, and thus excluded itself entirely; and that the sea air combining with the saline deposit or sediment, continued this incrustation.

The curious and interesting springs, before mentioned, are situated on the right or north side of this dry bay or river, about one hundred feet below the surface of the desert, and from three hundred and fifty to four hundred feet from the bed or bottom. There was not the smallest sign of their ever having overflowed their basins; thereby leaving it a mystery how they ever should have been discovered, as there was no rill to serve as a clue.

Our masters now hurried on to the eastward, to find a place to emerge from this dreary abyss, still more gloomy, if possible, than the face of the desert. As we passed along, the salt crust crumbled under the feet of our camels, like the thin crust of snow. We came at length to a spot in the bank at a kind of point, where we ascended gradually from one point to another until within, probably, two hundred feet of the top; here we were obliged to dismount, and drive, coax, and encourage the camels to go up. The ascent was very steep, though in zigzag directions, and the flat rock over which the camels were forced to climb, threw them down several times, when our masters would encourage them to get up again, by singing and making repeated trials; helping them over the bad places by a partial lifting, and begging the assistance of God and his prophet most fervently, as well as of all the saints.

Having at length reached the surface of the desert, they stopped a few minutes to let the camels breathe, and also that we might come up, for Mr. Savage and Clark could not keep pace with the rest of us, on account of their severe pains inconsequence of overcharging their stomachs with water. The desert here had the same smooth appearance we had before observed: no rising of the ground, nor any rock, tree, or shrub, to arrest the view within the horizon—all was a dreary, solitary waste, and we could not but admire and wonder at the goodness of Providence in providing a reservoir of pure fresh water, to quench the thirst of the traveller and his camel, in this dry, salt, and torrid region, and we felt an inexpressible gratitude to the Author of our being, for having directed our masters to this spot, where our lives had been preserved and refreshed by the cool delicious spring, which seemed to be kept there by a continual miracle.

We had not gone more than eight miles from the bank, (in a N.W. direction,) before we stopped for the night: here we found no lee to screen us from the strong winds, nor bush for the camels to browse on. I reckon we had travelled five hours this morning, at the rate of seven miles an hour, before reaching the bank, and five miles after getting down it, before we came to the spring; making it forty miles to, and ten miles from the spring to where we halted for the night, so that this day's march was altogether at least fifty miles.

The dry bed or bottom before mentioned, had probably been an inlet or arm of the sea that never was explored by Europeans, or any other civilized men; yet it must have had an outlet; and that outlet must be to the southward of us, and if so, its mouth must have been at least three hundred miles distant.

Here we ate the remainder of our camel's meat:—we had no milk; for neither of our masters' camels yielded any, and our share of meat was not more than about an ounce each.

I judged by the height of the north star above the horizon that we were about in the latitude of twenty degrees north. I now experienced that to have only one want supplied, made us feel the others as less supportable than before; for although we had drank as much fresh water as we could contain, and our thirst was in a great measure allayed, still we were rendered extremely uneasy by the gnawings of hunger, which, together with our sufferings from the cold and piercing winds, made this a long and restless night.

CHAPTER 11

Hospitably Entertained by Arabs

On the morning of the 30th we started very early; three of us rode, while the other two walked; taking our turns every three hours, or thereabouts. They let the camels walk all this day, but their long legs, and the refreshment they had enjoyed at the spring, enabled them to step along so fast and briskly, that those of us who were on foot, were obliged to be on a continual small trot in order to keep up with them: the wind at the same time blowing very strong directly against us, and our course being nearly N.W.

About two o'clock, p. m. Sidi Hamet said to me, "Riley, *shift Gemel;*" (I see a camel;) he was very much rejoiced at it, and so were his companions; but neither I nor my companions could perceive anything of the kind above the horizon for two hours after this. Our masters had altered their course to about east, and at length we all saw a camel, appearing like a speck in the horizon, but we did not reach the travellers, who were with a large drove of camels, until sunset. Having; come up with the men, they invited our masters to go home with them; the invitation was accepted, and we drove our camels along, following them as they went towards their tents:—it was dark and quite late before we reached them, which were four in number.

We stopped at a small distance from the tents, and were obliged to pluck up a few scattered shrubs, not thicker than a straw, to make a fire with. Our masters had given us neither meat nor drink this day. I begged for some water, and they gave us each a very scanty drink. We had travelled full fourteen hours this day, and at the rate of about three miles an hour, making a distance of about forty miles. We were now in a most piteous situation, extremely chafed and worn down with our various and complicated sufferings, and were now to lie on the hard ground without the smallest screen—not even a spot of sand on which to rest our wearied limbs; we had been promised, however, something to eat by our host, and about 11 o'clock at night Sidi Hamet called me and gave me a bowl containing some boiled meat, which I divided into five heaps, and we cast lots for them. This meat was very tender, and there was just enough of it to fill our stomachs: after eating this, we had scarcely lain down when they brought us a large bowl filled with milk and water. This was indeed sumptuous living, notwithstanding our pains and the severely cold night wind.

On the morning of the first of October we were roused up early to pursue our journey. Sidi Hamet then called me aside, and gave me to understand that this man had got my spy-glass, and wanted to know what it was worth. I requested him to show it to me, which he did: it was a new one I had bought in Gibraltar, and it had not been injured. The Arab owner, though he did not know the use of it, yet as the brass on it glittered, he thought it was worth a vast sum of money. Sidi Hamet had only seven dollars in money, having invested the rest of his property in the purchasing of us, and was not able to buy the glass;—his fancy was as much taken with it, however, as was that of the owner. They had also several articles of clothing in their possession, which gave me reason to infer that we could not be a great distance from the place where our vessel was wrecked; but there was no method of calculating to any degree of certainty, as they all move with such rapidity in their excursions, that they seem not to know whither, or what distances they go, nor could I find out anything from this man concerning the wreck. Taking our leave from this truly hospitable man, we pursued our course N. W. on the level desert.

Our masters had been very uneasy all the preceding day, on account of meeting with no landmarks to direct their course: they were in the same dilemma this day, directing their camels by the winds and bearing of the sun; frequently stopping and smelling the sand, whenever they came to a small sandy spot, which now and then occurred, but we did not come across any loose drifting sand. We took turns in riding and walking, or rather trotting, as we had done the day before, until the afternoon, when our masters walked, (or rather ran,) and permitted us to ride.

About four o'clock p. m. we saw, and soon fell in with a drove of camels, that had been to the northward for water, and were then going in a S W. direction with skins full of water, and buckets for drawing and watering the camels: their owners very civilly invited our masters to take up their lodgings with them that night, and we went in company with them about two hours to the south, where falling in with a very extensive but shallow valley, we saw about fifty tents pitched, and going into the largest clear place, unloaded and fettered our camels, to let them browse on the leaves and twigs of the small shrubs that grew there, or on the little low moss, with which the ground was, in many places, covered. As we went along near the tents, the men and women called me *el Rais*, and soon gathered around with their children to look at us, and to wonder. Some inquired about my country, my vessel, my family, &c.

Having satisfied their curiosity, they left us to gather sticks to kindle our masters' fire; this done, we found, after considerable search, a soft spot of sand to lie down upon, where we slept soundly until about midnight, when we were aroused, and each of us presented with a good drink of milk: this refreshed us, and we slept the remainder of the night, forgetting our sores and our pains. I reckon we had travelled this last day about forty miles, on a course of about N.W.

On the 2nd of October we set out, in company with all these families, and went north fifteen or twenty miles, when they pitched their tents, and made up a kind of a shelter for our masters with two pieces of tent cloth joined together by thorns, and supported by some sticks. Our masters gave us a good drink of water about noon, and at midnight milk was brought from all quarters, and each of us had as much as he could swallow, and actually swallowed more than our poor stomachs could retain.

The tribe did not move, as is customary, on the 2nd of October, waiting, as Sidi Hamet said, for the purpose of feasting us. They gave us as much milk as we could drink on the night of the second. Here our masters bought a sheep, of which animals this tribe had about fifty, and they were the first we had seen; but they were so poor, that they could with difficulty stand and feed upon the brown moss which covered part of the face of the valleys hereabouts, and which moss was not more than one inch high. This tribe, not unlike all the others we had seen, took no nourishment, except one good drink of milk at midnight, and a drink of sour milk and water at mid-day, when they could get it.

On the morning of the 3rd of October, our masters took leave of this hospitable tribe of Arabs, who not only fed *them*, but seemed desirous that *we, their slaves*, should have sufficient nourishment also, and gave us liberally of the best they had. Our masters had made a trade with them, and exchanged our youngest camel for an old one that was lame in his right forefoot, and one that was not more than half grown. The old one they called *Coho*, (or the lame,) and the young one *Goyette*, (or the little child.) The sheep our masters purchased was tied about the neck with a rope, and I was obliged to lead it until about noon, when we came to a low valley, with some small bushes in it: in the midst there was a well of tolerable good water. Here we watered the camels, and as the sheep could go no farther, they killed it, and put its lean carcass on a camel, after placing its entrails (which they would not allow me time to cleanse) into the carcass. This well was about forty feet deep, and dug out among the surrounding roots.

CHAPTER 12

Further Extreme Sufferings

Having watered our camels, and filled two skins with water, and drank as much as we needed, they mounted Horace on the young camel, and all the others being also mounted, we proceeded on towards the N.W. at a long walk, and sometimes a trot, driving the old lame camel before us until dark night, and I think we travelled thirty-five miles this day. The entrails of the sheep were now given us for our supper; these we roasted on a fire we made for the purpose, and ate them, while our masters finished two of the quarters.

We lay this night without any screen or shelter, and early in the morning of the 4th, we set off on our journey, all on foot, driving our camels before us, on the same kind of flat surface we had hitherto travelled over: but about 10 a. m. it began to assume a new aspect, and become sandy. The sand where we first entered it, lay in small loose heaps, through which it was very difficult to walk, as we sank in nearly to our knees at each step: this sand was scorching hot. The camels were now stopped, and all of us mounted on them, when on their rising up, we saw before us vast numbers of immense sand-hills, stretching as far as the eye could reach eastward, and from the north to the south, heaped up in a most terrific manner; we soon arrived among them, and were struck with horror at the sight:—huge mountains of loose sand, piled up like drifted snow, towered two hundred feet above our heads on every side, and seemed to threaten destruction to our whole party: not a green or even a dry bush or shrub of any kind in view to relieve the eye; here was no path to guide our footsteps, nor had we a compass to direct our course, obstructed by these dreadful barriers.

The trade winds, which had hitherto given us so much relief on our journey, by refreshing our bodies when heated by the rays of an almost perpendicular sun, and which had served, in some measure, to direct our course—even these winds, which now blew like a tempest, became our formidable enemy:—the loose sand flew before its blasts, cutting our flesh like hail stones, and very often covering us from each other's sight, while the gusts (which followed each other in quick succession) were rushing by.

We were here obliged to dismount, and drive the camels up the sandy steeps after our masters, who went on before to look out a practicable passage. The camels, as well as ourselves, trod deep in the sand, and with great difficulty ascended the hills; but they went down them very easily, and frequently on a long trot, following our masters. Sidi Hamet, Seid, and Abdallah, seemed full of apprehensions for their own and our safety, and were very careful of their camels.

Thus we drove on until dark, when coming to a space where the sand was not so much heaped up, being like a lake surrounded by mountains, we saw a few shrubs: here we stopped for the night, unloaded and fettered our camels, whose appetites were as keen, apparently, as ours, for they devoured the few leaves, together with the shrubs, which were as thick as a man's finger. We next prepared a kind of shelter with the saddles and some sand for our masters and ourselves, to keep off in some measure the fierce and chilling blasts of wind, and the driving sand which pierced our sores and caused us much pain. Having kindled a fire, our masters divided the meat that remained of the sheep:—It was sweet to our taste, though but a morsel, and we pounded, chewed, and swallowed all the bones, and afterwards got a drink of water:—then lying down on the sand, we had a comfortable night's sleep, considering our situation. I reckon we had made thirty-five miles this day, having travelled about eight hours before we got among the heavy sand-hills, at the rate of three miles an hour, and five hours among the sand-hills, at the rate of two miles an hour. We were all afflicted with a most violent diarrhoea, brought on, no doubt, by excessive drinking and fatigue.

At daylight on the morning of the 5th, I was ordered to fetch the camels, and took Mr. Savage and Clark with me; and the two old ones being fettered, that is, their two forelegs being tied within twelve inches of each other, they could not wander far; we soon found them, and I made the one I found kneel down, and having taken off its fetters, mounted it with a good stick in my hand for its government, as the Arabs of the desert use neither bridle nor halter, but guide and drive them altogether with a stick, and by words. Mr. Savage having found the big camel, took off his fetters, intending to make him kneel down in order to get on his back; but the old lame camel, which had hitherto carried no load, and which had occasioned us much trouble, in forcing him to keep up with the others, when on our march, now set off on a great trot to the south:—the young one followed his example, so did Abdallah's, and the big one started also, running at their greatest speed.

Seeing the panic of the other camels, I endeavoured to stop them by riding before them with my camel, which was the most active and fleet; but they would not stop—dodging me every way; my camel also tried to get rid of its load by running, jumping, lying down, rolling over, and striving to bite my legs; but I made shift to get on again before he could rise, and had got some miles from where I had started, keeping near, and frequently before the other camels, which appeared to be very much frightened. Our masters had watched us, and when the camels set off, had started on a full run after them; but had been hid from my view by the numerous sand-hills, over and among which we passed.—Finding I could not stop the others, and fearing I should be lost myself, I stopped the one I was on, and Sidi Harriet soon coming in sight, called to me to make my camel lie down. He mounted it, and after inquiring which way the other camels went, (which were now out of sight.) and telling me to follow his tracks back to our stuff, he set off after them on full speed:—Seid and Abdallah followed him on foot, running as fast as possible. I returned; and picking up a few skins that had jolted off from the little camel, I joined Mr. Savage and Clark, and we reached the place where we had slept, but much fatigued; and here we remained for two or three hours before our masters returned with the camels.

We had during this interval tasted the bark of the roots of the shrubs which grew on the sand near us—it was bitter, but not ill flavoured, and we continued to eat of it until the runaway camels were brought back; it entirely cured our diarrhoea. They had overtaken the camels with much difficulty, and the creatures were covered with sweat and sand. I expected we should receive a flogging as an atonement for our carelessness in letting the big camel go, that had been fettered, and in particular, that Mr. Savage would be punished, whom I did not doubt they had seen, when he let his camel escape.

So as soon as they got nigh, I began to plead for him; but it was all to no purpose, for they whipped him with a thick stick (or *goad*) most unmercifully. Mr. Savage did not beg as I should have done in our situation, and in a similar case, and they believed he had done it expressly to give them trouble, and continued to call him *Fonte,* (*i. e.* a bad fellow,) all the remaining part of the journey. Having settled this affair, and put what stuff they had on the camels, we mounted them and proceeded,—shaping our course as before, to the N.N.W. as near as the mountains of sand would permit. It was as late as nine o'clock when we started, and at eleven, having made about three leagues, winding round the sand-hills on a trot, we were obliged to dismount.

The hills now stood so thick, that great care was necessary to prevent getting the camels into an inextricable situation between them, and our masters went on ahead, two of them at a considerable distance, to pick the way, and one to direct us how to go:—the latter keeping all the time in sight. The sand was heated (as it had been the preceding day) by the rays of the sun, to such a degree that it burned our feet and legs, so that the smart was more severe than the pain we had before experienced, from our blisters and chafing:—-it was like wading through glowing embers.

During the whole of this day, we had looked for shrubs, or some green thing to relieve the eye; but not a speck of verdure was to be seen. We had no food; our water was nearly exhausted, and we saw no sign of finding an end to these horrid heaps of drifting sands, or of procuring anything to relieve our fatigues and sufferings, which were now really intolerable. We continued on our route, however, as near as circumstances would permit, N. N.W. until about nine o'clock in the evening, and stopped to rest among the high and dreary sand heaps, without a shrub for our camels to eat. I calculated we had gone this day from 9 to 11 o'clock, twelve miles, and from that time till we stopped, about two miles an hour, making in all thirty-two miles. We had nothing to eat; our masters, however, gave us a drink of water, and being fatigued beyond description, we soon sank down and fell asleep, I happened to awake in the night, and hearing a heavy roaring to the northward of us, concluded it must be a violent gust of wind, or a hurricane, that would soon bury us in the sand forever.

I therefore immediately awakened my companions, who were more terrified at the noise even than myself, for a few moments; but when we perceived that the sound came no nearer, I was convinced (as the wind did not increase) that it must be the roaring of the sea against the coast not far off. This was the first time we had heard the sea roar since the 10th of September; and it proved to us that our masters were going towards the empire of Morocco, as they had promised. My comrades were much rejoiced at being undeceived on that subject, for they had all along continued to suspect the contrary, notwithstanding I had constantly told them that the courses we steered could not fail of bringing us to the coast.

On the sixth, early in the morning, we started, and I found, by inquiring of Sidi Hamet, that our conjectures were true; that we were near the sea, and that the roaring we heard (and which still continued) was that of the surf: he added, "you will get no more milk," which I thought he regretted very much. We continued on our course, labouring among the sand-hills until noon, when we found, that on our right, and ahead, they became less frequent, but on our left there was a string of them, and very high ones, stretching out as far as the eye could reach. The sand-hills through which we had passed rested on the same hard and flat surface I have before mentioned, without being attached to it; for in many places it was blown off, leaving naked the rocks and baked soil between the towering drifts.

About noon we left these high sands, and mounting on the camels, proceeded along southward of them, where the sand was still deep, but not high, on about an east course. Near this line of sand-hills, our masters discovered two camels—they bore about N. E. and we made directly for them as fast as possible. On a near approach we observed they were loaded, and our masters now took off the sheaths from their guns and primed them anew; and upon coming near the camels, they dismounted and made us do the same. We saw no human being.

The camels had large sacks on their backs, made of tent cloth, and well filled with something; there was also a large earthen pot lashed on one of them, and two or three small skin bags. Seid and Abdallah drove these camels on with ours, observing strict silence, while Sidi Hamet was searching for the owner of them with his double barrelled gun, cocked and primed. Mr. Savage was on the young camel, and not being able to keep up, was a mile or more behind; when Sidi Hamet found the owner of the camels asleep on the sand near where Mr. Savage was. He went towards him, keeping his gun in readiness to fire, until he saw the other had no firearms, and was fast asleep; when stepping carefully up, he snatched a small bag from near the sleeper's head, and went slowly away with it until past the fear of waking him.

He then assisted in driving Mr. Savage's camel along, and they soon came up with us, where Seid and Abdallah had made the two loaded camels lie down between some small hillocks of sand. They untied the mouth of one of the sacks, and behold its contents were barley! This was the first bread stuff we had seen, and it gave us new hopes. They poured out about fifty pounds of it, I should guess, and put into a large leather bag of their own; then tying up the neck of the sack again, they made the camels get up with their loads. They now began to examine the contents of the small bags, and found them to consist of a number of small articles: but the one that was taken from near the Arab's head was partly filled with barley meal.

They were all overjoyed at this discovery, and immediately poured out some of it into a bowl, mixed it with water, and ate it; then giving us about a quart of water between us, with a handful of this meal in it, making a most delicious gruel, they hurried us on to our camels, and set off to the S. E. on a long trot, leaving the strange camels to themselves.

We had not proceeded more than half an hour, before we saw a man running swiftly in chase of us, and hallooing to make our masters stop; they knew he must be the owner of the camels they had robbed, and paid no other attention to him than to push on the camels faster. Sidi Hamet now told me that that fellow was a "poor devil—he has not even a musket," said he, "and he let me take this bag while he was asleep."

The man gained on us very fast. I was afraid he would get back what had been taken from him by our masters, especially the barley—so were my shipmates; one of whom wished he had a loaded musket—saying, "I would soon stop him if I had one, and thus save the barley."

Our masters made their signs for this man to go back, but he continued to advance, while our Arab masters, finding he would come up, kept their guns cocked in their hands, and ready to fire on him, though he had no other arms than a scimitar; and drawing near they halted; upon which the stranger, making an appeal to God, and bowing himself down and worshipping, declared that he had lost a part of his property, and that he knew they must have taken it; that he was their brother, and would rather die than commit a bad action, or suffer others to do it with impunity: "you have firearms" (*Celibeatahs*) said he, "and believe you can kill me in an instant; but the God of justice is my shield, and will protect the innocent; I do not fear you."

Sidi Hamet then told him to leave his scimitar where he was, and approach without fear, and then making our camels kneel down, we all dismounted. The stranger upon this came forward and asked—"Is it peace?"

"It is," was the reply of Sidi Hamet: they then saluted each other with—"Peace be with you—peace be to your house—to all your friends," &c. &c. and shaking one another in a most cordial manner by the hand, seated themselves in a circle on the ground. After a long debate, in which our masters justified themselves for having taken the provisions without leave, because we, their slaves, were in a state of starvation, which was very true, they added—"you would not have refused them a morsel, if you had been awake!" and it was thereupon finally agreed, to restore all that they had taken: so they made us clear a place on the ground that was hard, and pour out the barley from our bag. They also gave him up his bag of meal, which had been much lightened, and a very small bag, which I supposed to contain opium; this they said was all they had taken; then after they had prayed together, we all mounted our camels and proceeded on our journey. Religion and honour even among thieves, thought I!

CHAPTER 13

They Come Within Sight of the Ocean

This had detained us about an hour: Mr. Savage was put on the old camel, which still continued very lame, and Horace on the smallest. These camels could not keep pace with the others, and both Mr. Savage and Horace were severely flogged for what our masters called bad management: though the true reason I suspected was the loss of the stolen barley, whicn had put them in a bad humour. We kept on to the east as fast as the camels could go, until late in the evening; when hearing the voices of men hallooing to each other at a short distance on our left, our masters seemed much frightened; kept all still; and finding a deep hollow, we silently descended its steep bank, leaving our little camel with his legs tied on the level above, as he was so far worn down by fatigue that he could scarcely walk.

When we got to the bottom of it, we found a considerable number of small bushes, and having taken the saddles from off the camels and fettered their forelegs together, as usual, we let them go to feed. I calculated we travelled seven hours this day, at two miles an hour, among the sand-hills; then two hours on camels, until we came to the strange ones, at the rate of six miles an hour including two stops, say two hours; then from four until about ten p. m. six hours, at five miles an hour—total this day, fifty-six miles.

As soon as the camels were fettered, our masters examined their guns, and having ascertained that they were well primed, ascended the sand-hills in this valley, (for there was much drifted sand about it in scattering heaps, and it appeared to have once been a river, whose bed was now dry.) They bade us all follow them, and went first to the lowest part of the valley; then ascending the steep sides of the sand drifts, made us crawl after them on our hands and knees. After they had gained the top, and waiting for us to climb up, they set up the most tremendous howling I had ever before heard—one counterfeiting the tone of a tiger, the other the roar of a lion, and the third the sharp frightful yell of a famished wolf. Having kept up this concert for some time, they again proceeded, mounting and descending, and searching for tracks, &c.

I was much terrified, I confess, and expected they were hunting for the people we had heard halloo when we entered the valley, to rob and murder them, and that we were to share their danger and carry their spoil. But after they had kept us mounting and descending about two hours, they found a snug retreat surrounded on all sides by high sand drifts, where however a few small bushes were growing: they made us lie down in the deep sand, and after continuing their howlings for about half an hour, bade us go to sleep, which we much needed, as our fatigues were excessive; they had not suffered us to make the least noise since we reached the valley, nor did they themselves make any, except in imitation of wild ferocious beasts.

I was now fully persuaded that they were actuated by feelings of fear and not views of plunder in these manoeuvres; and taking a station with their guns in their hands around us, as if afraid they should lose their slaves, we soon forgot our troubles in the arms of sleep, and did not awake until the morning of the 7th, when we repaired to our camels and found everything safe. There were more camels, which we saw in the open valley, browsing upon the bushes, which grew higher here than any we had hitherto seen; they were of a different species, and not clothed with long thorns.

Just as we were ready to set off on our journey, an old woman and a boy came where we were; the woman appeared very friendly, made inquiries respecting our situation, and if our masters as well as ourselves were not hungry; and finding that we were indeed in want of food, she sent off her boy, who soon returned with the boiled remains of what I conceived to have been a sheep or goat, consisting of the entrails and a few bones; of these our masters ate the greatest part, but gave us the remainder—that is to say, the bones, which we were very glad to get, bare as they were, for our hunger was extreme.

Having gnawed and swallowed this hard food, and drank about half a pint of water each, coloured with sour milk, which the old woman kindly gave us, we proceeded on our journey, mounting this dry river's bed or gully, which had been acted upon by water at no very remote period. We here saw the first bushes that deserved that name, since we had been on this continent. They appeared to be of the willow kind, some of them as large as a man's leg, and about fifteen feet in height. It was with much difficulty the camels could ascend this bank, but when we did reach its summit we found ourselves on the same level desert as we had before travelled on: our view on every side was bounded only by the distant horizon, except on our left, where a long string of sand drifts of great height intercepted it.

Near these sand-hills we discovered a man mounted on a camel; he rode swiftly towards us, which our masters observing, while he was yet a great way off, dismounted from their camels to wait his approach. Myself and Mr. Savage were on foot, making the best of our way along. We saw our masters dig holes in the sand, and bury two small bags which they had stolen from the stranger the day before, at the time they helped themselves to the barley. The man on his camel soon came up, and we recognized him as the same our masters had plundered; he had followed us on, and now told them they had stolen his goods and deceived him besides.

Our masters denied the charge, and after showing him that they had nothing about them of the kind he described, told him to satisfy himself fully, and to go and search their stuff on the camels; protesting, at the same time, that he accused them wrongfully, and calling God to witness that they had nothing of his in their possession. The man seemed satisfied with their protestations, and rode off without further examination. We were going on during this time, and they remained on the spot to dig up the treasure after its owner had left them. When they came up with us, Sidi Hamet said to me, "That fellow wanted his bags and things, but he has not got them yet:" he then showed me the bags and their contents. There was a small box in one of the bags, containing opium and several hollow sticks of the thickness of a man's finger, and six or eight inches long; these were filled with what I supposed to be gold dust.

The other bag contained tobacco stalks, and the roots of a herb, which I afterwards understood to be a specific remedy for *evil eyes*, or witchcraft; this they esteemed as of great value, even more than the gold dust and opium: the natives smoke this root through the leg or thigh bone of a sheep or goat, they having no other pipes, and then conceit themselves invulnerable. I confess I was not pleased at the discovery of our masters' propensity to thieving, and could not help being apprehensive of the consequences that might result from such licentiousness, affecting our safety and prospects of release. We travelled fast most of this day, and must have made thirty-five miles on about an E. N. E. course. It was late when we stopped for the night: we were on a hard surface, and had neither shrub, nor indeed any other thing to fend off the cold night wind, which blew extremely fierce from the N. N. E.

October the 8th, we started very early and rode on rapidly until the afternoon, when some camels' tracks were discovered, at which our masters seemed very much rejoiced, for they were extremely hungry and thirsty. We followed these tracks until about four p. m. (they being nearly on our course,) when we came in sight of a large drove of camels feeding on the scattered shrubbery in a small shallow valley, with a few sheep and goats, which were nibbling a short brown moss, not more than an inch in height, that grew round about in spots. After due salutations, which were very long and tedious, the owners of the flocks and herds invited our masters to remain with them for the night, which may well be supposed was readily accepted; we having travelled this day about forty-five miles. They showed our masters the way to their tents, who, after bidding us to follow, set off for them on a full trot.

We reached them in about half an hour: there were about twenty in number—pitched in a little valley, near a small thicket of thorn trees. I call them trees, because they were much larger than any vegetable productions we had yet seen in this country—a few of them might be eight inches in diameter. Our masters had already killed a kid they had bought, and were employed in dressing it; which being prepared and boiled soon after dark, our masters gave us the entrails, which we immediately devoured, though not cleaned, and nearly raw, as we had not patience to wait till they were roasted sufficiently: they then offered some of the meat to the Arabs, who were sitting around them on the ground; but as they only came to gratify their curiosity in viewing us, they did not accept of any. This was the first time I had known any of them refuse so tempting an offer; and I could not but consider it as a favourable omen, and that the land was becoming more fertile and productive as we advanced on our journey, and that we must shortly escape from this horrible desert.

After we had swallowed our morsel, these people gave each of us a good drink of water, and at midnight (the hour set apart by the Arabs for taking their refreshment) they awaked me and gave me a bowl, containing probably four or five pounds of a kind of stir-about, or hasty pudding, in the centre of which, in a hole made for the purpose, there was poured a pint or more of good sweet milk: we quickly seated ourselves in a circle around the bowl, and though it was quite hot, we swallowed it in a moment. This was the most delicious food I ever tasted; the effect it produced on my palate has never since been effaced from my memory, and my companions agreed with me that nothing half so sweet had ever before entered their mouths; and as we all took it up with our hands, each one accused the other of eating like a hog, and of devouring more than his equal share. I endeavoured to convince them that it could not be more equally divided, as each put his hand to his mouth as fast as he could.

Notwithstanding every one, by the irresistible impatience of hunger, burnt his mouth and throat, yet this dish was unspeakably grateful, for hunger, sufferings, and fatigue had absolutely reduced us to skeletons: it warmed our stomachs, and checked the dysentery, which had been extremely distressing for several days past. This was the first kind of bread we had tasted since we left the wreck.

Our masters had been very much out of humour (probably owing to hunger) for several days, and beat my shipmates oftentimes most unmercifully, who, in their turn, smarting under the lash, and suffering incredibly from their sores, fatigues, and privations, became as cross as wild bears, notwithstanding I did all in my power to lighten their burdens, relieve their fatigues, and intercede for and beg them off when our masters were about to beat them, and frequently walking that they might ride; yet one of them would often curse me to my face, and load me with the most opprobrious epithets.

My kindness seemed but to inflame his petulance, and to excite in him a strange animosity, so that in the ravings of his distempered imagination, he declared that he hated the sight of me, and that my very smiles were more cutting to him than daggers presented to his naked breast; he seemed indeed to be transformed into a perfect savage in disposition, nor did this rankling humour forsake him until I shewed him in Suze the letter I there received from Mr. Willshire, assuring me he would shortly redeem us from slavery.

Early on the morning of the 9th, we set forward in a north-easterly direction, and having travelled about ten hours on the camels, at the rate of four miles an hour, we came to a deep well, situated in the midst of a cluster of high bushes; here was a large company of men watering many droves of camels that were round about. These people saluted our masters in a friendly manner, when they came up. I was preparing to assist in drawing water for our camels, but Sidi Hamet would not permit me or my companions to work; indeed we were so extremely reduced and weak, that we could not without difficulty stand steady on our feet, though (from what cause I know not) our sores were fast healing, and our skins uniting in all parts over our bodies.

While Seid and Abdallah were busied in drawing water for our camels, an Arab came up with one, and led him to our masters' watering tub or bowl, which Seid observing, bade him desist; but the strange Arab swore his camel should drink here, and he (Seid) should draw water for him. This kindled the resentment of Seid; he left his bucket, ran up to the Arab, and gave him a heavy blow on his face with his fist, which staggered him near to falling; but recovering himself, he drew his scimitar, and made a powerful thrust at Seid, who saved his life by springing suddenly from him, and the scimitar out slightly pricked his breast. Sidi Hamet had by this time seized and unsheathed his gun, and presented it to the Arab's breast within a yard's distance, ready to blow him through.

When he was about to fire, his hand was seized by one of the bystanders, and others of them rushing between the combatants to prevent bloodshed, laid hold of Seid and his antagonist, and having separated them by main force, they removed the Arab to the other side of the well, where some of the company drew water for his camel, which having drank its fill, they sent the fellow off, muttering curses as he went away. Our masters, during all this time, were so exasperated at the conduct of this man, that nothing less than the strength of superior numbers would have prevented them from putting him to death; and all the company agreed that they had been grossly insulted, especially as they were strangers.

When our camels had finished drinking at this well, the water of which was very brackish, we were mounted, and proceeded further east for about one hour's ride, where we found two more wells, which appeared to have been lately dug, and the water they contained was very salt. Here was a large drove of camels (probably one hundred) to be watered, and they obliged me to assist in drawing water until they had all finished; my master encouraging me, by saying, "their owner was a very good man, and would give us food." It was about sunset when we had finished drawing water, and we followed the valley in which we were for about three miles east, when we came to the tent we had been in quest of: here was no lee to keep off the cold wind, nor did we get anything to eat, notwithstanding our masters had praised the liberality of our host, and tried by every means to obtain some provisions from him. I soon found his goodness was like that of many others; (*i. e.*) he was no longer liberal than while there was a prospect of profit. I presume we travelled forty-five miles this day.

As soon as daylight appeared on the morning of the 10th. we set forward, all mounted on the camels, and kept on steadily until night over this most dreary desert, and came to a halt long after dark, without any thing to keep off the wind, which was blowing a strong gale. We travelled this day about thirteen hours, at four miles an hour; as the camels went all day on a quick walk, we must have made at least fifty-two miles E. N. E.

October 11th, we set off very early on a full trot, and went on until about noon, seven hours, at six miles an hour, when the land before us appeared broken, and we descended gradually into a deep valley, whose bottom was covered with sand; and on both sides of us, at a great distance, we saw very high and steep banks like those of a river, and followed the tongue of land that separated them. Our course was nearly east. At about two p. m. our masters said they saw camels ahead, but *we* could not perceive them for a long time after, when keeping on a great trot, we came up with a drove about six p. m. We could however find no owners, nor in fact any human being; for all had fled and hid themselves, probably from fear of being robbed, or that contributions might be levied on their charity for some provisions. We searched some time for the owners of these camels, but not finding them, we continued on, and having come to the abrupt end of the tongue of land on which we had been travelling, we descended into the river's bed, which was dry and soft.

Pushing forward, we reached a large cluster of bushes, which appeared like an island in a lake when seen at a distance, and I suppose it was ten o'clock at night before we arrived at the spot, though we saw it in the distant horizon long before dark. As we entered among the bushes, our masters preserved a profound silence; and having found a clear spot of about twenty yards in diameter, encircled by high bushes, which kept off the wind, we stopped there for the night; having travelled that day for the space of about fourteen hours, at the rate of five miles an hour, making a distance of seventy miles. We had nothing this night wherewith to allay our hunger: our fatigues and sufferings may be more easily conceived than expressed; yet as we were sheltered from the night winds, we slept very soundly until we were roused up to continue our journey.

On the 12th of October, as soon as daylight appeared, we watered the camels at a well of brackish water near the bushes before mentioned. Our masters had been careful not to make the least noise during the night, nor to kindle a fire, fearing they should be discovered and surprised by some more powerful party; but neither foe nor friend appeared; and having filled a skin with some of this brackish water, we descended a second steep bank to the bottom or lowest part of this river's bed, which was then dry, sandy, and incrusted with salt; it appeared very white, and crumbled under the feet of our camels, making a loud crackling noise.

The reasons of this bed being then without water, appeared to be the recess of the tide: its left bank rose very high in perpendicular cliffs, while its right was sloping and covered with sand, evidently blown by the winds from the sea beach, and which lay in drifts up to its very summit. This bay (for it can be nothing else) ran into the land from near a S.W. to a W. direction, and was not more than eight or ten miles wide here, which I afterwards found was near its mouth, but was very broad within, and extended a great distance into the country; for since we entered its former bed we had travelled twelve hours, at the rate of five miles an hour, making sixty miles, and it then extended farther than the eye could reach to the S.W.

The steep banks on both sides, which were four or five hundred feet high, showed most evident signs of their having been washed by sea water from their base to near their summits, (but at a very remote period,) and that the sea had gradually retired from them. Our masters being in a state of starvation, their ill humour increased exceedingly; when about nine o'clock in the forenoon we saw two men, driving two camels, come down the sand-hills on our right. Our masters rode off to meet them, and having made the necessary inquiries, returned to us, who had continued going forward, accompanied by Abdallah. Sidi Hamet informed us that there were goats in an E. S. E. direction not far distant, and that we should soon have some meat; so we commenced climbing over the high hills of sand, in order that we might fall in with them. In ascending these hills, which were extremely difficult and long, our old lame camel gave out, having fallen down several times, which caused much delay; so finding him nearly expiring, we abandoned him and proceeded on; though this circumstance of losing the camel, also helped to increase the rage of our masters, who now behaved like madmen.

As we were climbing up we perceived a hole dug in the sand, and we were told that the entrails of a camel had been roasted there, which Seid discovered by applying his nose to the surrounding earth. Sidi Harriet having gone on before us with his gun, we had already ascended several miles of this steep and sandy bank; and on arriving near the level of the surrounding country, we heard the report of a musket fired, at no great distance from where we were, and soon perceived Sidi Hamet, accompanied by another Arab, driving a flock of goats before them. This Arab was much intimidated at the sight and report of a gun, for my master had fired off one of the barrels to frighten him.

When the goats came near us, our masters, who considered possession as a very important preliminary, ran in among the flock, and seized four of them, which they gave into our charge, until they should settle about the price with their owner, who was alone and unarmed, but at this moment he was joined by his wife:—she had not been at all frightened, and commenced scolding at our masters most immoderately and loudly:—she said, she would not consent to part with the goats, even if her husband did, and insisted on knowing Sidi Hamet's name: this he told her, and she then began to abuse him for being so cowardly as to rob an unarmed man; said the whole country should ring with his name and actions, and she did not doubt but she could find some man who would revenge this injury.

Her husband all this time strove to stop her tongue, but to no purpose; nor did she cease scolding until Seid presented his gun to her breast, and threatened her if she spoke another word, to blow her to pieces. This compelled her to pause a moment, while our master (taking advantage of her silence) informed them that he had left a good camel a little distance behind, which being only tired, could not proceed with them, and that he would give them this camel in exchange for these four goats. I could plainly discover, however, that these people did not believe him. Sidi Hamet nevertheless spoke the truth in part; a camel was indeed left behind, but not a good one; yet as there was no alternative, they were necessitated to submit: the woman however insisted on exchanging one goat we had for another, which our masters assented to, merely to gratify her caprice.

This business being thus settled, which had taken up nearly an hour's time, our goats were tied fast to each other by their necks, and given into my charge; leaving Mr. Savage and Horace to assist in driving them. Clark and Burns were ordered to drive the camels, whilst our masters, a little less fretful than before, went forward to pick out a practicable passage for them and the goats, while my party brought up the rear. The goats were difficult to manage, but we continued to drive them along, and generally within sight of the camels, though with great fatigue and exertion. Our hunger and thirst were excessive: the direct heat of the sun, as well as that reflected from the deep and yielding sands, was intense. Mr. Savage found here a very short green weed, which he pulled and ate, telling me it was most delicious and as sweet as honey; but I begged him not to swallow any of it until I should ask our masters what was the nature of it, for it might be poison and I refused to touch it myself, though it looked tempting.

In our distressed condition, however, he thought a green thing that tasted so well could do him no harm, and continued to eat whatever he could find of it, which (happily for him) was not much: but in a short time he was convinced of the contrary, for he soon began to vomit violently:—this alarmed me for his safety, and I examined the weed he had been so delighted with, and after a close investigation, I was convinced it was no other than what is called in America the Indian tobacco, (*Nicotiana*.) Its effects were also similar; but how these plants came to grow on those sands I cannot conceive.

Mr. Savage continued to vomit by spells for two hours or more, which, as he had very little in his stomach, strained it so excessively as to bring forth blood. I could not wait for him, because both our masters, their camels, and our shipmates, were already out of sight. When he could proceed no further, he would stop and vomit, and then by running (though in great distress) as fast as he was able, come up with us again. I encouraged him all I could—told him what the herb was, and that its effects need not be dreaded.

Ever since we had been coming near the summit of the land, we had discerned the sea, though at a great distance ahead and on our left; but as it appeared dark and smooth in the distant horizon, I supposed it to be an extensive ridge of high woodland, and hoped we should soon reach it, as our course bent that way, and that this would prove to be the termination of the desert. Horace, however, thought it appeared too dark and smooth for land, and regarding it attentively, I discovered it was in fact the ocean, and I could planely distinguish its mountainous waves as they rolled along, for it was greatly agitated by fierce winds. This was the first view we had of the sea since we were made slaves: it was a highly gratifying sight to us all, and particularly so, as it was quite unexpected; and it very much revived the spirits of myself and desponding companions.

CHAPTER 14

Travel in the Night for Fear of Robbers

Discerning the tracks of our camels, which we had lost sight of for a time, as they had crossed over rocks, where they had descended through a rent or chasm, partly covered with high drifts of loose sand, towards the sea shore, we followed them down immensely steep sand-hills, to a tolerably inclined plane, between the first and second banks of the sea; which, from appearances, had once washed the upper bank, but had long since retired:—the inclined plane had also been a beach forages, where the stones, that now covered its surface, had been tossed, and rounded by striking against one another.

From this beach the ocean had also retired, and now washed other perpendicular cliffs of one hundred feet or more in height, at a distance of six or eight miles to the northward of the former ones, which appeared to rise in abrupt, and in many places overhanging cliffs of rocks to the height of three hundred feet. We had made our way through these cliffs, by means of a hollow, seemingly formed on purpose for a passage, as it was the only one in view; and as I did not know which way our masters went, I had stopped to view the surrounding prospect, and now give what was then my impression. I was at a loss which way to steer my course, but our masters, who were concealed behind a small hillock on our left, discovering my embarrassment, now called to me, where I soon joined them.

It was then nearly dark, and there were three or four families of Arabs near, sitting under a shelter made of skins extended by poles; here our camels were turned up to browse, and we were ordered to collect brush, which grew on the steep side of the banks, to make a fire, and to keep off the wind during the night. Mr. Savage was entirely exhausted, and I requested him to lie down on the ground, whilst the rest of us gathered the bushes required; but when I came in with my handful, Seid was beating him with a stick to make him assist. I begged he would permit Mr. Savage to remain where he was; told him he was sick, and that I would perform his share of the labour.

Sidi Harnet now returned and killed one of the goats, of which they gave us the entrails—a seasonable relief indeed, and we were allowed to drink a little of the soup they were boiled in, and a small piece of meat was divided between us; and each received a drink of water: I had before stolen a drink for Mr. Savage, whose bloody vomit continued. In the course of the night, they gave us a small quantity of the same kind of pudding we had before tasted, but as Mr. Savage was sick, they refused to give him any, saying, "he has already eaten too much of something, but they did not know what," Sidi Hamet, however, saved a little of the pudding in a bowl for him, and as he seemed unwilling to die with hunger, I gave him part of the pudding I had, and saved my share of meat for him until the morning. Our hunger and thirst being somewhat appeased, we slept this night pretty soundly. We had travelled this day about thirty miles.

October the 14th, early in the morning, we took leave of these Arabs; but while we were busied in getting off, Abdallah seized on Mr. Savage's pudding in the bowl as a good prize, and swallowed it in an instant; so that nothing but my care for Mr. Savage saved him from fainting and consequent death on this day. Our masters had purchased two more goats from those Arabs, which increased our number to five; these we were forced to drive, and we kept along the seashore the whole of this day. On our right the original seashore (or bank) rose nearly three hundred feet perpendicularly, and in many places in overhanging cliffs. The inclined plane on which we travelled was from three to six or eight miles wide, and very regular; covered with pebbles and many round stones; among which grew here and there a few dwarf bushes of different kinds from what I had seen before in various parts of the world.

A little to our left the plane broke off abruptly, and the ocean appeared. The bank was from one hundred and fifty to two hundred feet high above the level of the sea, and mostly perpendicular, against which the heavy surges dashed with great fury, sounding like loud peals of distant thunder. Our course and that of the shore was about east, and near dark we fell in with four families of Arabs who were about pitching their tents near the seashore. Our masters went and introduced themselves to the one who appeared to be their chief, or the principal character among them, and whose name was Hassar. They soon became acquainted, and it was ascertained that Hassar and his wife, together with four men that were with him, and their families were going the same route that we were; upon which our masters agreed to join company.

Hassar's wife, whose name was Tamar, and who appeared to be an uncommonly intelligent woman, addressed me in broken Spanish and Arabic mixed:—she said she had saved the lives of some Spaniards who had been wrecked on that coast a great many years ago; that a vessel came for them, and that she went to Lanzarote (one of the Canary islands) to get some goods which the Spanish captain promised to deliver to her father, who retained three of the men until the Spaniard should have fulfilled his contract, and brought her back. She represented to me the manner in which the houses in Lanzarote were built, and described the forts and batteries with their cannon, &c. so very clearly and accurately, that I had no doubt she must have seen them, and I gave her to understand I had been there also. She said Lanzarote was a bad country, and assured us, we should not die with hunger while we remained in her company.

We travelled on the 14th about twenty miles. In the night our masters killed a goat, and gave us a part of the meat, as well as of the entrails: Hassar's wife also gave us a small quantity of the pudding before mentioned, which the Arabs call *Lhash*; and here we had a good night's sleep. October the 15th, early in the morning, Hassar and his company struck their tents, and all these families proceeded on with us until near night; when we came to a very deep gully, which we could not pass in any other way than by going down the bank on to the sea beach, and at low tide; there was a kind of pathway where camels had gone down before us. We descended, and there found a tent with an Arab family in it, just below the high bank; so sending on the camels, Sidi Hamet made us stop here a few moments.

The owner of the tent pretended to speak Spanish, but in fact knew only a few detached words of that language: he mentioned to me that he knew I had promised Sidi Hamet that my friend in Swearah would pay him the amount I had bargained for, stating the sum: now, said this Arab, "Have you a friend in Swearah?" I answered I had.

"Do not lie," said he, "for if you do you will have your throat cut; but if you have told him so merely that you might get off of the desert, so as to procure something to eat, he will pardon that pretext and deception so far as only to sell you and your comrades to the highest bidder, the first opportunity, provided, however, that you confess the deceit now. In a few days" added he "you will find houses and a river of running water, and should you persist in deceiving him, you will certainly lose your life."

I made him understand that I was incapable of lying to Sidi Hamet; that all I told him was true; that he was the man who had saved my life, and he should be well rewarded for his goodness by my friend, and by our Almighty Father. This seemed to satisfy Sidi Hamet, who was present and understood me better than the other did, and he told me I should see Swearah in a few days. We now went forward, accompanied by the Arab, who piloted us across a small arm of the sea that entered the before mentioned gully. We here found a pair of kerseymere pantaloons that had belonged to Mr. Savage in the possession of one of this man's little sons:—I pointed them out to my masters, and begged them to buy them, which after a long barter with the boy, Seid effected, by giving him in exchange a piece of blue cotton cloth which he had worn as a kind of shirt: they wished me to give the pantaloons to Clark or Horace, but I gave them to Mr. Savage, although they insisted he was *fonte*, or a bad fellow.

Having got up the steep bank again, after wading through the salt water, which was nearly up to our hips, and one hundred yards broad, we encamped for the night on high dry land; and at dark our masters, taking Horace and myself with them, went near a few tents lose by the sea, where we were presented with a quantity of dried mussels, which, though very salt, we found excellent; these we divided among our shipmates. I conjecture we had made twenty-five miles this day. Here our masters killed their remaining goats, boiled and ate their entrails and most of their meat, as all present were hungry, and would have some in spite of every opposition; so that our share was seized and swallowed by others.

October the 16th, we made ready and started very early, but went on slowly, keeping near the seashore, and mostly in the broken grounds, caused by its former washings. Our masters seemed very fearful all this day, and told me there were many robbers and bad men hereabouts, who would endeavour to seize and carry us off, and that they could throw large stones with great force and precision. We had not travelled more than fifteen miles before sunset, and nigh coming on, our masters, who had mounted Mr. Savage, Clark, and Burns on the camels, drove them on at a great rate, while myself and Horace were obliged to keep up with them by running on foot.

All this time they had their guns in their hands unsheathed, and when Horace and myself were obliged occasionally to stop, one of them always stayed with us, and then hurried us on as fast as possible. In this manner we proceeded until about midnight, when coming to a deep gully, Mr. Savage and Clark were dismounted, and Horace and myself placed on the camels. Descending the valley, we found it full of high sand drifts, and proceeded without making the least noise: the valley was wide, and the sand lying in it had, no doubt, been driven from the sea beach by the wind. All the women and children at this time were running on foot. After reaching, with much labour, the other side of the valley, and the summit beyond it, we found the whole surface of the ground making an even inclined plane, covered with deep drifts of loose sand. I had been riding, I think, about two hours, when Clark, who was a considerable distance behind, called to me, and said, "Mr. Savage has fainted away, and they are flogging him with sticks."

I instantly slipped off my camel, and ran to relieve him as fast as my legs could carry me. Seid was striking his apparent lifeless body, which lay stretched on the ground, with a heavy stick: Hassar had seized him by the beard with one hand, and with the other held a sharp scimitar, with which he was in the act of cutting his throat. I laid hold of Hassar, jerked him away, and clasping the body of Mr. Savage in my arms, raised him up, and called for water. Hassar would have run me through with his scimitar, but Sidi Hamet arrested and prevented him I expected to lose my life, but had determined to save Mr. Savage's at all hazards. Our masters and the whole company of men, women, and children, were around me: they were possessed with the belief that he was perverse and obstinate, and that he would not exert himself to proceed at a time when they were in haste to go on, lest they should fall into the hands of robbers; for which reason they had determined to kill him.

I made Sidi Hamet, however, and the others understand, that he had fainted through hunger and excessive fatigue, and that he was not perverse in this instance. This surprised them exceedingly: they had never before heard of such a thing as fainting. Sidi Hamet ordered a camel to be brought, and a drink of water to be given him, and when he revived, this Arab shed tears; then putting him and Clark on a camel, one to steady the other, they proceeded. Sidi Hamet desired me to get on with Horace and ride, saying, with a sneer—"the English are good for nothing—you see even our women and children can walk and run." I told him I could walk, that I was not a bad fellow; and began to run about and drive up the camels: this pleased him excessively, and he bade me come and walk with him, leaving the camels to the care of others, calling me "good Riley—you shall again see your children, if God please."

We continued our journey eastward along the south side of a high string of sand-hills, when hearing a dog bark before us, we turned the camels suddenly off to the north, setting them off on a full trot, but passing over the sand-hills without noise: we kept this course for about an hour, until having got near the sea bank, and north of the sand-hills, we resumed our former course. Near daylight we lost our way, and fearing to go amiss, as it was very dark, they made the camels lie down in a circle, placing us within it—when they kept guard over us with their muskets in their hands, while we took a nap. I should guess we travelled fifty miles this last day and night.

October the 17th, early in the morning, we set forward again, still on the same inclined plane, between the first and second banks of the sea. The high banks on our right, whose pointed rocks, where they had been washed by the ocean, were still visible all the way, began to be overtopped with high hills rising far into the country, and presenting to our view a new aspect; so that I was convinced we had left the level desert.

CHAPTER 15

Black Mountains Appear in the East

The black tops of high mountains appeared in the distant horizon to the eastward about noon, and the camel paths were very much trodden. We kept on until near night, when meeting with a deep valley, we wound our course through it to the southward, and then went down south-eastwardly through another deep valley, where there was a good path. The black bare mountains on both sides of us gave us great hopes that we should soon come to running water and cultivated lands; and in reality near night we came to a stream of water, with high grass and bushes growing on its margin. The water, however, was very brackish, and could not be drank: but on its opposite bank we saw a company of men at some wells, watering about forty fine looking horses and some camels. Our masters saluted those men, and crossing the stream, which in this part was about two feet deep and thirty feet wide, we watered our camels also at the same place.

This river, whose water was as clear as crystal, was literally filled with beautiful large fish, which were jumping above the surface every moment; but the Arabs did not seem to want them, for they could have been caught very easily. The company with horses and camels left the wells, and went on to the south, riding at a full trot along the river's side: they were armed only with scimitars. Our company then went towards the sea, and Hassar's women pitched their tents for the night; here they cooked a goat, which they divided among all the party, and what fell to our share cannot be supposed to have been much. I believe we made thirty-six miles this day, as we rode nearly all the time.

October the 18th, we ascended the hill, climbing up in a zigzag path on the steep side of the east bank of this river; and having gained the surface, we found it to be a continuation of the same inclined plane on which we had before been travelling. The bank on our right, to the south, still continued to give indubitable proofs of its having been washed by the ocean; whose surges had worn in under the shelving rocks, which hung in immense masses of from two to three hundred feet high over the surface of the inclined plane below, while the plane itself adjoining the cliffs was covered with fragments that had fallen from above, and with other stones that had been washed and worn round by the ocean's waves, leaving the most positive marks of its having retired to its present bed.

These observations, with those I had made before, and was enabled to make afterwards, fully satisfied my mind, that the sea had gradually retired from this continent;—I must leave it to philosophers to account for the cause. The only green thing we had seen for several days past, except what grew immediately on the bank of the river, (which were some bushes resembling dwarf alders and bulrushes,) was a shrub that rose in a small bunch at the bottom, having frequently but one stock, from three to twelve inches in thickness; the limbs spreading out in every direction, like an umbrella, into innumerable branches, making a diameter of from fifteen to twenty feet, and not more than six feet in height; its leaves very green, smooth, pointed, and about four inches long, by one and a half broad; its bark resembled that of the hard or sugar maple tree; its branches terminated abruptly, the point of each twig being nearly as thick as the end of a man's finger: this shrub, or weed, was very tender, and as we broke off the twigs, a great many drops of glutinous liquid, resembling milk, flowed from them, but its odour and taste were of the most disagreeable kind, and the camels would not feed on it.

We saw a good deal that had grown up before, and had died and become dry: on breaking it off, I found it was hollow, and almost as light as a common dry weed. Neither our masters nor the other Arabs would light a fire with it, on account of its disagreeable smell when burning; the taste of the milk issuing from this plant was the most nauseous and disgusting in nature, though very white and beautiful to behold. About noon we came to the foot of the high mountains we had seen the day before, and turned in between two of them to the southeast, leaving the sea entirely. We went up through a chasm in the bank, over rocks and through a narrow footway, formed by the treading of camels and horses; for we had seen many horse tracks, and also the tracks of one animal of the kind called neat cattle.

As we proceeded on foot, winding upwards, we discovered on our left a few stones piled up in the form of a wall, round a pit of ten or twelve feet across, and six feet deep, dug in the earth by art. There were lying on the ground around the wall, several earthen pots that would contain from three to four gallons each, and which appeared to have been made for and used as boilers.

One of our young men directly took up one of them, and was lashing it on his camel as a good prize, when Hassar and Sidi Hamet, observing the circumstance, made him untie and carry it back again to the spot where he had found it. As I already knew the propensity all had for plundering, I could not but imagine that they now restrained themselves through fear. About sunset we came to a small spot of land that had been cultivated, and fell in with a heap of barley straw. Here was the first sign of cultivation we had seen on this continent, and we hailed it as the harbinger of happier days. We had travelled full thirty miles this day, and our masters now gave us the putrid remains of the goat which had hung on one of the camels for four days: this we roasted, and found it a delicious morsel; it was tender, and needed no seasoning.

Some of my comrades, as if their taste had become depraved by the rage of hunger, declared that putrid meat was far preferable to fresh; that it wanted neither salt nor pepper to give it a relish, and that it ever they got home again, they should prefer such food to any other. Having finished our savoury supper, we lay down on the straw, and enjoyed a most charming, sound, and refreshing sleep. To us, who for so long a time had been obliged to repose our wearied limbs and wasted frames on the hard-baked bosom of the desert, or the dead sides of the barren sand drifts, this solitary heap of fresh straw seemed softer and sweeter than a bed of down strewn over with the most odoriferous flowers.

October the 19th, we resumed our journey very early in the morning, and travelled on foot, all except Burns, who was so far exhausted as to be unable to walk. Our course rounded from S. E. to E. N. E. keeping the bottom of the valleys, most of which had been cultivated by the plough at no very remote period, but only in a narrow strip. The sides of the mountains were entirely barren and naked of foliage, and we kept on winding as the valleys permitted, until about two o'clock p. m. when, suddenly through a deep valley before us, a few rough stone huts broke upon our view, and a moment afterwards we beheld a stream of clear water purling over a pebbly bottom, and meandering through banks covered with green bushes and shrubs in full blossom.

On the farther side, cows, asses, and sheep, were feeding on green grass, and a number of date trees adorning and shading the margin of the rivulet. This was a sight none of us expected to behold, and I poured out my soul in rapturous effusions of thankfulness to the Supreme Being. Excess of joy had so far overpowered our faculties, that it was with difficulty we reached the water's edge, but urging forward to the brink with headlong steps, and fearlessly plunging in our mouths, like thirsty camels, we swallowed down large draughts, until satiated nature bade us stop. The rivulet was fresh, and fortunately not so cold as to occasion any injurious effects: it was quite shallow, and not more than about five yards in width; it appeared, however, very evidently, that when the rain falls in the surrounding country, it flows with a much deeper and broader current. It is called by the Arabs, *el Wed noon*, or the River Nun; comes from the southeast, and runs from this place to the sea in a northerly direction.

We had arrived on its right bank, where some barren date trees grew, and which offered us nothing but their shade: hungry, however, as we were, our fatigue got the better of every other want, and as these were the first trees we had met with during our distressing pilgrimage, we embraced the kindly offer, and enjoyed about two hours of refreshing sleep: I was then awakened by Sidi Hamet, who directed me to come with my companions and follow him: this we instantly did, and going near one of the small houses, he divided amongst us, to our inexpressible joy, about four pounds of honey in-the comb. This was indeed a dainty treat; and with the hungriness of greedy bears, we devoured it, comb and all, together with a host of young bees just ready for hatching, that filled two-thirds of the cells; our hearts at the same time swelling with gratitude to God, and tears of joy trickling down our fleshiest cheeks.

Hassar's men pressed around, and endeavoured to snatch from us this delicious food, of which they had no share; but Sidi Hamet placing the bowl on his knees, passed the honeycomb to us piece by piece in one hand, while he held his gun in the other, ready to fire on any one who should attempt to deprive us of our meal. The eyes of these fellows seemed to flash fire at the preference we enjoyed, and we dreaded the effects of their malicious envy; for the Arabs set no bounds to their anger and resentment, and regard no law but that of superior force. Having finished our luscious repast, we were told by our masters to go to rest, which we did, and soon fell asleep in the shade formed by a beautiful umbrella palm-tree.

About dark we were called up and ordered to gather fuel, and were afterwards presented with some pudding of the same kind we had before eaten, though mixed with oil, that I afterwards ascertained was the *argan* oil, which, though fresh, had a very strong smell, and my stomach being cloyed with honey, I declined eating any. My companions, however, relished this oil very much, and preferred it afterwards to butter during our stay in Africa. We found a good shelter this night near a burying place with a small square stone building in the centre, whitewashed and covered with a dome; and I afterwards learned that this was a sanctuary or saint house: it was fenced in with thorn bushes, and was the first burying place we had seen in this country. I computed we had travelled this day (Oct. 19th) about eighteen miles.

On the morning of the 20th we did not go forward, and a number of Arabs and Moors came to see our masters and us. This place appeared to be a great thoroughfare: large droves of unloaded camels were passing up to the eastward from the way we had come, as well as from the southward, and also great numbers of loaded camels going towards the desert. Their loading consisted principally of sacks of barley, some salt and iron, together with other merchandise.

During the fore part of this day, several parties of men, in all from sixty to eighty, passed us; all mounted on handsome horses of the Arabian breed, well-bred and high-spirited: their riders were covered with cloaks or *sulams*, and everyone had a single barrelled musket in his hand, the stocks of which were curiously wrought and inlaid with small pieces of various coloured wood and ivory, arranged and fitted in a very particular manner. The locks of these muskets were of the Moorish kind, and very unhandy, though substantial, and they seldom miss fire, although their powder is bad and coarse grained. This and a good scimitar slung on their right side constitute the whole of their weapons: they depend more upon the scimitar for close quarters in battle than upon their musket, for, say they, this will never miss fire; being similar to the practice which it is said the Russian General (Suwarrow) used to inculcate on his soldiers—"*The ball will lose its way, the bayonet never: the ball is a fool—the bayonet a hero.*"

A Moor is ashamed to be without his scimitar; their scabbards are made of brass, and plated on the outside with silver, but those worn by the Arabs are made of leather: these weapons both of the Moors and Arabs, are suspended from the neck by cords made of woollen yarn dyed red, or a strong braided leather thong. They call a scimitar or long knife *el skine*.

These natives were of a different race of men from any we had hitherto seen: they wear a *haick* or piece of woollen cloth wrapped about their bodies, which covering them, falls down below their knees; or else a cloak called *gzlabbia*, made in a similar manner, cut with short sleeves, and one fold of the *haick* generally covered the head; but those who had not their heads covered with their haick, or the hood of their *gzlabbia* or *sulam*, wore a kind of turban: the cloak or *sulam* is made of coarse black cloth, very shaggy, and much in the form of the European cloak, with a hood or head-piece to it; it is, however, sewed together part of the way down in front, so that to get it on, they slip it over their heads, and it covers their arms. They are generally stout men, of five feet eight or ten inches in height, and well set; their complexion a light olive. They wear their beards as long as they will grow, and consider a man without a great bushy beard an effeminate being, and hold him in great contempt.

Their saddles were well made and very high, at least eight or ten inches, fitted before and behind so as almost to make it impossible for the horse to throw his rider; their bridles are of the most powerful Arabian kind; their stirrups are made of broad sheets of iron that cover almost the whole foot—many of them are plated with silver. All the men wore slippers and spurs, and had their stirrups tied up very short.

While we remained here, a very respectable looking old man, who spoke a few words of Spanish, after learning from our masters who we were, came to me and inquired about my country and my friends in Swearah; said he knew all the consuls there, and told me their names were Renshaw, Joseph, Estevan, and Corte. He said he was going to Swearah, and should be there in ten days, and would carry a letter for me if my master would let me write; but we had no paper. I informed him that my friend was named Renshaw, guessing him to be the English consul. This old man told my master he believed I spoke the truth, and that I had been at Swearah, which from his discourse I understood to be the same as Mogadore. He then set off eastward on his mule, which was a very large and handsome one.

All the people that passed here appeared very friendly to our masters; they wished to know our story, and requested my opinion of their horses, saddles and bridles, muskets, scimitars, and accoutrements in general, &c. all of which I declared to be of the best possible kind. This morning Sidi Hamet bought a hive of honey, and undertook to give some of it to us, but was not able to carry his kind intentions into effect, for at the moment he was handing some to me, Hassar's men rushed on him and got possession of the whole, which they devoured in a minute: there was no getting it back, and after a long and violent dispute with Hassar and his company respecting it, he procured another hive, and being assisted by the man from whom he bought it, and a number of strangers, he succeeded in distributing amongst us about three pounds of the poorest part of the comb.

Chapter 16

Their Masters are Attacked by a Band of Robbers

After we had eaten this, our masters prepared the camels, and Hassar's company divided, that is to say, two men and all the women and children took the plane great route which led east in a deep valley, driving off about one half of the camels; Hassar and the others drove off the rest (including ours) in a N. E. direction, and we with our masters, accompanied by two other men, proceeded along the river's eastern bank to the northward for a short distance, and then ascended the high, steep, and craggy mountains eastward of us. The labour in clambering up these steep precipices is indescribable; we continued mounting them as fast as possible for about four hours, and I was fully convinced our masters took that route for fear they should be followed and surprised in the night by some who had seen us, and thus be robbed of their slaves and other property.

After climbing over the highest peaks of these mountains, we saw Hussar and part of his company who had driven the camels, and had gotten up by another and more practicable path. It was now near night, and we travelled along the craggy steeps, assisting one another over the most difficult parts, while Hassar sought out the easiest places for the ascent of the camels. Coming at length to a small level spot of ground, we saw some tents, and directed our course towards them: the tents were twelve in number, and placed in a semicircle. Having approached to within one hundred yards in front of the largest one, our masters seated themselves on the ground with their backs towards the tents, and a woman soon came out bringing a bowl of water, which she presented to them after the usual salutations of *Labez*, &c. &c.

Our masters drank of the water, and Sidi Humet was soon after presented with a bowl filled with dates lately plucked from the trees and not fully ripe: these he gave to us; though Seid, Abdallah, and Hassar snatched each a handful, to which we were forced to submit: we found them excellent, but did not know at that time what sort of fruit they were. Here we remained during the night, and rested our emaciated bodies, which were, if possible, more fatigued than they ever were before.

October the 21st, we set off to the northward very early, and made down towards the sea through numerous steep gullies, and got on to the inclined plane below the former seashore, about mid-day; here were the same sort of marks in this bank that we had before observed, and the same signs of its having been laved by the ocean. We went along through the same kind of thick bushes as those I have before described, near to the cliffs that at present formed a barrier to the mighty waters, where we discovered a number of tents, and soon reached them. Here our masters Sidi Hamet and Hassar, were recognized by some of the men, who were in all about twenty, with their families: these people had large sacks of barley with them, which they had procured far eastward up the country. Sidi Hamet was now sick with violent pains in his head and in all his limbs.

These people (who were Arabs, as all are who live in tents in the country) took compassion on him, and cleared a tent for him to lie under, where having made up a large fire, he kept his head towards it, turning about and almost roasting his brains, but obtained no relief from this manner of treating his disorder. He next had recourse to another singular remedy: he had a large knife put into the fire and heated red hot; then made his brother draw the back of it, hot as it was, several times across the top of his head, making it hiss (as may well be supposed) in all directions:—when it had in some measure cooled, he would again heat it as before, then making bare his legs and arms, he went through with the process of striking its back along them at the distance of three or four inches, scorching off the skin; and though it made him twitch and jump at every touch, he continued to do it for the space of an hour or more.

Burns had been very ill for some time, and was so weak that he scarcely was able to stand, and could not walk—he was, therefore, always placed on a camel, and as Sidi Hamet was now applying to himself a remedy for what he thought a stroke of the moon, he undertook to administer the red hot knife to the limbs of poor Burns, who from mere want of bodily strength was not able, poor fellow, to jump, but would at every touch cry out, "God have mercy upon me." As I was hungry, I begged of my masters to let me go and search for mussels on the sea beach, (for there was a hollow at a little distance, through which we might gain it,) but they refused, saying, "tomorrow, if God please, we shall be on the sea beach; there are no muscles on this part of the coast:" here, however, we received a good supper of *lhash*, or pudding, and rested our wearied limbs under the tent with our masters.

October the 22nd, we went forward, driving our own camels only: as Hassar had taken the young one, we had but three remaining; so we rode by turns, crossing the deep hollows which had been worn down by the rains or other causes, until afternoon, when we were forced to have recourse to the sea beach to get past one of these deep places, whose sides were so steep as to render a passage down it impracticable. When we gained the beach, we found ourselves on a narrow strip of land, which was then dry, the tide being out; this extended in length eight or ten miles, but from the water's edge to the perpendicular cliffs on our right, not more than ten yards: these cliffs appeared to be one hundred and fifty feet in height. When we came to the sea water, I went into it, and let a surf wash over me, that I might once more feel its refreshing effects; but my master, fearing I should be carried away by the receding waves, told me not to go near them again.

As we proceeded along this narrow beach, and had passed over half its length, the huge cliffs overhanging us on our right, with the ocean on our left— just as we were turning a point, we observed four men, armed each with a musket and scimitar, spring from beneath the jutting rocks, to intercept our march. Our masters were at this time on the camels, but they instantly leaped off, at the same time unsheathing their guns: to retreat would betray fear, and lead to inevitable destruction—so they determined to advance, two against four, and Sidi Hamet, though still in so weak a state as to be thought incapable of walking before he saw these men, now ran towards them with his musket in his hand, while Seid, that cruel coward, lagged behind—so true it is, that the most generous and humane men are always the most courageous.

The foe was but a few paces from us, and stood in a line across the beach. Sidi Hamet, holding his gun ready to fire, demanded if it was peace? while he eyed their countenances to see if they were deceitful: one of them answered, "it is peace," and extended his hand to receive that of Sidi Hamet, who gave him his right hand, suspecting no treachery; but the fellow grasped it fast, and would have shot him and Seid in a moment, but at that critical juncture, two of Hassar's men came in sight, running like the wind towards us, with each a double barrelled gun in his hand, all ready to fire; the robbers saw them as they turned the point, and the fellow who had seized Sidi Hamet's hand, instantly let it go, turning the affair off with a loud laugh, and saying he only did it to frighten him: this excuse was deemed satisfactory, merely because our men did not now feel themselves sufficiently strong to resent this insult, and we proceeded on: but these fellows, who were very stout and active, hovered around us, slaves, endeavouring to separate us from our masters, as it appeared, in the hope of seizing on us as their own, which Sidi Hamet observing, ordered me with my men to keep close to the camels' heels, while he and his company (now strong, though none of them armed with scimitars) kept between us and the *banditti*.

When they found that our masters were too vigilant for them, they took French leave of us, and ran along the beach with incredible swiftness, chasing each other, and taking up and throwing stones, that I should suppose would weigh from six to eight pounds, with a jerk that made them whiz through the air like cannon balls: they threw them against the cliffs of rocks, which resounded with the blow, and many of the stones were dashed, to pieces as they struck. I could see the marks they aimed at, and that the stones went with great precision, as well as force. I had before no idea that it was possible for men to acquire by practice such enormous power of arm; for they threw these stones with such velocity, that I am convinced they would have killed a man at the distance of fifty yards at least.

Having come to the end of the beach, we ascended the bank again, leaving these formidable ruffians masters of the shore, where they, no doubt, got some plunder before they left it. After we had mounted the bank and were clear, Sidi Hamet told me that the fellows we had met were very bad men, and would have killed him and Seid, and would have taken us away where I could never have hoped to see my wife and children again, if the great God had not at that time sent to our relief the two men: he then asked if I would fight to save his life? I told him I would, and that no one should kill him while I was alive, if it was in my power to prevent it: "Good Riley," said he, "you are worth fighting for; God is with you, or I must have lost my life there."

CHAPTER 17

Meet With Robbers on Horseback

Near evening we met and passed a man driving an ass laden with fish, probably of from ten to twelve pounds weight each: they had much the shape and appearance of salmon, and our masters endeavoured to procure one from the owner for me, as I gave them to understand I was very fond of fish, and that it would be good for Burns, but the man would not part with one of them on any terms. At evening we found Hassar's and his family's tents already pitched on a little hill near the cliffs, and we joined this company. Soon after, Seid, Abdallah, and two of Hassar's men, went out with their guns:—in about two hours, those with us, namely, Sidi Hamet, Hassar, and two others, hearing footsteps approaching, seized their muskets, and springing forward from their tents, demanded, who came there? It was Seid and his company, who came towards me, and unfolding a blanket, turned out four large fish of the same kind we had seen before. "Riley," said Sidi Hamet, "are these good to eat?" I answered in the affirmative—"take them and eat them, then," said he, "but be careful not to choke yourselves with the bones."

I took three of them, cut them into pieces, and put them into an earthen pot that belonged to Hassar, (this pot the Arabs call *giderah*,) added some water, and boiled them directly, and we ate till we were satisfied. We drank the soup, which was extremely grateful and invigorating, and helped to check the dysentery, with which we were all much troubled since eating the honeycomb. We had travelled this day, I think, about forty miles, and slept at night within a circle formed by our masters and their camels, out of which we were not suffered to go, as Sidi Hamet told me there were many robbers in this place, who would seize on us, and carry us off in a minute, without the possibility of my ever being restored to my family.

October 21st, at daybreak, we set forward on our journey, all in company, (except Hassar and the women and children.) The fresh fish we had eaten the night before, had made us very thirsty; and about noon we came to a kind of cistern, or reservoir of water, on the pathway side: this reservoir was built of stone and lime; its top was arched like a vault, rising about four feet from the ground, and the cistern was at least eighty feet in length, eight or ten feet in breadth in the inside, and appeared to be twenty feet deep. It was now nearly full of water, which had been led into it by means of gutters, formed and arranged so as to receive and conduct the rain water when it descends from the neighbouring hills, and is collected in a stream in this valley.

I understood this water was the common property of all travellers along this route, and that the cistern was built by a very rich and pious man, solely for the purpose of refreshing the weary traveller, and that it contained water the whole year round, even though there should be a continued drought for a twelvemonth; but no person of our party ventured to water his camel from it, considering it as sacred for the use of man alone. We were still travelling on the slope between the first and second banks of the sea, which in these parts was much cut up, occasioned by the waters which had from time to time poured down from the neighbouring mountains, and formed steep and very deep gullies, across which we were obliged to climb. The path on this inclined plane was not much frequented, and the margin of the bank on our right hand had been newly ploughed in many places here and there, in the nooks or fertile hollows.

On the high lands we saw two small wailed towns, with prickly-pear bushes planted around them. Near these towns or walled villages, some men were employed in ploughing with a pair of beasts, generally a cow and an ass yoked together in a very singular manner, which I shall hereafter describe, and others were watching flocks of sheep and goats on the surrounding eminences, while the women were seen lugging down wood on their backs from the tops of the lofty hills, and large jars or pitchers of water from a distant valley. They generally had a child on their backs, clinging with its arms round the neck of the mother, and the jar or pitcher rested on their shoulders in a manner that reminded me of the story of the beautiful Rebekah, in holy writ, coming to the well with her pitcher.

About noon, we came near a considerable walled village, that stood close by the road; it had gardens close by the walls on all sides, and there was one near the gateway planted with prickly-pear. These gardens were defended by heaps of dry thorn bushes, which served as an outward defence to the town: these heaps were about six feet high, and the walls fifteen feet. Our masters stopped near the gate for some moments, and no one seemed disposed to give them a drink of water, contenting themselves with gazing at them over the walls; so on they went, cursing the inhospitality of these villagers. Near night we descended into a delightful valley, whose bottom was level and well disposed into handsome gardens, fenced in with thorn bushes and stone walls, and divided into numerous separate plots. Round about them, and at their corners, stood many fine fig-trees, which looked healthy, though they were leafless, owing to the lateness of the season: we saw also a few pomegranate-trees. These gardens or plots were planted with different kinds of vegetables, such as turnips, cabbage, onions, &c.; they were watered by a small stream that flowed from the hills at a short distance above, and was conducted round and through the whole of them by gutters dug for that purpose.

The owners of these gardens lived in two little walled villages, near the top of the bank on the east side, but they offered us no refreshment. We passed; in the course of the day, three beds of streams or rivers, which were now dry, and one whose mouth was filled with sand, so as to stop its communication with the sea, though there was some water in it, where people from all quarters were watering their cows, sheep, goats, asses, and camels, and carrying it off in skins and pitchers. In the afternoon, a company of ten men on horseback, and well armed, rode towards us on the plane, making a loud jingling with their spurs against their stirrups, and crying out, *Hah! hah! hah! hah!* Our company consisted of our two masters, and two of Hassar's men, Abdallah, and one stranger, who had joined us that day; and being armed with five double barrelled muskets, and some scimitars, they all sprang from their camels on the approach of the strangers, drew their guns from their sheaths, primed them anew, and took a station in front of their properly, in a line ready for action.

The horsemen rode up to within five yards of our men at full speed, and then stopped their horses short. I expected now to see a battle, though I rather feared our men would be trampled to death by the horses; for their arms could not have saved them from the shock of this impetuous onset, yet they were on the point of firing the moment the horses stopped. The chief of the horsemen then demanded, in a very imperious tone, who our masters were? where they came from? if they knew Sidl Ishem? what countrymen we, their slaves, were? and where they had found us? Sidi Hamet replied to all their questions in a sharp quick manner, and as briefly as possible, and in his turn demanded, "who are you? where do you come from? and, what right have you to ride up to me in such a manner, and stop me and my slaves on the road?"

This is as near as I could understand what they said. A loud dispute was kept up on both sides for half an hour, when it ceased, and we were allowed to proceed; while the others rode off to the southward among the mountains. The force on both sides was so nearly equal, that I have little doubt this was the only circumstance that prevented a battle.

We travelled on till long after dark, when we came to a number of tents, and stopped for the night, and here we were treated with some dried mussels and barley pudding. Hassar and his family had not travelled with us the last day, but the two men who had assisted in relieving us from our critical situation on the beach, were in company, and we had also been joined by one more Arab, and two camels. Ever since we had come to the cultivated country off the desert, we had found the people sickly; many of them were afflicted with swelled legs, and some with what I took to be the leprosy; and also with pains in different parts of their bodies and limbs; though when on the desert we did not see the smallest sign of sickness or disorder among its inhabitants.

They now considered us as skilled in medicine, and consulted me wherever I came; one of the women here had a swelled breast, which was astonishingly large, and very much inflamed: she was in such pain as to cry out at every breath. They wished me to examine it, and prescribe a remedy, which I did by recommending a poultice of the barley *lhash*, or pudding, to be applied, and renewed often until the swelling should subside or burst. The woman was very thankful, gave me a drink of water and a handful of mussels, and requested I would examine a swelled leg of her brother; this was also inflamed, and very painful:—perceiving no skin broken, I directed a thick plaster of coarse salt to be bound round it, so as fully to cover the afflicted part; this they did immediately, and the man thought he felt instantaneous relief.

From the great expedition we had used, I think we must have travelled this day about fifty miles, as we were almost continually on the camels, and they going a great part of the time on a trot. In the afternoon of this day, we discovered land that was very high, a good way eastward of us, stretching about north as far as the eye could reach. We saw it when on a high hill, and at an immense distance; looking over the ocean, which was near us, it appeared like a high and distant island: "There is Swearah, Riley," said Sidi Hamet, pointing to the northernmost land in view: it was a great way off. I asked him how many days it would take us to get there? He answered, "Ten, at our slow pace."

CHAPTER 18

Sidi Hamet and His Brother Seid Fight

October the 23rd, we were awakened without making any noise, two hours before daylight, and went on our journey. I suspected there was some roguery going on, because we had never before started in the night; and we had not travelled more than two leagues, when, just at the dawn of day, we heard the sound of horses' feet coming up at full speed behind us: the clanking of the arms of their riders against each other, and spurs against their stirrups, made a great noise. Our masters stripped the covers from their guns, and gave them to me to carry. The horsemen, four in number, came up by this time, and passing us at a short distance on our right, rode round before our camels and stopped them. Our men were five in number, with four double barrelled guns; and bidding me to keep as close to them as possible with my men, they ran at their greatest speed to the encounter, whilst we followed on as fast as we could, fearing to be separated from them, (as it was still quite dark,) and falling into the hands of the *banditti*.

They approached each other with loud cries; the voices of those on horseback sounded like trumpets, and those of our masters were very little lower, so that the mountains near rang again with the sound. I expected every moment a slaughter would commence: each one strained his throat to speak, or rather to yell louder than his opponents. I had approached near my master, and could distinctly hear one of the horsemen accuse him of a breach of hospitality, and reproach him in the most opprobrious terms, for some wrong which he alleged had been done to him; the others were at the same time wrangling with our other men. This war of words having subsided a little, one of them asked my master his name, and after considerable delay on account of *punctilio*, (each insisting that the other should tell his name first.) my master told him his name was Sidi Hamet; the other then said his name was Ali Mohammed:—then ensued a long dispute between them, they mutually charging each other with perfidy, &c.

During this interval, and as daylight appeared, our adversaries gained strength, for they were joined by many armed and unarmed men, running on foot, and according as they increased in force, our party lowered their tone; but the clamour was still so loud that I frequently could understand nothing of what was said. The Arab who had joined our company with two camels the day before, did not set out with us this morning, but he now came running up: our masters had driven off his camels, and this was the cause of the uproar that was now raging. The purloined camels were then in our drove, and while the others were quarrelling about the matter, the owner ran round and drove his camels back. When our *honest* masters found they could not keep what they had feloniously taken, they began to lower their voices.

By this time the sun had made its appearance, and for two hours prior I had every moment expected a bloody scuffle. I knew our masters were brave, but I had no doubt they would be overpowered by numbers, in which event we should fall to the lot of the conquerors, who were strangers to us; and it was not probable that these men would be as humane to us as Sidi Hamet had been; nor was I indeed certain that we ourselves should not be killed in the contest, both parties being much enraged. I felt our situation to be dreadful indeed; but at length Sidi Hamet spoke to Ali Mohammed in a low tone of voice, and requested he would ride apart from the others with him, with which he complied, and they came near where I sat, trembling with apprehension.

Sidi Hamet now told Ali that his party had not the least intention of driving off any camels but their own, and that the mistake had been occasioned entirely by the darkness of the night. He then went on protesting that he was incapable of committing an unworthy action; that he abhorred a robber and a thief, and that as he was entirely innocent of intentionally driving off the man's camels, he would not acknowledge he had done wrong designedly, but would rather lose his life in maintaining his character, and would sell it as dearly as possible. Ali Mohammed on this appeared to be satisfied, and said to him, "I am *el Rais*, (the chief,) and am your friend, because you are a brave man:" so making Sidi Hamet's excuse to those about him, and the lost camels being recovered, they left us to pursue our journey.

We had gone up from the sea-board, and were passing between high mountains towards the southeast, when the late affray happened, but about noon we reached a plane, and took an eastern direction. Hassar's men with their camels, and Abdallah with his camel, now filed off to the left, leaving us with our masters and their own camels only, and were soon out of sight among the bushes. The mortifying result of the morning's enterprise, had rendered Seid uncommonly ill natured: he had claimed Horace as his slave from the very beginning, and Mr. Savage also belonged to him. He had always doubted my word to his brother, and would not believe that a miserable wretch like me could find a friend to advance money for my ransom, though both he, Hassar, and all the company, had a high opinion of my courage, since I put my own life in jeopardy to save that of Mr. Savage, at the time he fainted;—Seid had endeavoured to sell his slaves at every place we came to, after leaving the desert.

Hassar, as well as others, took a particular fancy to Horace, and had offered a large sum for him in camels and other merchandise, but the interference of Sidi Hamet, who had sworn that Horace should not be separated from me, aided by my often renewed entreaties and my tears, whenever I heard it suggested, had saved him thus far. As we were now approaching the Moorish dominions, powerful chiefs, with large bodies of armed men intent on plunder, were riding about and scouring the country in every direction, and Seid had come to a determination to take his slaves and make the most of them. Seid was a younger brother of Sidi Hamet, and had, until now, submitted in some degree to his counsel, though they had many slight quarrels at different periods of the journey. Where we stopped the preceding night, the Arabs strove hard to get possession of Horace. Seid had, to my knowledge, made a bargain to sell him in the morning, but was dissuaded from fulfilling it by his brother.

We, slaves, were now five in all, travelling on foot, but moving forward very slowly, for we were worn to the bones by our various and complicated sufferings. It seemed that the breath of hope alone had kept the vital spark from being totally extinguished. Sidi Hamet was riding on his big camel before us, when Seid ordered us to halt, but the other desired us to come on; upon which Seid laid hold of Mr. Savage and Horace, and stopped them. It was now that Sidi Hamet's wrath was kindled—he leaped from his camel, and darting like lightning up to Seid, laid hold of him, and disengaged Mr. Savage and

Horace from his grasp. They clinched each other like lions, and with fury in their looks, each strove to throw the other to the ground. Seid was the largest and stoutest man; they writhed and twined in every shape until both fell, but Sidi Hamet was undermost: fire seemed to flash from their eyes, whilst they twisted around each other like a couple of serpents, until at length Sidi Hamet, by superior activity or skill, disengaged himself from his brother's grasp, and both sprang up on their feet.

Instantly they snatched their muskets at the same moment, and each retiring a few paces with great rapidity and indignation, tore the cloth covers from their guns, and presented them at each other's breast with dreadful fury:—they were not more than ten yards asunder, and both must have fallen dead, had they fired. Horror had seized and chilled my blood, so that I could neither get from them, nor move, indeed, in any direction. My mind was filled with inexpressible apprehensions—"My God," I cried aloud, "have mercy on these unfortunate brothers, I pray thee, for our sakes, and suffer them not to spill each other's blood."

In the midst of this ejaculation, I was started by the report of two muskets, and imagined that both the brothers had fallen; but on turning my eyes again to this direful scene, I perceived that Sidi Hamet had fired the contents of both his barrels into the air, having had a moment's reflection, whilst priming and cocking his piece. He now threw it on the ground, then making bare his bosom, he advanced with a firm step towards Seid, and with an energetic voice exclaimed, "I am now unarmed, fire! your brother's heart is ready to receive your balls; glut your vengeance on your benefactor." He stopped short: Seid hesitated, Mr. Savage and Horace were near Seid, who threatened them with instant death if they moved.

Sidi Hamet, finding his brother's mind wavered, ran to Horace, and sent him towards me, telling his brother, he should have Clark in Horace's stead, whom he ordered to come near; but Seid would not consent to the exchange, whereupon my master added Burns; that is, two for one. Seid had made Mr. Savage sit down, and had placed one of his feet on his thigh, to keep him there; while his brother ordered me to go with Horace, first to the south and then to the eastward, following the camels; still resolving that we should not be separated, and bade Mr. Savage follow us; but Seid, presenting his gun, told him if he offered to go, he would blow his brains out.

As Sidi Hamet, however, bade him run, he obeyed, and when he came near me we were all ordered to stop, and our masters seated themselves on the ground to settle the dispute by figuring on the sand with their fingers. Here they calculated it every way. Clark and Burns were again offered for Horace, but Seid would not take them; he would keep the slave he had bought with his money.

"You shall not separate him from his father," said my master, "I have sworn it."

"Then I will destroy him," exclaimed Seid furiously, and springing up, he seized Horace by the breast and dashed him on the ground with all his might. The force of the blow beat the breath from his body, and he lay stretched out apparently dead. Overwhelmed with the most heart-rending emotions, I sank to the earth in an agony of despair. My master, observing my anguish, said, " Go, Riley," pointing to the east.

With tears and sobs, I told him I could go, for Horace, my son, was dead. After a flood of tears had relieved my swelling heart, I reflected that it was useless to bewail the fate of my adopted child, as I did not know how soon it might be my turn to suffer a similar, or perhaps a more cruel death. Seid's passion now began to subside a little, and my master then went to Horace, and taking him by the hands, raised him upon his seat: his breath returned, and he revived. Sidi Hamet melted into tears at the sight: I saw the big drops roll down his cheeks, while in a tender tone, he said to Horace, "Go to Riley." The spot where his head fell happened to be clear of stones, which entirely covered the ground on every side, otherwise his brains must have been dashed out.

I went up to him as quick as I could, and folding him in my arms, asked him if he was much hurt; but being in great pain, and his breathing being not yet perfectly restored, he was incapable of answering me: his heart, however, was in unison with mine, in thanking the Author of our being that his life was spared, and in imploring his future protection. Our masters again seated themselves, in order to discuss this affair thoroughly, and began to speak very loud, when, fortunately for us, some strangers came in sight, which reminded them that their united force was necessary for the defence of themselves and their property; so they agreed to seek a village, and take counsel as to what was best to be done.

Then turning to our left up a hill, we soon came in sight of a village, and entered it by passing between high walls. Having come to its farthest extremity, an old, but a very respectable looking man, (a

Moor,) of a light olive colour, came out of his gate, and welcomed our masters, saluting them, (as is customary,) and seeing us behind, told us to sit down in a shade formed by his wall, and rest ourselves; adding, "I will give you some food." We accordingly all seated ourselves, and while the food was preparing, our host inquired much about me and my men, and wished to know how I could make myself understood, (being a Christian.) Our owners told him all our stories, together with my promises, which they made me repeat in his presence. They wanted again to know in what my property consisted; if I had any money in my own country, or a house; how much money, how many horses, cows, sheep, goats, asses, camels, &c.; and lastly, what number of wives and children I had.

Having answered all these interrogations to their satisfaction, they made me tell what Mr. Savage, Horace, Clark, and Burns, were worth to me; how much property I thought they had in their own country; and our host, who spoke a few words of broken Spanish, asked me if Swearah was not called *Mogdola* by the English? I answered in the affirmative:—this was the first time I had heard this name mentioned on this continent, though I had endeavoured, by inquiring of all the people I had spoken with, to ascertain the point; but it appeared they had never heard of the name.

One bowl of boiled barley unhulled, was brought out to our masters, and one for us—this last was a very large one, and the old host told us to eat, saying, "*Coole, Rais*" (eat, captain.) We had now before us, for the first time, enough of this food, and falling to with keen appetites, we filled our stomachs, and were satisfied, leaving some in the bowl, which they tried hard to make us finish, but we could not. Sidi Hamet would not trust himself again with his brother, without having some person in company to take his part; so he hired a stout young fellow, named Bo-Mohammed, to go along with us to another place or village, not far distant, and we set off for it, travelling at first down towards the sea-coast, and passing along a kind of sandy beach where the salt water flowed in at high tides: we saw there, under the side of a shelving rock, two boiling springs of fresh water, which formed a considerable stream. This was the first spring I had seen in this country, and having taken a good drink and watered our camels, we proceeded towards the southeast among sands that had drifted from the sea-beach; there we remained until it was nearly dark, our masters fearing, as it were, to go forward.

About dark we resumed our course, and soon afterwards arrived at a village, where, while the barking of numerous dogs announced to their owners the arrival of strangers, a grave looking man came out, and silencing the curs, bade our masters welcome, and invited both them and us to sit down near his walls, until he should prepare some supper. We had no desire, however, for food, some of us having oppressed our stomachs to such a degree with the boiled barley, as to be racked with pain, and scarce able to breathe, particularly Mr. Savage.

Our present host, (whose name I soon learned was Sidi Mohammed,) after causing a mat to be spread near his wall, seated himself and our masters thereon, and desired me to come and do the same. He now made similar inquiries to those made by the former persons we had met, and I satisfied his curiosity as well as I could. He then informed me he had been many times in Swearah, and had seen the consuls, and wished me to repeat my promise to Sidi Hamet, which I did. He had a lamp for a light, so that he could see every motion that I made well enough to comprehend me entirely. By this time some cakes had been baked, which were presented to our masters, and of which they gave us some: these cakes were made of barley meal, ground coarse; yet it was bread, and it being the first we had seen, we ate a little of it, though our stomachs were not yet prepared to enjoy the treat.

After they had eaten and washed their hands and feet, and talked over their affairs, Sidi Hamet again called me to him, and told me he should set out in the morning for Swearah, in company with our host, Sidi Mohammed, where he hoped, with God's blessing, to arrive in three days, for he should travel on a mule, (*bugelah,*) and push on night and day: that I must write a letter to my friend, which he would carry; and, said he, "if your friend will fulfil your engagements, and pay the money for you and your men, you shall be free—if not, you must die for having deceived me, and your men shall be sold for what they will bring. I have fought for you," added he, "have suffered hunger, thirst, and fatigue, to restore you to your family, for I believe God is with you. I have paid away all my money on your word alone. Seid and Bo-Mohammed will stay and guard you during my absence: they will give you as much *khobs* (bread) and *lhash* (pudding) as you can eat; so go and sleep till morning."

This night was spent on my part in a state of anxiety not easy to conceive:—to whom should I write? I knew nobody at Mogadore, and yet I must take my chance. I remembered my remarkable dream—it had literally come to pass thus far—why should I doubt its whole accomplishment? yet I could not rest.

CHAPTER 19

The Author Writes a Letter

Early the next morning we were called up, and directed to go within the gates. My master said to me, "Come, Riley, write a letter," giving me at the same time a scrap of paper, not so wide as my hand, and about eight inches long; he had also got a little black staining liquid and a reed to write with. I now begged hard to be taken along with him, but he would not consent, though I told him I would leave my son, whom I loved more than myself, behind me as an hostage, and three men; but all would not do, the thing was determined on. He then told me, that what I had agreed to give him was not sufficient; that I must tell my friend, in the letter, to pay two hundred dollars for myself, two hundred for Horace, two hundred for Aaron, one hundred and sixty for Clark, and the same for Burns, adding, that I had promised him a good double barrelled gun, and I must give him that, and one to Seid also. "Seid is a bad man," said he, "but helped to save your life, and must have a gun." So I took the reed, and wrote on the slip of paper, as near as I can recollect, the following letter.

Sir—The brig *Commerce*, from Gibraltar for America, was wrecked or Cape Bajador, on the 28th August last; myself and four of my crew are here nearly naked, in barbarian slavery: I conjure you by all the ties that bind man to man, by those of kindred blood, and everything you hold most dear, and by as much as liberty is dearer than life, to advance the money required for our redemption, which is nine hundred and twenty dollars, and two double barrelled guns. I can draw for any amount, the moment I am at liberty, on Batard, Sampson & Sharp, London—Cropper & Benson, Liverpool—Munro & Burton, Lisbon, or on Horatio Sprague, Gibraltar. Should you not relieve me, my life must instantly pay the forfeit. I leave a wife and five helpless children to deplore my death. My companions are Aaron R. Savage, Horace Savage, James Clark, and Thomas Burns. I left six more in slavery on the desert. My present master, Sidi Hamet, will hand you this, and tell you where we are—he is a worthy man. Worn down to the bones by the most dreadful of all sufferings—naked and a slave, I implore your pity, and trust that such distress will not be suffered to plead in vain. For God's sake, send an interpreter and a guard for us, if that is possible. I speak French and Spanish.

    James Riley, late Master and
      Supercargo of the brig *Commerce*.

  While I was writing the above, they procured an additional scrap of paper, being a part of a Spanish bill of lading, on which I wrote a part of my letter, that could not be written legibly on the first scrap. Having folded them up, I directed them to the "English, French, Spanish, or American consuls, or any Christian merchants in Mogadore or Swearah." I purposely omitted mentioning that we were Americans, because I did not know that there was an American agent there, and I had no doubt of there being an English consul or agent in that place. My master was hurrying me while I was writing, and both he and my host, Seid, and the young man, and many others who stood by, were surprised to see me make the Arabic numerals; for the characters we use in arithmetic are no other than the real ancient Arabic figures, which have served them for thousands of years; they remarked to each other that I must have been a slave before to some Arabian, who had taught me the use of them, contrary to their law, because he had found me to be a smart active fellow. My master taking my letter, then mounted one mule, and Sidi Mohammed another, and rode off together very fast to the east.

  We remained here seven days, during which time they kept us shut up in the yard in the day time, where the cows, sheep, and asses rested, and at night they locked us up in a dreary cellar. Seid and Bo Mohammed guarded us all the day, not because they feared we would attempt to escape, but because some of the neighbouring people might steal and run off with us, and in the night time they lay on their arms outside the door, to prevent a surprise. We had as much bailey bread twice a day as we wanted, *lhash* once a day, and plenty of water. This food, though palatable, produced and kept up a continual dysentery;

our bowels seemed to ferment like beer, and we were tortured with cholics. Our numerous sores had now time to heal, and our bodies became mostly skinned over before our masters returned; but the haemorrhoids distressed us extremely.

All the inhabitants who lived near, and all those who heard that Christians were in the place, (for they call all Europeans Christians,) came to see us. Some were very familiar, and all wished to know if we were mechanics: from that circumstance I concluded that mechanics were very much wanted, and of great importance among these people, and that there would be no possibility of getting clear of them, if once they should find out our usefulness in that way. I therefore told them that we were all brought up sailors from our childhood, and knew no other business. One tried to make me lay out and hew a pair of posts for a door to a house that was building within the walls of the village, and gave me a line to measure the length of them, and tried to teach me to span it off; but I would not understand him.

They next put a kind of adze into my hand, and bade me fit the posts in. I took the tool, and began to cut at random, gouging out a piece here, and splitting it there, doing more hurt than good; and, at the same time, by my awkward and clumsy manner, taking care to make them believe that I could do no better. Some were satisfied that I had done my very best, but by far the greater part of them were of opinion that a smart application of the whip would put my mechanical powers into complete operation, and really expected they would apply this stimulus; for one of them ran and fetched a stout stick, and was about to lay it on, when Bo-Mohammed, who represented Sidi Hamet, interfered and saved me from a cudgelling. Mr. Savage, Clark, Burns, and Horace, were each tried in their turns, who, following my instructions, were soon relieved from all further requisition.

From this circumstance it is evident, that the less useful a Christian makes himself when a slave to the Arabs, especially in a mechanical way, the less value they will set upon him, and he will not only have a chance of getting ransomed, but it may be effected on easier terms than otherwise; for I am fully convinced, that if we had shown ourselves capable in those arts which the Arabs highly prize, such as carpenters, smiths, shoemakers, &c. &c. we should have been sold at high prices, and soon carried away beyond the possibility of redemption.

Four days after Sidi Hamet's departure, some papers were shown to me by one of the men who lived in the neighbourhood, which I found, on examination, to be, first, the register of the Spanish schooner *Maria*, issued by the custom-house at Cadiz, in May 1814; second, a bill of sale of the same schooner, made out at the island of Grand Canary in 1812, of the same date with the register. Many articles of clothing that had belonged to her crew were also shown me; and the topmast, jib-boom, and other small spars of a vessel, served to support the floor over our nightly prison.

I made inquiries as far as it was possible, in order to find out something respecting this vessel, which I presumed must have been wrecked near this place; and was informed that the preceding year a schooner anchored on this part of the coast to catch fish, and to trade; that these people found means to get alongside of her in the night in boats, and after killing the captain and three men, got possession of her; when having taken out the money and other valuables, they cut her cables, and ran her on snore: that they then made the surviving part of the crew assist in tearing the wreck to pieces, and in carrying; it up to build houses with. I asked how many people were on board her, and where the remainder of the crew were; and was informed by a serious looking old man, that it consisted of seventeen souls at first; that four were slain in the conflict when she was captured; that five more had died since, and that the remaining eight were a great way off to the southeast, where they were employed in working on the land and making houses.

Others said, they had gone to Swearah, and from thence to their own country; but I could easily perceive by their looks that those poor fellows had either been massacred, or were now held in slavery, where neither the voice of liberty, nor the hand of friendship, was ever likely to reach them. The people here, both old and young, could speak many words of Spanish, though they did not know their meaning, but made use of them at a venture at all times—these were a set of f the very coarsest and most vulgar words the Spanish language affords, and had been uttered, no doubt, by poor unfortunate slaves, natives of Spain, when they were suffering the greatest misery, and when execrating these savages.

One young fellow spoke several words of English, such as "good morning—good night," &c. and was master of a considerable list of curses. He one day came up to Mr. Savage, and said—"button, cut it wit a nif," and at the same time laid hold of a button on his pantaloons. Mr. Savage was very much surprised to hear a language he could understand; but these words and the oaths and curses, constituted the whole of his English education. Every person here had either a long knife or a scimitar always slung by his side. Among the rest, several negroes came to look at us, some of whom were slaves and some free, and they were all Mohammedans: these were allowed to sit on a mat beside our masters, and make remarks on us as we were placed among the fresh manure at a short distance. Seid desired to know what we called black men: I told him *negroes*; at which name the negroes seemed very indignant, and much enraged.

On the sixth day of my master's absence, a man arrived and took up his lodging with our guards: he was about six feet in height, and proportionably stout; his colour was something between that of a negro and an Arab: when he came in he was saluted by Seid and the others in company by the name of Sheick Ali, (or Ali the chief.) This man possessed talents of that superior cast which never fail to command the greatest respect, and at the same time to inspire dread, awe, and reverence. He appeared to be only a guest or visitor. In his deportment he was grave and dignified: he raised his voice on occasions terribly, and spoke in tones almost of thunder; yet when he wished to please by condescension and courtesy, it thrilled on the ear like sounds of softest music: his manner and air were very commanding, and his whole aspect and demeanour bore the stamp of the most daring courage and unflinching firmness.

He was the most eloquent man I had ever heard speak; persuasion dwelt upon his tongue; while he spoke, all the company observed the most profound silence, and with open mouths seemed to inhale his honeyed sentences. He pronounced with the most perfect emphasis; the elegant cadence, so much admired in eastern oratory, seemed to have acquired new beauties from his manner of delivery: his articulation was so clear and distinct, and his countenance and actions so intelligent and expressive, that I could understand him perfectly, though he spoke in the Arabic language. He would settle all controverted points among the disputants when applied to, in an instant, and yet with the upmost gracefulness and dignity.

This extraordinary chief was often conversing in a low tone of voice with Seid respecting me and my men: he said he believed me to be a very artful fellow, and capable of any action either good or bad; and said he did not doubt but my friends would raise any sum of money that might be demanded for my ransom. He regretted very much that he had not seen Sidi Hamet before he set out for Swearah, and concluded to remain with us until his return. He questioned me very particularly as to my country, my friends, family, property, &c.;

he also wished to know all the story of my shipwreck, and was very curious to find out what quantity of money and what other property fell into the hands of those who first met with us after the vessel was wrecked, and what crime was committed to induce these Moslemin to kill Antonio.

He next examined our bodies all over, and on one of Clark's arms his attention was arrested by a cross, and several other marks of Christian insignia that had been pricked in with Indian ink, in the manner of the Spanish and other sailors: the stain remained entire, though the skin had many times been changed, and now seemed drawn tight over the bone. This being a conclusive proof in the *Sheick's* mind of *Christianity*, he pronounced him "a Spaniard," and said he should not be redeemed, but must go to the mountains and work with him. Everything that this man said, seemed to carry with it a weight that bore downfall opposition.

We had, during Sidi Hamet's absence, (after the fifth day,) been in constant expectation of receiving news from him, or that he himself would return, and our keepers inquired of every stranger who came from the eastward, if they had seen him, but obtained no news until the seventh day, when one of the most fierce and ill looking men I had ever beheld, approached the wall, and hailed Seid by name, ordering him in an imperious tone to open the gate directly. Seid demanded to know who he was: he replied, Ullah Omar; that he came from Swearah, and had met Sidi Hamet near that place, who requested him to call and tell Seid where he was, and that God had prospered his journey so far.

The gate was now opened, and the stranger entered he was of a dark complexion, nearly six feet in height, and extremely muscular; had a long musket in his hand, a pair of horse pistols hanging in his belt, and a scimitar and two long knives slung by his sides, with the *haick* or blanket for a dress, and a large white turban on his head; he had a pair of long iron spurs, which were fastened to his slippers of yellow Morocco leather; he rode a beautiful horse, which seemed fleet and vigorous, and he appeared to be about forty years of age. This was the first man I had seen harnessed in this way. Sheick Ali knew him, and shook him most cordially by the hand, and after exchanging salutations all round, hearing I was the captain, he addressed me and told me he had seen my friend, Sidi Hamet; that he met him within one day's ride of Swearah; that he would no doubt be here on the morrow, for that God had prospered his journey on account of me; and added, that he hoped my friend in Swearah or Mogdola would be as true to me as Sidi Hamet was: he then spoke to all my men, who though they did not understand him, yet were rejoiced to hear through me, that there was a prospect of my master's returning soon.

This man had two powder horns slung from his neck, and a pouch in which he carried a wooden pipe and some tobacco, besides a plentiful supply of leaden balls and slugs. My shipmates waited some tobacco very much, and I asked him for a little, upon which he gave me a handful of very good tobacco, and seemed exceedingly pleased to have it in his power to administer comfort to such miserable beings. I imagined from his whole deportment that he resembled one of those high-spirited, heroic, and generous robbers, that are so admirably described in ancient history. Seid furnished him with some food, which I now learned they called *cous-koo-soo*, with some slices of *pumpion* or squash spread over it in the bowl, and well peppered, This dish, which is made of small balls of flour, boiled with a fowl and vegetables, looked (for I had not the pleasure of tasting it) like a very nice dish. After they had washed, drank water, eaten, washed again, and prayed together, Ullah Omar took his leave. During the whole of the time we remained here, our keepers washed themselves all over with water twice a day, before mid-day and evening prayers, and always washed their hands before and after eating.

The state of my mind, in the meantime, can be more easily conceived than described: during this day and the next, which was the eighth, I longed to know my fate; and yet I must own, I trembled at the thoughts of what it might be, and at the conditions I had myself proposed at my last purchase, and had so often since confirmed. If my master should find no one who should be willing to pay the money for my redemption, my fate was sealed. I had already agreed to have my throat cut! this could not be prevented; yet when I made this agreement I was naked and on a vast and dreary desert, literally without a skin; my remaining flesh was roasted on my body; not a drop of fresh water to quench my burning thirst, nor even an herb nor any other thing to satisfy the cravings of hunger: my life was fast wasting away, and there was not even a hope remaining, or a possibility of existing long in my then forlorn condition: both myself and my companions would have sold our lives for a drink of fresh water or a morsel of bread.

In that most dismal and desperate situation, I imagined that if I could once get to the cultivated country beyond the desert, I should find some food to support nature, and fresh water to allay our thirst. My remarkable dream had also given me courage to hope for redemption; but if I was not redeemed myself, I felt it my duty to exert myself to the utmost to preserve the lives of my shipmates; they might some of them, I fancied, possibly survive, even though I should not, and be at length restored to their country and friends, in consequence of my exertions, and convey to my distressed family the sad tidings of my wretched fate. Circumstances were now changed; I had passed the dangers of the desert, and arrived in the cultivated country; we had now plenty of good water, and some food and shelter; and though my flesh was nearly all wasted away, yet a new skin had succeeded and nearly covered my bones. My desire to live kept pace with the increase of my comforts; I longed for the return of my master, and yet I anticipated it with the most fearful and dreadful apprehensions. I could not sleep; alternate hope and fear kept me in a state of continual agitation. I calculated on the moment of his arrival as decisive of my fate; it would either restore me to liberty, or doom me to instant death: I trembled at every noise occasioned by the opening of the gate on any new arrival.

FAC SIMILE of an Arabic Letter, written on one square of Mr Willshire's letter, by Sidi Hamet when in Mogadore, to his brother Seid, in Suse, having under his charge Capt. Riley & four of his Companions. The letter was handed to Capt. R. by Rais Bel Cossim & is inserted in the Narrative.

CHAPTER 20

The Letter

The eighth day of my master's absence passed tediously away; when, after dark, we heard a trampling outside the walls. Seid went forth to learn its cause, and soon returned with Sidi Mohammed, followed by a well looking Moor. They came directly to that part of the yard where we were sitting on the ground, trembling with apprehension and with cold. When they came near me, the Moor called out and said in English, "How de-do, *Capetan*." This raised me and all my men from the ground; I felt as if my heart was forcing its way up into my throat, and it entirely obstructed my breath. I eagerly seized his hand, and begged to know who he was, and what was my doom, and if Sidi Hamet had come back: he then asked me in Spanish if I spoke that language, and being answered in the affirmative, he informed me in Spanish that he came from Mogadore; that my letter had been received by one of the best of men, an Englishman, who was his friend, and who had shed tears on reading my letter; that he had paid the money to my master immediately, and had sent him (the Moor) off, without giving him scarcely a moment's time to take leave of his wife, and that he had been on his mule ever since he left Swearah, travelling on as fast as possible, night and day.

The anxiety of my companions by this time had risen to such a pitch that they broke in upon his story, on which I communicated to them the thrice welcome and happy intelligence, that we had a friend who would redeem us from slavery. Our souls were overwhelmed with joy, and yet we trembled with apprehension lest it might not be true: alas! perhaps it was only a delusive dream, or some cruel trick to turn our miseries into mockery. At this moment, however, the Moor handed me a letter: I broke it open; but my emotions were such, that it was impossible for me to read its contents, and I handed it to Mr.

Savage; for my frame trembled to such a degree, that I could not stand, and I sank to the earth, but, thank God, not senseless; while by means of the light of a fire, he read as follows:—

Mogadore, October 25, 1815.

My Dear and Afflicted Sir,

I have this moment received your two notes by Sidi Hamet, the contents of which, I hope you will be perfectly assured, have called forth my most sincere pity tor your sufferings, and those of your companions in captivity.

By a Gibraltar paper I discover, under the arrivals from the 5th to the 11th August, the name of your vessel, and that she was American, from which I conclude both you and your crew must be subjects of the United States: had it not been for the paper adverted to, some delay would have occurred, as you do not state in your notes to what nation you belong.

I congratulate you most sincerely, on the good fortune you and your fellow sufferers have met, by being in the hands of a man who seems to be guided by some degree of commiseration.

I can in some measure participate in the severe and dangerous sufferings and hardships you must have undergone; but, my dear sir, console yourself, for, thanks be to God, I hope they will soon have a happy issue; for which purpose I devoutly pray the great Disposer of all things will give you and your unfortunate companions health and strength once more to visit your native land.

This letter will be delivered you by Rais bel Cossim, in whom you may place the fullest faith: he speaks Spanish, and has directions to pay attention to your orders, and render you every care your severe misfortunes may require. Be pleased to write me an immediate answer, slating every particular relating to yourself, your crew, and vessel, as I have given orders to the Moor to forward it to me without delay.

I have agreed to pay the sum of nine hundred and twenty hard dollars to Sidi Hamet, on your safe arrival in this town with your fellow sufferers: he remains here as a kind of hostage for your safe appearance.

I have been induced to trust implicitly to your word, and the respectable references you have given, in confidence that those gentlemen, or yourself, will readily reimburse me the whole of the expenses that may be incurred in obtaining your redemption.

I have the most sincere pleasure to acquaint you, you will be at liberty to commence your journey for this town on the receipt of this letter, and make what stages you please on the road, as I do not advise you, in the eagerness all of you must feel, to run into danger by over exertion and fatigue: I would, therefore, recommend the greatest precaution on this point. I have sent under charge of Rais bel Cossim, shoes and cloaks, which I have no doubt you will find very useful in preserving you from rain or cold on the road. I have also forwarded you some provisions and spirits, that you may enjoy a foretaste of returning liberty.

I beg to recommend the greatest secrecy of your circumstances until your arrival here, for should the Moors suppose you able to pay more, they would throw difficulties in the way, and thereby much retard your redemption.

I shall send off an express tomorrow to the United States' Consul General at Tangier, and a letter to Mr. Horatio Sprague of Gibraltar, informing them of your loss, and of the favourable hopes I entertain of your immediate release.

I have appointed with Rais bel Cossim, on your arrival at a short distance from Mogadore, to wait at the garden of a friend of mine, and send me notice of the same, when I shall immediately set out to meet you.

I trust there is no occasion for me to say how truly I commiserate and enter into all your misfortunes: when God grants me the pleasure to embrace you, it will be to me a day of true rejoicing. I beg you will assure everyone with you of my truest regard; and with sentiments embittered by the thoughts of the miseries you have undergone, but with the must sanguine hope of a happy end to all your sufferings I subsonic myself, with the greatest esteem, my dear sir, your friend,

      William Willshire.

P. S. I willingly agree to advance the money, considering a month or more must elapse before I could receive an answer from Mr. Sprague. I therefore concluded you would prefer being at liberty in this town, to experiencing a prolongation of your sufferings during that period. I shall be happy in rendering you every comfort that my house and this country can afford.

      W. W.

My feelings, during the reading of this letter, may perhaps be conceived, but f cannot attempt to describe them; to form an idea of my emotions at that time, it is necessary for the reader to transport himself in imagination to the country where I then was, a wretched slave, and to fancy himself as having passed through all the dangers and distresses that I had experienced: reduced to the lowest pitch of human wretchedness, degradation, and despair, a skinless skeleton, expecting death at every instant: then let him fancy himself receiving such a letter from a perfect stranger, whose name he had never before heard, and from a place where there was not an individual creature that had ever before heard of his existence, and in one of the most barbarous regions of the habitable globe: let him receive at the same time clothes to cover and defend his naked, emaciated, and trembling frame, shoes for his mangled feet, and such provisions as he had been accustomed to in his happier days—let him find a soothing and sympathising friend in a barbarian, and one who spoke perfectly well the language of a Christian nation; and with all this, let him behold a prospect of a speedy liberation and restoration to his beloved, family:—here let him pause, and his heart must, like mine, expand near to bursting with gratitude to his all-wise and beneficent Creator, who had upheld his tottering frame and preserved in his bosom the vital spark, while he conducted him, with unerring wisdom and goodness, through the greatest perils and sufferings, by a continued miracle, and now prepared the heart of a stranger to accomplish what had been before determined.

The letter being finished, we could only raise our eyes and hearts to heaven in adoration and silent thankfulness, while tears of joy trickled down our haggard cheeks.—Amidst these joyful and heart- thrilling sensations, my attention was aroused by the thundering voice of Sheick Ali, who stormed away most furiously on being informed that Sidi Hamet had given up me and my companions for such a paltry sum:—he said, Sidi Hamet must be a fool and a madman to put himself in the power of a villainous Christian, who would undoubtedly murder him and take back his money so soon as we should arrive in Swearah. The Moor, who had hitherto remained silent, now spoke out in a very spirited manner, and told the *Sheick* in a very firm, but eloquent and persuasive tone, that he. had bought me and my companions with his own money, which he had paid to Sidi Hamet before he left Swearah; and that he (Sidi Hamet) remained there voluntarily as a hostage for his (Rais bel Cossim's) safety, as well as security for the delivery of the slaves.

"We are of the same religion," added Rais, "and owe these Christian dogs nothing; we have an undoubted right to make merchandise of them, and oblige them to carry our burdens like camels. That fellow" said he, pointing to me "calls himself the captain of a vessel—he has deceived his master and you; for he was nothing more than a cook on board, and the captain has long been dead."

This the *Sheick* would not believe; if it was so, how could I write a note to induce a stranger to pay so much money for me and my men? "It was only a short one," added he, "and its writer must be a man of much consequence, as well as knowledge. I fear you (though a Moslemin) have leagued with a Christian against Sidi Hamet, first to rob him of his slaves, and then to take his life."

"No, by *Allah!* I am incapable of such an act of treachery," retorted Rais, and told the *Sheick* I was indeed the cook, but being a stout fellow, had been able to endure fatigues better than the others: "but" added he "give them paper, pen, and ink, and they will soon convince you they can all write, and much better than Riley."

This controversy continued a long time, and I found that Rais bel Cossim was a man of great courage, as well as knowledge and eloquence; and he certainly displayed great address and management in checking the avaricious calculations of the *Sheick*, by insisting on my not being a captain, and thus depreciating my value as a slave. Seid seemed to have sunken into a kind of sullen silence: it was now late, and Sidi Mohammed conducted the whole company into an apartment that had served, from appearances, as a stable for mules. They had loudly insisted that we should lodge in the same place where we had been before confined, but Rais would not consent, and declared that his slaves should stay by his side, both night and day. They had cost him a great deal of money, he said, and he was determined not to lose them. Having thus got into comfortable quarters, our cloaks were produced from a basket, and we put them on.

Our friend had sent us some hard biscuits and boiled neats' tongues—he had also forwarded tea, coffee, and sugar, and a few bottles of rum, with a tea-kettle, tea-pot, cups and saucers, all nicely packed up in a small box. Rais then procured a lighted lamp, and I gave each of my men a slice of tongue, some biscuit, and a drink of rum: this revived their spirits exceedingly, and we all felt as if new life was infused into our hearts, which at the same time swelled with gratitude to God for his infinite mercy and goodness. We were next regaled with a very fine watermelon; and having put on our new shoes to make our feet warm, and wrapped ourselves up in large cloaks or *gzlabbias*, we stretched ourselves on the ground to sleep, whilst Rais, Seid, and his companion, Bo-Mohammed, and Sheick Ali, laid themselves down on a platform made of boards that must have been brought from the wreck of some vessel, and was raised two feet from the ground. The food which I and my companions had eaten, together with the melon and liquor, caused us such violent griping pains in our stomachs and intestines, that we could with great difficulty forbear screaming out with agony, and we found no relief till morning, after having passed a sleepless night.

Early in the morning, Rais desired me, in Arabic, to make some tea: so I took out the kettle, had it filled with water, made a fire with a few sticks, and soon had the tea ready for drinking. The men and boys in and near this village, hearing of Sidi Mohammed's return to his family, came now to congratulate him, and to see the Moor, who directed me to pour out a cup of tea for each of the men, which he made thick with sugar. None of the people had ever before seen such a thing as a tea-cup, nor knew what the taste of tea was, and it was with difficulty that several of them could be persuaded to drink it, and they appeared to be reconciled to it only on account of the sugar. I waited on them all until they had finished; when Rais, turning to Sheick Ali, said, "I told you before that Riley was the cook, and now you see with your own eyes that he is the only one that can wait upon us." I next made a strong cup of tea for ourselves, which had a most remarkable effect in composing and restoring the tone of our stomachs.

All our things being soon packed up and loaded on mules, we set forward at about eight o'clock. The Moor had tried to procure mules for us to ride on; but they could not be had in this part of the country at any price. Our company consisted of Sheick Ali, Sidi Mohammed, (who had been to Swearah on our account,) Seid, our master, Bo-Mohammed, (who had assisted in guarding us,) and Rais bel Cossim, all well armed. Though he could procure no beasts exclusively for our use, yet Rais managed in such a manner as to let us ride by turns, and Burns all the time, for he was so feeble as not to be able to walk. So soon as we were on the road, Rais bel Cossim begged me to give him an account of my misfortunes and sufferings, and by what miracle my life and the lives of those who were with me had been preserved. I satisfied his curiosity as well as I could, by a short narration of the most prominent occurrences.

When I had finished, he raised his eyes towards heaven with an air and expression of true devotion, and exclaimed, in Spanish, "Praised be God, the most high and holy! for his goodness:" then addressing himself to me, he remarked, "You have indeed been preserved most wonderfully by the peculiar protection and assistance of an overruling Providence, and must be a particular favourite of heaven: there never was an instance" added he "of a Christian's passing the great desert for such a distance before, and you are no doubt destined to do some great good in the world; and may the Almighty continue to preserve you, and restore you to your distressed family. Sidi Hamet" added he "admired your conduct, courage, and intelligence, and says they are more than human—that God is with you in all your transactions, and has blessed him for your sake." I mention this conversation to show the light in which my master had viewed me; and this will account for the interest he took in my restoration to liberty, over and above his motives of gain.

I now inquired who Sheick Ali was, and why he was going on in company; and said, I much feared him. Rais informed me that all he knew about him he had learned from Sidi Mohammed, which was, that he is the chief of a very large and powerful tribe of Arabs, who inhabit the hills south of us, and near the borders of the great desert; that Sidi Hamet had married one of his daughters, but had since been at war with him, and that in the contest his father-in-law had destroyed Sidi Hamet's town, and taken back his daughter, but afterwards restored her again on making peace; that this *Sheick* could bring ten or fifteen thousand men into the field whenever he pleased, and that he was a man of the greatest talents and capacity in war, as well as in peace; but why he was going on in our company in this manner, he could not tell, and agreed with me in suspecting that it could be for no good purpose; yet he observed, "God could turn his evil intentions to our good, and that that power which had protected me thus far, would not forsake me until his will was accomplished."

Chapter 21

Lodge in a City

We travelled on in a southeast direction through a very sandy country, with, however, here and there a small rising, and a few cultivated spots, for about five hours, at the rate of five miles an hour, when we came opposite the shattered walls of a desolate town or city that stood not far from our path on the right. These walls appeared to inclose a square spot of about three hundred yards in extent on each side, and they seemed to be at least fifteen feet in height. They were built of rough stones, laid in clay or mud, and partly daubed over with the same material. On the north side there was a gateway handsomely arched over with stone, and furnished with a strong heavy looking wooden gate that was now shut.

Over the gate there appeared to be a platform for the purpose of defending the gate, for the wall was not quite so high in that part as elsewhere. Two battering machines were standing against the western angle of the wall, opposite to which a large practicable breach had been made by means of one of those machines. They were both very simple in their structure, but calculated to be very powerful in their effects. I could distinctly see and examine with my eyes the one nearest to us.

It was formed, as it appeared to me, in the first place, by laying down two large logs of wood at right angles with the wall, and about fifteen feet apart, the ends of the logs butting against the wall. Into the upper side of each of these logs a nitch or mortise was cut, to receive the thick ends of two uprights, consisting of two rough trunks of trees, of about twelve inches in diameter at their base, of equal lengths, and rising to the height of about twenty-five or thirty feet. Each upright had a crotch in its upper end, formed by the natural branching of the two principal limbs of the tree, like a common country well-post in

America.

These crotches being rounded out by art, a stout piece of knotty timber, of about from twelve to eighteen inches in thickness, was placed horizontally in them. To the centre of the cross-piece, a pole often or twelve inches in circumference was lashed with a strong rope, and to the lower end of this pole a huge rough rock was fastened, weighing from appearances several tons. The rock was slung and fastened to the pole by means of thick ropes, formed by braiding many thongs of camels' skins together. After the machine had been fitted together on the ground, it had been raised all in a body by the help of long shores or sticks of timber, not so thick as the uprights, but nearly twice as long; these shores were tied fast to the uprights, near their crotches, by ropes, and served to raise and lower the machine at pleasure, and also acted as braces to support it when in action. Two short props or braces were fixed between the uprights and the wall, with one end resting against its base, and the other in a notch cut on the inner side of the uprights, to help to keep them steady, and to prevent them from falling against the walls. The rock hung within two or three feet of the ground, like a huge pendulum; and having a long rope fastened to its slings, stretching off from the wall at least one hundred and fifty feet.

The manner of applying it, was by the assailants laying hold of this rope in great numbers, and then hauling off the rock to its greatest extent; all let go at the same instant, and the rock swung back with such impetuosity against those ill constructed walls, that its repeated strokes soon opened a breach, through which the besiegers entered, sword in hand. The other machine was made of four rough sticks of timber, of nearly equal lengths, lashed together at their smallest ends, and raised in form of a common triangle, or rather a quadrangle; from the point of juncture, a large rock was suspended by a rope of camel's skin, braided to the thickness of a man's leg, and slung in such a manner as to be struck against the wall in the same way as the one first described.

My companion, Rais bel Cossim, gave me all the information I desired, relative to these machines. The ground about the breach and near the gate was strewed over with dry human bones; and my curiosity being much excited to know the history of this melancholy scene of carnage and desolation, I requested Rais to communicate to me the particulars; but not being, it seems, acquainted with them himself, he applied to Sidi Mohammed on the subject, who thereupon gave the following relation, while Rais translated into Spanish for me such parts as I did not perfectly understand in Arabic, by which means I was enabled thoroughly to comprehend the whole narrative.

"That city" said Sidi Mohammed, pointing towards it with his staff, "was built by Omar Raschid, about forty years ago; he named it Widnah. He was a very brave and pious man; and the number of his family and friends, consisting at first of no more than five hundred souls, when the city was built, increased so rapidly, that in a few years they amounted to several thousands: they planted those fig, date, pomegranate, olive, and other trees which you now see near the walls; they cultivated the fields round about, and made gardens; had abundance of bread, beasts, and cattle of every kind, and became exceedingly rich and great, for God was with them in all their transactions.

"They were respected, loved, and feared by all their neighbours, because they were wise and just. This man was called Omar el Milliah, (or Omar the good;) he was my best friend when living," said Sidi, "and helped me when I was very low in the world; but the best men have enemies—so it was with Omar; he had an inveterate enemy from his youth, who lived among the mountains to the southward of his city, whose name was Sheick Sulmin. This *Sheick*, about twenty years ago, came down with a great host and invested the city of Omar; but Omar, taking advantage of the darkness of the night, sallied out of his city at a private passage, with all his forces, and falling upon his besiegers unawares, killed a great number, and put the remainder to a shameful flight: from that time until the time of his death, (which happened two years ago, [as at time of first publication]) he enjoyed a profound peace on every side.

"After Omar's death, his eldest son, Muley Ismael, (for he caused himself to be called a prince,) took upon him the government of the city. He was a very effeminate man, entirely devoted to sensual pleasure, and had a great number of wives and concubines. The people had long enjoyed a profound peace, and confided in their strength; when, about a year ago, one of the brothers of Ismae named Kesh-bah, who was very ambitious, and being fired with resentment at the conduct of Muley Ismael, in taking away from him his betrothed wife, left the city and repaired to the mountains, where having found his father's old enemy still living, he stirred him up to war against the city.

"The old *Sheick* soon collected a powerful army of hungry and rapacious Arabs on the borders of the desert, and came down the mountains, bringing on their camels the battering machines you now see standing there. When this host approached the city, it was in the dead of the night, and all within were asleep, for they dwelt carelessly and dreamed of no danger, and felt so secure, that they did not even keep a watch. The *Sheick* and his host drew near the walls in perfect silence, and raised their battering machines undiscovered: it was now nearly daylight, when both machines were put in operation at the same instant, and the gate was also attacked by means of large stones hung from the upper extremities of long poles by ropes, which poles stood up on end, and were managed by the hands of the Arabs.

"The first strokes against the walls and gate, shook them to their very foundations, and awakened the slothful inhabitants, who flew to the walls in order to make a defence; but it was too late; the enemy were thundering against them; all was confusion within; those who attacked the gate were repulsed with great slaughter by those who mounted the platform over it, but the walls were already shattered to pieces, and the assailants entered the bleaches over heaps of their dead and dying enemies.

"It was now daylight, and an indiscriminate slaughter of the inhabitants ensued; all was blood and carnage; every male was put to death, except two, who escaped over the wall to carry tidings of the fate of the town to their friends and neighbours. All the women and children shared the same fate, except two hundred virgins, who were spared for the use of the conquerors. They next plundered the slain of their clothing and ornaments; gathered up all the spoil, and drove off the oxen, sheep, camels, and asses, and departed, leaving the city before mid-day a heap of ruins, covered with the mangled carcasses of us once highly favoured inhabitants: they were in such haste as to leave the battering machines standing, and made off by way of the plane southward.

"The inhabitants of the neighbouring towns soon collected, and pursuing them with great vigour, came up with them on the side of the mountain the next morning, while the invaders sending forward their spoil, took a station in a steep narrow pass, and prepared for battle. It was a very long and bloody fight, but Sulmin's men rolled down great stones from the precipices upon their pursuers, who were at last forced to retreat, leaving about half their number dead and wounded on the ground."

Sidi Mohammed was one of the pursuers, and now showed me a very large scar from a wound he then received on his breast by a musket ball. Sidi Ishem, a very powerful prince, had in the meantime

VIEW OF A TOWN IN SUSE BEING SACKED BY THE ARABS

heard the news, and assembled a very large army, and pursued the enemy by another way; but they had fled to the desert and could not be overtaken. The dead bodies in and about the city had become so putrid before the pursuit was over, that none could approach to bury them, and they were devoured by dogs, and wild beasts, and birds of prey.

"They had offended the Almighty by their pride," observed Sidi Mohammed, "and none could be found to save them. Thus perished Widnah and its haughty inhabitants."

I was at that time riding along on a mule next to Rais bel Cossim and Sidi Mohammed, whilst the latter recounted the transaction in a most solemn tone. My sensations at beholding the desolate ruins of a once populous town, whose inhabitants had all been cut off in a few hours by the unexpected irruption of a ferocious and unsparing foe, may easily be conceived. I was at first induced to consider the story as fictitious, but my eyes warranted the belief of it, and the sight of the battering machines, together with the breaches in the wall, and the dry human bones scattered around, afforded conclusive evidence even to the minds of my fellow prisoners, who did not understand the narrative, that here had once stood a town, which had been sacked and destroyed.

After leaving these ruins, we continued on about an east course for three hours, when we came to the bank of a stream, or fresh water river, which was now no larger than a brook, owing to the dryness of the season. It flowed from the southeast, and bent its course through a broad valley in a crooked channel, nearly north, towards the seashore. On its left bank, which was very high land, stood two considerable walled villages, and a great number of small square-walled enclosures on the same bank southward, some in ruins and some apparently in good repair. The walls were made of rough stones laid in clay, and the houses had flat' roofs. On the margin of the brook were a great number of gardens fenced in with dry thorn bushes, placed on the ground, and planted chiefly with the prickly-pear; but some with squashes, cabbages, &c.

At a distance on both sides of this stream, we saw a number of square stone sanctuaries, or saint houses, with round domes: they did not appear to be more than ten or fifteen feet square, and were all nicely whitewashed. This bank of the river bore strong marks of having been washed to a very great height from the place where the stream then flowed; and on inquiring of Sidi Mohammed, I was informed that the whole of the valley between the two high banks (which from appearance must be five or six miles wide) was entirely covered with water during some part of the season, or when great rains fall; at which times travellers were obliged to go up the banks three days' journey to a fall, before they could cross it: that he himself had once been that way, but for the last five years the land had been so cursed with droughts, that it had not once overflowed its present bed where we crossed it, and where it was not more than twenty yards wide and one foot in depth.

As we passed along close to the prickly-pears, which hung over the thorn bushes, bearing yellow fruit, some of my men plucked them and put them in their mouths, without regarding the sharp prickles with which these pears were covered, so that their tongues and the roofs of their mouths were literally filled with them: on the first touch, they were extremely painful, and were extracted afterwards with much difficulty. There were also on both sides of this river near where we crossed it, numerous herds, and many inhabitants. We travelled along the right bank of the river for several miles, until it became both wide and deep, for it met the tide water from the sea; when coming within sight of a city on the high right bank, we made towards it.

On our approaching within two miles of its walls, we passed large fields of Indian corn and barley, and gardens filled with most kinds of common vegetables. The borders of these fields and gardens were planted with date, fig, pomegranate, orange, and other fruit trees in great numbers, and many clumps of grape vines: the soil of this spot appeared to be of the richest black mould. As we passed along in a high foot-way, formed by throwing up the turf from the enclosures, (apparently to make them perfectly level, or all of a gentle descent,) we saw hundreds of the inhabitants busily employed in gathering the Indian corn and barley into heaps, for it was now their harvest time, while others (men and boys) were loading it in sacks and baskets on camels, mules, and asses, and driving them, thus loaded with the rich products of the soil, into their city.

These several enclosures contained, I should judge, one hundred acres of land, divided from each other by mud walls, strewed with dry thorn bushes; the whole were watered by means of a considerable stream, brought from the heights near the city in a large ditch, and carried round each enclosure in small gutters dug for the purpose; so that any one of the owners could either water the whole or any part of his field or garden, at pleasure. Hundreds of oxen and cows, sheep and goats, were feeding in the newly cleared fields, whose thin and famished appearance proved they had been forced to feed on scanty and dried up herbage during the summer months, and that on account of the long and excessive droughts, they had merely been able to exist. Rais also informed me, that the locusts had nipped off and destroyed nearly every verdant thing in the whole country; and that for the last five years they had laid waste whole provinces in the empire of Morocco.

We now arrived at the city, and entered it at a very large gateway, with our camels and mules, and took up our quarters in a smith's shop, near the gate. It was after sunset when we entered this town, and I could observe one broad street that appeared to run its whole length. The houses were built of rough stones, principally laid in clay, but some in lime—all of one story high, and flat roofed: there were no windows next the street, except a small aperture in each one not a foot square, for the purpose probably of admitting light. They had each a stout plank door strongly made, and furnished with a big clumsy iron Jock. The corn continued to pass into the city till dark; all the camels, oxen, cows, sheep, goats, and asses, belonging to the inhabitants, and which were very numerous, were also driven into the city, and the gate shut and barred with four large pieces of timber: this was about eight o'clock, and a watch was then stationed on the wall.

On entering the city, Rais bel Cossim and Sheick Ali waited on the governor or chief, and obtained permission to remain in his town over night; and a few dates were brought by Rais for our suppers. The shop in which we were permitted to stay was about twenty feet square; a kind of forge was fixed in one corner; two skins were curiously applied, so as to form a bellows to blow this fire with, which was of charcoal; a man stood between them with a hand on each skin, which he raised and depressed alternately, and thus kept up a small and irregular stream of air. They had a large piece of iron for an anvil, which lay so low on the ground, that when they worked on it with the hammer, which was a very clumsy sort of one, they were obliged to squat down. I believe every man and boy in this town came to look at us by turns, and ask questions concerning ourselves, our country, &c. so that we were surrounded with people during the whole night, chatting with each other, and asking our Arab guides an endless string of questions.

These people were of the same nation we had been in the habit of seeing since we came to the River Nun, yet they appeared to be more civilized. Several of them asked me in Spanish how I did, and uttered many other words in that language, the meaning of which they did not seem to understand, the most of them being vile oaths and execrations; which proved satisfactorily to me that they had frequent communications in some way or other with people of that nation. Sheick Ali had all the day after we left Sidi Mohammed's house been lost in a seeming reverie: he would seldom speak, and when he did, it was in a low voice apart with Seid, and I strongly suspected that some plot was in preparation between them. We had travelled the last day about five hours, at the rate of four miles an hour, before we came abreast of the ruins of the city I have described, and we had proceeded five hours afterwards at the same rate, making together forty miles.

On the 30th of October, we made ready to start before daylight, and as soon as it dawned the gate was opened, and we proceeded on our journey. The walls of this city or town, were built of rough stone laid in clay, and were four feet thick at their base in the gateway, and about twenty feet high, but had no outer ditch to defend them, nor any cannon mounted. It appeared to cover a space of about three hundred yards in length along the river's bank, north and south, and one hundred and fifty yards in breadth from east to west. The channel of the river at low stages of the water is about one mile west of the town: this river is called by the natives *Woed Sehlem*, or River Sehlem, and the town, Rais told me, bore the name, *i. e. Sehlemah*: it is, I should judge from its appearance, fifty yards in width opposite the town at high water, and proportionably deep.

I was now informed by Rais bel Cossim and Sidi Mohammed, that there was once a large and flourishing Christian town and settlement near the mouth of this river, and only thirty miles from us; that the town was taken by storm about eight centuries ago, and all the Christians massacred. An Arabian century contains forty lunar years, and is called *Zille*, and they reckon twelve moons to the year. Both Rais bel Cossim and Sidi Mohammed said they had been to the spot, and seen some of the remains of the walls, which were still standing, though nearly all buried up in sand drifted from the seashore. They further stated, that there was now a village at a little distance from the ancient ruin, inhabited by fishermen; that the old Christian town was situated on a bay or arm of the sea, and five or six miles broad at its entrance, and that it is an excellent harbour both for large and small vessels; that there was no bar across its mouth, but that the usual bar was formed of sand a few miles below the town we had left.

From my own observations on the increasing breadth of the river, I am inclined to think that this bay may contain a fine harbour, particularly as Rais and his companion could have no motive for deceiving me. Rais bel Cossim had been many times in Europe, as captain under the Moorish flag, in the grain trade, and insisted that this was a better harbour than Cadiz: if so, it is the only one on that coast, from Cape Spartel, in latitude 34. 30. to the latitude of 19. north.

Travelling on at a great rate, we entered on a vast plane, over whose surface a few shrubs, and weeds, and clumps of trees were thinly scattered: the boughs of these trees were bending under the weight of a bright yellow fruit, and I learned from Rais that it was the *arga* tree, from the nut of which is extracted the *argan* oil, very much esteemed by the natives; and it was also highly relished by my companions. This nut, when ripe, much resembles the ripe date in appearance; so much so, indeed, that seeing some of them scattered on the ground, I took one up and bit it, when I found out my mistake, as its bark was extremely bitter. The trees generally grew in clusters of from three to ten trunks, that seemed to spring from the same seed; these rise in a shaft of from ten to fifteen feet in height, and then branch off in all directions, forming a diameter of at least one hundred feet; the trunks are from one to three feet in diameter; the branches are covered with thorns, which fall and lie so thick on the ground, as to make it almost impossible to approach them near enough to shake or knock off the nuts, and they are consequently left to ripen and drop off spontaneously.

We were now going on at a small trot, mostly all mounted on the camels, mules, and two asses that were in company. The Atlas mountains were now full in view, stretching as far as the eye could reach from northeast to southwest, at some distance on our right. We had seen these mountains for several days past, in the distant horizon, when we were on the high ridges, which we were obliged to pass; but we now beheld them from this wide spreading plane in all their awful magnitude: their lofty summits, towering high above the clouds in sharp peaks, appeared to be covered with never melting snows. This sight was calculated to fill the mind of the beholder with wonder and astonishment. The cold and chilling blasts of wind which blew directly from the Atlas, almost congealed our impoverished blood, and made our feeble frames shake almost to dissolution, notwithstanding the good cloaks and shoes with which we were provided.

Seid and the other Arabs were also shivering with cold, and ran on foot to make themselves warm, for the sky was overcast and obscured by thick and heavy clouds, portending torrents of rain. I was now sure we were very near the emperor of Morocco's dominions, and began to imagine myself a free man—I felt myself at peace with all mankind; my mind expanded with gratitude towards the great Author of my being, and I viewed this stupendous ridge of mountains as one of the strongest proofs of Divine goodness to his creatures; for I considered that all the rivers, and streams, and springs, that water and refresh the northern part of Africa, from the borders of that immense and thirsty desert over which I had travelled, to the straits of Gibraltar, and which empty into the Atlantic ocean, or into the Mediterranean sea, westward of Tripoli, and from the 26th to the 35th degree of north latitude, must either take their rise or have their sources in this vast chain of Atlas. On these burning coasts, seldom refreshed by rains, (and that only in small quantities, and during the winter season,) the great bodies of accumulated snow on these mountains, tend in the summer season to cool the atmosphere in their vicinity, as well as to supply water for the use of the animal and vegetable creation.

In the course of this morning, Thomas Burns became so weak (being benumbed with cold) that he could no longer hold on the camel, and tumbled off over the beast's tail with great violence, falling on his head and back, which deprived him for a considerable time of all sensation: with much exertion, however, on our part, he at length revived, and was again placed on his camel. Proceeding on the plane, we saw a large number of cities, or walled towns, I should reckon at least fifty, some on one side of our path, and some on the other; but mostly on our right, and extending as far as the eye could reach towards the mountains. Those near the path appeared to be three or four hundred yards square: the walls were built of rough stones laid in clay, and with only one gate; they were from twenty to thirty feet in height, and crowned with short turrets about three yards apart all around; at each corner on the top was built a kind of circular sentry box, also of stone, something in the manner of all European castles.

Most of the land, at some distance from the vicinity of these towns, was prepared for sowing, and many of the inhabitants were engaged in ploughing. A little nearer, were numerous orchards of fig, date, and other fruit trees; and close to the walls, many gardens of fine vegetables, such as onions, cabbages, turnips, squashes, &c. Round about these gardens, we saw many dung-hill fowls, and at a distance, herds of neat cattle, asses, and flocks of sheep and goats, were feeding upon the scanty and dried up herbage, under the eye of their respective keepers or herdsmen. These beasts were very poor, yet the whole seemed to promise abundance of food to the apparently industrious inhabitants, and brought to my mind the ancient Jewish history.

Sheick Ali had been very attentive to me all this morning: he had in imitation of Rais bel Cossim, called me captain, and endeavoured to convince me that I had better go with him to the mountains southward, where he had large possessions, and would give me one of his daughters for a wife, and make me a chief in his nation. He had stopped the whole company two or three times to talk over his own affairs, and I now supposed that Seid was leagued with him, and bent on doing me and my men some mischief. We had travelled on thus for ten hours, (say from four in the morning till two in the afternoon,) at the rate of five miles an hour, making a distance of fifty miles, when turning aside from our path, as if by choice, we approached the gate of a city.

We were both hungry and thirsty, and we seated ourselves down by a very deep well, within one hundred yards of the city gate: Seid and Sheick Ali went immediately into the town, as I supposed, to get some provisions—Sidi Mohammed and Rais bel Cossim were soon invited in also, to partake with them, leaving us on the outside, and under charge of Bo-Mohammed, who stood in Sidi Hamet's stead, and two others. A great many men, and I believe all the boys belonging to the place, now came out to look at and make remarks on the slaves; most of them, no doubt, from mere curiosity. The boys, by way of amusement, began to throw stones and dirt at, and to spit on us, expressing, by that means, their utter contempt and abhorrence of us and of our nation. Burns and Clark were so far exhausted as to be unable to support themselves sitting, and were obliged to lie down on the ground; but one man brought a bucket from the town, and drew water, that we might allay our thirst; this revived us in some measure.

Mr. Savage, Horace, and myself, were in so weak a state, that I much feared we should not be able to keep on for the remainder of this day. Burns' fall had proved him to be too weak to hold on the camel, and had besides bruised him very much. I tried my utmost to encourage them and keep up their spirits, by representing to them that we were now free, and would soon be in the emperor's dominions, where I presumed we should be out of the reach of the rapacious Arabs; for I had been informed by Rais bel Cossim, that in the space of one day's journey we should be within the territories of the emperor.

Whilst Rais bel Cossim and the rest of his company remained within the walls, the winds from the mountains, driving before them thick masses of dark clouds, loaded with vapour, brought on a copious discharge of rain, and we were directed to enter under the gateway for shelter, which we did, supporting each other in our weakness, and seated ourselves in the gate. This was the first rain I had witnessed in this country; and it continued to fall for about an hour. I had for a long time looked for Rais bel Cossim and his companions to come out, and began to apprehend some disaster or treachery on the part of Sheich Ali, whose harsh and loud voice I now heard roaring within.

This tremendous clamour between the *Sheick* and other persons, continued for about two hours, when Rais bel Cossim made his appearance, escorted by a number of men: his intelligent countenance bespoke fear, grief, and indignation—he called me aside from my companions, and told me that Sheick Ali was the intimate friend of Muley Ibrahim, (or prince Abraham,) the king or governor of the city; that Sheick Ali had claimed us as his property, alleging that Sidi Hamet was his son-in-law, and owed him a great deal of money, and that he (Sidi Hamet) was now held as a hostage or slave to a Christian in Swearah; that he had insisted we should not proceed one step further until fifteen hundred dollars were produced, together with Sidi Hamet, the husband of his daughter; and that in conjunction with Seid, he had contrived to stop us hereby the power of the prince. This news was to me like a clap of thunder; it bereft me of all my fortitude: the fair prospects I had entertained of a speedy liberation from slavery, particularly for the last two days, were now suddenly darkened.

Rais bel Cossim further informed me, that he had argued the matter every way, but all to no purpose—that he had promised the money required, namely, six hundred dollars, as soon as we should get to Santa Cruz, in the emperor's dominions, and that he would agree to have the prince and *Sheick* go along with him and receive it there, and there wait for the return of Sidi Hamet; "but they will not listen to me," added he, "and I must set off immediately and carry this discouraging news to Mr. Willshire, leaving you here until I return, which will be in six days; and may God preserve you in the meantime from their evil machinations."

This was more than I could bear:—tears of anguish, which I had not the power to control, now gushed from my eyes, and my almost bursting heart vented itself in bitter groans of despair. My companions heard my distress, though at a considerable distance from me, and turning fearfully on me their almost extinguished eyes, begged for an explanation of the cause.

Rais bel Cossim was just in the act of mounting his mule to ride off, when Sidi Mohammed, who went in the first place with my master to Swearah, came near him and said, "Rais,—Muley Ibrahim and Sheick Ali have determined you shall not go to Swearah; they fear you will cause a war to break out between them and the *Sultan*." Observing me in tears and in great affliction, he took me by the hand, and said, "Don't be cast down, Riley, I will go to Swearah, and carry a letter from Rais, and one from you to Willshire; and if he wants a hostage, I will stay with him. I have two wives and seven children to leave, and houses, and lands, and herds of cattle; and shall be a more valuable hostage than Sidi Hamet—he is your friend, and will come immediately down and relieve you. God is great and good, (added he,) and will restore you to your family."

I kissed his hand in gratitude, and called him father, and hoped the Almighty would reward aim for his benevolence. Rais now joined Sheick Ali and the prince, who with many attendants were seated on the ground in a circle, outside of the city gate—here they debated the matter over again. Rais insisted we were his slaves; that neither the prince nor *Sheick* had a right to detain what he had bought with his own money, much less to stop him like a criminal; that it was contrary to their religion (which made them all brothers) to commit such an outrage en hospitality Sheick Ali, on the other hand, contended, that Sidi Hamet and Seid owed him money to a large amount; that we were their joint property, and that consequently he had an undoubted right to detain and to carry us off into his own tribe or family, and there to keep us until Sidi Hamet should return and pay his debt.

Rais insisted he had paid his money for us, and had nothing to do with Sheick Ali's claim; however, after extolling the justice and virtue of the prince to the highest pitch, they both at last agreed to leave it to Muley Ibrahim to decide what should be done. Muley Ibrahim now asked Sidi Mohammed and Bo-Mohammed what they knew concerning this business, and they gave testimony in favour of Rais bel Cossim's previous claim: thus prepared, Muley Ibrahim said—"You, Sheick Ali, my old friend, and Rais bel Cossim, both of you claim these five Christian slaves as your own property, and each of you has some reason on your side—yet, as it is not in my power to decide whose claim is the best founded, I am resolved, with a strict regard to justice, and without going into further evidence, to keep the slaves in my own city, carefully guarded, until messengers can be sent to Swearah, who shall bring down Sidi Hamet, when you three being confronted, may settle your claims as shall be found most consistent with justice." He then proposed that Rais should remain with him, like a friend, and without having anything to fear. This plan was agreed to by all parties, and they shook hands upon it like friends.

This done, we were conducted into the city, and into a house adjoining that where the prince lived. A mat was spread for the *Sheick* and Rais, and their companions to sit on, while we were placed in a narrow corner on the ground, among the saddles and other stuffs: sentinels with muskets and scimitars were stationed at the door of our apartment and the other doors, and at the city gate. It was after dark when the dispute was settled, and soon afterwards a dish of *cous-koo-soo* was brought in, of which all partook after due ablutions; and they then performed their evening prayers most devoutly. My companions were very much cast down, and their bodies and minds were so much exhausted and debilitated by their sufferings, that they had become like children, and wept aloud.

I was certain that it would have been impossible for Clark and Burns to have proceeded further on that day, and I tried to persuade them all that it was better for us to be detained a little, as it would give us an opportunity of taking some rest, without which we should be in danger of fainting on our route. Muley Ibrahim, the Sheick, and Rais, were conversing during the whole night, and when daylight appeared, (the 2nd of November,) Rais furnished me with pen, ink, and paper, and told me to write to Mr. Willshire, stating our present situation as near as I was able: this I accordingly did, while a *talb* or scrivener was employed in writing a letter for him, as he could not write himself. At an early hour Seid, Sidi Mohammed, and Bo-Mohammed set out for Swearah, taking our letters, and promising to return as soon as possible. Sheick Ali also, soon afterwards left us, promising to return in four days.

CHAPTER 22

Sheick Ali's Plans Miscarry

Being now left alone with Rais bel Cossim, I questioned him concerning our detention: he said it would be but for a few days, and that we needed a little time to refresh ourselves, in order to enable us to bear the fatigues of the remainder of our journey; that he trusted we should make a friend of the prince, in whose power we all now were, and that he hoped to be able to effect this by making him a small present. I told him I almost despaired of living to regain my liberty, as I was extremely feeble, and must soon perish.

"What!" said he, "dare you distrust the power of that God who has preserved you so long by miracles? No, my friend," added he, "the God of heaven and of earth is your friend, and will not forsake you, but in his own good time restore you to your liberty and to the embraces of your family; we must say, 'his will be done,' and be contented with our lot, for God knows best what is for our good."

To hear such sentiments from the mouth of a Moor, whose nation I had been taught to consider the worst of barbarians, I confess, filled my mind with awe and reverence, and I looked up to him as a kind of superior being, when he added, "We are all children of the same heavenly Father, who watches over ill our actions, whether we be Moor, or Christian, or Pagan, or of any other religion; we must perform his will."

Rais then called Muley Ibrahim, and had a long conference with him. This prince Ibrahim was a man of very mild aspect, of a light complexion, about five feet ten inches in height, and rather thin: his countenance was intelligent, and he was very active, though apparently sixty or seventy years of age. By the tenor of the conversation, I could understand that Rais was flattering him highly, but in a delicate way: he asked very affectionately about the prince's wives; and understanding he had but one, he inquired if she had any children; and was answered, she had none: he next wished to know if she had any tea or sugar, and was answered in the negative. We had not seen the faces of any of the women since we arrived at the town where Sidi Mohammed dwelt. Rais now managed to get a little wood and some water, and we made a fire and boiled some coffee; this was done by the help of a small negro girl who was a slave to Muley Ibrahim, and during the absence of the prince.

Rais, by giving the girl a small lump of loaf sugar, persuaded her to carry a large lump to her mistress, and also a cup of coffee thick with sugar. The prince had gone out before Rais attempted to bribe the girl. After carrying in the coffee and the sugar, the girl returned and told Rais that her mistress was much obliged to him, and would keep the cup and saucer, for she had never seen one before, and thought them very pretty, and begged to know how she might serve him in return. Rais sent back word that she could serve him most essentially by striving to make the prince his friend.

About one hour after this, Muley Ibrahim entered our apartment, and asked Rais what he had been doing with his wife? saying, at the same time, "you had no need of gaining my friendship through her influence, for you had it already;" but I could perceive a very great difference in his manner. He wished to know if Rais did not want to go to the mosque, which he said was not far distant. Rais accompanied him thither, and I discovered at his return, about two hours after, that all was right between him and the prince, and that he had all the liberty he required. I had in the meantime made some coffee, of which my companions and myself drank as much as we wanted, and nibbled our biscuits; for our Arab friends had before taken care to eat up all our boiled tongue. We were all of us so excessively weak, that we were not able to fetch water for ourselves, and our diarrhoea also continued with the most distressing haemorrhoids; this day, however, had passed away more smoothly than I had expected.

In the evening the prince came, and prayed in company with Rais, and appeared very friendly. After the prince retired, Rais informed me that he (Rais) had sent off to a rich man, an old acquaintance of his, who lived about one day's journey south of us, for money to pay Sheick Ali's demand, and that he expected his friend would come to him the next day—"but" said Rais "God has made Muley Ibrahim my firm friend; and he has given his princely word that he will protect both me and my slaves, and in case force is necessary, he will provide a sufficient escort for us into the emperor's dominions; he will also provide some fowls and eggs for you in the morning, and you may tell your shipmates they have nothing to fear, for tomorrow *M. Shallah,,* (*i. e.* if it is God's will) they shall have plenty of good food." This news cheered their spirits, and as our apprehensions had in some measure subsided, we rested comfortably.

Early in the morning of November the 3rd, Muley Ibrahim brought in some eggs, which we boiled for our breakfast: he gave us salt to season them with, and soon after brought half a dozen fowls, and Rais taking the fowls' wings in his left hand, and turning his face towards the east, after saying aloud, *Besmillah,* (in the name of the most holy God) he cut their throats, and we soon dressed them after our fashion, and put them into an earthen pot with water, and set it a boiling. The prince had furnished us with wood, and brought us water with his own hands; he next went into his garden, and pulled some onions, turnips, and small squashes, with which we enriched our soup; and he also gave us salt and green peppers to season it with. We put in four fowls, and this soup would have been thought good in any country. A more grateful and wholesome dish could not possibly have been prepared for our poor disordered stomachs, that had been so long harassed with the most cruel griping pains, and felt as if they had lost all power of digestion.

The prince and Rais had a bowl of the soup, with a part of the fowls, and seemed to relish it exceedingly. The prince insisted on my eating from the same dish with them: inquired concerning my wife and children, wished to know their sex: and continued from that time during our stay in his city to administer all the relief and comfort in his power, both to me and my desponding and wretched companions, whose last ray of hope had faded away on our being stopped here; although in fact they were not in a condition to continue their journey, particularly Burns and Clark, for they had sunken into a lethargic state, bordering on dissolution.

Yet, when I was enabled to explain the causes of our detention, and to inform them that the prince was our friend, and gave them nourishing soups, their spirits came again, and hope raised them from the ground. To the circumstance of this stoppage alone, and the friendship and protection of this good chief, I attribute, under Providence, the salvation of our lives. On the second day of our detention, in the afternoon, the old man, Rais bel Cossim's friend, to whom he had written for assistance, came to see him; he had been riding all night to be with Rais in time. Their meeting was a friendly one; the old man had two mules, on one of which were two baskets, containing a dozen of fowls, and some dry *cous-koo-soo;* these he presented to Rais, and said he had brought five hundred dollars for his use, as he requested, and that he would bring it in: but Rais had now become the friend of Muley Ibrahim, and therefore did not need the money; yet this old friend insisted on his taking the fowls as a present, with some eggs he had also brought with him: these Rais accepted, for he said they were meant as a present to me.

I had some fowls cooked already, and the old man sat down and ate with Rais, and would have me to be one of the company: he told Rais that if he would but say the word, he would go and collect his friends and take the slaves by force of arms, and in spite of Sheick Ali's opposition, would carry us safe to Santa Cruz, and beyond his power: but as Muley Ibrahim had given his word, on which Rais said he could depend, to see us all safe to Santa Cruz, and to use all his force and influence, if that should be necessary, the old man, whose name I am sorry to say I have forgotten, left us and returned to his home. We now lived for three days as well as we could wish.

On the fourth day after Seid's departure, a kind of fair was held at a short distance from our city, and Rais told me he was going to it, and would try by some manoeuvre to liberate us, and to get us on towards the *sultan's* dominions.—A man of great influence lived about five leagues distance from that city. He was called a son of the holy prophet, or Shariff; had been to Morocco, and was also called *el ajjh*; (the pilgrim:) he was looked upon by all, far and near, as possessing supernatural powers, and was obeyed and almost worshipped as a superior being; and his word or dictate was equivalent to a law. Rais went to the fair and from thence to the place of worship, and did not return until the afternoon, when he informed me he had bought a bullock at the fair, the best and fattest he could find, though it was but a small one. He had sent one half of it to the son of the prophet (or *Shariff*) by the hand of a messenger, on a mule, saying, " when you deliver the flesh to the *el ajjh*, and he asks you who sent it to him, ell him a pious man, who has lately come from Swearah, and is now a guest with Muley Ibrahim, and wishes to be remembered in your prayers."

This, Rais said, was all the message he sent, but he was sure that if the Shariff accepted the present, he should see him before the sun went down. Rais had given the other half to Muley Ibrahim, and remarked, that it was not so much the real value of a present that was taken into consideration by the Moors, but the manner of giving it, which laid the receiver under such an obligation as to make him your friend forever. This notion I was at a loss to understand, and therefore supposed it to be some peculiarity in the customs of these singular people. Rais went out to prayers about sunset, and returned in a short time, when he mentioned that he had been waited upon by the Shariff, who had asked him what favour he wanted, that made him send such a present to a stranger. Rais told him our story, and that he had paid his money for myself and my companions, and begged his assistance to force Sheiek Ali (whose power all dreaded) to consent to have us removed quietly to Santa Cruz, where Rais thought his property would be safe: this the Shariff promised to do, and even to exert all his power and influence, if necessary, to remove and protect Rais and his property by force of arms, and requested to be informed without delay when Sheick Ali returned.

On the following day (November 4th) the *Sheick* did return; and, relying on the friendship of Muley Ibrahim, had only one attendant: the Shariff was immediately informed of his arrival by express, and came to see him as an old friend; then taking him aside, he advised the *Sheick* to remove his slaves to Santa Cruz as soon as possible, asserting, at the same time, that he was certain that Sidi Ishem, whom the *Sheick* well knew and dreaded, would set out from his city on the morrow with a force, in order to seize upon the slaves, whom he had before strove hard to purchase for money without success, and if they were not in the dominions of the emperor before he came, another day would place them in his hands, when the *Sheick* would not only lose them, but it must also kindle a war between him and that powerful chief, which would set the whole country in a blaze, and after all it would be impossible to deliver them from his grasp by force.

When the *Sheick* heard the advice of the *Shariff*, he returned to our prison, and Rais contrived to find out what had passed between them, by again meeting the *Shariff* at the city gate alone, as had been before agreed upon. Rais being thus fully informed and let into the secret, came into the apartment and informed me how matters stood. Sheick Ali, in the meantime, was unfolding his plan to Muley Ibrahim, and trying to gain his consent to let the slaves be carried off in the night by surprise, but the prince would not consent; they were now within his walls, and he had given his word they should not be removed until the disputed right of property was settled by all parties face to face: this he should insist on.

Finding that plan would not answer any good purpose, and fearing Sidi Ishem's expected arrival, and wishing to make a merit of necessity, this crafty chief addressing Rais bel Cossim, told him, in a flattering way, that he had found him to be a good and an honourable man, and wished to be called his friend; that he did not doubt Rais's word, since he knew his character, and would therefore consent to go on with the slaves on the morrow morning, as far as Santa Cruz, where they would wait for the arrival of Sidi Hamet, and settle the right of property amicably. Rais, on the other hand, as crafty as the *Sheick*, took care not to evince any desire of going; and being in the whole secret, now told Sheick Ali, that he had stopped him and his Christian slaves at first contrary to the laws of justice and hospitality, and that as he had kept them so long a time, he had no wish to remove them at present, but would wait with patience until Sidi Hamet should come down and convince the *Sheick* that he had done wrong in detaining him.

At last, however, he suffered himself to be persuaded by the united voices of Sheick Ali and Muley Ibrahim, but on the express condition of being escorted to Santa Cruz by the prince, who was a party in the whole secret. He was also to procure camels for us to ride on, and went forth to engage, and have them ready for a start at daylight the next morning. Rais bel Cossim now informed me, that Muley Ibrahim had previously agreed to accompany us; that we were to ride on camels, and that two hundred horsemen were to guard us on the road, in order to prevent any treachery on the part of Sheick Ali, who might already have troops stationed on the way to seize and carry us off to the mountains: he had also given private orders to his friends and his *vassals*, to hold themselves in readiness in case of an alarm. The two hundred horsemen were to take stations, so as to keep us in continual view without exciting suspicion, and to be ready to carry intelligence. Rais then bade me kill and boil what fowls and eggs remained, which I did, with the assistance of my men, who had very much recovered.

Character of Sidi Ishem.

While the fowls and eggs were cooking, I asked Rais who this Sidi Ishem was, as his name alone had seemed capable of inspiring such dread. "This Sidi Ishem" said Rais, "is a descendant of the former kings of Suse, before it was conquered by the Moon;—he is a man of between fifty and sixty years of age, possessed of great wealth and power; is very crafty, and very brave, but rapacious and cruel , he has under his command fifteen thousand horsemen, well armed, they are of the race of the ancient inhabitants of the country, from whom the whole country derives the name of Berberia, corrupted by the Europeans into Barbary;—these Berberians are extremely fierce and warlike, and are joined by all the *renegado* Moors, who escape from the emperor's dominion, to evade punishment for crimes they had committed.

"These men are always ready to join him in any of his enterprises, for they always get a share of the spoil. He lives in the gorge of a mountain, near the town of Widnoon, on the great route from Morocco across the great desert, to Soudain, the country beyond the desert, and the city of Tombuctoo. All the caravans that travel either to or from the desert, are obliged to go close to Widnoon, and as the Atlas mountains are on the one side, and the ridge next the sea on the other, they find it highly necessary to secure his friendship and protection by presents. Between this chief and the emperor of Morocco there exists the most implacable hatred, and a continual jealousy, which a few years ago broke out into an open war. The emperor sent a powerful army against him, (said to be 30,000 strong,) but Sidi Ishem was apprised of its approach in time, and sent off all the women, children, and old men, with all their substance, to the south foot of the Atlas mountains, and on the great desert.

"The emperor's army entered his territory, where they found nothing to subsist upon: yet as they met with no resistance, they carried on their work of destruction, by burning all the towns and everything that was combustible, tearing down the houses and walls of their cities, so that nothing escaped their violence and rapacity. They continued pursuing Sidi Ishem (who hovered about them with most of his men) until they were exhausted by fatigue and hunger; when this chief fell upon them by surprise with his infuriated followers, who had been rendered doubly desperate by the sight of their ruined cities.

"They slew more than ten thousand on the spot; those who escaped this dreadful carnage, and fled, were hunted down, and nearly all destroyed, before they could reach the city of Tarudant, (the southern and westernmost town in the emperor of Morocco's dominions,) where the few that were left found shelter, and spread such terror and dismay throughout that part of the empire, by the horrid accounts they gave of their disasters, as to render it impracticable to raise another army for the purpose of reducing Sidi Ishem and his men to submission. All the inhabitants were soon recalled by their chief from the mountains and deserts—took possession of their country anew, rebuilt their cities and dwellings, and are at this time more powerful, more feared and respected, than they were previous to that event."

This is the account Rais bel Cossim gave me in Spanish, as nearly as my memory served me, when I took it down at Mogadore:—he also said that we had escaped falling into his hands only by groping our way along a private path on the seashore. The substance of this account of Sidi Ishem was confirmed, after my arrival at Mogadore, by Mr. Willshire and others.

Our food being prepared, and everything packed up tight for a start, we took a snort nap, and at daylight on the morning of the 4th of November, we were placed on five camels, which were saddled much better than any we had hitherto rode: they had on them also bags of barley, and empty sacks, made of tent cloth, that would hold I should suppose, ten or twelve bushels; these all together made quite a comfortable seat, though rather a wide one, and we could hold ourselves on by the ropes that secured the lading. They placed me on the largest camel I had yet seen, which was nine or ten feet in height. The camels were now all kneeling or lying down, and mine among the rest. I thought I had taken a good hold to steady myself while he was rising, yet his motion was so heavy, and my strength so far exhausted, that I could not possibly hold on, and tumbled off over his tail, turning entirely over.

I came down upon my feet, which prevented my receiving any material injury, though the shock to my frame was very severe. The owner of the camel helped me up, and asked me if I was injured? I told him no: "God be praised," said he, "for turning you over; had you fallen upon your head, these stones must have dashed out your brains; but the camel," added he, "is a sacred animal, and heaven protects those who ride on him! had you fallen from an ass, though he is only two cubits and a half high, it would have killed you; for the ass is not so noble a creature as the camel and the horse."

I afterwards found this to be the prevailing opinion among all classes of the Moors and the Arabs.—When they put me on again, two of the men steadied me by the legs until the camel was fairly up, and then told me to be careful, and to hold on fast: they also took great care to assist my companions in the same way.

Being now all mounted, we set off to the northeast, leaving Stuka, (for that was the name of the place where we had been confined,) accompanied by Rais bel Cossim, Muley Ibrahim, and his two servants, and Sheick Ali, with his attendant, all riding on mules and asses: the five owners of the camels went on foot, each driving his own camel, and taking care of its rider. Stuka is built in a quadrangular form; its walls would measure about three hundred yards on each angle; they are built of rough stone, laid in clay, and appeared to be four or five feet thick at their base, and twenty feet in height, tapering off to two feet thick at the top, and were crowned with turrets all around. It has but one gate, which is at its north angle, very strongly made, and swinging on the ends of its back posts, which are let into large stone sockets at the bottom and at the top: the gate consisted of two folding leaves, and at night was secured by four heavy wooden bars.

The town was divided within into as many compartments as there were families in it, which I should think might amount to three hundred, probably containing in all five thousand souls. The houses are built of the same materials as the walls—only one story high, and flat roofed: excepting the door, they looked like heaps of mud and stone: even that of the prince bore the same appearance, without any other distinction or ornament than being closer jointed, and more bedaubed with mud. All the flocks and herds were driven within the Walls every night, and each owner makes those that belong to him lie down in his own yard or enclosure.

As we travelled on, we passed between a great number of cities or towns, similar in appearance to Stuka, with which this truly vast plane is chequered. The whole plane seemed very fertile, was planted with numerous groves and orchards of fig and other fruit trees, with here and there a clump of the *arga* tree, yellow with fruit. The inhabitants were busied in ploughing up the soil, with a kind of plough which I shall hereafter describe. We proceeded on very rapidly, keeping those on foot running constantly, and had been travelling about six hours, when we came to the ruins of many towns on our left, similar in appearance to Stuka; near the shattered walls of some of which stood several battering machines, but they were at the distance of a mile or more from us.

These places appeared to have been recently inhabited; for the gardens near the walls were still green with vegetation. Wishing to know what had been the cause of such desolation, I was informed by Muley Ibrahim and Sheick Ali, through Rais bel Cossim, that a family quarrel happened about one year ago between the chiefs of two of these towns, which soon broke out into the most dreadful kind of warfare: each party engaged their friends to assist them in fighting what each termed their *righteous battles*: the neighbouring towns joined, some on one side, and some on the other, and the plane was deluged with blood. This quarrel being only of a family nature, Sidi Ishem did not interfere, and it was finally settled by the destruction of seven of those small cities, and most of their inhabitants. These ruins were now entirely abandoned, and their environs laid desolate, though the war continued only one month.

I could scarcely believe it possible for such devastation to have been committed in so short a time, or on such trivial grounds; but Rais bel Cossim (who was born near Santa Cruz) assured me that nothing was more common than such feuds between families in those parts; that he had known many himself, with every circumstance attending them, and that they were very seldom finished until one family or the other was exterminated, and their names blotted out from the face of the earth.

We continued our journey until about mid-day, still on the plane, when Santa Cruz or Agader was distinctly seen, and pointed out to me. It is situated on the summit of a high mountain; its walls are white, and can be descried at a great distance. The plane on which we travelled was nearly level; not a brook or stream of water had we passed since leaving the last mentioned river, but the towns and villages had many deep wells near their walls, from which the inhabitants drew water for themselves and their numerous cattle.—Innumerable clumps of the ever-green *arga* tree, loaded with the rich oil nut, were scattered over the plane in every direction. Vast numbers of leafless fig trees, and enclosures of grape vines with date, pomegranate almond, orange, and other fruit trees, promised abundance in their seasons, and delightfully variegated the scene. Hundreds of the inhabitants were busied in ploughing the soil (which appeared rich, though dry) and sowing their barley; while their herds were browsing on the shrubs round about, for the want of grass.

Many unarmed men, with droves of camels and asses loaded with salt and other merchandise, were meeting and passing us almost continually. We saw also from time to time, bands of armed men on horseback, of about fifty in each band, most of whom I learned from Rais were the friends of Muley Ibrahim, whom he had requested to ride guard, as I before mentioned, and to be ready to act in our behalf in case of treachery, or of any emergency whatever. Our path led us in a N. E. direction, and the camels were kept most of the time on a great trot, while their drivers were running on foot, and kept up with us, seemingly, with great ease; though I compute we rode at the rate of seven or eight miles an hour.

About two p. m. approaching the coast, we fell in with huge drifts of loose sand on our left, which extended to the seashore. This sand had been driven from the sea-beach by the constant trade winds, and as the sea had retired, (for it was clean coarse beach sand,) it had undoubtedly for ages been making its way gradually from the coast, (which was now about twenty miles distant,) and had buried, as I was informed, several flourishing villages, towns, and cities, the tops of whose walls were still visible; the circular domes of a considerable number of saint-houses, or sanctuaries, whose bodies were entirely enveloped, were yet to be seen among these barren heaps of overwhelming sands; for the inhabitants take great care to clear away around them, and to give them a whitewashing every year.

Muley Ibrahim informed me, that a large town called Rabeah, whose ruins we had passed in mounting over the sand-hills, was a flourishing place within his remembrance; (probably fifty years ago;) that he himself was born in it—but that large bodies of sand had already encroached upon its northern wall; that as soon as it was overtopped it fell in, and the whole city was filled with sand in the course of one year after, and its inhabitants forced to seek a new shelter. These drifts extended as far as we could distinguish sand on our right.

Having got past the high heaps, which filled a space of eight or ten miles in width, we came to the high banks of an apparently once large river, now called by the natives *el Woed Sta*. This river's ancient bed, and the high banks, which are still perfectly distinct, bear the strongest marks of having been once laved by a stream of four or five miles in breadth, and nearly one hundred feet in depth, or by a part of the ocean. The steep, barren, and craggy mountains, rising before us to the eastward and southward, though very high, appeared to serve only as a base to the mighty range of Atlas, whose towering height and grandeur filled my mind with awe and astonishment.

Notwithstanding my frame was literally exhausted, yet my imagination transported me back to a time when this region might have been inhabited by men in a higher state of civilization, and when it was probably one of the fairest portions of the African continent. My reasons for imagining this are, first, that it is well known by historians, that the Romans had settlements along this coast as far south as Salee at least, and no doubt much further. Second, that the Portuguese and Spaniards had possessed the settlements of Mamora, Mazagan, Asbedre, Santa Cruz, &c. Third, by the traditional information obtained from Rais bel Cossim and Sidi Mohammed, I have no doubt that a large city and settlement of civilized men existed at a former period near the mouth of the River Schelem, from sixty to one hundred miles west of Santa Cruz, and I am firmly of opinion, that the convenience of these harbours, the luxuriancy of the surrounding soil, and the commercial advantages this part of the country offers, were a sufficient inducement for colonization.

We had now approached to within two miles of Santa Cruz or Agader, (the lower town or port,) when rising an eminence, the ocean opened to our view at a distance, and nearby appeared Santa Cruz bay. which was then quite smooth. Nearly one hundred good looking fishing boats were hauled up on the beach out of the reach of the surf, and numbers of long fishing nets were spread out to dry on the sand and over the boats. This view gave a most favourable idea of the importance of this bay as a fishery.

The sun had not yet set, and Rais informed me he did not wish to enter the lower town till dark, and did not mean to go nearer the fortress than he could help, for fear of insult and detention; so we stopped about a mile short of it, to the southward, where I had an opportunity of examining this bay with a seaman's eye. It is spacious and perfectly well defended from the common trade winds, say from N. N. W. all around the compass by the east, and as far as S. W.; thence to N. N. W. it is entirely open, and of course is a very dangerous anchorage in the winter months, when westerly winds prevail on these coasts, at which times, as there is no possibility of getting to sea, vessels at anchor in this bay must remain where they are; not, however, without the greatest risk of being driven on shore in spite of the best of anchors and cables, and large vessels must ride too far out to make it a good harbour for them at any season of the year. The port of Santa Cruz, or, as it is called by the natives, Agader, has been shut by order of the *Sultan* for many years; yet there are parts of the wrecks of vessels still visible, sticking up through the sand on the beach.

A little while after sunset we entered the lower town, or port, as it is called: this village is situated on the steep declivity of the mountain's base, on which the upper town is built, and near the sea, which washes the south end of the principal street. The steep side of the mountain on which this village is erected, has been apparently sloped down by art, so as to make it practicable to build on it; has one principal street, and several small alleys: the houses are built of rough stone laid in lime mortar, and are but one story in height, with flat roofs terraced with lime and pebbles. We could see the tops of many houses below us, and the whole made but a miserable appearance.

It was not quite dark when we entered the village. The street was soon filled with Moors, (men and boys,) and they saluted us by spitting on us, and pelting us with stones and sticks, accompanied with the Spanish words "*Carajo a la Mierda le Sara, perro y bestias*" and many other chosen phrases, equally delicate and polite; but some of the old men now and then uttered a "How de do, *Christianos?*" in broken English and Spanish. We were conducted through the street to its further extremity towards the north, where we took up our quarters for the night in the open air, alongside a smith's shop; our camels and asses were then fed with barley. Some of the inhabitants kindled a fire for our company, whilst others were preparing a rich repast for them of boiled and baked fish, and *cous-koo-soo*, of which, after they had eaten, they gave us the remains, and we found it excellent food.

Numbers of men, driving asses before them, loaded with fish, had passed us going into the country, the day before, and they were of the same kind as those we had tasted soon after our entrance into Suse, and we had also seen the same kind of fish at Stuka: they carry them from Santa Cruz, or Agader, about the country in every direction, where they sell them for a good price, being much in request. This fish very much resembles the salmon, both in size, shape, and flavour—weighing, from appearance, from eight to sixteen or twenty pounds; and is extremely fat and delicate. I then recollected to have seen in my several voyages to the Canary Islands, numbers of small vessels arrive from the coast of Africa, laden with this species of fish, and to have been told they were caught near that coast: they are highly esteemed in the Canaries, where they call them *Bacalao Africano*, or the African codfish, and are sold at from five to ten dollars per quintal, or at least one-third higher than the best of American codfish: they are dried, without salting, on the vessels' decks, and their scent is so strong as nearly to suffocate the crews of merchant vessels that lie near them while discharging.

I have been told that no less than one hundred *barks*, of from fifteen to fifty tons burden, are continually employed in this fishery near the African coast, from the Canary Islands, and that scarcely a year passes without more or less of them being driven on shore by tempests or other accidents, when the crews either perish with the vessel, or upon their reaching the shore are massacred by the natives, or else carried off into the interior as slaves, where they are never after heard from. After my arrival in Mogadore, or Swearah, I was informed that the crew of a *bark* of this description landed imprudently on the beach not far from Santa Cruz, about two years since, where they were surprised by a sudden attack, but all escaped into the boat except one man, who was seized and carried off.

On the return of the bark to Teneriffe, the wife of the man who had been left, upon inquiring for her husband, was informed that he was made a slave: distracted by this shocking event, she ran, raving as she was, to the archbishop, and begged of him either to take her life, or restore to her arms her lost husband, the father of five helpless children: she was poor, but her case excited general pity—a subscription was opened, and the sum of about five hundred dollars soon raised. The archbishop in the meantime wrote to Alexander W. Court, then Spanish agent at Mogadore, to ransom this unfortunate man, which he effected with much difficulty; but as the money did not come on in time, or from some other cause, this poor Spaniard, whose name was Fermin, remained in Mogadore for nearly a year without being permitted to go home, when Mr. William Willshire and Don Plabo Riva, of Mogadore, and Mr. John O'Sullivan, of New-York, interfered in his favour; furnished him with clothing; procured for him a passage, and sent him to his disconsolate family. This is said to be the only Spaniard who has been redeemed in that part of Barbary for many years past.

Chapter 23

They Set Off in the Night

After supper, Rais bel Cossim told me to keep a good lookout; that he would watch the motions of Sheick Ali, who he still feared was plotting against our liberty. After I had informed my enfeebled and desponding companions that we were now out of danger from the Arabs, (having come about fifty miles from Stuka,) and in the emperor of Morocco's dominions, and, consequently, sure of being liberated, and that too in a very few days; and after telling them that we must bear up under our fatigues with fortitude, and exert our remaining strength and spirits, in order to reach Mogadore, we all laid ourselves down to rest; and my companions, though they had the bare ground for their bed, yet as they were wrapped up in cloaks, and had their stomachs well filled with good and nourishing food, soon fell asleep.

As for myself, fear, hope, and various other sensations, kept me awake, and I could not close my eyes, but waited with extreme anxiety for the appearance of Rais bel Cossim. Soon after midnight Rais came, and finding me awake, he roused me and the owners of the camels, and requested them to get ready to go on speedily, and then told me that on entering this place, while he was busied in feeding his mule, Sheick Ali had stolen off privately to the town, and visited the governor, who had agreed, on his representation, to take us into custody in the morning at daybreak, and assist in extorting what money the *Sheick* demanded; or to connive at our being stolen and carried back by Sheick Ali's men to Suse.

"I have learned this" said he "from an old friend of mine, whom I met and commissioned to watch Sheick Ali's motions when we were coming into this place: awaken your shipmates: you must depart this instant: the drivers know the road: it is very rocky: you must tell your men to hold on as tight as possible; and remember, if you are four leagues from this town before daylight, your liberty is secured, if not, you will be again the most miserable of slaves. Encourage your men to use their utmost exertions, and I hope, with God's blessing, in three days more you will be in Swearah with your friend. I will join you as soon as possible."

The camels were by this time ready: we were placed on them, and proceeded up the rocky steeps as fast as possible, but with the most profound silence. Sleep seemed to have literally sealed the eyes of all the Moors in the lower town, and in the batteries near the path through which we passed; these batteries rose one above another like an amphitheatre towards the fortress. The quadrangular walls of the town and fortress of Santa Cruz, or Agader, crowned the summit of this mountain on our right, and stand, from appearance, not less than fifteen hundred feet above the level of the sea. We went fast forward, in profound silence, which was not in the least disturbed by the tread of the camels, because their feet are as soft as sponge or leather: only the hoarse roaring of the surf breaking among the rocks below us, startled the ear, and excited in my mind frightful images of direful shipwrecks, and the consequent miseries of the poor mariner driven on this inhospitable coast.

We had been hurrying on as fast as possible for about two hours, and had gained the distance of probably three leagues from Santa Cruz, when our ears were struck with the clinking sound of iron against the stones, which announced the approach of horses or mules that were shod; and in an instant, though dark, we discovered close by us on our right, a considerable number of men riding on mules, and passing the other way. Not a word was uttered on either side, nor could the faces of any be distinguished, though we were not more than three or four yards asunder.

A thought darting across my mind, suggested to me that it was my old master: I instantly called out, "Sidi Hamet!" and was quickly answered, "Ascoon Riley?" (who is it, Riley?) The whole company stopped in an instant, and the next moment I had the joy of kissing the hand of my old master and benefactor. Sidi Mohammed, Seid, and Bo-Mohammed, where in his company, together with three or four Moors, whom our kind friend had sent down, charged with the money and mules for our ransom and conveyance.

The principal Moor, and who had charge of the money until we were delivered over according to the wish of Sidi Hamet, spoke Spanish fluently: he wanted to inquire of me where Rais bel Cossim was:

I told him at Santa Cruz. Sidi Hamet wished to question me himself, and asked me "Where is Sheick Ali?" and when I informed him that I had left him in Santa Cruz, in company with Rais bel Cossim and Muley Ibrahim, he was satisfied: and said Sheick Ali was a bad man, and did not fear God.

Seid also pretended to be much rejoiced at our being on the road to Mogadore, and yet I thought I could discover that he was trying to play a deep game of artful duplicity: but old Sidi Mohammed was in truth rejoiced to find us in the emperor's dominions.—Having now been absolutely delivered over to Bel Mooden, the Moor who had charge of the money, he paid it over to Sidi Hamet, and three of us were mounted on mules, and proceeded on, while all those whom we met went towards Santa Cruz, except the three Moors who owned and brought the mules down for us to ride on, and who remained and proceeded northward with us.

All the time we had stopped to make the necessary arrangements above mentioned, the owners of the camels were urging us to go forward, thereby showing a disposition to obey the orders of Rais bel Cossim, and would not for a long time believe that those who stopped us were not our enemies. The backs of the mules were covered with large saddles made of coarse cloth, stuffed with straw, and formed very broad, so as to fit their shape, and reached almost from their heads to their tails: this kind of saddle is too broad for a man to attempt to stride. Over the saddles were placed what the Moors and Arabs call a *shwerry*, which is made like a double basket, and formed of palm leaves woven together like mat work: each of these baskets might contain about two bushels; they are attached together by a mat woven in with and like the rest, of about a foot and a half in width, sufficiently strong to bear a burden, and long enough to let them hang down easily on the sides of the mules: the outer part of this *shwerry* is held up by means of a rope passing through the handle on one side, and tied to that on the other, passing over the mule's back.

In this *shwerry*, they carry their provisions, merchandise, and spare clothing, (if any they have,) when on their journeys. The rider sits on the saddle above the *shwerry*, with both legs on one side, balancing his body exactly, and rides extremely easy, as he can shift his position at pleasure, and the mule's gait is an easy, fast ambling walk, which they are taught when very young; their motion is very slight, and was a seasonable relief to our almost dislocated limbs: the change, with respect to jolting, was so great from the camel to the mule, that we could not keep our eyes open from mere drowsiness, and Burns getting asleep, dropped off his mule, and was so badly hurt as to be from that time incapable of supporting himself; so that a Moor was obliged to sit before or behind him, and keep him on, driving the mule at the same time: and this was continued during the remainder of our journey.

We had proceeded in this way until about ten o'clock, when we were joined by Raisbei Cossim, Sidi Kamet, Seid, Sidi Mohammed, and Bel Mooden. I now inquired of Rais what had become of Muley Ibrahim and Sheick Ali, with their attendants, and he told me they had set out for their respective homes. I wanted to know all the particulars of their proceedings, and Rais promised to satisfy me after breakfast, which we now stopped to eat (*viz.* biscuit and butter) near a well that afforded us good water, though nearly on a level with the sea. After we were again mounted, he began to relate as follows:—"When my friend told me of Sheick Ali's plan, I stole away softly, and came and sent you off without the *Sheick's* knowledge; but Muley Ibrahim was in the secret, and remained with the *Sheick* to prevent alarm if he should awake during my absence."

Rais bel Cossim further told me in substance, that as soon as we were on our journey, he returned and laid himself down to sleep across the doorway, where Sheick Ali slept, and in such a manner as to make it impossible for the *Sheick* to go out without alarming him; the *Sheick* awoke at the dawn of day, and finding himself blockaded in the house, awakened Rais, and told him that they had better wait on the governor this morning, to which Rais consented, but wanted to see the slaves first, so as to have some coffee made: this was agreed on; but when they came where we had slept, and found none of us there, nor the camels, nor their drivers, Rais broke out into the most violent passion apparently; accused the *Sheick* of having robbed him of his slaves during the night, and said he would instantly have him seized and delivered up to the governor, to be punished according to the Moorish law.

Muley Ibrahim, who knew the whole affair, joined with Rais, protesting he could no longer hold friendship with a man who was capable of committing such an act, which he considered to be one of the worst breaches of faith that ever disgraced a man of his (the *Sheick's*) high character. Sheick Ali was thunderstruck by this unexpected event—declared, in the most solemn manner, that he knew nothing about our escape; begged he might not be delivered up to the governor; acknowledged he had laid a plan the preceding evening for our detention; wished Rais to leave the governor a small present, and proceed on the road towards Mogadore in the hope of finding us, saying, we must have gone that way, as the gates were shut on the other side, and there was no possibility of turning back by any other route.

The *Sheick* added, "I am in your power, and will go on with you and my friend Muley Ibrahim, without any attendants, to prove to you that I am innocent, and that I place the greatest confidence in your friendship." Thus they agreed to pursue and endeavour to overtake the supposed runaway slaves; but soon after they had mounted the hills north of Santa Cruz, meeting our former masters, with Bel Mooden and Sidi Mohammed, who had seen us, (as I before mentioned,) they stopped and talked over their several affairs. Sheick Ali insisted that Sidi Hamet had treated him very ill: that he and Seid owed him four hundred dollars, which they were to pay him on their return from the desert, but that they had passed by his lands three days' journey with their slaves, without even calling on him to eat bread: he added, he would have gone with them himself, and with an armed force through Sidi Ishem's country, to prevent that chief from taking their property—"but you wished to cheat me of my money, as you did of my daughter," said he, addressing himself to Sidi Hamet.

Sidi Hamet, whose voice had been very high before, now lowering his tone, said, it was better to settle their disputes than to quarrel; so he acknowledged he owed his father-in-law three hundred and sixty dollars for goods, but asserted that they were not worth half the money: he would, however, pay the principal, but no interest, which would have swelled the amount of debt to more than five hundred dollars: the *Sheick* agreed to take the principal, which was counted out in silver, as he would not take gold *doubloons* in payment, because he did not know their real value. He then delivered up Sidi Hamet's bond, and said he would return to his tribe. Rais bel Cossim gave Muley Ibrahim a present in cash, and they separated, having first vowed everlasting friendship, and joined in prayer for the success of their several journeys.

Our company now consisted of Rais bel Cossim, Bel Mooden, Sidi Hamet, Seid, Sidi Mohammed,, and three muleteers, all armed with muskets, swords, or daggers—the five Bereberies with their camels, who had brought us on from Stuka, and myself and four shipmates. We proceeded along the coast, sometimes on a sand beach, now climbing an almost perpendicular mountain of great height, by a winding kind of zigzag road that seemed to have been cut in the rock in many places by art; then descending into deep valleys by this kind of natural steps; the rocks on our right for a great distance, rising nearly perpendicularly.

The path we were now obliged to follow, was not more than two feet wide in one place, and on our left it broke off in a precipice of some hundred feet deep to the sea—the smallest slip of the mule or camel, would have plunged it and its rider down the rocks to inevitable and instant death, as there was no bush or other thing to lay hold of by which a man might save his life. Very fortunately for us, there had been no rain for a considerable time previous, so that the road was now dry. Rais told me when it was wet it was never attempted, and that many fatal accidents had happened there within his remembrance; though there was another road that led round over the mountains far within the country.

One of these accidents he said he would mention.

A company of Jews, six in number, from Santa Cruz for Morocco, came to this place with their loaded mules in the twilight, after sunset; being very anxious to get past it before dark, and supposing no other travellers would venture to meet them, or dare to pass it in the night, they did not take the precaution to look out, and call aloud before they entered on it; for there is a place built out on each end of this dangerous piece of road, from whence one may see if there are others on it: not being quite half a mile in length, a person by hallooing out can be heard from one end to the other, and it is the practice of all who go that way, to give the signal.

A company of Moors had entered at the other end, and going towards Santa Cruz at the same time, and they also supposing that no others would dare to pass it at that hour, came on without the usual precaution. About half way over, and in the most difficult place, the two parties met: there was no possibility of passing each other, nor of turning about to go back either way: the Moors were mounted as well as the Jews: neither party could retire nor could anyone, except the foremost, get off of his mule.

The Moors soon became outrageous, and threatened to throw the Jews down headlong: the Jews, though they had always been treated like slaves, and forced to submit to every insult and indignity, yet finding themselves in this perilous situation, without the possibility of retiring, and being unwilling to break their necks merely to accommodate the Moors, the foremost Jew dismounted carefully over the head of his mule with a stout stick in his hand: the Moor nearest him did the same, and came forward to attack him with his scimitar: both were fighting for their lives, as neither could retreat—the Jew's mule was first pitched down the craggy steep, and dashed to atoms by the fall—the Jew's stick was next hacked to pieces by the scimitar; when finding it was impossible for him to save his life, he seized the Moor in his arms, and springing off the precipice, both were instantly hurled to destruction: two more of the Jews and one Moor lost their lives in the same way, together with eight mules; and the three Jews who made out to escape, were hunted down and killed by the relations of the Moors who had lost their lives on the pass, and the place has ever since been called "the Jew's leap."

It is, indeed, enough to produce dizziness, even in the head of a sailor, and if I had been told the story before getting on this frightful ridge, I am not certain but that my imagination might have disturbed my faculties, and rendered me incapable of proceeding with safety along this perilous path. The danger over, however, and the story finished, we found ourselves mounting the first bank from the sea on Cape Geer. When we came on the height, at the pitch of the Cape, I rode up to the edge of the precipice to look down upon the tumultuous ocean. The present Cape is about one hundred feet in height, and appeared to have been much shattered and rent by the waves and tempests: huge masses of rocks had been undermined, broken off, and tumbled down one upon another, forming very wild and disorderly heaps in the water all around it.

I could not help shuddering at the sight and sound of the surf as it came thundering on, and burst against the trembling sides of this rocky Cape, which is about a mile in length, and is already undermined in a such a manner, that the whole road along which we passed will very probably soon tumble down among the assailing billows. On our right, the land rose gradually like an inclined plane, and was covered with pebbles and other round smooth stones that bore strong marks of having been tossed about and worn by the surf on the sea beach: it rose thus for about two miles, when it was interrupted by perpendicular and overhanging cliffs of craggy and broken rocks, three or four hundred feet in height: these rocks, and the whole face of the upper Cape, bore as strong marks of having once been washed and beat upon by the ocean, as did the cliff below us, against which it was now dashing with dreadful violence.

Along most parts of the inclined plane, and particularly near the upper cliff, were large mounts of loose sand in form of snowdrifts. This sand was now flying up from the beach below, being blown out from among the rocks by the strong trade winds at every low tide, and almost as soon as the dashings of the waves among them had prepared it: this sand, and in fact all we had seen since we came to the cultivated country, was the same in appearance as that which we saw and passed through on the desert, and must have been produced and heaped up by the same causes. After passing the Cape about one hour's ride, we came to the high bank of a river, and descending to its left shore, we found its mouth was filled up with sand that had been washed in by the sea, though the river was about a half a mile wide at its end, and appeared quite deep: here we stopped to take some food, namely, biscuit and butter.

Bel Mooden had also brought some dried figs, dates, and nuts. Having finished our repast, we were again placed on our beasts, and proceeded round the mouth of the river on a sandy beach, about one hundred yards wide, and twenty feet above the level of the fresh water within, and thirty feet above the sea water on the beach at high tide. Our guides informed me that this river was called "*el woed Tensha;*" that it had formerly been a very wide and deep one, and used to empty itself into the sea; that in the rainy season it was impossible to pass it without going twenty miles up the country; but for the last few years there had not been rain enough in this part of the country to force open its mouth.

Having left the margin of the river, we entered on a plane, and struck off to our right in a direction nearly east, and we went forward as fast as possible towards the high land. We had passed many sanctuaries, but had not observed a single dwelling house, nor even a tent, since we left Santa Cruz. We now beheld several square walled places, which answer the double purpose of dwelling house and castle, crowning the top of the high mountain, which appeared very dry and sterile, mostly composed of layers of huge rocks and very steep, with a few dry shrubs scattered thinly about the crevices and small fiat spots or spaces.

Approaching the foot of the mountain, we came to a very deep hollow, apparently formed by the washings of a small stream of water, assisted by rains that have poured through it from time immemorial. Our way wound up through this steep hollow, and alongside of the little brook before mentioned. As we entered it, the eye was delighted with the beauty of the scene. The bottom of the hollow had been made level by art, and was covered from its base with gardens, which rose one above another in the form of an amphitheatre: they were kept up to a level by means of solid stonewalls laid in lime, and had been filled in with rich soil: the longest was not greater in extent than twenty yards by ten.

The sides of the hollow were so steep, that the upright walls were not less than ten or fifteen feet in height between each garden: they were well stocked with most kinds of vegetables cultivated in kitchen gardens, and with melons: gutters were curiously disposed around these gardens, to convey water to every part, at the pleasure of the proprietor: they had growing on their sides an abundance of fig and date trees, and grape vines running up the sides of the rocks; and a little higher up, hundreds of the dwarf *arga* tree, whose yellow fruit contributed to enliven the prospect. We were at least two hours in gaining the summit, when it had become dark, and we had to pass down the mountain on its east side through another hollow, though not a fertile one; for here was no running water. The narrow path we travelled in, had been worn into the lime-stone rock, by the feet of mules and horses that had passed along it, no doubt, during the course of many centuries; and, assisted by the rain water streaming through it from above, it was in some places channelled out to the depth often or fifteen feet, and just wide enough for a camel or mule to pass.

In one place it became necessary, for the want of sufficient room to get through, to take the hiding from the mules and carry it down by hand. After descending about three hours we came to a plane, and kept on in an eastern direction until about, midnight, when we approached the walls of a small city, or dwelling- place, and took up our lodgings near it on the flat top of a long cistern, which afforded plenty of water. The chief men of the city, alarmed by the barking of their dogs, soon came out and welcomed their visitors by the well known Arabic salutation, "*Salemo Alikom, Labez*" &c.

They furnished our company with a supper of *cous-koo-soo*, while I and my men ate some dates and dry figs. The night was damp and cold, and this, with my fatigues, rendered it impossible for me to sleep. We stayed here for about three hours, when daylight appearing, (October the 6th,) we were again mounted, and proceeded on our journey. My companions, as well as myself, were so weak, being really worn out, and completely exhausted, that it was with the greatest difficulty they could be supported on the mules.

As daylight increased, we saw a number of towns or dwellings handsomely enclosed with high walls of stone, cemented with lime: the land on the plane was divided off and fenced in with rough stone walls made with great labour: numerous flocks of goats were feeding on the oil nut; some herds of cattle, with a few old horses, asses, and camels, were nibbling off the green leaves and branches of small shrubs, for the want of grass: we also saw many regularly planted orchards of fig trees; and the land was in many places ploughed and ready to receive the seed barley, so soon as rain should fall sufficient to ensure its vegetation.

We went forward to the north-eastward, and on rising a hill, we saw two mountains before us to the north, over which I was informed we must pass: the farthest one north appeared to be twenty miles distant. We soon began to climb the nearest, and when we reached its summit, looking to the east, the Atlas was fairly in view, and all its lofty peaks covered with snow. Descending this mountain, we met large droves of camels, mules, and asses, laden with salt and other merchandise, and driven by a considerable number of Moors and Arabs. The Moors were easily distinguished by their dress: they had each, besides his *haick*, a *caftan* or close jacket next his skin, and the most of them had turban on their heads. They were armed with daggers, or scimitars, suspended from their necks by a cord of red woollen yarn thrown over the left shoulder: the scabbards were such as I have before described.

The dagger is worn outside of the *haick*; its handle is made of wood, handsomely wrought. The point of the dagger hooks inward like a pruning knife: when they have occasion to use it, they seize it with their right hand, the lower side of the hand being next to the blade, and strike after raising it above their heads, ripping open their adversary: they never attempt to parry a stroke with their daggers.

The valley between these two mountains had been well cultivated and would be very productive with seasonable rains, but at this time those dreadful scourges, severe droughts, and myriads of locusts, had destroyed almost every green thing: even the leaves of the trees and shrubs had not escaped their devastations. I was informed by Rais bel Cossim that we were now in the province of Hah hah, and that the locusts had utterly laid waste the country for the last six years, so that the land now groaned under a most grievous famine; nor could our company procure any barley or other food for their beasts. This province must be naturally a very strong military country; it is very mountainous, and rendered almost inaccessible by the craggy steeps and narrow roads, or defiles, through which an army would be under the necessity of marching.

The cities, or rather castles, in which the inhabitants reside, are built strong with stone and lime, and are fifteen or twenty feet in height, generally of a quadrangular form of from fifty to two hundred yards square, and the tops crowned with turrets: within these walls all the flocks and herds are driven every night for safe keeping. All the men in these parts are well armed with long Moorish muskets, and with sabres, or daggers, by their sides: there are no Arabs dwelling in this part of the country, as they always live in tents, and will not be confined within walls; nor had we seen a tent since our arrival at the dwelling of Sidi Mohammed.

The valley now spread out to the right, and might be termed a considerably extensive plane, on which but few castles or dwellings appeared, and we saw no river or stream of water, though there were high mountains on both sides. The little herbage that had sprung up, in consequence of the recent rains, was destroyed by the locusts, which were to be seen thinly scattered over the ground, and rose in considerable numbers on our approach, skipping like grasshoppers. Rais bel Cossim informed me that the flights of locusts, from which these few had strayed, had gone to some hitherto more favoured part of the country to continue their ravages.

While we were tranquilly travelling along, I asked Rais in what manner the oil was extracted from the nuts that grew in such quantities on the *arga* tree, which entirely covered the sides of the hills. He told me that in the country these nuts were swallowed by the goats, (and in fact we saw these animals picking them up under the trees;) that the nut passes through, after being deprived of its bark, which, though very bitter, was highly relished by the goats, and when voided, the women and children, who tend them, pick up the nuts and put them into a bag, slung about them for the purpose, and carry them home, where they crack them between stones, get out the kernel, and expressing the oily juice from them, they boil it down in a jar until it becomes of a proper consistence, when it is poured off and fit for use. The appearance of this fruit growing thickly on the trees, different in size, and variegated in colour from green to red, and from that to bright yellow, had a pleasing effect: the ground beneath the trees was also covered with them.

Having come to the foot of the high mountain, we ascended it, winding up its steep side in a zigzag path very difficult of ascent, and indeed almost impracticable, On our left was a deep gully, with a considerable stream of water running down through it, like a small mill-stream: it poured over the precipices, making a loud roaring, that might be heard at a great distance; though the whole stream seemed to lose itself entirely in the sand before it reached the bottom of the mountain. The sides of this gully were shaded by the *arga* and bean tree, and many other bushes; and near the water I discovered a few yew or hemlock bushes, that reminded me of scenes I had been familiar with in my own country. As we rode near the top of the mountain, this gully assumed the appearance of a rich valley, filled with gardens one above another, supported by strong stone walls in the same manner as those I have already described, though much larger, and they were apparently well watered by the stream that was carried around them in gutters fitted for that purpose.

These gardens looked as if they were well cultivated, and stored with vegetables; and numbers of men and boys were at work tilling and dressing them. On the highest part of the mountain that we reached, I was much surprised to find a considerable plane spot, nearly covered with stacks of salt, which stood very thick, and must, I think, have amounted to several hundreds. To see marine salt in such quantities on the top of a mountain, which I computed to stand at least fifteen hundred feet above the surface of the ocean, excited my wonder and curiosity; but we stopped short of them, for the camels we had started with from Stuka, were to carry loads of this salt back; so that after Rais had paid the owners of them for their trouble and assistance, they went towards the salt heaps, wishing us a prosperous journey.

While we were stopped to settle with them, we were taken from the mules and seated on the ground, when many of the inhabitants came near to have a look at us, *Christian slaves*. They brought with them a few raw turnips, which they distributed among us: they were the sweetest I had ever tasted, and very refreshing. We were soon placed upon the mules again, and I rode a little to the left, in order to find out in what way this great quantity of salt had been procured and deposited in this singular situation; and on a near approach, I saw a great number of salt pans formed of clay, and very shallow, into which water was conducted by means of small gutters cut for the purpose in the clay.

The water issues in considerable quantities from the side of the mountain, in the northwest part of the plane, (which has been levelled down, and regulated with great labour,) and is very strongly impregnated with salt: the pans or basins being very shallow, the water is soon evaporated by the heat of the sun, and a crystallization of excellent salt is the result. It is small grained, and tinged by the reddish colour of the clay of which the pans are formed. The highest peak of the mountain did not appear to rise above the salt spring more than about one hundred feet. A great number of men and boys were employed in raking and heaping up the salt, and numbers more in selling and measuring it out, and loading it on camels, mules, and asses Rais bel Cossim informed me that this spring furnished the greatest proportion of the salt that is made use of in the Moorish dominions, and in Suse; and I should estimate the number of camels, mules, and asses that were there at that time waiting for loads, at from four to five hundred. We had met hundreds on the route since we left Stuka, loaded with this article, and I afterwards saw many loads of the same kind of salt enter Mogadore, Saffy, and Rabat.

We proceeded to the northward down the mountain, which is not so steep on its north as on its south side. The country, after descending it, was tolerably smooth, with much of the *arga* wood flourishing on every side. Soon after dark we came to a wall that enclosed a space of ground forty or fifty yards square: it was built of stone and lime, six or eight feet in height, with an open space like a gateway on its northern side, through which we entered, and took up our lodgings on the ground, which was very smooth. A walled village was near this yard on the west, and on the north, outside of both walls, stood a mosque, or house of worship: the inhabitants were chanting their evening or eight o'clock prayers when we entered the yard; yet none of them came out to look at us, their attention being wholly confined to their religious duties.

We were taken from the mules and placed near the wall, which kept off the night wind, and after we had nibbled a little biscuit and drank some water, we thanked God for his goodness, and tried to get a little sleep. The wind did not molest us, and we rested until about midnight, when we were awakened by the noise occasioned by a company of men with loaded camels and mules: they had already entered the yard without ceremony, to the number probably of thirty men, with three times as many camels, mules, and asses. I was awakened by the bellowing of the camels, as they were forced to lie down with their heavy loads. The men did not speak to ours, and as soon as they had tethered their mules by tying ropes round their footlock joints, and fastening them to pegs driven into the ground for that purpose, they laid themselves down to sleep, wrapped up in their *haicks*.

Our whole company being awake, they saddled their mules, put us thereon, and we proceeded on our journey. It was very dark, and the path lay through a rough stony country. We were so weak, that we could not sit on the mules without one being behind to steady our tottering frames: at daylight we found ourselves near some substantial buildings, and I begged of Rais to buy some milk if it was possible: he rode near the gates and asked some of the inhabitants for milk; but they would not sell any. This to me was a sore disappointment, as I was benumbed with cold, and so much fatigued that I thought it would be impossible for me to ride much further; which Rais observing, said to me, "Keep up your spirits, Captain, only a few hours longer, and you will be in Swearah, if God Almighty continues his protection."

I was so reduced and debilitated, that I could not support even good news with any degree of firmness, and such was my agitation, that it was with the utmost difficulty I could keep on my mule for some moments afterwards. We had been constantly travelling for three days and most of three nights, and though I concluded we must be near Swearah, I did not think we should reach it before late in the evening. Passing along a narrow footway between high bushes, we came to a long string of sand-hills on our left, drifted up like the sand heaps on the desert, and along the coast: it was then about eight o'clock in the morning, when mounting the side of one of those hills, the city of Swearah broke suddenly upon our view, with the island of Mogadore forming a harbour, in which was a brig riding at anchor with English colours flying:—"Take courage, Captain" said the good Rais; "there is Swearah," pointing towards the town; "and there is a vessel to carry you to your country and family: if God please you will soon see the noble Willshire, who will relieve you from all your miseries. I thank my God your sufferings are nearly at an end, and that I have been found worthy to be an instrument in the hands of the Omnipotent to redeem you from slavery."

He next returned thanks to the Almighty in Arabic, with all that fervour and devotion, so peculiar to Mohammedans, and then he ejaculated in Spanish, "May it have pleased Almighty God to have preserved the lives of my wife and children."

We now proceeded down the sand-hills towards the city—but very slowly. Sidi Hamet had been for some time missing: he had gone privately forward, to be first to carry the news to our deliverer of our approach; and now Bel Mooden and Sidi Mohammed left us for a similar purpose, and made the best of their way towards the city. It would be idle for me to attempt to describe the various emotions of my mind at this exquisitely interesting moment: I must leave that to be conceived by the reader. We soon approached the walls of an imperial palace, which is situated about two miles southeast of Swearah, or Mogadore. The walls are built in a square of probably one hundred yards at each side, and about twenty feet in height—they enclose four small square houses, built at the four corners within, and which rise one story above the walls: the houses have square roofs, coming to a point in the centre, and handsomely covered with green tiles—they, as well as the other walls, are built with rough stone, cemented with lime, plastered over and whitewashed.

Near the western angle of the walls we stopped, and were taken off our mules and seated on the green grass. A small stream of fresh water, running from the east, was spreading over the sand near its northern wall, flowing and meandering slowly towards the bay over the beach, in a number of small rills. The water in the bay was quite smooth; small boats were moving gently on its glassy surface, or were anchored near its entrance, probably for the purpose of fishing, this, together with the sight of great numbers of men driving camels, cows, asses, and sheep, and riding on horses, all at a distance, and going different ways, together with the view of the high steeples in Mogadore, infused into my soul a kind of sublime delight and a heavenly serenity that is indescribable, and to which it had ever before been a stranger.

The next moment I discovered the American flag floating over a part of the distant city: at this blessed and transporting sight, the little blood remaining in my veins gushed through my glowing heart with wild impetuosity, and seemed to pour a flood of new life through every part of my exhausted frame. We were still seated on the green sward near the western wall, and the mules that brought us there were feeding carelessly before us at a little distance.

Our deliverer, who had received news of our coming from Sidi Hamet, having first directed the flag of our country to be hoisted as a signal, had mounted his horse, ridden out of the city, and came to the eastern side of the palace walls, where Rais bel Cossim met him—unknown to me. I expected him soon, but did not think he was so near. He had dismounted, and was prepared to behold some of the most miserable objects his imagination could paint. He led his horse along the south angle, and near the wall: Rais was by his side, when opening past the corner, I heard Rais exclaim, in Spanish, *"Alla estan"*—"there they are:"—at this sound we looked up and beheld our deliverer, who had at that instant turned his eyes upon us. He started back one step with surprise. His blood seemed to fly from his visage for a moment, but recovering himself a little, he rushed forward, and clasping me to his breast, he ejaculated, "Welcome to my arms, my dear sir; this is truly a happy moment."

He next took each of my companions by the hand, and welcomed them to their liberty, while tears trickled down his manly cheeks, and the sudden rush of all the generous and sympathetic feelings of his heart nearly choked his utterance: then raising his eyes towards heaven, he said, "I thank thee, great Author of my being, for thy mercy to these my brothers." He could add no more; his whole frame was so agitated that his strength failed him, and he sunk to the ground. We, on our part, could only look upwards in silent adoration, while our hearts swelled with indescribable sensations of gratitude and love to the all wise, all powerful, and ever merciful God of the universe, who had conducted us through so many dreadful scenes of danger and suffering; had controlled the passions and disposed the hearts of the barbarous Arabs in our favour, and had finally brought us to the arms of such a friend. Tears of joy streamed from our eyes, and Rais bel Cossim was so much affected at this interview, that in order to conceal his weeping, he hid himself behind the wall; for the Moors as well as the Arabs, hold the shedding of tears to be a womanish and degrading weakness.

After a short pause, when Mr. Willshire had in some measure recovered, he said, "Come, my friends, let us go to the city; my house is already prepared for your reception."—The mules were led up, and we were again placed on them, and rode off slowly towards Mogadore. Mr. Savage and Clark were on one mule, and Burns and Horace on another, for the purpose of mutually supporting each other; but their debility was such, that they fell off on the beach two or three times before they reached the city;—however, it was on the soft sand, and as they were very light, they seemed to have received no material injury: they were again placed on the mules, and steadied until our arrival at the gates of Swearah, by Moors walking beside them.

The gateway was crowded with Moors, Jews, and negroes—the news of our coming having spread through the city, and a curiosity to see Christian slaves, had brought them together in great numbers; and the men and boys of the rabble were only restrained from committing violence on us, by the gate-keepers and a few soldiers, who voluntarily escorted us to Mr. Willshire's house, and in some measure kept off the crowd: there we were taken from our mules: but some soldiers coming in at that instant, said it was the *Bashaw's* orders that we should appear before him immediately, and we were constrained to obey: it was but a few steps, and we were enabled to walk there by supporting one another. When we came to the door, we were ushered into a kind of entry-way, which served as an audience chamber, by Mr. Willshire's Jew interpreter, who in token of submission, was obliged to pull off his cap and slippers before he could enter.

We were ordered to sit down on the floor, and we then saw before us a very respectable looking Moor, of about sixty years of age: he was sitting cross-legged on a mat or carpet that lay on the floor which was terrace work, drinking tea from a small cup—his dress was the *haick*. After he had finished his cup of tea and looked at us a moment, he asked me, through the interpreter, what countryman I was? where my vessel was wrecked? how many men I had in all, and if the remainder were alive? how long I had been a slave, and if the Arab, my last master, had treated, me kindly? He wanted, further, to know how much money from my vessel fell into the hands of the Arabs, and what other cargo she had on board. Having satisfied his inquiries in the best manner I was able, he said we were now free, and he would write to the emperor respecting me and my men, and hoped he would give us leave to go home to our country: he then dismissed us. Mr. Willshire was with us, and answered all the questions the *Bashaw* chose to put to him, and then assisted us in returning to his house.

CHAPTER 24

The Kindness of Mr. Willshire

Upon our arrival at Mr. Willshire's house, some Jews were ready to shave off our beards; and as the hair of our heads was also in a very unpleasant condition, being literally filled with vermin, that, as well as our beards, underwent the operation of the scissors and razor: the hair was cut off at least as close as the horrible state of our skin and flesh would admit of: this may be imagined, but it is absolutely too shocking for description. Our squalid and emaciated frames were then purified with soap and water, and our humane and generous friend furnished us with some of his own clothing, after our bodies, which were still covered with sores, had been rubbed with sweet oil.

Mr. Willshire's cook had by this time prepared a repast, which consisted of beef cut into square pieces, just large enough for a mouthful before it was cooked; these were then rolled in onions, cut up fine, and mixed with salt and pepper; they were in the next place put on iron skewers and laid horizontally across a pot of burning charcoal, and turned over occasionally, until perfectly roasted: this dish is called *Cubbub*, and in my opinion far surpasses in flavour the so much admired beef-steak; as it is eaten hot from the skewers, and is indeed an excellent mode of cooking beef. We ate sparingly of this delicious food, which was accompanied with some good wheaten bread and butter, and followed by a quantity of exquisite pomegranates: for our stomachs were contracted to such a degree by long fastings, that they had lost their tone, and could not receive the usual allowance for a healthy man.

A doctor then appeared, and administered to each of us a dose of physic, which he said was to prepare our stomachs for eating. He was a Jew, who had been bred at Moscow in Russia, had studied medicine there, and had since travelled through Germany, Italy, and Spain; he spoke the Spanish language fluently, and I was convinced, before I left Mogadore, that he possessed much medical as well as surgical skill. He had only been in Mogadore two months, and there was no other physician in that city, or in that part of the country, except jugglers or quacks. Good beds had been fitted up for myself and Mr. Savage in the same room, and after being welcomed by Mr. John Foxcroft and Don Pablo Riva, who had heard of our arrival, we retired to rest.

My mind, which (though my body was worn down to a skeleton) had been hitherto strong, and supported me through all my trials, distresses, and sufferings, and enabled me to encourage and keep up the spirits of my frequently despairing fellow sufferers, could no longer sustain me: my sudden change of situation seemed to have relaxed the very springs of my soul, and all my faculties fell into the wildest confusion. The unbounded kindness, the goodness, and whole attention of Mr. Willshire, who made use of all the soothing language of which the most affectionate brother or friend is capable, tended but to ferment the tempest that was gathering in my brain. I became delirious—was bereft of my senses, and for the space of three days knew not where I was.

When my reason returned, I found I had been constantly attended by Mr. Willshire, and generally kept in my room, though he would sometimes persuade me to walk in the gallery with him, and used every means in his power to restore and compose my bewildered senses: that I had remained continually bathed in tears, and shuddering at the sight of every human being, fearing I should again be carried into slavery. I had slunk into the darkest corner of my room; but though insensible, I seemed to know the worth of my friend and deliverer, and would agree to, and comply with his advice and directions.

In the mean time, this most estimable and noble minded young man, had neither spared pains nor expense in procuring for us every comfort, and in administering, with his own hands, night and day, such relief and refreshment as our late severe sufferings and present debility required. He had sent off persons on mules to the vicinity of the city of Morocco, more than one hundred miles, and procured some of the most delicious fruits that country can produce, such as dates, figs, grapes, pomegranates, &c. He gave us for drink the best of wines, and I again began to have an appetite for my food, which was prepared with the greatest care. My men were furnished with shirts, trowsers, and jackets, and being fed with the most nourishing soups and other kinds of food, gained a considerable degree of strength.

Captain Wallace, of the English brig *Pilot*, then being in the port, furnished us with some pork, split peas, and potatoes, and seemed very friendly. Clark and Burns were but the skeletons of men: Mr. Savage and Horace were nearly as much reduced, but not having been diseased in so great a degree, they were consequently stronger. Many of my bones had appeared white and transparent through their thin and grisly covering, like dry bones, when on the desert; but they were now nearly covered again with skin, though we still might with some reason be termed the dried skeletons of Moorish slaves. At the instance of Mr. Willshire I was weighed, and fell short of ninety pounds, though my usual weight for the last ten years had been over two hundred and forty pounds: the weight of my companions was less than I dare to mention.

The sight of my face in a glass called to my recollection all the trying scenes I had passed through since my shipwreck. I could contemplate with pleasure and gratitude the power, and wisdom, of the Supreme Being, as well as his mercy and unbounded goodness. I could planely discover that the train of events which, in my former life, I had always considered as great misfortunes, had been directed by unerring wisdom, and had fitted me for running the circle marked out by the Omnipotent. When I studied the French and Spanish languages, I did it from expectations of future gain in a commercial point of view. All the exertions I had hitherto made to become acquainted with foreign languages, and to store my mind with learning and a knowledge of mankind, had procured for me no wealth; without which acquirement a man is generally considered on the stage of the world as a very insignificant creature, that may be kicked off or trampled upon by the pampered worms of his species, who sport around him with all the upstart pride of (in many instances) ill-gotten treasure.

I had been cheated and swindled out of property by those whom I considered my friends; yet my mind was formed for friendship;—I do not speak of this in the way of boasting. My hand had never been slack in relieving the distresses of my fellow men whenever I had the power, in the different countries where I had been; but I had almost become a stoic, and had very nearly concluded, that disinterested friendship and benevolence, out of the circle of a man's own family, was not to be found; that the virtuous man, if poor, was not only despised, by his more fortunate fellow creatures, but forsaken almost by Providence itself. I now, however, had positive proof to the contrary of some of those hasty and ill-founded opinions; and I clearly saw that I had only been tutored in the school of adversity, in order that I might be prepared for fulfilling the purpose for which I had been created.

In the midst of those reflections, I received, by a courier from Consul General Simpson, at Tangier, to Mr. Willshire, the following letter:—it speaks the soul of the writer and needs no comment.

Gibraltar, 13th November, 1815.

My Dear Riley,
I will not waste a moment by unnecessary preamble. I have wrote to Mr. Willshire, that your draft on me for twelve hundred dollars, or more, shall be duly paid for the obtainment of your liberty, and those with you. I have sent him two double barrelled guns to meet his promise to the Moor.—In a short time after the receipt of this, I hope to have the happiness to take you by the hand under my roof again. You will come here by the way of Tangier. Your assured friend,

Horatio Sprague.

My sensations on reading this letter, and on seeing that written by Mr. Sprague to Mr. Willshire, I must leave to the reader to imagine, and only observe that my acquaintance with that gentleman was but very slight, (of about ten days,) while I remained at Gibraltar, immediately before my disaster—It was sufficient for him to know his fellow creatures were in distress, and that it was in his power to relieve them. Mr. Sprague is a native of Boston, the capital of the state of Massachusetts, and had established himself as a respectable merchant in Gibraltar a little before the breaking out of the late war. In the early part of that war a number of American vessels were despatched by individuals with cargoes of provisions, &c. for Spain and Portugal—these vessels were navigated under enemies' licenses, but from some cause or other, many of them were seized on the ocean by British ships of war, and conducted to Gibraltar, where both the vessels and their cargoes were condemned, and their crews turned adrift in the streets without a cent of money in their pockets, and left to the mercy of the elements.

Mr. Gavino, the American consul, would not act in their behalf, because (as he stated) his functions had ceased by reason of the war;—when this humane and generous gentleman took them under his protection, hired an old vessel for them to live in, furnished them with provisions and other necessaries and comforts for the term of one whole year or upwards, and in this manner supported for the greater part of that time as many as one hundred and fifty men: this he did from his own purse, and out of pure philanthropy: of this I was informed by Mr. Charles Moore, of Philadelphia, and other gentlemen of respectability and veracity. He also furnished and sent a considerable sum of money to Algiers, which bought from hard labour our unfortunate countrymen, comprising the officers and crew of the brig, Captain Smith, of Boston, who were made slaves by that regency; in this he was assisted by Messrs. Charles H. Hall & Co. merchants at Cadiz, and several other worthy and respectable Americans; but the loss of the United States' sloop of war the *Epervier*, (this ship was spoken with, when homeward bound, by a Genoese schooner eighty miles from Mogadore, all well, and was probably wrecked and destroyed, on the iron bound coast of South Barbary,) having on board all the redeemed slaves after the peace with Algiers, rendered it impossible for them to communicate their sense of gratitude for Mr. Sprague's humanity. These facts were stated to me by several respectable individuals in Gibraltar, and can be fully authenticated.

After my mind had been again tranquillized by a refreshing night's sleep, my reflections returned to my providential preservation. When my vessel was wrecked, I was endued with presence of mind, judgment, and prudence, whereby my whole crew was saved in the first instance, and safely landed. When I was seized on afterwards by the Arabs, a superior intelligence suddenly suggested to my mind a stratagem by which my life was saved, though one of my unfortunate companions was sacrificed to glut the brutal rage of the natives, whilst I was conducted to the wreck in safety through a tremendous surf that rolled over me every instant. The ways of Providence were next traced out to my wondering eyes in the smoothing down of the sea, so that we were enabled to row our shattered boat out with safety to the ocean, and in our preservation in an open boat amidst, violent gales of wind, though her timbers and planks seemed only to hold together by the pressure of the sea acting upon their outer side.

When destitute of provisions and water, worn down with privations and fatigues, we were again landed on the coast, carried on the top of a dreadful wave over the heads of craggy rocks that must have dashed us and our boat to atoms, without a particular divine protection. We were next forced to climb over the most formidable precipices and obstructions, before it was possible to arrive on the dreary desert above us: these delays were necessary to bring us, at a proper time, within sight of fires kindled by Arabs, who had arrived there that day, (and who were the first, as I was afterwards informed, who had

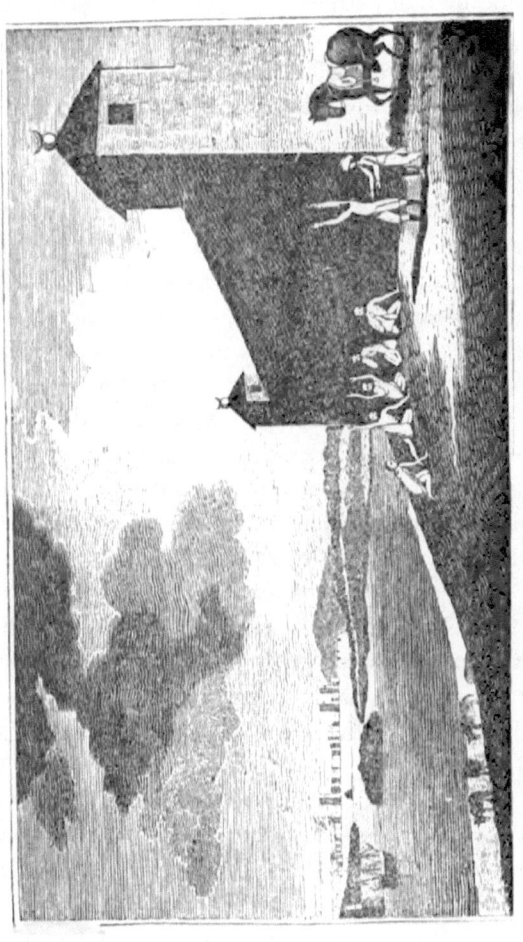

THE AUTHOR AND HIS MEN'S FIRST INTERVIEW WITH MR. WILLSHIRE, WITH MOGADORE IN THE BACKGROUND

been there to water their camels within the last thirty days,) and who were providentially sent to save our lives, as we could not have existed a day longer without drink.

Though my skin was burned off by the sun's rays, and myself given a slave to those wandering wretches——the same Almighty power still preserved my life, endowed me with intelligence to comprehend a language I had never before heard spoken, and enabled me to make myself understood by that people, and in some degree respected. Sidi Hamet (though a thievish Arab) had been sent from the confines of the Moorish empire before I left Gibraltar: he was conducted by the same unerring wisdom to my master's tent; his heart was softened at the recital of my distresses, and instead of trading in the article of ostrich feathers, (which was his whole business there, as he believed,) he was persuaded by a wretched naked skeleton of a slave, merely retaining the glimmering of the vital spark, against his own judgment, and whilst directly and strenuously opposed by his brother and partner, who insisted that if even I told the truth, and had a friend in Morocco to purchase me on my arrival there, yet my death must certainly happen long before it was possible to get me to that place: yet this same brother, one of the most barbarous of men, was forced, though against his will, to agree, and to lend the aid of his property in effecting the purchase, and to exert himself to support and to defend myself and four companions, through the desert, whilst all his schemes for selling and separating us had constantly proved abortive.

A Spanish *barque* had been destroyed by the natives on the coast of Suse, north of Cape Nun, and nineteen men had been either massacred by the natives, or were then groaning out a miserable existence in the worst kind of barbarian slavery—this event had furnished a piece of paper on which I wrote the note, at a venture, to Mogadore: my note fell into the hands of a perfect stranger, whose name I had never even heard of, and who was as ignorant of mine.

This excellent young man was touched by the same power who had hitherto protected me: he agreed to pay the sum demanded without reflection, though his utter ruin might have been the consequence, trusting implicitly to the written word of a wretched naked slave; a person of whom he had no knowledge, and who was then three hundred miles distant, and even out of the power of the government that protected him; and his impatience to relieve our distresses was so great, that he instantly paid the money demanded by my master, on his simply agreeing to stay in Swearah (Mogadore) until we came up, but without the power to keep him one instant if he chose to go away; nor would he allow time to the magnanimous Moor, who kindly volunteered to go down after us. at the imminent risk of his life, scarcely to take leave of his family: mounting him on his own mule, and begging him to hurry on, day and night, until he reached us, and to spare neither pains or expense in fetching us to Mogadore.

I cannot here omit mentioning the manner in which Mr. Willshire got my first note. Sidi Hamet (the bearer of it) was one of those Arabs belonging to a tribe, surnamed by the Moors, sons of lions, on account of their unconquerable spirit; when he came to the gate of Swearah, or Mogadore, he providentially was met by Rais bel Cossim, who, though a perfect stranger, asked him, "From whence come you, son of a lion?" Upon which Sidi Hamet stopped, and made known his business. This Moor was the only one which Mr. Willshire placed confidence in, or treated as a friend: he conducted Sidi Hamet to Mr. Willshire's house, and offered to leave his family, who were then sick, and to do his utmost to restore me and my men to liberty. Providence had also caused us to be stopped at Stuka, where we had time to recover, in part, from our illness, and to gain strength enough to support us through the remainder of our journey; had turned the contrivances and wisdom of Sheick Ali into nothingness, and finally provided for us such a friend as Mr. Sprague of Gibraltar, one of the most feeling and best of men.

This providential chain of events, thus planned and executed, even against the will of the principal agents employed, filled my mind with unutterable thankfulness and wonder at the wisdom, the goodness, and the mercy of God towards me; and the emotions which these reflections excited, kept me almost constantly bathed in tears for the greatest part of a month. When I retired to rest, and sleep had closed my eyes, my mind still retaining the strong impression of my past sufferings, made them the subjects of my dreams. I used to rise in my sleep, and think I was driving camels up and down the sandy hills near the desert, or along the craggy steeps of Morocco; obeying my master's orders in putting on the fetters, or beckets, on the legs and knees of his camels, and in the midst of my agonizing toils and heart-sickening anxieties, while groping about my room, I would hit my head against something, which would startle and awaken me: then I would throw myself on my bed again to sleep, and dream, and act over similar scenes.

Fearing I should get out of my chamber and injure myself in my sleep, I always locked the door, and hid the key before I went to bed. There was a grating to the windows of the apartments I slept in, and I often awoke and found myself trying to get out. My mind at length became more composed and serene, as my strength increased, and by the first of December I was able to ride out, and to walk about the city. Mr. Willshire, whose whole attention had been shown to me and my companions, tried every means to divert my mind from the subject of my reflections, and would ride out with me to a garden two miles out of the city, accompanied by a Moor, where we passed away many pleasant hours, which were endeared by every feeling and sentiment of gratitude and esteem on the one part, and of generous sympathy and godlike benevolence on the other.

In this garden stood a venerable fig tree, whose body and boughs were covered with the names, and initials of the names, of almost all the Europeans and Americans who had visited Mogadore, carved out with knives in the thick bark, accompanied with the dates of their several visits, &c. This was a kind of monument I delighted to examine; it seemed to say that Mogadore was once a flourishing city, when as commerce was fostered by the Moorish government; but now, that superstition, fanaticism, and tyranny bear sway, they have swept away, with their pernicious breath, the whole wealth of its once industrious and highly favoured inhabitants;—have driven the foreigner from their shores, and it seems as if the curse of Heaven had fallen on the whole land, for in spite of all the exertions of its cultivators, and the fertility of the soil, severe droughts, and the ravages of the locusts, have frequently caused a famine in that country, from whence wheat was exported in immense quantities but a few years past for Spain and Portugal, at half a dollar per bushel. Not a single bushel had been shipped for some years past, and at this time none was to be had at any price, except now and then a few bags, brought from the province of Duquelia, which could only be purchased by the most wealthy: the others were provided with scanty portions of barley, of which they made their *cous-koo-soo*.

CHAPTER 25

His Former Master's Narrative

From the time I had a prospect of being redeemed from slavery, I had determined (if that should ever happen) to write an account of our sufferings, which I considered greater than had ever fallen to the lot of man, and also to embody such observations as I had been enabled to make while a slave, in travelling the great desert, &c. &c. for the satisfaction of my family and the friends of my fellow sufferers. My late master was yet in Mogadore, for he remained in the house of my deliverer about two weeks after our arrival, and he now mentioned to me, that he and his brother had been three times to Tombuctoo (as he had before informed Mr. Willshire) with caravans, and had crossed the desert in almost every direction. I felt interested in making every inquiry that could suggest itself to my mind, respecting the face and the extent of the desert and the countries south of it: and although I was convinced, by my own observations, that both he and his brother, probably in common with the Arabs of the desert, knew the courses they steered, notwithstanding they had no compass or any other instrument to direct them in their journeys, yet wishing to be fully satisfied in this particular, I took them up upon the roof of the house (which was flat and terraced with stones laid in lime cement, and smooth like a floor) one clear evening, and then told them that I wanted to know by what means they were enabled to find their way across the trackless desert.

Sidi Hamet immediately pointed out to me the north or polar star, and the great bear, and told me the Arabic names of the principal fixed stars, as well as of the planets, then visible in the firmament, and his manner of steering and reckoning time by the means of them. His correct observations on the stars, perfectly astonished me: he appeared to be much better acquainted with the motions of the heavenly bodies than I was, who had made it my study for a great many years, and navigated to many parts of the globe by their assistance. To convince me that he knew the cardinal points, he laid two small sticks across at right angles, one pointing directly towards the polar star—he next placed two others across, dividing the circle into eighths, and then in like manner into sixteenths, so that I was satisfied he knew the requisite divisions of the compass: and on the next day I requested him to give me a narrative of his journeyings on, and across the desert, with which he very readily complied, and related as follows;—while I sat in my room with pen, ink, and paper, and noted it down, having the Moor Bel Mooden to interpret and explain to me in Spanish such parts of the narrative as I did not perfectly comprehend in Arabic.

I give it to the reader as nearly as possible in the words of the narrator, and do not hold myself responsible for Sidi Hamet's correctness, or his veracity, though, for my own part I have no doubt he meant to, and did tell the truth as near as his recollection served him; and as he had a retentive memory, and the incidents related were calculated to impress themselves strongly on his intelligent mind, I have no doubt that his whole narrative is substantially true.

Section 1
Sidi Hamet's narrative of a journey

"The first time I set out to cross the great desert, was several years ago, (about nine or ten,) being in the vicinity of Widnoon, where I had the year before been married to the daughter of Sheick Ali, (a beautiful woman, who is now my wife, and has two fine boys and one girl.) I, with my brother Seid, joined the caravan at Widnoon, by the advice of Sheick Ali: we had four camels loaded with *haicks* and some other goods. The whole caravan consisted of{ about three thousand camels and eight hundred men, with goods of almost every kind that are sold in Morocco.

"The men were all armed with good muskets and scimitars, and the whole under the command of Sheick ben Soleyman of Waldeleim, (Woled Deleim on the map,) with four competent guides. We set out from Widnoon in Suse, which is a great place of trade, late in the fall of the year, and travelled six days to the west, when we came to the last mountain—there we stopped ten days, and let our camels feed on the bushes, while half the men were employed in getting wood from the mountain, and burning it into charcoal, which we put into bags, as it was light, and laid it on the camels over the other goods; then setting off for the desert, we mounted upon its level, which is a great deal higher than the country near it to the north, and travelled four days on the hard level; we then passed amongst the high sand-hills, which you saw when we were coming up, in order that we might keep along by the great sea, so as to be sure of finding water: we travelled through and among these great mountains of sand, which were then very bad to pass, because the wind blew so hard we could scarcely keep together, being almost covered up by the flying sand: it took us six days to get through them; after which the ground was smooth, and almost as hard as the floor of a house, for ten days more, when we came to a watering place, called Biblah; there we watered our camels, for they were very thirsty, and eight of them had died and served us for food.

"We stopped at that great well seven days, and afterwards kept on our journey to the S. W. twenty days, to another well, called Kibir Jibl, but there was no water in it, and we were obliged to go six days' journey to the sea coast, where there was a well close to the sea, the water of which well was very black and salt: here we were forced to unload the camels, and get them down the bank to the water, and after drinking, they yielded us some milk, which had been almost dried up before: we found, however, nothing for them to feed on, and had been obliged to give them of the coals to eat once a day for many days: this kept them alive, but it made their milk almost as black as the coals themselves; yet it was good, and we were glad to get it. It took up six days to water the whole of them, when we set out again and travelled near the sea, where we found wells about every ten days, like the one we had already visited, but very few green leaves on the little bushes, in the few small valleys we saw; for no rain had fallen for a great while on that part of the desert.

"After a journey of four moons, we came to the south part of the desert, and went down into the country of Soudan, where we found a little stream of good running water, and some bushes, and grass, and a very large tribe of Bessebes Arabs, (Libdessebas on the map,) who had plenty of barley and maize or Indian corn, of which we bought some and made bread, and stopped here one moon. We lost on the desert more than three hundred camels, which died of fatigue, and the want of water and food, but not one man. All the tribes of Arabs we came near, took their stuff on their camels, and rode away as fast as they could, so as not to be robbed, and we did not find any party strong enough to attack us, although we saw a great many tribes, but they were very poor on the Zaharah, or great desert."

I then asked him how the face of the desert looked in general, as he passed over it, taking the whole together, or if there was any material difference in different parts of it, near the sea coast? to which he answered:—

"The whole extent of the desert near the sea coast, is like that we came over in bringing you up here, except in one place, where we travelled for nearly one moon without meeting with so much as a valley with green bushes in it for the camels to feed on: the whole is a trackless waste. Close by the sea we were obliged to pass mountains of sand that was blown up from the shore before the wind, but the guides always went before us, to show which way the caravan must go, and to find a place to stop in. Our camels had eaten up all the coals we had laid upon them before we got off the desert, and two of them had died, so that my brother and I had only two remaining, but we kept all our goods.

"After we had rested one moon, and got our camels recruited, we set off to the east on the border of the desert, close by the low country, with mountains in sight to the south, most of the way, and in two moons more we came near Tombuctoo, where we stopped in a deep valley with the caravan, and went every day close to the strong walls of the city with our goods (but without our guns) to trade them off with the negroes, who had gum, and gold rings, and gold powder and great teeth, such as are sold in Swearah, (*i.e.* elephant's teeth,) and slaves, and fine turbans: they had plenty of cows, and asses, and a few sheep, and barley, corn, and rice: but the little river that runs close to the wall on the west, was quite dry, and all the people in the city were obliged to fetch water for themselves to drink, with asses, from the great river south of the city, (about one hour's ride on a camel,) and we were forced to go there to water our camels, and get our drink.

"After staying near Tombuctoo one moon and a half, the season being far advanced, we set out again for Widnoon. I had not been in the city all the time we stopped here, because I was chosen captain of two hundred men that kept guard all the time about the caravan, to keep off the thievish Arabs and the bands of negroes that were hovering around us to carry off our camels, if any of them strayed away: but we lost only twenty during our whole stay at Tombuctoo, and the *Sheick* gave me for my trouble a fine young negro girl slave, which I carried home with me, and she now lives with my wife. We set out for home from Tombuctoo, in the month of *Rhamadan*, after the feast, and went back by the same route we had come—that is to say, we went first to the west one moon, along the border of the desert.

"We durst not take anything without paying for it, because we were afraid of the inhabitants, who were a mixture of Arabs and negroes, and all of them Mohammedans, but very bad men: they had also many white men slaves. I saw sixteen or eighteen myself, and a great many blacks. These true believers have very fine horses, and they go south to the country of the rivers, and there they attack and take towns, and bring away all the negroes for slaves, if they will not believe in the prophet of God; and carry off all their cattle, rice, and corn, and burn their houses; but if they will adopt the true faith, they are then exempt from slavery, and their houses are spared, upon their surrendering up one half of their cattle, and half of their rice and corn; because, they say, God has delivered their enemies into their hands.

"The negroes live in small towns, fenced in with reeds or bushes, and sometimes with stones, but the Arabs live only in tents, and can move off in a minute on their horses, whilst their wives and children ride on camels and asses. Before we struck off N.W. on the desert for the sea coast, we stopped in the hill country and fatted our camels, and burned wood to make charcoal to carry with us: we were encamped on the bank of a little river, one day's journey from a large town of negroes, named Jathrow. I did not go to it, but the *Sheick* went and bought some corn and barley, and forty oxen for our provisions.

"After we had prepared our coals, and laid in our provisions, we went up on to the level desert, and set off to the N.W. and in three moons and a half more we reached Widnoon again, having been gone almost a year and a half. We had lost about five hundred camels, that either died, or were killed to give us meat; and while we stayed at Tombuctoo, and were coming home, thirty-four of our men had died, and we lost eighty slaves." I asked him what were the goods they carried down at that time? he answered:—

"We had about one hundred camels loaded with iron and knives, and two hundred with salt; all the others carried *haicks*, and blue and white cloth, and amber, and tobacco, and silk handkerchiefs, and *chilly weed*, and spices, and a great many other articles. Seid and myself had lost two of our camels, but had got two negro slaves, and some gold dust, worth six camels, and ornaments for our wives; but Sheick Ali was not satisfied because I did not give him two slaves; so that he made war against me, and battered down my town which I built, (it was but a small one;) and took away all I had, together with my wife, because he said I was a bad man, and he was stronger than me: I myself, however, escaped, and after one year I asked him for my wife again, and he gave her to me with all he had taken, for he loved his daughter: but I had no house, so I removed into the *sultan's* dominions, near the city of Morocco, close by the Atlas mountains, and lived there with my father and brothers two years without going forth to trade."

Section 2
another journey for Tombuctoo

"About that time one of our party, when we first went to Tombuctoo, named bel Moese, came to see me—he was going to join the caravan at Widnoon again, and persuaded Seid and me to go with him; so we bought eight camels between us, and sold off our cattle and sheep, and bought goods and powder, and went with him to Widnoon, and joined the caravan. Sheick Ali came to meet me like a friend, and gave me two camels laden with barley, and wished me a safe journey. The Sheick who was chosen by all the people to command the caravan, was named Sidi Ishrel; he was the friend of Sidi Ishem, who owned almost one half of the whole caravan, and we set out from Widnoon with about four thousand camels, and more than one thousand men, all well armed.

"We laid in an abundant store of barley, and had a great many milch camels, and it was determined to go south across the desert, nearly on a straight course for Tombuctoo, by the way the great caravans generally travelled: though there had been several of them destroyed on that route, that is to say, one within every ten or twelve years. We went to the south, around the bottom of the great Atlas mountains, six days' journey; then we stopped close by it, and cut wood and burned coals for the camels, for the caravans never attempt to cross the desert without this article: four hundred camels out of the number were loaded with provisions and water for the journey, and after having rested ten days, and given the camels plenty of drink, we went up on the desert and steered off south-easterly.—We travelled along, and met with no sand for fifteen days; it was all a smooth surface, baked together so hard that a loaded camel could not make a track on it to be seen: we saw no tracks to guide us, and kept our course by the stars, and sun, and moon.

"We found only one spot in all that time where our camels could satisfy their appetites by eating the shrubs in a shallow valley, but the great well in it was filled up with stones and sand, so we could procure no water there; at the end of fifteen days, however, we came to a very fine deep valley, with twenty wells in it; but we found water in only six of them, because the desert was very dry: here we watered all our camels, and replenished our bottles or skins, and having rested seven days, we departed for the south-eastward, our camels being well filled with leaves and thorn bushes.

"We travelled along three days on the hard sand, and then arrived among innumerable drifts of fine loose sand; not such coarse sand as you saw near the sea; it was as fine as the dust on a path, or in a house, and the camels' feet sunk in it every step up to their knees: after travelling amongst this sand (which in the daytime was almost as hot as coals of fire) six days, there began to blow a fierce wind from the southeast, called the wind of the desert, bringing death and destruction with it: we could not advance nor retreat, so we took the loading from off our camels, and piled it in one great heap, and made the camels lie down.

"The dust flew so thick that we could not see each other nor our camels, and were scarcely able to breathe—so we laid down with our faces in the dust, and cried aloud with once voice to God—'Great and merciful God, spare our lives!' but the wind blew dreadfully for the space of two days, and we were obliged to move ourselves whenever the sand got so heavy on us that it shut out all the air, and prevented us from breathing; but at length it pleased the most High to hear our supplications: the wind ceased to blow; all was still again, and we crawled out of the sand that had buried us for so long a time, but not all, for when the company was numbered, three hundred were missing—all that were left having joined in thanks to God for his mercy in sparing our lives;—we then proceeded to dig out the camels from the sand that had buried their bodies, which, together with the reloading of them, took us two days.

"About two hundred of them were dead—there was no green thing to be seen, and we were obliged to give the camels a little water from the skins, to wash their parched throats with, and some charcoal to eat: then we kept on twenty-four days as fast as we could through the dry, deep, and hot sand, without finding any green bushes worth noticing for our camels to eat, when we came to a famous valley and watering place, called Haherah. All our camels were almost expiring, and could not carry the whole of their loads; so we threw away a great deal of the salt before we got to Haherah, where we intended to stop twenty days to recruit our beasts, but who can conceive our disappointment and distress, when we found there was no water in any of the wells of this great valley: not one drop of rain had fallen there for the last year.

"The caravan, that amounted to upwards of one thousand men and four thousand camels when we set out, was already reduced to about six hundred men, and thirty-five hundred camels. The authority of Sheick Ishrel could now scarcely restrain those almost desperate men; everyone was eager to save his own life and property, and separately sought the means of relief by running about the valley in a desultory manner, looking for water; this disorder continued for two days, when being convinced that nothing could be done without union, they became obedient, and joined together in great numbers in digging out the different wells. After digging five days without the smallest sign of water, all subordination was entirely at an end.

"The *Sheick*, who was a wise and a prudent man, advised and insisted that all the camels should be killed but three hundred, so that the little water found in them, together with their blood, might keep the rest alive, as well as all the men, until, by the aid of Providence, they should reach some place where they could find water; but the company would not hearken to this advice, though the best that could possibly be given; no one being willing to have his own property sacrificed. Sheick Ishrel, however, directed thirty of the oldest and most judicious men to pick out the three hundred camels that were to be spared, who accordingly selected the most vigorous; but when they began to kill the others, a most furious quarrel and horrible battle commenced.

"The *Sheick*, though a man of God, was killed in a moment—two or three hundred more were butchered by each other in the course of that dreadful day; and the blood of the slain was drank to allay the thirst of those who shed it. Seid was badly wounded with a dagger in his arm. About five hundred camels were killed this day; and the others drank the water from their bodies and also their blood.

"Fearing there would be no end to this bloody conflict until all had perished, and as I had been a captain in the other caravan, and knew how to steer a course on the desert; and as both Seid and myself were very strong men, we killed four out of six of our own camels that remained, in the first part of the night, and gave their water and blood to the other two: we saved a small package of goods, and some barley, and some meat, and persuaded thirty of our friends privately to do as we had done, and join us, for we meant to set off that night. This was agreed on, for to stay there was certain death, and to go back was no less so.

"We were all ready about midnight, and without making any noise, we moved off with our company of thirty men and thirty-two camels. The night was very cloudy and dark, and it thundered at a distance, as if the Almighty was angry with us for fighting together; hut there was no rain. We went towards the southwest, in the hope of reaching Tishlah, another watering place, before our camels died: the desert was dry and hard, and as we went along, we found only now and then a little hollow, with a few prickly shrubs in it: these the camels devoured as we passed among them; but many died, so that on the twelfth day we had only eighteen camels left; when the g eat God saved our lives by sending a tempest of rain, but he thundered so as to make the whole earth tremble, because of our sins, and we all fell upon our faces and implored his forgiveness.

"The rain that fall upon the ground gave plenty of water to our camels, and we filled thirty skins with it; when we steered to the south towards the borders of the desert. Nine of our company had died, and many of our camels, before we went down from the desert to the cultivated land, and we then made to the south towards a little river of fresh water, to which some Arabs whom we met with directed us, after they had first given us some rice and some milk, for all our milch camels had died on the desert."

Section 3
Sidi Harriet's journeyings

"Those of us who had escaped with our lives from the desert, only twenty-one in number, with twelve camels, out of a caravan of one thousand men and four thousand camels, stopped near a small town, called Wabilt, on the bank of a river about half as broad as from the city of Mogadore to the island, that is to say, fifty yards We had no provisions, but the negroes seeing us in distress, came out and gave us some meat, and bread made of barley-corn: here we remained ten days to recruit ourselves and our camels, which were just alive. The river on whose bank we remained, was called by those who spoke in Arabic, *el Woed Tenij*, and by the negroes, *Gozen-Zair.* A very high ridge of mountains, great like Atlas seen from Suse, (but not capped with snow,) lie to the south-westward, and at a distance. After resting ourselves and our camels for ten days, we set forward for Tombuctoo. We travelled for four days to the eastward through Soudan, a hilly country, but of a very rich soil, and much of it cultivated with the hoe."

I then asked him what he meant by Soudan? and he said,

"The whole country south of the great desert from the great ocean, a great way east, and including the district of Tombuctoo, is called by the Arabs and Moors, Soudan; of which Tombuctoo is the capital. Having watered our camels again, and finding the hill country tedious to get through, by reason of the trees, we bought some barley-corn, and killed two cows, and went northward to the border of the desert, and travelled on to the eastward for eight days, when we fell in with the great path used by the caravans, and in two days more came near to the walls of Tombuctoo.

"We had seen a great many negroes near the river: they live in small towns, fenced in with large reeds, to keep off enemies and the wild beasts in the night; they dwell in small round huts made with cane standing upright, are covered with the same materials, and daubed with mud, to fill up the openings between them. The negroes were afraid of us when we came near their little towns, and those who were outside ran in and blocked up the passage in a minute; but finding we did not come to rob them, as the large companies of Arabs often do, but that we were poor and hungry, they were willing to exchange barley-corn and meat for some of our goods. Nearly all the few things we had were expended to keep us alive until we came near Tombuctoo.

"The king and the people of that city had been looking out for the caravan from Widnoon for two moons, but not one soul had arrived before us, and we were permitted to go into that city after delivering up our guns, powder, and lead, to the king's officers to keep until we should wish to depart. Tombuctoo is a very large city, five times as great as Swearah: it is built on a level plane, surrounded on all sides by hills, except on the south, where the plane continues to the bank of the same river we had been to before, which is wide and deep, and runs to the east; for we were obliged to go to it to water our camels, and here we saw many boats made of great trees, some with negroes in them paddling across the river. The city is strongly walled in with stone laid in clay, like the towns and houses in Suse, only a great deal thicker: the house of the king is very large and high, like the largest house in Mogadore, but built of the same materials as the walls: there are a great many more houses in that city built of stone, with shops on one side, where they sell salt, and knives, and blue cloth, and *haicks*, and an abundance of other things, with many gold ornaments.

"The inhabitants are blacks, and the chief is a very large and grey-headed old black man, who is called *Shegar*, which means *sultan*, or king. The principal part of the houses are made with large reeds, as thick as a man's arm, and stand upon their ends, and are covered with small reeds first, and then with the leaves of the date trees: they are round, and the tops come to a point like a heap of stones. Neither the *Shegar* nor his people are Moslemins, but there is a town divided off from the principal one, in one corner, by a strong partition wall, and one gate to it, which leads from the main town, like the Jews' town, or Millah in Mogadore: all the Moors or Arabs who have liberty to come into Tombuctoo, are obliged to sleep in that part of it every night, or go out of the city entirely, and no stranger is allowed to enter that Millah without leaving his knife with the gate-keeper; but when he comes out in the morning it is restored to him. The people who live in that part are all Moslemin.

"The negroes, bad Arabs, and Moors, are all mixed together, and marry with each other, as if they were all of one colour: they have no property of consequence, except a few asses: their gate is shut and fastened every night at dark, and very strongly guarded both in the night and in the day time. The *Shegar* or king is always guarded by one hundred men on mules, armed with good guns, and one hundred men on foot with guns and long knives. He would not go into the Millah, and we only saw him four or five times in the two moons we stayed at Tombuctoo, waiting for the caravan: but it had perished on the desert—neither did the yearly caravan from Tunis and Tripoli arrive, for it had also been destroyed.

"The city of Tombuctoo is very rich, as well as very large; it has four gates to it; all of them are opened in the day time, but very strongly guarded and shut at night. The negro women are very fat and handsome, and wear large round gold rings in their noses, and flat ones in their ears, and gold chains and amber beads about their necks, with images and white fish-bones, bent round, and the ends fastened together, hanging down between their breasts; they have bracelets on their wrists and on their ankles, and go barefoot. I had bought a small snuff-box filled with snuff in Morocco, and showed it to the women in the principal street of Tombuctoo, which is very wide: there were a great many about me in a few minutes, and they insisted on buying my snuff and box; one made me one offer, and another made me another, until one, who wore richer ornaments than the rest, told me, in broken Arabic, that she would take off all she had about her and give them to me for the box and its contents.

"I agreed to accept them, and she pulled off her nose-rings and ear-rings, all her neck chains with their ornaments, and the bracelets from her wrists and ankles, and gave them to me in exchange for it: these ornaments would weigh more than a pound, and were made of solid gold at Tombuctoo, and I kept them through my whole journey afterwards, and carried them to my wife, who now wears a part of them. Tombuctoo carries on a great trade with all the caravans that come from Morrocco and the shores of the Mediterranean sea.

"From Algiers, Tunis, Tripoli, &c. are brought all kinds of cloths, iron, salt, muskets, powder, and lead, swords or scimitars, tobacco, opium, spices, and perfumes, amber beads, and other trinkets, with a few other articles; they carry back in return elephants' teeth, gold dust, and wrought gold, gum senegal, ostrich feathers, very curiously worked turbans, and slaves; a great many of the latter, and many other articles of less importance: the slaves are brought in from the southwest, all strongly ironed, and are sold very cheap; so that a good stout man may be bought for a *haick*, which costs in the empire of Morocco about two dollars. The caravans stop and encamp about two miles from the city, in a deep valley, and the negroes do not molest them: they bring their merchandise near the walls of the city, where the inhabitants purchase all their goods in exchange for the above mentioned articles; not more than fifty men from any one caravan being allowed to enter the city at a time, and they must go out before others are permitted to enter.

"This city also carries on a great trade with Wassanah (a city far to the southeast) in all the articles that are brought to it by caravans, and get returns in slaves, elephants' teeth, gold, &c. The principal male inhabitants are clothed with blue cloth shirts, that reach from their shoulders down to their knees, and are very wide, and girt about their loins with a red and brown cotton sash or girdle: they also hang about their bodies pieces of different coloured cloth and silk handkerchiefs: the king is dressed in a white robe of a similar fashion, but covered with white and yellow gold and silver plates, that glitter in the sun; he also has many other shining ornaments of shells and stones hanging about him, and wears a pair of breeches like the Moors and Barbary Jews, and has a kind of white turban on his head, pointing up, and strung with different kinds of ornaments; his feet are covered with red Morocco shoes: he has no other weapon about him than a large white staff or sceptre, with a golden lion on the head of it, which he carries in his hand: his whole countenance is mild, and he seems to govern his subjects more like a father than a king.

"The whole of his officers and guards wear breeches that are generally dyed red, but sometimes they are white or blue; all but the king go bareheaded. The poor people have only a single piece of blue or other cloth about them, and the slaves a breech cloth. The inhabitants in Tombuctoo are very numerous; I think six times as many as in Swearah, besides the Arabs and other Moslemin or Mohammedans, in their Millah, or separate town; which must contain nearly as many people as there are all together in Swearah."

NOTE BY THE AUTHOR.

Swearah or Mogadore contains about thirty-six thousand souls; that is, thirty thousand Moors and six thousand Jews: this may be a high estimation for Tombuctoo, making it two hundred and sixteen thousand inhabitants; yet considering the commercial importance of the place, and the fertility of the country around it, there can be no doubt but it contains a vast number of inhabitants; and I must also observe, that if it was a small town, and contained the riches attributed to it, they would require a very strong force to prevent the Arabs from the desert, together with the caravans, from taking it by surprise or by storm.

"The women are clothed in a light shirt or under dress, and over it a green, red, or blue covering, from their breasts to below their knees—the whole girt about their waists with a red girdle: they stain their cheeks and foreheads red or yellow on some occasions, and the married women wear a kind of hood on their heads, made of blue cloth or silk, and cotton handkerchiefs of different kinds and colours, and go barefooted. The king and people of Tombuctoo do not fear and worship God, like the Moslemins, but like the people of Soudan they only pray one time in twenty-four hours, when they see the moon, and when she is not seen they do not pray at all: they cannot read or write, but are honest, and they circumcise their children like the Arabs: they have no mosques, but dance every night, as the Moors and Arabs pray.

"The *Shegar* or king had collected about one thousand slaves, some gums, elephants' teeth, gold dust, &c. to be ready for the yearly caravans; but as three moons had passed away since the time they ought to have arrived, he gave them up for lost, and concluded to send a caravan with part of his goods that came across the desert; *viz*. some salt, iron, clothes, &c. to a large city at a great distance from Tombuctoo: and having formed a body of about three thousand men, well armed with muskets, long knives, and spears, and three thousand asses, and about two hundred camels, which were all loaded with heavy goods, such as iron, salt, tobacco, &c. he hired my brother Seid and myself, (with ten more of our companions,) to carry loads on our two camels to, Wassanah, for which he was to give us, when we came back, two *haicks* each and some gold.

"As we were completely in his power, we did not dare to refuse to go, and he put us under the care of his brother, whose name was Shelbaa, who had command of the whole caravan. It was in the month of *Shual* (——) when we departed from Tombuctoo for a place we had never before heard of. We had in the company about two hundred Moslemin, but the master of the caravan would not permit us Moslemin to keep our guns, for fear we should turn against him, if he was obliged to fight."

Section 4
Sidi Harriet sets out for Wassanah

"All being prepared, we went from Tombuctoo about two hours' ride, towards the south, to the bank of the river which is called at that place Zolibib, and was wider than from Mogadore to the island; (*i.e.* about five hundred yards;) here was a miserable village built with canes, and mudded over: it had about two hundred small houses in it, but no walls. We then set off near the side of the river, and travelled on in a plane even country for six days, every day within sight of the river, which was on our right hand, and running the same way we travelled, and our course was a little to the south of east; when we came to a small town called Bimbinah, walled in with canes and thorn bushes, and stopped two days near it, to get provisions and rest our beasts: here the river turned more to the south-eastward, because there was a very high mountain in sight to the eastward: we then went from the riverside, and pursued our journey more southwardly, through a hilly and woody country, for fifteen days, when we came to the same river again. Every night we were obliged to make up large fires all around the caravan, to keep off the wild beasts, such as lions, tigers, and other animals, which made a dreadful howling.

"Here was a small town of black people belonging to another nation, who were enemies to the king of Tombuctoo, but were friendly to the king of Wassanah; and not being strong, they did not molest us, but furnished us with what corn we wanted, and twenty oxen. We saw a large number of armed black men, nearly naked, on the other side of the river, who seemed to be hostile, but they could not get across to attack us: we also saw two very large towns, but walled in like the others we had passed.

"We stopped here and rested our camels and asses five days, and then went onward again in about a S E. direction, winding as the river ran, for three days; and then had to climb over a very high ridge of mountains, which took up six days, and when we were on the top of them, we could see a large chain of high mountains to the westward; those we passed were thickly covered with very large trees, and it was extremely difficult to get up and down them; but we could not go any other way, for the river ran against the steep side of the mountain; so having gotten over them we came to the river's bank again, where it was very narrow and full of rocks, that dashed the water dreadfully; then finding a good path, we kept on to the S. E. winding a little every day, sometimes more to the east, then to the south again. We kept travelling this way for twelve days after leaving the mountains, during which time we had seen the river nearly every day on our right hand, and had passed a great many small streams that empty into it: it was now very wide and looked deep—here we saw many trees dug out hollow, like the boats at Tombuctoo, and they were used to carry negroes across the river, and were pushed along with flat pieces of wood: we also saw the high mountains on the west side of the great river, very planely.

"Having rested seven days at the ferrying place, we then travelled on for fifteen days, most of the time in sight of the river. When we came close to the walls of the city of Wassanah, the king came out with a great army, consisting of all his soldiers, to meet us, but finding we had only come to trade by the orders of, and with the goods of, his friend *Shegar* of Tombuctoo, he invited the chief, and the whole of the caravan, to abide within a square enclosure near the walls of the city: here we remained two moons, exchanging our goods for slaves, gold, elephants' teeth, &c.

"The city of Wassanah is built near the bank of the river, which runs past it nearly south, between high mountains on both sides, though not very close to the river, which is so wide there that we could hardly see a man across it on the other side: the people of Tombuctoo call it *Zolibib*, and those of Wassanah call it *Zadi*. The walls of the city are very large, and made of great stones, laid up like the stone fences in the province of Hah Hah, in Morocco, but without any clay or mud amongst them: they are very thick and strong, and much higher than the walls of Tombuctoo.

"I was permitted to walk round them in company with six negroes, and it took me one whole day: the walls are built square, and nave one large gate on each side. The country all around the city is dug up, and has barley, corn, and other vegetables planted on it: and close by the side of the river all the land is covered with rice, and there are a great many oxen, and cows, and asses, belonging to the city, but no camels, nor horses, mules, sheep, nor goats; but all about and in the city speckled fowls abound, and there are plenty of eggs. The people of the caravan were allowed to enter the city, but only twenty at a time, and they were all obliged to go out again before night.

"We had been there more than a moon, when it came to my turn to go in. I found almost the whole of the ground inside of the walls was covered with huts made of stones piled up without clay, and some reeds, laid across the tops, covered over with the large leaves of the date or palm tree, or of another tree which looks very much like a date tree, and bears a fruit as large as my head, which has a white juice in it sweeter than milk; the inside is hard, and very good to eat: the trees that bear this big fruit grow in abundance in this country, and their fruit is very plenty: their huts have narrow passages between them. The king or chief is called *Oleeboo*, which means, in the negro talk, good *sultan*: he is a very tall, and quite a young man: his house is very large, square, and high, made of stone, and the chinks filled up with something white like lime, but not so hard: they would not let me go into his house, and told me he had one hundred and fifty wives, or more, and ten thousand slaves: he dresses in a white shirt, that looks like the one worn by Mr. Willshire, and long trowsers made like them you have on, and coloured like an orange."

Those I then had on were common wide sailor trowsers.

"He has over his shirt a *caftan* or robe with sleeves to it, made of red cloth, tied about with a girdle that goes from his breast to his hips, made of silk handkerchiefs of all colours, and has slips of fine coloured silk tied round his arms and legs: his hair is also tied in small bunches, and he wears on his head a very high hat made of canes, coloured very handsomely, and adorned with fine feathers: he has sandals on his feet, bound up with gold chains, and a great gold chain over his shoulder, with a bunch of ornaments made of bright stones and shells, that dazzle the eyes, hanging on his breast, and wears a large dagger by his side in a gold case. He rides on the back of a huge beast, called *Ilfement*, three times as thick as my great camel, and a great deal higher, with a very long nose and great teeth, and almost as black as the negroes: he is so strong, that he can kill an hundred men in a minute when he is mad; this is the animal that the teeth grow in which we bring from Tombuctoo to Widnoon, which you call elephants' teeth, and this was the only one of the animals I ever saw, but they told me these creatures were very plenty down the river from Wassanah."

This answers to the description of, and no doubt is, the elephant.

"The king of Wassanah has a guard of two hundred negroes on foot, one hundred of them armed with muskets, fifty with long spears, and fifty with great bows and arrows, with long knives by their sides: they always attend him when he goes out on his beast: he has also a very large army: they fight with guns, spears, and bows and arrows. The city has twice as many inhabitants in it as Tombuctoo, and we saw a great many towns near it on the other side of the river, as well as several small settlements on the same side below. The king nor the people do not pray like the Moslemins, but they jump about, fall down, tear their faces as if they were mad when any of their friends die, and every time they see the new moon, they make a great feast, and dance all night to music made by sinking and beating on skins tied across a hollow stick, and shaking little stones in a bag or shell; but they do not read nor write, and are heathens. Though the free people in this place do not steal, and are very hospitable, yet I hope the time is near when the faithful, and they that fear God and his prophet, will turn them to the true belief, or drive them away from this goodly land.

"The principal inhabitants of Wassanah are dressed in shirts of white or blue cloth, with short trowsers, and some with a long robe over the whole, tied about with a girdle of different colours: the free females are generally very fat, and dress in blue or white coverings tied about their waists with girdles of all colours: they wear a great many ornaments of gold, and beads, and shells, hanging to their ears and noses, necks, arms, ankles, and all over their hair; but the poorer sort are only covered about their loins by a cloth which grows on the tree that bears the big fruit I have told you about before." This fruit, I imagine, must be the cocoa-nut, and I have often in the West-Indies, and elsewhere, observed the outer bark of this singular palm-tree: it is woven by nature like cloth, each thread being placed exactly over and under the others. It appears like regular wove coarse bagging, and is quite strong: it loosens and drops from the trunk of the tree of its own accord, as the tree increases in size and age. I had long before considered that this most singular bark must have suggested to man the first idea of cloth, and taught him how to spin, and place the threads so as to form it of other materials that have since been used for that purpose, and this first hint from nature has been improved into our present methods of spinning and weaving.

"The male slaves go entirely naked, but the women are allowed a piece of this cloth to cover their nakedness with: they are very numerous, and many of them kept chained: they are obliged to work the earth round about the city. The inhabitants catch a great many fish: they have boats made of great trees, cut off and hollowed out, that will hold ten, fifteen, or twenty negroes; and the brother of the king told one of my Moslemin companions who could understand him, (for I could not,) that he was going to set out in a few days with sixty boats, and to carry five hundred slaves down the river, first to the southward, and then to the westward, where they should come to the great water, and sell them to pale people, who came there in large boats, and brought muskets, and powder, and tobacco, and blue cloth, and knives, &c.: he said it was a long way, and would take him three moons to get there, and he should be gone twenty moons before he could get back by land, but should be very rich."

I then asked him how many boats he supposed there were in the river at Wassanah?

He said, "A great many, three or four hundred, I should think; but some of them are very small: we saw a great many of these people who had been down the river to see the great water, with slaves and teeth, and came back again: they said the pale people lived in great boats, and had guns as big as their bodies, that made a noise like thunder, and would kill all the people in a hundred negro boats, if they went too near them. We saw in the river and on the bank a great number of fish with legs and large mouths, and these would run into the water in a minute, if any man went near them, but they told us they would catch children, and sometimes men, when in the boats: (these are, no doubt, crocodiles or hippopotamus.) The negroes are very kind, and would always give us barley, corn, or rice, milk or meat, if we were hungry, though we could not speak a language they understood. While we stopped at Wassanah, it rained almost every day.

"Having traded away all the goods we carried there, Shelbar took three hundred slaves and a great many teeth, dazzling stones, and shells, and gold—with these we set off again, and went the same way back to

Tombuctoo, which took us three moons, and we were gone from the time we left it, to the time we returned, eight moons. On my arrival at Tombuctoo, we were paid by the chief of the caravan according to promise, and a few days afterwards a caravan arrived there from Tunis, which we joined, to return by that way to our own country."

I must here beg the reader's indulgence for a moment, in order to make some remarks, and a few geographical observations that this part of the narrative has suggested. This narrative I, for my own part, consider strictly true and correct, as far as the memory and judgment of Sidi Harriet were concerned, whose veracity and intelligence I had before tested: he had not the least inducement held out to him for giving this account, further than my own and Mr. Willshire's curiosity; and his description of Tombuctoo agrees in substance with that given by several Moors, (Fez merchants,) who came to Mr. Willshire's house to buy goods while Sidi Hamet was there, and who said they had known him in Tombuctoo several years ago. From these considerations combined, and after examining the best maps extant, I conclude that I have strong grounds on which to found the following geographical opinions, *viz.*

1st, That the great Desert is much higher land on its southern side (as I had proved it to be on the north by my own observations) than the surrounding country, and consequently that its' whole surface is much higher than the land near it that is susceptible of cultivation.

2ndly, That the river which Sidi Hamet and his companions came to within fourteen days' ride, and west of Tombuctoo, called by the Arabs el Woed *Tenij,* and by the negroes *Gozen-Zair,* takes its rise in the mountains south of, and bordering on, the great desert, being probably the northern branch of that extensive ridge in which the Senegal, Gambia, and Niger Rivers have their sources; and that this river is a branch of the Niger, which runs eastwardly for several hundred miles to Tombuctoo, near which city, many branches uniting in one great stream, it takes the name of *Zolibib,* and continues to run nearly east, about two hundred and fifty miles from Tombuctoo; when meeting with high land, it is turned more southeastwardly, and running in that direction in a winding course, about five hundred miles, it has met with some obstructions, through which it has forced its way, and formed a considerable fall: for Sidi Hamet, having spent six days in passing the mountains, came again near the river, which was then rilled with broken rocks, and the water was foaming and roaring, among them, as he observed, "most dreadfully." This must be a fall or rapid.

3rdly, That from these falls, it runs first to the south-eastward, and then more to the south, till it reaches Wassanah, about six hundred miles where it is by some called *Zolibib,* and by others *Zadi.*

4thly, That as the inhabitants of Wassanah say they go first to the southward, and then to the westward, in boats to the great water; this I conceive must be the Atlantic Ocean, where they have seen pale men and great boats, &c. These I should naturally conclude were Europeans, with vessels; and that it takes three moons to get there, (about eighty-five days,) at the rate of thirty miles a day, which is the least we can give them with so strong a current: it makes a distance from thence to the sea of about two thousand five hundred miles: in computing this distance, one-third or more should be allowed for its windings, so that the whole length of the river is about four thousand miles, and is probably the longest and largest on the African continent.

5thly, That the waters of this river in their passage towards the east, have been obstructed in their course by high mountains in the central regions of this unexplored continent, and turned southwardly; that they are borne along to the southward, between the ridges of mountains that are known to extend all along the western coast, from Senegal to the gulf of Guinea, and to round with that gulf to the south of the equator; that they are continually narrowed in and straightened by that immense ridge in which the great River Nile is known to have its sources, and which mountains lie in the equatorial region; that this central river receives, in its lengthened course, all the streams that water and fertilize the whole country between the two before mentioned ridges of mountains: the waters thus accumulated and pent up, at length broke over their western and most feeble barrier, tore it down to its base, and thence found and forced their way to the Atlantic Ocean, forming what is now known as the River Congo. In corroboration of this opinion, some men of my acquaintance, who have visited the Congo, and traded all along the coast between it and the

Senegal, affirm, that the Congo discharges more water into the Atlantic, taking the whole year together, than all the streams to the northward of it, between its mouth and Cape de Verd.

Section 5
Sidi Hamet takes his leave, and sets out to join his family.

"The caravan we joined at Tombuctoo, was a very large one, belonging to Algiers, Tunis, Tripoli, and Fez, four united together. They remained near that city two moons, and bought two thousand slaves, besides a great deal of gold dust, and teeth, and turbans, and gold rings, and chains, and gum; but Seid and I had only our two camels, and they were but partly loaded with gum, for account of Ben Nassar, the *Sheick* of the Tunisian part of the caravan, for there were three *Sheicks* in it. When everything was ready, we set off from Tombuctoo, and travelled east-northerly twenty days through the hilly country, crossing a great many little streams of water that ran to the south and west towards the great river, it having rained very hard almost every night whilst we were at Tombuctoo.

"When we were going amongst the hills and trees, we saw a great many small towns or cities, most of them fenced in with good stone walls, but some with cane and thorn bushes. The land of that country is very good, and plenty of corn grows on it, and some rice and dates, and we saw some oxen, sheep, and asses, and a few horses.

"The inhabitants are Moors and Arabs mixed with the negroes, and almost as black as the latter; all of our own religion: they are very stout fierce men, but they did not attempt to molest us, and sold us everything we wanted at a cheap rate: they wear no clothing but a strip of cloth about their middles, and a ring of bone or ivory round the women's ankles and wrists, and some beads in their hair; they are peaceable people, and never attack the caravans unless the latter attempt to rob them: they are armed with muskets, and with long knives, and with bows and arrows. When they are forced to fight, they do it with the greatest fury, and never take prisoners or receive quarter, and only defend their rights.

"Some of the people in our caravan told us, that a few years ago a caravan, going from Tombuctoo to Tunis, Algiers, &c. in passing through this country, surprised and stole about four hundred of the inhabitants for slaves, and a great number of cattle and much corn, and went towards the desert; but these people assembled a large host, and came up with them in the night near the edge of the desert, and cut the whole of them to pieces, though they were more than two thousand men strong, and well armed; only about fifty of the people of the caravan escaped and got back to Tunis to tell the news, and they only by riding on the swiftest camels without any loads. After having refreshed our camels for ten days in a beautiful valley, where there was a good stream of water for them to drink, and filled the sacks with coals, we mounted up to the desert, and steered on the flat level away to the north.

"As we went along we came to some small valleys, where the Arabs feed their camels and live on their milk, and think themselves the most learned, virtuous, and religious people in the world, and the most happy too, though they have neither bread, nor meat, nor honey, nor any clothing but a rag tied round their waists, and live in tents, wandering about. We steered about north for eighteen days, when we came to the usual watering place, called Weydlah; here was a great deal of water in a pond, but it was black and quite salt, like the water in the wells close by the great sea: it was very dead and stinking, and tasted of sulphur: it is in a very deep pit and difficult to get at, there being only one place by which we could lead the camels down to the water: it is said to be very deep in the middle, and was never known to be dry: it was almost covered over by a thick green scum: we could see the tracks of wild beasts, such as tigers and lions, near the water.

"We had seen a great many of these animals in our travels to Wassanah, and when we were coming from Tombuctoo to the eastward. Our caravan consisted of about fifteen hundred men, most of us well armed with double barrelled guns and scimitars, and we had about four thousand camels. It was a long journey to the next well; so we stopped here six days peaceably, having encamped in a valley a little distance west of the pond or lake. We had always made the camels lie down in a circle, placing the goods in the centre, and the men between the camels and the goods: we had two hundred men on guard, and always ready for any emergency.

"In the night of the sixth day, about two hours after midnight, we were attacked by a very huge body of wandering Arabs: they had got to within a few yards of us before they were discovered, and poured in a most destructive fire of musketry, at the same time running in like hungry tigers, with spears and scimitars in their hands, with dreadful yellings: they threw the whole caravan into confusion for a moment; but we were in a tight circle, formed by the camels, which with the guards kept them off for a short time, till the whole of our men seized their arms and rallied.

"The battle now raged most furiously: it was cloudy and very dark, the blaze of the powder making only a faint light, whilst the cracking of musketry, the clashing of swords, the shouts of the combatants, and the bellowings of the wounded and frightened camels, together with the groans of the wounded and dying men, made the most dreadful and horrid uproar that can be conceived. The fight continued for about two hours, hand to hand and breast to breast, when the assailants gave way and ran off, leaving their dead and wounded on the field of battle. We remained with our arms in our hands all night. I was wounded with a ball in my thigh, and Seid with a dagger on his breast."

They then showed me their scars.

"In the morning we numbered our men, and found that two hundred and thirty were killed, and about one hundred wounded: three hundred of the camels were either slain or so badly wounded that they could not walk, and so we killed them. We found seven hundred of our enemies lying on the ground, either dead or wounded; those that were badly wounded, we killed, to put them out of pain, and carried the others that could walk along with us for slaves; of these there were about one hundred. As the enemy fled, they took all their good camels with them, for they had left them at a distance, so that we only found about fifty poor ones, which we killed; but we picked up two hundred and twenty good double barrelled guns from the ground: the gun which Seid now uses is one of them; we got also about four hundred scimitars or long knives. We were told by the prisoners that the company who attacked us was upwards of four thousand strong, and that they had been preparing for it three moons.

"We were afraid of another attack, and went off the same day, and travelled all the night, steering to, the N. E. (out of the course, the caravans commonly take) twenty-three days' journey, when we came to a place called the Eight Wells, where we found plenty of good water. Fifty of our men had died, and twenty-one of the slaves. We remained near these good wells for eleven days; our camels feeding on the bushes in the valleys near them, when we again travelled to the north-westward ten days to Twati, a good watering place. For the last three days we waded through deep sands, like those we passed among while going from Widnoon. We rested here two days, and then went down north, into the country of dates, and came to the town of Gujelah, a little strong place belonging to Tunis—there we found plenty of fruit, and good water, and meat and milk: we stopped there ten days, and then the part of the caravan going to Tripoli left us and went towards the east, by the mountains, and the rest went on north-easterly twelve days to Tuggurtah, close by a mountain near the River Tegsah, that is said to go to the sea near Tunis; here we stopped twenty-five days, and the caravan for Tunis left us. Tuggurtah is a very large city, with high and thick walls, made tight, and has a great many people in it, all of the true religion, and a vast number of black slaves, and a few white ones.

"After stopping here twenty-five days, we set off to the northwestward through a very fine country, full of date and fig trees, and cattle, and goats, camels, sheep, and asses; we then travelled ten days to the high mountains, where the caravan for Algiers parted from us, and we remained with about two hundred camels and eighty men going to Fez. We then travelled over the great mountain, which we were told belongs to the same ridge we see close to Morocco and in Suse; (the Atlas;) and in two moons more we passed through Fez, where what remained of the caravan stopped, and we returned to our father's house, and our families, on the side of the Atlas mountains, near the city of Morocco, having been gone more than two years. We brought back only one camel, and a small load of merchandise, out of the eight camels richly loaded when we set out; yet we thanked God for having preserved our lives; for the whole caravan with which we started had perished on the desert, and out of the twenty-eight men who left it with us, only four reached their homes, and they on foot, and entirely destitute of property.

"I found my wife and all my children and my father's family in good health. Sheick Ali came to see me as soon as he got the news of my arrival, and after staying with me one moon, he invited me and Seid to go with him to his place, which invitation we accepted, and he furnished us with one camel and some *haicks* and blue cloth, and advised us to go up on the desert and trade them away for ostrich feathers, to sell in Morocco or Swearah; so, being poor, we accepted his offer, bought his goods and his camel, and. he was to have been paid when we came back. We set off for the desert, and had passed a great many tribes of Arabs without finding any feathers of consequence, when the great God directed our steps to your master's tent, and I saw you.

"I was once as bad a man as Seid, but I had been in distress and in a strange land, and had found friends to keep me and restore me to my family; and when I saw you naked and a slave, with your skin and flesh burnt from your bones by the sun, and heard you say you had a wife and children, I thought of my own former distresses, and God softened my heart, and I became your friend. I did all I could to lighten the burden of your afflictions: I have endured hunger, thirst, and fatigues, and have fought for your sake, and have now the high pleasure of knowing I have done some good in the world; and may the great and universal Father still protect you: you have been true and kind to me, and your friend has fed me with milk and honey; and I will always in future do what is in my power to redeem Christians from slavery."

Here Sidi Hamet finished his narration: he then said he wished to go and see his wife and children, and that as soon as he had rested for a few days, he would set off again with a large company to seek after the rest of my men. The next morning I made him a small present, and Mr. Willshire also gave him some fine powder, and many order small articles. After he was prepared to go, he swore by his right hand, he would bring up the remainder of my crew if they were to be found alive, and God spared his life: he then took his leave of me by shaking hands, and of all my companions, wishing us a happy sight of our friends, and set off for his home. I did not part with him without feelings of regret and shedding tears; for he had been a kind master to me, and to him I owed, under God, my life and deliverance from slavery; nor could I avoid reflecting on the wonderful means employed by Providence to bring about my redemption, and that of a part of my late unfortunate crew.

CHAPTER 26

An Account of the Face of the Great African Desert

In giving an account of the great western desert, or Zahahrah, and of its inhabitants, &c. it must be remembered, that in journeying across, or on the desert when a slave, I did not go over, but a very small part, comparatively speaking, of that extensive region; I cannot therefore undertake to describe what did not come under my own observation. I can, however, state, without fear of future contradiction, the following facts, *viz.* that the face of this desert, from about the latitude of 20 to 22 degrees north, where we were forced ashore in our boat, to near the latitude of 28 degrees north, and from the longitude of Cape Barbas, about 19 to 11 degrees west, is a smooth surface, consisting partly of solid rocks, of gravel, sand, and stones mixed, and in some places of what is commonly called soil, this mass is baked down together in most places, by the extreme heat of the sun, nearly as hard as marble, so that no tracks of man or beast are discoverable; for the footstep leaves no impression.

The whole surface is as smooth, when viewed on every side, as the plane of the ocean unruffled by winds or tempests, stretching out as far as the eye can reach; not a break that might serve as a landmark, or guide to the traveller; not a tree, shrub, or any other object, to interrupt the view within the horizon; the whole is in appearance a dreary waste: the soil is in colour of a light reddish brown: not a stream of water (at least for many centuries past) has refreshed this region, which is doomed to eternal barrenness; but as we went forward on this flat hard surface, we met from distance to distance with small valleys or dells, scooped out, in appearance, by the hand of nature, from five to thirty feet below the plane—those we saw and stopped in were ten, fifteen, and twenty miles apart, and contained from one to four or five acres each—they seem to serve as receptacles for the little rain water which falls on the desert; for the inhabitants always expect some in the winter months, though they are frequently disappointed; and none had fallen on those parts on which we were thrown for the last two years.

It was already September, and they were offering up prayers to the Almighty every day, and most fervently imploring him to send them refreshing rains. These little valleys appear mostly in the form of a bowl, though in some the sides are steep, and bottoms nearly level, and the whole irregular. Here grows a dwarf thorn bush, from two to five feet in height; it is generally scattered thinly over the valley. The leaves of this shrub, which is almost the only one that is to be found on that part of the desert, are a fourth of an inch in thickness, one and a half inches in width, and from two to two and a half inches in length, tapering to a sharp point, and are strongly impregnated with salt, so much so, that neither myself nor my companions could eat them, though nearly perishing with hunger and thirst, and a green fresh leaf would have been a great relief to us, when neither meat nor drink was to be procured.

Such is the face of the desert over which we passed, until we came within a short distance of Cape Bajador, where we fell in with immense heaps of loose sand, forming mountains of from one to three or four hundred feet in height, blown and whirled about by every wind, and dreadful to the traveller, should a strong gale arise from the southward whilst in the midst of them; for he and his beasts must then inevitably perish, overwhelmed by flying surges of suffocating sand.

The face of this part of the desert is still the same as that before described, when laid bare and seen between the sand-hills, by reason of the sand being blown off. This sand has evidently been driven from the seashore, and in the same degree as the ocean has retired, by means of the trade wind blowing constantly on to the desert, and that too very strongly in the night time, through a long succession of ages. The heavy surf dashing perpetually among the rocks, gradually reduces them to grit, which then mixes with the sand that is washed up upon the shore, where it is left by the tides that rise on this coast to the height of twelve or fourteen feet, and only once in twenty-four hours; this becomes dried by the excessive heat of the sun, and is whirled about and driven before this constant gale, upon the surface, and then into the interior of the desert.

Such have unquestionably been the causes which have produced such astonishing accumulations of sand on that part of the desert; and I am further confirmed in this belief by the enormous strings of sand-hills to be found all along the coast of Suse and Morocco, near the seashore. These accumulations are in many parts so great, as to have raised new bounds to the ocean some miles beyond its original limits, which have evidently been washed by the sea at a former period, and the intermediate spaces are filled up with loose sand-hills; which circumstances all together amount, in my opinion, to a demonstration of the origin of the sand on this part of the desert.

Some authors have supposed that there were many fertile spots on the great western desert which were cultivated, &c. &c. but this is, I think, an impossibility: the whole desert being a level plane, it can produce neither spring or stream of water, and no herbage can consequently grow unless by means of rain, and this falls on the desert so seldom, and is so soon evaporated, as to render even a passage across it with a caravan of Arabs and camels, at all times dangerous in the extreme, as is proved by Sidi Hamet's narrative of his journeys, connected with my own observations. That there are more shrubs growing in some parts than in others, is true, from natural causes. This smooth dry surface can produce no vapour, and if it did, there are no breaks or mountains to arrest it, and it flies off to the north or south, where more is produced: the neighbourhood of mountains condenses the atmosphere and produces the rain, which is driven sometimes only from thence on to the desert by strong gales, and even then in scanty quantities.

The small valleys or dells which now furnish a scanty subsistence for the hardy camel, and that only by feeding on the coarsest shrubs and leaves, serve as basins to catch the little water that sometimes falls there: this is immediately dried away by the intense heat of the sun, which beats down upon the surface in all parts most violently, and scorches like actual fire;—yet that moisture, little as it is, causes the growth of the dwarf thorn bush, and of two or three other prickly plants, resembling weeds; these grow only among sand, and there are spots on the desert which produce a shrub that grows up in a bunch at the bottom as thick as a man's leg, and then branches off in every direction to the height of two feet, with a diameter of four or five feet.

Each branch is two or three inches in circumference, and they are fluted like pillars or columns in architecture, and almost square at their tops: these are armed with small sharp prickles all over, two or three inches long, and yield, when broken off, a whitish liquid that is very nauseous, and bites the tongue like *aqua-fortis*, so that the camels will nip it off only when they can find nothing else: they are so numerous in some places, that it is difficult for the camels to get along amongst them, and they are obliged to dodge about between these bunches. This plant resembles a chandelier in appearance: the barren mountains of Suse are nearly covered with it: I believe it is a species of *euphorbium*, and each of the branches were surmounted at that time with a red blossom of three or four leaves, half an inch long, resembling in some degree the blaze of a candle; from this flower the bees that are found in such quantities in Suse extract their honey.

In many valleys the thorn bushes furnish a few snails. A few ground nuts are also to be found, resembling in shape and size of small onions; and there are also to be seen under the shade of the thorn bushes, an herb known by the name of shepherd's sprouts in America; but like the other things before mentioned, they are very rarely to be met with. These are, as far as came within my knowledge, the whole of the productions of the desert.

It has been imagined by many, that the desert abounded in noxious animals, serpents, and other reptiles; but we saw none, nor is it possible for any animal that requires water to exist on the desert of Zahahrah, unless it is under the care of, and assisted by man in procuring that necessary article. I saw no animal that was wild, except the ostrich, nor can I conceive how that animal exists without fresh water, which it is certain he cannot procure, nor what kind of nourishment he subsists on. There are neither beasts, nor birds, nor reptiles, to be seen on that dreary waste on which we travelled, and it is certain that there are other districts still worse, bearing not the smallest herb nor bush wherewith the camel can fill his stomach; but near the borders of the desert, where more shrubs are produced, sheep and goats are fed in considerable numbers, and we saw many of those light-footed and beautiful animals called the *Gazelle*, tripping across the sand-hills, and near watering places; some tigers also now and then made their appearance. Such is the great western desert, or Zahahrah, which can only afford a description as dry and as barren as its dreary surface. For its extent, see the map.

Nearly all parts of this vast desert are inhabited by different tribes of Arabs, who live entirely on the milk of their camels and wander from valley to valley, travelling nearly every day for the sake of finding food for their camels, and consequently food for themselves: they live in tents formed of cloth made of camels' hair, which they pull off by hand, and spin with a hand spindle; this they twist round with the fore-finger and thumb of the right hand, after they have pulled out the thread sufficiently long from a bunch of camels' hair, which they hold in their left hand, whilst the spindle descends to the ground, when they take it up in their hand again, and wind off the yarn in a ball, and then spin another length in like manner: they afterwards double and twist it by hand, making a thread as thick as a goose quill.

When they have spun a sufficient quantity, and have agreed to stop for two or three days in one place, (which they always do when they can find sufficient food for their camels,) they drive into the ground two rows of pegs, in parallel lines, sufficiently wide for a tent cloth, that is, about two and a half feet apart: they then warp the yarn round the pegs, and commence weaving it by running a kind of wooden sword through the yarn under one thread and over another, in the manner of darning: this sword they carry with them, and it appears to have been used for ages: they then tuck through the filling by hand, after turning up the sword edgeways, haul it tight, and beat it up with the sword.

They weave it the whole length which they intend the tent to be, and then roll up the pieces or length, until they have made enough to finish a tent. This, in my opinion, must have been the very first method of weaving practised in the world, and the idea, I imagine, was taken from a view of the outer bark of the cocoa-nut tree, as I have before observed. The tent is then sewed together with the same kind of twine, through holes made with an iron bodkin. After it is sewed together to a proper width, from six to ten breadths, they make four loops on its ends, by fastening short crooked sticks to the cloth, and two on each side. When they are about to pitch the tent, they spread it out, stretching the cords by which it is fastened, and driving a stout peg into the ground for each cord; this is done with a hard smooth stone, which they always carry with them, in place of a hammer; then getting under the tent and raising it, they place a block, whose top is rounded like a wooden bowl, under its centre, and set the tent pole into a hole made for that purpose, and set the pole upright, which keeps the tent steady in its place.

After the tent is raised, all the ropes that hold and steady it (ten in number) are tautened: these ropes are made of skins partly dressed, or of camels' hair, so that the tent is suspended in form of an oblong umbrella, and the lower edge is about two feet from the ground. In

Arab tents in the Desert of Sahara

the day time they raise up the south part of their tents (as those on the desert are always pitched facing the south) with two small stanchions fixed under the cords that hold it in front, so that they can go under the tent by stooping: this tent serves all the family for a shelter. Each family has a mat, which serves as a bed for the whole: they lie down on it promiscuously, only wrapped up in their *haick* or blanket, if they have one; if not, in the skin that covers their loins only, and lie close together, to keep off the cold winds which blow under the tents in the night: the children lie between the grown persons; their heads are as low, and frequently lower than their feet, and their long bushy hair, which is never combed, and resembles a woollen thrumb mop, serves them instead of a pillow. The families consist of the father, and one or more wives, and the children that are unmarried, (generally about four to a family, but sometimes six or eight,) and their slaves, who are blacks.

The rich Arabs have one, two, or three slaves, male and female; these are allowed to sleep on the same mat with their masters and mistresses, and are treated in all respects like the children of the family in regard to apparel, &c.; they are not, however, permitted to marry or cohabit with the Arab women, under pain of death, and are obliged to take care of the camels and follow them, and to do other drudgery, such as getting fuel, &c. but they will not obey the women, and raise their voices higher than their master or any of his children in a dispute, and consequently are considered smart fellows. They marry among their own colour while they are slaves, with the consent of their masters, but the children remain slaves. After a slave has served his master faithfully for a long time, or has done him some essential service, he is made free: he then enters into all the privileges that the free Arabs enjoy, and can marry into any of their families, which he or she never fails to do, and thus become identified with the families of the tribe in which they were slaves, and may rise to the very head of it.

The negroes are generally active and brave, are seldom punished with stripes, and those who drive the camels do not scruple to milk them when they are thirsty, but take care not to be discovered: they are extremely cunning, and will steal anything they can get at to eat or drink, from their masters, or indeed anyone else. If they are caught in the act of stealing, they are only threatened, and promised a flogging the next time, (this being the common practice of their masters!) The father of the family is its absolute chief in all respects, though he seldom inflicts punishment: his wives and daughters are considered as mere slaves, subject to his will or caprice; yet they take every opportunity to deceive or steal from him: he deals out the milk to each with his own hand, nor dare any one touch it until it is thus divided: he always assists in milking the camels, then puts the milk into a large wooden bowl, which has probably been in the family for ages: some of the largest bowls will contain five gallons: they are frequently split in every direction, and the split parts are fastened together with small iron plates, with a rivet at each end, made of the same metal.

All the milk is thrown into the great bowl; then, if in the old man's opinion, there is a sufficient quantity for a good drink round, he takes a small bowl, (of which sort they generally have two or three,) and after washing or rubbing it with dry sand, he begins to distribute the milk, by giving to each grown person an equal share, and to the children in proportion to their size, measuring it very exactly, and taking a proportionate quantity to himself. If there is any left, (which was very seldom the case with those I lived among,) he has it put into a skin, to serve for a drink at noon the next day: if there is not a sufficient quantity of milk for a good drink all round, the old man fills it up with water (if they have any) to a certain mark in the bowl, and then proceeds to divide it as before related.

The camels are driven out early in the morning, and home about dark, when they are made to lie down before the tent of their owner, very near, with their tails towards it: a doubled rope with a large knot in one end is then put round the knee joint when the leg is doubled in, and the knot being thrust through the doubled part at the other end, effectually fastens the knee bent as it is, so that the camel cannot get up to walk off, having but the use of three of his legs. This kind of becket is also fixed on the knees of the old camels that lead the drove; and the others remain quiet when their leaders are fast: in this manner they are suffered to lie until about midnight, when they have had time to cool and the milk to collect in their bags—the becket is then taken off, and as soon as they get up, the net which covers the bag to prevent the young ones from consuming the milk, is loosened: this is fastened on by two cords, that go over the back of the camel, and are knotted together.

As each camel is milked, the net is carefully replaced, and she is made to lie down in the same place again: here they lie until daylight, when all the camels are made to get up; a little milk is then drawn from each, and the young ones are suffered to suck out the remainder, when the net is put in its place again, not to be removed until the following midnight. While the head of the family is busied milking the camels and suckling the young ones, assisted by all the males, the wife and females are striking and folding up the tent, selecting the camels to carry the stuff, and bringing them near, where they make them lie down and pack on them the tent and all their other materials. This being done, they fasten a leather or skin basket, about four feet wide, fitted with a kind of tree, like a saddle, on the back of one of the tamest camels, in which the women place the old men and women that cannot walk, and young children, and frequently themselves, and proceed forward according to their daily custom.

The women take care of the stuff and the camels that carry it, and of the children: the other camels are driven off by slaves, if they have any, if not, by some of the boys, and kept where there are some shrubs to be found, until night. The old man, or head of the family, generally precedes the women and stuff, after having described to them the course they are to steer. He sets off on his camel, with his gun in his hand, at a full trot, and goes on until he finds a fit place in which to pitch the tent, when he gives the information to his wife, who then proceeds with all possible despatch to the spot, unloads her camels, and lets them go; then she spreads her tent, puts all the stuff under it, clears away the small stones, and spreads her mat, arranges her bowls, hangs up the skins containing water, (if they have any,) on a kind of horse or frame that folds together, &c. &c. They start long before sun-rising in the morning, and calculate to pitch their tents at about four o'clock in the afternoon, if they can find a convenient spot; otherwise a little sooner or later.

When one family sets off, the whole of that part of the tribe dwelling near travel on with them; and I have frequently seen from five hundred to one thousand camels in one drove, all going the same way, and I was greatly surprised to see with what facility "they could distinguish and separate them; each knowing his own camels, even to the smallest: they would sometimes march together for half a day; then in a few minutes they would separate, and each take his own course, and would generally pitch within a few miles of each other. As soon as the place is agreed on, the men go out on their camels, with their guns, different ways, to reconnoitre and see if they have enemies near.

When they rise in the morning, after having first milked their camels, and suckled the young ones, they next attend to prayers, which is done in the following manner: they first find a sandy spot, then unwrap themselves, and take up sand in both their hands; with this they rub their faces, necks, arms, legs, and every part of their bodies, except their backs, which they cannot reach: this done, as if they washed with water, they stand erect, facing towards the east; wrap themselves up as neatly as they can in their blankets or skins; they look up towards heaven, and then bow their heads, bending their bodies half way to the ground, twice, crying aloud at each time, *Allah Hooakibar.*

They next kneel down, and supporting themselves with their hands, they worship, bowing their faces in the dust, twice successively; then, being still on their knees, they bend themselves forward, nearly to the ground, repeating, *Hi el Allah-Sheda Mohammed—Rahsool Allah*; then rising, they again repeat, *Allah Hooakibar*, two or three times; and this is the common mode of worshipping four times a day. In addition to this, at sunsetting, they implore the Almighty to send rain to moisten the parched earth; to cause the food to grow for their camels; to keep them under his special care, with their families and tribes; to enrich them with the spoils of their enemies, and to confound and destroy them that seek their hurt: they thank the Almighty for his past mercies, for food, raiment, and his protection, &c. &c.; they then repeat part of a chapter from the *Koran*, in which God's pretended promises to the faithful are made known by their prophet; and repeating at all times the *Hi el Allah*, or, "Great is the Almighty God, and Mohammed is his holy prophet."

Their times of prayer are, before sunrising in the morning, about noon, the middle of the afternoon, about sunsetting, and again two or three hours after the sun has set: this makes five times a day, washing themselves (at least their faces and hands, when they have water) before praying; when they cannot get water, (which is always the case with those on the desert,) they perform their ablutions by substituting sand. Mohammed, their prophet, when he arrived with an army on the deserts of Arabia, found that there was no water either for himself or his followers to wash in; yet by the laws he had already promulgated, ablutions could not be dispensed with; a new chapter, however, of revelation, soon relieved him from this dilemma, and he directed his followers to use sand, when no water was to be had. In the ninth chapter of the *Book of Numbers*, it appears that Moses, in a similar dilemma, found it necessary to apply for a new command from the Lord on a particular subject.

The Arabs always wash when it is in their power, before they eat, nor does any business divert them from the strict observance of their religious ceremonies: and with respect to particular stated times, while pursuing their journeys, and going on in the greatest haste, when the time for prayers arrives, all stop, make the camels lie down, and perform what they conceive to be their indispensable duty; praying, in addition to the usual forms, to be directed in the right course, and that God will lead them to wells of living water, and to hospitable brethren, who will feed them, and not suffer them to perish far from the face of man; that he will enrich them with spoils, and deliver them from all who lie in wait to do them mischief: this done, they mount again cheerfully, and proceed, encouraging their camels by a song, a very lively one, if they wish them to go on a trot; if only to walk, something more slow and solemn.

The Arabs who inhabit the great western desert, are in their persons about five feet seven or eight inches in height; and tolerably well set in their frames, though lean: their complexion is of a dark olive: they have high cheek-bones, and aquiline noses, rather prominent; lank cheeks, thin lips, and rounded chins: their eyes are black, sparkling, and intelligent: they have long black hair, coarse, and very thick; and the men cut theirs off with their knives, to the length of about six or eight inches, and leave it sticking out in every direction from their heads: they all wear long beards: their limbs are straight, and they can endure hunger, thirst, hardships, and fatigues, probably better than any other people under heaven: their clothing in general is nothing more than a piece of coarse cloth, made of camels' hair, tied round their waists, hanging nearly down to their knees; or a goatskin so fastened on, as to cover their nakedness; but some of the rich ones wear a covering of linen or cotton cloth over their shoulders, to their knees, hanging something like a shift or shirt, without sleeves; and some have, besides, a *haick* or a woollen blanket, about four feet wide, and four yards long, which they wrap about them; but this is the case only with the rich, and their number is very small.

These *haicks* and blue shirts they get from the empire of Morocco, in exchange for camels' hair and ostrich feathers; the only commodities in which they can trade. The Arab women are short and meagre, and their features much harder and more ugly than those of the men; but they have long black hair, which they braid and tuck up in a bunch on their heads, and fasten it there by means of thorns. They generally wear strings of black beads round their necks, and a white circular bone, of three inches in diameter, in their hair, with bands of beads or other ornaments around their wrists and ankles. Their cheek bones are high and prominent; their visages and lips are thin, and the upper lip is kept up by means of the two eye-teeth. They take great pains to make these teeth project forward, and turn up quite in front of the line of their other fore-teeth, which are as white and sound as ivory. Their eyes are round, black, and sparkling, very expressive, and extremely beautiful, particularly in the young women, who are generally plump and lascivious.

The women wear a dress of coarse camels' hair cloth, which they manufacture in the same way they make their tent cloth: it covers their shoulders, leaving their arms and breasts naked; it is sewed up on each side, and falls down nearly to their knees; they have a fold in this, like a sack, next their skin on their shoulders, in which they carry their little children; and the breasts of the middle aged women become so extremely long, lank, and pendulous, (being in appearance not unlike a wrinkled stocking with a small bunch at the bottom,) that they have no other trouble in nursing the child which is on their backs, when walking about, than to throw up their breasts over the top of their shoulders, so that the child may apply its lips.

All the Arabs go barefoot; the children, both male and female before they come to the age of puberty, run about entirely naked, and this exposure to the sun is one great cause of their black colour. The miles are all circumcised at the age of eight years, not as a religious rite, but because it is found necessary as a preventive of a disease incident to the climate, (the venereal.) The men are very quick, active, and intelligent—more so, taken collectively, than any other set of men I had ever come across in the different parts of the world I had before visited. They are the lords and masters in their families, and are very severe and cruel to their wives, whom they treat as mere necessary slaves, and they do not allow them even as much liberty as they grant to their negroes, either in speech or action: they are considered by the men as beings without souls, and consequently, they are not permitted to join in their devotions, but are kept constantly drudging at something or other, and are seldom allowed to speak when men are conversing together.

They are very filthy in their persons, not even cleansing themselves with sand, and are covered with vermin. The continual harsh treatment, and hard drudgery to which they are subject, have worn off that fine edge of delicacy, sensibility, and compassion, so natural to their sex, and transformed them into unfeeling and unpitying beings; so much so, that their conduct towards me and my companions in distress, was brutal in the extreme, and betrayed the extinction of every humane and generous feeling.

The Arab is high-spirited, brave, avaricious, rapacious, revengeful; and, strange as it may appear, is at the same time hospitable and compassionate: he is proud of being able to maintain his independence, though on a dreary desert, and despises those who are so mean and degraded as to submit to any government but that of the Most High. He struts about sole master of what wealth he possesses, always ready to defend it, and believes himself the happiest of men, and the most learned also; handing down the tradition of his ancestors, as he is persuaded, for many thousands of years. He looks upon all other men to be vile, and beneath his notice, except as merchandise: he is content to live on the milk of his camels, which he takes great care to rear, and thanks his God daily for his continual mercies.

They considered themselves as much above me and my companions, both in intellect and acquired knowledge, as the proud and pampered West-India planter (long accustomed to rule over slaves) fancies himself above the meanest new negro, just brought in chains from the coast of Africa. They never correct their male children, but the females are beat without mercy. The men were not cruel to us farther than they thought we were obstinate, and always gave us a small share of what they themselves had to subsist on.

I never witnessed a marriage among them, but was told that when a young man sees a girl that pleases him, he asks her of her father, and she becomes his wife without ceremony. Polygamy is allowed, but the Arabs of the desert have but very seldom more than one wife, unless amongst some of the rich ones, who have need of servants, when they take another wife, and sometimes a third.

They all learn to read and write: in every family or division of a tribe, they have one man who acts as teacher to the children: they have boards of from one foot square to two feet long, and about an inch thick by eighteen inches wide: on these boards the children earn to write with a piece of pointed reed; they have the secret of making ink, and that of a very black dye: when a family of wandering Arabs pitch their tents, they set apart a place for a school: this they surround with broken shrubs in the desert to keep off the wind: here all the boys who have been circumcised of from eight to eighteen or twenty years old, attend, and are taught to read and to write verses from the *Koran*, which is kept in manuscript by every family on skins: they write their characters from right to left— are particular in the formation of them, and make their lines very straight: all the children attend from choice or for amusement.

The teacher, I was told, never punishes a child, but explains the meaning of things, and amuses him by telling tales that are both entertaining and instructive; he reads or rehearses chapters from the *Koran* or some other book, for they have a great many poems, &c. written also on skins: when the board is full of writing, they rub it off with sand, and begin again: they enumerate with the nine figures now in use among all European nations, and in America, and were extremely astonished to find that I could make them, and understand their meaning, saying one to another, "This man must have been a slave before to some Arabian merchant, who has taught him the manner of using the Arabic figures, and contrary to his law, unless indeed he is a good man and a believer."

The boards on which they wrote seemed to have lasted for ages—they had been split in many places, and were kept together by small iron plates on each side, fixed by iron rivets: these plates, as well as their rude axes, of which each family has one, are made of tempered iron by the smiths which belong to and journey with the tribe: I saw several of them at work: they burn small wood into charcoal, and carry it with them on camels: their anvil is made of a piece of iron a foot long, and pointed at the end—this they drive into the ground to work on; the head of the anvil is about six inches over: they make their fire in a small hole dug in the ground for that purpose, and blow it up by means of two skins curiously fixed: so that while one is filling with air. they blow with the other, standing between them—with a hand placed on each, they raise and depress them at pleasure.

By means of a clumsy hammer, an anvil, and hot irons to bore with, they manage to fix the saddles for themselves to ride on, and to make knives and a kind of needles, and small rough bladed axes. This forge is carried about without the smallest inconvenience, so that the Arabs even of the desert are better provided in this respect than the Israelites were in the days of Saul their king, *Samuel*, chapter xiii. verses 19 to 23—"*Now there was no smith in all the land of Israel; for the Philistines said, Lest the Hebrews make them swords or spears.*"

There appeared to be no kind of sickness or disease among the Arabs of the desert during the time I was with them: I did not hear of, nor see the smallest symptom of complaint, and they appear to live to a vast age: there were three people I saw belonging to the tribe in which I was a slave, namely, two old men and one woman, who from appearance were much older than any I had ever seen: these men and the woman had lost all the hair from their heads, beards, and every part of their bodies; the flesh on them had entirely wasted away, and their skins appeared to be dried and drawn tight over the sinews and the bones, like Egyptian mummies: their eyes were extinct, having totally wasted away in their sockets, the bones of which were only covered by their eye-lids: they had lost the use of all their limbs, and appeared to be deprived of every sense, so that when their breath should be spent and their entrails extracted, they would in my opinion be perfect mummies without further preparation; for from their appearance there was not sufficient moisture in their frames to promote corruption; and I felt convinced, that a sight of such beings (probably on the deserts of Arabia) might have given the Egyptians their first idea of drying and preserving the dead bodies of their relations and friends.

An undutiful child of civilized parents might here learn a lesson of filial piety and benevolence from these barbarians: the old people always received the first drink of milk, and a larger share than even the acting head of the family when they were scanted in quantity: whenever the family moved forward, a camel was first prepared for the old man, by fixing a kind of basket on the animal's back; they then put skins or other soft things into it, to make it easy, and next lifting up the old man, they place him carefully into the basket, with a child or two on each side, to take care of and steady him during the march, while he seems to sit and hold on, more from long habit than from choice.

As soon as they stopped to pitch the tents, the old man was taken from his camel, and a drink of water or milk given him, for they take care to save some for that particular purpose. When the tent was pitched, he was carefully taken up and placed under it on their mat, where he could go to sleep:—this man's voice was very feeble, squeaking, and hollow. The remarkably old man I am speaking of belonged to a family that always pitched their tent near ours, so that I had an opportunity of witnessing the manner of his treatment for several days together, which was uniformly the same.

After I was redeemed in Mogadore I asked my master Sidi Hamet of what age he supposed this old man to have been, and he said about eight *Zille,* or Arabic centuries. Now an Arabic century, or *Zille,* is forty lunar years of twelve moons in each year, so that by this computation he must have been nearly three hundred years old: he also told me, that it was very common to find Arabs, on different parts of the great desert, five *Zille* old, retaining all their faculties, and that he had seen a great many of the ages of from seven to eight *Zille.* He further said, that my old master from whom he bought me had lived nearly five *Zille* or centuries, though he was very strong and active; and from the appearance of a great many others in the same tribe, I could have no doubt but they were much older.

I then asked him how they knew their own ages, and he answered, "Every family keeps a record of the ages and names of its children, which they always preserve and pack up in the same bag in which they carry the *Koran*." Each family had a bag as large as a camel's skin, full of manuscripts, written on skins prepared for the purpose, resembling parchment, but not stiff; they were whole goat or sheep skins, covered on all sides by writing: one skin, I understood, contained the whole *Koran*. I told him that few people in other parts of the world lived to the age of two *Zille* and a half, and the people of those countries would not believe such a story.

"The Arabs who live on the desert (said he) subsist entirely on the milk of their camels; it is the milk of an animal that we call sacred, and it causes long life: those who live on nothing else, have no sickness nor disorders, and are particularly favoured by heaven; but only carry the same people off from the desert, and let them live on meat, and bread, and fruits, they then become subject to every kind of pain and sickness when they are young, and only live to the age of about two *Zille* and a half at the most, while a great many die very young, and not one tenth part of the men or women live to the age of one *Zille*. I myself (added he) always feel well when I live on the milk of the camel alone, even though I do not get half as much as I want, for then I am strong and can bear heat, and cold, and fatigue, much better than when I live on flesh, and bread, and fruit, and have plenty of good fresh water to drink, and if I could always have as much camels' milk as I could drink, I would never taste of meat again; but I love bread and honey very much."

This account from an Arab who was my friend and the preserver of my life, and one who had traversed the desert in many directions, and who was also a good scholar for an Arab, and on whose veracity I could rely, together with what fell under my own observation, has removed all doubt from my mind on that subject, and I am fully of opinion, that a great many Arabs on this vast expanse of desert, actually live to the age of two hundred years and more of our calendar. My reasons for this belief, in addition to those already given, are,

1st. That their lives are regular, from the day of their birth to the day of their death.

2nd. That there is no variation in their food, which is of the most pure and nutritive kind, and cannot cause in them disorders originating from indigestion, &c. &c.

3rd. That the climate they inhabit, though hot, is perfectly dry, and consequently must be healthy for those born there; and,

4th. That in their wandering life they are never subjected to hard bodily labour, and their daily movements afford them sufficient exercise to promote a due circulation of the fluids; nor do they ever taste wine or any ardent spirits, being entirely out of the way of those articles, and are besides strictly forbidden by their religion. I am no physician, and cannot therefore enter into any learned disquisition on this subject, but merely give my own impressions respecting it, without pretending to be less liable to err in judgment than others. It cannot be doubted but that the Arabs existed as a wandering race long before the tine of the Greeks, and it is possible that they possessed in those early ages the art of writing, and reckoned time by the same method they to at this day, (as at time of first publication), say forty lunar years for a *Zille* or century, and that in translating or quoting from their writings, a *Zille* may have been taken for a hundred of our years.

The tribe of Arabs to which I belonged owned four horses, or rather mares: they were the general property, and were fed on milk, and watered every two days: with these animals they hunt the ostrich, and with this view, having agreed on the time and place, the whole of the men assemble before daylight on their camels, and surround a certain spot of ground where they calculate on finding ostriches, with the horses to windward, and their riders with loaded muskets in their hands: they then approach each other until they start the ostriches, who seeing themselves surrounded on all sides but one, run to the southward before the wind, followed by the horses, which it is said run extremely swift, and pressing on the ostrich very hard, the bird runs himself out of breath in about three hours, when the men on horseback come up and shoot him: but let these birds run against the wind, and no horse can overtake them, for then they do not lose their breath.

After my arrival at Mogadore, I heard of the *Heirie*, or small swift camel of the desert, but I never saw any camel that differed from the common one either in size or shape, and can only suppose that it may be a camel of the same race trained for running swift, and fed on milk like the horses. The common camel can easily travel one hundred miles in a day. A good new milch camel gives at one milking when on the desert about one quart, which is very rich and good: this is besides what suffices to sustain the young camel, and is drawn at midnight— they only draw about a gill in the morning.

Most of the Arabs are well armed with good double barrelled French fowling pieces, (which have excellent locks,) and with good scimitars and knives: each has a kind of bag to carry his slugs, &c. in, slung by his neck and hanging down to his waist on the left side: their big powder-horn is suspended in like manner: this contains coarse powder, and is used for loading the muskets, but they all have a little horn in which to carry their fine powder for priming. Many of the gun barrels that I saw were worn through, and the holes were stopped up by brazing: they have procured many of their guns, no doubt, by shipwrecks on the coast of the desert; many more from caravans that they have overpowered, and others in the way of trade from the French settlements of Senegal, and from Tunis, Tripoli, and other ports on the Mediterranean sea, and Morocco.

I did not see a single Moorish musket or lock during the time I was among the Arabs of the desert: they were all made in Europe, and generally in Paris, with the maker's name on the locks. They have tolerably good powder, which they say they know how to manufacture, but do not make it fine, so that the first rate English or French musket powder is much in request, and looked upon as invaluable for priming. Their swords or scimitars they most probably obtain by the same means as their muskets, or from Turkey: they are ever ready to attack an inferior, or even an equal force, and fight for the sake of plunder.

Their language is the ancient Arabic: is spoken with great fluency, and is distinguished for its powerful emphasis, and elegant cadence. When they converse peaceably, (and they are much given to talking with each other,) it thrills on the ear like the breathings of soft wind-music, and excites" in the soul the most soothing sensations; but when they speak in anger, it sounds as hoarse as the roarings of irritated lions, or the most furious beasts of prey. They attack the small towns in the vicinity of the desert, on all sides; which are walled in to ward off their incursions: if they are successful, they put all to the sword, burn the towns, and retire again to the desert with their spoil. Such is the wandering Arab of the great African desert: his hand is against every man, and consequently every man's hand is against him.

Description of an Arabian Camel or Dromedary.

The Arabian camel, called by the ancients and by the naturalists the dromedary, is, perhaps, the most singular, and at the same time one of the most useful animals in nature. He is, when full grown, from eight to nine feet in height, and about twelve or fourteen feet in length, from the end of his nose to the root of his tail: his body is small, compared with his height: his neck resembles in shape that of a goose more than any other animal, being long and slender, and it seems to grow out of the lower part of his body, between his forelegs he raises his head to the height of his back, poking his nose out horizontally, so that his face looks directly upwards, and his nose bone so high as to be on a line with the top of the bunch on his back: his head is small, his ears short: his eyes are of various colours, from a black to almost a white; bright, and sparkling with instinctive intelligence, and placed on the sides of his head in such a manner that he can see before, behind, and one very side at the same time.

His tail is short, and hangs like that of a cow, with a small bunch of hair at the end: his legs are long and slender, though their joints are stout and strong: his feet are divided something like those of an ox, but he has no hoof except on the extreme points of the toes—in other parts they are only covered with skin, and are soft and yielding: the soles of his feet are not thicker than stout sole leather: he is generally of a light ash colour, but varying from that to a dark brown, and sometimes a reddish brown: many of them are also marked with white spots or stripes on their foreheads, and on different parts of their bodies: the hair on his body is short and fine, like the finest of wool, and serves the Arabs instead of that necessary article, with which they make their tent cloth and coarse covering: it is pulled or else falls off once a year: the hair about the throat and on the hump is eight or ten inches in length, and hangs down: he has a high bunch on his back, which rises from his shoulders, and comes to a blunt point at about the centre of his back, and tapers off to his hips: this bunch is from one to two feet high above the back bone, and not attached to it nor to the frame of the camel, so that in skinning him the Arabs take off the bunch with it, which is larger or smaller, as the camel is fat or lean.

He who rides on a camel without a saddle (which saddle is peculiarly constructed, so as not to touch the bunch) is forced to get on behind it, where the breadth of the body keeps the rider's legs extended very wide, while he is obliged to keep himself from slipping off over the beast's tail, by clenching both hands into the long hair that covers the bunch.

The camel is a very tractable animal; he lies down on his belly at the command of his master, folding his legs under him something like a sheep; there he remains to receive his rider or his burthen, when he rises at a word, and proceeds in the way he is driven or directed, with the utmost docility and readiness, while his master encourages him by singing. The Arabs use neither bridle nor halter, but guide and manage the camel (whose head is quite at liberty) by means of a stick, assisted by words and sounds of the tongue; having one sound to urge him on faster; one to make him go slower; and a third, which is a kind of cluck with the tongue to make him stop. He chews his cud like an ox, and has no fore teeth in his upper jaw; but his lips are long and rough, so that he nips off the rugged shrubs without difficulty, on which he is obliged to feed.

The camel seems to have been formed by nature to live on deserts: he is patient, fleet, strong, and hardy; can endure hunger and thirst better than any other animal: can travel through deep and dead sands with great ease, and over the flinty parts of the desert without difficulty, though it is hard for him to go up or down steep hills and mountains, and to travel on muddy roads, as he slips about and strains himself; but he is sure-footed, and walks firmly on a hard dry surface, or on sand. I have never made the natural history of animals my study, and it cannot be expected that I should be acquainted with the particular formation ot their interior parts; but I will venture to say a few words in regard to those of the camel, without fear of contradiction from anyone who shall see and examine for himself, having assisted in butchering three camels while a slave.

The camel is described by naturalists as having, besides the four stomachs common to ruminating animals, a fifth bag, exclusively as a reservoir for water, where it remains without corrupting or mixing with the other aliments: this is a mistake—for the bag that holds the water contains also the chewed herbage, and is in the camel what a paunch is in an ox. into this bag all the rough chewed herbage enters, where it is softened by the water, thrown again into the mouth, chewed over, and passes off by another canal, and the faeces are so dry that the day after they are voided, the Arabs strike fire on them instead of touch-wood or spunk.

Having to draw water for these animals, I am certain that the largest sized ones drink at least two barrels of water at one time, when they have been long without it, and that the whole of the camels belonging to the tribe by whom I was made a slave, which were then at a well, did not again get a drop of water within twenty days: these camels were at least two thousand in number, and were then on one of the hottest and dryest parts of the great western desert, where there was scarcely a green leaf or shrub to be found, and their owners knew how far it was back to the same watering place at which myself and crew were seized, and to which they drove them again at the end of that period—and even that water was almost as black as ink, owing probably to its stagnant state in the well, and very brackish, because it filtered through the sand beach from the ocean, which was not more than three hundred yards from the well; and these camels went twenty days without water under such circumstances; and I have not the smallest doubt that they can go thirty or forty days without water before they would die with thirst.

At the end of fifteen days after watering the camels, my old master, Mohammed Bessa, killed an old and very poor camel, and I was obliged to assist in dressing, though not in eating it, for its flesh, bones, and intestines, were divided among the whole tribe; a small piece to each family: they cut open the paunch of this camel, (for he had no other bag to contain water,) and dipped out the contents, though thick with faeces, in order to boil the intestines in it, as well as to drink. When my master, Sidi Hamet, killed a camel to give me and my companions some meat, and procure something to sustain us on our journey across the desert, the paunch was rolled out of the camel, and the water taken from it, thick as it was, to boil the uncleansed intestines.

After drinking this stuff, we put the remainder (about two gallons) with the filth it contained, into one of our bottles, or goat skins, and it served to sustain life, though the most rank and nauseous both to the smell and taste that can be imagined. These bottles sufficiently explain why Christ said, "*Put new wine into new bottles,*" in order to preserve both, as an old skin bag, being in scripture termed a bottle, is evidently weaker than a new one, and more liable to burst during the fermentation of its contents.

The camel is considered by the Arab as a sacred animal: with him he can transport a load of merchandise of several hundred weight with certainty and celerity through deserts utterly impassable with any other animal: on him the wandering Arab can flee with his family from any enemy, across the trackless waste, one hundred miles or more in a single day if he wishes, and out of the reach of his pursuers, for the desert, like the ocean, neither retains nor discloses any trace of the traveller. Its milk is both food and drink for the whole family, and when they have a sufficiency of that article, they are contented, and desire nothing more: with his camel the Arab is perfectly independent, and can bid defiance to all the forces that civilized or uncivilized foes can send against him: with him they collect in strong bands, all well armed, and fall upon the caravans, slaying without mercy all they can overpower, and divide their spoil: should they meet with a repulse, they can flee and soon be out of sight: they also attack the settlements and small walled towns in the cultivated country near the desert, and if strong enough, destroy all the inhabitants, and drive off the cattle: all the goods of the slain they carry away on their camels, and return to the desert, where no force can pursue them without meeting with certain destruction.

The camel's motions are extremely heavy and jolting: his legs being long, he steps a great distance, and though he appears to go slowly when on a walk, yet he proceeds at about the rate of four miles an hour, and it is difficult for a man to keep pace with him without running. When the camel trots, he goes very fast; the small trot being about six, and the great one about eight miles an hour—this they can do with great ease with light loads for a whole day together, and will replenish their stomachs at night with the leaves and twigs of the sullen thorn-bush, that is barely permitted by nature to vegetate in that most dreary and desolate of all regions. The flesh of the camel is good for food; and that of the young ones is esteemed preferable to that of the ox: they bring forth a single young one at a time, and generally once in about two years, their time of gestation being about one year.

When the camel is in heat, he is extremely vicious, so that none dare come near him: they are said to pair like doves, and not to have promiscuous intercourse like horses, neat cattle, &c. The formation of the camel, in one particular, resembles that of a horse, but it has a contrary direction, so that the water is voided behind; and when obeying one of the most important instincts of nature, he is obliged to make his approach in a retrograde manner.

In the year 1804, I was in the island of Lanzarote, one of the Canaries, and loaded my vessel (the brig *Eliza and Mary*, of New-York) with *barilla*, which I carried to Belfast, in Ireland;—the *barilla* is brought from the interior of the island to the port, on camels, from whose backs I received and weighed it. Their common loads were from nine to twelve quintals of one hundred pounds; but many loads overran that weight, and one load in particular weighed over fifteen hundred pounds. Those were the same kind of camels used in Barbary, and on the desert, and indeed I never saw any other kind: they are said to come to their full growth in six or eight years, and to live in many instances, to the age of fifty or sixty.

CHAPTER 27

Some Account of Suse

The country of Suse, or South Barbary, is bounded by the Moorish province of Hah-Hah, on the east, by the Atlas mountains and the great desert, south, and by the Atlantic ocean on the north and west: its length from east to west is about two hundred and fifty miles; its breadth from north to south one to two hundred miles. In coming from the desert, its principal towns are, Waldeleim, which is said to be very large and strong, and to contain ten thousand inhabitants. Akka is much the largest town in Suse, and its inhabitants are computed by the Arabs at thirty thousand. Widnoon is said to contain twenty thousand. Schelem contains four thousand. Stuka, where I was shut up a slave, does not appear to be a principal town, but is made up of a cluster of small ones, nor could I learn the names of the many little towns or castles, in sight of which I passed coming up.

Suse was formerly a kingdom, and was afterwards united to those of Morocco and Fez, which now forms the Moorish empire: it has, however, become entirely independent, for though the emperor of Morocco claims jurisdiction over the whole of Suse, and indeed of the whole desert as far south as Soudan, yet all those countries are in fact independent, and the emperor's power extends only a few leagues south and west, from a line drawn through Santa Cruz or Agader, and Tarudant, southeast to the Atlas.

The soil of this country is very rich and fruitful: here wheat, barley, and Indian corn, or maize, are cultivated, and most kinds of kitchen garden vegetables thrive with great luxuriance; the date, fig, pomegranate, olive, orange, lemon, sweet and bitter almond, *arga*, and many other fruit and forest trees, thrive exceedingly well, and produce, it is said, great abundance in their seasons: the *gum arabic* and *sanderach* are also produced there in great quantities. The country being speckled over with small cities, towns, and castles, all strongly walled in with stone, laid in clay, is calculated to remind one of the times of the feudal system; each place is under the government of its own chief, who is by common consent the head of the family: they are under a kind of patriarchal government, and each individual feels himself perfectly free and independent.

In case of attack or danger, all unite for the general defence, under such leaders as shall have proved themselves brave, enterprising, and worthy of command: and by this means they are enabled to secure themselves, in some measure, against the frequent inroads and insults of the wandering Arabs, who inhabit the great desert in their vicinity, and to repel the more formidable attacks of the forces of the Moorish emperor. They raise great numbers of camels, horses, asses, mules, oxen, goats, and sheep, which are guarded by their negro slaves, (of whom they have many) or by the young boys, and they are driven into their towns or castles every night, to prevent their being surprised and carried off by the Arabs, or other predatory neighbours: their horses are very handsome, strong, and fleet, of the real Arabian kind, and very high spirited

The inhabitants are of a tawny colour, like the Moors, though not quite so dark, and I was informed they were principally descendants of the ancient inhabitants of the country before it was overrun by the Arabs or Saracens: they are in their persons about five feet eight or nine inches in height, stout built, robust, and athletic, and are very straight limbed: they have rather a round visage, with prominent features, black hair, sharp pointed noses, and great bushy beards: their eyes are black, but not so lively, expressive, or intelligent, as those of the Arabs: their mouths are wide, and their lips plump. Their dress consists of a kind of shirt made of blue Guinea or linen cloth, or coarse white muslin, that passes over their shoulders, and falls down near their knees, but without sleeves: over this, they wear a *haick* or blanket made of woollen cloth, of about five yards in length, and an ell in width: this they wrap round them; some of them also wear the cloak, or *sulam*, and Moorish trowsers; and have on their heads either turbans or white cotton cloth, or a fold of their *haick*.

The heads of the men are generally shaved smooth, at least once a month: their women, like those of the Moors, are not to be seen by the men, except their husbands or fathers: the men are very industrious, and work their land by ploughing it up with a plough formed out of the trunk of a tree, hewn sharp to a point that projects about two feet forward, from a stout crooked limb, that serves as a beam to the plough; while a smaller, and particularly formed limb, is used as a handle to steady and govern it.

In order to fix their animals to the plough, they first attach them together, say a cow and an ass, (for this seemed to make a favourite pair, and I observed a great many such pairs, yoked together) by fastening a rope round the horns of the cow, and about the nose of the ass, in form of a halter: they next place a short piece or stick of wood, hollowed out like one end of an ox yoke across the neck of each animal, and fasten it by means of a rope tied to one end of the stick; this going round under their necks, is made fast to the other end of the short yoke; they then run a long pole through under their bellies, just behind their forelegs, and fasten it there by means of two ropes, like the draw ropes or traces of a horse's harness: these are fixed to the rope that goes round the animal's neck at one end, and the pole under their bellies serves for a yoke, and projects out a foot or two on each side: to the centre of this pole, the end of the plough beam is lashed fast.

The point which enters the ground, is hewn in a triangular shape, but the edges soon wear off, so that it becomes nearly round. In loamy and sandy soils they plough with the naked wood, but in stony places they point it with a round piece of iron, tapering to a sharp point that lets on with a socket: it turns up the earth on both sides, and goes into the ground about eight inches deep. The people of Suse. and those of Morocco, use only one pair of beasts, whatever they may be, and have lines leading from the heads of the animals into the hands of him who steadies the plough, by means of which he directs and governs them: he also carries a thick stick sufficiently long to reach them with a sharp-pointed iron like a spear in its end; by the help of which he pricks and goads his beasts along at pleasure.

This instrument is an ox goad, and no doubt is similar to those spoken of in *Sacred Writ*—1st Samuel iii. 1. But these Moors do not obey that part of the law of Moses; "*Thou shalt not plough with an ox and an ass together.*" See 22nd chapter of *Deuteronomy*, 10th verse, except by sometimes substituting a cow instead of an ox. This, I imagine, was the primitive plough, or something very near it, and the first method hit upon for using it.

I have also promised to treat of the primitive churn, and manner of making butter, which is simply this. The Arabs, or people who inhabited the country near the River Euphrates, as long ago as the time of Abraham, the father of the Jews, and probably much earlier, knew the use of the camel, and actually kept him in a domestic state: they would very naturally feed on its milk, and they, no doubt, in those days, made use of the same means to carry their milk about with them, that the wandering Arabs do at present—that is, whatever milk is left of what the family has been using over night or in the morning, is put into a goat skin, or some other skin, and slung on a camel to serve for drink in the heat of the day; thus equipped, they set off together: and when they stop to take refreshment, or to pitch their tent, they find a lump of butter in the milk; for the violent and continued agitation, occasioned by the heavy motions of the camel, has churned, or forced it to produce butter: this simple method was suggested to my mind by seeing a lump of butter in my old master's milk bag, when we were wandering on the desert, and this must, without doubt, have been the first mode found out by chance of making butter; for what reason would he have, who had never seen such a thing as butter, for supposing milk could be converted into that substance, more than any other fluid? (For a further illustration of this subject, and a view of the camel, see page 287, copied from an original drawing by the author).

The country of Suse, altogether, resembles the narrow country as described in Holy Writ, called the land of Canaan: its vast number of small cities, or rather castles, with high and strong walls, with gates and bars, each under its own sovereign, must be similar to the cities there described, as taken and destroyed by the Jews, (together with their kings) soon after they emerged from the deserts of Arabia, under the command of their chieftain and prophet, Joshua, and have, doubt-less, been constructed for the same purpose; *i. e.* to guard against the irruptions of the wandering inhabitants of the contiguous deserts, &,c. The inhabitants are brave and warlike: all well armed with single barrelled muskets, stocked and mounted in the Moorish manner, and with Moorish locks; they have also knives, daggers, scimitars, and swords, and are the best of horsemen: they seldom or ever go out of their little cities unarmed; but like the wandering Arab on the desert, they are completely equipped either for offence or defence, even when they go to visit their nearest friends. They are said to be, like the Arabs, warm and sincere in their friendship; in their enmities implacable, cruel, and revengeful; and in trade, cunning and deceitful.

The whole number of inhabitants in Suse, including white and black slaves, is estimated at more than *one million*: they are all strict observers of the Mohammedan doctrine and ceremonies, and appear to be enthusiasts in religion, though like the Moors they are not generally taught the arts of reading and writing, and are in consequence considered by the wandering Arabs much beneath them in acquirements, as well as in point of natural abilities. Their language is the corrupt Arabic, not easily understood by the Arabs of the desert, who pretend to speak and write that ancient and beautiful language in its greatest purity.

CHAPTER 28

The Bashaw of Swearah is Seized and Put in Irons

There had been an insurrection in the province of Duquella the last year, (1815) which had spread itself into the provinces of Abdah and Siedmah, and was said to have originated from a false report of the emperor's death. The governor or *Bashaw* of these provinces, whose name was Mohammed ben Absedik, resided in Swearah, and had been a *Bashaw* and a man of great power during nearly the whole reign of Muley Soliman, the present emperor—he was the officer before whom I was carried on my arrival at Swearah, or Mogadore. I was informed that he had used all the means in his power to quell this insurrection, but could not succeed until the emperor joined him with an army of thirty thousand men, when a most desperate battle was fought, which terminated in the destruction of more than fifteen thousand of the rebels, and the remainder were reduced to unconditional submission.

The whole of their flocks, herds, and substance, fell into the hands of the *Sultan*, or rather his black troops, who showed them not the least mercy, but seized on the wretched fugitives wherever they could be found, massacred many thousands, and carried those that remained of the revolters, with their families, into the provinces that had not rebelled, where they were distributed as slaves.

This war being thus terminated, Mohammed ben Absedik had returned in triumph to Mogadore, or Swearah, a few days previous to my arrival there, when he caused presents to be made to him, as if he had taken possession of a new government. In the meantime the death of the *Sultan's* first minister, named Ben Slowy, was announced: he had been the firm friend of Mohammed ben Absedik, and with the aid of

Muley a Tea, (the *Sultan's* princely tea maker,) who was always about his person, managed the whole affairs of the Moorish empire. Ben Slowy being dead, and Muley a Tea sent to Fez to transact the imperial business in that quarter, the emperor then at Morocco, the enemies of Mohammed ben Absedik, (for he had been long in power, and had a host of them) found means to transmit heavy complaints to the *Sultan* against him, (Ben Absedik) and his administration, who perceiving the cloud lowering upon him, set out for Morocco about the 20th of November, 1815, hoping by an early interview with the emperor, to dispel the impending storm—he had only been gone from Mogadore, or Swearah four days, when late in the evening a new governor arrived, accompanied by six hundred horsemen.

The gates had been shut for the night; the brother of the *Bashaw* was civil governor of the city and port: the emperor's order was sent to him over the wall;—the gates were soon opened, and the new governor, or *alcayd*, entered amidst the general and joyful acclamations of the inhabitants, both Moors and Jews. These ignorant and discontented people (ever fond of change) flattered themselves that this arrangement would be for the better, and in the morning all were ready to prefer complaints against their former governor, when they waited on the new one, and made their customary presents. This governor took charge of the civil affairs of the city and the custom-house, in the room of Ajjh Hamet, (or Hamet the pilgrim,) the *Bashaw's* brother, who was ordered to repair with his family to Morocco, and set out for that city the next day, accompanied by a strong guard of black troops. In the evening of the same day, a commander of the troops, or military governor, arrived: he was a black man, and had three hundred horsemen for an escort, all of the same colour: he was received with considerable pomp, and took on himself the immediate command.

We now learned that Mohammed ben Absedik had been put in irons on his arrival at Morocco, and sent off to Fez, and that all his property was seized by order of the *Sultan*, as soon as it could be found. "*New lords, new laws,*" says the old adage:—a small vessel had arrived from Gibraltar—no goods could be landed—new duties were announced, and new regulations, by which no vessel was allowed to be supplied with provisions except for daily consumption: the duties and impositions to be paid every day amounted to more than the first cost of the articles consumed.

The Moors, who had rejoiced at the fall of the old *Bashaw* and civil governor, or *alcayd*, soon changed their tone, and began to wish them back again: all the Moors in the town, up to that time, were considered as imperial soldiers or sailors, and accordingly received a monthly allowance out of the *Beetle mell*, or treasury—this was now ordered to be stopped from the white Moors, but that all the black Moors, or negro troops, should be paid double: new officers were appointed, and many of the old ones confined and sent to Morocco, or despoiled of their property. The Christian merchants residing there, four in number, were obliged to make costly presents to the new governor.

The Christians are, William Willshire, Esq. my deliverer, of the house of Dupuy and Willshire, the most respectable there in point of property, as well as on every other account, being connected in business with James Renshaw & Co. of London, and George Allardyce & Co. of Gibraltar, both houses of long standing and great respectability;—Don Estevan Leonardi, and his nephew, Don Antonio, French, Portuguese, and Genoese consular agents;—Don Pablo Riva, a respectable Genoese, and Alexander W. Court, and Mr. John Foxcroft. The Jews, that were overjoyed at the recent change, soon turned their joy into mourning, when they received, a day or two after, an order to pay their *Gazier*, or yearly tribute to the *Sultan*: the order was for about three thousand five hundred dollars, including expenses, (for the Moor who brought the order must be paid,) in a gross sum to be raised directly: the gates of the Jews' town, or Millah, were immediately closed upon them, nor were any suffered to go out until the money was forthcoming.

The whole number of Jews here does not probably exceed six thousand souls, and they are very poor: the priests or *rabbies* soon convened them in their synagogues, and apportioned the tax according to their law; they were classed thus: the four Jew merchants, Ben Guidallas, Macnin, Abilbol, and Zagury, formed the first class, and I was told their share was two thousand dollars or more; the few petty traders the second, the mechanics the third, and the lowest order of miserable labourers the fourth class: the priests and *rabbies* (who are a great proportion of their number) were of course exempted, as the other classes support them at all times: not a Jew, either man, woman, or child, was allowed to go out of their town for three days, except they were wanted by the Moors or Christians to work, and not then without an order from the *alcayd*.

During this period I visited the Jews' town several times, but never without seeing more or less of these miserable wretches knocked down like bullocks by the gate-keepers, with their large canes, as they attempted to rush past them, when the gates were opened, to procure a little water or food for their hungry and thirsty families. On the fourth day, when the arrangements had been made by the priests and elders, they sent word to the governor, and the three first classes were ordered before him to pay their apportionment. I knew of it, because I was informed by Mr. Willshire's interpreter and broker, who was a Jew of considerable understanding, named Ben Nahory—he was one of the committee of arrangement to wait, on the governor. I wished to see the operation, and went near the house of the *alcayd* for that purpose.

The Jews soon appeared by classes; as they approached, they put off their slippers, took their money in both their hands, and holding them alongside each other, as high as the breast, came slowly forward to the *talb*, or Mohammedan scrivener, appointed to receive it; he took it from them, hitting each one a smart blow with his fist on his bare forehead, by way of a receipt for his money, at which the Jews said, *Nahma Sidi*, (thank you, my lord,) and retired to give place to his companion.

Thus they proceeded through the three first classes without much difficulty, when the fourth class was forced up with big sticks: this class was very numerous, as well as miserable: they approached very unwillingly, and were asked, one by one, if they were ready to pay their *gazier:* when one said, yes, he approached as the others had done, paid his money, took a similar receipt, and then went about his business; he that said, no, he could not, or was not ready, was seized instantly by the Moors, who throwing him flat on his face to the ground, gave him about fifty blows with a thick stick upon his back and posteriors, and conducted him away, I was told, into a dungeon, under a *bomb proof battery*, next the western city wall, facing the ocean: there were many served in this way—the Jews' town was all this time strongly guarded and strictly watched.

At the end of three days more, I was informed that those who were confined in the dungeon were brought forth, but I did not see them: the friends of some of these poor creatures had made up the money, and they were dismissed; whilst the others, after receiving more stripes, were remanded and put in irons. Before the next three days had expired, many of them changed their religion, were received by the Moors as brothers, and were taken to the mosque, and highly feasted, but were held responsible for the last tax notwithstanding. The four above-named Jew merchants, in Swearah or Mogadore, live in high style; are absolute in the Jews' town, and manage nearly all the English trade at Mogadore: at present, their stores are allowed to be kept in the fortress part of the town, or *el Ksebbah*. where Guidallas and Macnin are permitted to reside and stay at night, by paying a handsome sum to government: Guidallas wears European cut clothing, the others the Jew dress.

I had the pleasure to see two brigs arrive from England, and to receive a letter from Mr. Simpson at Tangier, and a kind letter from Mr. Sprague at Gibraltar, which are before mentioned and inserted. Two days after the arrival of these vessels from London, the one commanded by captain Mackay, and the other by Captain Henderson, I went down to the water port to see these gentlemen when they should land in the morning: on my arrival there, I saw a great concourse of soldiers, and on inquiring the cause, found that an execution was about to take place, and some malefactors were at the same time to be maimed. The governor arrived at this moment, and the prisoners were driven in with their hands tied: the order for punishment was read by the *Cadi* or Judge, and the culprits told to prepare themselves, which they did by saying, *Hi el Allah Sheda Mohammed Rahsool Allah*, and worshipping.

They were then made to sit down in a line upon their legs on the ground: a butcher next came forward with a sharp knife in his hand; he seized the first in the line on the left, by the beard, with his left hand; two men were at the same time holding the prisoner's hands: the butcher began cutting very leisurely with his knife round the neck, (which was a very thick one,) and kept cutting to the bones until the flesh was separated; he then shoved the head violently from side to side, cutting in with the point of the knife to divide the sinews, which he seemed to search out among the streams of blood, one by one: he finally got the head off, and threw it on a mat that was spread to receive the mutilated limbs of the others.

There were eight more who were sentenced to lose a leg and an arm each, and nine to lose only one arm. The butcher began to amputate the legs at the knee joint, by cutting the flesh and sinews round with his knife, which he sharpened from time to time on a stone: he would then part the joint by breaking it short over his knee, as a butcher would part the joint in the leg of an ox. Having in this manner got off the leg, and thrown it on the mat, he proceeded to take off the arm at the elbow, in the same leisurely and clumsy manner; he seemed, however, to improve by practice, so that he carved off the hands of the last eight at their wrists, in a very short time—this done, they next proceeded to take up the arteries, and apply a plaister, which was soon accomplished by dipping the stumps into a kettle of boiling pitch that stood near, or something that had the same appearance and smell. Is not this last circumstance an improvement in surgery?

They then carried the lifeless trunk and mutilated bodies, with the head and other limbs, to the market: the head and limbs were carried on a mat by six men, who were making as much sport as possible, for the spectators: the bodies were thrown across jackasses, and they were exposed in the most public part of the market place, nearly the whole day. The two governors, and other officers who were present during the execution of the sentence, were sitting on the ground next to a wall, appearing quite unconcerned, and were conversing gaily on other subjects. The Moors, who came from mere curiosity, did not shew the least mark of disapprobation, or any signs of horror: they jested with the butcher, who seemed highly gratified with the part he was acting.

I now asked Rais bel Cossini, who attended me, concerning the mode of procuring an executioner, &c. &c. He told me, that when an order came to execute or maim any culprits, it generally embraced several at the same time, so as to make but one job of it: that the butchers were called on by the *alcayd* or governor, and forced to find one out of their number to do this work: that they then made up a purse agreeably to a rule, made among themselves in such cases; that is, two and a half *ducats* per man for cutting off heads, and two *ducats* per man for maiming; (two and a half *ducats* make one dollar, or forty cents per *ducat*;) they then question each other to know who will accept of the money, and do the job: if no one appears willing, they cast lots, and the one on whom it falls, is obliged to undertake it: this man is protected by the governor for twenty-four hours after the execution, when he is left to take care of himself, brave the public odium, and the revenge of the friends of the sufferer; or else to fly: he generally goes off the first night afterwards to some other place, and never returns: his wife, if he has one, can be divorced from him by applying to the *Cadi* or Judge, and swearing, that as her husband has served as an executioner, she is afraid to live with him, lest he should be tempted to commit some violence on her, in a similar way.

The butcher who acted on the present occasion, was a voluntary executioner for forty-eight *ducats*, and he decamped the next night, leaving, as I was informed, a wife and seven children to shift for themselves: he was poor, and carried away his wages of death with him. Mr. Willshire and Don Pablo Riva, confirmed this statement, substantially.

Taking a walk round the walls of the city one day, to make observations on it at low water, in company with Mr. Savage, and being escorted by a Moor, in order to protect us from insults, we came to the Jews' burial place: it is situated a little without the walls, and on the north side of the city, near the ruins of a couple of windmills, which I was informed, used to do all the grinding for the city; but this work is now performed in the town by horse-mills. On our approach, we observed a great concourse of Jew women, and heard a great outcry: curiosity led us to the spot where they were collected: here was a newly dug grave, and the dead body of a man lying on the ground near it, enveloped in a cotton wrapper, with his face partly covered: some men were busied in clearing out and preparing the grave; others had brought and were bringing lime, mortar, and stones, to fill it up with: whilst upwards of one hundred women were standing in a circle eastward of the grave, howling in an extraordinary manner.

On a nearer approach, I observed about a dozen women ill raftered garments, who formed an inner circle. As I gazed with pity on this spectacle, these twelve women, who were before quiet, seemed to be seized with a sudden paroxysm of grief, and they began to approach each other with their hands uplifted above their heads; stretching the palms towards each other's faces, and commenced howling, at first moderately, but which soon increased to wailings the most violent, and yellings that it is impossible to describe; they tore their faces with their long finger-nails, and made the most hideous contortions of their features: the mania was now communicated to all the women present, who joined in the lamentation, but the others did not tear their faces like the twelve, who kept it up, stamping with their feet, and going round in their circle; their blood and perspiration mixing together, and streaming from their faces, ran all over their filthy garments, and dyed them red in streaks from head to foot: this paroxysm lasted fifteen or twenty minutes, when they were so much exhausted as to be under the necessity of ceasing for a few moments, to take breath, when they commenced again, and went over the same ceremony, seemingly with redoubled vigour.

The grave being at last ready, the body was put in by the men, who then built up over it a wall of mason work, even with the surface of the ground. The grave was dug in a direction north and souths the head was placed towards the south, and space enough left on one side of the body to support the weight of the mason-work, without bearing upon the corpse: they next rolled a stone on it, formed of lime and small pebbles about two feet square, and as long as the grave; this they placed level on a bed of lime mortar, and then retired without speaking, except as much as was necessary to prompt mutual assistance: the women all this time keeping up their howlings.

After the men had retired, the women ceased their wailings, and seating themselves alongside the windmill, were refreshed by eating cakes, and drinking copious draughts of aniseed, Jew brandy, which had been previously prepared for the purpose, and they soon became as merry in reality, as they had before appeared to be sad. While these women were regaling themselves in this manner, I observed an old woman washing the corpse of a child of about two years old, in the surf: she then wrapped it up in a dirty piece of woollen cloth, and carried it to a man who had been digging a hole for it in the side of another grave, where he shoved it in; put a flat stone before it; filled up the hole with stone and lime, and went away: one woman only attended the burial of the child, besides her who wrapped it up; and this must have been its mother, as I judged from her emotions: she sobbed aloud, while an abundance of tears trickled down her woe-worn, and furrowed cheeks.

I concluded she was poor and a widow: not a soul seemed to join her, or pay the least attention to her grief: after a short pause, she kissed passionately the stone that covered, I presume, the remains of both her husband and child; wet it with her tears; wiped it with a clean white cloth she had in her hand, and returned weeping, amid the brutal scoffs of the Moorish boys, as she dragged herself along towards her cheerless abode. The women who had assisted at the other burial, had by this time ended their repast, and they went round amongst the graves many kissed their hands and laid them on the grave-stones of their deceased relations, while others kissed the rude resemblance of a face carved on the stone: others plucked up the weeds and grass that encroached on the grave, or replaced the earth and small stones which had been dug out by the rats, or broken off by the corroding tooth of time.

On my way home to Mr. Willshire's house, I learned that the corpse of the man that was buried, was that of a *rabbi*, who was poor, and had not been able for a long time to perform the duties of his office, and was buried by charity; I also learned from Ben Nahory, Mr. Willshire's interpreter, that a priest, or *rabbi*, had arrived from Jerusalem, to gather the tribute paid yearly by all the Jews in Barbary, towards the support of the few Jewish priests, or Levites, who are permitted to reside in Jerusalem, by paying a tribute to the *Grand Seignior*, or *Sultan* of the Turkish empire, and for purposes of traffic: this is called a voluntary contribution for the support of Jerusalem.

All the Jews in these countries believe that their nation is one day to sway the sceptre of universal dominion, and that Jerusalem must be kept as a kind of possession until the time arrives predicted by their prophets, when the little stone is to be cut out without hands from the mountain of Jerusalem, and is to fill the whole earth. This and other predictions, constantly and adroitly handled by their crafty teachers, together with the miseries inflicted on the Jews in Barbary by the merciless Moors, tend to nurse their natural superstitions, and render them completely subservient to the will of those who are considered their spiritual guides, and who rob them without mercy, under the pretext of applying the money to good purposes.

A schooner arrived from Gibraltar under the English flag, though a Genoese vessel, as the Barbary powers were at war with Genoa: she brought a cargo of dry goods, iron, steel, cotton, &c. to Ben Zagury, a Jew: one of his sons came passenger in the vessel; his name was Elio Zagury; he was a young Jew, was dressed in the European fashion, had been educated in England, and spoke the English language fluently. As soon as he had seen his father, he called on Mr. Willshire, and to see me; expressed great joy at my deliverance, and invited Mr. Willshire, myself, and Mr. Savage, to dine with him at his father's the next Saturday: the invitation was accepted, because I wanted to learn some of the Jewish customs, and get acquainted with the priest from Jerusalem, who was a guest in his father's house.

On our arrival there, I was presented to the priest: he was a man of middling stature, dark complexion, short hair, and a most venerable, manly beard, that reached down nearly to his *ceinture*, or girdle: his dress was a brown striped mantle, that buttoned close round his neck, and fell loosely to his feet, on which he had a pair of black slippers, down at the heel, as is the custom of Moorish Jews: his head was covered with a *camblet* coloured turban, very high: in his hand he held a string of very large beads, which he was continually counting or telling over: his mantle was girt above his hips with a brown silk girdle that took several turns round him; and was about six inches wide. I accosted him in Spanish, which he spoke very fluently—and made inquiries of him respecting the present city of Jerusalem and its inhabitants.

From his answers (as he was very intelligent) I learned that Jerusalem now contains thirty thousand Turks, and twenty thousand Jews, Armenians, and Greeks: that a very brisk trade is carried on there, principally by Jews, between it, Persia, Constantinople, and Jaffa, which Jews are permitted to reside there and trade, on paying a tribute to the *Grand Seignior*: that the language mostly spoken by the Jews and Christians at Jerusalem is the Spanish: that there is a convent of Christian monks near it, containing a number of St. Francisco's order, &c.

The walls of Jerusalem are strong and well built: all religious denominations are there tolerated by paying contributions, and protected by order of the *Grand Seignior,* provided they pay the soldiers well for their trouble. The name of this priest was Abraham ben Nassar: he said he should get about twenty thousand dollars from the Jews in the Moorish dominions, and carry the amount of contributions in gold, embarking again at Tangier for Gibraltar, where he should deposit the money while he went to England, France, Holland, and Germany, for the same purpose: that there were six more associated with him on the collecting expeditions. One of them had gone to Alexandria, and other parts of Egypt, to collect from the Jews there, from whence he would return by way of the different islands in the Archipelago: one had sailed for Tripoli, who would take money from the Jews there and at Malta; thence to Italy and back; one had gone to Tunis and its various towns, and would go from thence to Sicily and Sardinia, and back; one had gone to Algiers and the towns in that regency, and would go from thence to ancient Greece, including Venice, and that part of Germany bordering on the Venetian gulf; one had gone over land to Russia, and would meet him in Germany, after passing through Poland, Sweden, Denmark, Prussia, &c.

I wished to have an estimate of the sums likely to be collected in all those places, and then he began to be a little reserved. However, after considerable conversation and solicitation, he one day gave me what he stated to be the amount of collections as per the last returns of 1813, which he had with him in Hebrew, and I set it down as he interpreted, after he had first brought the several sums into Spanish dollars; it made up in the countries already mentioned, five hundred and eighty thousand dollars; this was exclusive of the expenses of collecting, and travelling out and returning again to Jerusalem. Many individuals of the priests also came from Jerusalem to Barbary, begging on their own account. Out of this fund a yearly tribute is paid to the *Grand Seignior*, besides impositions in the form of presents to the Turkish officers; and the remainder serves to support the *rabbies*, who are very numerous in Jerusalem, and for commercial purposes: thus the superstition and credulity of the ignorant Jews in all Europe and Africa, as well as in Asia, are made subservient to the purposes of the elders of that singular people, who still reside, by permission, at Jerusalem.

The city of Jerusalem lies from thirty to forty miles east of Jaffy, a small port on the Mediterranean sea: from thence to Jerusalem the road is good, and the priest told me he had walked the distance in two days. Jaffy is the port anciently called Joppa: it has a small town and fortress, and considerable trade with Jerusalem, the islands in the Archipelago, and with Egypt, and some with Malta and Italy; here the Jewish priests, who are sent out on begging expeditions, embark, and return by way of the same place, generally in Greek vessels of small burthen, but very well built and manned.

The priest asked me many questions respecting America, of which he knew but very little, and thought it was a wilderness or a desert. After I had put him right in regard to those points, and informed him we had many Jews in America, where they enjoyed every kind of privilege in common with people of other religions; that they could hold landed estates, &c. and that many of them were very rich, he declared that as soon as he should have finished his present tour, which would still detain him more than a year, he would try to obtain leave to visit America, and collect the dues there. I informed him that our Jews were not so superstitious, nor in such bad repute, as those in Africa or Europe, where they were looked upon as a set of sharpers and villains: "That may be, (said he,) but if they are Jews, they must conform to the laws of Moses, and must contribute towards the support of those of their nation who reside in the Holy Land, in order to be ready for the future conquest of Jerusalem, which would be the fulfilment of God's promises to his people."

I asked him in what manner they collected this contribution? and he told me, that "having letters from the chief *rabbies* and elders at Jerusalem, the collectors (who are always *rabbies*) were kindly received and well treated by all Jews wherever they came; that soon after their arrival in any place where synagogues are established, they convene all the Jews together, and having laid before them the authority by which they make the demand, they then proceed, with the assistance of the priests and chief Jews of the place, to class them, and apportion

THE ORIGINAL PLOUGH AND MODE OF USING IT

the sum to be raised amongst them according to their ability: when this is done, the tax must be paid without delay: it takes up six or eight months time to make up the sums and finish the collections in the empire of Morocco."

The Jews in West Barbary are as completely under the control of the Moors, as if they were slaves, though they fancy themselves in some measure free: even their dress is regulated by a Moorish law; that of the men consists of a shirt, without a collar, and wide petticoat drawers that come tight below the knees; the sleeves of the shirt, which are of the full breadth, of coarse muslin cloth, fall a little below their elbows, and are not plaited in any way, but hang flowing: they wear above the shirt, a jacket with short sleeves to their elbows—the jacket is generally made of green woollen cloth, with a small collar, buttoned tight round the lower part of the neck; it is sometimes wrought with needle-work from the collar to the waist in front, with which, and small round buttons, made from the same materials, it is almost covered: they hook this together with wire hooks; and again over this, those who can afford it have a black cotton mantle, which comes over their shoulders, and falls down to the calves of their legs.

This is so contrived, that one end can be thrown over the left shoulder in such a manner as to discover the drawers: they are girded with sashes of various colours over the mantle round about their loins: they wear long beards, and black woollen caps on the back part of their heads, leaving the forehead uncovered, which: s shaved often, and kept smooth. The four merchants that lived in Mogadore, wore coloured silk handkerchiefs on their heads, covering their caps, and tied loosely under their chins: they also go bare legged, and wear black slippers on their feet, as the luxury of coloured slippers is forbidden them. In riding, they were formerly restricted to the ass alone, but now they use mules, which they are not, however, allowed to mount or ride within the gates of the city. When Jews or Jewesses are about to pass a mosque, or place of worship, they must take off their slippers, and carry them in their hands, going barefoot past it, and that too, until they enter another street.

The dress here described, is that of the wealthy who can afford it. but the greater part of the Jews in West Barbary, are poor, miserable, and covered with rags and vermin. A Jewess of the first class, is clad with a shirt made of muslin, that is very wide; the sleeves, not less than a yard, hang loosely down to the elbow, when the two hinder parts are doubled and fastened together behind their backs; the bosom of this shirt is wrought with fine needle-work on both sides; it laps over before, and covers part of the breasts: a white waistcoat, wrought in like manner, is superadded: the lower extremity of this is covered by a wrapper, in form of short petticoats, wrapped around above the hips, and just laps over in front; this is commonly made of green broadcloth, and falls down below the knees: the two lower corners in front, are covered with a fancifully cut. piece of red broadcloth—the whole is fastened together by a girdle round the hips, to which are suspended behind a number of red woollen cords of different lengths, hanging down with a piece of plated silver, or other metal, bent round each at its lowest end; these make a kind of tinkling when they walk by, striking against each other. Their hair is long, coarse, and black, and the principal part turned up, and fastened on the top of the head, while two small braids from behind each ear, are attached together at their extremities, and fall down to their girdles.

Married women of the first class, cover their heads with a flowing silk handkerchief. Both married and single women, are extremely fond of ornaments, and are generally corpulent: they wear amber and pearl necklaces, with golden hearts, set about with fine diamonds and other precious stones: many other ornaments are also hung to heir necklaces, which are frequently connected by golden chains: they wear silver or gold bracelets around their wrists and ankles, from one to two inches wide, enriched with enamel and precious stones. I examined several of these ornaments: they are made of the finest gold, silver, and stones, and the best amber: the weight of the four bracelets on the wrists and ankles of a young girl, (a broker's daughter,) was fourteen ounces, and they cost, together with her necklaces, ear and finger-rings, and other ornaments, about two thousand dollars. Those of the Jews who can get money, are excessively fond of ornamenting their wives and daughters, and setting off their charms to the very best advantage; but there are very few of them that have the ability: not more than twenty Jews in Mogadore can afford this expense; and but few of the rest can furnish their wives and daughters with bracelets of even base metal, washed over with silver or gold; yet every woman feels as if she were naked, without some ornaments of this description.

The Jews are forced to live in a town by themselves, called *el Milluh*, but the Moors enter it whenever they choose, without the smallest restraint. Should a Jew attempt to resist a Moor on any occasion, he is sure of getting a sound drubbing, and as his testimony cannot be taken against a Moor, any more than that of a negro slave in the

West Indies and the southern states of America, can be given against a white man; he is forced to pocket every affront, and content himself therewith.

The Jews' Sunday begins on Friday evening at sunset, after which time no Jew can even light a candle or lamp, or kindle a fire, or cook anything until Saturday night, at the same hour; so that they heat their ovens on Friday; put in their provisions before night, for their next day's meals, and let it stand in the ovens until Saturday noon, when it is taken out, and set on the table, or on the floor, by Moors, whom they contrive to hire for that purpose. Every Jew who can afford it, has brass or silver lamps hanging up in his house, which are lighted on Friday and not extinguished until Sunday morning: they burn either olive or *argan* oil. Their principal and standing Sunday dinner, is called *skanah*; it is made of peas baked in an oven for nearly twenty-four hours, with a quantity of beeves' marrow bones, (having very little meat on them) broken to pieces over them: it is a very luscious and fattening dish, and by no means a bad one: this, with a few vegetables, and sometimes a plum-pudding, good bread, and Jews' brandy, distilled from figs, and aniseed, and bittered with wormwood, makes up the repast of the Jews who call themselves rich.

The poor can only afford *skanah* and barley-bread on their Sunday, and live the rest of the week as they can. The men and boys attend their synagogues, (on their Sundays,) but these are no more than small rooms, where all join in jabbering over prayers in Hebrew, as fast as they can speak, everyone in his own natural tone of voice, making altogether a most barbarous kind of jargon.

The Jewish women are considered by the men as having no souls, nor are they allowed generally to enter the synagogues, nor do the women partake of their sacraments. The sacraments consist of bread and wine, and of circumcision. While in Mogadore, I attended a Jewish circumcision. The child being ready, and the friends present, the priest took him on his left arm, having a pair of silver tongs in his left hand, with which he gauged and prepared the parts, and performed the operation with a sharp knife he had in his right hand, cutting off a piece of the flesh, as well as all the foreskin: this appeared to me to be a painful and cruel operation, and it made the infant scream out most piteously.

The Jews circumcise at the age of eight days, and the Moors and Arabs at the age of eight years; the Arabs cut the foreskin and flesh off square, as well as the Jews; but with the Arabs, as I have before

A Jewish circumcism witnessed by the author in Mogadore

observed, it is a preventive of venereal disease, and not a religious rite. (For a view of the Jewish costume, and mariner of performing this ceremony in West Barbary, see page previous.)

During my journey towards Tangier, we put up at Sally, during the Jews' Sabbath, having two Jews in company, who had friends or relations in that place that entertained them, and furnished a supper. Before eating, they brought forward a cup in the form of a tankard, and some white bread, in which some green herbs had been chopped up, and mixed with it before baking: they all arose at once, formed a circle round the supper dish, consisting of boiled fowls, which was set on the floor, and when standing, all began to chant over their prayers in Hebrew, as fast as they could speak: there were about twenty in all, relations and visitors.

As I was ignorant of the Hebrew language, which they spoke, and which I am told, differs materially from that taught in the schools and colleges of our country, I could not join with them. This chant, discordant enough to be sure, to my ear, took up at least a quarter of an hour.

When they were about to finish, they passed round the bread, of which each one took a piece, and not to be singular, I took one also and ate it. After saying over a few more words, they handed round the cup to all, and each took a drink, keeping up their chant all the time—when it came round to me, I took it and drank a little: it was wine, made by steeping dry raisins in water, and to me not very palatable, being somewhat sour and bitter.

After the cup had gone round, all turned their faces to the east, bowed thrice, bending their bodies more than half way to the ground, still going on with their chant. As soon as they had done worshipping, they resumed their places round the dish, seized each other by the hand, giving it a convulsive grasp, and stamping at the same time with their feet: this terminated the ceremony.

The chant being finished, all took their seats around the dish as near as they could get, on their legs and on the floor, having first washed their hands; some vigorously seized the boiled fowls, which they soon carved, by pulling them to pieces, and then passed those pieces round to the company.

Their bread was made of barley-meal; this they dipped in the dish, after each bite, and called it a sop: the gravy in which they dipped their bread, was the liquor in which the fowls had been boiled, mixed with vinegar. This was on Friday evening, January the 6th, 1816, about 9 o'clock, p. m. On the next evening, they repeated the same ceremonies. After supper, they amused themselves by singing songs in Arabic, and telling stories, which they kept up with great glee until near midnight, when, at my entreaty, they retired for the night, as I wished to get some rest.

CHAPTER 29

Mr. Willshire is Grossly Insulted by Moors

About the last of November, a courier came to Mogadore from the emperor to the governor, ordering him not to suffer a Moor to serve either a Christian or Jew, under any pretence whatever, or to live in their houses, under the severest penalty: this letter was no sooner read, than the news flew to every part of the town. In consequence of this order, Rais Bel Cossim, Bel Mooden, and a Moor of the name of Soliman, who had been constantly in and about Mr. Willshire's house, durst not return even to take their leave: the life of a Christian previous to this was hardly safe, even in the city, without a Moor in company to ward off the insults of the boys and those of the Moors who were vicious or fanatical. New orders had also been given to the guards of the water-port, not to allow any ne to go on board vessels, except the captains and crews, without a special order from the governor.

On New-Year's day, captains Mackay and Henderson, of whom I have before spoken, dined with Mr. Willshire: when they went down to go on board their vessels, Mr. Willshire and myself went to take a walk round the water-port, it being low tide: the guards ran after us, seized hold of Mr. Willshire, and turning him round, bid him, in an insulting tone, to go back, uttering the most abusive language; and drawing their scimitars, they threatened to cut him down. We had no Moor with us to witness this insult, but Mr. Willshire's spirit could not brook this indignity, and he rebuked these fellows in a very resolute manner, bidding defiance to them and the *alcayd*, and told them that if they offered to touch him again, he would revenge himself instantly, and at any rate would complain to the emperor, and would cause them to lose their heads for insulting a consul and a merchant.

I advised him to return to the port, which he did; but the Moors were so enraged, that they ran with all speed to the *alcayd*, and told him that Mr. Willshire had beat them; that he called them hard names, and defied the power of the *Sultan*. Immediately soldiers were sent after him, who came up with us before we got to his house: they insisted on taking him before the *alcayd* forthwith by force, if he would not go without; he told them, however, that he must and would wait for his Jew interpreter, Nahory, ,and that then he would come: this answer was carried to the *alcayd*, and in a few moments Ben Nahory made his appearance, and they went before the *alcayd* together.

The *alcayd* reprimanded Mr. Willshire for having cursed the *Sultan*, and advised him to settle the business, by giving a present to the guards, as they would depose against him before the Cadi, which if they should do, he would be obliged to go up to Morocco to the emperor, and he (the governor) said he could not be answerable for the result. Mr. Willshire defended himself so well by the help of his interpreter, who was a cunning Jew, that his accusers began to lower their tone a little: he stated that he had the *Sultan's* letter, which ordered the governors and *alcayds* to see his person protected from insult, as well as his property, and that the late order had deprived him of the aid and evidence of a Moor, to which he was entitled by that letter: he added, that he would write the *Sultan* an account of the insult immediately, and of the villainy of the port guards, but would not pay a *blanquille*, (*i. e.* a farthing) to anyone.

The *alcayd* said he was ordered to protect him and the other Christians in the port, and wished them to be respected, but they must respect themselves, and byway of an excuse, remarked that the consuls at Tangier did not go down with the captains that have the honour of dining with them, to their boats after dinner; that this was derogatory to the etiquette due to their office; but, at the same time, calling the guards, he told them that Mr. Willshire was the *Sultan's* Consul; that they must never lay a finger on him; but if he should wish to go off in one of the boats of the vessels in port, they must permit him to get into the boat, but prevent it from going off until they sent him information, in order that he might give a permit for him to go on board. He further told the guards that they had done very wrong, and if they were not careful in future he should dismiss them.

The guards were very angry, and said it was intolerable for a Moor to be insulted with impunity by a Christian dog; that they would swear against him before the *Cadi* that instant; that they did not fear his (the governor's) power, and theu would appeal to the *Sultan* and abide his decision. As they were going to the *Cadi*, the *alcayd* told them if they did contrary to his orders it would cost them their heads, and bid them return to their duty immediately; and in order that there might be no further complaint on their part, he would make inquiry, and have justice done to them as well as to the consul: thus ended the affair, which I at first was apprehensive would be attended with more serious consequences. Mr. Willshire, however, took care to send presents to the *Addals*, or four assistants of the *alcayd*, who took occasion to convince the *alcayd*, that the guards were in the wrong—however, we durst not go out walking or riding as formerly, but were obliged to restrict ourselves to the city, and I had time to examine it within and round about.

The city of Mogadore, called Swearah by the Moors and Arabs, or *the beautiful picture*, is situated on the Atlantic ocean, in latitude 31. 15. (thirty-one degrees, fifteen minutes) north, and longitude 9—(nine degrees) west from London. It is built somewhat in form of an oblong square: its length from north to south is about three-fourths of a mile, and its greatest breadth is not more than half a mile: it stands on a peninsula that has been recovered from the sea, which washes its walls on the W. N. W. and south sides every tide, and is sometimes completely surrounded by water at high spring tides. The walls are built of stone and lime, generally six feet thick at their base, and about twenty feet in height, surmounted with small turrets; and have batteries of cannon on them at every angle: the walls generally are made of rough stone and small sea pebbles, mixed and cemented together by liquid lime-mortar, filling up every crack solid; they are plastered over with this kind of stucco within and without, and are thick, solid, very firm, and hard.

On the eastern angle, as you approach the gates, there is a round tower built of hewn stone, thirty feet high, mounted with about forty pieces of brass and iron cannon, that command the approaches of the city on the east side, assisted by the four batteries on the N. E. angle, and a heavy battery on the water-port. It is divided into three parts—*el Ksebah*, or the strong and lion-like fortress, is the southernmost, and is surrounded by a double wall on the east and south sides; a single wall, but very thick, next the sea, where there is a strong bomb-proof battery, mounting about forty pieces of cannon of different calibres, and most of them are of brass: this is its whole defence on the seaboard. Vessels of war might anchor, in smooth weather, within half cannon shot of the town, in thirty fathoms water, rocky bottom. This town is separated from the main town by a strong wall, whose gates are regularly shut at 8 o'clock every evening, and not opened until broad daylight the next morning.

The Christian merchants reside in the fortress, and the four Jew merchants keep their goods in it. The next is the main town, where the market is held, and where the artificers live: there is a very handsome square set apart in that section of the town for a grain market, surrounded by small shops, kept by Moors and Jews: these shops are on the ground floor, have a door, but no window to them, and are so very small that the keeper can sit at his ease in the centre and reach nearly every article in them. They, among other things, manufacture at Mogadore large quantities of *haicks*, which are made of woollen yarn, spun by hand with a common iron spindle, and wove in common rough looms similar to such as we made use of, even in America, not more than fifty years ago—they throw the shuttle by hand, and weave their pieces about five yards long and five feet wide, and they are sold from the looms at about two dollars each, but are not allowed to be exported by sea: they also make axes and many other iron tools, such as adzes, scimitars, knives, &c.

East of the main town is the town occupied by the blacks, in a corner or kind of a triangle made by the outer wall: it is said to contain two thousand free blacks: this part is also walled in by itself, and has its gates shut every night. The negroes that are free enjoy nearly all the privileges of the Moors, being of the same religion; still they are not allowed to live together with the Moors promiscuously.

The fourth division is the Jews' town, or Millah: it is very confined, and occupies the northwest angle of the city: the sea washes its outer wall every tide, and has nearly beat it through on the west side: it is divided from the principal town by a high strong wall. The Millah has but one outer gate, which is on its eastern side, near the north city gate; this is always strongly guarded by Moors, and has a governor or *alcayd* to adjust and settle disputes between the Jews, and between them and the Moors. The water-port is two hundred yards south of the city, within the outer wall—this is a wall built of hewn stone, with several broad and lofty arches, through which the tide flows and ebbs: the wall is about twenty feet thick, and has a strong battery of heavy cannon well mounted on it, for the defence of the harbour: it is extremely well built; its arches are well turned, and the whole work would bear a comparison with a European fortress.

The harbour spreads itself before the town to the south, and is shielded from the sea by an island about two miles long, and half a mile broad, only distant from the water-port point about five hundred yards. Between the island and the water-port, the vessels enter, keeping the island side close on board, until they run down half the length of it, when they may anchor in two and a half fathoms at low water, within a cable's length of the island, and with good cables and anchors ride safe during three quarters of the year; but vessels drawing over fourteen feet water cannot ride secure on account of the shallowness of the harbour.

In the months of December, January, and February, strong gales prevail from the westward, which heave in such heavy swells round the two ends of this island, that what seamen call the send or swing of the sea, breaks the strongest cables, and forces all the vessels in this port on shore, in the winter of 1815, an English brig was driven on shore with a full cargo, and totally lost; another parted her cables, and was driven fast towards the water-port, when the master and crew deserted her in their boat, in hopes of saving their lives; but the boat was upset, and all hands were either drowned or dashed to pieces against the rocks; the brig's cables, however, caught round some craggy rocks, which held her through the remainder of the gale, though within a few feet of the rocks astern.

An American schooner's crew were also lost in this port a few years ago, together with her supercargo, in consequence of quitting the vessel, and taking to their boat, while the captain, who was soliciting assistance from the other vessels in port, was saved, and the schooner was also finally saved, though she had been totally abandoned: it is in the winter a very dangerous port, and any vessel entering it should have three good cables and anchors, to moor her head and stern by, and should strike her yards and topmasts immediately.

The island is called Mogadore by the Europeans, and was thus named by the Portuguese or Spaniards, when they first partially surveyed this coast, and thence the European name of Mogadore, is derived for the town, and not from the sanctuary or saint-house near it, which in Arabic is called *Milliah*. This island serves as a State Prison for the Moorish empire: it is fortified and strongly guarded, commonly containing not less than one thousand state prisoners, who have mostly been *alcayds* and military men, and who are frequently pardoned and restored to their former posts again, after a few years' trial of their fortitude and patience there in irons. Provisions are sent to the island twice a week in good weather. All communication with the island is forbidden to strangers, under pain of death.

On a rocky point, without the water-port, nearest to the island, stands a circular battery, to defend the entrance of the harbour, and protect the island: on the east side of the harbour, near the *Sultan's* palace, there is also a circular battery, well built of stone, calculated to mount twenty guns, but the guns that had been mounted on it were taken away, under an impression that they might fall into the hands of the Arabs, who attacked Swearah during the quarrel for the succession, which was terminated in the elevation of the present Sultan, Muley Soliman, to the Moorish throne.

Swearah or Mogadore was built by Sidi Mohammed, the father of Muley Soliman, who spared no pains or expense in making it correspond with its name: it is the only tolerable seaport in the Moorish dominions, except Tangier, and the only one in which foreign vessels are allowed a kind of free trade, or one without special licenses: the houses are built of rough stone and lime; are from one to three stories high, and nearly all have flat terraced roofs: the streets are narrow, and some of them almost entirely covered with houses arched or projecting over them, particularly in the fortress part: the buildings at first, it is said, were erected under the inspection of artisans, who were brought from Europe for the purpose: it is by far the neatest town in the empire, and is computed to contain about thirty thousand Moors and blacks, and six thousand Jews.

During the contest for the succession, at the death of Muley Eitzid, who reigned a short time after the death of Sidi Mohammed, Swearah was attacked by surprise in the night, and about three thousand of the assailants entered the fortress part over the walls, and actually got possession of the streets; but they were soon destroyed by the garrison and town's people, from the roofs of their houses; and the army before it, consisting of field-Moors and Arabs, were put to flight, it has been since visited and nearly depopulated twice by the plague, which spread terror and devastation in all the western part of the empire. Mercantile trade was here encouraged by its founder, and flourished to a great extent; large quantities of wheat were sent from hence to Spain and Portugal; sheep's wool and the gums were also shipped in great abundance; namely, *gum-sandarach, arabic,* &c. &c.—almonds, olives, dates, dried figs, and large quantities of olive oil, bees-wax., and honey—*annis, cummin,* worm, and other medicinal seeds—pomegranate peel, and many other drugs—goat, calf, and a few camels' skins, and camels' hair—*haicks* for the Guinea trade, and many other articles.

Their imports were bar-iron and steel, knives, and other cutlery, raw cotton, and many kinds of manufactured cotton goods, woollen cloths, silks, and silk handkerchiefs, teas, sugars, spices, gold and silver ornaments, pearls, amber beads, small Dutch looking-glasses, German goods, *platillas, nankeens,* lumber, &c. &c. There were at one time no less than thirty Christian mercantile houses established there: the duties on imports are ten *per centum*, taken in kind when the goods are landed, except on the articles of iron, steel, and cotton, on which the duties are paid in cash at the same rate: (the government allowing the importer a short credit on the duties:) this is the duty the *Sultan* is entitled to by the *Koran* as tithes, or tenths, according to their sacred code, for he is the religious, as well as the temporal sovereign. The duties on exports are regulated by an imperial order, and are not steady.

Trade has been depressed of late years by enormous duties on exports, and by prohibitions, so much so, that there are now only two or three respectable Christian establishments in Mogadore, and those who conduct them are forced to put up with frequent insult and imposition: they do little business to a profit, and must, if it does not soon alter for the better, quit the place altogether. It is the policy of the present emperor, who is absolute, to keep the people as poor as possible, that they may not have it in their power to rebel; for a rebellious army cannot be supported there without money, or kept together without an immediate hope of plunder, and the Moorish government has very little to fear from a partial and ill organized insurrection, the chiefs of which must have money as well as bravery, and display good conduct, or they will soon be forsaken.

The *Sultan* commenced his system by shutting the ports of Santa Cruz, Saffy, Rhabat, Azamore, Darlbeida, &c. and ordering the foreign merchants residing in them to go to Mogadore or Swearah, where he said they should be protected. Soon afterwards they began to prohibit the introduction of some articles, then the exportation of many— such as wool, wheat, olive oil, &c. and laid a duty that amounted to a prohibition on several other articles of exportation; when the people murmured, they were told it was a sin to trade with men who did not follow the true and only holy religion on earth: that their prophet had strictly forbidden such traffic as would be liable to corrupt their morals and defile them in the sight of God: that this sin had been committed, and that God was now taking vengeance of his people by sending the locusts and the plague that followed them, laying waste the country, and unpeopling so many fine cities.

These were arguments which had great weight with the superstitious Moors, aided by the plague which at that time raged with dreadful fury, and swept off three-fourths of the inhabitants of Mogadore, Sally, and several other towns; the whole garrison of *el Ksebbah*, on Tensift River, &c. &c. Several of the Christian merchants died also of the plague, and many of the most respectable mercantile Moors: this caused an almost total stagnation of business, which stagnation has been increasing, if possible, ever since, owing to these causes and other heavy commercial restraints imposed by the present emperor.

Should any of the maritime nations declare war against the Moors, Mogadore might be easily taken and destroyed, though the place could not be retained any length of time: a few sloops of war of a light draught of water might enter the harbour and sail down near the south end of the island, where they might land troops and take possession of it, which being high, commands the town; here they might construct batteries, and beat down its walls at their leisure. The country near it is covered with nothing but drifts of sand for a distance beyond cannon shot. The Moors are very awkward gunners, though as brave as men can be, believing that if they venture even up to the very mouth of a cannon, they cannot die one moment before the time appointed by fate, nor in any other manner than that which was predestined by the Almighty before they were created, and even from the foundation of the world.

CHAPTER 30

Horsemanship

The Moors are a stout athletic race of men, and are generally of about five feet ten inches in height. They sprung from the Bereberies, or old inhabitants of the north and western parts of northern Africa, together with the descendants of the Carthagenians. and various Greek and Roman colonies on those coasts, conquered by and commixed with the Arabs or Saracens who passed the isthmus of Suez, and subjugated the north of Africa under the caliphs of the pretended prophet Mohammed. Fez is at present the great capital of the empire, and chief residence of the emperor, who is styled by the Moors and Arabs *el Sultan*, (the *Sultan*,) or as they pronounce it, *Sooltan*. Suse has become independent of the Moors.

The Moors are all strict followers of the Mohammedan doctrine, and firm predestinarians. I call the doctrine Mohammedan instead of Mahometan, because the name of their prophet is pronounced, both by the Moors and Arabs, Mohammed, and both of them pronounce their letters very distinctly, and with their mouths open like the Spaniards, giving to every letter its full sound; for though they write with characters, and do not know how to form a Roman letter with a pen, yet a person understanding letters, who hears them speak, would say they were perfectly familiar with the Roman alphabet, and laid more emphasis and stress on the letters, by means of which they speak their language, than any other people on earth.

The Moors, in general, do not learn to read and write, but their *Talbs* are learned men, who take great pains to become acquainted with the principles of their own and the ancient Arabic language, and with the laws of the *Koran*, which is held by them, as the *Bible* is by Christians, to be a sacred book, and to contain nothing but divine revelation. The *Talbs* transact all the business that requires writing, and serve alternately as scriveners, lawyers, and priests. The Moors use no bells for their places of worship, but in the towns and cities, their religious houses have high minarets or steeples, with flat tops &nd a kind of balustrade round them: to the tops of these the *Talbs* ascend to call the people at stated times to prayers, and as the steeples are very high, and the *Talbs* are accustomed to call aloud, they are heard at a great distance, particularly when all is still in the city.

Their times of prayer are before daylight in the morning, at about mid-day, about the middle of the afternoon, at sunset, and again before they retire to rest, about 8 or 9 o'clock in the evening. The *Talbs*, who are on the steeples before daylight in the morning, commence by calling all the faithful to prayers: their voices sound most harmoniously, and thrill through the air in a singular manner. I was always awakened by them myself while I staid at Mogadore, and often went to the window to hear them; their call reminded me of my duty also. After they summoned all the faithful to attend prayers, they either rehearsed particular passages from the Koran, or sang some sacred poetry with a loud and piercing, but at the same time a very melodious and pleasing tone of voice. The Moors who live near the places of worship go in, join with the *Talbs*, and pray aloud together; but by far the greatest number perform their devotions in their own rooms.

The *Talbs*, I am informed, perform their religious duties, which are very fatiguing, merely from motives of piety—they do not receive the smallest remuneration either from the prince, or people, in any shape or way whatever. All worship by turning their faces to the east, and bow their heads in the dust like the wandering Arabs: they wash their bodies all over with water before prayers, as well as their hands and faces, for which purpose, within the walls of their mosques or churches, they have wells or fountains of water, and large stone basins in which to bathe. When they appear before God (as they call it) in their places of worship, they divest themselves of all superfluous ornaments and clothing, and even of their breeches; after purifying with water, they wrap themselves decently up in their *haick* or blanket only, and go through their ceremonies with signs of the most profound devotion.

If a Christian enters a Mohammedan place of worship, without one of the *Cadi*, or with a guard, he must either change his religion, by having his head shaven, undergoing the operation of circumcision, and confessing there is but one God, and that Mohammed is his holy prophet, &c. or suffer instant death—but I have ventured to look into them from the street. The court leading to the mosque was paved with tiles, and kept very clean, with stone basins filled with pure water on each side for the purposes of purification; though I durst not approach so near as to see in what manner the interior part was arranged, but I was informed they were entirely free from ornaments.

The women are not generally permitted to enter their houses of religious worship, nor even to appear in the streets, unless they are completely covered by their clothing, which going over their heads, is held m such a manner by their hands on the inside, as only to permit them to peep out with one eye, to discover and pick their way; so that no Moor or Christian can see their faces. In the streets, they are very seldom seen, and are so extremely fleshy, that they waddle, rather than walk along, like fat and clumsy ducks.

No Moor will marry a wife until she is well fatted by her father; and if it is not in the husband's power afterwards to keep her in the same good case and condition, or rather, to improve upon it, he is dissatisfied, and endeavours to get clear of her, which he very often effects, for he will not keep a wife unless she is very fleshy, or bed with what he calls "*a death skeleton.*" The women visit each other, and walk together on the tops of their houses, but even the husband cannot enter the room they are in when uncovered, or get a sight of his neighbour's wife or daughter, being strictly forbidden by his religion to look on any other woman than his own wife or wives:—thus the Moors, when they receive company, sit down with them on the ground outside of their houses, where they converse together; but notwithstanding all these precautions, as the women are very amorous, they manage to introduce their gallants by means of the female covering, and the privilege they enjoy of visiting each other, and get their lovers off by the same means undiscovered.

The Moors go off in large numbers every year, forming a great caravan, on a pilgrimage to Mecca, and return in three or four years; every Moslemin being by law obliged to visit the tomb of his prophet once in his lifetime, if he can afford to pay the expenses of his journey. The men who have been to Mecca and returned, are dignified by the name of *el ajjh*, (or the pilgrim,) and the women who go and return, (for there are a few who venture,) are allowed the privilege of wearing the *haick*, or man's blanket; of walking the streets uncovered, like men, and of conversing with them promiscuously, as they may deem fit, being considered holy women, and as possessing souls by special grace and favour.

Every Moor who is born an idiot, or becomes delirious, is considered a saint, and is treated with the greatest attention and respect by everyone; is clothed, and fed, and taken the greatest care of by the whole community; and, do what he will, he cannot commit a crime in the eye of their law.

Soon after my arrival at Mogadore, about the 15th of November, 1815, the feast of expiation was celebrated by the Moors, at which every Mohammedan is by law obliged to kill a sheep, if it is possible for him to procure one; if not, each kills such other animal as he can obtain: the rich (if liberal) kill a number proportioned to their wealth and inclination, and distribute them amongst their relations, or the poor who have none to kill. Rais bel Cossim (*i. e.* Captain bel Cossim) killed seven sheep: they had been bought long before, and were well fatted for the purpose.

The first day of the feast was spent in visiting, and in giving and receiving presents or gifts; and the second in military parade. On the morning of that day, I accompanied Mr. Willshire to the top of a house, formerly occupied by a Mr. Chiappi, deceased, who was the Portuguese Consul at Mogadore for many years: this house was, before it went to decay, the largest and most elegant in that city: it stood near, and overlooked the eastern wall. From that place, we saw from thirteen to fifteen hundred Arabian horses, fleet as the wind, and full of fire, mounted by Moors and Arabs, who sat on strong Moorish saddles that came up high before and behind, covered with rich quilted scarlet broadcloth. They were paraded between the outer and main walls of the city:—the horsemen were dressed with red caftans or vests, not generally worn by them, except on great occasions: these were covered with worsted *haicks*, wove transparent like bunting for ships' flags: each rider was armed with a long Moorish musket, and had a knife or scimitar hanging loosely by his side: they wore on their heads either white turbans, twisted and wound many times around, or a red cap, in token of their being regular imperial soldiers, or else a fold of their *haick*: their bridle-bits were the most powerful of the Arabian kind.

The horses were all studs, and wore their whole natural quantity of main and tail unmutilated in any part, and consequently retained all their natural fire, beauty, strength, and pride: each horse was furnished with a head-piece, resembling the stall of a bridle at top, and a halter below—this stall or head-piece, was made of the richest scarlet cord and velvet, with fringe hanging down over, and nearly covering his eyes, and a large pendulous pad of scarlet velvet cloth under each ear: the neck of each was adorned with a very elegant scarlet cord, having a handsome knob and tassel underneath: these trappings were solely for ornament, and not for use, and put on before the bridle.

Each had besides, a small red cord about his neck, to which was fastened a number of little bags, made of fine red Morocco leather—these bags, I learned on inquiry, were stuffed with scraps of paper, covered with Arabic writing, furnished to the owner of the horse by jugglers; and, as they pretend, serve as a charm to ward off the effects of "*evil eyes*" or witchcraft, in which they all believe: the Moors and Arabs are so firmly attached to this superstitious opinion, that they believe both themselves and their horses are in imminent danger without this favourite charm.

The Moorish and Arabian saddle, which I consider to be the very best that can be invented by man to keep the rider steady in his seat, is fastened on by a strong girth under the horse's belly, and by one round his breast, but without any crupper: the stirrups are made of broad pieces of sheet iron or brass, and for the most part plated with silver—the bottom of them is as long as a man's foot, so that he can shift the position of his feet in them at pleasure: they are kept exceedingly bright, and are taken up short and tied to the saddle by braided leather thongs, so that in order to support himself firmly in his saddle, the rider has only to press his feet to the horse's sides, near his flanks, his knees on the lower part of the saddle; thus resting at five points at one and the same time.

The bridle is of that kind which will either stop the fiercest horse in an instant, or snap off his lower jaw—so that the rider has his horse under the most perfect command possible. This body of horsemen, thus mounted and equipped, were reviewed by the *Bashaw* and *Alcayd*, or military and civil governors. There were also five or six thousand foot soldiers assembled for the same purpose: these were dressed in *haicks* and red caps, and armed with muskets and daggers. After the review, the exercises began by a discharge of twenty-four pieces of cannon, mounted on the different batteries about the city, and then followed a kind of sham fight, which was begun near the northern gate, between two bodies of infantry: they marched forward to the attack, and each poured in an irregular fire, which was supported and kept up in almost one continual blaze by successive advancing lines, until it seemed necessary to bring forward the heavy cavalry, in order to arrest the progress of a solid column of men, that kept slowly and constantly advancing upon the opposing troops.

The expected signal was at length given: the whole of the cavalry was instantly in motion: it advanced in squadrons of about one hundred, in close order, and at full speed, and seemed to fly like the wind: the distance between the opposing forces was near one fourth of a mile: the horsemen shouting loudly, "*hah-hah! hah-hah!*" raised themselves on their stirrups, took a deliberate aim with their long muskets, when within five yards of the enemy's lines, and poured in their fire while going at their greatest speed. I expected they would inevitably dash in amongst the infantry, and trample many of them to death; but the moment the men had fired, they brought their horses down upon their haunches, and stopping them short, reined them instantly round, to make room for the next approaching squadron, while the horses of the first squadron walked steadily and leisurely back, giving time for the riders to reload their muskets at their ease: thus furiously attacked by numerous squadrons, in quick succession, and so closely, the infantry were soon broken and dispersed, by which means the cavalry remained apparent masters of the field.

Nothing of the kind could exceed the ardour, activity, and intelligence, displayed by those noble looking and well trained horses; they seemed almost to fly to the attack, and looked as if determined to rush through the opposing host, and trample it to atoms; but when the riders had fired their muskets, and the horses were turned about the other way, they were perfectly calm in an instant, and walked on leisurely until they were again faced round towards the enemy; then their eyes seemed to kindle with fire; they pawed up the dust, which they seemed to snuff up into their wide-stretched nostrils, and into which one might see, as they then appeared, nearly up to their eyes: they snorted and pranced about in such a manner, that nothing short of the heavy and true Arabian bridle could have been capable of checking or keeping them in subjection, and nothing short of the Moorish or Arabian saddle, could have prevented their riders from being dashed against the ground.

The long spurs of the horsemen had gored their flanks, so as to make the blood stream out, which, uniting with their sweat, formed a kind of streaked froth, that nearly covering their sides, dropped fast upon the ground, whilst the severe working of the bit upon their mouths, caused them to bleed profusely. The dazzling of their stirrups and arms in the sun, the rattling of their spurs against their stirrups, and the clashing of their arms against each other; the beautiful appearance of the squadrons of horses; the cracking of musketry, and continual shouting of the mock combatants, produced an effect truly imposing, and I was of opinion that no lines of infantry, of equal numbers, however well formed and commanded, would be capable of withstanding their impetuous and repeated shocks, when actually attacked: this was truly a superb school for horsemanship.

Sidi Hamet, my old master, had borrowed and mounted Mr. Willshire's fine horse, and seemed to be in all his glory while exercising him like the others. After they had nearly finished the sham-fight, he, together with a line of Moors, consisting of about fifteen or twenty, commenced their last career towards the enemy: they had a. quarter of a mile to ride, and all with long muskets in their hands: they set off their horses at full speed, in a line when on their seats; then turning over, they placed their heads upon their saddles, and rode with their feet in the air. and their backs towards the horse's heads, for a considerable part of the distance; then regaining their seats by a sudden movement, they rose in their stirrups, fired off their pieces close to the wall, reined their horses around, and returned again to their post. Many of these horses were extremely fleet and beautiful, and seemed as much to exceed in spirit, strength, and courage, the first-rate race horses I had ever seen in Europe or America, as those fine animals excel the common plough horse.

The Moors soon wear their horses down by hard service, and then put them into mills to grind their grain, as there is scarcely such a tiling as a wind or water-mill, wherewith to grind their breadstuff, to be found in the Moorish empire. The mares are never rode or worked, and are kept solely for the purpose of breeding; and I found that what I had considered as an exaggerated account of the good qualities attributed to the Arabian horse, fell far short of his real merits; for though the most proud, fierce, and fiery of the horse kind, he is, at the same time, the most docile of those noble animals.

The true Arabian horse is about fourteen to sixteen hands in height; his body is long, round, and slender; his limbs small, clean, and straight; he is square- breasted and round-quartered; his neck well set and slender, with a beautiful natural curve; his head small, with a face inclining to a curve, from the fop of the head to the nostrils, with eyes full, bright, quick, and intelligent—many of them are of a beautiful cream colour, and frequently spotted with black, and vary in colour from a light sorrel, through all the shades of bay and chesnut, to the deepest jet black: they are strong-jointed, and full of sinew—naturally docile, and very active; but. if they become in the least vicious, they are doomed to the mill for the remainder of their days. It was with much regret I learned that these beautiful and serviceable animals could not be exported from either the Moorish dominions, or any 'other of the Barbary states, without a special permission, as a private favour from the reigning prince, which is very seldom granted, and only on particular and important occasions.

The Arabs inhabiting Morocco, live in tents, in a wandering state; for the true Arabs will not be confined within walls, and are a distinct race of men from the Moors. They keep large herds of cattle, horses, camels, sheep, goats, and asses, making use of the milk of all the females for butter and for drink: they supply the cities with butter, which they make by the simple process of putting the milk into a goatskin, the hair side in, hanging it up by the legs, and shaking it by the help of a rope, by which it is fastened: when the butter is made, they pack it, hair and all, into earthen jars that hold from two to four pounds each, and in that state, carry it to market without salting, selling the butter, jar, and all, for a mere trifle: they cultivate nearly all the plane land that is cultivated in the empire of Morocco, (as the Bereberies till the hilly country and sides of mountains,) except the grounds in the immediate vicinity of the cities, which they do not approach for the purposes of agriculture, those being cultivated and dressed by the Moors and their slaves.

They live in families or sections of tribes, and pitch their tents in companies of from twenty to one hundred and fifty tents, each tent containing one family: these tents when pitched, are called a *Douhar*: they elect a chief to each of these *douhars*, whom they dignify with the title of *Alcayd* or *Sheick*, for the time being; their authority, however, is rather of an advisory than mandatory kind. Near seed time, they remove and pitch their *douhar* (or encampment) near the spot they mean to cultivate, and plough and sow the land with wheat, barley, corn, or peas: they fence in some parcels of land with good high stone fences, particularly orchards of fig-trees, but for the most part they are entirely open: the sowing being finished, they remove again, for the sake of pasture, to other parts of the same province, in which they continue to reside, as they cannot move out of a province without leave being first obtained from the emperor: thus they wander from place to place, until near harvest time, when they return and gather in their crops which they have sowed, and which are considered safe from the flocks, herds, and hands of other tribes, by common consent or interest, as all rove about in a similar way, having no fixed habitations; yet sometimes one tribe sows, and another reaps the fruit of its labour, but that is only done by force of arms.

The Moorish Arabs are rather below the middle stature: of a dark complexion, resembling that between the *mulatto* and a white man, with long black hair and black eyes: they are strong and healthy: they wear round their bodies a woollen *haick*, which does not cover their heads, and go without any other clothing: their legs and feet are generally bare; their beards long; their cheek-bones high; their noses regularly hooked; their lips thin; and they are as hardy a race of men as exists; perhaps, indeed, with the exception of the wandering Arabs.

The women wear a kind of a garment made of a *haick*, through the midst of which they thrust their head and arms to keep it up—it hangs down to their knees, and nearly covers their breasts; they have a fold behind, like those living on the desert, in which they carry their young children; they all stoop forward very much; are treated by their husbands as mere necessary slaves; are obliged to milk the cows, camels, mares, goats, sheep, and asses; make the butter, and spin and weave the tent-cloth and clothing by hand for themselves and families. They both spin and weave in the same manner as the Arab women of the desert, and bring all the water they use in large pitchers on their shoulders, let the distance be ever so great: they take care of, and help to draw the water for the flocks of sheep, and goats, and herds of cattle; but the men manage the camels and horses.

They grind their wheat and barley in their hand-mills, which are the same as on the desert and in Suse, as already described, and they make cakes, which they roast in the fire. The women are, in fact, complete slaves: they are obliged to strike their tents when they remove, and pack them on camels, with all the other stuff that is possessed by the family—to pitch the tent again, and pack away the stuff, &c. &c. while the men take upon themselves to lord it over them, and drive them about at pleasure, only looking after the flocks and herds, and punishing the women and girls, if any are lost: the men also plough and sow the land, and attend to the reaping and threshing out the corn. The sickle they reap with is nothing more than a knife with a blade of about a foot long, with the point bent inwards: the principal part of the labour in this business, they also oblige the women to perform.

Their law permits them to have seven wives, but it is recommended to them by their prophet to have only one, in order to prevent contention in the family. When they increase, however, in wealth or substance, they need more help, and instead of hiring or buying slaves, they take more wives; and on this economical and agreeable plan, they make out to manage the affairs of their household.

They are the same race of people in appearance and manners, as the Arabs of the desert, and have bartered their liberty for the comforts afforded by a country susceptible of cultivation. The Arabs are said to have continued migrating gradually from the deserts and other parts of Arabia into Africa, ever since the irruptions of the first Saracens, by joining themselves in small numbers to the returning caravans which go yearly from Morocco, Algiers, Tunis, Tripoli, &c. on a pilgrimage to visit the tomb of their prophet at Mecca. These caravans carry large quantities of goods with them, and make a trading trip of it, as well as a religious duty; and many of the pilgrims return home very rich for Moors.

CHAPTER 31

The Present Arabs and Ancient Jews Compared

Soon after I was seized on as a slave by the wandering Arabs of the great Western Desert, I was struck with the simplicity of their lives and manners, and contrasted the circumstances of their keeping camels, living in tents, and wandering about from day to day, with the simplicity of the lives of the old Jewish patriarchs, who also lived in tents, had camels, and wandered about from place to place; possessed men-servants and maid-servants—that is, they owned slaves; but as they for the most part lived in countries where the soil was capable of culture, they also had flocks of sheep and goats, and herds of cattle, and asses; yet the patriarchs lived in a thirsty land for a part of the time, and were often in want of water, as well as of bread. My mind was also strongly impressed with the similarity between the patriarchal form of government, and that prevailing among the Arabs at the present day, (as at time of first publication), which is, in the strictest sense of the word, paternal; the father of each family being its supreme and absolute head: the wandering Arabs will submit to no other control, and they actually reverence their fathers and the old men of their tribe next to the Deity himself, and pay, without the least apparent compulsion, the most cheerful and implicit obedience to their orders and wishes.

When I became more acquainted with the Arabs, I observed that the manner of salutation between strangers was very much like that of the Jewish fathers, as recorded in *Holy Writ*, and which also prevailed among the inhabitants of the country where they sojourned. When a stranger approached an Arab's tent, he first finds out which way it is pitched; then, going round until he gets directly in front, he draws near slowly, until within about one hundred yards and stops, but always with his weapon in his hand, ready for defence, and then turns his back towards the tent: when he is perceived by those in and about the tent, (who are always upon the lookout,) and they come forth, he bows himself nearly to the earth twice, and worships: upon which one from the tent takes some water in a bowl, and advances towards him; this is done by the head of the family, if he be at home, or by his eldest son: if none of the males are present, one of the women goes forward with her bowl of water, or something else, either to eat or drink, if they have any; if not, they take a skin, or roll of tent-cloth, to make a shelter with for the stranger.

As they come within a few yards of the stranger, they ask, "Is it peace?" and being answered in the affirmative, they mutually say, "Peace be with you, with your father's house, your family, and all you possess;" then touching the fingers of the right hands together, they snap them, and carrying them to their lips, kiss them, which is the same with them as to kiss each other's hand; and thence, I presume, is derived the compliment now in such general use among the polite Spaniards, which is to say, in saluting a gentleman, "*Beso de usted las manos*"—I kiss your hands; if a lady, "I kiss your feet."

The Arab manner of worshipping the Deity, as I have already described, is by bowing themselves to the earth, and touching their faces to the ground: after bowing to the ground six times, they say, "God is great and good, and Mohammed is his holy prophet:" this is their confession of faith. After that, they offer up their petitions, that God will keep them under his special protection; that he will direct them in the right way; that he will lead them to fountains or wells of living water; that God will scatter their enemies, and deliver them from all those who lie in wait to do them mischief; that he will prosper their journeys, and enrich them with the spoil of their enemies, &c. and they afterwards recite some poetry, which they call sacred.

Since my being redeemed, I have been told that the form of worship now in practice among those people, was taught them by Mohammed; but as these forms do not differ materially from the forms of worship practised by Abraham and the other old patriarchs, and those of the people among whom they dwelt in the land of Canaan and elsewhere, I am inclined to believe that the artful prophet did not change their ancient mode of worshipping the Deity, but on the contrary, simplified and sanctioned their long established customs, which had continued among that singular race of men ever since the time of Abraham; and that the only innovations or alterations he ventured to make in that respect, were in appointing set times for performing those religious duties; enjoining, besides, frequent purifications, by washing themselves with water, and thus inculcating cleanliness, so indispensably necessary to preserve health in hot countries, as a religious duty.

When travelling along the great desert, near its northern border, we fell in with flocks of sheep and goats, which were kept by the women and children, who were also obliged to water them; and when, after our arrival in Suse, while we were travelling on its immense plane, and many small cities or towns were in sight at the same time on every side, with nigh stone walls, gates, and bars, and I learned that each one was independent, and under the command or government of its own chief, who generally styled himself a prince; and when I heard the story of the destruction of Widnah, and other devastations committed by the wandering Arabs in their vicinity, I could not avoid figuring to myself, and observing to my companions at the same time, that the country of Suse must now resemble in appearance the land of Canaan in the time of Joshua, both in regard to its numerous little walled cities; its fertile soil; and in many other respects; and that the frequent irruptions of the hordes of wild Arabs from the desert, destroying and laying waste the country, and the cities they are able to overpower, bore a strong resemblance to the conduct of the ancient Israelites, when led from the deserts of Arabia into the cultivated country near them; with this difference, however, that the Israelites were then particularly guided, supported, and protected by Divine power, and consequently were enabled to act in unison, and with decisive effect against those small, feeble, and ill-constructed cities.

In travelling from Mogadore to Tangier, in the empire of Morocco, and coming to those parts of the provinces of Abdah and Duquella. which are entirely peopled by Arabs living in tents, and in a primitive or wandering state, (their tents being formed of the same materials, and pitched in the same manner as those of the Arabs on the desert,) I observed, that these people were of a much lighter complexion than those on the desert; but that circumstance, in all probability, was owing to the climate's being more temperate; to their being less exposed to the rays of the sun, and better clothed; yet their features were nearly the same, and those of both bear a strong resemblance to those of the Barbary Jews, who also have black eyes and Arab noses, lips, hair, and stature, and whose complexion is but a shade or two lighter than that of the Moorish Arabs, which is chiefly occasioned by their different modes of life, the Jews all living in cities, and the Arabs in the fields: the Jews, however, are stouter men than the Arabs, owing, most likely, to the unrestrained intercourse between the lusty Moors and Jewesses, &c.

That these Arabs and those who live on the desert, are the same race of men, I have not the smallest doubt: their height, shape, eyes, noses, and other features, together with their customs, manners, and habits, being essentially the same. Between the Barbary Jews and the present Arabs, there is only a slight difference in their religious ceremonies and belief, and both very much resemble those forms which were followed by the old Jewish patriarchs, and their fathers and brethren, as recorded in the Book of Genesis. There is one more singular coincidence between the customs of the old Israelites and present Arabs, which, though seemingly unimportant, I shall, nevertheless, mention. The Arabs, both on the desert and in Morocco, when they have occasion to go abroad from their tent, m order to obey one of the most pressing calls of nature, always carry a stick or paddle with them, in the manner and for the same purpose as is mentioned of the ancient Israelites in the twenty-third chapter of *Deuteronomy*, the twelfth and thirteenth verses. The men always sit close to the ground to urinate, and compelled us, while slaves, to do the same: the men never touch the virile member with their hands.

In journeying through the province of Duquella, I learned from ocular demonstration what was meant when certain personages are described in Holy Writ as having an abundance of flocks and herds, &c. We stopped and pitched our tent one night within a *douhar*, which I found in the morning to consist of one hundred and fifty-four tents: they were pitched in form of a hollow square, and about fifty yards apart, occupying a large space of ground, and all of them facing inwards: before each of these tents, the owner had made his beasts lie down for the night. I felt a desire to know the number of animals each man possessed, and in order to make an estimate of the whole with correctness, I stopped, counted, and set down the whole number that lay in separate flocks before thirty of the tents nearest to where I was, and then made an average of their numbers for each tent, which were nineteen camels, eleven head of neat cattle, six asses, fifty-five sheep, and fifty-two goats: the whole of the horses within the *douhar*, I counted separately; they amounted to one hundred and eighty-six.

I think the flocks I counted were a fair average of the whole, and I compute them accordingly; that is, two thousand nine hundred and twenty-six camels; one hundred and eighty-six horses; eight thousand seven hundred and seventy sheep; eight thousand and eight goats; and nine hundred and twenty asses:—they had besides a considerable number of dung-hill fowls, and a great plenty of dogs. I also counted the number of inhabitants occupying fifty tents, which averaged, including slaves and children, nine to a tent, or one thousand three hundred and eighty-six in all.

These Arabs lead a pastoral life, and though the amount of their flocks, at first sight, appears great, yet when it is taken into view that their only employment is to feed cattle, in which consists their whole riches or wealth, and their daily support, the number will not be considered as unreasonably great. This *douhar* was said to belong to the Sheick Mohammed ben Abdehla, a very old man, (whom I saw,) and to consist of his family only; if so, this Arab must have been very rich and powerful, even like Abraham the patriarch, who had three hundred and eighteen servants born in his own house, able to go forth to war, (*Genesis* xiv. 14,) or like pious Job, who was pre-eminently blessed with flocks and herds, and was also, most probably, an Arab.

CHAPTER 32

Villainy of His Jew Companion

Having recovered my strength, so as to be able to undertake a journey by land, and being desirous of viewing that part of the empire of Morocco which lies between Mogadore and Tangier, and also to visit the American Consul General residing at that place, in order to make effectual arrangements for the redemption of the remainder of my unfortunate crew, should they be yet alive, I shipped my companions on board a Genoese schooner that navigated under the English flag, bound for Gibraltar, where I intended to meet them. I drew bills on my friend, Mr. Horatio Sprague, of Gibraltar, for the amount of cash actually expended by Mr. Willshire in obtaining our redemption, and in furnishing us with clothing, though he had given, both to me and my men, many articles of his own clothing, for which he would not receive payment, nor would he accept of any compensation for his trouble, for our board, nor for the extraordinary expenses incurred in consequence of his exertions to render us every assistance, as well as every service and comfort in his power, during the whole of our stay with him for about two months.

Elio Zagury, the Jew whom I have before mentioned, was also going to set out for Tangier by land, and as my friend did not wish me to be troubled with the arrangements for provisions, &c. on the road, he agreed with Zagury, for him to furnish me everything necessary during the journey, except a bed, and paid him the amount agreed on beforehand, which was a handsome sum.

On the 4th day of January, 1816, all being previously prepared, the schooner sailed with Mr. Savage, Burns, Clark, and Horace on board. After seeing her safe out of the harbour, I went, accompanied by Mr. Willshire, into the Jews' town, to the house of old Zagury, where I took my leave of the Jew priest before mentioned, and we proceeded without the northern city gate, where the Jews are permitted to mount their mules or asses. I then found that the mule on which I was to travel, was already loaded with two large trunks, one mattress, and provisions in proportion, and was told by Zagury that I must get on the top of this cargo, and ride the best way I could, as he should procure no other mule on my account.

I was not at all pleased at this plan, but my friend told me it was only a Jew's trick, and such a one as every man may expect to be served who has any dealings with those villains: he then ordered his own mule to be brought for me, which was ready saddled in the gateway, and kept there, I believe, for the purpose, anticipating deceit on the part of the Jew; though in this, as in every other instance, he endeavoured to lighten as much as possible, the weight of the obligations he had laid me under. His mule was one of the handsomest and finest I had ever seen: to have refused riding it at that time, would have been to doubt his friendship; so I mounted the mule, and proceeded northward in company with Mr. Willshire and his trusty friend, Rais bel Cossim, on horseback.

We rode on, conversing together, for about two hours, along the sand beach, when we stopped a few moments, and took some refreshments. It was there I took my leave of my benefactor. This painful parting I shall not attempt to describe: a last look was at length taken, and a final *adieu* uttered, when he rode back towards the city, and I proceeded on my journey. We went silently along, and mounted up the bank. Our company consisted of young Zagury, an old Jew named David; a Jew servant; two Moors, who were the muleteers, and an imperial soldier for our guide, well mounted on a high spirited horse, and fully armed: he was a fine looking fellow, though half negro, and possessed all that suavity of manners so conspicuous in a first rate Moor or Arab. From these soldiers the emperor chooses his *alcayds* and officers for the army; if they only possess talents and bravery, their colour is disregarded. The Jews called him *alcayd*, by way of making themselves appear more respectable, and me they styled *el Tibib del Sultan*, or the *Sultan's* doctor.

We proceeded on till near dark through a dreary country, when we came to the *Omlays*, or three springs; there we found a number of travellers watering their camels, mules, and asses. Having let our beasts drink, we turned aside a little to the south, in a ploughed field, near a few stone houses, and pitched for the night. We had a bell tent, which was a very good one, made of two thicknesses of canvass; it was large enough to contain two beds spread out, and very tight, and left plenty of room besides for our other things. We had with us a box containing tea, coffee, sugar, &c. coals to make a fire, and all the utensils necessary for cooking: so we had a cup of tea, and ate some *coos-koo-soo* for our supper, and went to sleep very comfortably.

The soldier and the muleteers slept outside the tent on the ground, wrapped up only in their *haicks*: this is the constant practice of the Moors and Arabs when travelling, and they wonder that people of other nations do not prefer that method to any other; they carry this custom so far, that many of the male inhabitants of the cities sleep on the tops of their houses (which are flat) in preference to sleeping on their mattresses under cover.

At daylight on the morning of the 5th, all our company were in a bustle, being busily engaged in striking our tent, and loading the mules, while a cup of coffee was preparing, and some eggs boiling for our breakfast; and we set off on our journey long before sunrise. We travelled along this day on uneven ground, through groves of *arga* trees, which grew thereabouts spontaneously, and were then loaded with the oil-nut of various sizes and colours, from a deep green through, to a lively yellow. The very shrubs and bushes among which our path lay, were in blossom, and diffused a most delightful fragrance. We still heard the roaring of the troubled ocean dashing against this inhospitable coast, and which had been constantly dinning my ears for more than two months; for it being urged towards this coast by the continual trade-winds, it never ceases its loud roarings, which may generally be heard at the distance of from twenty to thirty miles from the sea.

The Atlas mountains were still in view, whose pointed tops, now covered with snow, seemed to glitter in the sun, though at a very great distance. About sunset we came near a village consisting of about twenty stone houses, flat roofed, one story high, and as many more built with reeds or sticks, in form of a sugar-loaf, with a small mosque or place of worship in the midst. Near this village, which was not walled in, the first I had seen of the kind, we pitched our tent, and soon after this was done, a great number of unarmed Moors, probably four or five hundred, came by turns to look at us, and inquire who I was.

At the same time the owner of the village sent to tell us we were welcome, and that he was sorry it was not in his power to furnish barley for our mules, for his whole crops had been cut off by the locusts for the last three years: that he had bought twenty ducats worth that day, but it was all gone, as an unusual number of travellers had called on him; however, he sent us a loin of good mutton, which I was pressed to accept, and about two dozen of eggs; our Moors were also supplied with *coos-koo-soo*.

I learned from Zagury, that this man was esteemed a great saint by all the Moors; that his name was Mohammed Ilfactesba; that he taught all pious Moors who wished it, to read in the *Koran*, and the Mohammedan laws: that he generally had from one to three hundred scholars or students, who came from every part of the empire; that he taught all who came, and supplied them with provisions *gratis*; that his wife and one daughter prepared the victuals and cooked for all those people, without any assistance whatever, which was considered by the Moors a continual miracle, and this, Zagury assured me, he for his own part, firmly believed; that he entertained all travellers who chose to call on him, free of expense: but, added he, where all his property comes from to enable him to pay these enormous expenses, nobody knows.

It was soon reported about that an English doctor was in the tent, and the old saint sent and begged me to call and see him: so taking Zagury with me to act as interpreter, I was conducted by some Moors to his presence, where I was welcomed by a withered old man, who was seated on a mat on the outside, and leaning against the wall of his house—it was the saint: he requested me to sit down near him, and then inquired of Zagury who I was: Zagury satisfied him on that point, and gave him besides a short sketch of my late disasters: the saint said he was a friend to Christians, and men of every other religion; that we were all children of the same heavenly Father, and ought to treat each other like brothers: he also remarked that God was great and good, and had been very merciful to me, for which I ought to be thankful the remainder of my life.

He next informed me, that he was very lame in his legs, occasioned in the first place by a stone falling on one of his feet, that had lamed and laid him up for three or four months, and when he had so far recovered as to be able to ride out on his mule, the animal fell down with him, and injured his lame foot and leg so much that he had not since been able to use it: this, he said, happened about a year ago, and within the last few months, his other leg had become affected, and he had now lost the use of both of them, which was extremely painful: he said he did not murmur at his lameness, because he knew it came from God, and was a punishment for some of his sins; yet he hoped the Almighty would be merciful, and pardon his offences, and permit him to walk again, so that he might take care of his guests, and do more good in the world: he also told me that the number who were then studying the *Sacred Writings* with him, amounted to about three hundred.

I examined his legs; they were very thin, and yet seemed to be consuming with a feverish heat; no skin was broken, and I concluded that he laboured under an inveterate chronic disorder, particularly as the joints were much swelled. I asked him if he had ever applied anything as a remedy, or taken any medicine for this disorder: he said, no, except that he had bound some Arabic writing round them, furnished by a man eminently skilled in the science of witchcraft; that he had also kept them wet with oil, but had received no benefit whatever from either of those applications: he further said, he knew some men were endowed with the gift of healing, and hoped that I could prescribe something that would ease his pains.

I told him that I felt disposed to render him all the service in my power; that I would see what medicine I had, and would consider of his case: then assuming the air of a quack doctor, I retired to my tent with a very thoughtful countenance. Our conversation was carried on by the help of Zagury as an interpreter. I really wished to administer some relief to this good man, who was afflicted with such a painful disorder, and accordingly prepared some soap pills, which was the only medicine I had with me, and sent them to him, with directions how to take them. I also advised him to discontinue the use of oil; to rub his limbs frequently with flannel cloths, in order to promote the circulation of the fluids; to endeavour to walk every day with the assistance of two men using his legs as much as possible, even if they did pain him, and to bind them up in fine salt every night, while the heat continued: this, I fancied, might allay the fever. I also directed a drink to be made for him, by boiling the roots of some particular herbs in water, and thus forming a kind of decoction.

Having explained the nature of his disorder to him, in the best manner I was able, which gave him. some encouragement, I retired to my tent. Many of the Moors came and wanted me to prescribe something for their various disorders, which I did according to the best of my judgment, and the medicines I had within my power. Among the rest, was a poor old grey-headed man; he came near, and thrusting his head under the tent, cried out—*Tibib, Tibib*: (doctor, doctor:) my guard was going to drive him away, but I told him to let him alone, mat I might find out what ailed him, for he seemed to be in great distress—so I told Zagury to ask him what his disorder was: this he made known without ceremony—he said, he had been a husband to three wives; that two of them, who had died, loved him exceedingly; that his present wife was very young, fat, and handsome, and yet she was so cold, that notwithstanding all his caresses, she could not return his love: his case was, indeed, a very plane one, but to prescribe a remedy, needed some reflection—so the Jew told him to go away, and return in half an hour.

When he returned, I pretended to, and did sympathize with him in his afflictions, and recommended that he should set her about no kind of work; that he should entreat her kindly; feed her on the dish called *shanah; i. e.* peas baked in an oven, and swimming in beef's marrow, with a plenty of soft boiled eggs and rich spices in her *cooskoo-soo*, &c. &c.—that he should join with her in all her repasts, and chew opium himself, if he could procure any, and by no means to lodge in the same, room with her oftener than once in two weeks. He promised very faithfully to obey my directions, though he did not seem to relish the last item of advice; but I assured him, with much gravity, that I had done my very best; so he left me with a shower of blessings for my kindness, after having bestowed two dozen of fresh eggs on my Jew interpreter for his trouble. The Moors who were the pupils of the saint, joined in prayer, and chanted over sacred poetry for about an hour, on account of his disorder, begging of God to heal their benefactor, &c.

January the 6th, we started early in the morning, after I had taken leave of the good old man. We proceeded on our journey, descending the hills to the north about half an hour, when we saw one of the Moors who waited on the old man the night before, running after us, and hallooing very loudly to make us stop, which we did, and he soon came up, bringing Zagury's gold watch, which he had put under his head the night before on the ground where our tent was pitched, and had left it through forgetfulness and haste: this watch, together with an elegant gold seal, chain, and trinkets, was worth at least three hundred dollars. The Moor generously refused any compensation for his trouble, and I told Zagury it was well for him that the people where he left it were not Jews: to this he assented, and said that he believed that the saint was the most honest man in the world.

After travelling about two hours in a northerly direction, we came near the ruins, or rather the walls of an old town or fortress—it was situated on the left bank of the River Tensift: the walls were built in a square form; were about one mile in circuit, and flanked with thirty small towers, with embrasures, where cannon might have been mounted. Apart of the southern wall had fallen down; it was very thick, and within was nothing but a heap of stones and ruins.

On inquiry, I was told by my guard that this town was built by the former Sultan, Sidi Mohammed, in order to secure a passage across the river, when the people of the province of Abdah rebelled against him; that it was well garrisoned and mounted with a great many cannon, and called *el Ksebbah*, or the strong lion-like fortress; that it was dismantled by the present emperor, who took away the cannon; and that the garrison, and all the inhabitants were destroyed a few years ago by the plague, since which no soul has ventured to live in it. We rode on, and crossed this stream, dignified by the name of river, but which, in fact, is no more in the dry season than an American brook. The country, in its valley, which is very wide, is rich and level; is said to be overflowed in a rainy season, and was at this time cultivated in many parts. We went along its right bank, and saw the site or ruins of what is called old Swearah, on its left bank, near its entrance into the sea: there are now only a few huts and four saint-houses to be seen; all the other parts of the town are buried in sand, blown from the seashore.

The river, near its mouth, is both deep and wide, and the soldier said, it was once a considerable port, where vessels could enter, but its mouth is now entirely dammed up with sand; only leaving a small passage for the water, which runs off in a shallow stream to the sea, over a beach of two hundred yards in breadth, and so high that the tide cannot enter the river's mouth. From the banks of this river, we proceeded towards the seashore, and descending the high steep bank, we entered between it and the first bank from the ocean, and travelled along a delightful inclined plane, about four miles in breadth: the surface of this plane was covered with verdure, and flowers of all the variegated colours of the rainbow, resembling in appearance the richest Turkey carpet.

About the middle of the afternoon, we met a courier fourteen days from Tangier: having an inkhorn and paper with me, I wrote by him a few lines to my friend Willshire, and we proceeded along towards Saffy, pronounced by the natives *S'fee*. This inclined plane was the most beautiful that can be imagined; speckled over with herds of cattle and numerous flocks of sheep, which were quietly grazing on its rich herbage. As it was the sixth day of the week, and the Jews with me were obliged by their religion to stop the seventh, during their

Sabbath, I had a mind to pitch our tent on this delightful plane, and pass the Sabbath of rest, by reposing on its downy bosom, and inhaling its delicious fragrance: but Zagury assured me it was not safe to lodge there, and that he must enter S'fee in order to recruit his stock of provisions, for that a Jew could eat no kind of meat except it was killed by a priest of his nation.

He was exceedingly superstitious, though educated in England, and we kept on towards Saffy. When in sight of the walls of that city, we came near a large saint-house, on a cliff near the sea's brink—here our soldier and muleteers made the Jews dismount, and pass this house barefooted, though at half a mile's distance from our path: he told me that the house was built over the remains of a great saint; that every man who was not a Moslemin must walk past it barefooted: mat people came to visit it from all quarters to be cured of their diseases: but, added he, as you are a good man. and very weak, you may ride past, but must pay the saint one dollar towards keeping his house in repair. I did not much relish this mode of giving away my money, and told the soldier so; but he replied, that no Christian must pass it without this tribute, and that it would be demanded from him on his entrance into S'fee. I was convinced it was only a trick of his to extort money; but there was no getting off, and so I paid him the dollar, telling him at the same time I should set it down as a debt due to the saint's account, and presumed he would have no objection to repay me in another world: "No," said he, "that saint was very liberal in this world, and will, no doubt, pay you both principal and interest in the other, and intercede for your admission into paradise in the bargain:" he was a shrewd fellow, and understood my feelings on the subject perfectly.

After the Jews had walked about a mile, they were again permitted to ride. We approached the city on its southeast or fortress side: some ruins of its ancient walls were still visible, which proved it to have formerly been, at least, four times larger than at present. It was near night, and we went round the fortress, which appeared to be very strong, and was defended by a double wall: it is situated on an eminence, which not only commands the city that is attached to it below, but is also well situated for defending all the entrances into the town, and has a good number of cannon mounted on it: the whole appears extremely well calculated for defence, and I imagine it must originally have been constructed by some eminent European engineer.

A small brook of water runs from the east near the northern wall of the city. We entered it at the eastern gate, and proceeded through a crowd of spectators to the house of Zagury's Jew friend. The Jews were obliged to dismount, and walk into the city, but they allowed me to ride. Having entered the court, (for the building was very spacious, but had very much decayed, and was fast crumbling to the ground,) we ascended a broken staircase to the gallery of the first storey and were conducted to a small room that had been shut up, apparently, for a long time: the unhinged door and shattered window-shutter were, however, removed to accommodate our company, and I took a peep into the apartment: it was about ten feet square, and nearly filled with filth of almost every description; the whole fermenting in rancid *argan* oil, which far exceeded in scent the most stinking fish or blubber oil.

The effluvia arising from this newly opened bed of nastiness entering my olfactory nerves, was immediately transmitted to my stomach, and brought on an instantaneous vomiting, which continued for about two hours without intermission, until my stomach was completely empty, and it threw up besides a considerable quantity of fresh blood: this abominable stench caused a nausea even in the Jews' stomachs; however, as there was no other place to lodge in, and the weather looked likely for rain, they cleared out this chamber, washed it with hot water, and fumigated it afterwards with burning charcoal and brimstone; Zagury taking care to observe, by way of recommendation, that this house was built by a Christian, and that its occupants, who were his father's friends, were the most respectable Jews in S'fee.

The house was, indeed, large, and had been very commodious; but its tenants, consisting of about twenty miserable dirty families, did not choose to lend nor let to us a better apartment, and after refreshing myself with a cup of strong tea, my stomach became composed, and I went through, in the course of the evening, with their religious ceremonies, in company with the Jews, as I have before described.

In Saffy the Jews live in company with, *i. e.* promiscuously among, the Moors in adjoining houses. On their Sabbath, all the men belonging to the house went to the synagogues, and the women, in the mean time, decked themselves in their best attire; they had already stained the insides of their hands and fingers, between every joint, and then finger-nails, yellow; had borrowed and put on fine ear-rings and necklaces of pearl and amber, and golden chains, golden hearts, and other trinkets; these hung down upon their naked bosoms: they wore bracelets on their ankles and wrists. Their hair, which was long and black, was newly braided, and greased over smoothly with *argan* oil: they had painted their eyes and eyebrows black, and the most of them wore slippers; thus tricked up in all their finery, two of the most handsome and stylishly dressed damsels, with a number of the second-rate, came round to that side of the gallery where I sat quietly and alone, writing down notes for my journal: they first expressed their wonder at my manner of writing from left to right; then at the letters I formed, &c.—and having, by this method, succeeded in diverting my attention from what I was about, the two smartest looking girls, who were about sixteen and eighteen years of age, with quite pretty faces, and richly dressed, invited me to go with them, and see their father's room: my curiosity prompted me to comply, and I suffered them to lead me along into their chamber, where their mother, a very fleshy middle aged woman, was sitting on a mattress; and as they had no other seat, they invited me to sit down on the same bed beside her.

After due salutations, the old lady left the room, shutting the door after her. The object of these sirens was to get money from me; but finding I was able to withstand all their temptations, they at last permitted me to retire, but not before they had tried every indelicate art and enticement, of which they were complete mistresses, to effect their purpose. After I had withdrawn from the room, I was shown into all the other apartments on that floor, in succession, and their artifices were still played off to win my cash, until, at length, finding that all their wiles proved abortive, they next had recourse to begging for money, but I had none to spare them.

The Jews in Saffy are very poor and miserable; they were generally about half clothed, and that with filthy rags. Saffy is a small place, and has no trade; so that the Jews are hard put to it, and are obliged to resort to every base expedient in order to gain a mere subsistence. I could not but pity their condition, and lament the depravity to which they all seemed to be prone, though, perhaps, oftentimes plunging into guilt from sheer necessity.

This day I went in company with my guard to view the town and port of S'fee: the town is small, and strongly walled in on all sides: the walls, for the most part, are made of rough stone and lime, like those of Mogadore or Swearah, except that part next the sea, which is laid up with large hewn stone, and appears very strong: the walls are flanked with four towers, besides the *el Ksebbah*, on which cannon are mounted, and a battery at the water-port. The town lies very low, and is surrounded on all sides by hills, and appears to be the receptacle of all the filth of the country near it. Its streets are very narrow, crooked, irregular, and not paved: the houses are built of rough stone and lime;

have few windows next the streets; are from one to three stories high, and flat roofed; but, like the houses in the cities in Spain, have a court, the interior of which serves for a stable.

The public buildings are three mosques, with high square towers, and a large hewn stone building, formerly occupied as a customhouse, but now uninhabited and falling to pieces. The Jews have also twelve small rooms, for the purpose of worshipping, which they call synagogues. The number of inhabitants in Saffy is computed at twenty thousand, that is, sixteen thousand Moors and four thousand Jews. The walls of the present town, including the fortress, are about one mile in circumference. The inhabitants of the city are supplied with good water, brought in kegs on asses from the brook that washes its northern walls. All the cattle, sheep, &c. that are owned in and feed near S'fee, are driven within the walls every night, and from its appearance, no dirt is ever carried out of the city: the filth in the streets was in many parts two feet deep at the least, so that it was quite impossible for me to get along through the mire without being besmeared with it up to my knees. Passing along one street as well as I could pick my way, I lost both my shoes in the mud, but some Jew boys, recovered them again; for which service I had to pay them half a dollar.

The bay of Saffy is formed by the projection of Cape Cantin; is very spacious, and well defended by that cape from the common trade winds. Vessels visiting that place are obliged to anchor very broad in the offing, and where the ground is said to be very foul: the landing-place is either on a sand beach, upon which the surf breaks with considerable violence, or else in among some rocks, where there was formerly a kind of basin, which is now nearly filled up with sand. There were about twenty fishing boats on this beach, which were in a bad state of repair. The port of Saffy has been shut, by order of the Sultan, for several years. A circular fort stands on a hill to the north, and within half cannon shot of the town, and which completely commands it: it had been lately dismantled, and the cannon carried into the city, for fear it would be taken possession of by the field Moors and Arabs during the late rebellion. The land in the vicinity of this city is foi the most part uncultivated.

CHAPTER 33

Continuation of the Journey

We left Saffy early on the morning of the 7th of January, and found the country, as we proceeded northward, more open, but not much cultivated: the ground was covered with flowers of different kinds, and every shrub was also in full blossom, and seemed to vie in beauty with its neighbour, while their blended fragrance rising, with the exhaling dews, and wafted along by a gentle land breeze, conveyed to the soul sensations of the most exquisite delight. We travelled along during this whole day on uneven ground, frequently meeting large droves of loaded camels and mules, and passing many groups of tents, some formed of woollen cloth, and pitched in the same manner as the Arab tents on the desert, and others with reeds; regaling ourselves occasionally with milk, which we found to be excellent, and in great abundance, and at night pitched our tent near one of those flying camps which are here called *douhars*.

On the morning of the 8th, we started very early, and after riding about three hours, came to the walls of an old Portuguese town and fortress, now called Asbedre, but in ruins and deserted. It is situated on the second bank from the sea, one hundred feet above a beautiful harbour or small port and sound, formed by an opening through the first bank, which resembles the entrance of a dock: it appeared shallow, and one vessel only can enter at a time. This port seems to be capable of containing a vast number of small vessels, where they might ride in perfect safety in all seasons of the year: here is also, near the walls of the ruin, a small Moorish settlement of badly built houses and tents.

Passing this, we entered into one of the richest valleys ever formed by nature: the face of the earth here was smiling with cultivation, and speckled over with flocks and herds: here thousands of oxen, sheep, goats, and camels, horses, and asses, were peaceably feeding in concert, while hundreds of the inhabitants were busied in tilling the rich soil, in sowing wheat and barley, and cutting down, with a common sword, the weeds that grew where they had reaped their last crops, higher than their heads, and some of them more than an inch in thickness, in order to admit the plough. This valley is bounded on the west by a long sound or narrow arm of the sea, in which the tide ebbs and flows many feet: the sea water enters it near Asbedre, and on its right: the valley is bounded by a hill of easy ascent: its mean breadth is about four miles, and its length about twenty miles. The valley contains hundreds of wells of excellent water, fitted with solid stone basins around their mouths, which were covered with large stones; these serve to give drink to their flocks, and to quench the thirst of the weary labourer and traveller. Some of these wells were immensely deep, and a windlass was rigged to them to draw the water.

Near the middle of this valley we stopped to take our dinner: my mind was absorbed in contemplating the riches and beauties of bountiful nature, when I observed something that appeared like a cloud of thick smoke rising over the hill at the northeast, and with the wind approaching us rapidly. I remarked to my Jew, that there must be a monstrous fire in that quarter; no, said he, they are only locusts. In the mean time, the flight was fast approaching, and soon came within a short distance, and directly towards us. Every labourer's attention was instantly turned from his plough and other employment; the oxen were stopped, and every one stood aghast with apprehension and dismay painted in strong colours on his anxious countenance, fearing his field was to become the prey of this devouring plague.

The locusts began to descend, and alighted to the northward of us; very few passing where we sat: we soon mounted and rode on, and as we proceeded we found the whole surface of the ground covered with them as thick as they could stand, and all busy in the work of destruction. As it was necessary for them to clear our road to avoid being crushed to death by the trampling of our mules, those in and near the path rose as we passed along, filling the air around us like one continued swarm of bees; whilst thousands came in contact with our faces and bodies. In this situation, fearing my eyes would be injured, I covered my face with a transparent silk handkerchief, and pushed on my mule as fast as I could; we were about two hours in passing this host of destroyers, which when on the wing made a sound, as finely described in *Holy Writ*, "*like the rushing of horses into battle.*"

The space covered by this flight extended in length for about eight miles along the road and three miles in breadth. After they had fairly alighted, the Moors, each resuming his labour, left the locusts in the full enjoyment of their repast, assuring us, that when they had filled themselves, which would be in the course of that day and the night, they would move off in a body with the wind, probably one day's march further, where they would again repeat their ravages, leaving the remainder for other successive flights; but which they hoped, by the blessing of God, would not destroy the whole of their crops and all the herbage, as they had done some years within the last seven, during which space they had continued to lay waste the country.

To see such fair prospects of crops thus blasted in a moment, would fill the inhabitants of more refined countries with feelings of despair, and their fields would be left untilled; while the Mohammedan considers it either as a just chastisement from heaven for his own or his nation's sins, or as directed by that fatality in which they all believe;— thus when one crop is destroyed, if of wheat, they sow the same ground over again with barley, or plant it with Indian corn or peas, so as to have every possible chance for subsisting.

These Arabs, while at their labour, are entirely naked, except a small piece of woollen cloth about their loins:—they make use of the same plough and harness as the people of Suse, already described, but in this part of the country they plough with a pair of oxen:—and here let me beg the reader's indulgence for a few moments, while I undertake to give him a description of that wonderful insect, the destroying locust, that so often lays waste the fertile planes of Asia and the northern regions of Africa. I call him the destroying locust of Africa, because, as far as my memory serves me, he is first described in *Holy Writ* as a destroyer in the land of Egypt.

DESCRIPTION.

The locust of Africa is a ringed insect, which resembles both in size and appearance at the first view, the largest sized grasshopper of America; but on a close inspection, diners from him very materially: the shape of his head and face is similar to that of a common sheep, or goat, being crowned with two long and tapering protuberances, which turn backwards like the horns of a goat. He has attached to his muzzle a pair of smellers or feelers, by the help of which he feels and gathers up the herbage about him, which he nips off, making a champing noise like a sheep when eating: he has four wings, and the hinder pair are quite transparent: he has six legs, with two claws to each foot, which are divided something like the hoof of a sheep, but are more spread in proportion to their size, and pointed: he is stout about the neck, breast, and body; the hinder part of which is forked, and armed with a hard bony substance, by the help of which he can make a hole in the ground.

The largest African locust is above three inches in length, and nearly one inch in diameter: he has the most voracious appetite of any insect in the world, and devours grass, grain, the leaves of trees, and every green thing, with indiscriminate and merciless avidity. They go forth by bands or flights, and each flight is said to have a king, which directs its movements with great regularity. Locusts can only fly when their wings are perfectly dry; and when they rise they always fly off before the wind, and fill the air like an immense cloud of thick smoke: when the leader alights upon the ground, all the flight follows his example as fast as possible. They are at times so numerous, that they may be said to cover the whole face of the country; then they devour every spear of grass and grain, even eating it into the ground, dislodging it root and branch, cutting off all the leaves from the shrubs and trees, and sometimes all the *bark* from tender trees in a whole province, and that too in a very short space of time.

The present African locusts are of the same race of insects that are mentioned in the Bible, as one of the plagues sent upon the land of Egypt, by the Almighty: they have always been considered in the countries where they usually commit ravages as a scourge from heaven, and as a punishment for the sins of the people. The locust has been described as being produced by some unknown physical cause, different from the ordinary mode of animal production: this is a mistake: when I was in Mogadore, Mr. Willshire told me that the locusts were produced by a very well known and natural cause; that the female, a little before the flights disappear for the season, thrusts her hinder parts into the surface of the ground up to her wings, first having found a suitable spot of earth for that purpose: here she forms a cell in shape like that made by the bee, but from one to three inches in depth, and one to two inches in diameter.

Having made the sides of the cell strong by means of a glutinous matter, which she has the power of producing, she deposits her eggs, which are blackish, and so small as scarcely to be distinguishable with the naked eye: each cell is filled full, and contains an immense number of eggs: she then seals it over carefully with the same kind of glutinous matter of which the inside of the cell is formed, and covering it over

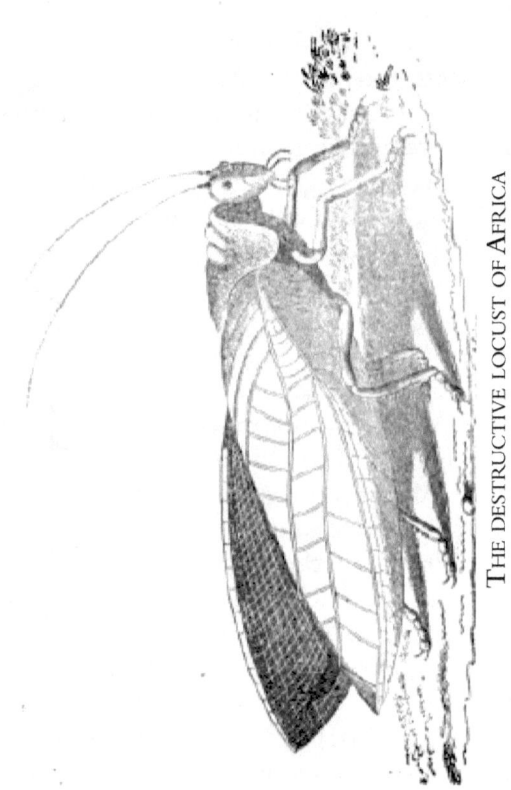

The destructive locust of Africa

with earth, she leaves it to be hatched out by the heat of the sun in due time, which generally happens in the month of January: the eggs in one cell alone produce a host of locusts, amounting to near a million. I opened and examined several cells in and near a garden, two miles from Mogadore, and was much surprised to see the eggs lie thick together in one mass, like the spawn of fishes. I took up some of it on the tip of a sharp pointed penknife, and separating and counting the eggs, by means ot a microscope, as accurately as possible, I enumerated seven hundred and forty-one.

Admitting that every egg would produce a locust, and that the number contained in the small portion on the point of the penknife was the one thousandth part of the whole mass, (which is a low estimate,) it proves that a single locust could produce in one season, even if she fills but one cell, upwards of half a million of her species. When the locust is hatched, he crawls out of the earth a little worm, of a light brown colour, and the whole cell of them are said to hatch about the same time. This host of worms creep forth from the ground, and commence their march, all going one course, generally towards the north or west, devouring everything green that comes in their way, and leaving behind them a dismal scene of desolation.

These reptiles grow so rapidly, that within the space of one week they are prepared for their transformation, when they climb up a stout spear of grass or a twig, attach their skin fast to it, and by a sudden effort, burst the skin asunder at its head, and come forth a four-winged insect, with six legs; they remain a short time in the sun to dry themselves and their wings before they attempt flying, which they commence by trying separately to fly a short distance at a time, and continue fluttering and skipping like grasshoppers for two or three days; next they set off in a body on the wing, and fly from five miles to one hundred, without stopping, just as the country seems to please their taste, and they then go on, as I have before described.

Dry warm seasons are favourable to the breeding of locusts, and a very wet cold one is sure to destroy them in the empire of Morocco until the flights come again from other parts. I do not know precisely the months in which the female locust makes her deposit of eggs, only that it is in the latter part of the summer, or first of the fall months. The old locusts having done their share of mischief, are either driven off by the winds into the sea, or die a natural death; thus making room for a new and more hungry swarm. When all have disappeared in the Moorish empire, a few flights are seen to come from the borders of the desert, or from the coasts of Egypt, which again lay waste the whole country, until they are in their turn destroyed by frequent rains and cold damps, or strong gales from the land, which sweeps them into the ocean.

It is said at Mogadore, and believed by the Moors, Christians, and Jews, that the Bereberies inhabiting the Atlas mountains, have the power to destroy every flight of locusts that comes from the south and from the east, and thus ward off this dreadful scourge from nil the countries north and west of this stupendous ridge, merely by building large fires on those parts of the ridge over which the locusts are known always to pass, and in the season when they are likely to appear, which is at a definite period, within a certain number of days in almost every year. The Atlas being high, and the peaks covered with snow, these insects become chilled in passing over them, when seeing the fires, they are attracted by the glare, and plunge into the flames. I do not know what degree of credit ought to be attached to this opinion, but it is certain that the Moorish *Sultan* used to pay a considerable sum of money yearly to certain inhabitants of the sides of the Atlas in order to keep the locusts out of his dominions.

The Moors and Jews further affirm, that during the time in which the *Sultan* paid the aforesaid yearly stipend punctually, not a locust was to be seen in his dominions north and west of the Atlas, but that about six years ago the emperor refused to pay the stipulated sum, because no locusts troubled his country, and he thought he had been imposed upon; but it so happened that the very same year the locusts again made their appearance, and have continued to lay waste the country ever since.

Locusts are esteemed very good food by the Moors, Arabs, and Jews, in Barbary, who catch large numbers of them in their season, and throw them, while jumping alive, into a pan of boiling *argan* oil: here they hiss and fry until their wings are burned off, and their bodies are sufficiently cooked, when they are poured out and eaten. I have seen many thousands cooked in this manner, and have had the curiosity to taste them: they resemble in consistence and flavour, the yolks of hard boiled hen's eggs. After my arrival at Tangier, on conversing with our Consul General, Mr. Simpson, respecting the locusts, he confirmed the substance of what I had before heard and observed myself in Barbary concerning them. This ravenous insect had actually caused a famine in that part of the country, so that Mr. Simpson, and the other Christian Consuls at Tangier, were obliged to send to

Gibraltar, and buy American flour for the ordinary consumption of their families; inferior American flour was then selling at Tangier for fifteen dollars per barrel, although before the scarcity occasioned by the locusts, the finest Barbary wheat used to be sold for one dollar and a half per barrel.

Mr. Simpson further stated, that in the year 1814, (to the best of my recollection as to the time,) being with his family at his house on Mount Washington, near Cape Spartel, and where the locusts covered the whole face of the ground at night, when he arose the next morning, he could not perceive a single one, and observed to his lady, that all the locusts which had remained with them for a long time, and destroyed most of the herbage about the country, had disappeared; he wondered at first what had become of them; but after the fog in the strait was dissipated, looking at a vessel through his glass, that was passing out, he observed that the whole surface of the water was covered with something that appeared like a reddish scum, and on reflection, it struck him, that the locusts had attempted at night to migrate across the straits into Spain, flying before the wind, which was fair, and blowing from the southward; but that they were either lost in the fog, or checked on their passage by contrary winds, (which generally prevail at night, particularly in the summer time,) in the middle of the strait; and were thus forced by fatigue and the humidity of the atmosphere, to settle upon the surface of the water, from whence they could not rise, and were, consequently, all drowned.

That two days afterwards, a vessel arrived at Tangier from Gibraltar the captain of which confirmed his conjecture, by assuring him that vast numbers of dead locusts had been driven ashore on the rock of Gibraltar, and along the coast of Spain, from Algeciras to Tariffa, a distance of nearly twenty miles, and that there were still greater numbers of their carcasses floating in the straits, near the Spanish shore. I was also informed, that several years ago, nearly all the locusts in the empire, which were at that time very numerous, and had laid waste the country, were carried off in one night, and drowned in the Atlantic ocean; that their dead carcasses a few days afterwards were driven by winds and currents on shore, all along the western coast extending from near Cape Spartel to beyond Mogadore, forming, in many places, immense piles on the sand beach: that the stench arising from their remains was intolerable, and was supposed to have produced the plague which broke out about that time in various parts of the Moorish dominions.

I have thus faithfully embodied what information I could obtain regarding the locusts, from living authority, which I deem indubitable, and to which I have added such facts and circumstances as fell under my own observation, unassisted by books; and I trust the whole will be found essentially correct. As I do not profess to be a naturalist, it cannot be expected that I should undertake to give a description of his interior formation, &c.—but for a side view of this famous and formidable animal, see page 332. To return to my Journal:

Leaving this beautiful valley, embellished and enriched by many thousands of fig and other fruit trees, as well as many clumps of grape vines that seemed to thrive exceedingly well, we ascended the hill on our right, and about dark approached a *douhar* or encampment that was surrounded by a stone wall: the chief of the *douhar* was not willing to let us enter within the walls, but our soldier telling him that I was the *Sultan's* doctor, and must go in, he reluctantly consented, telling my guard, however, we must take care of our baggage ourselves, as the whole of the people in the *douhar*, both men and women, were ill of the venereal disease. They offered us milk and eggs, and asked my advice in regard to their disorder. I told them, I had no medicine with me—I, however, recommended a milk or light diet, and a drink to be made by steeping a certain root, having an affinity, in appearance, to sarsaparilla, that is common in this part of the country; and to let all drink plentifully of this decoction, for ten weeks, not doubting but it would prove beneficial.

We slept here without molestation, started early on the morning of the 9th, and passed, in the course of the day, many *douhars* of tents in the open fields; many orchards regularly planted, consisting of several hundred fig-trees, fenced in with stone walls very thick, and from five to six feet in height: the land on both sides of the path was principally cultivated. Zagury had despatched our guide on to Azamore before us, to a Jew in that town, in order to engage him to prepare some provisions against our arrival; for they are so superstitious, that they would not even eat bread that had been baked in any other but a Jew's oven, and received the priest's blessing, for which, of course, he has his tithe.

Proceeding forward, at about ten, a. m. we saw at some distance on our left, what David and Elio told me was the famous old town of Mazagan: stopping here to take refreshment, a large number of Arab women came from some neighbouring *douhars*, to stare at me and my dress: some of them were quite young, and Zagury began to rally them in a very coarse and rude manner, asking them if they loved Christians, &c. upon which one very old woman said to him, "there is Mazagan; (pointing towards the distant town;) when that place was taken from the Christians, I helped to cut off one of their heads, and yet I love Christians better than the mean, cheating, *infidel* Jews." Zagury, not relishing this retort, dropped the conversation.

Riding on. briskly, we arrived at Azamore about 3 o'clock, p. m. On our approach, our Jews were obliged to dismount, and walk for about two miles to pass a saint-house, which the Moors hold in high veneration: this was the fiftieth saint-house I had seen since I left Swearah. Azamore is a town strongly walled in: it lies on the left bank of the River Ormorbear, one league from its mouth: it is built in the form of an irregular quadrangle, and is about one mile hi circumference: the river washes its eastern wall, while the other sides are defended by a deep ditch. We did not enter it, but from it appearance, it is an old-fashioned Portuguese town, badly built, and within and about the walls, very dirty.

This stream was the only one I had yet passed on this continent, that deserved the name of river: it has a dangerous bar at its mouth, which is said to be navigable only for vessels drawing six feet water at high tides and in smooth weather; these may come alongside the walls of Azamore, where there is a very neat water-port for the reception of their cargoes, but it has now no external commerce whatever: there are, however, some large manufactories of Morocco leather, and coarse earthen ware, in the suburbs outside the walls. We passed this river, which is here about two hundred yards wide, in a good boat, built after the Spanish manner, large and well managed by expert hands.

We found here a good shad fishery: there were ten large nets, and about one hundred and fifty stout Moors employed in this business at that time, and in the proper season, which is from the first of January to April: they catch large quantities of shad, which are much esteemed in this country, and are sold at the landing for about six cents apiece: they are carried from hence to Fez, Mequinez, Morocco, Mogadore, and all the adjoining country. We remained on the bank of this river until dark, waiting for our provisions, which came at last, and we pitched our tent under three date trees, about one mile from the bank. We had bought some shad, which, when roasted, afforded us an excellent supper, as they were very fat and delicious.

On the 10th, at two o'clock in the morning, we started from this place, and owing to the darkness, lost our path, and wandered about for two hours before it was found: we rode all the day through a fine even country, passing many *douhars*, and travelling as usual: and at night pitched our tent in the midst of one of the *douhars*, which I shall here describe, (having made mention of them frequently before,) and this description will answer for the whole of them, with little variation.

On our approach to within fifty yards, we halted, and were soon met by the chief, for they all have one head man, whom they honour by the title of *Sheick*: he welcomed us in very handsome terms; invited us to advance; pointed out a place which was the safest within the *douhar* for our tent; and furnished us with milk and eggs gratis, while the Moors that accompanied us were plentifully regaled with bread, water, and *coos-koo-soo*. This *douhar* was composed of one hundred and fifty-four tents, pitched in the form of a hollow square; the tents being placed about fifty yards apart; an equal number occupying each side, and at equal distances—all made of very coarse strong woollen cloth, of the same colour, and set up in the same manner as those on the desert, and all facing inward. Before each tent, and at a very short distance from it, all the camels, cattle, goats, and asses, are made to lie down, where they are taught to remain until they are roused up to be milked in the morning, when the shepherds or herdsmen drive them out into the open country to feed, and return with them again at nightall.

They milk the mares, camels, cows, asses, goats, and sheep; and in order to effect this with the two last mentioned animals, which are very tame, they divide the sheep and goats into two rows, facing each other; as soon as they approach so as to interlock their necks, they are caught by two ropes which are ready strung for the purpose, and by this means they are kept close together, while the women and girls go behind and milk them between their hind legs; the lambs having been previously tied or secured in a similar way. A good ewe will yield a pint of milk in a morning, and a goat more: sheep's milk is reckoned the richest by the natives, but I preferred that of the goat or the camel to any of the others, though asses' and mares' milk is very rich and good. They make butter by putting the new milk into a goatskin, the hair on the inside; the butter is of course a little hairy, but they can pick it clean with their fingers, and they generally have white-haired goatskins for churns.

The Arabs who inhabit exclusively these *douhars*, are extremely hospitable, and not only furnish the traveller with the best they have to eat and drink, but also set a watch over his tent and baggage, which they strictly take care of: the *Sheicks* themselves at s responsible for every article that may be missing in the morning, and which if not immediately found, they pay the stranger his own price for it in money without hesitation. Thus the Moorish and Arab travellers can pass from one end of the empire to the other without expense, and at their leisure, and transact their commercial business in a cheap way, only buying the barley for their beasts which carry their burdens when they travel on mules or horses, being obliged to feed them on barley and straw; but when they use camels, which is by far the most common method, these hardy beasts live on the herbage and shrubbery which they nip passing along the road, taking a bite now and then as they continue walking, and as soon as they stop, their two fare legs are tied within a foot of each other, and they are turned out to feed.

Without this precaution, the camel is such a wandering creature, not unlike his Arab master in that respect, that be the herbage ever so good and plentiful where he is turned out, he is continually restless, and keeps moving on, so that in the course of an hour or two he will stray many miles from the place where he was first turned loose.

On the 11th, at daybreak, we left this *douhar*, and proceeded over a smooth beautiful plane, everywhere covered with fields of grain or grass and flowering shrubs, with numerous herds of cattle, camels, asses, and flocks of sheep and goats; while the road, or rather foot path, (for such they all are in this country,) was covered with loaded camels travelling each way to and from Darlbeda, and at about 8 o'clock, a. m. we reached that city. Darlbeda is a walled town of about two miles in circumference, situated at the bottom of a broad bay; its port is tolerably good for landing cargoes, although the bay where vessels lie is very rocky, and can only be approached with safety in the summer months and in mild weather. Large quantities of wheat were formerly shipped at this port for Spain and Portugal.

I peeped into it for a few minutes; it is much on the decay; the houses, which are built chiefly of stone and clay, as well as the walls, are falling down in every direction, and even the gateway is in a tottering condition: it is a very dirty place: the houses are from one to three stories high, and the streets very narrow: there still remains an open aqueduct, that used to convey water for a distance of several miles into this town; it is in good repair, being built of stone and lime; the water runs in it to within two hundred yards of the wall, where it has been cut off for the convenience of roads: thus the destructive hands of the Moors are employed in marring and spoiling even their own town, which must soon become no better than a heap of ruins.

We passed Darlbeda, and came to Afidallah, a town built by Sidi Mohammed: this town is enclosed by a tolerable mud and stone wall, and is situated about one mile from the sea. The whole coast from Darlbeda to far beyond Afidallah, is lined with huge heaps of beach-sand, hove up by the almost constant trade winds, blowing direct on shore.

Afidallah stands on a beautiful plane: it was built for the purpose uf receiving and storing the large quantities of wheat and barley that usually grew near its site; and its harbour, only one mile distant from it, is sheltered by a long and narrow island, within which vessels of a small size can anchor, and be tolerably safe. This is said, by Mohammed, one of our muleteers, and an old sailor, to be by far the safest open harbour in the empire during the winter months; but the landing is bad, and can only be effected in light winds and good weather. Large quantities of wheat, barley, big acorns, fruit, &c. were shipped from Afidallah during the reign of Sidi Mohammed, and a part of the present reign; but Muley Soliman, the present *Sultan*, has of late become so bigoted, that he thinks, or pretends it is a sin for his subjects to trade with the Christians; he has, therefore, forbid the exportation of almost all the articles of commerce, and rendered, by this means, his people poor; ruined most of his towns, and involved himself in many broils with his subjects, while he is straining every nerve to take away the little remains of their property, in contributions and presents extorted from them by rapacious officers appointed for the purpose.

The goods for shipping were carried from Afidallah on camels, across the sand-hills that shelter the town from the violent sea-gales. This place is about six hundred yards square, flanked by four square forts joined to each corner, and so constructed as to be able to rake the whole length of the wall on the outside, with cannon and musketry.

We passed on, and pitched our tent at night within the walls of an old town called Sebilah; there is no house standing in it, except a part of a large mosque, and a tall well-built tower, though it was once a considerable place. Within these walls, in one corner, was a large garden, well stocked with vegetables, and about a hundred tents were pitched, as if in the open field; so we pitched our tent near the walls of the mosque. There were several women here that wanted medicines, and though I had none to give them, yet my mere advice, which was thought important, procured milk and eggs sufficient for our suppers.

Soon after sunset, all the flocks and cattle belonging to the inhabitants were driven within the walls, and disposed of as in the common *douhars*, when the stout gate was shut and strongly barred. Many travellers arrived in the evening, and wished to enter, but found no admittance, and they took up their lodgings outside of the walls.

January the 12th, at daylight, our soldier had the gate opened, and we went forward: there were outside of the gate several large droves of camels with their owners, which had put up there in the night—they were principally loaded with sacks of salt or barley, and going towards Rhabat. We rode on fast, and passed three considerable streams, which the Moors call rivers, and say they are not fordable in the rainy season; but we got over without difficulty, being then only brooks": the country was level and well cultivated, and we passed innumerable droves of light and loaded camels, mules, and asses.

At about eight o'clock, a. m. we saw a high tower east of us, which stands at the head of the aqueduct that conveys water to Rhabat: and at about three, p. m. we came to the outer wall of that city, which stands half a mile from the main wall, and encloses a great number of fine gardens of fruit and vegetables, besides some wheat fields: it extends from the palace (which is spacious, and situated on the left upon the bank of the sea between the outer and main walls) round to the river eastward of the city: here the Jews were obliged to dismount before they could enter the town, and there I left them, and proceeded with my guard, followed by my muleteer into the city. My friend Mr. Wiltshire, had given me an introductory letter to Mr. Abouderham, the English Vice Consul at Rhabat, and we proceeded directly to his house, which is situated in the principal town.

On my arrival, I was received by that gentleman with every mark of politeness and respect I could wish: he furnished me with a room and everything I needed for my comfort. The next day being the Jews' Sabbath, I had time to visit different parts of the city, and the Jews' town, or Millah.

Rhabat is situated at the mouth of the river Beregreb—on its left bank, within a mile of the sea; it is defended on the south by a double wall and some batteries of cannon; on the west, facing the sea, by a very strong fortress; and along the river on the north, by very high and steep cliffs, a wall, and a number of strong batteries. I should compute the circumference of the outer walls at six miles, but the inner one not more than three.

The city is situated on uneven ground: is very well built for a

Moorish town, though the streets are narrow, crooked, and dirty; yet the houses in general are in good repair, and two stories high, built of stone and lime mortar, and flat roofed, with an inner court; a few windows next the streets, which are only air holes, and secured with wooden shutters and grates, without glass. There are in this city ten mosques of different heights and shapes: it is the largest seaport town in the Moorish dominions, though at present the bar at the river's mouth is so heaped up with sand, as only to admit of vessels drawing six feet water, and yet the tide rises within it about ten feet, and runs very rapidly.

The Millah, or Jews' town, is walled in separately, to prevent the Jews from mixing with and defiling the Moors, and that they may more easily be kept in subjection with the aid of the *bastinado*. This Millah has been built only about six years; has but one gate, which is guarded and kept by Moors; and there are some very good houses in it. It is said to contain eight thousand Jews, who are (for the most part) very poor, miserable, and depraved, and live in the most degraded condition: they worship in twelve rooms called synagogues, and I was told that nearly one half of the male inhabitants were *rabbies*.

Rhabat is very well peopled: the whole number of its inhabitants is computed by Mr. Abouderham to exceed sixty thousand. Many of the Moors here are rich, and live in great luxury, keeping large *seraglios* of women, and having beautiful gardens. Vast quantities of *haicks*, and other woollen and cotton cloths, are here fabricated, and great quantities of sole and Morocco leather, and coarse earthen ware, such as pots, bowls, jars, &c. are also manufactured in this city. It carries on a brisk inland trade, and the Moorish inhabitants seem to be more civilized than in any other town I passed through. Here is the principal navy-yard of the emperor, where his ships are built; for the Moors have none for commerce.

Here was one new frigate lying by the walls, partly fitted; she appeared to be about five hundred tons burden; was pierced for 32 guns, and the Moors said she would be ready to go round to Laresch, where their ships of war are fitted out, in two or three months: to get them over the bar at the mouth of the river, they are obliged to go out perfectly light; to buoy them up as much as possible, and lay them sideways on the bar, at high tide, and in mild weather, where they are steadied by means of cables and anchors, until the yielding sand is washed away, and they are forced over by the power of the ebb tide, which runs like a mill-race.

Rhabat is supplied with water by a considerable stream led into the city by means of an old fashioned aqueduct from the south, that is four or five leagues in length: the aqueduct was either built or thoroughly repaired by the old and liberal emperor Sidi Mohammed. I wished to visit the town of Salle, so famous in history for its piracies on the ocean, situated on the other side of the river, and directly opposite Rhabat, but I was dissuaded from making the attempt, by Mr. Abouderham and my guide, who said that the whole people of Sallee still retained their ancient pride, prejudices, and natural ferocity: that no Christian, or even a Barbary Jew in a Christian dress, could enter their walls if he was ever so well guarded by imperial soldiers, without being in imminent danger of losing his life. Mr. Abouderham said he had visited it twice; that it contained about forty thousand fierce and haughty Moors, and four thousand miserable Jews.

CHAPTER 34

Arrival at Tangier

On Sunday, the 14th January, 1816, being anxious to get forward on my journey, I went into the Jews' town to make the necessary preparations; for I intended to proceed without my Jew's company whom I had found out to be deceitful and dishonest, having already manoeuvred me out of most of my money. The soldier and muleteer went along with me: this muleteer, as I before observed, had been a sailor; had visited Spain and Portugal, and spoke the Spanish language so that I could understand him; his name was Mohammed, soon after our entrance into the Millah, we saw a concourse of people, consisting of Moors and Jews, crowding about one of the single storied houses, which stood alone. Going near it, I inquired the cause of this assemblage, and was informed that a couple of that kind of Moors, called serpent-eaters, were about to amuse the Moors and Jews with a sight of two of the most venomous serpents on earth; together with their manner of attacking the human species: and that each one who chose to see the exhibition through the windows, (for it was to take place in that room,) must pay half a dollar.

Being desirous of having a look, I offered a dollar for a station at a window; but all the windows were already occupied, and the places paid for. My guard, observing my disappointment, asked me if I wished for a berth? which I answered by putting two dollars into his hand: whereupon he called out to the Jews at one of the windows to clear a place for *el Tibib del Sultan*. (The *Sultan's* doctor.) Those, however, who had paid their money, not liking to lose their places, were unwilling to move: upon which my guard brushed them away with his big cane without ceremony; giving me a whole window to myself, saying he would keep guard; and I looked into the room without interruption: it was about twenty feet long, and fifteen feet broad, paved with tiles, and plastered within. The windows had also been secured by an additional grating made of wire, in such a manner as to render it impossible for the serpents to escape from the room: it had but one door, and that had a hole cut through it, six or eight inches square; this hole was also secured by a grating. In the room stood two men who appeared to be Arabs, with long bushy hair and beards; and I was told they were a particular race of men that could charm serpents.

A wooden box, about four feet long and two feet wide, was placed near the door, with a string fastened to a slide at one end of it: this string went through a hole in the door. The two serpent-eaters were dressed in *haicks* only, and those very small ones. After they had gone through with their religious ceremonies most devoutly, they appeared to take an eternal farewell of each other: this done, one of them retired from the room, and shut the door tight after him. The Arab within seemed to be in dreadful distress: I could observe his heart throb and his bosom heave most violently; and he cried out very loudly, "*Allah houakibar!*" three times, which is, as I understood it, "God have mercy upon me!"

The Arab was at the farthest end of the room: at that instant the cage was opened, and a serpent crept out slowly; he was about four feet long, and eight inches in circumference; his colours were the most beautiful in nature, being bright, and variegated with deep yellow, a purple, a cream colour, black and brown spotted, &c. As soon as he saw the Arab in the room, his eyes, which were small and green, kindled as with fire: he erected himself in a second, his head two feet high, and darting on the defenceless Arab, seized him between the folds of his *haick*, just above his right hip bone, hissing most horribly: the Arab gave a horrid shriek, and another serpent came out of the cage. This last was black, very shining, and appeared to be seven or eight feet long, but not more than two inches in diameter: as soon as he had cleared the cage, he cast his red fiery eyes on his intended victim, thrust out his forked tongue, threw himself into a round coil, erected his head, which was in the centre of the coil, three feet from the floor, flattening out the skin above his head and eyes in the form and nearly of the size of a human heart; and, springing like lightning on the Arab, struck its fangs into his neck, near the jugular vein, while his tail and body flew round his neck and arms in two or three folds.

The Arab set up the most hideous and piteous yelling, foamed and frothed at the mouth, grasping the folds of the serpent, which were round his arms, with his right hand, and seemed to be in the greatest agony—striving to tear the reptile from around his neck, while with his left he seized hold of it near its head, but could not break its hold: by this time, the other had twined itself around his legs, and kept biting all around the lower parts of his body, making apparently deep incisions: the blood, issuing from every wound, both in his neck and body, streamed all over his *haick* and skin.

My blood was chilled in my veins with horror at this sight, and it was with difficulty my legs would support my frame. (Notwithstanding the Arab's greatest exertions to tear away the serpents with his hands, they twined themselves still tighter, stopped his breath, and he fell to the floor, where he continued for a moment, as if in the most inconceivable agony, rolling over, and covering every part of his body with his own blood and froth, until he ceased to move, and appeared to have expired. In his last struggle he had wounded the black serpent with his teeth, as it was striving, as it were, to force its head into his mouth; which wound seemed to increase its rage.

At this instant, I heard the shrill sound of a whistle; and looking towards the door, saw the other Arab applying a call to his mouth: the serpents listened to the music; their fury seemed to forsake them by decrees; they disengaged themselves leisurely from the apparently lifeless carcass; and creeping towards the cage, they soon entered it, and were immediately fastened in. The door of the apartment was now opened, and he without ran to assist his companion: he had a phial of blackish liquor in one hand, and an iron chisel in the other: finding the teeth of his companion set, he thrust in the chisel, pried them open, and then poured a little of the liquor into his mouth; and holding the lips together, applied his mouth to the dead man's nose, and filled his lungs with air: he next anointed his numerous wounds with a little of the same liquid; and yet no sign of life appeared. I thought he was dead in earnest; his neck and veins were exceedingly swollen; when his comrade, taking up the lifeless trunk in his arms, brought it out into the open air, and continued the operation of blowing for several minutes, before a sign of life appeared: at length he gasped, and after a time recovered so far as to be able to speak.

The swellings on his neck, body, and legs, gradually subsided, as they continued washing the wounds with clear cold water, and a sponge, and applying the black liquor occasionally: a clean *haick* was wrapped about him, but his strength seemed so far exhausted, that he could not support himself standing; so his comrade laid him on the ground by a wall, where he sunk into a sleep. This exhibition lasted for about a quarter of an hour from the time the serpents were let loose, until they were called off, and it was more than an hour from that time before he could speak.

I thought that I could discover that the poisonous fangs had been pulled out of these formidable serpents' jaws, and mentioned that circumstance to the showman, who said that they had indeed been extracted; and when I wished to know how swellings on his neck and other parts could be assumed, he assured me, that though their deadly fangs were out, yet that the poisonous quality of their breath and spittle would cause the death of those they attack: that after a bite from either of these serpents, with all their fangs, no man could exist longer than fifteen minutes, and that there was no remedy for any but those who were endowed by the Almighty with power to charm and to manage them, and that he and his associate were of that favoured number.

The Moors and Arabs call the thick and beautiful serpent *El Effah*, and the long black and heart-headed one *El Buschkah*. I afterwards saw engravings of these two serpents in *Jackson's Morocco*, which are very correct resemblances: they are said to be very numerous on and about the south foot of the Atlas mountains, and border of the desert, where these were caught when young, and where they often attack and destroy both men and beasts. The *Effah's* bite is said to be incurable, and its poison so subtile as to cause a man's death in fifteen minutes. When I saw the *Effah*, it brought to my mind the story of the fiery serpents that bit the children of Israel in the deserts of Arabia, near Mount Hor, as recorded in the 21st chapter of the *Book of Numbers*; merely because the *Effah* resembled in appearance a brazen serpent: the two serpent-eaters said they came from Egypt about three years ago.

This exhibition of serpents, (the first, I was told, of the kind that had lately taken place at Rhabat,) and our preparations, detained us the whole day; however, I had made all the necessary arrangements, got the tent, provisions, &c. in order to be ready for a start the next morning, and on January the 15th, very early, I took my leave of Mr. Abouderham, who, though a Jew, was nevertheless a man of feeling, and much of a gentleman: he is a native of Leghorn, had received a good education, and spoke the French language fluently.

We crossed the river, which is here about half a mile wide, and proceeded towards the walls of Sallee: the river has entirely left the Sallee side, which is now filled up with sand and mud, leaving the town nearly a mile from the water: there were still to be seen some remains of its ancient docks, and wrecks of vessels. I looked attentively at Sallee, in passing its walls, which are high and strong, built of stone, and well cemented; they had been repaired lately, and are flanked by many circular and square towers, on which about two hundred pieces of cannon are still mounted, of all calibres; and it appeared that it must have formerly been mounted with seven hundred pieces more.

Near its walls, on the east, north, and west sides, are beautiful gardens that appear to be extremely fertile, well laid out, and cultivated: great numbers of orange, lemon, and sweet lemon trees, were bending under their loads of rich yellow fruit: hundreds of fig, pomegranate, almond, and other fruit trees, were now leafless, but budding forth, and thus promising abundance in their season. Many of the gardens are of great extent, and planted with the cotton tree, which is small, and produces cotton inferior to the American, called Georgia Upland, and only in small quantities.

As we proceeded on our road, we came to the aqueduct which supplies Sallee with fresh water: this aqueduct serves as an outer wall to the city on the north: it is nearly a mile from it, and about thirty feet high where we passed through it: here are three large arches resembling gateways, and marks are still to be seen, where gates were once hung: the wall is eight or ten feet in thickness, and the aqueduct appears to be about four miles in length. The canal for conducting the water is near the top, but uncovered; this aqueduct is said to have been built by the Romans; it is formed of large hewn stones and is extremely solid.

We travelled on through a fine Champaign country, everywhere cultivated, until two, p. m. when we saw on our left, and passed a lake of fresh water, about two miles in length, and half a mile in breadth: this was the first lake, or indeed pond, I had ever seen in this country; and soon afterwards we arrived on the bank of the River Mediah. On the left bank of this river, near its mouth, stands, though mostly in ruins, the ancient Portuguese town and fortress of Mamora the fortress is situated on a high hill that overlooks the surrounding country, commands the ruins of the town, and is now garrisoned by about three hundred black troops.

The town was built close along the bank of the river, and its northern wall was washed by every tide; and though very old, has not yet sustained much injury. The river enters the sea over a bar in a N. W. direction: the lower wall has an excellent circular battery, built of large hewn stone, and was calculated for mounting thirty heavy guns for the defence of the harbour; though now dismantled. This town wall is about half a mile in length along the river, and the ruins two hundred yards in breadth; the place was once very strongly walled in on the land side, but this wall is now in ruins: not a soul inhabits this town at present. Here some of my former opinions were confirmed; for it is certain that the sea has receded from this coast: the evident marks of the water high on this wall, and on the point of land near which the town stands, that must from appearance have been worn in by the dashing of the sea, together with the situation of the present bar, prove to an observer, without any possibility of doubt, that the ocean has receded since this place was built, for more than a mile distance, and that its perpendicular height has decreased at least fifteen feet since that period. I do not pretend to account for this fact, but leave it to be explained by philosophers.

We were to cross this river in a good boat that took over fifteen camels with their loads at a trip; but there were on the bank, waiting for their turns to cross, at least five hundred loaded camels, besides mules and asses, chiefly with burdens of wheat and barley, going on to Tangier and Tetuan, where all kinds of bread-stuffs were said to be very scarce and dear. I told my soldier that it was necessary to inform the boatman that I was the emperor's surgeon, and himself an *alcayd*; that we could not wait, but must pass over immediately, for the wind blew fresh from the S.W. and they had but one boat, which could not make above six trips in a day; and it would not be our turn, from the then appearances, in less than a week: this, with an offer of two dollars to the boatman, had the desired effect, and we were ferried over with the second boat-load, though not without much opposition and dispute between my guard and those who were waiting before us, and which was only settled by the interference of the black garrison; for my guide had the address to persuade them that he was indeed an *alcayd*, and I the *Sultan's* doctor. After crossing the river, we mounted the sand-hills, and at 10, p. m. pitched our tent in the midst of a *douhar*, where we got some milk and eggs for our money.

Tuesday, the 16th, we started very early: it had rained hard with heavy squalls of wind most part of the preceding night, but my tent being sound, kept off the storm: it was now clear and serene; nearly the whole face of the ground was covered with violet and pink coloured flowers, not more than an inch or two in height, which seemed to have sprung up during the night, and as the sun exhaled the dews from around them, the fresh air of the morning was filled with the most delightful fragrance. The country on our right was a low morass, partly covered with water, which soon grew into a lake of considerable breadth. We travelled, during the whole day, along its left margin: its surface was spotted over with innumerable wild ducks and other aquatic birds, which some of the inhabitants were shooting at.

In lieu of boats they use a kind of *catamaran*, which is made by lashing three small *palm tree logs* together by means of cords made of the bark of this useful tree; they have a crotched stick set up near one end of their float for a rest to their guns, and instead of oars, use long poles to force it along: when the gunner gets on his raft, he leaves his *haick* behind him for fear of wetting it, and shoves out entirely naked: their guns are very long and clumsy, with Moorish locks; so that mode of fowling supplies them with but little game, though the lake is nearly covered with it.

The sight of this catamaran brought to my mind those made use of in the Atlantic ocean along the coast of Brazil, and in some other parts of the world: the fishermen on those coasts form a raft by laying three rough logs alongside of one another, thirty feet in length, and pinning them together with wooden tree nails; they then place two more logs partly on the upper side of the exterior logs, and pin them on fast; sharpen the two ends of all the logs, and the float is finished. To make it manageable, they raise a four-legged bench in it, near the centre, which serves to steady a mast, on which they hoist a shoulder-of-mutton sail, and go out to sea. I have seen them twenty leagues from land. These boats are perfectly safe, for they can neither leak, upset, nor founder, and sail remarkably fast, and are steered with a stout oar.

There are several islands in this lake, on one of which there is a very spacious sanctuary, many fruit trees, and several apparently good gardens. Since leaving Darlbeda, we had seen no high land, only moderate acclivities, no more than to make it agreeable to the cultivator. This afternoon we discovered the ridge of mountains which lie behind Fez and Miquinez, stretching from the Atlas to the straits of Gibraltar, and forming one of the far-famed pillars of Hercules. At first they were scarcely visible in the distant horizon, and appeared like the tops of high islands, when approaching them on the ocean: not a tree or bush of any magnitude had we seen for several days, except the fig, palm, or other fruit trees, which were generally planted in clusters, or in gardens near the towns: at night we pitched our tent at a *douhar* near the border of the lake.

Wednesday, January the 17th, we started early, and went down the bank near the sea, to pass round the former outlet of this lake, which was now dammed with sea-sand very high; and on the sides of the bank which formed the outlet, stood four saint-houses, nearly covered up with sand-drifts. Continuing our journey until about noon, we began to come among trees of considerable size; they looked like a species of oak with a thick shaggy bark, but are an evergreen: this wood is very brittle, and the trees produce a kind of acorn of a very large size, which the Spaniards and Portuguese used to carry away in large quantities from this country: they were as highly esteemed as the chesnut, and used for food by the people of those nations: they also fed their swine on them.

Passing through a large forest, we came to a small lake on our right, and, at sunset, approached the walls of Laresch. Having heard that some Spanish friars resided here, I inquired for them, and was soon conducted to their dwelling, a very good house of European construction. The principal friar came out to meet me; and after I had given a short account of myself in Spanish, said he would lodge me for charity's sake; and then conducted me into a tolerably well furnished room: and, as he had lived in Mogadore, he asked me many questions concerning that city, and his old acquaintances there, some of whom I happened to know. He treated me with some wine, which he said was of his own manufacture; it was none of the best, however: and, at 10 o'clock at night, an excellent supper of fowls and salads, dressed in the Spanish style, was served up.

This *Padre*, whose name is Juan Tinaones, told me that he had lived in Barbary for ten years, four of which he had spent at Mogadore, three at Rhabat, and three here, secluded from the civilized world; that the court of Spain allowed a large premium to those *Padres*, or Fathers, of good character, to be approved of by the Archbishop, who are willing to spend ten years in Barbary as missionaries, and a stipend of three thousand dollars a year for the remainder of their lives. I asked him of what use he could be in Barbary to the cause of Christianity, since he dare not even attempt to convert a Moor or an Arab, or mention the name of the Saviour as one of the Godhead to either, or even to a Jew?

"None at all," said he, "but still we bear the name of missionaries at home, to convert the heathen: our allowance of money is ample: we live well, as you see, (he was indeed fat and in fine order,) laugh at the folly of our countrymen, and enjoy the present as well as we can."

(The circumstance of there being two young and pretty Jewesses in the house, and plenty of good cheer, did not tend, in any great degree, to discredit his representation.) "When this ten years expire," continued this pious *Padre*, "we get leave to return to our country, where we are received as patterns of piety, that have rendered vast services to the Christian world: every respectable house is open to receive us: our company is much sought after: our yearly salary of three thousand dollars affords us many gratifications; and, for these ten years spent in such privations and severe gospel labours, we are allowed absolution for the remainder of our lives, which, you will readily believe, we try to make as comfortable as possible."

Padre (*i. e.* father) Tinaones wanted to know if I was a Catholic? To this I answered in the negative. He said it was a pity; and that, unless I came within the pale of the Church, he feared my precious soul would be forever miserable. Our conversation next turned upon the Jews: he said, "there were about two hundred miserable families of them in Laresch, who, though they are, in a manner, slaves to the Mohammedans, will not believe in our holy religion: there were two Jews who applied to me, and said they were converted to the true Catholic faith, and believed Jesus Christ to be the Son of God, and the Saviour of mankind: they were accordingly baptized as Christians; yet, as soon as they had obtained a loan of four hundred dollars from me, in small sums, and found they could get no more, they turned back to Judaism again, and left me no means of redress; which fully convinced me that their pretended conversion to Christianity was nothing more than a premeditated scheme to rob me of my money; and that, whenever a Jew professes to become a Christian, it is but a false pretence, and he is actuated entirely by mercenary motives.

"The Jews," added he, "hold Christ and his followers in the greatest possible contempt, and pretend to believe that all men, who are not Israelites, will be doomed, at the day of judgment, to eternal punishment." This night was principally spent in conversation with the *Padre*, on various subjects.

Thursday, January 18th, I made ready to go on early, but the tide ran so rapidly at that time, that it was impossible to pass the river without the risk of being driven into the sea; so I had time to make observations.

Laresch is handsomely situated on the left bank of the River Saboo, near its entrance into the sea: the town lies along the river's bank, and is half a mile in length, but very narrow: it is strongly walled in all around, and has two gates, one on the east, and the other on the south side: the fortress is on a hill south of the town, from which it is only separated by a wall; it is strongly built, and flanked by eight towers; has about one hundred pieces of cannon mounted on its battlements, and stands too high to be battered down by the shipping, even if they could get into the river. This town is said to have been built by the Portuguese originally, and only occupies the same space it did formerly, that is to say, about one mile in circumference: it contains about eighteen thousand inhabitants, *i. e.* sixteen thousand Moors, and two thousand Jews, who are all very poor, as no trade is carried on here by sea or by land: they are obliged to work hard in the adjacent gardens, and till the impoverished fields, in order to gain a scanty subsistence.

This is the only safe port the Emperor of Morocco has for fitting out his large cruisers, from whence they can get to sea with their armament: the river here is very narrow, runs close along the walls of Laresch, and is very deep opposite the town: there is said to be on the bar at its mouth eighteen feet of water at high spring tides. The river within the town is both broad and deep; the tides run very rapidly both at flood and ebb, so much so, that we were obliged to wait until it was nearly spent before it was deemed safe to cross: directly in the ferrying place, an old brig lay sunk, which had been captured under the Russian flag, and the crew kept as slaves or prisoners for about a year.

The Emperor's navy was now lying alongside of the opposite bank, consisting of one frigate-built ship, coppered to the bends, of about 700 tons burden, and mounting 32 guns, apparently 13 pounders, on the main deck; and a brig, called the *Swearah*, also coppered—a beautiful vessel, mounting 18 guns, said to sail, and from her appearance, would sail very fast: she was built in England, and there fitted in the best possible manner, and presented to the emperor by a Jew of Mogadore, named Macnin, a most notorious character, but called a very rich merchant: this Jew has a brother in London, who, it is said, has heretofore managed to get goods on credit to very large amounts, and he then sends them to Mogadore, where his brother loads back the ships with less, generally, than half the value of the outward cargo, and thus continues to gull the English merchants in the true Barbary style: the principal in London fails—his creditors compound with him: he begins anew; obtains, from some quarter or another, all the credit he wishes; sends out the goods to Barbary; gets no returns; fails again, and again compromises, and commences the old business.

The emperor, some time ago, attempted to give this worthy Jew merchant a gentle squeeze, and seized his goods, houses, cash, and everything valuable that his officers could lay their hands on; upon which Macnin, to conciliate his majesty, and to get a part of his ill-gotten property back again, made him a present of this fine brig, which could not have cost him much, for "*los Inglesis lo pagan*," (the English pay for it,) is his motto. These two vessels and the new frigate at Rhabat, now constitute the whole of the emperor's naval force: his maxim is to be at war with every nation who has not made a treaty with him, or which has not a Consul General residing at Tangier, to make him the customary presents on his annual holidays, or pay him tribute agreeably to the terms of his treaties.

According to this system, he sends out his cruisers from time to time, who, if they find a vessel bearing a flag, whose nation has not made a treaty of peace with him, they capture her, bring her in as a good prize, and retain the crew as slaves or prisoners. About eighteen months ago, this brig *Mogadore*, then on a cruise, captured the Russian brig before mentioned, and carried her into Laresch: now the emperor of Russia had not stipulated for a peace with his Moorish majesty, and had no Consul residing at Tangier; so the vessel's cargo was soon disposed of as a prize, and her officers and crew, ten in number, were thrown into prison, and frequently compelled to work on board the vessels of war. After about a year's captivity in this manner, finding no Christian power claimed the men, and having no use for them, the emperor ordered them to be removed to the prison at Tangier. Padre Tinaones told me these facts, and said he had done all he could for the Christians while they were in Laresch prison, and that their brig had sunk, in the ferrying-place for want of care.

Proceeding on our journey, we soon mounted the high hills on the right bank of this river, where we found many huts constructed of stones and mud, with steep roofs thatched with straw, after the manner of the Scotch and Irish hovels: these were the first buildings of the kind I had seen in Africa, and contrary to the Moorish custom, they were quite defenceless. Continuing our journey through a long wood, and over a hilly, sandy soil, all this day as fast as possible, we pitched our tent at night in a deep valley, near a small *douhar*, where we obtained some milk for our suppers. It commenced raining in the evening, and continued to pour without intermission, attended with strong gales and squalls, until daylight, but as our tent was t:ght and strong, I experienced from it no material inconvenience.

Friday the 19th, soon after daylight, it ceased to rain, and we proceeded on our journey. After passing many *douhars* and some huts of the construction mentioned near Laresch, we entered a deep valley, the breadth of which was about six miles: the rain had soaked the soil so much, as to render it almost impassable, so that the mules sunk into the mud nearly up to their bellies, and we were obliged to dismount and wade through it on foot.

This valley contains two small rivers, which are not fordable at high tides: the little town of Azila stands at their mouth, and lay about ten miles to our left: the quantity of rain that had fallen the preceding night, had rendered them quite deep even at low water, so that in attempting to ford one of them on my mule, he was carried away by the current, and I was forced to swim; however, I held the mule by the bridle, and landed safely. My soldier and muleteer seeing I had got safe across, at length ventured in different places, and also succeeded in getting over. Our way now became very mountainous and woody, and the deep valleys, through which a number of brooks ran winding along in very serpentine courses, rendered our path muddy and slippery.

At 3, p. m. we gained the summit of a mountain, when I saw distinctly the bay of Tangier, part of the straits of Gibraltar, and to my great joy, the coast of Spain; it was the hospitable shore of civilized Europe! The crowd of sensations that rushed upon my mind at this grateful sight, can be more easily conceived than described. It brought to my recollection the trials and distresses I had undergone since leaving it, as well as my great deliverances: all these sensations together so overcame my faculties, and agitated me in such a manner, that I had not power to keep myself steady, and I actually fell from my mule no less than three times in travelling from thence to Tangier, a distance of five or six miles.

As I had not before fallen from my mule during my whole journey from Mogadore, the soldier who guarded me thought it very extraordinary, nor could I persuade him that I was not too ill to ride: he, therefore, after helping me on again the third time, gave his horse to the muleteer, and walked by my side, holding me on for some time: my head, however, became so dizzy from the state of my feelings, that I was obliged to alight and walk with his assistance for about a mile, until we came near the walls of Tangier, when he again, at my request, placed me on my mule.

It was in the dusk of the evening when we arrived at the gate, and the soldier having announced me to the guards, I was conducted directly into the city, and before the governor, who ordered me to be escorted to the American Consul's house, where I soon arrived, and was received most hospitably by James Simpson, Esquire, the American Consul General, who immediately introduced me to his amiable lady and family, and requested me to consider his house my home. I accordingly took up my day-quarters with him, and remained under his truly hospitable roof during my stay at Tangier. I having made a present to my guard and muleteer for their attention and fidelity to me on the journey, and made up a packet for my friend Willshire, I despatched them with his mule, &c. on the 22nd of January, 1816, back for Mogadore.

CHAPTER 35

Embarks for America

During my stay at Tangier, I was made acquainted with Mr. Green, the English Consul General, a gentleman of talents, high respectability, and worth; and with Mr. Agrill, the Swedish Consul General, who had lately arrived there from Sweden. On his arrival, he found the crew of the before mentioned Russian brig, in Tangier prison, and finding there was no one to claim or redeem them, and that they were natives of what once was Swedish Pomerania, he purchased them from the Sultan for about two thousand dollars, which he paid out of his own private funds, and set them at liberty. I saw and conversed with the master and most of the crew of that vessel, who told me they had been imprisoned at Laresch about a year; had been robbed of most of their clothing, and then brought to Tangier, where Mr. Agrill had the charity and humanity to redeem them, though they were captured under the Russian flag, and did not owe allegiance to the Swedish government. Mr. Agrill kept them in his own house, waiting for a Swedish vessel of war, which was daily expected, and by which he meant to send them to their country. The captain mentioned to me that his vessel was in fact English property covered by the Russian flag, in order to avoid capture by the American cruisers. I had before known Mr. Agrill in St. Petersburg, Russia—then in a public character: he is a man of much real worth.

Tangier bay is said to be the best harbour in the Moorish dominions: its bottom is clear, and it might contain at one time one thousand sail of large vessels, which would ride in safety, being sheltered from all but the northerly winds, which have only the rake of the breadth of the strait, and the holding ground is excellent: the best anchorage is in seven and a half fathoms water; where the Portuguese flag-staff (which is the westernmost, and near the water) is on a line the American flagstaff, which latter is high, and can always be known by having its flag hoisted when an American vessel approaches the bay. The city of Tangier is built on the west side and near the mouth of the bay, on the declivity of a hill, two miles east of Cape Spartel, rising like an amphitheatre; the houses are built of stone, and whitewashed, and the town, when seen from the bay or strait, has a very handsome appearance; but it is badly built; the houses being generally small, and but one story high, with flat terraced roofs: the streets are narrow, crooked, badly paved, and commonly very dirty.

There are, however, some handsome buildings in Tangier; among which are the Spanish, Swedish, Dutch, French, Danish, and Portuguese consular houses: the old English consular house has been lately abandoned on account of its bad construction, but they are now building a very elegant one, that is said to have already cost the British government ten thousand pounds sterling, and will cost nearly as much more by the time it is finished and furnished. The American government has no consular house at Tangier; the consul general resides in a house that was formerly attached to that of the Swedish consulate: it was purchased by Mr. Simpson, on his own private account, for his own use, and for an office for the use of the United States, in order to save the expense of house rent; and the dwelling part is so small and inconvenient, that when his own children visit him from abroad, he is forced to hire lodgings for them in Jews' or other houses.

I believe every government having a consul residing at Tangier, except that of my own country, has either built or purchased a mansion for the accommodation of that officer. Mr. Simpson's eldest son, with his lady, were now on a visit to their parents; and the consul had to hire apartments in a Jew's house for a few days to accommodate them: he was also under the necessity of procuring lodgings for me in a Jew's house during a few nights of my stay there.

Tangier is an irregularly built walled town of about one mile in circuit, including the fortress which overlooks and commands it: it is well supplied with water by a covered aqueduct, and generally well furnished with provisions: the several batteries are lined with many pieces of ordnance, among which are two pieces of long brass cannon of about fourteen inches calibre; they are mounted on carriages, and stand in a battery near the landing without the city gate: these two enormous brass pieces were made by the Portuguese, and are (judging by the eye) about eighteen feet in length.

Tangier was taken from the Moors in the year 1441, by the Portuguese, who gave it to King Charles the II. of England, in a dowry for Catharine of Portugal, his queen. The English kept possession of it for about twenty years; but, finding it subject to the continual attacks of the ferocious Moors, from whom it was with great difficulty defended, they blew up its fine mole or basin, (which had before rendered it a safe harbour for small vessels,) to low water mark, together with some of the fortifications, and abandoned the place: the mole has not since been rebuilt.

I walked over it at low water: a great quantity of the large blocks of hewn stone are now to be seen lying on the solid foundations, which still remain almost entire. On the east side oft and near the bottom of the bay, are to be seen the ruins of an old town, which is said to have been built by the Romans. It must formerly have been very extensive, from the present appearance of its ruins and was watered by a small river that runs into the bay near its site. There are several forts and batteries on the eastern shore of the bay, and on Cape Malibat, but they are so badly garrisoned as not to be formidable to their enemies, if any should chance to take shelter in the bay during bad weather: they have only to keep out of the reach of the shot from Tangier. All the Christian consuls near the Emperor of Morocco reside at Tangier, where their persons are protected by order of the *Sultan*. Those at Tangier are—for the United States of America, James Simpson, Esq.; Great Britain, Mr. Green; France, Mr. Sourdian; Sweden, Mr. Agrill; Spain, Don Orne, vice-consul; Denmark, Mr. Scomboe; Holland, Mr. Nijsoin; and Portugal, Mr. Coloso.

The consuls at Tangier keep up a sort of etiquette, in celebrating the memorable epochs in the history of their respective countries, and their particular national holidays, which custom is peculiar to Tangier. They also keep up the long established custom of giving consular dinners all in turn round on the arrival of any new consul, or when an old one is recalled, &c. These customs are extremely expensive, but have now become absolutely necessary in order to impress the minds of the Moors with respect for the dignity of the respective nations which those consuls represent. The Christian Consuls general, near the Emperor of Morocco, are, generally speaking, men eminent on account of character, talents, and learning, and have a large salary; for, like foreign ministers plenipotentiary, they are not allowed to derive any emolument whatever from commerce.

By accepting of this appointment, they exclude themselves from the society and comforts of the civilized world, and live besides in exile, and in continual jeopardy, being always in the power of real barbarians. They are under the necessity of sending to Europe for all their clothing, liquors, stores, furniture, &c. except a few articles of provisions, and those who have families are obliged to send their children to other countries for their education, though at a very heavy expense.

Mr. Simpson left a lucrative commercial establishment at Gibraltar, in 1798, and went to Tangier, merely to serve our government, at a time when war was intended by the Moorish *Sultan* against our commerce. He succeeded in averting the threatened blow, and in establishing our present treaty with that sovereign. He is a gentleman of unblemished character and pleasing manners, and has expended a handsome fortune in the service of the United States, over and above his consular salary. He has passed the best of his days in the service of his adopted country, and, in my opinion, deserves a handsome maintenance from government during the remainder of his life, free from the cares, vexations, and anxieties that are always attached to a consulate in such barbarous countries. Mr. Simpson is a native of Scotland, but a firm American in principle, and an enthusiastic admirer of our excellent institutions.

The whole sea force of the Emperor of Morocco, as I before observed, consists of two frigates of 32 guns each, and the brig *Mogadore* of 13 guns: the only port he has which can shelter and secure them from the reach of an enemy, is Laresch, which they can neither enter nor sail from when equipped, except at high-water spring tides. There are no *corsairs* or small vessels belonging to individuals as formerly, nor is there even a merchant vessel belonging to the Moors. In order to show how much value the present *Sultan* sets on his ships of war, I must relate in what manner he sometimes disposes of them.

About two years since, the *Bashaw* of Tripoli sent as a present to the Emperor of Morocco, a beautiful Circassian girl: she was a virgin and possessed charms with which the old *Sultan* was so enraptured, that he asked the ambassador who escorted her from Tripoli, what he could send to his friend, the *Bashaw*, in return for this jewel? I have nothing but wheat, said he, of which the *Bashaw*, your master, can always have as much as he pleases. The *Bashaw*, my master, said the ambassador, is always in want of wheat: but, replied the Emperor, I would send him something more valuable; he has made me a most superb present, and I wish to return the compliment in a handsome manner. Your majesty has frigates, said the ambassador:—so I have, indeed, answered the *Sul-*

tan, and that gives me much pleasure; go to Laresch, and make choice of one from among my navy: I will have her fitted out in the best manner, and sent round to your master directly: the ambassador did not wait a second bidding, but went in haste to Laresch, for fear the sovereign might change his mind; chose a fine new frigate of 32 guns that had but a short time previous been coppered to the bends, which was immediately fitted according to promise, and sent to Tripoli, with the ambassador on board, and where she arrived in safety, being escorted by an English vessel of war.

Both Mr. Simpson and Mr. Green assured me, that this statement was in substance correct. The Emperor's squadron might be blockaded, at all times, by a very small force; his large ships are, therefore, not at all to be dreaded by any maritime power who has timely notice of his hostile intentions, as they are badly equipped and manned, having now no maritime commerce, and consequently no nursery for se men. The only port from which he could do any mischief of importance to Christian commerce, is Tangier. Should this or any future Sultan, think proper to declare war against any maritime state, he has only to send money over to Cadiz, Algeciras, or Gibraltar, and purchase fast sailing lateen rigged boats; fit and man them in Tangier immediately, and send them to cruise in the mouth of the straits: thus they might seize on the unsuspecting and unarmed merchant ships, as they pass along—conduct them into Tangier bay, or to any place along the coast, where they would soon unload and run the vessels on shore, keeping their crews as slaves.

In this light alone can the Emperor of Morocco be reckoned formidable to commercial states, and this game could only be played for a short time, until the nation thus attacked could send a force sufficient to destroy the marauders. It would be good policy, however, to keep at peace with the Moorish sovereign, as his rovers, lying at the door of the Mediterranean, might do much mischief; and to be a slave to the Moors, is, indeed, dreadful to a Christian.

Tangier has but little commerce with Europe, and this is chiefly carried on by the Jews; but the English government get their supplies of cattle and other fresh provisions for the garrison of Gibraltar, from that place and Tetuan: this and the other trifling trade is carried on in Gibraltar boats and Spanish small craft. There is a considerable coral fishery along the Moorish coast, about Cape Spartel; and while I remained at Tangier, two Spanish boats came into the port with what coral they had been able to procure for the last six months: it was of a beautiful colour, and of an excellent quality; I was informed by one of the boatmen, that in order to get the coral, they anchor in deep water, amongst the rocks, and let down their nets, which soon become entangled amongst the coral, and they then draw it on board: this man said that they came over from Tariffa, and obtained leave from the *Alcayd* of Tangier to fish on the coast, by agreeing to give him *one-third* of the coral they should obtain; that he put two Moors on board their boats (one each) to assist them in procuring provisions, water, &.c. and serve as safeguards: he said, the whole of the coral they then had was to be divided the next day, when they should sell their share at public sale to the highest bidder; and I afterwards understood from Mr. Simpson, that the French Consul purchased it for *twelve hundred dollars*, and there were twelve fishermen to share the money.

On the 29th of January, 1816, a small schooner being ready to sail for Gibraltar, I took my leave of Mr. Simpson and family, and proceeded on to the mole, in order to embark. This vessel had been hired by a certain Jew, named Torrel, to carry his family across to Gibraltar, which, with two or three other families of European Jews, who would not conform to the dress in which all Jews in Moorish Barbary had been ordered to appear, nor pay the tribute lately levied on them by the *Sultan*, were ordered to depart forthwith from his dominions.

These families came out of the gates of the city, in order to embark together, and proceeded with their baggage to the ruins o. the old mole, to go off in the boat, it being low water: they were accompanied by a considerable number of Jews and Jewesses: a few of the latter, very decently dressed, wished to escort them to the boat, and there to take their leave, &c.; but the Moorish captains of the port, without ceremony, began to brush them back with big staffs they carried for the purpose: these sticks were about five feet in length, and one inch in diameter, and they applied them so unmercifully, and with such singular dexterity, peculiar to the Moors, as to lay many decent looking Jewish females, as well as males, prostrate upon the beach; when they renewed their blows, in order to raise them on their feet again, and drive them into the city gate, like so many of the brute creation.

At about 8 o'clock, a. m. I got on board this vessel, in company with Mr. John Simpson and his lady, who were on their return from a visit to their parents; and after waiting nearly three hours for a letter which the Governor wished to send to Gibraltar, we set sail and left the bay with a fair but a light breeze. The scene of inhumanity and oppression I had just witnessed, prompted me to thank my God again that I was once more free from a country inhabited by the worst of barbarians.

Passing up the strait, which in one place is only eight miles broad, we arrived safe in Gibraltar bay in the evening; but as we did not get up before the town until the gates of the garrison were closed, we were obliged to remain (forty in number) on board the vessel during the night. On the 30th we were visited very early by a boat from the health office and permitted to land. I went on shore immediately and was received by my friend Sprague with demonstrations of unfeigned joy, and heartily welcomed to that portion of the civilized world, and treated with all the attention that flows from the warmest friendship, and the tenderest commiseration. The American Consul was also attentive to me, and he had previously paid attention to the wants of my companions in distress, who had arrived there from Mogadore by sea a few days before me.

An acquaintance told me that Mr. Sprague had received Mr. Willshire's letter, informing him of my captivity, on one Monday morning at the moment of his return from Algeciras, a famous Spanish town on the opposite side of the bay, about ten miles from Gibraltar, where he generally spent the Sabbath; that he opened the letter in the presence of, and read its contents to Mr. Henry, United States Consul, a Mr. Kennedy of Baltimore, and some other American gentlemen: that Mr. Henry suggested that a subscription should be opened and sent up to all the Consuls in the Mediterranean, in order to raise money as soon as possible, and transmit it to Mogadore to release us: that Mr. Sprague made no answer whatever to this proposition, but sent a trusty young man out with orders to purchase two double-barrelled guns, while he hastily wrote a few lines to Mr. Willshire and myself, as before mentioned: that there was but one double-barrelled fowling-piece to be procured in the garrison; this was bought at the price of *eighty dollars*, and taking it, together with his own, which was a very highly finished and favourite piece, he mounted his horse and proceeded as fast as possible to Algeciras, carrying the guns along with him; from whence he immediately despatched a courier to Tariffa with the guns and his letters, ordering them to be sent by an express boat to Tangier, and to the care of Mr. Simpson, to be again forwarded by express to Mogadore.

Such disinterested goodness, and such prompt and animated exertions to relieve a fellow-creature in distress, have seldom been recorded, and are above all praise: they are examples of pure benevolence, that do honour to human nature; and ever honoured and beloved shall he be, who has the heart and the spirit to imitate them.

Mr. Sprague had already paid the bills I had drawn on him in Mogadore for my ransom, &c. and he now furnished me with provisions and stores for my voyage home, I having determined to go by the first vessel for the United States. The ship *Rapid*, of New-York, Captain Robert Williams, being in readiness to sail for that port, I embarked in her, accompanied by Mr. Savage and Horace; Clark, and Burns, having been previously accommodated on board the ship *Rolla*, Captain Brown, of Newburyport, that was to proceed to the United States by way of Cadiz. We set sail for our native country on the 2nd of February, 1816, with a fair breeze, and on the 3rd were safe without the straits.

As Gibraltar has been so frequently mentioned in my narrative, a few descriptive observations respecting it may not be uninteresting to some of my readers. Gibraltar is situated at the entrance of the Mediterranean sea, and is attached to the continent of Europe by a low and narrow neck of sandy land which, as it lies neither in Spain nor Gibraltar, is called the neutral ground. The rock appears to me to have been originally an island, and the beach or neutral ground to have been formed by the heaving up of sand and gravel from the Mediterranean sea on the one side, and from the bay of Gibraltar or the other.

The rock is about two miles in length from north to south, and one mile in breadth from east to west. It rises from the south point in abrupt cliffs, one above another, for about half a mile, when it comes to its extreme height, which is said by some to measure fourteen hundred feet, and by others, seventeen hundred feet from the surface of the water: the top extends, in uneven craggy points, for about one mile to the northward, when it breaks off in one sudden cliff, which is nearly perpendicular, to the neutral ground, forming a face nearly as wide as the rock itself, and completely inaccessible. This rock forms probably the strongest fortress in Europe: it has been long in the hands of the English; and is surmounted with batteries of heavy cannon in every direction, and is strongly walled in at every accessible point, so as to be considered impregnable.

The western side of the rock, near its base, is more flatted and less inaccessible: here the town is built, which consists of about two thousand stone houses, and it is said now to contain thirty thousand inhabitants, who may be said to compose a very heterogeneous mass;

for, as it is a free port, where the vessels and subjects of all nations who are at peace with England, enter with their goods, traffic and depart at pleasure, and are wholly free from governmental duties and impositions, people of all nations, tongues, and kindred, are there to be found. The bay is very spacious, and is capable of containing a vast number of shipping, which may ride in safety, except in heavy gales from the east or south.

This fortress is held by the English government as a key, or rather a lock and key to the Mediterranean sea, the door of which the Moors and Spaniards consider as their property. Its garrison is composed of native English troops, which, in time of war, ought to be seven thousand strong: it is commanded by a military governor, and is always under martial law. The British, with indefatigable industry, and immense labour, have formed roads up its steep western side, and constructed batteries, which are mounted with heavy artillery, on its very summit. Its eastern side is steep and inaccessible. In its northern side, next the neutral ground, but some hundred feet above it, excavations have been formed in the massy rock, in which heavy artillery is placed, and pointed through port-holes penetrating the solid front: these batteries completely command the land side, and are of course bomb proof—they are called the upper and lower galleries, and are of great extent.

Among its natural curiosities, St. Michael's cave is the most remarkable: this commences near the top of the rock, and no bottom to it has ever yet been found by the English, though it has been explored (such is the popular story) for many miles, and the Moors have a notion that it forms a passage under the strait to the coast of Morocco. Thousands of monkeys also inhabit the summit and recesses of this singular and barren rock, but which in time of war is the emporium of the Mediterranean trade.

After beating about for several days, near Cape St. Vincent, with heavy gales of wind from the westward, we steered to the southward into the latitude of Madeira, and I found that the reckonings of the officers on board were up fifty miles before we saw that island, though they had good opportunities to got meridian and other altitudes, which further confirmed me in the opinions I had already formed respecting the Gulf Stream, as elucidated in the Appendix. After passing Madeira, we made the best of our way into the latitude of the constant trade winds, say from 25 to 28 degrees, and ran down as far as about the longitude of 70°: then steered northward, and arrived in New-York on the 20th of March, 1816, where I was received by my friends and fellow-citizens with demonstrations of joy and commiseration.

I hastened to Middletown, Connecticut, to visit my family, whom I found in good health. Our meeting was one of those that language is inadequate to describe. I spent only a week with them, our hearts beating in unison, and swelling with gratitude to God for his mercies; when what I owed to my friend Sprague, and the remainder of my fellow-sufferers, called me to the seat of government. On my arrival in Washington, I was introduced by the Hon. Samuel W. Dana, Senator in Congress, to the Hon. James Monroe, Secretary of State, who received me in the most kind and feeling manner.

The administration paid from the treasury my own and my crew's ransom, thus far, amounting to *one thousand eight hundred and fifty-two dollars and forty-five cents,* and assured me that provision should be immediately made to meet the amount that might be demanded for the remainder of the crew, should they ever be found alive. The Secretary, together with many distinguished members of both houses of Congress, advised me to publish a Narrative of my late disasters, which I have faithfully performed, and shall now close my labours with a few brief remarks.

I have spent my days, thus far, amidst the bustle and anxieties incident to the life of a seaman and a merchant, and being now fully persuaded that the real wants of human nature are very few, and easily satisfied, I intend henceforth to remain, if it is God's will, in my native country. I have been taught in the school of adversity to be contented with my lot, whatever future adversities I may have to encounter, and shall endeavour to cultivate the virtues of charity and universal benevolence. I have drank deep of the bitter cup of sufferings and woe; have been dragged down to the lowest depths of human degradation and wretchedness; my naked frame exposed without shelter to the scorching skies and chilling night winds of the desert, enduring the most excruciating torments, and groaning, a *wretched slave,* under the stripes inflicted by the hands of barbarous monsters, bearing indeed the human form, but unfeeling, merciless, and malignant as demons; yet when near expiring with my various and inexpressible sufferings; when black despair had seized on my departing soul, amid the agonies of the most cruel of all deaths, I cried to the Omnipotent for mercy, and the outstretched hand of Providence snatched me from the jaws of destruction.

Unerring wisdom and goodness has since restored me to the comforts of civilized life, to the bosom of my family, and to the blessings of my native land, whose political and moral institutions are in themselves the very best of any that prevail in the civilized portions of the globe, and ensure to her citizens the greatest share of personal liberty, protection, and happiness; and yet, strange as it must appear to the philanthropist, my proud-spirited and free countrymen still hold a million and a half, nearly, of the human species, in the most cruel bonds of slavery, many of whom are kept at hard labour and smarting under the savage lash of inhuman mercenary drivers, and in many instances enduring besides the miseries of hunger, thirst, imprisonment, cold, nakedness, and even tortures.

This is no picture of the imagination: for the honour of human nature I wish its likeness were indeed nowhere to be found; but I myself have witnessed such scenes in different parts of my own country, and the bare recollection now chills my blood with horror. Adversity has taught me some noble lessons: I have now learned to look with compassion on my enslaved and oppressed fellow-creatures; I will exert all my remaining faculties in endeavours to redeem the enslaved, and to shiver in pieces the rod of oppression; and I trust I shall be aided in that holy work by every good and every pious free, and high-minded citizen in the community, and by the friends of mankind throughout the civilized world.

The present situation of the slaves in our country ought to attract an uncommon degree of commiseration, and might be essentially ameliorated without endangering the public safety, or even causing the least injury to individual interest. I am far from being of opinion that they should all be emancipated immediately, and at once.

I am aware that such a measure would not only prove ruinous to great numbers of my fellow-citizens, who are at present slave holders, and to whom this species of property descended as an inheritance; but that it would also turn loose upon the face of a free and happy country, a race of men incapable of exercising the necessary occupations of civilized life, in such a manner as to ensure to themselves an honest and comfortable subsistence; yet it is my earnest desire that such a plan should be devised, founded on the firm basis and the eternal principles of justice and humanity, and developed and enforced by the general government, as will gradually, but not less effectually, wither and extirpate the accursed tree of slavery, that has been suffered to take such deep root in our otherwise highly-favoured soil: while, at the same time, it shall put it out of the power of either the bond or the released slaves, or their posterity, ever to endanger our present or future domestic peace or political tranquillity.

Appendix

Being safely at sea on board a good ship, and on my way to join my family, my mind was more tranquillized than it had before been since my redemption, and I turned my thoughts to the natural causes which had produced my late disaster. Upon taking a full view of the subject, according to the best of my capacity, I felt convinced that not only my own vessel was driven on shore by a common current, but that most of the others that are known to have been wrecked from time to time on the same coast, have been operated upon by the same natural causes.

In order briefly to illustrate my position, I shall begin by stating, that to men who are conversant with maritime affairs, and, particularly, practical navigators, who have for a number of years traversed the Atlantic ocean to Madera and the Canary Islands, the West Indies, or Cape de Verds; who have sailed along the African coast—from thence south-eastward towards the negro or Guinea settlements, and to those who have been accustomed to navigate towards the continent of South America, sailing along the coast of Brazil, and between that coast and the west coast of Africa, and north of the Cape of Good Hope to the equator, it is well known that when sailing southwardly from Europe near the coast of Africa, and in fact nearly across the northern Atlantic ocean, the trade winds, as they are called, set in and generally prevail, blowing from north to northeast or east, from about latitude 32. N. on the African coast;—that farther westward, they only begin in the latitudes from 30. to 26.—in the last mentioned latitude near the coast of America.

They generally blow from the northeast to the parallel of 23. of north latitude, when they turn more to the eastward as you gain the offing from the African continent. The coast of Africa from Cape Spartel, in latitude 34. 40. to Cape Blanco, in about latitude 33. tends about southwest, thence about south-southwest to Santa Cruz de Berberia, or Agader, the southern and westernmost port in the empire of Morocco, in about the latitude 30. north, and longitude 10. west, from London—it then turns abruptly off to the west-southwestward, to Cape Nun, and continues nearly the same course, about west-southwest, with little variation to Cape Bajador, about latitude 26. north, longitude 16. west.—The whole length of this coast the winds blow either diagonally, or directly on shore perpetually; the reason of this I take to be, that the empire of Morocco west of the Atlas ridge of mountains is very dry and very hot, having few rivers, and those very small during the greatest part of the year.

There are no lakes of consequence, except one near Laresch, to cool the atmosphere, nor any showers of rain, except in winter, to refresh the thirsty earth. From Santa Cruz west, through what was formerly the kingdom of Suse, it blows right on shore, from the same causes operating in a stronger degree together, with a variation in the rending of the coast, and thence to Bajador, and along the coast of the great desert to the latitude of 17. north, and the trade wind continues to haul round, and actually near the land blows eastward into the gulf of Guinea.

This desert is scorched for about one half of the year by the rays of a vertical sun: here nature denies the refreshing rains that fall in other regions; the smooth even surface strongly reflecting the rapid sun's beams, while there are no trees or other objects to intercept the rays and prevent the most powerful accumulation of solar heat, which consequently becomes so excessive during the day time that it scorches like fire, and the air you breathe seems like the dry and suffocating vapour from glowing embers: here the wind ceases in the day time, being literally consumed by the sun; the whole surface thus becomes heated and baked in the day time, and when the sun disappears from above the horizon, the cooling wind rushes on to the desert from the ocean to restore the equilibrium of the atmosphere-

The sea breeze begins about six o'clock in the evening, and continues to increase gradually all along this coast until four o'clock in the morning, at which period it has risen to a strong gale, so that vessels navigating near the land are frequently forced to take in all their light sails by midnight, and to reef down snug before morning, when it begins to lull a little, and about mid-day becomes very moderate, and sometimes quite calm. Every practical man knows that the winds drive a current before them on the bosom of the ocean, as well as along its shores, that becomes more or less strong in proportion as the gale is light or heavy, and of long or short duration.

On this coast the current sets before the wind against the shore—it there meets with unconquerable resistance, and is turned southward: it is always felt from about Cape Blanco, (lat. 33.) southward, and grows stronger and stronger until it passes Cape Bajador, because it is more and more compressed—thence it strikes off, one part to the southwest towards the Cape de Verd Islands, and the remainder keeps along the coast to Cape de Verd, whence it spreads itself towards the equator, and some part follows the windings of the coast round the gulf of Guinea.

The southeast trade winds blow almost continually from the latitude of 30. south in the Atlantic ocean to the equator, and often to the 5th degree of northern latitude—these southeast trades assist those from the northeast in heaping up the water in the equatorial region, when both the northeast and southeast winds uniting, blow from the east- ward, bearing the whole mass of water on this surface towards the American continent: it strikes that continent to the northward of Cape la Roque, between the parallels of 6 degrees south latitude and the equator, on the coast of Brazil, where the coast turns to the westward;—being much compressed, it runs strongly along this coast to the mouth of the mighty river Amazon, with whose current it is united and borne down along the coast of Cayenne, Surinam, and Guyanna, receiving in its way all the waters brought against those coasts by the constant trade winds from the east and northeast, and all the great rivers which flow in from the southward, among which is the Oronoko, one of the longest on the continent of South America, and that rolls, in the rainy season, an immense body of water to the ocean: I have ascended that river five hundred miles.

The current runs so strong at times towards the west along this whole line of coast, (which is mostly low land, and has principally been made on the seaboard by the alluvial qualities of the waters in the rivers, brought down by freshes, which are then thick with mud, like those of the Mississippi,) as to render it impossible for any vessel to get to the windward or eastward by beating against the wind and current. Its velocity has been known to exceed three miles an hour. This great current is driven westward along the coast between it and the West India Islands, a great part of it entering the Gulf of Paria, south of the island of Trinidad, where it receives and is strengthened by the waters of the western branch of the Oronoko River;—here the high land, that evidently joined this island to the continent formerly, has been burst asunder, perhaps indeed assisted by an earthquake, or some other convulsion of nature: there are here several passages for the current, I think four, (for I write entirely from memory,) through the same mountain, which is of an equal height on the islands and on the continent, and the fragments of rocks which have been torn out and rolled away by this tremendous shock or current leave no doubt in the mind of the beholder of the reality of such an event.

The widest passage is not more than two miles over; the narrowest not more than one fourth of a mile: these passages are called by the Spaniards, who first explored and settled that part of the country, (as well as the island of Trinidad, *i. e.* Trinity,) *Las Bocas del Dragon*, or the Dragons' Mouths. This body of water rushes through these passages with such force, that it is next to impossible, at times, for a fast sailing vessel to enter against the current, with a strong trade wind in her favour, and I have known many vessels bound to Trinidad, obliged to bear up and try for the Leeward Islands, and scarcely able to fetch Hispaniola or Jamaica. This, with what passes northward of Trinidad, is pent in and forced against the Spanish coast of *Terra Firma*, following its windings round the Bay of Honduras to Cape Catoche: by the constant trade winds which blow from the N. E. to east, they are then driven through between that Cape and Cape St. Antonio, or the western part of the island of Cuba, into the Gulf of Mexico.

From the similarity in the appearance of Cape Catoche and Cape St. Antonio, the lowness of the land on both sides, the strait that divides them being only about sixty miles wide, and the fact of soundings being round nearly or quite across the channel, it has been thought, and with every probability of truth in its favour, that the Island of Cuba was once attached to this point of the continent, and the waters heaped up by the foregoing causes in that great bay south of Cuba, at some remote period broke over the low sandy land, tore it down, and formed for themselves a free passage into the great Gulf of Mexico.

The circumstance of the island of Cuba stretching nearly east and west about seven hundred miles in length, and in many places very high, with the well known fact of the powerful currents already mentioned setting it upon the coast south and west of it, and the constant easterly winds that prevail on its southern side, leaves very little room to doubt that these strong trade winds, opposing the passage of the current up the south side of that once vast peninsula, have raised them to such a pitch that they have formed a channel for themselves.

This immense mass of water, thus forced into the Bay of Mexico, runs to the N.W. to its northern border, and strikes that shore a few leagues west of the Mississippi River's mouth—thence taking a circular direction round south towards Vera Cruz and along the south coast of the gulf, seems to lose itself near where it entered at Cape Catoche. In sailing in the Gulf of Mexico, you meet with whirlpools and very strong currents in every part of it, sometimes setting one way, and sometimes another; the gulf being of a circular form, there is no certainty in the currents. During the summer months it is visited by the most dreadful squalls of thunder and lightning, and by water-spouts that have often destroyed vessels.

Storms or hurricanes are also very frequent, and calms of a month or two often occur: here that astonishing body of water is joined by that of all the rivers that empty into the gulf, particularly those borne down by that father of rivers, the Mississippi;—thus accumulated and become much higher in the Bay of Mexico than in any other part of the Atlantic ocean, it forces its way eastward between Cape Florida and the northern side of the island of Cuba, until meeting the great bank of Bahama in its front, with its numerous keys and rocks, it is turned nothwardly along the coast of Florida. Its velocity there in the narrowest part, where it is only about forty miles wide, has been ascertained (and, indeed, I have known it myself) to exceed five miles an hour at some particular seasons.

After leaving this narrow passage, it keeps its course northwardly, spreading a little as it proceeds, until it strikes soundings off Savannah and Charleston—the coast then narrows in its western edge again until it approaches Cape Hattcias, where the stream is not more than fifty miles broad, and frequently runs with almost as great rapidity as between the Bahama Bank and Florida shore. From Cape Hatteras its course is N. E. to the shoals off Nantucket Island and George's Bank, where its velocity is about two miles an hour; these obstructions give it a more easterly direction, until it strikes the Great Bank of Newfoundland in the latitude of 42. N. or thereabouts: here it meets with the resistance of the bank, and is turned by it to the E. S. E.

There is in this part of the ocean a current which perpetually sets from the northward, south-eastwardly along the coast of Newfoundland; it is this current which brings from the coast of Labrador and Hudson's Straits the islands of ice that are so often met with by ships on and about the grand Newfoundland Bank in the first part of the summer, and which have proved fatal to so many ships and their crews:

the appearance of these islands proves beyond a possibility of doubt the existence of that current which pressing upon, is joined to that of the Gulf Stream, and the whole sets away together towards the Azores, or Western Islands, a the rate of from one to two and a half miles an hour:—this current is felt by all vessels bound from the United States to the Western Islands and Madeira, or the Canaries, that sail in the parallels of the Azores, which all those vessels bound to Madeira, the Canaries, or the coast of Spain and Portugal, and the Mediterranean sea, generally do.

Those vessels that make the Western Islands, when bound to Europe generally feel it until they lose sight of those islands; when in standing away for the northern or central ports of Europe, they feel it no more, and it has therefore generally been thought to lose itself near the Azores, in the ocean. This is a mistake—for it continues its course for the coast of Africa, making no account of the island of Madeira, though the most of it passes northward of that island in a southeasterly direction, and strikes the African continent from Cape Blanco to the latitude of 29° north. When it comes near this coast, it is again contracted as it feels the effects of the trade winds near the coast, and rushes forward at times with great velocity against the coast between Cape Blanco and the island of Lanzarote, the northern and easternmost of the Canary Islands, being attracted, as it were, by the vacuum occasioned by the trade winds and currents which have been before noticed, and which have in a measure drained the waters from the coast, and the continuation of the Gulf Stream increasing in velocity, restores the waters nearly to their former level, which still are kept rolling along before the wind, against and along the coast towards the equator, and are again driven by the same causes to the coast of America into the Gulf of Mexico and back again, in what is usually termed the Gulf Stream, to the coast of West and South Barbary, making their continual round.

Ships bound from Europe, say England, France, Holland, &c. to the West Indies, the Cape de Verd Islands, the coast of Guinea, Brazils, or India voyages, or to the west coast of America, generally steer southward along the coast of Portugal, until they cross the mouth of the straits of Gibraltar, where if they meet with southerly winds they are drawn towards the coast of Africa by a small indraught setting towards the strait, where a current always runs in; for the waters of the rivers which empty into the Mediterranean Sea are not sufficient to supply the loss from evaporations rendered necessary in order to moisten in some measure the parched earth and sand on its southern border, and to cool the heated atmosphere, and support by dews the scanty vegetation on the coast, during the greater part of the year, where no rain falls except a little in winter; so that the surface of the Mediterranean Sea is always lower than that of the adjoining Atlantic.

The same causes, *viz.* great evaporations, tend also to reduce the quantity of water in the open ocean near the west coast of Africa, and particularly that part bordering on the desert, where very little or no rain ever falls, and the smooth surface of which, baked almost as hard as stone by the heat of a vertical sun, is during the night in some degree refreshed by the strong winds and vapours which come from the sea, as before noticed. These reasons, together with the facts, which I have before stated, demonstrate to my understanding, satisfactorily, that in the offing all along this coast, the water must incline towards it, contrary to any general principle of currents; and this is proved, if any doubt did exist, by the vast number of vessels that have from time to time been wrecked on these wild and inhospitable shores, generally near Cape Nun, and from thence to Cape Bajador, and as far south as Cape de Verd.

Ships from Europe, bound round the southern capes of Africa and America, generally stop at Madeira or Teneriffe for refreshments, and are not unfrequently obliged to run for Madeira after they get in its latitude, and their reckoning by account is up one, and sometimes two degrees westward before they find that island; when, had they kept on the courses which they would naturally have steered to reach Teneriffe, they would have been sucked or drawn in by the current between Lanzarote and Cape Cantin, and driven ashore near Cape Nun, before they could suspect they had reached the latitude of that island, and in the firm belief that they were near the longitude of Teneriffe, and consequently two hundred and fifty miles from the coast where they in fact are, and where no human effort can save them from either perishing in the sea, or becoming slaves to the Bereberies, Moors, or Arabs, who inhabit this country.

Most merchant vessels steer courses that ought to carry them within sight of the Canary Islands when bound to the southward, or from the strait of Gibraltar; they generally experience a southerly current after passing the latitude of Cape Blanco, and have a fair wind when near the coast, with thick hazy weather, so that they cannot get an altitude of the sun: this is a sure sign they are in the southeast current, over which hangs a vapour similar to that observed over the

Gulf Stream near the American continent, and when these portending signs occur, they should stand directly off W. N. W. or N. W. until they reach the longitude of Madeira, and never pass the latitude of Teneriffe or Palma, without seeing one of them. Near these Islands the atmosphere is more clear, and they can be seen from sixty to one hundred miles distant in clear weather.

I am particular in advising those ship-masters who are bound that way, by all means to make the island of Madeira; it takes them but a little out of their route, and from whence they will be sure of making Teneriffe or Palma, in steering the regular courses, when by due precaution against indraughts southward of those islands, they avoid the dangers of this terrible coast, and the dreadful sufferings or deaths which await all that are so unfortunate as to be wrecked on them: I have learned from a long experience in trading and navigating from Europe as well as America, to the Madeira and Canary Islands, to the coast of Brazil and South America in general, thence northward across the southern Atlantic, all along the coast of Guyanna and *Terra Firma*, from the River Amazon to the Bay of Honduras, through the passages between Trinidad and the Main, Cape Catoche and the island of Cuba—in the gulf of Mexico, and in the Mississippi river, to Cuba;—through the Gulf Stream backwards and forwards—along the coasts of Florida to and from different ports in the United States, thence to and from all the West India islands, and to and from almost every part of Europe, and I can assert, without fear of contradiction from any practical man, that the particular currents I have here mentioned do in reality exist in all those parts of the ocean.

I have endeavoured to find out their causes, and now give the reader those I judge to be the correct ones. I presume no man ever took more pains to examine and ascertain the facts on which this theory is founded; having tried the currents whenever I had an opportunity, in different parts of the Atlantic, and very few men have had better opportunities: how far I have succeeded, must hereafter be determined. When I took my departure from Cape Spartel, bound to the Cape de Verd Islands, on my last voyage, I steered W. N. W. by compass, until that Cape bore E. S. E. distant four or five leagues, to give the coast a good birth; then I shaped my course W. S. W. and took care to have the vessel always steered her course—she was a very fast sailer, and steered extremely easy, and what little she did vary from her course was to the westward: we had a constant fair wind, and generally a good breeze, and were only three days northward of the Canary Islands.

I had frequently tried the compasses on the outward bound passage, and found them to be correct, their variation being no more than is generally calculated, *i. e.* nearly two points about the straits of Gibraltar; I therefore made all the allowance I could suppose necessary, and my courses steered ought to have carried my vessel to the westward of Teneriffe; but I was near the coast, and the indraught so strong, setting at the rate of at least two miles an hour E. S. E. or two and a half S. E. that my vessel was carried by it out of her course in three days nearly two hundred miles directly east broadside towards Africa, and she must have entered the passage between Lanzarote and Fuertaventura (the easternmost of the Canaries) and the coast of Africa, and so far from the islands that we could not discover them, though the island of Fuertaventura is very high.

The current here ran more to the south, sweeping my vessel along with great rapidity towards Cape Nun and the coast—but my course being so far westward, I was carried by the help of the current, which is turned by the coast to S.W. near to the pitch of Cape Bajador, before I could suppose it was possible that we were near it, and having been carried in three days one hundred and twenty miles of latitude.

Of the great number of vessels wrecked on this part of the coast, very few get as far down; almost all go on shore near Cape Nun, and before they believe themselves in the latitude of Lanzarote, being drawn in by this fatal current and indraught, when they think they are far to the westward, and are many times on the lookout for Teneriffe. The weather is always extremely thick and foggy along this coast within the vortex of this current. If the crews of vessels, even in the daytime, discover land to leeward, westward of Santa Cruz de Berberia, as it tends in some places nearly east and west, having always a strong wind, swell, and current, right on shore, and a tremendous sea rolling on, it is next to impossible for the fastest sailer to escape total destruction by running on shore, where the crew must either miserably perish in the sea, starve to death after tending, be massacred by, or become slaves to the ferocious inhabitants, the most savage race of men, perhaps, to be found in the universe.

These barbarians know and obey no law but their own will; their avarice alone sometimes prompts them to save the lives of their fellow mortals when in the deepest distress, in the hope of gaining by the sale, the labour, or the future ransom of their captives, whom, they say, God has placed in their hands as a reward for some of their virtues or good actions; and it is a sacred duty they owe to themselves, as well as to the

Supreme Being, to make the most they can by them. Not less than six American vessels are known to have been lost on this part of the coast since the year 1800, besides numbers of English, French, Spanish, Portuguese, &c. which are also known to have been wrecked there, and no doubt many other vessels that never have been heard from—but it is only Americans and Englishmen that are ever heard from after the first news of the shipwreck.

The French, Spanish, Portuguese, and Italian governments, it is said, seldom ransom their unfortunate shipwrecked subjects, and they are thus doomed to perpetual slavery and misery—no friendly hand is ever stretched forth to relieve their distresses and to heal their bleeding wounds, nor any voice of humanity to sooth their bitter pangs; till worn out with sufferings indescribable, they resign their souls to the God who gave them, and launch into the eternal world with pleasure, as death is the only relief from their sufferings.

I cannot omit to inform my readers, that on the 1st of January, 1816 when in Mogadore, I went in company with Mr. Willshire, to pay a complimentary visit to Don Estevan Leonardi, an old man, a Genoese by birth, who had lived a long time in Mogadore—he has, I was informed, exercised the functions of French Vice-Consul there for a number of years—he received us with the compliments of the season; congratulating me coldly on my redemption from slavery; inquired some particulars, &c. &c. after which, and when we had refreshed ourselves with a glass of wine, he told me, that "about the years 1810, 11, he received a long letter from Suse, brought to him by an Arab, written by a Frenchman: this stated that the writer and another Frenchman, whom he named, had escaped from a prison in Teneriffe a few weeks previously, where they had been long confined as prisoners of war, that they stole an open boat in the night, and set sail in the hope of escaping from the Spaniards, who had treated them with great harshness and cruelty.

"That they steered to the eastward, expecting to land on the coast of Morocco, where they trusted they might regain their liberty, and get home through the aid of the French Consuls; that they made the coast of Suse, and landed a few leagues below Santa Cruz or Agader, after great sufferings and hardships, where they were seized on as slaves, and stripped naked; and the letter concluded by begging of him to ransom them, and thus save the lives of two unfortunate men, who must otherwise soon perish, &c. &c.—but said Leonardi, I had no orders from the Consul-General to expend money on account of his government, and accordingly persuaded the Arab who brought the letter to stop with me a few days—his price was *two hundred dollars for the two*, and he was their sole proprietor.

"In the meantime I sent off a courier express to Tangier, for orders from the Consul-General, who returned at the end of thirty-five days, with leave to pay one hundred dollars a man for them, but no other expenses. The Arab stayed fifteen days with me, and then returned home in disgust; he could not believe I would ransom them, as I did not do it immediately; but when my express returned from Tangier, giving me leave to buy them, I sent a Jew down with the money to pay their ransom, but when he came to their master, he would not sell them at his former price, for he said he had found them to be mechanics, and demanded three hundred dollars for the two, or one hundred and fifty dollars each. The Jew said he saw the men; they were naked, hard at work, and appeared to be much exhausted, very miserable, and dejected:—he might have bought one for one hundred and fifty dollars, but would not, as he had no orders to do so.

"When the Jew was about to return, their master told him if he went away without the men, and the Consul wanted them, he must pay four hundred dollars for them:—now on the Jew's arrival at Mogadore with this news, (continued Leonardi,) I sent off another express to Tangier, who brought back leave to pay the four hundred dollars, at the same time cautioned me not to make any further expenses on their account. I sent down the four hundred dollars to Suse again, and ordered the messenger to buy one, if he could not get both; but their master said he had been played with and deceived until that time; that if I wanted them, I must pay *five hundred dollars*, and that he would then escort them up to Swearah, and be answerable for their safety until they arrived there, but he would not take the four hundred dollars, nor would he separate them; and so the messenger returned without them. I have expended (said he) about two hundred dollars that I shall never get again, and I suppose the men are dead, as I have not heard from them since."

This, if not in the precise words, was the substance of what he said, and I could scarcely suppress the indignation I felt at this recital, nor avoid contrasting the behaviour of this man with that of my noble friend Willshire. This old man is very rich; has no family but himself, and is one of the most zealous Christians, in professions at least, in Barbary; out a sordid wretch, who never knew the pleasure arising from the consciousness of having done a good deed, in my opinion.

While I remained at Mogadore, a schooner arrived there, as I have before observed, from Gibraltar: she was a Genoese vessel, but sailed under English colours, as the king of Sardinia was at war with all the Barbary powers, or at least they were at war with him: the captain, officers, and crew, were Genoese and Spaniards. She had been more than twenty days on her passage from Gibraltar, having been carried by the current down the coast below Santa Cruz or Agader. The captain told me he must inevitably have gone ashore near Cape Nun, had not God in his mercy favoured him with a south wind, out of the usual course of nature, on that coast, when he was close to the land: he had been beating for three days against the trade wind, nearing the coast every day, and could not fetch off either way, though his vessel was a fast sailer, and only in ballast trim.

He arrived at Mogadore about the 1st of December, after the wind had been blowing strong, with some rain from the south, for four days: it is only in December and January that these winds occur, and always bring a storm with them, either of wind or rain: this schooner was the vessel in which my second mate and three men went round from Mogadore to Gibraltar.

As the geography of that part of Africa lying in the equatorial regions eastward of that extensive ridge of mountains which borders its western coast from the latitude 18. N. to the Congo River, and westward of the Mountains of the Moon, in which the Nile has its sources, has excited much speculation and interest in the learned world, (though it does not come strictly within my province,) I will, nevertheless, make a few brief observations on the practicability of exploring those hitherto unknown countries, in the hope that they may hereafter be useful.

And first, it is my decided opinion, that no European or civilized armed force, however large or well appointed, can ever penetrate far into the interior of these wild and dismal recesses by and, either from the snores of the Atlantic ocean, or the Mediterranean sea; because an army on such an expedition, would not only have to encounter powerful hosts of savage enemies at every turn, and undergo the severest privations, fatigues, and hardships, but would besides have to encounter the raging heat of this scorching climate, surpassing anything they may ever have experienced, and the pestilential disorders incident thereto:—these circumstances taken together, could scarcely fail to produce its total annihilation in a short period, and thus frustrate the boldest and best planned military attempt.—Individual bravery, enterprise, skill, and prudence, in the ordinary way, by travelling unprotected, are also, in my opinion, entirely unequal to the task, and such enterprises must, I think, always prove abortive. Something might, perhaps, be done by black travellers, natives of that country, tutored expressly for that purpose, and sent off singly from different stations and on different routes; but owing to their confined education, and particular train of ideas, nothing very valuable could be expected from their researches.

Steamboats, strongly built, and of a suitable construction, well armed and appointed, might ascend the River Congo, (which I am induced from many considerations to believe is the outlet of the river Niger,) and traffic up that river, and other rivers, making important discoveries; but the whole of their officers, as well as all the men employed on board them, should first be inured to such climates, and be persons accustomed to fatigues, privations, hardships, and sufferings; and, above all, should be guided by the greatest degree of human prudence.

A plane and very simple method for visiting Tombuctoo in safety, and returning again, might be pointed out by either the American or English Consuls residing at Tangier, Algiers, Tunis, or Tripoli;—to accomplish this journey, the traveller, after being qualified, knowing the Arabic language, and being duly circumcised, has only to become a slave by his own consent, and a secret understanding with his hired master; being bargained away by the Consul to one of the principal merchants trading to that city in the yearly caravans, and who might be induced to enter into the project for an ample remuneration.

They're saved! They're saved!

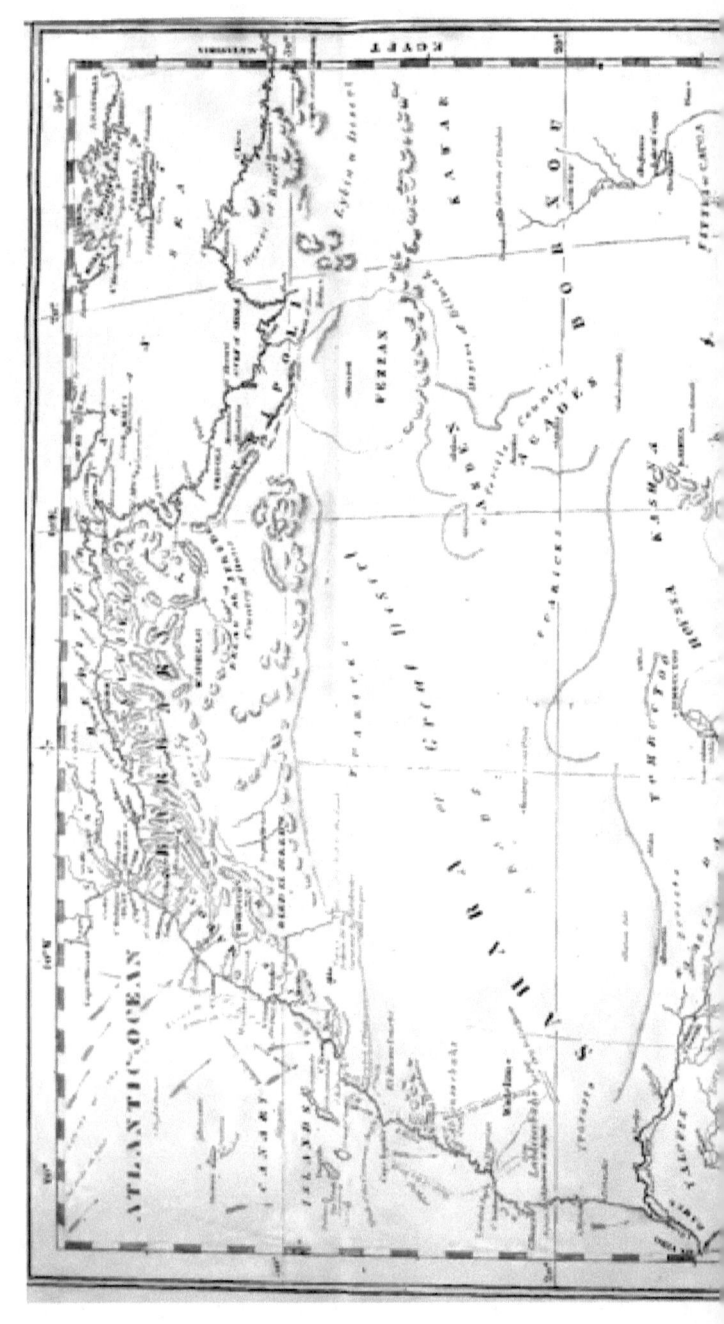

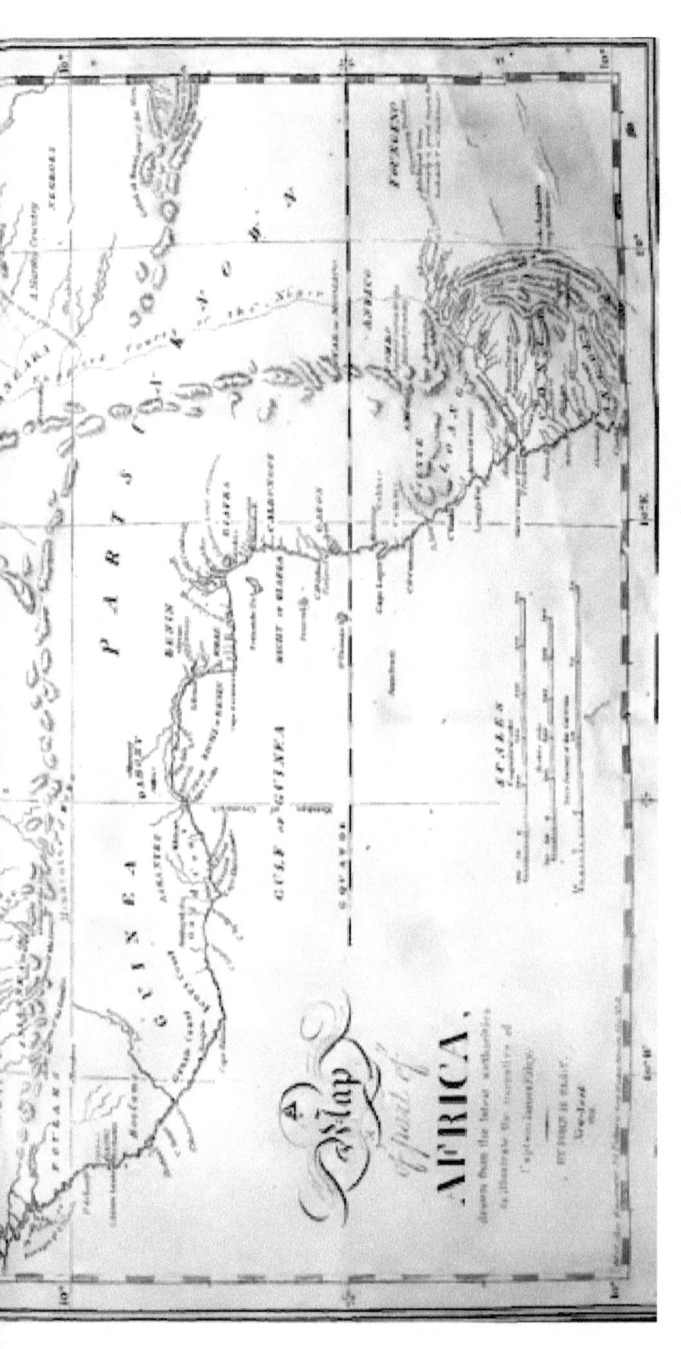

A Journal, Comprising an Account of the Loss of the Brig "Commerce", of Hartford, (Con.) James Riley, Master

Archibald Robbins

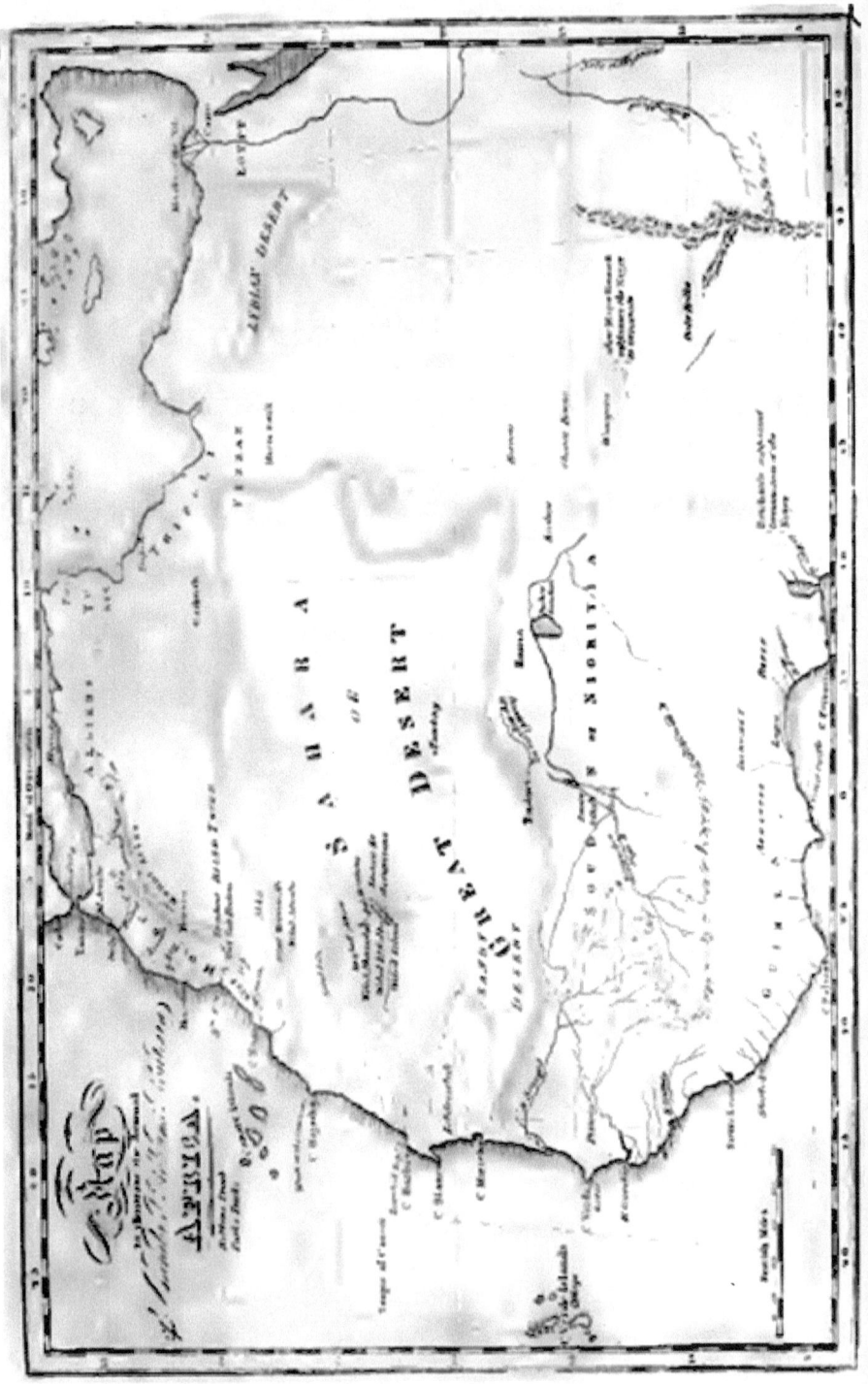

Contents

Preface	73
Introductoty Remarks	75
Recruit or Squad Drill	79
Setting-Up Drill	107
A Catechetical Examination, for the Use of Instructors	144

To the
Hon. James Simpson,
American Consul General
At Tangier,
And the
Hon. William Willshire,
British Vice Consul, and American Consular Agent
At Mogadore—Africa:—

Gentlemen—

Permit me to offer this little volume to you. I have, upon the ocean, endured the distress occasioned by the *elements*—upon land, the miseries inflicted by *man*, and from you have enjoyed the blessings of humane benevolence, which I can repay only by unalterable gratitude.

    With high Respect,
        and Consideration, I am, Gentlemen,
            Your grateful and ob't. servt.
                Archibald Robbins.

THE MAP.

The *Map* attached to this volume is added to illustrate the subject of it. It was not made to aid the geographer, but to assist the reader in tracing the eccentric course the author was compelled to travel with his Arab masters. The *Western coast of Africa* and the *Desert of Zahara* are represented with as much accuracy as was attainable from the observations of the author and from the most approved maps. The general situation of the different tribes is laid down upon the map, although their frequent wanderings almost precludes the idea of giving *locality* to them. The *great* station for caravans is designated, although there may be others unknown to the author. If errors should be detected in the map, by the acute examiner, the author can only say, "*to err is human, to forgive divine.*"

To the Public

I shall make no apology for offering to the public the following Journal. It would be affectation to pretend that in doing it, I have been influenced by motives wholly independent of personal emolument. My object in preparing and publishing this concise and simple narrative of my own sufferings, experience and observations, among a people, and in a quarter of the globe little known to my countrymen, was twofold—to obtain, if possible, a small remuneration for the unprecedented privations and sufferings, of which I have been the unfortunate subject, and to add to the scanty knowledge that exists with respect to this singular people, and extraordinary portion of the earth, such facts and information as I was enabled to obtain, during nineteen months of the most cruel and oppressive slavery which barbarism, and a blind and ferocious superstition could produce.

But although these were my principal objects, yet had they not been presented to my view, and strengthened by circumstances peculiarly favourable, I should never have been persuaded to have engaged in so arduous, difficult and expensive an undertaking. The wreck of the brig *Commerce*, and the distressing fate of the crew, was known throughout the United States; and in Connecticut, where most of them had lived, there was a lively and honourable sensibility felt upon the subject. Under these circumstances, on my return home in June last, it is not a matter of surprise that my friends, and others, should have felt anxious to have me publish the "sad tale of my sufferings."

In preparing this Journal, I have aimed to be correct—to give a faithful and accurate detail of *facts*; and although it will probably contain some errors even in this respect, yet I think it will be free from the charge to which works of this description are too generally and too justly exposed, that of containing *strange and marvellous accounts*. Not wishing to be deceived myself, I cannot, designedly, become the instrument of deceiving others. In describing the manners, customs, modes of living, religious ceremonies and worship of the Arabs, I have observed a minuteness which many may think unnecessary. But as the variance of a few shades changes the complexion and general appearance of a piece of painting, so a few minute, and apparently unimportant particulars, affect, essentially, the general characteristics of a people.

It was found impossible, in the course of the work, to avoid incorporating some of the proper Barnes of the Arabs; in doing which I have been obliged to adopt an English orthography, and the barbarous and guttural sounds of their words appear, if possible, still more harsh when put in an English dress. Wherever Arabic terms or words have been used, they have generally been explained; but the words *Wiled* and *Biled* which occur frequently in the work, not having been explained in the text, it may not be improper to inform the reader in this place, that the latter signifies country, and the former sons of; that is, denoting the first or primitive stock from whence the tribes have descended. These words, from the rapid speaking of the natives, are pronounced *Will'd* and *B'led*—as, *Will'd Abbousebah*—*B'led Mouessa Ali*.

Having had no other than a common education, and from the pursuits in which I have been engaged, it could not be supposed that I should make much pretension to literature. In preparing the work, I have been assisted by a gentleman of science and information, who has bestowed upon it considerable attention, and given it a shape and character which it could not have assumed if it had gone from my own hand, unassisted by literary skill or scientific acquirements.

                                                     Archibald Robbins.

Introduction

The narratives and journals of adventurers, the shipwrecked, the traveller, and the captive, are often told with exaggerations, and not unfrequently condemned by the discerning. Such narrations gratify those who are always seeking "to see or hear some new thing;" but they only raise the wonder of the credulous, and deceive the inquirer after truth. But it may be here remarked, that readers are readily disposed to disbelieve everything that goes counter to their own experience, that surpasses their own observations, or that represents the actions of men, and men themselves, in a manner that violates *their* ideas of human nature.

The author of the following Journal has seen life in a sphere uncommon to his countrymen:—he has endured miseries uncommon to human nature. But by the blessings of a merciful Providence, he has survived to relate them to his countrymen. However imperfect may be the *manner* in which he may give his relation, he is determined that the *matter* shall be founded on facts alone. If these facts are of a nature calculated to excite the doubts of his readers, he can only regret it; and will content himself with the reflection, that as he is incapable of deceiving his readers, he will not wound his own conscience by uttering a known falsehood. He hopes not even to be mistaken.

The narrative of my highly respected friend, Capt. James Riley, is already before the public. It has excited that interest which the history of human sufferings is calculated to produce among a humane people. For two months he was a captive among a race of beings, whose "*tender mercies are cruelties*." During that period, I, together with the rest of his unfortunate crew, was likewise a sufferer. At the end of this time, he was released from a cruel bondage, and was restored to his native country and anxious friends. A more cruel fate attended me. I was still detained as a captive among the wandering Arabs: and was compelled, for nineteen months, to endure as much as human nature can bear and yet survive. I have, however, abundant reason to rejoice that I am now among my friends, while the fate of some of this wretched crew is still unknown. The following journal shall be a faithful and accurate detail of all the knowledge I possess of this ill-fated crew.

CHAPTER 1

Short Biographical Sketch

The life of an humble individual is of but little consequence to a community, where the lives of the great are read as a common amusement. But as I am about to relate an interesting part of my own, I hope I shall escape the imputation of vanity by very briefly relating it from my birth. I was born in the town of Wethersfield, Conn.—a pleasant and fertile town, situated on the west side of Connecticut River, on the 10th day of November, 1792. I continued with my parents there until I arrived to the age of twelve years. At this time I went to reside in the town of Middlebury, Vt. In this flourishing village, in which is situated a University which begins to rank amongst the first in New-England, I spent the winters in obtaining a common school education; which, added to the little knowledge I had before acquired in my native town, gave me such rudiments of an English education, as is common with the young men of New-England. I returned to Wethersfield at the age of about fifteen years, and continued with my father until I became sixteen. Situated in a town where ship-building was then a leading business, and from which a great number of young men had gone to try their fortunes upon the ocean, I soon turned my attention from the peaceful and certain pursuit of husbandry, to the hazardous employment of a seaman.

My first voyage was made in a vessel, partly owned by my father, from Wethersfield to the island of St. Christophers. No incident happened to the vessel, to the crew, nor to myself, worthy of relation. No part of the cargo, nor any lives of the crew were lost.

The second voyage I made was in the same vessel to Wilmington, N. Carolina, from thence to the W. Indies—back again to Wilmington—from thence again to the West-Indies, and back to Wethersfield. A pleasant voyage.

My third voyage was mule from New-York to the West-Indies, from whence I returned to New-London in Connecticut.

Thus far I had met with no disasters uncommon to the pursuit of a sea-firing life. I became attached to it, as is common with the young men of New-England. The fascinating charms of the ocean, and the pleasing diversity of a sailor's life, led me along, like the song of the Syren, to the endurance of privations and miseries which, when I now review, call upon me for the most undissembled gratitude to that merciful Being, who suffers not a sparrow to fall to the ground without his knowledge; and who mercifully "*tempers the wind to the shorn lamb.*"

My fourth voyage was commenced in the month of February, 1813. The American canvass could no longer be spread with safety upon the ocean. Her proud and powerful mistress—wielding the trident of Neptune, would no longer permit the "striped bunting" of Americans to pursue its wonted course. We sailed from New-York for the neutral port of St. Bartholomews—were taken on our passage, by his B. M. frigate *Surprise*, and landed at St. Bartholomews, from whence, after a short detention, I returned in a cartel to New-York.

The fifth voyage I made, I sailed from New-Haven, (Ct.) for St. Bartholomews, in September, 1813, and was brought to by the British squadron lying off New-London. They took from our vessel about eighty barrels of provisions, and ordered us for Halifax. I remained there about two months. I then took a passage in a Swedish vessel for St. Bartholomews; having business entrusted to me at that island by a merchant in the city of New-York. I succeeded in accomplishing my business, and returned off New-London. The vessel, in which I was a passenger, was taken by the squadron, and I was put on board of the Borer, brig of war, and sent again to Halifax.

I remained a prisoner in the prison on Melville Island, until the conclusion of the peace by the treaty of Ghent. I hoped to have been in some measure compensated for this imprisonment, by receiving pay for eighteen months employ, and imprisonment occasioned by that employ, by the merchant at New-York.—His failure in the meantime cut me off from realizing this hope; but as he is a man of the strictest honour I have no doubt but I shall yet be compensated. On my return to America, I found myself destitute of property and employ, but not of resolution.

I now come to the relation of the sixth and last voyage I have made. In relating it I sensibly feel a high degree of responsibility. But, taking the pole-star of truth for my guide, I am determined to satisfy my conscience, and, if possible, my readers.

I felt anxious to pursue a business with which experience had made me acquainted. The brig *Commerce*, of Hartford, Con. being owned by Riley & Brown and the Messrs. Savages, was fitted for sea. She was a fine stout built new vessel. The acknowledged respectability of her owners. as merchants, and the long experience and reputation of Captain James Riley, as her commander, induced me to enter her in the capacity of an able seaman. Her principal mate was Mr. George Williams, of Middletown—her second mate was Mr. Aaron R. Savage, of the same place. The crew consisted of William Porter, Thomas Burns. James Clarke, and myself, seamen; Horace Savage, cabin boy; Francis Bliss, James Carrington, ordinary seamen; and Richard Delisle, (a man of colour.) cook.

This brig cleared out from Middletown for New-Orleans, with a small cargo—her ballast being brick. The object of the voyage to New-Orleans was to obtain a freight for a foreign market. We sailed on the 6th day of May from Saybrook, situated at the mouth of Connecticut River. Nothing material occurred until off Carysfort reef, on the coast of E. Florida. The vessel struck upon this reef, and excited great apprehension in our captain and crew for the safety of the vessel and ourselves. We clewed down all sails, and let go an anchor, which immediately brought her to; having passed the reef, and riding safe in about twelve feet water. We thou lowered down her stern boat; and the captain and four of the crew entered her—sounded below her for a safe passage—found one—weighed anchor, and passed through in safety.

We arrived at the city of New-Orleans upon the 1st day of June. We here discharged our cargo, and took in a cargo of flour and tobacco. The two ordinary seamen, Bliss and Carrington, objected to going a voyage to Gibraltar, to which place the vessel was bound, and were discharged. Two seamen were shipped in their room. *viz.* John Hogan and James Barrett. On the 24th of June, we sailed from New-Orleans for Gibraltar; and, after a passage of about forty-five days, we arrived at that place and landed our cargo. I was ordered, with three others, while lying in the bay, to go with Capt. Riley on board a schooner, from New-York. In performing this service, assisting the schooner in beating out of the harbour, and returning to the brig, it having become almost dark, our boat was upset; and while we were hanging upon it, we were relieved by Capt. Price, who returned with his schooner to our assistance; and having bailed the boat we returned to the brig.

We now took in part of a cargo of brandy and wine. An elderly man, by the name of Antonio Michel, was taken on board to work his passage to New-York. On the 23rd day of August, we set sail from Gibraltar for the Cape de Verd islands, to complete the cargo with salt. The usual course from Gibraltar to these islands is, to run down, and make the island of Madeira; but Capt. Riley, wishing to make the passage as expeditious as possible, run down between the Canary islands and the African coast. We continued our course, with all sails set. The weather being thick and foggy, we passed the grand Canaries without discovering them. It was noticed by the mates and some of the crew, on the 28th day of August, (sea account,) at meridian, that the water was coloured, indicating a near approach to land. This circumstance was mentioned to Capt. Riley; but he was of opinion that this appearance was occasioned by the fog and the thick weather; and he continued his course S. W. at ten knots an hour, until, at about 10 o'clock in the evening, we were wrecked on the coast of Africa, near Cape Bajador, between 26 and 27 degs. N. Latitude.

CHAPTER 2

Wreck of the Brig "Commerce"

To a seaman, the description of a shipwreck is familiar from his knowledge of a vessel, the tackle, and the nautical terms of seafaring men: but by that portion of readers who are not thus acquainted, no adequate conception can he formed of the appalling horrors of such a scene. When it is foreseen, and yet cannot be avoided, the mind is, in a degree, prepared to encounter it. It is fortified greatly by appealing to that Being who, "*on the wings of mighty winds*" directs the storm that is powerful enough to dash to pieces the strongest fabric of human invention. But when it comes upon the unsuspicious, who are riding in apparent security upon the element with which they have become familiar, the scene is doubly horrible.

Thus it came upon our worthy captain and his ill-fated crew. The gale, that we imagined was wafting us on our passage to our native shore, and the arms of our friends, dashed us upon the inhospitable coast of merciless barbarians. At a little past 10, on the night of the memorable 28th of August, our fine brig ran ashore with such violence as to start us from the deck, or prostrate us upon it. We immediately let go our sheet anchor, clewed down our sails, and used every exertion to save her. But her fate was decided, and our exertions were vain. The sea broke with tremendous power over the starboard quarter, and our stern boat, being in danger, we took her on board. We then broke open the hold, and exerted all our energies in filling small casks with water from our large water casks, knowing that the dismal coast on which fate had driven us, was almost destitute of that indispensable necessary of life.

We also secured all the provisions we could, as the vessel was now fast filling with water. At 12 o'clock, the weather became sufficiently clear to enable us to discover the beach off the larboard bow. The larboard bulwark was instantly cut away, to enable us to launch the boats with greater expedition and safety. The small boat was then lowered into the water, into which Capt. Riley and William Porter jumped, and carried a rope ashore which they made fast by means of sticks which had floated there from the wreck. We then got the long-boat overboard, and hauled her under our larboard bow. We threw over some barrels of water and wine, which floated ashore, and by those on shore were secured. We put into the boat two or three barrels of bread, and some beef and pork.

I jumped into the boat with James Barrett, and, veering her by means of a rope fastened on board the brig, we approached the shore. The surf immediately filled her. We instantly jumped overboard, and saved some of our wet provisions, and secured one barrel of bread wholly dry. Capt. Riley, Porter, Barrett and myself were now ashore. The long boat being bilged, and the small one unable to stand the surf, we could not return to the wreck. Our companions on board, in the mean time, were heaving overboard chests, beds, and every article that would float, that they could come at, and those of us on shore were securing them as they floated within our reach.

Daylight at length appeared. Capt. Riley hailed the mates, who were both on board, ordering them to make fast one of the ropes, that extended from the wreck to the shore, around his trunk containing some specie. This being done, we dragged the trunk ashore. The brig was now completely filled with water. Capt Riley ordered the masts to be cut away. This being done by those on board, our next attention was directed to the best means in our power, to rescue our companions from the imminent danger surrounding them. I had been ordered, with Barrett, to come ashore in the long boat with provisions, as before mentioned, and to return again. This was now impracticable, as the boat was bilged—the small boat would not have lived in the surf a moment—but a rope remained fastened to the wreck, and extending to the shore. This was loosened, and made fast to the hawser, by those on board, and by those who had landed, drawn to the shore, and made as fast as the slender means within our power would enable us to do it.

It was now high water. The brig lay from twenty-five to thirty rods from the shore; and between them, the surf was rolling and roaring in a manner calculated to produce consternation and despair in the stoutest heart. Capt. Riley, by signals, as he could not now be heard, motioned to those upon the wreck to come ashore upon the hawser.

He placed himself, together with Porter, Barrett, and myself at the hawser, as far in the water as we could stand, the surf all the while breaking over us. At length Hogan attempted the perilous passage. Suspended upon the hawser, between two worlds, uncertain to which every returning surge might waft him, he approached the shore. Before he reached it. he was so much exhausted, that he lost his hold—a surf washed him within our reach, and we saved him. The next that arrived and was received into our arms was Mr. Savage, second mate. Young Savage, (cabin boy,) Antonio, Mr. Williams, first mate, Clarke, Burns, and Dick, (man of colour,) came in succession, and landed at about sunrise on a coast containing a race of beings more merciless than the waves from which they had just escaped.

We now found ourselves with bodies exhausted, and minds agitated, stretched upon a desert shore. We saw, for nearly a mile on the shore, the fragments of a valuable cargo, which, twelve hours before, we thought safe. Our first attention was directed to the boats. We hauled them up from the surf, and gave Capt. Riley all the assistance we possibly could in gathering together the small amount of provisions and clothing which lay strewed along. This being done, our captain opened his trunk in which were two bags of specie of $1000 each. He told us all to take as much of it as we could conceal about our persons. I declined taking any part of it, as I had already more of my own than I could thus hide from the eye of an Arab. It is impossible to tell what would have been our fate, had not the Arabs discovered that we had in our possession the precious metals; but I verily believe it was the discovery of it that induced them to heighten their demands for our ransom, and increase their cruelty to our persons. The other bag was buried in the sand The sun was now rising over a sand-hill that stretched along a short distance from the shore.

Our attention was now attracted to the appearance of a human creature at the distance of nearly half a mile approaching us; if that creature can be called human whose appearance is nothing but a slander upon our species. As he discovered the wrecked articles and our wretched group, he manifested, by his actions, the commotions of a mind agitated by the mingled operations of joy and fear. He came perhaps within twenty rods of us; and then, by signs, showed an intention of departing, Capt. Riley walked gently towards him, and by every sign that could be resorted to, endeavoured to persuade him to come and take possession of some portion of the wrecked articles. After interchanging signs, in token of peace, this horrible figure, that defied description, left us to our reflections upon this adventure.

We were then endeavouring, with oars and the fragments of broken spars, together with two of our steering sails, which we had secured from the wreck, to erect a tent and secure our provisions and water; scarcely thinking of anything else, from the peculiar perils of our situation. While busily engaged in this service, the figure before mentioned reappeared; being joined by two aged females of the most frightful aspect, a boy, and two small girls, whom we supposed to be their children. More terrible visages never presented themselves to the astonished eyes and the agitated hearts of men. The gnashing teeth and opened mouth of the old man, stretching almost from ear to ear—his long grey beard hanging on his breast—his head covered with long bushy hair, standing in every direction—the red and flashing eyes of the old women, their tushes projecting from their jaws—and the more mild, though terrible appearance of their ferocious brood, imparted feelings to us, better imagined than described.

Although the old man, on his first appearance, showed evidence of fear, it was now changed to insolence. He broke open the chests, and plundered the clothing; and, approaching our tent, was about to wrest from us our provisions and water. We resolved that death should be his immediate portion, and that of his clan, if he attempted this; indeed, had it not been for the almost certain knowledge that the sand-hill concealed a numerous horde like his, they would soon have been deprived of the power of plundering us at all. They departed with their plunder, and left our wretched party either to despair, or to take measures for our future escape or safety. Capt. Riley proposed to attempt a repair of the long boat. Mr. Savage, Porter, Horace, and I, assisted him in doing this in the best manner we could.

The rest of our shipmates, from that despair which produces desperation, had deprived themselves of the power of joining us in this necessary duty, by too freely using the wine within their reach. Some of these natives had furnished us with some fire, with which we cooked some salted pork, by fuel procured from the beach. This, with some bread and butter, furnished us with the last meal we were to enjoy from the provisions yet saved from the wreck. The old man with his hideous followers had retired—the night came on—and although, on one side the ocean was dashing her surging billows upon the rocks we had just escaped, and on the other we were environed by the sand-hill concealing probably a horde of wretches preparing on the approaching morning to recommence the work of plunder, and perhaps become our executioners, I sunk down, with my shipmates, excepting a watch, into a profound and refreshing sleep upon the sand under our tent.

The next morning, the sun rose more gloomily to us than it did to Sterne's sick lieutenant. He was sinking into the arms of death, among his anxious friends;—we were in momentary danger of being devoured by demons, whose diabolical ferocity would have added a laurel to the escutcheon of Satan himself. The old man once more made his appearance with additional reinforcements. The women commenced a yell, that reminded me of the description of the wailing of the damned spirits. He ordered us to the wreck, pointing to a drove of camels descending a hill to the eastward. He approached our tent with an iron spear, and commenced an assault. We all fled to the small boat, while Capt. Riley defended himself with a piece of a spar with the most consummate coolness.

Our little boat immediately filled—bilged—and we relanded, and drove the old Arab some distance up the beach. The camels, with their armed riders, were pressing upon us. We flew to the long boat—turned her over, and committing ourselves to the waves, we all reached the wreck, and viewed these *banditti*, armed with spears and scimitars, showing us the tokens of defiance, and carrying off or destroying all they found upon the shore. Immediately upon getting aboard, we sought through the wreck to get what provisions we could. We found a few pieces of pork and a few bottles of wine, but no water. These we let down into the boat, which was in a leaky condition, requiring two men to bail her. Porter and I got a fore-top-mast-stay-sail, and put it into the boat.

We could find no oars; and as a substitute, we split two planks which we found floating in the hold. These we also put into the boat. We all let ourselves down into the boat, and attempted to put to sea. The surf nearly filled our boat, and drove us back to the wreck which we regained. The Arabs afterwards returned, unarmed, and by manifesting every appearance of peace, and offering Capt. Riley a goat skin, which will hereafter be described, filled with water, induced him to go ashore. The old man came aboard, and after seeking for firearms and money, in vain, he went ashore. We then witnessed the danger of Capt. Riley—he was seized by two of the clan, and we expected to be sad spectators of his death. We sent all the money we had on board in a bucket, to the shore, hoping to appease the vengeance of these merciless wretches.

We were disappointed. The danger of our captain increased. He hailed us. Mr. Savage once more descended on the hawser, and was approaching the beach, and was discovered by the captain, who intreated him by signs to return, and send Antonio ashore. He did so; but as Antonio carried no money, the vengeance of the Arabs apparently arose to the highest pitch. Capt. Riley made his escape to the wreck, followed by two natives, and Antonio was seized, loaded with plunder, and forced over the sand-hill. Since I have returned to America, I have read a small part of Capt Riley's narrative. I find that Capt. Riley expressed his regret at the death of Antonio, fearing that he was the cause of it. He may dismiss his regret upon this subject, as I, with many of my shipmates, are positive that he was not assassinated, as our captain states. We distinctly saw the Arabs load his back with plunder, and force him to carry it over the sand-hill. Afterwards, while at sea in our boat, it was a subject of conversation amongst us, that if we were all lost, as then seemed inevitable, Antonio would be the only survivor to relate our disaster, to our anxious friends, should he ever return to his native country.

Chapter 3
We Put to Sea in the Long Boat

We were now all on board the wreck, excepting poor Antonio, whose fate was mentioned at the close of the last chapter. A melancholy consultation was held by the captain and crew. Whether to go ashore and fall sudden victims to the Arabs, or drag out a miserable existence of slavery among them—or to entrust ourselves to the foaming billows, with our shattered boat, was a question, upon the decision of which hung, perhaps, "*our life, our death—our bane, our antidote.*" After long deliberation, we concluded once more to attempt our escape by sea. The weather had been moderating through the day—the wind a little shifted to the eastward, and the surf had, in a degree, subsided. To make our attempt with greater security, we rigged a spar over the stern of the wreck, making fast a rope to its outer end, to force the boat through the surf, and give her a good headway.

We then put aboard everything we had received from the wreck to begin our perilous voyage, which the boat could contain, in her leaky condition. These consisted of a few pieces of salt pork—a live pig—which we took from the wreck to the shore—and which, wonderful to relate, had voluntarily swum from the shore to the wreck—about four gallons of water, a few pounds of figs, soaked in salt water, and about a dozen bottles of wine. We likewise had aboard our small boat's sails, consisting of jib and main-sail, and the foretop-mast-stay-sail of the brig, and the splitted planks, before mentioned, which were to serve us for oars.

We now descended into the boat, out of which Porter waded to the shore, and brought aboard an oar which he found laying on the beach. On his own accord, he went again on shore and brought aboard about four or five hundred dollars which had before been buried. We now fixed ourselves at the oars, and at the rope bended from the spar provided as before mentioned. Capt. Riley placed himself at the stern of the boat to steer her with a plank, she having no rudder. We then, by an united effort, forced ourselves through the surf without difficulty, and passed off into a smooth sea; This was accomplished at nearly sunset. Capt. Riley returned thanks to Heaven, in which we all joined with uncovered heads, and, I trust, with sincere hearts, for our safe escape from the shore and from the surf.

Darkness now approached; and Cape Bajador being under our lee, the wind being partly ahead, we were under the most fearful apprehension lest we could not clear the cape. We spent the whole night in rowing and bailing, until our strength and fortitude were almost exhausted. At daylight, however, we were greatly rejoiced to find ourselves to the leeward of this fatal cape. It was like the transition from expected destruction to hoped-for safety.

On the morning of the 30th August, we ran moderately down the coast to the S. W.; during which time we were in consultation upon the question, whether we should run down to the Senegal River, upon which there is an European settlement near its mouth, or standoff, and endeavour to make some of the Canary Islands. The objections to going to the first mentioned place were, that we had no quadrant, no compass, and no chart of the coast. A further objection was, that if, in the night season, we should pass the Senegal and Cape Verd, without discovering either, we should then be in the open sea without *any* hopes. On the other hand, it was said, if we should stand off and attempt to make some of the Canaries, we should, with more likelihood, fall in with some European vessels.

We concluded to alter our course, and stand off for the Canaries. We this day put ourselves upon allowance, *viz.*—one bottle of water and half a bottle of wine amongst eleven of us, this being the whole crew. We also allowanced ourselves to two figs each; the pork not being particularly allowanced. We endeavoured to secure the boat from the breaking in of the sea, by fitting around her gunwale, waste-clothes about eight inches above it, composed of a part of the forestay-sail. We had a fresh breeze from N. E. during the day, and kept her close upon the wind; but made but little head-way, our sails being small, and a considerable sea running, which drifted us fast to the leeward.

On the 31st of August the weather moderated. We were in no immediate danger from the sea. notwithstanding our boat was in a most shattered condition, and we continued to stand out. Our pig, for the want of necessary sustenance, began to grow thin, and we concluded to kill him, while he was yet in an eatable state. His blood we carefully preserved to quench our thirst. His intestines we devoured for the same purpose. It was the painful sensations of thirst that we most dreaded; and to guard against it. we began to preserve our own urine, securing it in the bottles we had before emptied of their contents. As the night came on, it threatened darkness, and squally weather. The wind blew strong from the N. E. and by midnight the sea ran so high as nearly to fill the boat.

We endeavoured, with every instrument in our possession, to bail her; our buckets, our hats, and everything that would hold water, were used for this purpose; and although we all expected that every returning surge would send us to the bottom, we succeeded in keeping our boat alive until morning. No one can judge of our peril excepting those who have experienced something similar. The rocking of the boat had drawn most of her nails. We saw nothing of the dismal gloom that surrounded us, excepting what was presented to our affrightened view by the vivid lightning which kept constantly flashing. We could derive hope from no source but from the interposition of an over-ruling God, whose voice we hear in the thunder, and whose arrows we see in the lightning, and even this was despaired of. Capt. Riley and Mr. Savage alternately prayed with us, which had considerable effect in allaying our fears, and encouraging our dying hopes.

Daylight at length appeared, on the morning of the 1st September. No painter could adequately have described the appearance of this gloomy group of human beings. Despair was depicted upon every countenance, and fortitude deserted every heart. We supposed we were about to lose our last hold upon life, so dear to us all; and as our fate seemed remediless, we submitted to its decrees in silent horror. Soon after, however, the weather moderated considerably, and the wind hauled about to N. N. W. We continued to stand off; but we relinquished all hopes of fetching any of the Canaries, and our only remaining hope was of falling in with some sail that might be running down near where we were situated. Our thirst increased to a degree almost intolerable, and the scorching rays of the sun, being within the torrid zone, were nearly insupportable. We relieved our parched and thirsty frames a little, by making use of a few drops of wine and water, and the urine we had preserved.

On the 2nd, we continued to stand out for a considerable part of the day. Capt. Riley, with all the rest of us, gave up all hopes of descrying a sail; our provisions and water were growing short; our strength began to fail with our hopes, and by an unanimous voice, we concluded to stand in for the shore; lest, by getting farther out at sea, we should be wholly unable, from the state of the boat, our provisions, and our strength, to stand the sea or reach any shore whatever. We then, towards evening, put her head towards the coast, which we had left, and judging by the sun, began to steer a S. E. course.

On the 3rd of September, standing in, we were favoured with a fair wind, nothing very material occurring. Dismal as the prospect before us appeared, horrid as the recollection of the coast we had left was to our minds, we still felt a kind of desperate satisfaction in returning to it. Desperate, indeed, was the choice, as I trust my readers will find in the sequel of this Journal.

During the 4th, standing in, we were on the constant lookout for land, and feeling the deepest anxiety to discover it. The day passed off, and we beheld nothing but the surrounding ocean, expecting every hour to be swallowed up by it. We subsisted, as we before had done, without any water excepting a little urine to wet our parched lips, and stiffened tongues. In the night season, we obtained a little rest during the short intervals afforded us from the duty of rowing and bailing the boat.

On the morning of the 5th, we discovered land at a great distance to leeward. Why we should have rejoiced at beholding a coast from which we had so recently escaped with our bare lives, is difficult to determine. But, in the elegant language of the Poet—"*When grief overpowers us, a twine may lead us.*" The current drove us rapidly towards the shore. As we approached it, we found it bounded by perpendicular rocks, rising in majestic and destructive grandeur. We could discover no aperture, through which we might pass for some time. At length we saw something that had the appearance of a sand bank. We made for it with all our little strength; and, exerting ourselves with our oars, and rising upon a wave that elevated us mountain high, we were carried on to a beach of sand of very small extent.

As the wave retired we surveyed, in silent astonishment, the yawning grave of rocks we had just escaped. They looked like the jaws of a natural sepulchre, and we considered ourselves as rescued by Almighty power from the grave they seemed to have formed to receive our emaciated bodies. Thus, after seven days perilous navigation, in our frail boat, four days standing out and three standing in, we landed. Having stated that we were in the boat seven days, I must add, that this is according to my best recollection. During the time we were out, we little thought of reckoning *days*, when we all the while thought our *last day* had come; and it is from the most mature reflection that I have fixed it at the number of days mentioned. It would not be singular, after all, if a mistake, in this respect, should be made.

The place, where we thus landed, was to the northward of Cape Barbas; and between that cape and the River St. Cyprian, being at this time entirely dry; the coast running from E. N. E. to W. S. W. While Capt. Riley and Mr. Savage were seeking a passage to the land above the rocks, we made all the preparation we could for a night's repose, after having exerted all the remaining strength we had in digging for water in the sand, without finding it. They returned; and after partaking with us of a little refreshment, we committed our bodies to our bed of sand, and enjoyed undisturbed repose until morning. We then opened our eyes, and found ourselves again upon the land of barbarians!!

I had been taught in early life to believe in the doctrine of an overruling Providence; that the destiny of men is in His hands, and that, "*it is not in man that walketh to direct his own steps*" I was most sensibly convinced of the truth of these positions at this time. Although one misfortune had trod close upon the heel of another, for some years previous, until after a great variety of calamities I was now reduced to one which must be the greatest, excepting death, we can endure on earth, and which no possible change but that could make worse, I still felt the most perfect submission. Whether it arose from Christian humility, or from that kind of apathy, from long misfortune, which brings the minds of men to feel a contempt for even fate itself, I cannot certainly tell; but this I can assuredly say, I felt not the least disposition to murmur or repine at my fate, however awful it was, or might become.

CHAPTER 4

Interior of Africa

The readers of this Journal found the author of it, at the end of the last chapter, cast a second time, with his shipmates in misfortune, upon the western coast of Africa, and upon that part of it where the wandering Arabs inhabit. He wishes to relieve himself, and his readers, from the continued detail of human misery; and thinks he cannot do it better than by giving, very briefly, what scanty historical and geographical information he can collect concerning this quarter of the globe.

Although Africa holds the third rank in point of size among the four great continents that constitute our globe, in a moral, political, and commercial point of view, it is decidedly inferior to them all. While the continents of Europe and America have been making rapid progress in civilization, the arts and sciences, Asia may be said to have been, for the most part, stationary, and Africa retrograding. While the arts that conduce to the comfort of man, and the sciences that expand and elevate his mind, have, in the former, been advanced almost to perfection; in many parts of the latter, the same degree of barbarism prevails now, as prevailed at the birth of our Saviour. Indeed, for a considerable time before the Christian *æra*, the Persians, Medes, and Romans, had large and beautiful settlements upon the Niger, and in different parts of the African continent.

But upon the subversion of the Roman empire, in the fifth century, when the northern hive broke loose, and was precipitated upon Europe, the Goths, Vandals, Franks, Ostrogoths, Visigoths, and other barbarous tribes, made a war of extermination against civilized man, and of destruction against all the productions of the arts and sciences. The Vandals, always taking the lead in barbarity, passed from Spain into Africa, converted some of the most populous places in this continent to a barren wilderness, held uncontrolled dominion in all the north part of this continent for more than a century and were at last compelled to surrender a country which they had thus ruined, to the Mahometan Arabs, or Moors, who now, under different names, form the principal part of its population.

This immense continent, which has so long been the theatre of suffering humanity, is bounded north by the Mediterranean sea, having Europe on the north; west by the Atlantic ocean, having America on the west; south, by the southern ocean; east, by the Indian ocean, the Red sea, and part of Asia, to which it is united by the Isthmus of Suez, about sixty miles in breadth. This immense peninsula in shape resembles a triangle; its east and west sides being very irregular. From Cape Bona, on the Mediterranean, to the Cape of Good Hope, on the southern ocean, it comprehends seventy degrees of latitude, or about 4875 miles; and from Cape Verd 17° 33' W. long, to Cape Guardafui, 51° 20' E. long, it is something more than 4790 miles.

It is within the knowledge of every historian, that the present nations of Europe owe their origin to some one of the barbarous nations who overturned the Roman empire, about the middle of the fifth century. Breaking forth in myriads from the frozen regions of Scandinavia, where they had become inured to every hardship and privation, and pouring their countless legions upon the fertile, highly cultivated and delightful countries, bordering upon the Mediterranean, they lost the ardour of conquest, and the thirst for discoveries. The Ostrogoths and Visigoths, took to themselves the beautiful regions of Italy and Naples. The Gauls and Franks possessed themselves of France. The Moors, who came from the east, established themselves in Spain and Portugal. The Saxons overran the extensive German empire, including Prussia and Poland. This, the most brave, magnanimous and warlike of the northern clans, afterwards passed over to England. From them Americans may trace their origin. They continue to be brave and magnanimous, and, when necessary, can be warlike.

Although many of these tribes inhabited countries but a short distance from the continent of Africa, yet so completely had they destroyed every vestige of the arts and sciences, and with them so effectually checked the progressing knowledge of navigation, commencing the period which has been denominated the "dark ages," that this continent for a long period of time, remained to them, and to the rest of the world, almost unknown. At length the mariner's compass was invented; and about the middle of the fourteenth century, (1344) the Canary islands, near the western coast of Africa were discovered, and, by the Pope, erected into a kingdom, and bestowed upon a royal Castilian. The ardour for penetrating unexplored regions revived; and the fifteenth century may be called the age of discovery.

The Portuguese led the van in the path of navigating glory. An armament was fitted out by John I. of Portugal to attack the Moors, who had possessed themselves of the Barbary coast in Africa. The vessels that were sent forward to explore, proceeded as far as Cape Bajador, the dreadful place where Capt. Riley and his crew met their fate. This was 160 miles beyond the voyages of former navigators. The dreadful breakers, dashing upon the impending cliffs near that Cape, deterred them from approaching the coast, and they returned. Henry, son of John I. soon after fitted out a vessel, and entrusted the command to two gentlemen of his own household. Timidity made them merely coasters; but a gale of wind drove them out to sea, and they accidentally discovered Porto Santo.

The next year, he sent out three vessels to take possession of that island, and from that they discovered a fixed spot in the horizon; and upon approaching it, they found it to be the island of Madeira, so well known to our countrymen. Soon after. the dreaded Cape Bajador was doubled; and in a few years after they discovered the River Senegal, and the coast from Cape Blanco to Cape Verd, and, in 1446, the Cape de Verd islands. The equinoctial line was soon after passed; and Benin, Congo and Guinea, were discovered in succession. The Portuguese monarch, animated to enthusiasm by this success, and thinking there must be a southern termination to the African continent, despatched Bartholomey Diaz to find it.

He accomplished the object; but dared not approach the threatening promontory, which he named Cabo Tormentoso. or Stormy Cape. But the king, knowing that he had found a passage to India, gave it the name of the Cape of Good Hope. Towards the close of this century, (15th) he despatched a nobleman by the name of Vasquez de Gama, to double this Cape, and if possible proceed to India. He accomplished this great object, and landed in India the 22nd of May, 1498, and returned to Lisbon the 14th of September, 1499, about seven years after Columbus had discovered the continent of America.

The coast of Africa had now been thoroughly explored, while the interior was known only by the barbarians who inhabited it; to the geographer, it was nothing but a vastly extended blank; and it remained so until near the close of the 18th century. The reason for this may probably be found in the fact that all the great enterprises, set on foot for the discovery of unknown regions, have generally proceeded from a desire to accumulate wealth, or augment power; and the accumulation of the one is generally an augmentation of the other. The unpromising appearance of the coast of Africa afforded but little encouragement to the ambition of monarchs, or the cupidity of merchants.

To this it may be added, that De Gama, by discovering a passage to India round the Cape of Good Hope, had unfolded to European merchants the inexhaustible stores of wealth embosomed in that quarter of the globe. Columbus at the same time discovered a New World. The mines of Potosi and Peru were beginning to pour forth their rich contents into the coffers of European monarchs, and to stimulate the avarice of European merchants. To these, as the leading causes, may probably be imputed the ignorance in which the world remains of the interior of the continent of Africa to this day, (as at time of first publication).

We have, to be sure, a few books of travels in this continent. But they are the productions of individuals, whose romantic desire to obtain information led them to encounter every hazard, and surmount every danger. We can hardly expect a correct delineation of a country, or a description of its inhabitants, institutions, manners, and customs, by a solitary wanderer, who is every moment in danger of death. Surely, that head is poorly calculated to treasure up facts and detail them to the world, which is liable every hour to be taken from the shoulders. The travels of Vaillant, of Norden, and of Bruce, and what little of Park's is published, have been carefully examined by the writer of this Journal, with a view of enriching it with interesting extracts therefrom. But the design is relinquished, as they give us no information concerning the wandering Arabs, or of the immense desert of Zahara which comprehends a great proportion of the interior of North Africa. It may here be remarked, that we can expect correct information of this desert and of the Arabs, from none but European or American slaves.

The traveller, who is in pursuit of this knowledge, is in hourly danger of death or slavery. The slave is safe in the hands of his master. With him he traverses the desert; with him he reposes in a tent. Having leisure, he can record in safety the peculiarities of this peculiar people. If he becomes a slave to a settled resident in some of the towns, he can describe that, and the customs of the people. The author of this Journal was in both these situations, and hopes to give a correct account of this part of Africa, or that part of it which he saw.

But I cannot omit to incorporate into this work some portion of the doings of an *"Association for promoting the discovery of the interior parts of Africa"* This association was formed in England by a number of gentlemen of rank and learning, in the year 1788. The first adventurer that entered into its service, and proceeded upon a tour of discovery in Africa, was one of our own countrymen by the name of Ledyard.

The daring enterprise of Americans has been known to the world, and by the world applauded, ever since Englishmen became known by that name. Although the Portuguese first began the business of discovery, it was left for Americans and Englishmen to complete it; and from what they have already accomplished, it may be rationally expected, that the ardent spirit of discovery will not subside so long as an ocean or sea remains untraversed, or any portion of the earth continues unexplored. Our countryman, the indefatigable Ledyard, had been long engaged in traversing unknown seas, and exploring unknown countries, without the aid of governments, or the assistance of private munificence. He became known to this association, was adopted as their agent, and employed to accomplish their splendid objects. The readers of this volume will be better gratified by an account of this American, from the doing of this association, than from the imperfect manner in which it would be given by the writer; it is, therefore, presented in their own language:—

> Scarcely was this society instituted, when two gentlemen were engaged in the advancement of these schemes of discovery, whose talents and courage eminently qualified them for such an arduous service. One of them named Ledyard, by birth an American, feeling from his earliest youth an irresistible desire to explore those regions of the globe, which were undiscovered, or imperfectly known, had passed several years among the Indians in America, studying their manners and habits, and had thus learned how to recommend himself to the favour and protection of savages. He had accompanied Capt. Cook in his voyage round the world, descending to the humble situation of corporal of marines, rather than forego an opportunity so inviting to his inquisitive and adventurous spirit.
>
> He next resolved to traverse the continent of America, from the north-west coast which Cook had partly explored, to the east-

ern coast, with which he himself was already perfectly familiar. Disappointed in his intention of sailing in a voyage of commercial adventure to Nootka Sound, he crossed the British Channel to Ostend, with only ten guineas in his purse; determined to travel over land to Kamschatka, whence the passage is short to the western coast of America. When he came to the Gulf of Bothnia, he attempted to cross it on the ice, that he might reach Kamschatka by the shortest way; but finding that the water was not frozen in the middle, he returned to Stockholm; travelled northward into the arctic circle; and passing round the head of the gulf. descended on its eastern side to Petersburgh.

There his extraordinary appearance attracted general notice. Without stockings or shoes, and too poor to provide himself with either, he was invited to dine with the Portuguese Ambassador, who supplied him with twenty guineas on the credit of Sir Joseph Banks, and through his interest he obtained permission to accompany a detachment of stores which was to be sent to Yakutz, for the use of Mr. Billings, an Englishman, who was entrusted with the schemes of northern discovery, in which the Empress was then engaged.

From Yakutz, which is situated in Siberia, 6000 miles east of Petersburgh, he proceeded to Oczakow, on the Kamschatkan sea; but as the navigation was completely obstructed by the ice, he returned to Yakutz, intending to wait for the conclusion of the winter. Here, in consequence of some unaccountable suspicion, he was seized in the name of the Empress by two Russian soldiers, who conveyed him, in the depth of winter, through the north of Tartary, to the frontier of the Polish dominions; assuring him at their departure, that if he returned to Russia he should certainly be hanged; but if he chose to return to England, they wished him a pleasant journey.

Poor, forlorn, and friendless, covered with rags, and exhausted by hardships, disease, and misery, he proceeded to Konigsburg, where the interest of Sir Joseph Banks enabled him to procure the sum of five guineas, by means of which he arrived in England. He waited immediately on Sir Joseph, who, knowing his disposition, informed him that he could recommend him to an adventure as perilous as that from which he had just returned, and communicated to him the views of the association for discovering the inland countries of Africa.

Ledyard entered with enthusiasm into an enterprise which he had already projected for himself; and receiving from Sir Joseph a letter of introduction to one of the members of the committee appointed to direct the business, and promote the object of the association, he went to him without delay. The description which that gentleman has given of their first interview strongly marks the character of this hardy traveller. 'Before I had learned,' says he, 'from the note, the name and business of my visiter, I was struck with the manliness of his person, the breadth of his chest, the openness of his countenance, and the inquietude of his eye. I spread the map of Africa before him, and tracing a line from Cairo to Sennaar, and from thence westward in the latitude and supposed direction of the Niger, I told him that was the route by which I was anxious that Africa might, if possible, be explored. He said he should think himself singularly fortunate to be entrusted with the adventure. I asked him when he would set out? Tomorrow morning, was his answer.' From such zeal, decision, and intrepidity, the society naturally formed the most sanguine expectations.

Mr. Ledyard sailed from London on the 30th of June, 1788, and in thirty-six days, seven of which were spent in Paris and two at Marseilles, arrived in the city of Alexandria; and having there assumed the dress, and been instructed in the manners requisite for an Egyptian traveller, proceeded to Cairo, which he reached on the 19th day of August. Ledyard travelled with peculiar advantages. Endowed with an original and comprehensive genius, he beheld with interest, and described with energy, the scenes and objects around him; and by comparing them with what he had seen in other regions of the globe, he was enabled to give his narrative all the varied effect of contrast and resemblance.

His remarks on lower Egypt, had that country been less generally known, might have ranked with the most valuable of geographical records, and greatly heightened the opinion which his employers already entertained of his singular qualifications for the task which he had undertaken. Nor was his residence in Cairo altogether useless to the association. By visiting the slave markets, and by conversing with the *Iclabs*. or travelling merchants of the caravans, he obtained, without any expense, a better idea of the people of Africa, of its trade, of the position of places, the nature of the country, and the manner of travelling, than he could, by any other means, have acquired: and the communications on these subjects, which he transmitted to England, interesting and instructing as they were afforded the society the most gratifying proofs of the ardent spirit of inquiry, the unwearied attention, the persevering research and the laborious, indefatigable, anxious zeal with which their author pursued the object of their mission.

This interesting and elegant account of our wonderful countryman is extracted from the *Proceedings of the African Association* for 1790 It is incorporated into this volume with the highest pleasure, as it is an encomium, derived from our enemy, in favour of one of our native countrymen; from an enemy too, who have always used the small arms of the pen, and the artillery of the press, to diminish American genius—American courage—and American greatness.

This indefatigable association continued their laudable exertions. Mr. Lucas sailed for the African continent in October, the same year with Ledyard. In 1790, Major Houghton was employed in the same enterprise. In 1795, the celebrated Mungo Park began to explore the continent of Africa. Mr. Hernemann, a German, followed in 1797.

We might extend this chapter by giving short biographical sketches of these celebrated adventurers, but we now return to our Journal;—intending, in a future part of it. to give a brief Geographical view of Africa, embracing the principal places described by these travellers, and what may be gathered from other authentic sources.

CHAPTER 5

Capture by Arabs, and Separation

After having given our readers a compressed historical account of Africa, derived from the most authentic sources, we now return to the melancholy Journal of individual sufferings in this quarter of the globe. They were endured by the author for about nineteen months, that is to say, from the 5th day of September, 1815, when he landed from the boat near Cape Barbas, until the 8th day of April, 1817,—when the author left this quarter of the globe to return to America, that quarter of it in which he had his birth.

After we ran our boat ashore, as mentioned, north of Cape Barbas, our first object was to secure what provisions we had remaining. It had been many days since we ate bread; the wreck of the brig having ruined the whole, excepting what we got ashore at Cape Bajador, and that was soon consumed. Our wine was also exhausted, the last bottle having been drank just before we made our landing in the little sand beach among the rocks. We still had a little water, and some salt pork remaining; but could not transport them, together with our clothing, when ascending and descending rocks, whose perpendicular position and ragged sides seemed to defy the approach of human footsteps. We knew the impossibility of doing this from a view of the precipices that surrounded us,—and we left all our clothing excepting what covered our bodies—cut from our pork all that was lean—buried and threw away every piece of money in our possession, at the suggestion of Capt. Riley.

Most of us made small sacks out of the sail we had in the boat, with a penknife and some rope yarn. In these we deposited each of us a small quantity of fit pork and a porter bottle filled with water, it being all we had now remaining, excepting one extra bottle which we drank up on starting on our uncertain and hazardous journey. We now came to a solemn agreement to remain together as long as possible, and to render to each other every kind office in our power. It was not merely common danger that made us friends; we had become attached to each other by previous sufferings and mutual favours.

As we were doomed soon to be separated under circumstances the most painful to the human feelings, I must be indulged in naming the whole crew. James Riley, captain—George Williams, chief mate—Aaron R. Savage, second mate, all of Middletown; William Porter, James Barrett, and John Hogan, of Massachusetts, near Portland; Thomas Burns, of Lyme; James Clarke, of Hartford; and myself, seamen. Horace Savage, cabin-boy, of Middletown; and Richard Deslile, (man of colour) cook, of Hartford. Mr. Williams, Barrett, Hogan, Antonio, and Deslile. (called Dick) still remained unheard of, and probably are either starved, assassinated, or remain in bondage, from which the rest of us, heaven be praised, have escaped.

On the 6th of Sept. we started, scarcely knowing what object we had in view. We resolved, however, to follow the coast, hoping to espy some sail at sea—hoping to find water—hoping to reach the wreck—and hoping to find something more in it to sustain life a little longer; having at the same time no expectation of seeing either of those hopes realized; and in this we were not disappointed; we were defeated in all of them.

Porter and myself usually kept forward, sometimes seeing our companions in the rear, and sometimes they were hidden from us by projecting rocks. It is impossible for a stranger to this dreadful coast to conceive of the danger and fatigue we endured in this journey. Occasionally we found a short distance of beach on which we could walk without difficulty; we were then opposed by rocks projecting into the sea, upon which a surf was constantly beating. We had to wait for the surf to retire, and then clamber over the rock. For many rods we were obliged to ascend upon the broken cliffs of the rocks, the surge beating upon the base of them below in a manner calculated to make despair take the place of hope. During this day, we came to a narrow projection from, the almost perpendicular rock, for nearly thirty rods in length: not much wider than a stone step.

It was our only passage. It was as much as fifty feet above the surf below, and rising as many as five hundred feet above our heads. He must be something more or less than man, who could pass this track with unconcern. Porter and I being far ahead, found a small passage into the rock, where we could remain with safety, and we waited till the rest came up. The water had worn a hole into the rock, nearly in shape of a common kettle, which was filled with warm water. We bathed our heads in it which greatly refreshed us. We were soon joined by our whole party, who did the same, with the same effect. We continued to grope our way along the rocks until dark, when we came to a projecting one, around which we had to wade, or swim through the surf. We then ascended a cliff, and to our great joy, found a place where we could repose.

It ought to be here mentioned, that all the way we saw fresh dung, and tracks of animals, and during the night heard their howling; but we neither of us this day or night saw any animal. We lay down to rest with our clothes soaked, after eating a little raw pork and quenching our thirst with a sip of water. Notwithstanding our constant and unwearied exertions, we could not have travelled more than five miles during the whole of this day, judging from the objects in our rear which we had passed, and a harder day's travel was never made by man.

On the morning of the 7th of September, we found ourselves stiffened and almost unable to move from having slept the preceding night, which was chilly, in the open air, with wet clothes. In the morning we partook of the only food in our possession—cutting a thin slice of raw pork from what remained, and water enough only to wet our mouths. With this little nourishment, and with our debilitated bodies, we began our second day's journey. The difficulty of travelling was not diminished, but rather increased. We shortly came to a rock which projected a great distance over the sea. The water had worn under it from fifty to sixty feet; and the cliffs that had broken from the rock above, lay, in great masses, in the surf below. It seemed to us impossible to pass: but we resolved to attempt the dreadful passage. We let ourselves down from rock to rock until we reached those lying in the surf, and clinging to the one upon which we alighted, the dreadful surf broke over us with all its violence.

As the sea went out. we snatched the opportunity to pass a short distance over these craggy rocks, tearing our bodies in a terrible manner. In this way we travelled, from rock to rock, and through surf after surf, I should judge half a mile: in performing which we were as many as three hours. At length the party all came up, and we reached the sand beach which we had before seen ahead. Had it not been at low water, we could not have passed at all. For most of this distance, the water had worn under the rocks, as near as we could judge, from sixty to eighty feet, presenting to view a cavern, from whose frightful aspect the heart recoiled with horror. In this passage we found and ate a few salt muscles, which, although they afforded some nourishment, very much increased our thirst.

We also saw a large leopard; the first live animal we had seen on the African coast, excepting the camels, at Cape Bajador, where our calamities commenced. It was about 10 o'clock when we reached the beach. We immediately began to dig for water, and having no implements to do it with, we used our hands, scraping the sand into our hats and throwing it to the top of the well. Capt. Riley went in pursuit of a passage to the world above the rocks, if, by good fortune, he could find one, and we continued to dig, without the least effect, in various places for water. Capt. Riley gave us a gloomy account on his return, and his gloom was increased when he found that we had obtained no water. We all once more started, and at the end of the beach, it being about noon, we were completely exhausted.

Nature could do no more—we stretched ourselves upon the beach—under a shelving rock guarding us from the rays of the sun. *"Sleep, balmy sleep—nature's fond nurse, sweet restorer,"* came to our relief; we reposed, and our *"senses were steeped in forgetfulness,"* for two hours. I will not attempt to describe my feelings at the time I awoke, for it could hardly be said that I had any feelings. I had become so inured to misery, that she had adopted me as her child, and I felt no disposition to avoid her embrace. I knew I had done all I could to rescue myself and assist my companions in escaping from the army of calamities that surrounded us. This seemed to be a common sentiment among us.

Capt. Riley, in his pursuit of a passage over the rocks, had discovered that there was a beach for some ways ahead, and proposed that we should make one effort more to find our way to the land above, through this hitherto inaccessible precipice. With one accord we acceded to the proposition, and were once more on the march. We soon began to ascend, crawling upon our hands and knees, catching hold of every substance that would assist us in dragging our bodies forward. It was next to dragging ourselves to the scaffold—it was like becoming our own executioners. We at length ascended the top of the precipice, and, O merciful Heaven! what a prospect presented itself to our affrighted view! what despondency sunk into our hearts!

Had we been called to meet the dangers of the sea, or to fight the enemies of our country, we should, I know, like true American sailors, have encountered them without dismay. But, after having encountered and overcome almost all the varieties of human misery; after having rung all the changes of calamity; then to be cast upon a barren heath, a boundless plane, made up of burning sand and flinty stones, producing neither a green vegetable, or refreshing water; there to be famished with hunger, devoured by wild beasts, or become slaves to the most merciless of creatures that wear the form of man, was surely enough to appal the stoutest heart!

It seemed as if death was about to overtake us; and the outstretched plane before us seemed like the great Golgotha of the human race. Casting our eyes far to the southward, the plane, owing to the striking of the rays of the sun upon the dried sand, appeared like an immense lake. We even thought of going in pursuit of it; but having so long been betrayed by the illusions of hope, *this ignis fatuus* could not lead us. Some of us felt a disinclination to move at all. Hogan, at the mention of whose name I can hardly suppress a falling tear, however, the first one who ventured upon the hawser as before mentioned, was asked what it was best to do? He answered, with perfect apathy, "I don't know—but what's the use of lying down to die as long as we can stand up and walk."

The fortitude of a New-England sailor is certainly proverbial; but we are told that a continual dropping will wear away stones; and as our bodies wasted. our courage was diminished. We moved off in a body, keeping in with the coast; and as we wandered near the edge of the precipice, we were almost dizzied by the immense distance to the roaring surge at the base, which continually beat and wasted its force upon this iron bound coast. We occasionally saw a wild dry plant resembling a wild parsnip, or fennel stalk, which we dug up out of the hard baked earth with sharp stones and the knives we had with us. It afforded but little nourishment to us, and from the appearance of the earth around them, they had been sought after and ate by wild beasts. their tracks being visible around their roots.

We saw large heaps of muscle shells, and the appearance of a former fire where they probably had been roasted by the natives. Thus far, in this day's travel, we had found but little sand, the surface of the earth being chiefly covered with sharp stones. But towards night, coming to a more sandy ground, we discovered the tracks of a camel and those of a large human foot, travelling to the northward. These tracks appeared to be recently made: indeed they must have been, as the blowing of the dry sand would soon have filled them up. This circumstance convinced us that we were at no great distance from some of the natives;

and however terrible was the reflection, we now felt anxious to fall in with them, for we were famishing and thirsting to death. We still had a few drops of water remaining, with which we moistened our mouths, after sitting down near the precipice, where we enjoyed a cool breeze.

After travelling a little farther, we discovered a sandy beach; the precipice suddenly diminishing and filling back from the shore. We intended, if possible, to make this beach, and there to spend the night. It now became dark; and after travelling about an hour we discovered the light of a fire at a considerable distance ahead. This discovery excited in our bosoms the mingled emotions of joy and fear— joy, that we might obtain some- thing to satisfy the hunger that gnawed upon our frames, and quench the thirst which was parching us to powder— fear, that this relief would forever take from us the freedom which we enjoyed with our misery. We descended, with great difficulty, about halfway down to the beach, and upon a steep side-hill, surrounded by cragged rocks, we laid down upon the burning sand, after having scraped off the surface of it to make a cooler bed, and also a guard to prevent us from sliding down the hill. Here we slept until morning; and upon awaking, found ourselves chilled by the cold air and the dews which prevail herein the night season, notwithstanding the heat of the days.

The 8th of September had now come, a day memorable in the calendar of our crew; for upon this day we lost the exalted character of freemen, and became the most degraded of slaves.

About sunrise we were all assembled upon the sand bank upon which we had slept, and in a united manner, joined Mr. Savage (if I rightly recollect) in prayer. Standing uncovered upon the declivity of the hill, with the boundless ocean roaring on one side, and the immense desert stretching out on the other, we poured out our souls to that God who made them, imploring His protection and support in whatever situation we might be placed, in whatever scenes we might be called to act, and in whatever sufferings we might be compelled to endure.

We then mutually pledged ourselves to each other, that, as we should undoubtedly very soon be enslaved by the Arabs, and probably separated from each other, we would use every means to effect our own and each other's release, that should fall in our power; that if we could, by any means, convey the intelligence of our situation to any Christian power, we would avail ourselves of the opportunity. We now descended the hill to the beach, and continued our course along the same to the northeast.

After proceeding about two miles, as I judged, and rising a small sand-hill, we discovered at no great distance a drove of camels. We came to a sudden stop, and upon consultation, some were for going on, others for lying by. We concluded that this *might* be a *caravan* travelling to the northward; and *might* assist us on. We continued to approach them; and as we drew near, we concluded there must have been as many as seventy or eighty of the natives. We were now first discovered by six or seven of them, who had wandered from the clan; one of whom appeared to be a middle aged man, and who afterwards became Hogan's and Dick's master—the others were two women, the rest being children. As soon as they saw us, they run rapidly towards us. We immediately fell upon our knees, and, by signs, begging the man, who was armed with a drawn scimitar, to spare our lives, and bestow upon us a little water.

The first request he granted, but totally disregarded the second. The women, ten times more ferocious in appearance than the men, came up with the children, and with the greatest violence, stripped off all our clothes excepting trowsers. Some of us, however, were stripped entirely naked, although they left me my trowsers. The man, in the meantime, was constantly brandishing his naked scimitar around our heads, and darting it towards our breasts, seeming impatient to see us bleeding. The whole clan now discovered us, and came rushing on with many of their camels. The manner of their approach defies description; some were running on foot, armed with spears, some on camels, some with muskets, others with large clubs, others with scimitars, and all seemed anxious to be the first sharers in the plunder, when alas, they could find no plunder but our miserable bodies. As they came up, those who had possessed themselves of all our clothes, and of our persons also, began to throw sand into the air, and hooting somewhat like American savages.

A contest now began among themselves, of which we were spectators, all contending for their right to us as slaves. After this contest was ended, in which no lives were lost, although much heathen blood was shed, we were all led towards the well; each one of us having three or four Arabs hold of us, forcing us on, and each of them contending for his right to us, as his slave. We very soon reached the well, around which were a number of vessels filled with water, in which the camels were drinking. They were made of the skin of the camel. The top of them was a circular hoop, to which the skin was sewed, and which rested on three legs. Between these legs, the skin hung down in the shape of a common basket, holding generally about twenty gallons, from which five or six camels drink at one time; it being supplied from the well until the camels are satisfied.

As I came to the well, my masters released me from their grasp. I immediately plunged my head into the tub with the camels, to satisfy my raging thirst, regardless of the vessel or of the kind of liquid I was drinking. The camels were frightened by their new companion, and began to retire; the natives immediately drove me away, and restored to the camels, more humane than their masters, their previous right. During this time there seemed to be a contest among those who brought me to the well, the object which was to determine to whom of *right* I belonged. They seized me three or four at a time, and pulled me one way and the other, with so much force, that I concluded they were about to settle the dispute by making an equal distribution of my body among them.

During this scene, in which I was a passive actor, they kept constantly jabbering very loud and with great earnestness. At length one of them continued his hold, the rest having surrendered me to him; and he now became my sole master. His name was Ganus. He was about five feet eight inches in height; large and raw boned, as is indeed the case with all the wandering Arabs, and about forty years of age. It had now become about eight o'clock in the morning. My master led me off to his camels stationed at a small distance, in the keeping of two young women, who afterwards proved to be his sisters. I here fell in with Mr. Savage, Mr Williams, and Barrett, who were situated nearby. They informed me that they had been furnished with a small supply of milk and water. The girls then gave me some milk and water, in a bowl, which I shared with my companions in misery. The camels having been sufficiently watered, and the goatskins having been filled, preparations were made for a departure from the well.

CHAPTER 6

Separation of the crew

September 8th, 1815.—From this day I date my slavery among the Arabs, and my shipmates may also date theirs from the same time. We were now all in the possession of barbarian masters; although it is impossible for me to tell precisely how the crew were distributed. Just before my master started, which was between nine and ten o'clock a.m. I was permitted to take leave of Capt. Riley and all the crew, who were situated in different places around the well, excepting Mr. Williams and Barrett, who went off in company with me. As it is wholly impossible to describe the feelings of my bosom at this *adieu,* I will not attempt it. More poignantly distressing they could not have been, had I been about to leave this world for another. It left me in a state of horror and anguish which I then thought I could not, but for a short time, survive.

I was mounted upon a camel behind the hump, wholly destitute of clothing excepting my trowsers, and compelled to steady myself by clinching the long hair upon the hump, which is generally from four to six inches in length. The back of the camel, from the hinder part of the protuberance upon it. commonly called the hump, is entirely smooth: the back bone extremely sharp, and the hip bones projecting but a very little from the rump, which slopes very steeply, so that it is utterly impossible to keep your seat without inclining the body far forward, and constantly holding on by the long hair.

The camels commonly used for carrying baggage and passengers are from twenty to twenty-five hands in height; and although in riding at full trot the naked body of the miserable slave who is compelled to ride, is excoriated and torn to pieces, a sudden fall from them would endanger his life. If he falls off by accident, or voluntarily slips from his painful seat to relieve himself from excruciating torture. he is left in the rear, and is driven up to the party who have gotten ahead, by the scimitar, the spear, or the club of his master. After travelling in this way for some miles, I began to wonder why I had not been sunk in the ocean, precipitated from a rock, or in some sudden way been deprived of that life winch now became a burthen to me.

My body was naked, excepting my legs, under the almost vertical rays of the sun, being within the torrid zone, or tropic of Cancer, and my legs were constantly chafing and wearing away by constantly thumping upon the hard hips of an hard trotting camel. Poor beast, thought I, we both have the same unfeeling master, and must both submit to the capricious exercise of that power which absolute authority gives him, I almost imagined that the *camel* pitied me; and should have come to this conclusion absolutely, had it not been from the prevailing sentiment that men possessed more *humanity* than *brutes*. How often are we in the habit of making mistakes! The Arab is not the only being, among those called *rational*, whose direful cruelty would make even a tiger weep.

After we had ascended the precipice, and had gone some distance upon the plane, my master left his camels, his baggage and me, in the keeping of the girls, and joined the master of Mr. Williams and Barrett. They knew that we must have landed on this coast at no great distance off: and having asked me, by signs, where the boat or vessel lay in which we were wrecked, I satisfied them by signs as well as I could. They now both started upon a long trot, a camel seldom galloping, and went in pursuit of the boat or wreck. My master had about twenty camels, and the master of Mr. Williams and Barrett about the same number, and we were now all joined in one party, in the keeping of the women belonging to the two parties.

We now proceeded upon the plane towards the interior, in a S. E direction, travelling at full speed. We were compelled to keep up with the party, and although riding in the manner before described was excessively painful, we were under the necessity of enduring it, as we could not on foot do this. We however, occasionally dismounted, and run a short distance on foot, to obtain a little relief from our pain, occasioned by the hard trotting of the camels. At about 2 o'clock, two Arabs approached, with great speed, stole Mr. Williams and Barrett from their keepers, in spite of all their exertions to prevent it; placed them behind upon their camels, and made off to the south; and, in a few minutes, were out of sight. I was now left alone; no human creature to associate with; no bosom into which I could pour my own sorrows.

My captain and shipmates were all dispersed, and in different hands; and I was left, without any spectator of my distresses, excepting the wretches who took delight in increasing them. The girls now stripped off my trowsers, and gave me, in exchange, a strip of old blanket, about eighteen inches wide, which I made fast around my middle with thorns. I begged for some water, which they gave me in an old hat, which I was obliged to carry in my hand, out of sight of the camels, lest by wearing it, I should frighten them. We then started again; and, as the party slackened their pace a little, I was enabled to keep up on foot. We continued in a S. E. direction; and after travelling about two hours, I had the first view of the Arabs' tents. We halted at about a quarter of a mile distance from them, and I soon saw a female coming towards us, who came out to meet the returning party. She seemed to manifest a little feeling at my forlorn situation, and entreated the girls to give me a little water, which they did. She took hold of my hands and examined them very intently, showing at the same time signs of wonder and curiosity.

We then prosecuted our journey, some mounted on camels, and some on foot, till about five o'clock the sun appearing about an hour high. We now came near the tents belonging to the two masters of our party, situated in a small valley. The surface of the ground consisted of hard baked earth filled with small, sharp, flinty stones, and occasionally of a small vein of sandy ground There was not a tree nor vegetable in sight; and the earth had nothing verdant upon it, but a few small bushes thinly scattered, about two feet high. Upon these, the camels fed. They were distributed around the valley, and supported themselves by browsing upon these bushes. The camels loaded with water, which was contained in goat skins, were; driven up to the tent, and unloaded.

These skins, made to transport water from one part of the desert to the other, are fitted for this purpose by taking the skin whole from the goat. This is done, by cutting it around the neck; then by thrusting in the hand, it is taken whole from the animal to the end of its legs. The holes, at the end of the legs, are made fast. by tying an overhand knot with the skin of the legs. The Arabs have a kind of root which, dried and pounded, they apply to the inside of the skin, which cures and tans it, sufficiently to become a water vessel; leaving the hair on the outside in its natural state. The neck of the skin, into which they pour the water, is made water-tight by lashing a cord around it, which is also made fast to the skin of one of the forelegs; and in this way they keep the neck of the skin in a perpendicular position, while the body of it lies alongside of the camel horizontally; being made fast to the saddle by a cord extending from each leg. The camel is sometimes leaded with four of these skins, two upon each side. These skins are sometimes used for the transportation of milk, taken from the camel, although those used for this purpose are more thoroughly tanned, and the hair wholly taken off.

Before we arrived at the tents, my master's wife and three children came out about half a mile to meet us. They welcomed the return of the party, by enclosing their hands in those of the returning, and also throwing their arms about their necks and kissing them. The old lady wore a face that seemed to have something of humanity in it. She took my hand, and letting it go, put hers to her own mouth, motioning to me to do the same, with my own, which I did. The little children, by their signs, wished me to kiss their hands, which I did. They all manifested a kind of pleasure in having a slave in their family, to serve them, and more probably because they hoped to make a sum of money by the sale of me. I was then conducted to the tent; and after resting awhile, was sent out with one of the girls, who had a kind of hatchet in her hand, for what purpose I could not tell. I however soon learned it was to cut bushes for fuel.

After she had cut a few of them to instruct me, she handed the hatchet to me and bade me cut or dig them out of the ground. After gathering and carrying three handful s to the tent, I was told it was sufficient, and was bade, by signs, to sit down. They then dug a small hole in the ground in front of the tent, and struck tire with a flint and steel upon a kind of dried weed, which served for tinder. After the weed had taken tire, they gathered up a quantity of dried camel's dung, which is always to be found around an Arab's tent, and after rubbing it in their hands, placed it upon the burning weed, and blowing it, it soon set the dung on fire. They then put on a few dried sticks, and, as soon as they began to blaze, they were placed in the bottom of the hole. This is the universal method of building a fire among this people.

They then gathered some small stones and threw into the fire; commanding me to cut a small slice from the pork which they found in my sack, and the same being cut into small pieces, it was put into a small wooden bowl. They then, with two sticks, took from the fire in the hole the heated stones and dropped thorn into the bowl among the pork, which I kept from burning by stirring it round. It was very much for my benefit that my mistress was a Mahometan, for she would not *publicly* eat pork herself, although she dispensed so far with the articles of her faith, as to permit her children to partake with me of this unholy food. Before I began my supper, however, she made me pour my pork, fat and all, into my hat, as they will never permit a Christian to contaminate their vessels by eating or drinking in them: and I have often been deprived of a draught of water, because no vessel but theirs could be found to contain it. They commanded me to preserve part of this mess until next morning, as I could have no more food until the next evening.

Cooking, however, is an uncommon duty among the Arabs, as they seldom have anything to cook, living almost wholly upon the milk of the camel, which they sometimes warm with heated stones. Indeed, were it not for the camel, the immense desert of Zahara, sometimes called Zaara, and Saharah, must be wholly deserted by human beings. From the peculiar nature of the camel's feet, being somewhat of the nature of a puff-ball, and yielding to the smallest pressure, they are enabled to endure the sharp stones, and also to travel in the deep sand. By these animals, the Arabs are enabled to traverse the desert, and to transport their plunder, their persons, and their slaves, from one part of it to another. The country, producing no vegetable food of any consequence, the natives are enabled to sustain life by the milk of these animals and their meat when slain. Why they are permitted to live at all, as they do nothing to add to the common stock of human enjoyment, but everything in their power to diminish it, is a question which neither the dim light of nature, nor the imperfect reason of man can solve.

At about eleven o'clock at night, the usual time of milking the camels, I had perhaps a pint of milk mixed with a pint of water, which is the usual quantity afforded a slave. The reason for milking the camels near the middle of the night is to let their milk cool, which is always much heated by the exercise of the animal, and the burning sun of the preceding day. They suffered me to sleep upon the sand at one corner of the tent. In the course of the night my master Ganus returned from seeking after the boat. To me, it was next to a miracle, that he could have reached the boat, and have taken therefrom articles which I knew we left there, in this short space of time.

But afterwards, on seeing Porter, he told me that the next day after my master descended, he went down to the boat himself with his master. That the camels and an Arab would descend a precipice with ease, which an European or American could hardly pass without endangering his life. My master brought a bag of rice which we had left near the boat, the same being ruined by the salt water, and having turned as green as *verdigris*: he also brought some lean pork, which we could not carry with us upon the precipice; a part of a boat sail, pieces of ropes, and, what reminded me of our brig and my country, the colours of the brig.

September 9th.—This was the second day of my slavery. The family of my master consisted of himself, his wife, and two girls, and a boy; the oldest about twelve. His mother and his two sisters, before mentioned, lived in a tent nearby. and both seemed to constitute but one family. I now furnished myself with a long string, having no means to keep the day of the week, or of the month, the month itself, or even the year; and every day I tied a knot in it to keep my reckoning and have it correct. The family of my master could not be reckoned among the rich Arabs; he and his mother having between them but two small tents, and but about twenty camels, young and old.

At this time they milked but three, which produced but about six quarts of milk daily. This served for the support of the whole, being eight in number, besides myself; and my proportion of milk was of course the smallest in quantity, being sometimes not more than one pint, mixed with the same quantity of water, for twenty-four hours. They generally preserved a part of the milk they got in the night, in a goat skin, for the next day at noon; depending upon the small quantity they obtained in the morning for breakfast, of which I was sometimes deprived of any part.

The first thing the family do upon rising, which is invariably at daybreak, is to go to *Sulle*, or prayer. This they perform with great apparent solemnity. They begin this worship by pulling off what few camel-skin slippers are among them; then kneeling to the earth, rubbing sand upon their hands, arms and faces, a number of times. In whatever attitude, during this duty, whether standing, sitting, or kneeling, their faces are always turned to the east. The ceremony of rubbing their hands, arms and faces, with sand, is a symbol of ablution, or cleansing, as they have no water to perform this with. After this is done they stand up very erect, facing to the east; each repeating exclamations or orisons, in a manner so very peculiar, that it is almost impossible for a foreigner to *spell* the words made use of, however familiar he may become with the pronunciation of them.

It is equally difficult to obtain from them the precise meaning of the words used; as there is a kind of peculiar mystery in their language, as well as a peculiar solemnity in their deportment when worshipping. For nineteen months I was in the habit of witnessing the worship of the Arabs, in families and in larger bodies, generally four times in a day, and hearing the exclamations they made; and will attempt to enter down a few of their most frequently repeated expressions. Looking towards the east, they exclaim—"*Sheda el la lah, Hi, Allah!—Sheda Mahommed Rah sool Allah!*" They then throw their outspread hands forward, exclaiming "*Allah Hooakibar*" (Great God.) They then kneel down upon the earth, and, supporting their bodies with their hands, kiss the earth; and as they kiss it, exclaim again, "*Allah Hooakibar*"; then rising erect, repeat the same expressions.

They now, with a low and solemn tone of voice, casting their eyes occasionally towards heaven, repeat over a prayer from one to two minutes in length. From having afterwards learned the meaning of many of the expressions made use of in these prayers, I feel fully authorized to say that they return thanks for the favours received; for the food they eat; for the clothes they wear. They most earnestly pray for rain when the earth is dry; and for sufficient food for their camels. They pray for abundance of plunder, and that they may take numerous slaves. That, the Great God would destroy their enemies and protect them; that he would keep their children alive, and bless all their possessions. In the course of these prayers, they frequently mentioned the name of *Moolay Solimaan*.

During the repetition of this prayer, they stand perfectly erect. After the conclusion of it, they again exclaim, loudly, "*Allah Hooakibar!*", and again kiss the earth, in the manner described, two or three times, at each time repeating "*Allah Hooakibar!*" They then sit down upon the earth, and each repeats over to himself, probably some part of the *Koran*. During this, they hold in their hands, the most of them, a string of beads upon which they cast their eyes as though offering to them the most profound adoration. These beads they count over, stopping as they come to some particular one. They sometimes wear them upon their arms, and frequently carry them in their hands as they are walking or sitting. They close this ceremony by repeating the words, *Sulle Mulla*.

This is a description of family worship. When a larger number are together, the worship is conducted by arranging themselves in a single line, one of the oldest stepping out in front, and being the only speaker. They, however, all repeat with him, "Allah *Hooakibar*", and following his motions, bow to the earth and kiss it. When a family have closed their morning worship, they proceed to suckle the young camels, the bag of the old one being always secured from them, by a kind of basket made of a species of grass found in some of the northern parts of the deserts, which the women fasten over them. They then milk the remainder into a bowl, which is but a trifle, and divide and drink it.

The camels, unless they are to travel, are then sent off to feed upon the small shrubs or bushes already mentioned, being always in the care of some one of the family. My master remained in his tent through this day. Having obtained two pair of shoes, he gave one pair to me, they being part of the plunder they took from the crew the day before. He restored to me my trowsers, which his sisters the day before had torn from me, having cut them off at the knee, saying, all below the knee was *foonta*—*i. e.* good for nothing. He also gave me part of our boat sail, which his son fancied, and took from me, giving me a patched skin in exchange, which, tied in front, hangs over the back part of the body, covering it nearly as low as the knee. The family spent part of the day in examining their plunder, and I slept under the tent a considerable portion of it. I ate a little of my pork, with the milk allowed me for my supper, and nothing occurred until next morning.

CHAPTER 7

Meeting with Part of the Crew

On the 10th of September, 1815, at about 9 o'clock, a. m. my master took me with him, on foot, about five miles, where we came to a number of tents. No one can judge of my surprise, when I saw Capt. Riley, Clarke, Burns, and I think Horace, sitting near one of the tents. Although the interview with my shipmates was wholly unexpected; although it produced the most delightful feelings, they were mingled with the melancholy reflection that it could be but short, and probably would be the last. We spent nearly half a day together; and while we were in sad conference upon the subject of our fate, the Arabs, about twenty in number, were holding a council. These they frequently hold, but in a very confused and irregular manner, having no one in particular to preside over their deliberations.

Not at that time knowing any of their language, I could not tell, from that or from any signs, what was the subject under consultation; but I judged it was relative to the mode of disposing of us, their slaves, as Capt. Riley was telling them, by counting stones, how many dollars he would give for our ransom, if we could be carried to Morocco, or, as the Arabs call that country, *Marocksh*. Capt. Riley seemed to feel some hopes that we might yet get released, and advised us all to keep up good spirits. I took a painful leave of them, and, at about 3 p. m. returned with my master to his tent. I was sent to gather wood for the night.

The family built a fire, and cooked some of the damaged rice which was brought from the boat, by heated stones. This they did by putting a small quantity of rice, mixed with water, into a bowl; then throwing in the hot stones and covering it over, it became a kind of pudding, which they divided among themselves, leaving what little adhered to the atones for my share, which I was obliged to scrape from them with my teeth. This, with a little piece of lean, salt pork, which was cooked by the embers of fire mixed with sand, a little water, and, at 11 o'clock, a few drops of milk, made up my supper.

On the 11th, for the first time, I witnessed the manner in which the Arabs prepare for a journey It may here be remarked, that they have no particular places appropriated to particular individual. They pitch their tents in any unoccupied place; and when they strike them, they leave the place of their temporary abode, to the next occupant. They begin, by taking all their furniture, from the inside of the tent, which consists of two or three wooden bowls (*geddacks*) which they procure from the Moors; about the same number of water goat skins, (*gillabar*) and a small milk goat skin, (*s'cow*) both of which have been before described; a small axe, (*gaddo*)—a tent knife, made perhaps of an iron hoop, (*sekeen*)—a sleeping mat for the family, (*lassaia*)—a patchwork skin (*farrowa*) to cover them, and sometimes a few spinning implements, with which they spin camel's hair.

They all have a kind of female saddle of which no idea can be formed by an American without a description; and it is almost impossible to give an accurate idea of it by the most minute description. It is made by two crotches, not unlike the forward part of our saddle trees. One of these settles on to the backbone of the camel, forward of the hump, and the other back of it. From these, are extended two poles about four feet in length, and near the ends they are made fast to the two crotches which are padded inside to prevent them chafing the camel's back. Upon the top of these two poles, is placed a camel's hide, the outer edge of which is sewed to a rim rising about eight inches above the poles, making a sort of oblong basket, about three feet in length, and two in width, placed crosswise upon the back of the camel, and made fast to the poles. A girth is made fast to each of these poles either by buckles, which they can seldom procure, or a knot, passing under the belly of the camel. Another girth or rope passes from the hinder part under the tail of the camel, somewhat like our cruppers. Another one extends from the forward part around the breast of the beast, somewhat in the manner of our breast girths.

From each corner of this basket is raised a pole, meeting in the centre of it, and made fast at the top, over which they throw a blanket, a skin, a piece of sail, or whatever they have suitable for this purpose, to preserve their bodies from the rays of the burning sun. Into these, the mother generally places herself in the centre, having a child on each side to keep this saddle properly balanced. They also have a saddle which is placed upon the forward part of the hump for the owner, or a man to ride upon. This has a saddle-tree forward, which is padded inside, and goes on to the camel's shoulder bones, very near the neck, rising eight inches above the seat, which is circular, hollowed in the middle, and from the outer edge a piece of raw camel's hide is drawn over it. Around the whole of this circular seat, excepting where it is made fast to the tree, a small thick pad is fastened, a stud extending from each side of the circle, and resting upon the pad to support it. This saddle is made fast by a girth passing just back of the forelegs. The rider seats himself, and crosses his legs upon the descending part of the camel's neck. This is a description of the saddles generally in use, although others vary in some trifling respect.

They now strike their tent, and take therefrom all its long and short poles. These, with all the rest of the articles described, excepting the saddles, water and milk skins, they roll up in the tent, by putting part in one end of it, which is folded up in shape of a piece of cloth of different lengths. They roll up each end of the tent, each having a long tent poll in it. together with other articles, so divided as to make a balance. These poles are lashed together fore-and-aft upon the top of the camel, resting upon the centre of the hump. This is made fast to the animal by a rope extending over the top of it and around the body. Another rope passes from it under the tail, and another round the breast. All this preparation is made in half an hour, and often in less time. The tent and its contents are generally put upon a camel that is driven, although he is sometimes ridden.

We started this day at sun two hours high. I shall hereafter be less particular in stating the hour of the day upon which any event took place, unless it is a very interesting one. Indeed, time was of but little consequence to me, as I had nothing to interest me but the peculiar habits, manners, and customs of the Arabs, the immense deserts through which I was passing in almost every direction, and the distresses I there endured. This day we travelled moderately, alternately on foot, and mounted on camels. As we came to spots where bushes were thinly scattered, the camels were permitted to feed, as is generally the case. In the course of the day we saw great numbers of animals which the natives called *Gazelle*. Their appearance was very similar to that of a deer, although they were of a smaller size. They were extremely gaunt and had long legs.

Although they leaped and skipped about with great activity, they manifested but little fear upon our approach: and continued to browse at a short distance from us. I have seen them frequently upon different parts of the Zahara Desert; but I never saw the natives take any of them, although I have often seen their skins, and was at this time wearing part of one. I afterwards learned from the natives, that they were taken at a particular season of the year, probably on account of their condition as to flesh and hair, the latter of which is exceedingly beautiful; surpassing, in this respect, any animal I ever saw in America. We halted, towards night, amidst a small flat of bushes, more flourishing than any I had before seen, in sight of a number of tents.

It is not generally the custom, when on a journey, to pitch tents very near to each other, as each party requires a considerable adjoining ground to feed their camels upon during the night. I reckon we travelled about twenty miles this day, and, as I judged from the sun, in a S. E. direction. After pitching our tent, I was sent, as usual, to gather fuel for the night, then to the nearest tent to get fire, as this would save the trouble of striking one. In this tent I saw Mr. Williams and Barrett, who were stolen as before mentioned. Their legal master had regained them, probably, after a severe contest, as a slave is the last piece of property an Arab will relinquish; indeed, they are the only property except their camels, that is worth a contest. From what I could learn relative to their traffic, they would estimate a healthy slave, at the value of ten full grown camels; although as they approach near to a market for slaves, they rise in value.

These miserable shipmates were almost entirely naked. The skin upon their backs was very much blistered. They informed me that they had suffered very severely from rapid travelling, and from want of food; they still, however, had a small quantity of pork which their master, in company with mine, had gotten from the boat, and which neither dared to eat. Like me, they derived some benefit from the religious tenets of their master: and I think we might all say, without incurring the vengeance of Mahommed, their prophet, that this was the only benefit we ever derived from the faith of a mussulman. It is almost impossible in this place, to avoid remarking upon the different effect that the two systems introduced into our world by our divine Redeemer, and the impostor Mahommed, has upon the professors of these different systems.

The religion introduced by the one teaches *"Peace on earth, and good will to men. To do to others as you would have others do to you."* It teaches men to check the operations of passion, and depraved nature, and to become pure in heart. That of the other promises the full gratification of every propensity. His paradise is a region of gluttony, drunkenness, and debauchery. The one teaches men to love their enemies—the other to destroy them. The one teaches us "*to feed the hungry, and clothe the naked,*"—the other, to tear from the unfortunate being in their power, the last piece of raiment that guards him from the inclemency of the seasons, and to see, with perfect indifference, the famished slave die at their feet, when they become unfit for market.

I could spend but few minutes, and have but few words with my unfortunate friends. I hastened to my master's tent—built a fire—cooked a small slice of my pork, and, at the usual time, had my scanty portion of milk and water; and. in a corner of my master's tent, upon the sand, slept till daylight.

September 12th.—This day we started early, and continued south easterly. I sometimes rode behind my master, by securing myself, as well as I could, by means of my skin and rope, upon the hump of the camel. We halted a few minutes in the middle of the day, took a little milk and water, and the camels browsed upon the bushes. At about sun set we stopped for the night, having travelled, as I concluded, about fifty miles. Knowing the service I should be compelled to perform, I voluntarily set myself about it; procured a fire, fuel for it, assisted in unloading the camels, pitching the tent, &c. As it was in vain to resist the power of the unfeeling wretches, into whose hands fate had thrown me, I endeavoured to conciliate their favour, by performing, with apparent cheerfulness, all the irksome duties of a slave.

13th.—This was a day of but little travel and considerable rest; having stopped and pitched the tent about noon. An Arab's tent, folded up as before described, containing almost all the moveable estate of its. owner, is taken from the came l—separated from its contents, and pitched, ready to receive the furniture and the family, in fifteen minutes. The cloth, of which the tent is made, is wove of camel's hair, sheared from the hump and sides of this animal. Their mode of spinning this hair, which they prepare for doing by whipping it in the same manner Americans do oakum, is the most simple. They have no implement with which they twist this or anything else; seeming to have not the least idea of a wheel to facilitate motion. They hold a quantity of this hair in one hand, and with a spindle in the other, commence the operation.

The spindle is nothing more than a small stick made sharp at one end, and about eight inches in length. This they make fast to the hair, and with the thumb and finger begin to twist. After drawing the thread to the length of the arm, they let the spindle hang down, and by having affixed to the lower end a considerable weight, and giving it a twist with the thumb and finger, the weight below will turn the spindle sufficiently to twist a thread about three feet long. The thread is then wound round the lower end of the spindle, and in the same way they continue to draw out and wind up, thread after thread, until the spindle is filled, which they then wind off upon a ball.

When they have made two balls, perhaps of the size of a twenty-four pound cannon shot, they twist two threads into one, in the above manner, after having wound them into a single ball. In this tedious and slow process they manufacture all their yarn for tent cloth. When they get a sufficient quantity of yarn to make one tent cloth, which is longer or shorter, according to the size of the tent they intend to make, they proceed to weave it. They make the cloth about three quarters of a yard wide; and when they are prepared to weave, they must halt long enough to weave the cloth through, as they have no other loom than that which is made by driving into the earth a number of pegs at each end of the web, equal to half the number of threads they put into the warp. Then by turning the yarn around each of those pegs at each end, and drawing it very tight, the warp is prepared to receive the filling.

They have no idea of a reed, a harness, or a shuttle. They have a piece of hard wood, about three feet in length, about three inches in width, and about half an inch thick. This has a handle at one end, and is made pointed at the other, resembling a wooden sword. With the point of this instrument, they separate the threads of the warp, having half upon the upper side, and half upon the underside of it. Then, by turning it up edge-wise, they make a space sufficiently large to pass through the filling, which is always done with the hand, either from a ball, or from a stick, upon which they sometimes wind it. After passing through a thread, it is beat up, by taking hold of each end of this wooden instrument, and pulling it up two or three times with as much force as a female can conveniently exercise.

I have been thus particular in describing the mode of spinning and weaving, among the Arabs, to shew how stupidly ignorant this barbarous race of beings are, of the most simple arts of civilized life. The mode described is that in universal practice among the wandering Arabs; although at Wadinoon a mode somewhat different is adopted.

To make a tent for a family, the natives generally sew together from eight to twelve of the pieces of cloth manufactured as has been described. They are from twenty to thirty feet in length, and from eighteen to twenty-five feet in width. In the centre of this tent cloth, upon the inside, is sewed on a kind of socket, composed of the thrums of the camel's-hair yarn. When they pitch a tent, they insert into this socket, an oblong block, rounded upon the top, and in the underside of which is made two mortises. To each tent, are two long poles of about twelve feet in length, and two short poles of four feel. Upon each corner, is a loop made of iron, wood, or rope, and strongly fastened to the tent cloth, and upon each side and end two; making twelve in the whole. To each of these loops is fastened a tent-peg, about one foot in length, with a raw camel's-hide rope, six or eight feet long.

The first thing done in pitching a tent, is to spread the cloth flat upon the ground; then driving into the earth the twelve pegs. For this purpose, an Arab always carries with him a smooth round stone, lest he should come to a place where none could be found. In driving the pegs, the cloth is sufficiently slackened, to give it a proper height with the long poles; and constant practice almost invariably enables them to make a proper allowance for this. The next thing done, is to insert the upper end of the long poles, into the mortises in the central block. These poles stand one on each side of the tent.

After the upper end is inserted, a sufficient number of women (for the men are but spectators) are placed at the lower end of each pole; and raising them at the same time, they place the end, which is sharpened, into the earth; leaving them about eight feet apart at the bottom. This braces the tent, and prevents the wind from blowing it down. If this does not make the cloth sufficiently tight, it is made so by means of the ropes fastened to the loops and the pegs. This leaves the tent cloth about two feet above the ground. The entrance into the tent is made by the two short poles, being entered into the two side loops, and standing perpendicularly. This entrance is about four feet high, and is always opposite to the wind; for if the wind shifts before the tent is struck, these poles are shifted to the opposite side.

The space between the bottom of the tent cloth, and the earth, is generally closed upon the back-side and the ends, by means of spare cloths which are fastened to the tent cloth, with iron or wooden pins, and to the earth, by laying stones or any other heavy substance upon the edge of them. This preserves the people within the tent from the chilly easterly wind, which generally blows through the night season. During the afternoon of this day, I remained an idle and uninterested spectator of the stupid conduct, and beastly manners of the wretches with whom I was compelled to associate. But by this time I had learned that it was my best policy to conform to their whims, affect a cheerfulness which I could not feel, and submit to my fate without murmuring.

Notwithstanding their disregard for everything belonging to humanity, they were invariably punctual in worshipping *"something whom they call God."* Three or four times every day, let their engagements be what they might; let their violations of common justice be ever so enormous; they suddenly prostrate themselves upon the earth, exclaiming *"Sheda el la lah, Hi Allah—Sheda Mahommed, Rahsool Allah—Allah Hooakibar!"*—concluding with some part of the *Koran*, and, with the most solemn appearance and manner, exclaiming *"Sulle Mulla"* Happy may the wretched slave think himself, who, the next moment after this ceremony is ended, can feel safe from a stroke of the scimitar, the spear, or the club.

CHAPTER 8

Africans Enslave Each Other

September 14th, 1815.—This was a day of rapid travelling, having started very early, and not having halted 'till about dark; and I conclude we must have made as many as sixty miles. Our course was an easterly one, and no event of any consequence took place. I rode a considerable part of the day behind my master. To do this with the more ease, I took from my back my skin to secure myself from the sharp back of the camel. But while this preserved my seat and legs from being worn raw, my back was exposed to the almost vertical rays of a torrid sun, and the skin began to peal from my back from being blistered and parched. Judging from the course we had travelled from the place where I was captured, I conclude we must now have reached the 21st deg. N. latitude, the body of a tent, a camel, and a man, making but a very little shade. and that to the *south*, as it was now near the autumnal equinox.

This night our tent was not pitched, being unloaded, but not unfolded. At the time of stopping, I discovered a number of lights, from different tents. I learned from one of my master's sisters, whose name I had now found out was *Muckwoola*, that Mr. Williams and Barrett were in one of these tents. How she knew this I cannot tell; but this I know, that the different parties of Arabs generally know the situation of each other, and the slaves they have in their possession. She accompanied me to the tent; and on the way, said some things to me which I could not then understand. I found my shipmates near a large fire in front of a tent, it being pitched in a place where there were large dry thorn bushes. They were cooking some pork. Upon our shaking hands, the natives noticed it very particularly, laughing and sneering at our mode of salutation, at the same time going through their own mode, which is, by placing the inside of the open hands together, then bringing it to the lips, touching them, and dropping the hand. I think I shall always prefer the mode handed down to us from our brave Saxon ancestors, of clasping and squeezing the hand of a friend whom I love.

Mr. Williams was considerably emaciated; his body much blistered arid parched by the sun, and his, as well as the rest of our legs and feet, were much swollen, occasioned by the heat of the sun, and the irritation by thumping upon the almost bare bones of the camel, I can hardly, at this time, suppress the anguish I feel in remembering this, which was the last interview I ever had with this worthy man and good seaman. He had lost his fortitude by his misery; and despaired of life. He mentioned his family in the most affectionate manner; and continued to converse upon this interesting subject, until overwhelming grief forbade farther utterance.

Although this was the last time I saw Mr. Williams, I learned some time after, by Barrett, whom I saw at a fish place near Cape Mirik, that he had regained his health and flesh; was living better; had a very good man for a master, who was also his (Barrett's) master; and I console myself, and I think his friends may also console themselves with the hope, that he may once more see his native country, and be blessed with the society of his friends.

As to Barrett, he was at this time apparently less miserable than Mr. Williams. I took some fire from this tent, and returned to my masters. My pork still held out, as my Mahometan master would permit me to eat but little of it at a time: and, thanks to his Mussulman faith, would eat none himself.

On the 15th and 16th we prosecuted our journey at a moderate rate. The general view of this part of the Zahara desert is a boundless plane terminated by the horizon, although in travelling over it, the traveller meets with gently rising sand hills, and shallow vailies. Sometimes he sees a rock from which large pieces have fallen, in a very irregular shape, there seeming to be no seams or grain to this stone like most of the large bodies of rocks in New-England, These rocks are mostly covered with a whitish moss, similar to what is frequently seen upon the rocks in the District of Maine. This is sometimes eat by camels when nothing else can be found.

We occasionally met with clusters of tents, and some standing singly. Many of the Arabs have muskets, for which they have the highest admiration; seeming to esteem them next to their holy beads. The one they think will secure to them the favour of their prophet, and with the other they hope to procure or intimidate slaves, as they frequently took deliberate aim at my breast, which I as often laid open, telling them to fire; being then almost indifferent, whether I was laid dead upon the desert, food for wild beasts, or compelled to traverse with men as wild and as ferocious as the tigers or leopards that prowl over them also. They often put these muskets into my hands, asking me whether they were *Fransah* or *Inglisis*.

I sometimes saw valuable double-barrelled muskets, which they probably either procured from the European settlement upon the Senegal, or took from a black slave, which perhaps *he* obtained in exchange for one of *his* countrymen. These Africans, of every name and feature and complexion, take delight in enslaving each other; and although the slave trade, carried on by Christian merchants, on the coast of Africa, excites the just indignation of the Christian world, yet it can hardly be expected that an American, who has for months and years been enslaved by them, can feel so much compassion towards a slave *here* as those do, who have always enjoyed the blessings of humanity and liberty.

A description of the male wandering Arabs is: they are six feet in height generally; remarkably straight; large-boned; have very black, penetrating eyes; black hair, until age makes it grey, but of different qualities; some being soft and straight, and some coarse and bushy. They have high cheek bones; noses that incline more to the aquiline than Roman; thin lips; beautiful white teeth, and very regular; thick, black beards when in middle life, which hang down to the breast, increasing in length as they advance in years, which then become almost entirely white. When old, and some of them must be very aged, they have a gravity and solemnity of appearance which is seldom seen in Americans. The features of the men, unless when distorted by anger, or the prospect of plunder, are regular, and often display some marks that would induce a stranger to think that they belonged to the human family.

I would gladly omit a description of the female wandering Arabs; but it will leave a chasm in the description of the natural curiosities of this country. They are somewhat higher in stature than the American women, and, like the Arab men, remarkably straight when young. Their cheek bones are high; their eyes and hair similar to the men. Their teeth are also white; but the two eye-teeth often turn out of the mouth like a tush. They endeavour to make them project as far as possible, to furnish a resting place for the upper lip; and they constantly stand, like two faithful centinels, to protect it from an assault from the under one. They generally carry their young upon their backs; and their breasts, from constant exposure, and having no stays to support them, become relaxed, and hang down to such a length, that they can furnish the child upon their backs with food from these accommodating reservoirs, by thrusting them under their arms; the child, at the same time, hangs quartering upon the mother's back, and grabs them, one at a time, to draw therefrom the food they furnish it.

Among the young women, however, are many of very regular and interesting features. They generally have very long hair, which they braid behind, and turn up to the back part of the head, and confine with a kind of hoop placed upon the crown of the head, giving the back part of the head an elevation considerably above the forehead. Upon the forehead and temples are a number of small braids of hair, to which is fastened a great variety of the most beautiful shells; and sometimes large rings, made of white stone Over the whole of this apparatus is thrown a piece of blue cotton cloth, as a turban, concealing the whole head and face, excepting the forehead, the eyes, cheek bones, and nose; the variety of shells hanging around the edge of it. They also ornament their wrists and ankles, with strings of black beads, and sometimes of small shells. Their covering is generally a single blanket or skin of different lengths, and put on in different ways, depending upon the wealth, the whim, or the necessity of the wearer.

During these two days we were penetrating easterly into the interior. The reflection, that I was departing farther and farther from every trace of civilization, imparted feelings of the most gloomy kind. We, however, travelled moderately; advancing, perhaps, not more than sixty miles. I saw none of my shipmates, nor any other unfortunate slave.

September 17th.—We continued to travel in an easterly direction. I was reminded of my native land, and of the abundance of her blessings, by occasionally partaking of a little slice of pork which was there produced. It was a real comfort, notwithstanding it compelled me to draw a most disheartening parallel between my former situation, and the dismal prospects that then surrounded me. My master's water began to grow short; and although I was parched without by the burning sun, and within by dreadful thirst, I could not, by the most humble and urgent entreaties, move the obdurate heart of my master to afford me a drop. Amidst the most melancholy reflections, I recognized Mr. Savage in company with two Arabs.

This was the first time I had seen him since the commencement of our slavery. When I first saw him, he was in my rear. I slackened my walk, and he overtook me. My master's camels were travelling at a quick rate, which shortened my interview with him. He said he had neither seen or ate any food but milk and water, and that in very small quantities, since we first were separated. I lamented that I had not the small remains of my pork to divide with him, my master never suffering me to carry it myself. I hastened with all my power to overtake the camels. The country had become more barren and sandy, and the heat of the sun increased. We at length found a few thorn bushes, which is the only tavern an Arab ever finds, and we *put up*.

18th.—Having found this place of refreshment, my master and his retinue were determined, I suppose, to *eat it out* before he quitted: and during the whole of this day, we laid by.

19th.—For the four past nights, we had not pitched the tent; and sleeping upon the sand in the open air, I found myself every morning moistened with the heavy dews, and almost stiffened by the chilly air. It can easily be imagined what would be the sensations of a person, who, for a number of days, had been exposed to a scalding sun, and blistered with its rays; deprived almost wholly of food and water; hunger gnawing him within, and the heated sand irritating his blistered body, and the dews and cold chills operating upon him at the same time. We started early this morning at a moderate rate, and continued in an eastern course. At about 11 o'clock, we came to ascending ground; and the camels were halted while my master, having been joined by some other natives, went forward to make discoveries.

The camels browsed; the women laid down to enjoy the sand beneath, and the sun above, and I wandered off to a small bush to enjoy a little shade, and, what my debilitated and fatigued body greatly needed, a little rest. I fell into a kind of broken slumber and continued here, "*twixt wake and sleep*," until my master returned. I then discovered, to my very great joy, that they had unloaded the camels, and seemed to be making preparations to pitch the tent. I saw a number of other tents at no great distance, and again fell into a sleep. I slept till the middle of the afternoon, and was then awakened; not by the hoarse and menacing voice of a barbarian, but by the mild, and cheering accents of a friend.

It was Mr. Savage. To see him once more was a consolation that made me, for a moment, forget my misery; it was doubly consolatory to see my friend not wholly destitute of resolution. He said he was in a state of absolute starvation; and bestowed a string of the most bitter curses upon the inhuman wretches who were starving him to a skeleton. We went to seek something from our mother earth, and found a few snails, which Mr. Savage took. Notwithstanding we had the most vindictive feelings towards our tormentors, we retired to our shade; and after bewailing our hard fate, remembered that we had a Father in heaven, to whom we addressed a short prayer, and separated. I gathered wood for the night; the tent was pitched, and my master allowed me a little of my pork, a small quantity of water, and a less quantity of milk for my supper.

20th.—This was a day of repose. After having performed the usual ceremony of worshipping, which, as I have before stated, is always the first service of the day, whether on a journey or at rest, my master went off, as usual, about the desert or to the neighbouring tents. The camels were sent off to feed, which were always watched by the children, this service never having yet been enjoined upon me. When the natives are stationary, the men are constantly visiting each other at their tents, and sometimes are assembled in considerable numbers around them.

It ought to be remarked that the wandering Arabs consist of many distinct tribes, and not of one general one, as is by some supposed. The tribe to which my first master belonged is called Wiled Lebdessebah. From what I afterwards learned, when in possession of ether tribes, I found that this was considered by all, as the poorest, most ferocious, and contemptible of the whole. They wander farther over the deserts, and have the most uncertain and casual subsistence. This accounts, in some degree, for the total want of method or object which is perceptible among them. They wander from day to day, seeming neither to know where they are going, nor what they are going for. When assembled together, as mentioned, they jabber together in confusion, for a while, and then for a while gaze at each other with unmeaning vacancy.

The women at the same time saunter in and around their tents, with but little employ, although all the labour that is done, is done by them. While our brutal masters were thus employed, Mr. Savage and I, their wretched slaves, again met at the tent of his master. I found him alone, pondering upon his fate. Upon my approaching him, he seemed to affect a degree of cheerfulness. We thought it no great crime to steal a little water from a goat skin, as we were nearly choaked. After this, Mr. Savage recollected that early in the morning a wen or sore had been cut out of one of his master's camels; and we concluded to cook and eat this excrescence that was taken from a beast, which itself is not more palatable than our horses. It lay upon the sand in two pieces, and upon taking it up, it appeared not unlike a shad-spawn, and like that, was very tender.

A little fire remained, mixed with sand, into which we put our delicious morsel, and before we had half roasted it, we saw Mi. Savage's mistress approaching, and ate it down, almost at a mouthful, knowing that this was the only method we could take to secure it from being taken from us. I spent a considerable part of the day with my friend, and towards evening returned to my master's tent.

Chapter 9

Submission to Fate

From reading most of the productions of travellers, and all the narratives and journals of slaves, readers have their indignation excited to the highest pitch against the degraded race of beings among whom the author of this Journal was so unfortunate as to be enslaved. Before we conclude, however, to exclude them from the human family; before we denounce them as unworthy of the least consideration, as a part of human beings; the candid inquirer after truth will endeavour to trace their origin. He will try to learn what has been their course of life; what kind of government they have lived under, and what advantages they have enjoyed. It cannot be done in this little volume, which professes to tell what they *are*, and not what they *have been*. It may be briefly remarked, however, that a general sentiment prevails among historians, that the Arabs are the descendants of Ishmael.

In recurring to an authority which will not be doubted, we find that Ishmael was the son of Hagar, the handmaid of Sarai, Abram's wife; that Hagar was an Egyptian; that although Sarai, being childless herself, consented that Abram should go in unto Hagar, yet, when she found that Hagar had conceived, her wrath was kindled.

"*And when Sarai dealt hardly with her, she fled from her face.*" (*Gen.* xvi. ch.) "*And the angel of the Lord said unto her, Behold, thou art with child, and shalt bear a son, and shalt call his name Ishmael, because the Lord hath heard thy affliction. And he will be a wild man; his hand will be against every man, and every man's hand against him,*" &c. In chap. xxv. of *Gen.* we find it thus recorded:—"*And these are the names of the sons of Ishmael, by their names, according to their generations: The first born of Ishmael, Nebajoth, and Kedar, and Adbeel, and Mibsam, and Mishma, and Dumah, and Massa, Hadar, and*

Tema, and Jetur, and Naphish, and Kedemah. These are the sons of Ishmael, and these are their names, by their towns, and by their castles; twelve princes, according to their nations. And these are the years of the life of Ishmael, an hundred and thirty and seven years."

Thus it appears, that these miserable creatures owe their origin to a despised mother. That she herself was a wanderer, and her son "a wild man." The common chronology makes this tribe (or the descendants of Ishmael) 3995 years of age; and the best historical authorities called Profane History, in distinction from Sacred History, have always represented them as a despised, abused, degraded, and wandering race. They are now called wandering Arabs; and from many of their religious rites, they seem to have blended together some of "the law that came by Moses," with many of the ceremonies introduced by Mahommed. They circumcise their young according to the first—they worship the prophet according to the last. *Their hands are literally against every man, and every man's hand against them*—to this day, (as at time of first publication).

It is with "trembling solicitude," that the author of this Journal has attempted, very briefly, to trace the origin of a race of beings, whose existence and modes of life, excite the wonder of an inquiring world. It was not done so much to impart information, as to excite inquiry. It was with the same view he attempted to give a brief historical account of Africa. To give a gloomy. monotonous diary of human sufferings would "pall upon the senses;" he has, therefore, endeavoured to blend with it such accounts of this quarter of the globe, as he thought tended to illustrate the subject of his Journal.

It was now the 21st September. We had no possible means to determine in what latitude we were situated; but the sun was to the northward of us, and of course, what little shadow any object made, it was east to the south. The heat was excessive, and I could almost have envied the natives a tawny skin, that was made to endure it. To me it was distressing in the extreme. Although some of them seemed to pity me for the blistered and parched skin that slightly adhered to my flesh; yet their pity was mingled with contempt that *Inglesis* could bear no more. They glory in bearing everything—hunger, thirst, fatigue, and every privation, and pronounce that being *foonta*, or good for nothing, who cannot endure with them.

My master's water was nearly expended, and in the morning of this day, preparations were made to retrace the dismal desert over which we had before travelled. We started early, and travelled nearly in a north east direction. The sun was my only compass by day, and the north star by night. We travelled rapidly through this day, and I watched, with the utmost care, to see if I could recognize any object I saw as we went out; but I could not. At this time, almost all the parties were returning towards a well, and we were frequently in sight of different tents, some near to us, and some at such a distance, that the size of a camel seemed to be diminished to that of a small dog. It reminded me of a fleet of merchantmen, recently dispersed by a storm, and all endeavouring to make the same port. No singular object presented itself, nor any event took place upon this day, worthy of description.

On the 22nd, travelled same course, and very rapidly. Our tents were this night pitched. After I had assisted in making the usual preparations for the night, I cooked my remaining piece of pork, and as I was just about to enjoy the last piece of food of American growth, I was overjoyed to see my master enter his tent with Mr. Savage. My mistress cooked a little rice, and handed it to me. Mr. Savage and I partook of this pork and rice together, by the consent of my master and mistress. I must confess I felt a glow of gratitude to him for conducting my friend to his tent, and to her, for enabling me to partake of what we then deemed a rich repast. They familiarly called me *Robbins*, and Mr. Savage they called *Arrone*. It is always the first object of an Arab to learn the name of a stranger; and as they rarely have but one name themselves, they take either the given or surname of a stranger, as best suits their whim, or their organs of speech. After learning the name, they ask if he is *bono*-good, or *foonta*, which has already been explained. Mr. Savage retired to his master's tent, and I to my bed of sand.

The next day, (23rd) we prosecuted our journey, in company with eight or ten different families, making a large party. Mr. Savage's master bore to the northward, and I was separated from him. We travelled fast; our water being all expended, and we had no liquid or food except the milk of the camel, and that bring a very small quantity for the number of the family, and my pork being expended, I suffered very severely. Toward night we stopped, and the women, as is always the case, sought for a suitable place to pitch the tent, and pitched it. At night my master entered the tent. I inquired after Mr. Savage, and he told me he was but a little way to the northward, and that I should see him again the next day.

Upon this day, (24th) the camels having fed but a little for two or three days, and the family having eat nothing but a very little milk, we rested after travelling a short distance. The camels browsed upon bushes, and the children went in pursuit of a small root, sometimes found in the shallow valleys. I also went in pursuit of the same myself, and found a small quantity. This root resembles a small white onion, and is about the size of a walnut. The stalk or stem of it is five or six inches high, growing generally in a single blade. There is but little nutriment in it. I also found a vegetable that had the appearance of a shepherd-sprout, which I saw the natives eat, and ventured to eat myself. It had a bitter taste.

For two hours I sought for these roots and sprouts, and ate all I found, which were but few; but as I found any vegetable that was eatable in this ocean of burning sand, I snatched at it with the utmost avidity, and devoured it with the keenest appetite. The men during this time, had gone ahead. I was ordered to drive the camels together, and we proceeded on our journey, until about noon; then rising a small hill, we discovered the men seated in a small valley. They made the usual sign, of waving a blanket, for us to approach, with the camels, the tents, &c. loaded upon them. Upon our arrival, the camels were made to kneel, and were unloaded of everything, except the necessary implements to procure water. The goat skins were made ready to contain water for the family, and the skin basket, or watering tub, for the camels to drink in.

My master and his two sisters went off with the camels and their accoutrements in search of a well, leaving me with the rest of the family. I now went forth a solitary wanderer, famishing with hunger, parching with thirst, and almost scorching to powder with the dreadful heat of the sun. The camels were gone, and no milk could be had until their return; and the length of time they would be absent was unknown. Death seemed to stare me in the face; and death, too, in the very worst shape. To fall in the field of battle—to be drowned in the ocean, or to die suddenly with a raging epidemic, is not half so terrible to the imagination, as that of a lingering death by starvation. I found a few roots, and devoured them, and searching among the thorn bushes I once in a while discovered a snail, which I could obtain in no way, but by thrusting my naked arms through them, and by this I was lacerated and torn from my shoulders to my fingers' ends. I brought my snails to the tent, cooked some of them for my supper, which I was compelled to divide with my mistress and the children, having neither milk nor water for themselves.

On the 25th, I started, early in the morning, in pursuit of something to eat, being in a situation that would make me readily devour anything. My thirst led me to pursue the tracks of the camels, as they had gone in pursuit of water. I found nothing but a few of the roots mentioned, which the natives call *taloes*, to satiate my hunger, and nothing but my own urine to quench my thirst. I wandered about until noon, found a few snails, and returned, roasting and despairing to the tent. Toward night I discovered my master approaching with the camels loaded with three goat skins of water, holding about eight gallons each. The sight of camels, although the most odious and deformed looking beasts in nature, had, by this time, become as cheering to my view as a sumptuous feast is to the eye of an epicure; and well they might; for my very life itself depended upon them.

To see them coming with milk in their bags, and water upon their backs, produced a tumultuous joy bordering upon delirium. On being unloaded, my bowl (for I was not allowed to contaminate that of a Mussulman) was filled with water, holding two quarts. This I drank off at a draught without stopping, and almost without breathing. I had two motives for this, one to quench my thirst, the other to induce my master to give me more— my thirst was partially quenched, but no more water was to be had. I looked in vain among the Ishmaelitish daughters to find a tender hearted damsel, like Rebekah, who bade the servant of Abraham to drink, saving, "*I will give thy camels drink also.*"

I then proceeded to cook the few snails I had gathered in the gloomy morning that preceded this evening. This I did by pouring them into the sand at the bottom of the fire-hole, after having scraped away the coals, then covering them with hot sand, and building a fire upon the top. they were roasted in fifteen minutes. These I ate after my master had examined them, and fell asleep about sunset. I became very much distressed, probably from the roots, vegetables, and snails I had been driven to live upon for some days past, and drinking too much water at once. My mistress, having warmed a little milk with heated stones, presented it to me, which I drank, and found much relief.

It had now got to be 10 o'clock at night, as I judged from the stars, when my master called me up, and asked me if I wished to go and see *Arrone*, (Mr. Savage.) I answered yes. He took me on the camel, and started off at a long trot to the northward. Being naked, excepting my shortened trowsers, the cold air was very painful: but as I knew my master, if he was so inclined, could afford me no relief, I made no complaint. We rode till one o'clock in the morning. The camel was then permitted to feed upon the diminutive shrubs, and I to sleep naked upon the sand. After sleeping about two hours, I was again mounted on the camel. I began to conjecture that my master was about to offer me for sale, and my conjectures soon became reality.

September 26.—By my string, I found I had been eighteen days a slave to my master Ganus, and I must confess I did not then wish to run the risque of exchanging him for any other descendant of Ishmael that I had yet seen. But it was not for a slave to choose, to wish, or repine. I affected a total unconcern; and although I had but little of the *lamb* in my feelings toward the Arabs, I was determined to appear to be *"pleas'd to the last;"* and although I could not in Zahara *"crop the flowery food,"* I had almost got my mind prepared *"to lick the hand just rais'd to shed my blood."* Hard indeed was this mental submission to a free-born son of New-England; hard as the pain I endured in my body;—but I thought the philosophical advice of Hudibras to Ralpho was applicable to me at this time:

Ne'er be so dully desperate
To join against yourself with fate.

At about sunrise I discovered a number of tents ahead, and as we came to one, I saw some camel's meat. Delicious food! not much worse than that of an old horse; how I longed to devour it; but like Tantalus in the water, I was only aggravated by the sight of it, as I could not enjoy it. My master, however, begged some boiled blood for me, which I put into my hat, not knowing what it was. He bade me *cool, i. e.* eat. We again started, and at about eight o'clock came to a valley where we saw a number of camels crossing and passing over a small sand hill. We followed them; and on reaching another valley, I saw numerous tents. It looked like a great market for the sale of the sons of sorrow. On seeing an old woman, my master asked where the *kellup en-sahrau (Christian dogs)* were. She pointed to a hill to the eastward, and upon drawing near to it I saw the smoke of a fire, where they had been cooking camel's meat. I ran up to it, hoping either by begging, or stealing, to obtain a bite of it; but I forgot my hunger, my thirst, my misery, and almost myself, upon discovering Capt. Riley, Mr. Savage, Clarke, Burns, and Horace. Something whispered to me that my deliverance was near, that the day of my redemption had come.

After exchanging the common tokens of affection, with my beloved shipmates, I learned from them, that they had been bought.

Capt, Riley pointed to two Arabs, telling me that they had bought him, and those that, were with him, and had agreed to carry them to the *Sultan*, (the Arabs call the emperor of Morocco *Sooltaun*) where their redemption would be certain. He said Hogan, my friend, was with them the day before, and that he supposed the purchasers were waiting to take him also; and that if they did not, he hoped to persuade them to purchase me. My heart was immediately swollen with gratitude to my captain for his solicitude and kindness to me, as miserable a son of Adam as walked upon the footstool of Deity.

I exchanged a little of my boiled blood with Horace, for a piece of gristly camel's meat, which I swallowed almost whole. At a small distance off, I saw my master talking very earnestly with the two Arabs who had purchased all my shipmates just named. Hope lightened my heart and almost deprived me of reason. I almost saw my own country; I almost felt the embraces of my friends; although environed by the desert of Zahara, and held in bondage by barbarians. How soon was I dashed from the highest elevation of hope, to the lowest dejection of despair! The two Arabs hastily took my shipmates one way, and my master carried me off another.

Capt. Riley tried to console me; but why *"preach patience to those who wring under a load of sorrow?"* My brother sailors will excuse me, when I tell them that I burst into tears. I converted my eyes into two pumps, and in this way I was partially relieved from the bilge-water of sorrow which was about sinking my shattered vessel forever. I considered my shipmates as safe, and in the event it proved to be so. While I rejoiced at *their good fortune*, I grieved, in the very depths of sorrow, at *my own calamities*, I might with the utmost propriety, exclaim, *"How fortune deceives! I had pleasure in tow"*—but now I had it no longer. *"My life, steered by misery's chart"*—I was compelled to continue a captive among the most unfeeling, debased, and degraded race of creatures on earth, the tribe, as I have before mentioned, which now held me a slave, being so.

I separated from my shipmates about nine o'clock, a. m. and went with my master in pursuit of his tent. The camel, being a male, I had no milk; the goat skins being at the tent, I had no water; and subsisted through the day upon my camel's blood, which I carried in my hat, exposing my bare head to the rays of the sun. The tent was removed, and we did not overtake it till dark, and not having it pitched that night, I slept in the open chilly air.

Upon the 27th, we travelled E. S. E. as near as I could judge. By this time I had become acquainted with the meaning of some few of the words of the Arabs; and by means of these and signs, I asked my mistress why I was not sold? Why they did not travel toward Morocco? And many other questions. Her answer was, that they could not go until the rainy season sat in, which commences generally in January, or, at any rate, it did this year. She said they could not support their camels in the dry season, but still encouraged me with the hope that I should, some time or other, reach that empire. We travelled, I conclude, in the course mentioned about fifteen miles, and then shifted it to about N. E.

The country became more hilly than I had before seen it; and after passing a number of small hills, we ascended one of considerable height. To the N. E. of it, I saw the largest and deepest valley I had before seen in this country. It ran from N. E. to S. W. and might have been eight or ten miles in length and two miles in width. I regret exceedingly that I cannot inform my readers of the particular situation of the country I passed; but as I then had no means to ascertain it, no maps, charts, or instruments, and could derive no information from the illiterate Arabs, I will not attempt it. I could judge of the latitude only from the situation of the sun. and as to longitude, I could judge of it from nothing at all.

We must now have been near the tropic of cancer, it being September, and the rays of the sun being nearly vertical. We entered this valley at the S. W. end of it, and passed to the S. E. side of it, upon which I noticed a number of very deep gullies, on almost the whole length of the hill, which must have been occasioned by heavy rains. The surface in the valley was composed of sand, gravel, and small round stones, which were washed from the hill. the gullies having the same kind upon their sides. In one of these gullies, we saw two or three tents. The air was cooler here than it is generally found to be, and I even imagined I saw some appearance of comfort, and no one could need it more: for having been deprived of all my remaining hopes in the morning, it appeared to me through the whole day that it must have been my last, for *"hope was deferred,"* and *"my whole heart was sick."*

They left the camels with me, and the whole family went to the tents. It is an universal custom among Arabs, when the master of one tent or any of his family visits another, to offer them whatever they have to eat or drink; the whole bill of fare, however, consisting of earners meat, milk, and water. I saw my master and family drinking with them, and my thirst *"almost persuaded me"* to wish I was a Mahometan that I might have partaken with them. I was then ordered by signs, to drive the camels to the tents, and as I was approaching one, was met by a young Arab, who told me that there was an *en-sahrau* (Christian) in one of the tents.

The name of *en-sahrau* was as dear to me as was the name of Uncle Toby to a distressed soldier. I had not the most distant conception to what Christian nation he might belong, but it was enough to console me, that he was not a degenerate Mussulman. He was one of my shipmates—it was Porter! I came near rejoicing at his slavery, it gave me such joy to see him. With this worthy fellow, I had been particularly intimate; and I think my shipmates will all say that we went hand in hand in performing our duty like faithful seamen. He appeared less dejected than many of my shipmates whom I had before seen. His robust body and stout heart enabled him to bear anything within the compass of human endurance. He had on the remnants of an old coat, and his trowsers down to his knees, the rest of them, like mine, having been declared *foonta*.

I informed him of the good fortune of Capt. Riley, Mr. Savage, Clarke, Burns, and Horace; and the near fortune of Hogan. He then told me that Hogan and Dick were in the valley above, he having seen them the day before. My master hailed, *Robbinis!* and I was obliged to end my interview, although it was the first I had enjoyed with this good friend since we were enslaved. We passed to the top of the hill through one of the gullies, and travelled upon the top of it to near the upper end of the valley. Then discovering a number of tents, in the valley below, we descended through another difficult gully, I conclude as many as three hundred feet, and reached them. Here we pitched our tents in sight of, perhaps, thirty or forty others. The camels were put to feed in the valley, and I furnished the necessary fuel for the night. My fatigue was excessive.

After eating a little of my blood, (taken from the camel,) and having a scanty portion of milk divided out to me, I retired to a corner of the tent, and forgot myself and my miseries, in as sound a night's rest as ever a sailor enjoyed.

CHAPTER 10

American Flag Upon Zahara Desert.

September 28th, 1815.—As we progress in our volume, we feel a great degree of solicitude lest the detail of individual suffering should become tedious to our readers. The world more readily sympathizes with the *joyous* than the *sorrowing*. The joys of the author have been few, his sorrows have been numerous; but he will endeavour to blend with the narration of them, such delineations of the country and descriptions of the peculiar manners, customs, and habits of the natives of Africa, as have fallen under his immediate observations, or been derived from the most authentic sources.

This day we lay by. After the morning service was performed, and the camels milked, (the last service invariably following the first,) the camels were sent with the boy to feed upon bushes; my master went to visit his neighbours; the female children went in pursuit of roots and herbs; the women lounged in the tents; and I laid down under one to reflect or to sleep, just as reflection came to my sorrow, or sleep to my relief. After remaining here until about eleven o'clock, I saw my half-starved friend Hogan, lurking around the tents; and, judging from the appearance of his mouth, and the rest of his diminished body, I concluded that he had not *"fared sumptuously every day"* since we parted.

This was the first time I had seen him since I parted with him on the 8th at the well. I could hardly conceive that this sterling sailor, who first ventured to come from the wreck to the shore upon the hawser at Cape Bajador, on the 28th of the preceding month, could so soon have lost his firmness and his hope. He appeared depressed, melancholy, and hopeless. He entered our tent. This was attended with considerable difficulty, as my mistress at first refused him admittance; but upon informing her as well as I could, that he was almost naked, having nothing but a small skin and a piece of sail to wear, and almost melting in the sun, she gave him admission. We sat down together. Hogan's master was the first Arab that assailed us near Cape Barbas, where we first landed.

Hogan informed me that his sufferings had been too much for a Christian to bear from such cursed barbarians; that he had not been permitted to sleep under a tent since he was enslaved; that he had been almost starved ever since he had been among them; and that he expected to die soon unless he could escape. He told me that the two Arabs who bought Capt. Riley, bought him next, and paid for him; and that a dispute arose between his master Mahomet, and Porter's master, who claimed half of him, and that his master had returned the price paid for him (Hogan) and still kept him as a slave. Mahomet and Porters master continued to quarrel about him: had come to blows upon this subject; and the quarrel was not yet ended. Having the most painful feelings upon Hogan's melancholy relation, I entreated my mistress to permit me to give him some of my camel's blood, to which she, with some reluctance, consented, and we ate the whole I had remaining, which was but little, relying upon the mercy of my tyrants for my future support.

After we had eaten our food, my mistress, whom Hogan thought an angel of mercy in comparison to his, gave us a little milk and water. I did not altogether agree with him about the angelic qualities of my *mistress*, knowing that my *master* had more of the virtues attributed to those celestial beings than what she had. I inquired of Hogan about Dick. He said he was a fellow-slave with him to Mahomet, and fared much better as to living than he had; although he was often beaten by his master, and compelled to attend camels from daylight till dark. Hogan tarried with me till towards night, and we agreed to go next day to procure something to eat, either by stealing from the tents, or gathering from the earth, if haply we could find anything to steal or gather. I requested him to ask Dick to come and join us. but he said Dick would not be permitted to come. He went home; and I did the customary duties of a slave, and retired to all the rest I could enjoy upon sand.

Upon the 29th, early in the morning, my master and his family went out before the tent to worship, and took me with them; having for some days past expressed a wish that I should become a Mussulman, and no longer continue to be a *kellup en-sahrau*. I knew I might be a witness, and even a performer of their mode of worship, without becoming a proselyte to their *faith*; indeed, I was compelled to go, from the fear of vengeance if I refused. They were arranged upon the sand, in front of the tent. My master Ganus bade me follow his motions. He kneeled down, and *washed* his hands, arms, and face in the sand. I did the same. He then rose up, facing to the east, and loudly exclaimed. "*Sheda el la lah, Hi Allah—Sheda Mahommed—Rahsool Allah.*" They generally add, "*Hi eahrah sullah—Hi eahrah sullah.*" This I also repeated, having learned the pronunciation of it before, although not the meaning. They then cried aloud "*Allah Hooakibar.*" I followed them in this likewise. They then fell upon their knees, and, upon rising, said again, "*Allah Hooakibar.*"

I continued to follow their example, as often as they repeated it. They then went through a catalogue of words, which I could not understand, and could not repeat. They concluded with a loud voice, "*Sulle Mulla;*" I said so too. They seemed to be highly pleased with my *apparent* conversion to the Mahometan faith. This was the first time I ever worshipped in the manner of a Mahometan; and, lest I should be brought to make a *ceremony* of worship merely, I declined, as long as I remained in Africa, to *Sulle* in this way; telling him that an *en-sahrau*, or Christian, had a different mode of praying.

Soon after this ceremony (for it was nothing else) was through, Hogan came to my masters tent. I took my sack, which I had made upon landing from the boat, and hung it upon my neck to put snails in, if we should find any. We passed over the hill lying to the eastward of us into an adjoining valley where we found a few snails. At noon, the heat became so intense, that we could not endure it. We returned to within a short distance of my master's tent, where we cooked what few we had gathered, by some fire procured from a tent near us. My master was dissatisfied that I did not bring the snails home, and divide with him and the family. Hogan came to the tent, and spent part of the afternoon with me, where we had a little milk and water allowed us, and toward night I accompanied him to his master's tent

Upon the 30th, I wandered round with Hogan, as I did the day before gathering snails and bewailing our fate. The natives, unless engaged in spinning and weaving, which is but seldom, are listless, inactive, and stupid. They have nothing that serves for pastime or amusement, unless it can be called recreation for females to comb arid braid each other's hair, and divest it of the vermin that generally colonize it. They do this and sleep alternately. The men visit each other at the tents, apparently without object; although when a considerable number are assembled they converse together with earnestness, and sometimes go through with the customary worship.

When stationary, the men repair their saddles, goatskins, and watering tubs. The women have the entire control of the tent; they make the cloths for it, they put them together, they pitch, and strike and repair it. They have all the management of what may be called domestic economy; they apportion out the milk and the water, with the accuracy of a sergeant when making out rations, among the master, the children and the slaves, and from their decision upon this subject, there is no appeal.

October 1st.—Having added another day to the calendar of my captivity by making another knot in my string, I began to ponder with the most gloomy anticipations upon my future fate. As I have already mentioned, my pork was expended; the country where we were now situated was uncommonly barren even for the desert; my master's camels afforded but a very small quantity of milk, and one of them had become entirely dry. The little portion allowed me was hardly sufficient to sustain life; and my flesh began, moderately, to waste away. To see the gradual, although certain, approach of the king of terrors by the slow ravages of a consumption is indeed gloomy; but, in the enjoyment of health, as I was at this time, and with an appetite as voracious as the tigers of the desert that I inhabited, to waste away and go down to the grave for the want of food, was too much for the small portion of philosophy imparted to me, to endure with fortitude.

My own forebodings were rendered doubly aggravating at the situation of my shipmate Hogan, whose despair was as raging as his appetite. He called again this day. Having but little encouragement to seek even for snails, we lurked around the tents in the gloomy valley, which seemed like the valley of the shadow of death. We found some of the old bones of a camel which had first been scraped by the Arabs, next by their dogs, and the remaining part fell into our hands. We gnawed off what little dry gristle was remaining, in doing which, I almost dislocated my jaws, and very much injured my teeth. At night we returned to our tents.

October 2nd.—As I was standing near my master's tent, I saw Dick the cook, descending from the hill where he had been placed to watch camels. He came to the tent. For the first time I saw him since the day of our slavery. He was esteemed by the crew as a faithful, active cook, and always did all the duty assigned him with promptitude.

He looked pretty hearty, and had better clothing than Hogan. We had been together but a few minutes before he was hailed by his mistress to return. Anxious to see me longer he did not immediately obey. She came after him, struck him on the head with her claws, and pulled him up the hill to the camels. His master immediately knocked him down, and began beating him in the most unmerciful manner with clubs. The poor fellow hallooed and screamed aloud. Never did I more ardently pant to revenge the injury of a shipmate. Readily would I have become one of a body of American seamen that would number not more than *two* to *five* Arabs, and have commenced immediate war. I was desperate, but knew I must be humble, and see my shipmate mauled to pumice.

It is singular that the negroes, although Africans like the Arabs, should, even by their own countrymen, although of a different tribe, be used with such barbarity. This miserable race of beings seem to be left by their Creator to the cruelty of the whole human race. In every clime, unless, indeed, they become objects of curiosity, as did the negro in Russia, they are beaten, enslaved, and often murdered. What language, then, can be found equal to the grateful task of eulogizing the names of Wilberforce and Clarkson, who have devoted their whole lives and great talents to the endeavour of rescuing these miserable creatures from the inhumanity of man? And what language is adequate to express the indignation of the heart, at that portion of civilized and Christianized man, who continue to capture, enslave, and murder them?

I saw no more of poor Dick this day, nor did I ever afterwards see him. He has probably become a victim to the merciless Arabs of the tribe of Wiled Lebdessebah. I feel myself bound, however, to say that my master, although of this degraded and cruel tribe, was guilty of but little inhumanity to me. I suffered all but death to be sure when his slave; but from his situation, I know not how *he* could have helped it. He was a grave, thoughtful, and regular man; seldom inflamed with passion, and often bestowed favours upon me, which notwithstanding my distress when with him, I remember with gratitude. While I hope never to bear an injury with mean submission, I also hope, I never shall become so hardened as to forget a favour.

My master this day gave me a square piece of the colours of the brig, perhaps a yard and a half square. In the centre of it, I cut a hole to let my head through, and sewed up the sides, leaving armholes. By this, my body was considerably secured from the sun. This was probably the first *American* flag that was ever hoisted upon the deserts of Zahara. My mistress, like a true Amazon, determined that the "striped bunting" should not be monopolized by American tars *everywhere*, took the remainder of it, and "*covered herself with glory*." Toward evening I went to the tent of Hogan's master to shew him my new uniform, made of the colours under which we once sailed happily together. It excited feelings not to be expressed, or repressed; but his gloom made almost every object equally indifferent to him.

The day ended, as it began, in misery. Hogan told me that Dick, the day before, offered him some cooked snails, which his master would not suffer him (Hogan) to eat, and that he expected to starve.

Chapter 11

Arab Hospitality

October 3rd, 1815.—I went this day to the tent of Porter's master, about seven miles distance, and found him in it. After tarrying some time, Porter and I, together with his master, and another Arab, each of whom had a musket, went up the valley to a tent where a camel had been killed. The muskets were good double-barrelled pieces, which Porter and I carried. When we arrived at the tent, some meat was cooked, which the Arabs greedily devoured, and gave the bones to us, which we immediately, with our teeth and finger nails, scraped clean of every particle of gristle. The Arabs were also treated with milk and water, but none was allowed to us. Porter and his master toward night went home, and I to my master's tent.

October 4th.—Upon this day I saw what I had never before seen upon the desert—a shower As soon as it commenced, the women went to the rocks upon the hills, with their *geddacks* and sponges to gather water. This they did by taking the water from the rocks with a sponge, then squeezing it into the *geddacks*, or bowls. I laid down upon the rocks and licked and sucked all I could, but was unable to satisfy my thirst. The shower soon passed over, and the burning rays of the sun returned. The women nearly filled a water goat skin, which they call *gillabar*, with water, and carried it with them to the tent.

Upon the 5th, I remained in and about the tent. The women were engaged in ripping into pieces the garments they had found at the boat where we landed. They picked out the stitches with a large iron needle, and very carefully preserved every thread, being vexed when they broke one. They then took the different pieces of the garments, and cut them into small pieces of almost every variety of shapes. My mistress was preparing to make a garment of them for herself. The cloth was all of blue, brown, or black colour; and what possible object they had in cutting it to pieces, I could not imagine. They then proceeded to sew it together.

After about fifteen days' labour, she had gotten together enough to make a kind of loose frock, which was sewed to the colours, at her breast and back, and hung loosely down to her knees, her arms remaining naked to her shoulders. She assumed that kind of consequence when clad in this garment, which is sometimes seen in females that never saw or traversed these deserts. Her visitors admired it; and thought her peculiarly fortunate in having introduced a new fashion. My master, Ganus. with all his Mahometan gravity, was pleased with the comely appearance of his *amiable* bride. To see the flag of my country decorating the upper part, and the habit of a sailor the lower part of my mistress, made me smile myself,

The next morning, (6th) my master and his two sisters, Muckwoola and Ishir, went with all the camels, about twenty, young and old, after water; not having watered since the 24th of last month, or as the natives call a month, *Shahar*. They were gone during this day, and the 7th. and returned upon the 8th, early in the morning. During their absence, I sought for snails and found but few. There was but a small remnant of water in the tent; and the small quantity usually allowed me was diminished, so that I was obliged to beg at a neighbouring tent, in the name of my mistress, as this was the only way to obtain it. As I had wandered about five miles from the tent, entirely out of sight of all the tents, I saw a large Arab, with a drawn scimitar, approaching me with great rapidity. I leave it to the imagination to form an idea of my feelings, He said, "*Soo-mook en tar?*" what's your name?

I answered, *Robbins*,

"*Robbinis! Robbinis!*"

He then asked, "*Me-nane jate?*"

I answered, by pointing towards my master's tent.

He continued, "*Ille-mein en tar?*"

I answered, to *Ganus*.

He seemed by his conduct, to know my master, and said no more; but eyed me very sharply as I walked hastily from him. The tents began to move away from the valley, leaving my master's almost alone.

Upon the 8th, early in the morning, my master, with Muckwoola, Ishir, the camels, and the water, returned, and the tents were immediately struck, preparatory for a departure to some point in the compass, or, as I sometimes thought, to a point *not in the compass*; these unthinking creatures seeming to act, half of the time, without any discoverable motive. Our family started off with the two tents, in company with one of our neighbours, who also had two tents, and about fifty camels; so that four tents, sixty camels, about twenty Africans, and one American, formed quite a respectable cavalcade. We left the valley, and passed over the hill, bearing to the S. E.

Upon a journey the usual times of *refreshing*, eating generally out of the question, is about noon, and eleven o'clock at night. When they have meat, which is seldom, they partake of it once only, and that after dark, lest they should lose a portion of it from its being discovered. When they have nothing either to *eat* or *drink*, which is often the case, these particular *times* and *seasons* are dispensed with, and the time of refreshing is made up, by a rational creature, with "*the feast of reason*" and by Arabs, with jabbering and sleeping. We travelled moderately and pitched about sunset.

From the 9th, until the 12th, we travelled gradually forward in a S. E. direction. The travelling dress of the male Arabs, of the *Wiled Lebdessebah* tribe, if they have any at all, is a coarse white blanket as the principal article. It is about a yard and a half wide, and five yards long. The mode of putting it on, when done properly, is by pulling one corner of it over the left shoulder as low as the breast; then winding it around the back and under the right arm, holding it by the upper edge; then turning the body quickly round, until it comes under the left arm; then throwing the upper edge over the head; then behind the neck upon the right shoulder, the lower edge coming in front as low as the knee; the remaining part of it is thrown over the left shoulder, hanging loosely behind, some almost to the ground, or according to the length of the blanket. The blanket is made fast next to the body, by a belt of morocco leather with a buckle.

Over the whole is thrown a belt from the right shoulder, under the left arm, and sometimes another from the left shoulder under the right arm, crossing at the breast. To these are attached sheathes or powder horns, and in the sheath is put the scimitar, or long knife, such as the owner happens to have. This tribe seldom have any under-dress, being so miserably poor that many of them are unable to procure a decent blanket. If they have muskets, of which they appear excessively proud, they generally carry them in their hands, exhibiting them as an evidence of their wealth, or a proof of their skill in gunnery.

They all have a kind of leather pouch hanging before them, by a strap going round the neck, in which they carry their smoking furniture, and tobacco, or weeds, or anything else that will smoke. In these they also carry their flint and steel, to strike fire with. In one department they carry their tinder, made of a weed produced in the desert. Their pipes are also carried therein, some of steel and some of wood, and some smoke through the shin bone of the goat. The men are passionately fond of smoking if they can get tobacco; and if they cannot, they will smoke pieces of leather. My master, by little and little, smoked up nearly all his pouch. When a number form a circle, the pipe passes from mouth to mouth, each taking two or three whiffs, the last of which furnishes them with a number of puffs through the nose or mouth, as best suits their inclinations. They procure their tobacco from and near Wadinoon. The manner of cultivating it will hereafter be described.

Upon the 13th, continuing nearly the same course, we discovered a number of tents far ahead. My master, taking the most fleet camel in the drove, went forward. After an absence of four hours, he returned with the head, neck, and part of the entrails of a camel, but we could not enjoy a repast immediately, as there was not brush enough in sight to cook it. We halted at sunset, and it was not until ten o'clock at night, after the most diligent search, that I was able to procure fuel enough to dress it. It was a kind of feast day with the family; and I was permitted to rejoice for the bounties of the desert over a few of the guts, which were broiled upon brush, without being washed. They cooked their part of the feast by digging a hole in the earth, and putting the head therein; then building a fire upon the top of it, it was fitted for the supper-party at about one o'clock in the morning.

From the 14th to the 16th, nothing happened worthy of relation. On the last of these days, my master procured some water from a small valley into which the water, produced by a shower, had settled, it being thick, warm and muddy. We continued in a S. E. direction.

On the 17th, we shifted our course to the eastward; the country became more hilly, and as it became so, there were always more bushes for the camels to feed upon. In this part of this desert, we found a few trees about the size of our cherry-trees, resembling a large thorn bush, or tree. It produced a species of gum, for which the natives have a great fondness. It is light coloured and transparent, and is the real *Gum-Arabic*. In the afternoon we ascended a considerable hill, and after descending a part of the way down the opposite side of it, the party stopped, without pitching the tent. We spent the night in the open air, the northeast wind blowing chilly upon us. I felt very unwell, and laid down; and my master, knowing that my indisposition arose from want of food, cooked me a small piece of camel's hide, which, with a little warm milk, and some sound sleep, restored me to health by next morning.

Upon the 18th, having retired to the most secret place, an event of the greatest immediate importance to me took place; it was one that I had long wished to witness, and the temporary benefits of which, I hoped to experience—it was the butchering of a camel. A young man from our neighbouring tent came to my master's assistance, and, joining him and his sisters, assisted in catching a two-year old camel of the male kind. They cast him, and lashed his four legs together. They then made fast a rope around his nose, and drew his head nearly back to the tail, the beast lying upon the side. They then, with a large knife, cut the neck off, close to the shoulder blades—then turning him on his back, they divided the skin from the shoulder to the tail. The entrails were laid upon clean bushes, and the meat being equally divided, was disposed of in the same manner—one half for my master and his family, the other for his mother and sisters.

The mothers name was *Annbube*. They cut off pieces of the hump, which is somewhat like the brisket of an ox, and ate it raw. I had, in the meantime, gathered together a large quantity of fuel, and they immediately proceeded to cook the blood, and with the utmost voracity devoured the whole of it. This was at about two o'clock, and during the afternoon the women were employed in cutting the lean part of it into thin long slices, and hanging them in the sun to dry. Joy seemed to pervade every heart: and even the rigid features of the Arab were relaxed into something that resembled complacency. Supper time was looked for with delightful anxiety, knowing that we should then be regaled with the guts of the animal, boiled in the water found in the paunch. After this repast was disposed of, we all remained in the tent till about midnight, and then I retired to rest with a satisfied appetite; being the first time since my slavery that I could say the same.

Never, I think, did the most sincere Christian feel more grateful to the Great Giver of temporal blessings, than I did for this refreshment. It is a fact, worthy of observation, that the Arabs kill a camel with the utmost secrecy. When my master killed this one, we were upon a plane that seemed to be without limits, no tent nor human being in sight, excepting the four belonging to our party; yet, before the skin was off five or six Arabs came bounding over the sandy desert, to partake of it. This I noticed was invariably the case, so long as I continued a slave to the wandering tribes.

The next morning, (19th) I was employed in curing the camel's hide, or rather putting it in a situation to be preserved, until after the meat of the beast was consumed. It was cut into small pieces, and thrown into the fire, which, by singing off the hair, and drying it, prepared it to be deposited in the tent and carried upon a journey. The hoofs are disposed of in the same manner. They break all the bones to pieces, and eat all the marrow, uncooked. It is astonishing to see what a quantity of marrow is produced from an animal whose meat is so dry and lean.

At about ten o'clock, a. m. the master of Hogan, with him, and a number of Arabs, came to our tent; having discovered, either from the smoke of our fire, or the odour of the cooking meat, that a camel had been slain. Some meat was immediately cooked. I was rejoiced to see a pretty liberal portion allotted to my hungry friend Hogan—who ate as though the genius of famine had long had him in her keeping. He tore off the meat from the hard, unyielding neck of the camel like a tiger; and preserved a piece to carry home to his shipmate and fellow-slave Dick: although his own appetite was not satisfied. The visiters, in the mean time, were satiating their appetites. It has been before remarked, that the Arabs always treat their visiters with what they have; it is always expected— and if it is known that a camel has been slain, and the owner conceals the meat, or declines to impart a portion, the highest indignation is excited.

During these visits, the master and mistress never eat themselves, but wait upon their guests. Whether this practice arises from *real hospitality*, or from some *article of their faith*, I know not, but I strongly suspect the latter. Not having with me the *Koran*, I cannot ascertain it. Those of my readers, who are acquainted with the system introduced into the world by that wonderful production, may probably settle the question for themselves.

After the meat was eaten, the guests were served with milk and water, and retired highly gratified; not probably so much from a principle of gratitude, as from the relief obtained for their hunger.

Chapter 12

Impossibility of Escaping

From the 20th, to the 22nd of October, we travelled leisurely to the southward end westward. Every morning, after the sun had reached a considerable height, the party stopped, and hung out the slips of meat upon the tents or bushes to dry. The country became more hilly and more sandy. Those who have seen the sandy hills at Cape Cod, in a violent gale of wind, can form a faint idea of the country over which we were now passing. The trade wind Mew a gale almost constantly. The atmosphere was filled with hot sand, as ours is with snow in a snow storm. The vertical rays of the sun beating upon a body almost naked—the sand filling the eyes constantly exposed—the feet sinking, ankle deep, into the sand at every step, made travelling all but destruction.

My ears, and nose, and sometimes my mouth, were literally filled with sand—the one almost lost the sense of hearing—the other that of smelling, and the last that of tasting. The tent could not be pitched, as the sand would not hold the tent pegs. We had no water to spare for the grateful exercise of washing, and, as a most disgusting substitute, I was compelled to make use of my own urine, in washing my face, arms, and hands. A few more such day's travelling, I think, would have put an end to my life and my slavery.

Upon the 23rd, we travelled to the southward. The wind moderated considerably, and at about noon, we stopped, and unloaded the tents. My master's only son, about twelve years of age, named Elle, told me that Joe was in a tent at a little distance off I knew he meant Porter, and he and I went in pursuit of the tents to the northward. After travelling three or four miles, we called at a tent which was owned by Mr. Savage's former master. I also saw my master Ganus, who was assisting in butchering a camel. I was immediately sent to gather dry bushes which were scarce, and continued as much as three hours in this laborious service. By this time, the camel was dressed. They had procured a brass kettle, into which they threw some meat, entrails, &c. and boiled them in the paunch water.

Of this, they all partook liberally. As a compensation for my toil, they gave me the *foetus* of a young camel, found in the one they had killed, about the size of a rat. I pushed it into the fire and sand under the kettle, and after roasting it, was permitted to *swallow the whole camel myself.* Extreme hunger made this a delicious meal. Porter's master was also here, and asked mine to let me go to his tent to see Joe, as he was sick. Liberty was granted, and I visited him at nearly sunset. He had been sick a number of days with the headache, and had been bled in the head by the natives with a jack-knife, which they call *L'moose*. He looked sick, had lost much flesh, and was extremely dejected.

Although the common cant of advising in such a case rather aggravates than mitigates sorrow, I ventured to urge him to exercise all the fortitude he could; and as it was the will of our Maker that we must suffer, we ought to make the best we could of our situation, wretched as it was. I fully believe that it was from this sentiment, that my own life was preserved; and that by this, I was kept from perishing upon the deserts of Zahara.

We travelled, during the 24th, over deep sand; but upon the 25th, early in the morning, we all reached a boundless plane, stretching, apparently, an immeasurable distance to the south east, south west, and north west. The surface of the earth was hard, mixed with small stones, mostly baked in it. It appeared to be as hard as a pavement; and the hoof of the camel made not the least impression upon it. If could not be more dissimilar to the country we had just passed than it was. At sunrise, the camels were stopped, and, as usual, service was performed. I cannot call that *divine service*, which was performed in honour of Mahommed. Our water was wholly exhausted, there being not a drop remaining in either tent. A little dried meat was still left. We entered upon this plane, and to me the most gloomy entry I ever made upon any part of the earth.

The natives *must* have known that the course we were travelling would lead to a well, or they never would have ventured upon it. This was to me the only consolation. By about noon, having travelled very fast, we reached the centre of this plane. The country presented to my view the most melancholy prospect that I can possibly imagine can exist in nature. It appeared to be an exact water level. The sea, in a dead calm, never, to my eye, appeared smoother; and the earth was as destitute as that of every shrub, plant, or weed. It seemed as if the genius of *famine* and *drought*, held here their cheerless dominion. Neither man, beast, nor even insect, could subsist upon it, and neither were within sight, except our party. We fled across it as we would have fled from *the city of destruction*.

At nearly sunset we again reached a more sandy country. We continued to travel until ten o'clock at night; and having found a few bushes, the wearied camels were stopped to feed. Having started in the morning at about one o'clock, by the stars, as I judged, and travelling with amazing rapidity, until ten o'clock at night, we must have gone as many as ninety miles. The course we travelled was to the S.W. We only threw off the tents, and resting till nearly daylight, again started upon the journey. Not having drank a single drop of water the day before, nor during this night, my thirst was so excessive, that I thought I could not survive it. We, however, drove on as usual at a full trot; and did not, until the next day, (26th) at twelve o'clock, find any water. My master then procured a draft for us all, at a tent; and this, with a few of the roots and sprouts before mentioned, in some measure, satisfied me.

We stopped but a few minutes; and the country becoming hilly, and the night dark, we travelled, full speed, over hills and valleys, till twelve o'clock. We must have gone as many miles this day as we did the preceding one, being the most rapid travelling I ever witnessed upon camels. The tents were thrown off, and the camels fed; a little meat was cooked for the party, and as soon as this was finished, we started again. For the past day, our course was about west. We drove on with the greatest rapidity until the next day, (27th) at about noon, when, to my inconceivable joy, we reached a well. But upon attempting to taste the water, notwithstanding the extremity of my thirst, it was with the greatest difficulty I could force it into my throat, or retain it there when I had. It was more offensive than the most nauseous bilge-water—it had turned green by stagnation, and reddish by the quantity of camel's dung mixed with it; but it was our only resource, "*and we must drink or die*"

This was an interior well, which is seldom found far into the deserts. This well was one of great depth. When the natives begin to dig a well, they furnish themselves with all the largest bushes or trees in the adjoining country, some of which are of the size of a man's thigh. These they cut into poles of about six feet in length. After they have penetrated a small depth into the earth, they put three of these sticks into holes, made in the sides of the well, leaving a triangular hole in the centre, of a sufficient size to let down and draw up the water-bucket. These poles are placed thick at the top, and further apart as the earth grows harder. In this way they continue to descend into the earth, passing the earth up in bowls from one to the other to the top, and inserting the stakes as mentioned, when necessary.

After they have descended a considerable depth, they draw up the earth in leathern buckets, by means of a rope, having no windlass or sweep, to assist bodily strength in this laborious operation. Indeed, this tribe seemed to have no idea of *machinery* of the most simple kind, to facilitate the construction or manufacture of anything, or to save manual labour. They continue in this manner to descend, until they come to water. Looking down the well, as far as light will enable the eye to discern, the observer sees a regular triangle in the centre. These cross-sticks furnish a ladder, by which the natives descend to clear the well of sand, which is constantly blowing into its open surface; these stupid creatures seldom having sagacity enough to prevent this by covering the top. The water is drawn from the well in a leathern bucket, made of tanned camel's or goat's skins. The top of it is a circular hoop, over which the skin is sewed, forming a round vessel at the sides and bottom, holding about three gallons.

Three ropes are fastened to this hoop, equi-distant from each other, and these to the one by which it is let down. The country in which this well was situated was the deepest and most extensive valley I had yet seen; surrounded, excepting to the westward. by high rocky hills. On the east side, I saw and examined immense ledges of the most beautiful white marble. As I was descending into this valley, my distress could not suppress my admiration, at beholding an immense rock of white marble, standing perpendicularly, and entirely detached from the ledge, which formed the eastern limits of it.

On a distant view, I immediately imagined it to be some castle for the defence of an adjoining city, or the palace of some African prince. I felt confident that I was approaching some great city. I continued to approach; and almost forgot my hunger and thirst in the anticipated gratification of my curiosity. At length, I came to this astonishing monument—went round it—examined it as minutely as I possibly could, and could not discover upon it the least trait of human art.

My expectations were blown away by the wind that whistled round it, and my readers must excuse me for not saying anything more about it, only that it was, at the base, in the shape of a parallelogram, or oblong square, as near as I could judge, of one hundred feet in length, and sixty in breadth. Its height must have been from seventy to eighty feet. After stating the simple fact, I leave it to the curious, the philosophical, the inquisitive, and the wondering, to make conjectures for themselves. This valley was, to appearance, the most fertile place I had seen.

It was the first earth I had walked upon in Africa, that seemed susceptible of cultivation. It was mostly a clay-soil, and considerable grass was growing, or rather standing, as the excessive drought this season had dried up everything. The grass resembled that which grows in what is called, in New-England, *boggy meadows*. Toward night we left this valley, and passed through the opening hill to the southwest, having fitted but two goat skins with the offensive water found in the well. I carried a bowl full, however, four or five miles, fearing I should be destitute of water of any kind. We stopped for the night, and cooked a little dried meat, by putting small hard pieces into the fire, roasting it, taking it out and pounding it in a *maress*, or mortar.

Upon the 28th, we travelled moderately to the southwest, until noon, when the tents were pitched, for the first time, for a number of days Even the stomach of an Arab could no longer endure the water we had; and my master and his sisters having learned from a passing party, that water was at no great distance, went in pursuit of some of a better kind, if comparisons of quality are allowable between different sorts, all of which would nauseate a beast.

On the next day, (29th) Muckwoola and Ishir returned, bringing with them some fresh water. and some dried fishskins, or fragments of fish, which had before been deprived of the better part. Some of this was allowed me for supper; and as it was a rarity, having lived upon camel's hide, meat, and bones for some time, I ate it with the best appetite. My master Ganus did not return with his sisters. I was left under the command of the women once more; and, as usual, found my privileges abridged as female authority prevailed. We remained stationary until the next day, at noon, (30th) then started and bore to the N. W. and travelled moderately, during that and the next day, (31st.)

November 1st, 1815.—From this day until the 3rd, we continued to travel moderately, and as we passed along, the country became more hilly; nothing took place of any consequence. On our passage we saw a few small locusts, which we gathered and ate. Upon the 3rd, my master returned to his tent, after an absence of six days, it being his longest absence since I was his slave, bringing with him one piece of tent cloth. Having often mentioned that I wandered off at a distance, and frequent opportunities occurring to make my escape, it may excite wonder that I did not attempt it. The description I have attempted to give of the country seems to be a sufficient reason. Had I attempted it, starvation must have been the final result, if I had not been taken by another master before this took place. Let the reader imagine to himself a desert of eight hundred miles in width, and more than two thousand in length, furnishing nothing for the subsistence of human beings, but camels, and these always in possession of individuals, parties, or caravans. Let him also picture to himself a solitary wanderer upon this desert, without food or water, and without any means to procure either, and liable every day, and almost every hour, to be encountered by the natives, who are passing it in every direction, he will conclude that the means of escape were of the most unpromising nature. I might as well have escaped from a ship, by plunging into the ocean.

At Wadinoon I afterwards became acquainted with a Spaniard, who attempted, upon a male camel, to escape. He assured me that he travelled the desert thirty days without water, and without any food, excepting a fox which he killed. That at the end of this time, he and his stolen camel were taken by another tribe, and he became a slave to them. He was afterwards demanded by his first master; but absolutely refused to return again into the tribe of the Lebdessebah, and seizing a musket, threatened the life of him. His former master relinquished the attempt to reclaim him, and he continued a slave until the time he and I were, upon the same day, ransomed. He assured me that he had been in slavery seven years. I shall again have occasion to mention this Spaniard.

My master ordered the tents to be struck up on his return, and we proceeded to travel in a northern direction. I went ahead with my master, delighted again to be relieved from the thraldom and irksomeness of female government, which, wherever it prevails, being founded in less reason, is accompanied with more tyranny than that of men. Toward night, we overtook a sick woman upon a camel. She was the first female Arab whom I had seen dangerously sick; indeed it was rare to see even the slightest indisposition among them. I assisted her in dismounting, after the camel was made to kneel. My master's family overtook us, and the tent was pitched. After taking a little milk, I turned in.

The next morning, (4th), before daylight we were on the march for another watering-place. I was permitted to go with the party to the well, being the first time, since my slavery, that I was allowed so to do, being always before left behind with the tent. This variation from the usual custom excited a suspicion in my mind that I was to be sold; as the large watering-places are generally the market for slaves. In travelling toward it, we passed over hills of sand. When at the top of them, I saw the ocean! I knew it must be the Atlantic, from the course we had travelled. I ardently panted to be on the bosom of it, as the waves thereof might waft me to the regions of civilization—and *might* waft me to my beloved country. In the valley below, I saw a great multitude of camels around the wells, there being a number in this valley. The camels *knew* there was water below, as well as their riders; and after descending a part of the way down the steep hill, the forward camels began to run.

My camel followed the example; and as the mouth of this beast never submitted to the restraint of the bit, never having been bridled, I was precipitated down the hill with a velocity with which I had before been unacquainted; and when I arrived at the well, I might have said, as Gilpin did when he reached Ware, "*I came, because my camel would come.*" The wells were situated near each other; but from the number of camels that are constantly coming to drink, they are obliged to keep them off, if possible, till those drinking are satisfied. This is done with very great difficulty. After the camels are sufficiently watered, they are sent to browse.

The natives never bring their tents to a well, leaving them behind in the keeping of the women. I now had as much water as I wanted; and can say, that it was the first time my thirst was thoroughly quenched, since I became a slave to Ganus. The tents must have been as many as fifty miles back in the desert; for they always remain where they are left, when the owner goes in search of water, until he returns. We slept this night under a large bush with a large company, and kept a fire for the most part of the night.

Upon the 5th, early in the morning, the camels were all watered again, as they are sometimes compelled to go entirely without it for twenty days, and sometimes for a longer period My master Ganus expressed great anxiety that my short trowsers should be washed; and told me to take them off. This left my body entirely naked, excepting that part of it which was covered with the American flag, and which he did not attempt to compel me to *strike*. They were hung upon a camel to dry, and this was the last time I ever saw them, or Muckwoola and Ishir. who carried them off with them.

I was now taken on to a camel behind my master, who, in company with another Arab, went off full trot to the southward. Before noon, we met numbers of the natives who had fresh fish with them. We obtained a breakfast of them. By the middle of the afternoon, we came to the edge of an high precipice, limiting a considerable bay, a little to the north of Cape Mirik. We descended to the beach, at the head of the bay, which had in it a number of sand islands. The tide was now out, leaving it dry, and we passed along at the base of the precipice, and discovered a number of shallow wells, having brackish water in them. We continued to travel upon the beach until we came to a number of pitched tents, and here I first saw a kind of hut or *wigwam*, constructed by erecting two crotches about ten feet apart—laying a pole on them, and from this extending poles to the ground, and covering them with seaweed, giving them the shape of a thatched roof.

Within, the natives have a bed made also of seaweed; but lest they should blunder upon something that looks like the convenience and comfort of civilized life, they are careful to make them so low that a human being cannot stand erect in one of them. We dismounted near a hut. My master went off, and I sat down, in a kind of trance, gazing upon the bay before me, and upon the point of Cape Mirik, stretching into the sea. Soon after my master returned with three or four Arabs, one of whom was soon pointed out as my *second* master. He bade me stand up—told me to walk, and viewed me with the closest scrutiny. I suspected he was about to open my mouth to judge of my age by my teeth, and examine my feet to see if I had been *foundered* by *high living* with my master Ganus, mistress Sarah, misses Muckwoola and Ishir; but he dispensed with these ceremonies, seemed to be pleased, and said I was not *foonta*, but *bono*. He bade me follow him. We went some distance to one of the huts, where he begged some dried fish for me which I ate.

I now became the property of another Arab. I felt but little anxiety at this exchange, knowing that my situation could not be rendered much worse, although I was sensible that Ganus was not so bad as some of the Arabs I had seen. At first sight, I was pleased with my new master. He was a little over thirty, by his appearance. He had an open, ingenuous countenance, with but little of that fiery malignity so universally seen in the tribe of the Lebdessebah. His name was Mahomet Meaarah, of the tribe of the *Wiled D'leim*, his tent being some distance in the interior.

The readers of this Journal thus far will perceive, that the author has confined himself strictly to what passed under his immediate observations. He has absolutely prohibited himself from incorporating with his narration, any of the vague, and generally deceptive stories, which he had heard from the illiterate and brutish race of creatures, among whom he was enslaved. Had he done this, the volume would have already been filled. His steady object has been to give an accurate idea of that part of the Zahara Desert over which he travelled. It cannot have a *geographical* accuracy, because he had no means to ascertain the *latitude* of the country over which he travelled, or rather was transported, but by the situation of the sun, and by the shade which his own body cast upon the sand of this immense desert.

As to the manners, customs, and habits of the tribe, with which he had thus long continued, he hopes the reader has acquired some correct ideas. He has attempted to describe their implements of manufacturing, cooking, and travelling—their habitations, and particularly their mode of worship. The result of this relation and description is before the reader, and it is hoped it may at least furnish some amusement, if it is destitute of instruction. We now take leave of the wretched tribe of the *Wiled Lebdessebah*, and whatever has been seen among the *Wiled D'leim* of a similar nature, we shall not repeat, but merely allude to. Whatever was noticed of a different nature in this tribe, we shall continue patiently to detail, and faithfully to describe.

CHAPTER 13

Africa

The attention of the reader having been for some time devoted to that part of Africa called *Zahara*, or the *Great Western Desert*—to the peculiarities of the wandering Arabs who inhabit it, and to the sufferings of the author upon it; it may be a useful way to relieve it, by changing attention from a section of this continent to a general view of the whole. It is not intended to give a minute geographical description of each kingdom, as such more properly belongs to the geographer than the journalist. In our historical chapter we endeavoured, in a compressed manner, to trace the progress of discoveries, and settlements upon this continent. In this, it is intended merely to describe the relative local situations of the different countries or kingdoms, situated upon this immense Peninsula, comprising at least one quarter of the whole globe.

The most accurate information we can obtain of this continent is at best but imperfect; and our limits preclude us from giving anything but a general account. In our historical chapter, we attempted to assign the reason, why this portion of the world is so little known, while the other continents, even that of the new world, America, have been almost wholly explored and described. To that, we refer the reader; and also to that, we refer him for the boundaries of this continent (chapter 4)

Africa is divided, nearly in the centre, by the Equator; of course the greatest part of it is situated within the torrid zone. The whole of it is either exceedingly fertile, or extremely barren. Its fertility is occasioned by the great sources of vegetation, heat and moisture. Heat prevails everywhere; but moisture in particular portions. Where the latter prevails, this country is one of the most productive in the universe—where it is deprived of rain, it is "all barren." This continent differs from the other three great ones, in almost every respect. In the others, the sea coast is generally the most barren; in this, the interior is so. Upon the coast, are regions abounding with every luxury which nature pours into the lap of indulgence; much of the interior is a boundless waste of deserts. A vertical sun, pouring burning rays upon dry sand, defies the progress of vegetation. Even upon these deserts, a race of beings is found to subsist. With the curse of Ishmael upon their devoted heads, and sordid hearts, they flee the regions of fertility and civilization, and seem to delight in sterile barrenness, and human misery.

It has been remarked, that this continent, in shape, resembles a triangle, with irregular sides. Beginning at the northeast point, Egypt is situated, bounding east upon the Red Sea, and north, upon the Mediterranean, and the Isthmus of Suez, uniting this continent there with Asia. This section of Africa has long been celebrated, and is well known in sacred and profane history. Continuing west upon the northern boundary of this continent, and along the shores of the Mediterranean, Barca, Tripoli, Tunis, Algiers, Fez, and Morocco, are situated, reaching the northwest point, at the Straits of Gibraltar. All these countries are possessed by Arabs and Moors, although with them are intermingled other nations. It is generally termed the Coast of Barbary. The history of these distinct states, or kingdoms, is known to every historian, and their geographical situation to every geographer.

For centuries they have been, and still are, the terror of the civilized world. Nations, the most powerful by land and by sea, have condescended to pay them tribute, and to ransom their unfortunate countrymen who are there enslaved. They infest the adjoining oceans with their contemptible navies, and upon land they are invincible; not from their numbers or their military science, but from the facilities afforded them by their country, to avoid conquest by the best disciplined armies. Destroy their naval armaments, and batter down their capitals, they still have a safe retreat in their mountains and in their deserts, where a civilized army cannot subsist. The mention of Tripoli calls up the proud recollection of the infancy of the American Navy. It was upon the coast of that country, that Americans began to learn how to conquer upon the ocean. It was their achievements there that occasioned the prophetic Nelson to see, in the infancy of our navy, the future rival of that of Britain. The mention of Algiers makes us remember a recent achievement of this navy as she is approaching towards manhood.

Upon the Western boundary of Africa, are situated Suse, Azanaga, North-Guinea, or Senegal, embracing the country of the Jaloffs, Foulahs, Feloops and Mandingoes—South-Guinea, containing the Pepper Coast, the Ivory Coast, and the Gold Coast—East-Guinea, or the Slave Coast, in which is situated the kingdoms of Whidah, Ardra, and Benin. The next great division of the western coast is Congo, comprehending the kingdoms of Loango, Congo, Angola, Matamba, and Benguela, It is upon this coast that the Slave Trade has so long, to the indelible disgrace of the Christian world, been prosecuted. The inhabitants are described, by all historians, as mild and peaceable. Possessing a country of great fertility—having no means of making conquests, or extending dominion, they remain where nature has placed them, unmoved by the sordid demands of avarice, or the more splendid and guilty calls of ambition.

The different tribes. or kingdoms, sometimes make war upon each other; but they are urged on to warfare by European and American merchants, to capture each other to furnish slave-ships with their cargoes. With a few paltry toys, calculated to catch the fancy of untutored barbarians, they induce the natives to prey upon each other, and exchange their countrymen for baubles. After doing this, a Christian merchant, excuses himself by saying, the Africans enslave each other! This reasoning may be conclusive before a tribunal of slave-merchants, assembled in a princely mansion, that owes its splendour to human blood, but all the courts of Europe have very recently, by common consent, united to wipe the foul stain from the character of their respective nations, impressed upon them by this inhuman, detestable, and diabolical traffic. The Constitution of the United States is the first one that absolutely prohibited it.

Upon the western coast is also situated the country of the Namaquas, and of the Hottentots; which, together with the colony of the Cape of Good Hope, comprehends the southern point of the continent, and stretching quite across it to the eastern side.

Upon the eastern side of this continent are situated Inhambane, Monica, Sabia, Sofala, and Mocaranga. Continuing east, toward Cape Guardafui and the Straits of Babelmandel, the kingdoms of Mozambique, Mongolla, Quiloa, Montbaza, Melinda, and Monoemugi, the republic of Brava, and the kingdom of Magadoxa, are situated. Adel is an extensive kingdom, embracing an immense country around Cape Guardafui, the easternmost point of the continent. From this Cape, to the Isthmus of Suez, this continent is bounded easterly upon the

Arabian Gulf which reaches to that place.

We have now conducted the reader around the coast of this immense triangular peninsula. We have mentioned the principal countries as they succeed each other, beginning at Egypt, and following the coast along its northern, western, and eastern sides, until we again reached that place situated near the Isthmus of Suez. The geographical knowledge of the reader will readily enable him to supply that minute information which our limits preclude us from detailing.

The Interior of Africa is known more from vague conjecture than accurate description. Many hardy travellers have, at the hazard of life, (see historical chapter,) explored parts of it. Abyssinia has long been celebrated by the geographer, and the scholar. The one makes it the region of fertility, having the sources of the Nile within its limits—the other converts it into the region of romance. The classical Johnson, in his Prince of Abyssinia gives us an idea of a distinct world. His Rasselas has dressed this kingdom in all the charms, which the most fertile imagination and classical mind can impart to a terrestrial region.

The description of the country situated upon the Niger, under the general name of Soudan. transports the mind of the reader to a region entirely the reverse. This part of the continent, although watered by a majestic stream, and having an adjoining country of great fertility, seems to be that region where the wrath of Heaven, against man, is forever to be displayed. The denunciation against the descendants of Ishmael stands yet unreversed—the innocent blood of the Messiah yet rests upon the head of his murderers, and here, in the Great Desert of Zahara, and in other parts of the interior, they both remain a standing miracle.

The knowledge we possess of this desert is principally derived from the Christian slaves, who have there been suffering witnesses of the manners, customs, and habits of the wandering Arabs; and famishing wanderers themselves, through the widespread desolation pervading the country they inhabit. It has fallen to the unhappy lot of Americans to furnish most of the information the world possesses upon this subject. The ingenious Mr. Cock has given the world the narrative of the American sailor, Robert Adams, and the indefatigable Mr. Dupuis, has, by his notes, confirmed its accuracy. The crew of the Commerce seem to have been designed to suffer themselves, that the world, through them, might learn.

It is hoped this little volume will add something to the little knowledge already obtained of the desert of Zahara, and the western coast of Africa. As to that portion of the interior, situated upon the equator, and within the Tropic of Capricorn, even conjecture itself has almost omitted to exercise its uncertain and futile powers. In Soudan, are included the empires of Houssa and Tombuctoo, the country of the Agadez, the kingdoms of Ludamar, Rondou and Bambouk. also the kingdoms of Bornou, and Darfur. Nubia contains Turkish Nubia, Dongala, and Sennaar. North of the Zahara Desert, are situated the countries of Tafilet and Biled-ul-Gerid, lying south of the Barbery States.

The Deserts, which comprehend so much of the interior, are the Zahara or Great Western Desert. This region of desolation and barrenness stretches, by the best authorities, from 15° to 31° N. Latitude, and from 70° W. to 16° E. Longitude. The desert of Libya from 25° to 30° N. Latitude, and from 21° to 30° E. Longitude. The desert of Barca is small.

The Mountains upon this continent, are in ranges. The Atlas has been celebrated from the ages of antiquity to this time. According to the fabulous accounts of the ancients, it supports the firmament. The inimitable Addison resorts to it as the emblem of firmness. He makes his Cato, like that "glory in height." These mountains extend from the western coast of Africa, to the Gulf of Sydra. They commence in the 28° N". Latitude, and extend, in a N. E. course, to 34° N. Latitude; and from thence, in an east direction, to 14° E. Longitude. Although these mountains are more celebrated, being more known, yet the mountains of Kong, in point of extent, certainly exceed them. They stretch from the River Gambia, to 23° E. Longitude.

The Mountains of the Moon commence in 17° E. Longitude, and run east to 37° E. Longitude. These two ranges divide almost the whole continent into northern and southern divisions, and are situated between the fifth and thirteenth degrees of north latitude. The mountains of Lupata begin at the mouth of the River Quilimane, upon the eastern coast, and encircling the kingdom of Mocaranga, extend to the country of the Hottentots. The Chrystal Mountains are situated near the kingdoms of Congo, Angola, and Benguela. upon the western coast.

The Capes upon this continent are, upon the northern coast, or the Mediterranean, Cape Bon, in Tunis; and Cape Spartel, near Tangier. Upon the western coast, or the Atlantic, are Cape Geer, near Santa Cruz—Cape Bajador, upon which the *Commerce* was wrecked—Cape Barbas where the crew landed with the boat—Cape Mirik—Cape

Verd—Cape Mesurada—Cape Palmas—Cape of the Three Points—Cape Formosa—Cape Negro—Cape de Lasvoltas, and the Cape of Good Hope, at the southernmost point of the continent. Upon the eastern coast, or Indian ocean, are Capes Needle, St. Mary, Corientes, Sebastian, Delgado, Baxas, and Cape Guardafui, forming the easternmost point of the continent.

The rivers of this continent, when compared with those of Asia, are diminished to rivulets. When the Ganges is recollected, the Nile, and the Niger, are almost forgotten in the majesty of the former. When compared with the Mississippi, Missouri, Ohio, Amazon, and La Plata, of America, they then lose their consequence. The Tyber , the Danube, the Seine, the Tagus, the Vistula, the Thames, and the Don of Europe, in many respects, exceed them; but still, the Nile must be ranked with the great geographical and classical streams.

The sources of this river have been sought after with an assiduity, unparalleled in the history of the most romantic adventurers. It is supposed to have its source in the Mountains of the Moon, and is known to empty itself, through numerous mouths, into the Mediterranean, near Alexandria, after passing through Abyssinia and Egypt. The source of the Niger is not certainly known; and even the course it runs is yet a disputed point among geographers. Some contend that it runs eastward, and empties itself into lakes in Wangara, in the interior of the continent. Others feel confident that its course is westward, and that it loses itself in the regions of Guinea.

All we can say is, "Who shall decide when Doctors disagree?" The Senegal has its source not far from the mountains of Kong, and it empties into the Atlantic ocean in about 16° N. Latitude. The Nile, the Niger, and the Senegal, annually overflow their banks, dispensing fertility and luxuriance to the country adjoining them. The other principal streams of Africa are the Gambia, Morocco, Sierra Leona, Benin, Congo, Zuire, Coantza, Manica, Zambezi, Coavo, Zeta, and Magadoxa.

The principal islands, situated around this continent, have a consequence in sacred and profane history, almost equal to the continent itself. In the Mediterranean, are the islands of Cyprus, Candia, Malta, Sicily, and Sardinia. In the Atlantic are those or Madeira, the Canaries, and Cape Verds. These islands are well known to American navigators, and have greatly enhanced the wealth of American merchants. St. Louis is situated at the mouth of the Senegal. In the South Atlantic, above 1100 miles from the continent, is situated the island of St.

Helena; well known to the navigators to India, and now dignified by the residence of Napoleon. It is a small island; but the modern Charlemagne cannot become small by being in a little place. The Isles of Ascension and St. Matthew are nearly the same distance from the coast. Near to the coast are situated Fernando Po, Princess, St. Thomas, and Annobon. In the Indian Ocean, is the important island of Madagascar, about 800 miles in length, and 200 in breadth. Also the Isle of France, and Bourbon, the Comora, Islands, Zanzeba and Pomba. Near Cape Guardafui is situated the island of Socotra.

The Straits adjoining this continent are those of Babel-Mandel, uniting the Red Sea with the Indian ocean, and Gibraltar, which separates this continent from Europe.

The Gulfs are—the Gulf of Sydra, Goletta, Guinea, and Sofala. The channel of Mozambique, between the island of Madagascar and the coast of Mozambique, is the only one belonging to this continent.

This chapter is introduced for the double purpose of relieving the reader from the detail of sufferings and minute descriptions, and giving a mere bird's eye view of Africa.

Chapter 14

Second Tour into the Desert

November 5th, 1815.—My new master Meaarah's first inquiry was, if I had any clothes beside what I had on? I told him I had not, my whole wardrobe consisting of the piece of our colours, before mentioned, and a piece of the skin of the *gazelle* tied round my middle. I told him that Ganus had taken from me that day my trowsers and my shoes, the latter being worn out by travelling. He said Ganus was *foonta*, for taking them, and that he would regain them. He discovered the same resentment that the purchaser of a horse would, if the seller, after the sale, should slily take off the halter. He recovered the shoes and gave them to me, and a piece of blanket for my middle. He might, among the Arabs, be called a well dressed man; for he had a blue frockshirt hanging below his knees, and a good white blanket put on as described among the *Wiled Lebdessebah*.

He seemed to be a man of more than ordinary consequence among the natives; for, instead of joining them in the toil of fishing, he was examining and purchasing fish. He went away towards night, and left me at one of the huts in the care of an old Arab by the name of Abdallah, who furnished me with fish for food. They were of the size of the mackerel, nearly the colour of our salmon trouts, of the most delicious flavour, and very fat. They were sometimes taken in considerable abundance. The seine with which they were taken was made of well manufactured twine, apparently of a species of grass. They consisted of meshes of a small size, having both a cork rope and a lead rope. Through the meshes next to the cork rope, they run a pole of six feet in length, gathering up the seine from each end to the centre. This seine consists of any number they choose to unite together, each single one being about twelve rods in length, and owned by different persons. The whole seine being gathered upon two poles, two carriers walk into the water up to their armpits; and then one goes one way and the other another, slipping off the seine as they walk. When it is drawn out at full length, which is sometimes seventy-five rods, a number of other men go out with threshing-poles, and drive the fish into the seine as the two men at the ends approach each other. They then enter the circle made by the seine, and continue to thresh the water, until they suppose they have gilled all the fish. The separate owners then take each their net, and the fish gilled in it, and bring them ashore. They seldom catch exceeding an hundred by one drawing. The fish are of different kinds, although generally of that first mentioned. *L'hoot* is the name of fish with the Arabs.

The bay where I was now situated is formed by *Cape Mirik*, upon the south, and by high sand-hills, and a few small islands upon the north. At ebb-tide, the whole bay, excepting a narrow channel, which extends into it about five miles from the outermost part of the Cape, running near it, is entirely dry. Within the bay, are situated two small islands, composed wholly of sand.

From the north boundary of this bay, is a point of sand running into it towards Cape Mirik, nearly half its width, which forms the *inner bay*. From the termination of this point, to the Cape, is about five miles. From the islands, which form the mouth of the *outer bay*, upon the north to the Cape, is about twenty miles. From Cape Mirik, to the head of the bay, following the shore, it is about the same distance. This Cape is situated, according to the most approved charts, in 19° N. Latitude and 17° W. Longitude. I have been thus particular in describing this bay, so that if any unfortunate mariner should hereafter navigate the western coast of Africa in distress, he might make a temporary harbour in the channel running within it, near the Cape, which I think he might do with safety, excepting in a northwest and westerly wind.

Upon the 6th, after, the usual ceremony of worshipping, which was performed precisely in the manner of the *Wiled Lebdessebah*, my master asked me of what nation I was. It would have been in vain to try to convince him that I came from a continent three thousand miles to the west, the natives upon the desert, in general, having not the least idea of the existence of the *American* continent. I therefore told him I was *Inglisis*, which they understand. He then asked, *Soo-mook en tar?* what's your name? I told him Robbins. He pronounced it the same as Ganus, *Robbinis*. He asked if *Inglesis* be better than *Fransah?* I told him they were both *bono*. He continued to ask me if I had a father and mother, brothers and sisters, wife and children. I answered all in the affirmative, meaning to affect his feelings if he had any, which cannot more readily be done, than by talking of *wives* and *children*. I thought the deception a very innocent one; nor was it altogether without effect; as he immediately said, we will go to *Sweahrah*; it being the same place which we call *Mogadore*, and the place where all the ransoms are effected.

He then left me with another man, with whom I went out to see them fish and assist in the service. They start at low water, and cross over the neck or point running into the bay, to the outer bay, carrying with them the fishing utensils and a sufficient quantity of wood to cook a meal with, and a skin of water They sometimes return as the tide comes in, although they generally continue out for two tides, lodging upon the point of land, and cooking their fish upon the sand. Each one has a small net to carry hence the fish that are taken. I was loaded with them, and obliged to transport them as much as seven miles through the deep sand, sinking often to my knees. I sometimes sunk down with excessive fatigue, and was compelled to stop; while the natives, possessing strength almost beyond human, would bound over the sand with the greatest ease. For this I became an object of their scorn, and sometimes of their resentment.

Upon returning to the tents or huts, some fish are cooked. What remain, are dressed by splitting open the backs, and taking out the inwards; then gashing them cross-wise, and laying them out to dry. They rarely become tainted although they are never salted. Indeed, *salt* is scarcely ever used by Arabs in preserving or cooking anything. During the two preceding months, I had not used a particle of it. The rays of the sun are so powerful, that fresh meat and fresh fish are dried so suddenly that putrefaction is always prevented; unless, which is more generally the case, it is prevented by the immediate consumption of all the meat and fish that falls in the way of the natives. At this place, I saw many black Africans, from which I concluded we were not far from the Senegal River.

We remained at this bay, and at this employment, until the 9th. I began to think I was about to become a slavish fisherman during life; and by affecting ignorance of every part of the duty imposed upon me, and shewing a good portion of obstinacy, the natives soon found that the small benefit they derived from my labour cost more than it would fetch. Upon the last mentioned day, as I was returning with a load of fish, I discovered a number of the natives coming towards us in the bay. We stopped, and concealed our fish as well as we could.

The natives came to us; and although I had abandoned all ideas of ever again seeing any of my shipmates, I recognized Barrett among them. It was nearly two months since I had seen him. We could hardly persuade ourselves that we were actually in each other's presence.—Barrett had become fat, and looked as hearty as a Yankee seaman need to. He said he had been stationed at a fish-place about seven miles north of this place, for three weeks. He had been out into the deserts with his master's brother, and had been retaken, and was now returning with him. He said he had learned nothing of any of the crew, excepting Mr. Williams, since he saw me upon the 14th of September. I communicated to him the good fortune of Capt. Riley, Mr. Savage, Clarke, Burns, and Horace. He said he had but little hopes of getting clear himself, although he could not conceive why the cursed creatures wanted to keep him, as he was not of the least service to them. I told him *that* was the great grounds of *my* hope; and advised him to follow my present example, in being as useless as possible, to be ignorant and obstinate; and in this way, induce them to carry us to the great place of *sale*, and of *redemption*—Mogadore. I inquired after Mr. Williams. He told me he was much better than when last saw him; that his health and spirits had been in a considerable degree restored; that they both continued slaves to their first master, and would probably remain with him. Our interview was but a short one.

I have but little doubt, that Mr. Williams and Barrett, if living, still remain at the same fish-place. This is not a mere conjecture; for at the time of my redemption at Mogadore, sixteen months after this time, the Hon. William Willshire informed me, that he had learned that two Christian slaves were upon an island near a fish-place, far to the southward, upon the western coast of Africa; that he had sent an express, to find them, if possible, and bring them to him that they might be redeemed. The name of this gentleman will hereafter be mentioned in this narration; but I cannot, even here, omit to express my highest admiration of his exalted character. After we returned to the huts, I assured my master that I could not sustain life in the employment I was in, and he assured me that I should, the next day, go off with him.

At about this time, I dispensed with the use of my string by which I was enabled, in counting the knots I daily tied therein, to ascertain the day of the month and of my bondage; and as no possible benefit can be derived from a continuation of dates, excepting that of months, or general periods, I shall omit them. I had not at this time, from either the *Lebdessebah,* or *Wiled D'leim,* learned whether they had any regular manner of keeping the smaller divisions of time, as hours, days, weeks or months; but I afterwards became familiar with their calendar, when I became stationary at Wadinoon. The Arabs, at this place, are steady residents; as they have no means of travelling, neither tents nor camels, but have there erected the small huts or *wigwams* before mentioned.

They have among them considerable flocks of goats from which they obtain some milk, and small asses with which they transport fresh water for a short distance. These animals subsist upon the coarse sea grass that grows within the bay, and the small quantity of bushes that grow in the vicinity of it. I never saw either ass or goat upon the deserts, as they could not there subsist with- out a constant supply of water. The camel, as is well known, can subsist without that article from twenty to thirty days, from the immense quantity they receive into the chest at the watering places. There are, I learned, a number of these fish-places upon the coast from Cape Mirik to Cape Blanco, which are all occupied as the one just described by stationary Arabs. The wandering Arabs are constantly resorting to them for supplies of fish, and at the same places can furnish themselves with water.

Having remained at this fish-place for five days, my master *Meaarah* took me off with him to traverse once more the desert of Zahara. He commenced by travelling in a southeast direction, and upon the first night readied his own tent. We had a very fleet camel, and having started at daylight, and riding till dark without dismounting, we must have travelled at least sixty miles. Upon reaching the tent, I found that of my master and those situated near it were much larger and better than I had ever before seen. My master's return was welcomed by every demonstration of joy. This was increased by seeing a quantity of fish, and carried to the highest pitch when they found me there as a slave.

The whole family seemed anxious to make my situation as comfortable as possible; some offered me fish; some milk, and some water; and the joy of the party was so excessive, that they seemed to "*take no thought for the morrow,*" having devoured almost every eatable thing in their possession. Witnessing the animation and enjoyment of this family of barbarians, my mind was immediately transported to the regions of civilization. It was about the season of a *Connecticut Thanksgiving.* In imagination, I saw the festive board surrounded by my refined, grateful and happy friends. I could see the eyes of parents, beaming with benignity upon their visiting children, blessing heaven for the gift of them, as well as for the luxuries that loaded their hospitable board, rendering thanks that they had been blessed "*in their basket and in their store,*" and that they had been preserved once more to form the happy family.

My heart was near bursting at this recollection. Although I was not destitute of gratitude for an unexpected supply, I was compelled to reflect that all my enjoyments depended upon the capricious whims of an Arab, and that a transition from enjoyment to the lowest wretchedness might befall me in the next twenty-four hours. Well might I exclaim, "*hard, hard is my fate.*"

Upon the next morning, I found my master's family consisted of his wife, Fatima; one son, Adullah; one daughter, named Tilah; and another, Murmooah; his brother, about twenty, Mid-Mohamote. Another small tent was occupied by Fatima's mother, also named Fatima, and her brother, named Ill-Mecca. They also had a teacher in the family supported by Meaarah. wholly without labour, excepting the labour of teaching the family. His name was Mahomet. They also had a black female slave, of the Guinea tribe. My master was possessed of sixty-eight camels; some of which were of the most superior kind. Six of them gave milk, furnishing a tolerable supply for the family. As is always the case with a Christian slave, my portion was less than that of a member of the family.

Although in many different publications, the camel is minutely described, so important an animal must not be passed over without a brief description here. The natives, as a general name, call camels *Lillabilts*: the male, *Izhmael*: the female, *Naig*. The male camel of the larger kind is from twenty to twenty-five hands high. He measures from the nose, to the root of the tail, about eleven feet. The body is deepest from the shoulder to the brisket, and, unless recently filled with water, will girth the most just back of the forelegs. This admeasurement is not meant to include the hump, that being a kind of excrescence rising eight or ten inches above the backbone. The body gradually diminishes in size until it comes to the loins, which are very small for so large an animal. The neck is very low upon the breast, growing out between the shoulder blades; it then descends a little, then rises almost perpendicularly, being from the lower part of the bow of the neck, to the top of the head, about five feet.

The head is carried horizontally; the nose, top of the head, and hump, making a direct line. The eyes are very prominent, and so placed upon the side of the head as to discern objects in every direction. They have a peculiar mildness, and indicate great sagacity for an animal. The ear is very small, and stands nearly erect. The limbs are straight and smooth, but have large strong joints. The hoof is the greatest curiosity in this animal. It is soft and yields to the slightest pressure, having a very small split in the fore part of it, the points of which are of a harder substance. It has before been mentioned that these feet or hoofs are remarkably calculated to travel in deep sand and upon the hardest stones. The tail is smooth and short, and is carried between the legs.

The hair of the camel, excepting what grows upon the hump and neck, is fine, short, and smooth, having a very handsome appearance. That upon the hump and neck is coarser and curly, and from six to eight inches in length. This long hair is sheared off annually, and with it the natives make tent-cloth and coarse clothing. Their colour is from white to a reddish brown. He is an animal of the greatest docility; lies down and rises at the command of his master: at the same command slackens or hastens his pace. When alive, he transports his master, his baggage, his food, drink, and slaves, from one part of the desert to another; when dead, every particle of him furnishes food, excepting his bones, and his hide furnishes leather for almost every purpose. Indeed, it is melancholy to reflect that such a noble animal should subserve the purposes of the most debased of men.

In the morning, after reaching the tent of my master, the camels were distributed around in the adjoining country, and were generally in the keeping of *Illa Mecca*. The country had about the same appearance as those parts of the desert so often mentioned; small sand-hills and shallow valleys. The bushes were very small and thinly scattered, and it required a considerable extent of it to recruit the camels. We remained stationary at this place for six days. During this time my master seemed generally inclined to remain in, or near his tent. At about sunrise, the Mahometan service was invariably performed by the whole family. I was urgently invited to join in the service, but, adhering to my previous resolution, I always declined it, thinking it sacrilege to offer up worship to a prophet whose followers shew so little of humanity in their practice.

The teacher generally took the lead in this service; their teachers being generally of the Mahometan priesthood. He had a number of very old volumes into which I often looked, but the letters and characters were as unintelligible to me as the handwriting upon the wall was to Belshazzar. When he began to read, it was at what I should call the end of the volume, reading from right to left.

The mode of instructing the children in reading, is by writing with a reed a few characters upon a smooth, white board, about the size of a ciphering slate. He then, with an audible voice, pronounces them, and calls upon the child to do the same. In this manner the child is taught their alphabet. He then writes out words; spelling them, and the children follow his example. From this he proceeds to write sentences, and teaches the children to read them. After they have progressed thus far, the whole of the children, under instruction, are furnished each with a board, and read together aloud, keeping very exact time. The teacher corrects them when in an error, and administers punishment when obstinate. These sentences they are taught to commit to memory, and to repeat without the assistance of the board.

Many of the sentences, although I could not well understand the language, were the same as I often heard repeated over in their religious ceremonies. From the antiquated appearance of the volume from which they were taken; from the same being used in worship, and from the peculiar solemnity of the teacher and the pupil. while repeating them, but little doubt can exist but that they were taken from the *Koran* in the original tongue. This is the universal method of teaching children, when they are taught at all, upon the desert, and at the large schools at Wadinoon.

Writing is taught by drawing upon the board a few single characters. The pen is made with a piece of flat reed, hollowed upon the inside to contain the ink, and sharpened to a single point. The child is taught to imitate the characters set as a copy. Children at twelve, who have been taught regularly, can read and write with considerable facility. When at rest, the hours of instruction are three hours very early in the morning, and three toward night. When upon a journey, the lesson given must be learned either before or after the day's journey, the teacher being extremely strict; although the children seem to consider their task as a pleasure rather than a burthen. This was the first instruction I ever saw given among the Arabs. During my slavery with the Lebdessebah, I never saw even a book, and never witnessed the least attempt among them to impart instruction. Nor did I while with the *Wiled D'leim*, ever see but one instructor besides this one in Meaarah's family.

My master, during the time we were stationary, frequently endeavoured to initiate me into the mysteries of tending camels. As I have mentioned before, I found it best to perform the common and ordinary duties of a slave with apparent cheerfulness and alacrity; but, as I did at the fish-place, I was determined to resist any attempt to make me a camel tender, or to impose upon me any steady duty in the performance of which I might raise my value in their estimation, as this would probably lengthen my slavery; and in the same proportion as I became useless to them, would be their desire to get rid of me, and increase the chances of my redemption. I however went out with my master *one* day, and he tried to instruct me how to assist Illa-Mecca in camel keeping. Although it was nothing but standing on elevated ground, keeping sight of the beasts, and driving them back when straying off, yet I convinced my master that I could not possibly learn the duty, and would not perform it. He did not, at this time attempt again to impose it upon me.

Chapter 15

A Long Journey

After the expiration of six days, we started upon a journey, and continued generally to travel, upon an average, forty miles a day. This we continued to do for eight days. It is impossible to describe the different courses we travelled, as they were constantly shifting; but the general course led us easterly into the interior. To describe that portion of the Zahara desert over which we passed would be but a repetition, of what was said when travelling with the *Wiled Lebdessebah*. For some distance the country would have gentle hills and shallow valleys, intermixed with sand and stones; and then it would present to you a plane, apparently without limits, terminated on every part by the horizon. We subsisted, during this time, upon camel's milk and water, added to a few snails found upon the passage.

We were frequently met by tents, and large droves of camels; and almost every passenger of respectable appearance paid attention to my master Meaarah and mistress Fatima. She received many visits, and was particularly attentive to her guests. She, and indeed all the females belonging to this family, were elegantly dressed in the Arab style; having a redundancy of the most beautiful shells suspended from their braided hair, which was always covered with a blue turban. Their blankets were of a superior kind.

Upon the eighth day of travelling, we came to an immense country of sand. At night a camel was slaughtered in the same manner as before described; some part of it was sliced thinly and dried, and lasted for two or three days. Our course was now shifted a little to the northward, still carrying us into the interior. After travelling for four days we came to a small valley or basin, into which considerable water had settled from a recent rain. Our tent was pitched upon the rising ground, overlooking it. A great number of tents were situated in the valley, some belonging to the *Wiled Lebdessebah*, and some to the *Wiled D'leim*, these two tribes, at this time, being at peace with each other. Among them was Porter's master, and Porter himself. He had regained his health, and, like me, entertained some hopes that we might escape from bondage. He asked me the season of the year, having entirely forgotten it. I told him it was the last of November.

In and about this valley were great flights of locusts. During the daytime, they are flying around very thick in the atmosphere, but the copious dews and chilly air, in the night season, render them unable to fly, and they settle down upon the bushes. It was the constant employ of the natives in the night season to gather these insects from the bushes, which they did in great quantities. My master's family, each with a small bag, went out the first night upon this employ, carrying a very large bag to bring home the fruits of their labour. My mistress Fatima, however, and the two little children remained in the tent. I declined this employ, and retired to rest under the large tent. The, next day, the family returned loaded with locusts, and judging from the quantity produced by the eye, there must have been as many as fifteen bushels. This may appear to be a large quantity to be gathered in so short a time; but it is hardly worth mentioning when compared with the loads of then gathered sometimes in the more fertile part of the country, over which they pass, leaving a track of desolation behind them.

But as they were the first, in any considerable quantity, that I had seen, and the first I had seen cooked and eaten, I mention it in this place; hoping hereafter to give my readers more particular information concerning these wonderful and destructive insects; which, from the days of Moses to this time, have been considered by Jews and Mahometans as the most severe judgment which heaven can inflict upon man. But whatever the Egyptians might have thought in ancient days, or the Moors and Arabs in those of modern date, the Arabs who are compelled to inhabit the desert of Zahara, so far from considering a flight of locusts as a judgment upon them for their transgressions, welcome their approach as the means, sometimes, of saving them from famishing with hunger. The whole that were brought to the tent at this time were cooked when alive, as indeed they always are, for a dead locust is never cooked. The manner of cooking is, by digging a deep hole in the ground, building a fire at the bottom, as before described, and filling it with wood.

After it is heated as hot as is possible, the coals and embers are taken out, and they prepare to fill the cavity with the locusts, confined in a large bag. A sufficient number of natives hold the bag perpendicularly over the hole, the mouth of it being near the surface of the ground. A number stand around the hole with sticks. The mouth of the bag is then opened, and it is shaken with great force, the locusts falling into the hot pit. and the surrounding natives throwing sand upon them to prevent them from flying off. The mouth of the hole is then covered with sand, and another fire built upon the top of it.

In this manner they cook all they have on hand, and dig a number of holes sufficient to accomplish it, each containing about five bushels. They remain in the hole until they become sufficiently cooled to take out by the hand. They are then picked out, and thrown upon tent-cloths, or blankets, and remain in the sun to dry, where they must be watched with the utmost care, to prevent the live locusts from devouring them, if a flight happen to be passing at the time. When they are perfectly dried, which is not done short of two or three days, they are slightly pounded and pressed into bags or skins, ready for transportation. To prepare them to eat, they are pulverized in mortars, and mixed with water sufficient to make a kind of dry pudding. They are, however, sometimes eaten singly without pulverizing, by breaking off the head, wings, and legs, and swallowing the remaining part. In whatever manner they are eaten, they are nourishing food. All the while we remained at this valley, the natives were employed in gathering and cooking locusts.

I cannot omit an incident at this valley, which came nigh to ending my slavery and my existence. I was commanded to sling a large water goat skin upon my back, and carry it to the tent. Upon letting it down when I arrived, my fatigue, and its great weight, occasioned it to fall and burst open. My master, with savage ferocity, ran toward me with an uplifted Arab axe, and, aiming at my head, would, without the least doubt, have severed it from my body, had not my mistress Fatima, leaped between him and me, and warded off the intended blow. From this time my master, who had before shewn some tokens of feeling, began to exercise toward me a systematic cruelty.

We remained at this valley until the water in it was dried up, and then made preparations for departure. I often saw Porter, while there, and left him there when I was taken off. We travelled to the northwest from day to day. I began to grow weak, and my flesh wasted away. I had nothing to eat but fresh locusts, there being no salt with the family. The blanket around my middle, hanging down as low as my knees, wore the flesh entirely off from the cords of my legs, leaving them entirely bare. This was occasioned by constant travelling. After sleeping upon the sand, a few hours, and rising upon my legs, the blood gushed out of my excoriated and dried flesh. My master viewed this with the indifference of a savage, when witnessing the contortions of his victim.

After travelling with great rapidity for ten days in this manner, we arrived upon the coast, after passing the dried bed of a considerable river. This, from a careful examination of the best charts, I feel confident was the River St. Cyprian, near which we first landed in the boat. What confirmed this opinion was, the coast, in its general appearance, was very similar to that upon which we landed.

The time of our arrival there must have been about the 10th of December. Here our tent was pitched for the first time, since we left *the valley of locusts*. We remained here but one night, having obtained a supply of water. We then travelled two days, in a northeast direction, and pitched our teats. The country was of the same general description, as the other parts of the desert. We remained here six days. The *teacher*, during the whole time I had been a slave to the cruel *Meaarah*, assiduously continued his instruction, and maintained his dignity with the whole family.

Even my master stood in awe before him. He often, in the most urgent manner, pressed upon me the necessity of renouncing the heresy of *Christianity*, and becoming a good *Mussulman*. He manifested the most sovereign contempt for the Christian religion, and often denounced me as a *kellup en-sahrau*. He expressed the utmost horror at the idea of eating pork; considering a hog as possessed of the devil, and those who eat it, as possessed of him also. He laid every inducement before me to espouse his faith; promising me the possession of wealth, and power, and wives upon earth, and eternal felicity and sensual enjoyment in paradise with the divine prophet *Mahommed*.

While here, I saw, for the first time, an Arab blacksmith. He has his anvil carried upon the camel. It is about four inches in diameter upon the top, tapering down to a point. This he puts into a piece of a block, the largest he can find upon the deserts, where nothing but small timber grows. His fire is built in a shallow hole, dug in the ground, into which he puts his coal. His bellows is made of a goatskin, with a handle fixed to the top of it. As he pulls the handle up, the air enters it; as he forces it down, the air is pressed out at the point of it into the coals, which blows them up to a fire. He then puts in his iron, which is soon heated. He then, with a clumsy sort of hammer, draws out the piece of iron in his hand, to any shape which is necessary. With this, he makes irons for a saddle, an axe, or any other iron tool which the Arabs wish to make use of; the whole being made in the most bungling manner. In this way. he makes the needles with which the natives sew their tent cloths together, and do all the necessary sewing in the family, unless, by accident, they can procure needles better manufactured. They make their coal by digging a hole in the ground, and throwing into it the largest wood they can find. This is burned into charcoal.

The locust food was nearly exhausted. The water grew short, and the camels gave but little milk; and I hardly had a sufficiency of sustenance to support life. My debility and weakness was such, as almost to deprive me of the power of walking about. Upon the last day my master remained at this place, I wandered slowly off to a neighbouring tent, where I was supplied with some water. The owner of the tent was an old and rich Arab, having a tent abundantly furnished. He shewed me pieces of money of silver and gold, and asked me my opinion of their value. Among them were *doubloons*. I told him one *doubloon* was worth sixteen of the dollars which he shewed me. He told me they were taken out of a *sfenah* (a vessel) upon the coast. As some of the money was in *doubloons*, and as we had no such money aboard the *Commerce*, I concluded some other American or European vessel might have been lately wrecked upon the coast.

Upon the next morning our tents were struck, and preparations were made for a journey. I knew not how I could endure it; but I was compelled to travel, and run the risk of dying with fatigue, or remain and perish with hunger. We travelled in an eastern direction; and upon the first day's journey we passed a small deep valley, situated upon our right. The bottom of it was filled with water; but as my master told me it was salt, I did not attempt to drink it. Upon the borders of the basin that contained the water, was lying, in great quantities, very clear and white salt. It excited my astonishment, as we were, at least, one hundred miles from the sea. If a conjecture might be ventured, there must have been a subterranean passage from the sea to this valley; and as the water, which sometimes filled it, dried away, it was converted into salt.

I have been cautious, thus far, in making conjectures of my own, or repeating the stories of others;—and shall continue to exercise that caution, determining to relate nothing but what has evidence sufficient to induce a belief in its probability, if not in its certainty. In the evening of the first day's journey, Meaarah slaughtered a camel. My weakness increased; and travelling rapidly and sleeping in the open air without any covering, occasioned the most extreme distress. From recollecting the number of days we were upon different journeys, and also the number upon which we rested, this must have been the latter part of December, the cold having increased to a considerable degree. The next day we bore more to the northward, travelling moderately, until late in the evening. When we stopped, fuel was necessary to cook with, but no dry bushes could be readily found. After seeking some time for them, I returned to the tent, destitute of them, and almost wholly exhausted with fatigue. Meaarah came at me furiously with a knife, pointing it toward my throat. I fled out again and procured a few dry sticks. was compelled again to sleep in the cold air without the least shelter or covering. Upon the next day, I travelled till about noon, and dropped down upon the ground, and was left alone, gazed round, but from dimness and dizziness, could see neither tent, camel, nor human being. I attempted to walk, but was wholly unable to move.

My master at length came and led me to the tent, which was pitched. Some warm milk was given to me, into which was put a considerable quantity of dried weed, which the natives generally carry about with them; although it may be gathered in almost every part of the desert. It gave to the milk a sharp bitter taste, and relieved me from the costiveness with which I had been much troubled from eating hard boiled blood, and baked locusts. At night I was permitted to have a small piece of tent-cloth for a covering. The herb given to me operated as a cathartic. The next day I was placed upon a camel, with a rolled tent cloth upon one side, and a watering tub upon the other, to keep me from falling off. In this manner I continued to travel with the family seven days, during which time I was not allowed to eat meat of any kind, but was supplied with milk warm from the camel.

As there was a good supply of camel's meat, I conclude, the reason why it was refused to me was on account of my health, being already unfit for market from the leanness of my body. I, however, found an opportunity to roast a small piece of raw hide rope, and eat it. For these seven days we travelled a southeast course; at the end of which we came to a low piece of marshy ground, which had upon it bushes and staddles of considerable size, and also standing water. The tents were pitched, and in the vicinity were situated about forty other tents.

CHAPTER 16

An Expected Battle

January, 1816.—It was now from my best calculation, the first week in January. The tents remained stationary for four days, upon the first of which, a camel was slain; with the fat part of which Meaarah procured a small skin full of dates, the first I had seen. These the Arabs call *T'murr*. They are a sweet nourishing food, and the few allowed me tasted deliciously. I was now literally reduced to a skeleton. The irritation of the blanket around my middle, and sleeping upon sand and hard ground, had worn the skin entirely off my hip-bones, leaving them visible; indeed, this was the case with all the prominent bones in my body. I was completely dried up; and the skin was contracted and drawn tight around my bones. Although I had seen many human beings reduced to bones and sinews before, I certainly never saw one so poor as I was myself. I was in no danger of inflammatory diseases, as there was nothing about me to be inflamed, unless a conflagration should have been made of my dried carcass; and this I was in danger of from the mode of practice adopted by the *Ishmaelitish faculty*.

They heated the blade of a long tent-knife—stripped me bare—held me in a perpendicular posture—and, with the edge of the hot knife began to strike gently upon my shin-bones, and continued to chop the whole of the front part of my frame. I felt not the least pain from this operation; indeed I was no more a subject of pain than an actual skeleton in the office of a surgeon. They repeated this operation daily, and began to afford me a little meat. In the course of three or four days, I became able to move slowly about—the blood began to circulate, and strength began to return. This was the mode of practice, and this was the result of it. Whether it was *Galvanism* or *Perkinism*, I leave to the Italian and American faculty to determine.

At the end of four days, the tents were struck, and a journey commenced toward the northward. Upon the first day, we passed a hill upon our right, upon the shelving rocks of which, was trickling down salt water, leaving particles of salt upon the rocks. We were descending into a very long and deep valley, where the tents were pitched as we halted. The rainy season had commenced; and the wandering Arabs, of various tribes, were bending to the northward and eastward, in numerous parties. The valley looked like a city of tents; there being, at least, three hundred situated in it.

Toward night, Meaarah told me I should see Joe; and I soon after, once more, beheld my shipmate in misfortune. Porter had, a few days before, been sold to a trading Arab, and said he had then hopes of going to Swearah, (Mogadore) where his ransom would be certain. He said, he, a few days before, had seen Hogan and Dick; that they had also been sold to a trading Arab—that Dick was worn out and left, probably to perish, and that Hogan and his master went off in a southeast direction. This large valley ran nearly east and west, about half a mile in width; bounded upon each side by high ranges of hills. We continued in it for six days, moving moderately through it to the east, in company with two or three hundred tents. Among these were a number of trading Arabs, from Lower Suse, having blankets, tobacco, dates, powder, blue cottons, &c. One came to my master's tents, and examined me with a view of purchasing; but said I was too poor—that I should not live to reach Swearah.

I begged of him to buy me; but he declined. Meaarah told me to walk about and be active, or I never should be sold. I would gladly had I been able, have done this, or anything else to induce a sale. At the end of six days, we reached the east end of this wonderful valley, which then branched into two smaller ones. It was altogether the most fertile part of Africa that I had yet seen. It had, for the whole length, green grass, and bushes in abundance. Long hills of rocks and sand limited it upon each side. As I was passing through it, I thought it the most striking prospect I had ever seen. There must have been travelling through it, and at no great distance from our tent, as many as twelve hundred natives. As we passed along, the natives were constantly chanting a kind of harmonious song, cheering up the loaded camels like the perpetual jingling of bells. The camels had a supply of food from the grass and the bushes; and the natives also were furnished with their meat and their milk. The little streamlets from the hills supplied them with water.

The different families and parties interchanged civilities peculiar to themselves. They had a fruition of present enjoyments, and expectations of a future supply. They worshipped, in large parties, four times a day. Their tents were pitched with cheerfulness at night, and with cheerfulness were struck in the morning. I could not see how this life could afford more happiness than *they* apparently enjoyed. But *I* was a slave!! subject to their capricious whims, and barbarous cruelty. I was a *kellup en-sahrau*—and to slay me, might be thought as offering an acceptable sacrifice to *Mahommed*. Porter was also in the party. He and I were the only beings present, that ever enjoyed the blessings and freedom of civilization. Every appearance evinced the fact that this valley, in the midst of the rainy season, is filled to a considerable height with water.

After leaving this extraordinary valley, or rather ravine, we continued to travel in an eastern course for four days, through a level and sandy country, passing a small stream of fresh water, with which the skins were filled. I gained strength daily, and began to do the service of a slave, although yet very feeble. Upon the fourth day, I was sold to a trading Arab. Meaarah took me off to a neighbouring tent, near which I saw a quantity of goods. One of the traders asked me of what nation I was? I answered, as before instructed by Meaarah, *Fransah*. After a little conversation, I was delivered to him as a slave. I understood the price for me was five camels and two blankets.

My third masters name was Hamet Webber, of the tribe of *Wiled El Kabla*, a trading Arab. His articles of traffic were blankets, tobacco, and powder. Hamet had a trading Arab as a partner; and they and I constituted the family. They had here no tent, but received their food, once a day, from an adjoining one. They were not permitted to lodge in the tent. Indeed, it was an universal custom among all the tribes, I had yet seen, never to admit any one to lodge in a tent, but members of the family. This custom arises from the suspicion they entertain toward each other; thieving being a vice to which they are *all* addicted. I was here supplied with a species of food I had never before seen. It was a thick boiled pudding, called *Laish*, furnished each night at about 11 o'clock.

The next day I went off with Hamet, and his partner, who had two camels, upon which the goods were loaded. We travelled but a short distance; the goods were unloaded, and the camels, under my care, were put out to feed. I fell in with Porter, who was also keeping the camels of his master. During the next day, Hamet was engaged in gathering in the camels, for which he had bartered away his goods.

The third day of my slavery with my new master, we started upon a journey with twenty-five camels, and one black slave, travelling to the eastward. Three other natives, with fifteen camels, joined us, making five Arabs two slaves, and fifty camels. At night a camel was killed and cooked. From the next morning, for eight days, we travelled in an easterly course, at about twenty miles a day.

Upon the journey. we lived as well as men could upon camel's meat and milk. Hamet was very kind to me, supplied me with some additional clothing, and allowed me a sufficiency of food. My health improved and my flesh increased. At the end of the eight days, we halted; and Hamet went forward in pursuit of his tent, not having seen one since we started. We remained here two days: at the end of which orders were sent to change our course to the northward. At the end of the first day's travel, we reached the tents belonging to the tribe of the *Wiled El Kabla*. There had been slight falls of rain for the ten days past. This tribe, in every respect, was the most wealthy I had yet seen. They had great numbers of camels, some goats, sheep and horses; besides considerable quantities of African and European merchandise. The European goods must have been taken from the English brig *Surprise*, which I learned, upon arriving at Wadinoon, was wrecked to the southward of that place, about the 1st of January, 1816.

We remained at this place. and in the vicinity of it, for thirty days. My master was generally employed in trading among the natives, situated in the adjoining country. There were great numbers of tents, and the country was well calculated for keeping camels. They gave milk in abundance, and I had a full supply. It was the season when the camels foal their young, and my chief employ was to attend them. Being at rest, and well supplied with *lillabent*, (milk) I regained my flesh rapidly. The tents of the tribe to which I belonged were situated near the base of a considerable hill, which I often ascended to pick a sort of green vegetable, totally different from any plant which I had ever seen. It grew out of the earth from three inches to a foot high in a square shape, without the least leaf attached to it. It was always green, and had a short beard or roughness upon its four corners. It had a very palatable acid in its taste, and the natives had the greatest fondness for it.

The mode of worship in this tribe, was precisely the same as that among the *Wiled Lebdessebah*, and *Wiled D'leim*; and always performed with great devotion, four times each day. I was by this tribe, as by the two others, urged most vehemently to espouse the *Mahommedan* faith; but, as I always had before, I positively refused a compliance, and do not know that I suffered any additional cruelty from this refusal. The tribe of *Wiled El Kabla* were much better armed, than either of the others to which I had belonged; having many valuable double-barrelled muskets, and many single-barrelled Moorish muskets. They were more warlike as a *tribe*, and less cruel as *individuals*, than any Arabs I had seen.

After remaining at this place a number of days, great alarm and consternation was excited, in this tribe, by the approach, from the southeast, of a large armed caravan. Our camels were all upon the opposite side of the hill, feeding, and it was supposed that this armed body of men were coming with a view of capturing them. An universal alarm was immediately spread throughout the whole encampment of tents, stretching five or six miles upon the west side of the hill. There must have been as many as six hundred tents, and three thousand natives. They had no warlike instrument with which they could sound an alarm; but this was well supplied by the hooting and screaming of the female Arabs. The echo of this universal hooting, over the hills, was to me, the most wonderful operation of sound. The Arab men, in the meantime, were sounding dreadful "notes of preparation." The muskets, spears, scimitars, knives, and clubs, were all in readiness. They rushed, without the least order or command, to the top of the hill, ascending rocks to get a sight of the enemy, or concealing themselves behind them for safety.

I supposed, and even hoped, I should see an engagement in which these Ishmaelites, who prey upon all the rest of the world, would make havoc of each other: and I ascended the hill. I was disappointed; for immediately the universal shout of *Labez* (all's well) echoed along the hills. Some of our tribe went down to the caravan, and I soon witnessed tokens of peace. Upon returning to the tents, I found the female jaws as nearly closed as nature would permit them to be, and tranquillity was restored. This tribe is remarkable for its skill in gunnery. Shooting was a common, and indeed the only amusement among the male Arabs. To manifest their skill, they place a small stone upon the top of a bush. They stand about eight or ten rods from the mark, and fire at arm's length. They certainly exceed Americans in this exercise. I very often saw them, at the first shot, and at a number in succession, knock off a stone with a single ball. I was sometimes a spectator; and the Arabs undoubtedly concluded that as I was a Christian, I was totally ignorant of firing.

As I was one day witnessing their astonishing skill, Hamet, and many others, insisted upon my making a shot. They permitted me to select my musket, thinking I could not distinguish between one that was *bono* or *foonta*. Universal attention was paid; and *William Tell* was not more applauded for taking an apple from the head of his son, than I was for fetching the stone from the bush. *Bono Robbinis! Bono Robbinis!* resounded through the valley, and I immediately became great. Hamet slapped me on the shoulder, in token of approbation, and thought he had done well in buying me.

The dress of this tribe, although in the great article of the long blanket, put on as before desribed, it is similar to the others; yet, they almost all wear a blue or white frock-shirt, falling below the knees. They wear the usual belts, and most of them slippers, and some of them fine rich turbans of white cloth. The female blankets are coloured red at the ends, with a thick fringe. They wear a belt around the waist, fastening one end of the blanket, over which the other end is thrown after passing over the shoulders, hanging upon one side, full at the bottom, and plaited at the waist. Upon that part of the blanket which covers the breast, they wear large silver breast-plates, upon which are engraved various figures and hieroglyphics, always kept exceedingly bright.

In their ears, they wear silver hoops, some of which are as large as the top of a coffee-cup. Upon their arms, they also wear silver rings, some going on whole over the hand, and some fastened together with clasps. Upon their hair, wrists, and ankles, they have a redundancy of beautiful shells. Some of the young females have the most perfect symmetry in their forms, and when full dressed, bounding over the planes, or riding upon a camel, also ornamented with red breast-girths, and red strips of cloth, hanging from the elevated saddle, they might attract the eye, even of an American. With a weed produced upon the deserts the females paint their nails, their hands, and faces a reddish colour, in various figures. With black lead they draw a circle round their eyes.

The teachers in this tribe are numerous; the mode of instruction the same as that practised with the *Wiled D'leim*. The children, belonging to this tribe, are almost all of them educated. Like the teachers in other tribes, they exercise great authority over the parents and children; and confirmed my belief, that they are of the Mahommedan priesthood. They also, in this tribe, take the lead in their mode of worship.

Chapter 17

Arrival at Wadinoon

From the best calculation I could make from the number of days we had travelled, and the time we were stationary, it had become about the 1st of March, 1816. Preparations were made by Hamet for a journey. He started with two camels, having before disposed of all his merchandise. He however had with him a number of bags for grain and goods, never having carried a tent while I was with him. One of his neighbours accompanied us. Hamet and I generally rode one camel and he another. Our course was, for a few miles, to the north, when we came up with a large collection of tents that were pitched. The Arabs were preparing to form a caravan. They consist of different numbers of natives and camels. Some have fifty men and five hundred beasts, and they sometimes amount to five hundred men, and two thousand camels.

The armed Arabs take the command of the whole, and travel or rest at pleasure. They generally go forward forming the van, although some of them are mixed with the unarmed ones, giving orders concerning the camels, the travellers, and the goods that are with them. They always travel in compact order. An Arab chief, armed for a caravan, presents to the eye of the beholder, a figure of the greatest boldness. He is six feet high. A long, black, bushy beard hangs from his chin to his breast. He has a fierce, black eye, sunk deep into his head, with thick, black eye-brows projecting over them.—His long white blanket is drawn close around his body, leaving his legs bare from the knee. Over this are cast, his red belts, crossing at the breast and at the back. To one, is suspended a large transparent powder-horn. decorated with bands of shining brass; to, the other, a leathern pouch, containing balls, flints, and a screwdriver. To the other belt, is fastened the scabbard, containing a long, broad, and burnished cutlass or scimitar.

Around his waist is buckled a broad, red, morocco belt, of many thicknesses, confining the belts, that support the cutlass and the horn. His head is generally naked, excepting a dress of black, bushy hair, although sometimes covered with a turban. His Moorish musket is always in his hand. Thus aimed, he is ready, at any moment, to encounter a foe. A caravan is formed from various tribes, and from men inhabiting different parts of the continent of Africa. When individuals wish to travel to any particular place, and can find a caravan bound to it, they join it; and agree to submit to the regulations of it. and are entitled to all the protection it can afford. In this way, they are safe, unless they should be overcome by a more powerful caravan. At this place, are formed many of the great caravans that travel, in various directions, across the desert. I learned, from the natives, that many large caravans go from this place to Soudan, and smaller ones to Wadinoon.

Upon leaving this place, we travelled west, inclining northerly, and in the course of the day. came to a range of black mountains, stretching to the southwest as far as the eye could discern; extending also a great distance to the northeast. These mountains we passed, sometimes in valleys intersecting them, and sometimes we ascended to their summits. Between these mountains we came to small patches of cultivated land, upon which was growing a species of barley, which will hereafter be described. This was the first cultivated land I had seen in Africa, although I had, seemingly, travelled in every point in the compass. Without stopping to inquire what Ishmaelite it belonged to, our party, consisting now of eight persons, deliberately cut and roasted a sufficient quantity for present refreshment.

Continuing on our journey, until sunset, we reached a long range of tents, containing two hundred, situated upon the side of a hill, where we tarried through the night. The next day we found that we had came to a part of the tribe of *Wiled Abboussebah*. I learned, that this was the original tribe of the *El Kabla*, from which the latter was formed into a new one. The number of camels, in the neighbourhood of the tents, was immense. Judging from droves which I had before seen, the numbers of which I knew, there certainly must have been five thousand. While I was here, I saw great consternation excited at the approach of a small party of Arabs, supposed to be a clan in pursuit of camels. They were driven rapidly together to be guarded. We started early in the morning, and travelled through a bushy and grassy country.

At about noon, we came to a piece of ground having thin low grass. We were travelling very moderately upon a walk, when my attention was attracted by a large shining black snake. He was coiled round regularly like a cable; his head rising from the centre about four inches high. Upon coming very near to the serpent, he directed his eyes towards me, and flattened his head. I told Hamet what I saw, and he immediately alarmed me, telling me to sheer off in an instant; which I did, without waiting to give him a farther examination, which I was about to do.

From what I soon learned, I found that by acquiring a minute knowledge of this venomous reptile, I should certainly have lost my life. I cannot tell its length, from the situation it was in, no otherwise than by saying that it was about the size of a chair pummel, and coiled, as it was, it made a circle about as large as the top of a half bushel. At eight or ten miles distance, we saw another of the same size and appearance, but I was no ways disposed to add to the little knowledge I had previously obtained of African serpents. At night we put up amidst a great number of tents, situated near a small stream of water. The next day we discovered a small caravan coming from the southeast toward the tents where we lodged. It had about two hundred and fifty camels, and fifteen armed Arabs, mounted upon fleet Arabian horses. Our party joined it; and as it passed the tents, the owners of them assailed the caravan, cutting from the camels the meat, bowls, and other articles loaded upon them. The armed Arabs of our caravan, with drawn scimitars, soon dispersed them.

I was mounted upon a good camel, and put him into full speed; not wishing to be stolen from my worthy master Hamet. The whole caravan bounded over the plane with amazing velocity, the savages firing upon us from the tents, till we were out of sight. No lives were lost in our party; but without doubt, the Mahometans at the tents had to perform the funeral service over the bodies of some of their companions. We travelled through the day, upon the dry bed of a river twenty or thirty rods wide. Such dried beds are frequently found in this part of the Zahara Desert, made probably by the heavy rains, and the torrents descending from hills which are always near them. These beds are always chosen for a passage, as they are entirely smooth, and furnish considerable grass. Our course was to the northwest.

At night, the whole caravan stopped near a field of grain; and, as before mentioned, without the least hesitation, the human beings fed all night upon that, and the beasts upon the grass. We here found a pond of stagnant water, which furnished us with beverage for our entertainment. The next day, highly refreshed, we rose with the rising sun, and started with high animation upon our journey. My life now became happiness itself, in comparison with the misery I had long endured. Hamet was uniformly kind. I had become familiarized with the modes of an Arab's life; and were it not from the consideration that I was a slave, I should have enjoyed happiness in reality.

At about 10 o'clock, a. m. we came to the bed of a river at least half a mile wide, having a small stream upon one shore of it. In passing the water, our camels waded mid-sides high; and in going over the rest of the bed, they sunk in the moist clay-ground, slipping at almost every step, having no hard hoofs to make a hold. This was the rainy season in this part of the continent of Africa. It sets in at different seasons, in different portions of it. While *Abyssinia* is almost inundated, *Soudan* will endure a most dreadful *drought*, and the country adjoining *Wadinoon* will enjoy the luxuriance of the *growing season*.

After passing this stream, we ascended a considerable hill, and came into a country where description must surrender its power. All that can be said is, it was a world made up of sand-hills and mountains, with narrow zigzag passages through, and over them. Travelling was excessively fatiguing to the poor loaded camels, and to their owners. It was still harder for the horses, ridden by the armed Arabs. We accomplished the passage by sunset, and found a few tents, but lodged, as a caravan always does, in the open air. Through the next day, we travelled over a country, consisting of small hills and planes, barren sands, and cultivated grounds alternately intermixed. It rained gently all the while. We saw a beautiful *gazelle*, which an Arab attempted to shoot, but the sprightly animal defied even the musket, by his agility, and escaped.

Toward night the caravan was broken up; the natives and camels composing it having reached the place of their destination. This night Hamet and I were welcomed to the tent of one of his connections, as I concluded, because, as before remarked, Arabs will permit none but family connections to lodge in their tents. I remained at this tent three days. Hamet, early in the first day, told me that he was going to *Sweahrah*. I had been too often deceived to believe it; and my suspicions proved to be true when, at the end of three days, he returned with Bel Cossim Abdallah, from Wadinoon. While here I found I was with the tribe of the *Wiled Adrialla*, and by them was treated with the greatest kindness; probably from the circumstance of belonging to Hamet, a merchant tribe of *El Kabla*, which, as before mentioned is a branch of the powerful and wealthy tribe of the *Wiled Aboussebah*.

I soon found that I was to be separated from Hamet; whose uncommon goodness for an Arab, made me esteem him. He and Bel Cossim came to the tent where I was situated, and began to talk about me. Hamet asked me, in the hearing of Bel Cossim, "*Ash soo-mook B'led cum?*" (whats the name of your country?) I answered, supposing that he, like the rest of the Arabs, had no idea of *America*, "*Fransah.*"

He smiled, and said, "*Arrah en tar murkan, Fransah en tar Americane.*" He gave me to understand, that he had learned I was an American, a day or two before at Wadinoon. It was a frequent inquiry made about me, whether I belonged to the vessel that had so much money in it, meaning the *Commerce*. They always insisted upon it, that great quantities were buried at Cape Bajador where she was wrecked. I always denied it, fearing I should be sent there to dig for it, which would remove me farther from the hopes of being redeemed. The next day after the return of Hamet from Wadinoon, I was taken off by my new master Bel Cossim.

Our course from this place to Wadinoon was about northwest. Toward night, we stopped at a tent, where we remained until the morning. I here saw a wounded Arab who had a musket ball shot deep into the middle of the thigh. Upon seeing me, they supposed I was a doctor, as they have many foreigners who reside upon the coast, as practitioners in surgery and medicine. Bel Cossim and others urged me to attempt to extract the ball, offering me a great reward to effect it. I scorned the idea of becoming a quack, even to deceive an Arab, and declined to *operate*. No patient ever needed assistance more to relieve him from the wound a ball had made, and from the more terrible gashes and incisions made into the top of the thigh in the bone, by the harsh knives of the Arabs. In the evening, I saw the Spaniard, I have before mentioned, who attempted to escape, and had some conversation with him in the Arab language, in which I could now *converse* tolerably well, however difficult it is to *write* it with accuracy, after a long acquaintance with it.

We travelled moderately on foot for three days, passing from one cluster of tents to another, until we reached the celebrated town of Wadinoon. Upon the passage, Bel Cossim purchased a small copper kettle, and a quantity of tow-cloth, which I had to carry. The name of the country through which we passed, was called *B'led-Mouessa Ali*, and the natives call themselves *Misse-le-mene*. We passed, upon the last day, a very small village situated upon an elevated piece of ground, from which we had a view of Wadinoon. This place is called *Wahroon*.

I have mentioned the method I adopted to keep my reckoning of time, *i. e.* by the string, in which I daily tied a knot until I disused it: by remembering the number of days we were upon the numerous journeys, and the number of days we rested.

From this method of calculation, for six months, I made the day of my arrival at Wadinoon the 12th of March. But I there found, upon ascertaining the actual time of the year, that I had lost four days, the day of my arrival being the 16th day of March, 1816. The day after my arrival was a market-day, which is held weekly. I found this to be upon the *Christian Sabbath*; and that the *Mahommedan Sabbath* was upon Friday, according to our calendar.

The family of Bel Cossim consisted of his wife, who was his third one, by whom he had two sons and a daughter. His first wife left a son and a daughter; his second wife a daughter. His oldest son, Hamada, was married, and lived in the same house with him, being himself an aged man. A married daughter lived in an adjoining one. He had five black slaves. He had other wives living in tents whom he occasionally visited.

CHAPTER 18

Cruelty of Bel Cossim

I now became a settled resident in what may be called the capital of the northern desert of Zahara. To my inexpressible satisfaction, I found Porter a resident here also. He had become the slave of a wealthy merchant, and was what might be called a well dressed man anywhere. He lived as well as could be wished, and it may be said, enjoyed "leisure with dignity." He informed me that he had written to Mogadore, and that Abdullah Hamet, his master, had received a letter concerning him—that he was in daily expectation of receiving one himself, and considered his ransom as certain, and that he had heard of the arrival of Capt. Riley at Gibraltar. A few days previous to my arrival here, the crew of the British brig *Surprise* left this place, and were in the keeping of *Sidi Hesham*, of Suse, for the purpose of being ransomed.

The town of *Wadinoon* is situated upon the western coast of the continent of Africa, about thirty miles from the sea, and upon the northern border of the Great Desert of Zahara, it is in that part of the continent called *Suse*, sometimes distinguished by *Upper* and *Lower Suse*. It is in 28° 15 minutes N. Latitude, and 11° W. Longitude. A range of mountains, of considerable height, lies along between that and the sea, upon the north, and a similar range upon the south, leaving between them a valley of about six miles in width. This valley diminishes in width toward the east, and is ended by the termination of the *Atlas Mountains*. Upon a rising piece of ground near the middle of this valley is built the town of Wadinoon. From this place may be seen the village of Wahroon, to the west, at seven miles distance; another village to the southeast, at twelve miles distance; and *Akkadia* to the northeast, at fifteen miles distance

From the mountain, upon the north, issues a small stream from a boiling spring, running into the town, and furnishing water for the whole of it. It is the finest water imaginable. The whole of it is absorbed in the place for necessary purposes, and watering the gardens. The other villages also have small streams to afford them water. The number of houses included within the town of Wadinoon, while I resided there, which was eleven months, reckoning two new ones, built while I was there, is forty-five. Some of these, however, being large, contain a number of distinct dwellings for different families. The number of families, statedly residing here, was between ninety-five and an hundred, almost every one of which, during my residence, I had some acquaintance with, from the service I had to perform for my master Bel Cossim, who was a trader and also a farmer. Families here will average five individuals each, exclusive of slaves; the slaves in the town, amounting to an hundred and fifty of African blacks. The only Christian slave at the time I arrived was Porter, and I made the second. Of the black slaves, the *Sheick*, or governor of the place, was possessed of twenty.

The cattle in this place were horses, (*l'hile*) a few cows, (*l'bugrau*) asses, (*hermah*) mules, (*bugalah*) sheep, (*kipps*) and goats, (*launims*.) Camels are seldom kept within the town, unless it be a few *Naigs* to furnish milk, when the cows become dry. The residents in the town, many of them, possess large droves at keeping in different parts of the adjoining country. Bel Cossim had several hundreds. They have fowls similar to our dung-hill fowls.

The inhabitants are generally descendants of the tribe of *Wiled Aboussebah*; although with them, are intermixed many of different tribes. Being much better educated than the wandering Arabs, they are much more refined in their manners than they are, although many of them manifest the ferocious nature, and vindictive spirit, common to all the descendants of Ishmael.

The mode of dressing is similar to that of the Arabs of the desert; although very much exceeding theirs, in the quality of the cloth. In addition to the dress of a wanderer, they have an outward garment, covering the whole body from the top of the head to the knee. It is woven whole of fine camel's hair and wool, is remarkably thick, and will shed rain for a very long time. These are not manufactured there, but are obtained from the trading Moors. When on, they look like a riding-hood; the head-piece of which is ornamented at the top with a tassel. They are of various colours, some of them having a very rich appearance; and those that are black have a large oval piece of orange coloured cloth, woven into the back, toward the bottom. The female dress differs but little from that before described, only in richness of quality. Some of the silk turbans are really elegant; having a broad piece of rich silk hanging from them to the hip. They invariably conceal their faces when walking in public.

The gardens are chiefly situated in the borders of the village. They are fenced in by a wall, composed of mud. upon the top of which are placed thorn-bushes, secured to it by laying large stones upon the stocks, leaving the bows to project over the outer edge of the wall to keep out intruders; stealing being a vice as prevalent here, as upon the desert. These gardens are cultivated with the greatest attention, and produce a great variety of vegetables.

The ingenuity of laying out gardens here must excite the admiration of every beholder. Let the surface of the ground be what it may, the beds, in which the vegetables are to be planted, are always made an exact water-level. They each have a ridge of earth upon the outer edge, ten inches high, which remains through the season. Each garden has a sluice-way, through which the water is conducted into the alleys. From the alleys, the water is conducted into the beds, through an aperture in the ridge, which is closed as soon as the bed is filled, leaving the water to soak into the ground. In this way, they go on, filling one bed after another in the garden, however numerous they may be.

Every garden in the place is watered in this manner. The water is supplied from the spring in the mountain, before mentioned. As it descends toward the town, it is drawn off in different directions for the accommodation of the people. Three reservoirs have been made by digging large basins in the ground, and bordering them with a wall composed of mud and stones. These being situated in different parts of the town, furnish a sufficiency for all the gardens. These reservoirs are owned by a number of proprietors, each having the privilege of drawing off the water, a number of days proportionate to the size of his garden.

The vegetables produced in these gardens are the following:—The Arabic names are *spelled* as *pronounced* at Wadinoon.

Arabic.	English.
Bishnall-suffarah,	Yellow-corn.
Bishnall-hamerah,	Red or Guinea-corn.
Liffett,	Turnips.
Keizah,	Carrots.

Bessal,	Onions.
C'shash,	Pumpkins, squash, and gourds.
Lyroom,	Cabbage,
Dillaa,	Watermelons.
Fijfil,	Peppers.
Tobac,	Tobacco.
T'murr,	Dates.
Zurrah,	Barley.
Carmoose,	Figs.
Arromann,	Pomegranates.
Tafferrez,	Pears.
Tack-nerrite,	Prickly-Pears.
Nornipps,	Grapes.

Henneh is a small leaf taken from a shrub, and dried, of which a powder is made, by mixing which with water a beautiful colouring is made for the hair, This is an article of great traffic. These different kinds of vegetables, in appearance and in taste, are very similar to those of the same species produced in New-England. Barley and wheat are raised in fields as well as in gardens; the reason why the Arabs sow *any* in gardens is, the fear that the fields will dried up where they cannot water them as they do in gardens. Wheat is raised but in small quantities.

At the time of my arrival at Wadinoon, the barley was ripe for harvesting. I was immediately put upon instruction to learn the art of reaping; but shewed as much ignorance and obstinacy in that art, in this place, as I did in that of fishing near Cape Mirik, and lending camels with Mearah. On the second day, I loitered around the fields, not knowing where the black slaves were at work. Bel Cossim ransacked the town to find me in vain, but his son Hamada found me. Bel Cossim approached me in a rage, struck me with his fists a number of blows, and then threw a heavy stone, which hit me upon the side, the effects of which I severely felt for two months. I longed for revenge in vain. Had it taken place upon the deck of a vessel, I should soon have obtained ample satisfaction.

I found resistance was in vain, and finally submitted to perform easy tasks. This ultimately proved a benefit, rather than an injury; for while other Christian slaves were wearing away life in listless indolence, in the houses of their masters, pondering upon their fate, I was constantly traversing the town and the adjoining country; in a degree forgetting my miseries, and daily acquiring knowledge of the place, and the manners, customs, and habits of the people. I found amusement and instruction, in the midst of my services. The barley harvest was not all gotten in until the first of June, one field becoming ripe after another, having been sowed at different times. This barley more nearly resembled oats, than barley, the hull adhering to it.

At one time, I was reaping with thirty Arabs, who gave my master, what is called a *spell* in N. England, and a *tuezar* at Wadinoon. We partook of our dinner, (*loader*) consisting of *Keskoosoo* and *El ham* in the field, having water from a spring. The sickles are of Moorish manufacture, not dissimilar to ours. The grain grows two feet and an half high, and very thick. As they reap it each handful is bound into a sheaf, and it is very soon stacked in the field. When the whole field is reaped and stacked, the grain is transported upon the backs of camels and mules to the common threshing ground near the town, which is entirely hard, and generally composed of smooth rocks. The grain is beaten out with horses, asses, and mules. By this operation, the straw and berry is all beaten together, leaving the straw as fine as that which is cut with a machine. The grain is separated from the chaff and fine straw. by throwing it up into the wind with a wooden fork of three flat tines; this being continued until the berry is entirely cleaned from everything.

With a good wind, a man in this manner will clean fifty bushels in a day. The grain is dried in earthen pots by fire, to prepare it for grinding. Every family grinds a portion of barley every day. This is done between two stones, the under one lying permanently upon the ground—the upper one having a hole in the centre. With one hand, the grain is thrown in, with the other the stone is turned round: the flour coming out all round the bottom of it. It is then sifted through a sieve, made of sheep's skin, when green, by pricking holes through it, and drying it suddenly with embers. This is put into hoops similar to our sieves. The flour is then put into a large shallow bowl, and by sprinkling water upon it in small quantities, and rolling the flour upon the bottom of the bowl with the hand, it is soon formed into small balls of the size of pepper corns.

An earthen pot (*gidderah*) is filled with water, and when boiling, the little balls, being put into a grass basket, (*kessikas*) set upon the top of the pot, into which the steam of the boiling water ascends and cooks it. When it is cooked, it is called *Keskoosoo*, before mentioned, and is the principal food of the inhabitants; although they often have vegetables with it, and sometimes a little meat (*El ham*.) The different sexes never eat in company; but both partake of their food, sitting upon the ground, and eating with their hands from wooden dishes, always washing their hands before they eat.

It had now become the 1st of June; the barley harvest was through, and the gardens occupied the chief attention. They were filled with the various vegetables enumerated before, many of which were ripened, and required great care. Bel Cossim appointed me *El Rais*, or Captain of this part of his dominions, and authorized me to expel intruders and punish aggressors. In the exercise of this power, I one day saluted an *Arrabere*, as the wandering Arabs are called by the citizens of Wadinoon, with a heavy stone, having caught him stealing grapes. He immediately turned, and aimed his musket toward me, which I totally disregarded; and, in a tone of authority, commanded him to flee, which he instantly obeyed. My master urged me to accept of a musket, which I declined, knowing that he would soon have compelled me to bear arms, in defence, against the numerous marauders who often infest the town, and render everything insecure.

The *markets* and *fairs* at this place are steadily holden once a week, upon the *Christian sabbath*, the *Mahommedan sab*bath being upon Friday, At these markets, are exposed for sale, almost every species of vegetables produced in the country—Olive oil and Argan oil are also offered, and purchased in greater or smaller quantities by almost every one. *Zate* is a common term for every species of oil. These oils are manufactured and sold by a race of natives called Berrebers, in distinction from Arabs and Moors, occupying the western coast of Africa, extending from *Morocco*, south to the dominions of *Sidi Hesham*.

These natives will be more particularly mentioned hereafter. Another kind of thick, white oil, made from small red berries, is also sold, which is called *d'hent*. Some kind of oil is always eaten with *koskoosoo*. Honey is also exposed for sale. Various meats are also in market, among which are beef, mutton, camel's and goat's meat; and sometimes cooked locusts. Bread, called *khobz*, is also sold. It is in heavy, black cakes, about the size of a sea-biscuit. Grain is also retailed. The foregoing articles include all that is sold for food.

At the *fairs* are offered for sale almost every article of *clothing*, necessary to cover or ornament the body. Blankets, or *haicks*, blue cottons, slippers, belts, turbans, and almost every species of trinkets. Occasionally, spices are exposed for sale—also powder, tobacco, and tar—the last article being in great use among the wandering Arabs fox healing camels, which are also sold here, and killing camel bugs. The persons resorting to these markets, as sellers and purchasers, embrace almost every different race of Africans. A duty or compensation is always demanded by the town, and paid by the sellers, for the use of the markets.

The mode of building houses may be reckoned among the peculiarities of these people. They have not sufficient wood to burn their clay into bricks, nor have they timber of sufficient size to saw into boards. There seems to be no other mode in which they could erect habitations but that resorted to. The houses are built of mud and stones. They begin the wall by placing a framed box, ten feet long, three feet high, and two and an half feet wide, upon the ground. This they fill with moistened earth, occasionally mixing flat stones with it. As it is thrown in, two persons standing within the box, pound it down as hard as possible. When the box is filled, it is taken apart, carried forward, and placed in an exact range with the piece of wall thus begun, The same process is carried on, until the whole foundation is raised three feet high—this making the lower tier—Any number of tiers are placed upon the top of each other that the owner chooses, sometimes extending to seven.

In one corner of the house, is carried up from the bottom, a wall ten feet square, having an apartment within it and rising from fifteen to twenty feet above the top of the four side-walls of the house. This makes the battlement or tower, for the defence of the house. These walls are covered upon the top by thorn bushes, in the same manner that garden walls are, there being upon the top of the house, no manner of roof. To secure the people and furniture, within these walls, from rain, there are small rooms, about six feet wide, and sometimes extending around the whole main wall about eight feet high, but sometimes raised two stories high. In these, the people sleep upon mats. The roof is composed of rafters made of date-trees, extending from the main wall to the inner one.

Upon these are placed reeds in thick order, and then covered with mud. The centre of the house is left exposed to rain, and the water is conducted off by a sluice through one of the outer walls. There is but one door or gate, which is made very strong by riveting together timbers of date-tree with iron bolts. This is fastened at night with a wooden lock of the most curious manufacture. The cattle, of various kinds, occupy the open area within the walls during the night season. Some of these houses have two or three different families occupying them, in different apartments.

The *Sheick's* house is the largest in the place, standing a little distance from the compact part of the town. In addition to the common walls, he had a wall about six rods from the house walls, entirely surrounding the house, enclosing as much as two acres of ground. Within it, he has a small church for his own devotion?, and that of his visitants, which are very numerous. His battlement is twenty feet high, in which are placed one of the guns of the British brig *Surprise*, which has been mentioned as lately lost upon the western coast of Africa. The houses are built promiscuously, without forming any regular streets.

CHAPTER 19

Sidi Hesham, His Appearance and Power

The religious ceremonies of the *Mahommedans*, in families and small parties upon the deserts, has already been minutely described, and frequently mentioned. In the town of Wadinoon, is a *place* consecrated for the sole purpose of performing their solemn rites, and manifesting their faith by their external ordinances. The building, in which they worship, has outward walls', built in the same manner as other houses, already described; but this has a flat roof, covering the whole at the top. The roof is supported by pillars in the inner side of the building, built with stone and mortar. It is arched upon the top; and upon the arches are painted, very coarsely, the sun, moon, and stars, and some other figures, which cannot be described particularly, as an *en-sahrau* was not permitted to enter it; and the only way I ever got within it, was by exercising secrecy to gratify my curiosity.

Before they enter the temple, they wash themselves in warmed water prepared in the yard, as they do with sand upon the deserts. Their mode of worship, after they enter, I cannot describe, as I never witnessed it; although they *sulle* in the same manner upon the roof as upon the deserts. The building is small, but large enough for so small a place as Wadinoon; and sufficiently capacious to enable its few inhabitants of the male sex to worship; females never being allowed to assemble with them. In the same house, the public-school is kept; the mode of instruction the same as before described.

The *fasting season* was a time of the greatest solemnity. It lasted for a whole moon, beginning when the new moon first made its appearance, in June, 1816. I conclude this must be the season of the annual fast, it certainly was in the season I resided at Wadinoon. During the continuance of this season, the natives never ate or drank between the rising and setting sun; but indulged themselves in both, with great voracity, during the darkness of the night. As I was resolved to show not the least conformity to the faith of *Mussulmen*, I made this a feasting season. having a full supply of *tack-nerrites* and *nornipps*.

The day after the fast concluded, the *feasting season* commenced. A spectator would have concluded that a month's abstinence was amply satisfied by a day of gluttony. The whole cooked dishes in the town were all brought to the market-place. Those who brought many changes of dishes fared no better than those who brought none. It was "*fall to and spare not*;" and whether the system of Mahomet requires it or not, the law of nature would dictate that a *fast* should *follow*, as well as *precede* a feast. These feasts frequently occur, as the Mahommedans have many holydays in honour of their different saints. Besides the general fast, single fast days frequently occur among different individuals, at different times, and for different judgments.

The feast was concluded a little past noon, and, after some sports in firing, the ceremony of *circumcision* commenced. From the most frantic and boisterous mirth, the whole multitude became, as if by a shock of electricity, immediately solemnized. The *Jews* invariably circumcise their children at eight days old; but among the *Moors* and *Arabs*, no particular age is regarded; but it is performed as circumstances make it convenient. Two of *Bel Cossim's* children were this day circumcised, one aged nine, the other fourteen years. The ceremony was performed in the yard adjoining the *Zham*, or the place of religious worship. That, and the adjoining grounds, were crowded with spectators. I, however, mingled with the rabble in such a manner as to witness the ceremony, notwithstanding I was not a *Mussulman*. It was performed by a Mohammedan priest, with the most profound solemnity.

The child was presented to the priest by the father, holding him in his arms with his private parts exposed. The priest drew the foreskin as far forward as possible without giving pain, then, with an *l'moose*, (knife) he cut the skin off without touching the fleshy part, leaving that forever afterwards entirely bare. This operation causes the child to shriek; upon which, a number of muskets are fired. At this time, a number were circumcised from the age of about five years, to that of eighteen. Two of the grandchildren of Bel Cossim were circumcised, the youngest of which was between five and six years of age. At every ceremony the muskets were discharged.

The circumcised children were kept in for a month, and prohibited the use of every species of fruit, unless it was prepared. Within that time, they generally recovered; and during my residence in Africa, I never knew death occasioned by circumcision. The black Africans, that are brought to Wadinoon from the country of Soudan, are sometimes uncircumcised. The fasting-season ended the 24th July, 1816, and the feasting and circumcision took place on the 25th, the new moon having appeared.

At about this time, I became acquainted with a Christian slave, who, a short time before, arrived at Wadinoon. His name was Thomas Davis, and he informed me that he was an *American*; that he formerly belonged to the privateer *Romp*, of Baltimore; that he was one of the prize-crew on board a Spanish vessel, that had been captured by the *Romp*, bound to Buenos Ayres. The vessel was wrecked upon the western coast of Africa in about 19° North Latitude, in May, 1816. The captain of the prize was drowned, and the remaining crew, five in number, were enslaved by a tribe of wandering Arabs. Their names, besides Davis, were Smith, (drowned) prize-master; John Brown; George Hall; John, a Spaniard, and an American gentleman, who, I was informed, had been a major in the late United States Army, and had, when wrecked, a commission in the Army of the Spanish Patriots, and was bound there, as a passenger, to join them. He and Brown were slaves to Sheick Ali, chief of a tribe of wandering Arabs. Brown, after his arrival at Wadinoon, which was in December, 1816, informed me that this gentleman died upon the desert, a few days before he arrived there, from absolute starvation, and that he buried him I published an article upon this subject soon after I returned to America.

About this time I learned, by the arrival of Sidi Hesham, at Wadinoon, that the crew of the British brig *Surprise*, who have before been mentioned as detained by him for the purpose of being ransomed, were released at Mogadore, through the instrumentality of the Hon. William Willshire, a philanthropist, to whom a very great proportion of the Christian slaves in Africa have, for some time past, been indebted for their emancipation from the most cruel and hopeless bondage.

The appellation *Sidi* is applied indiscriminately to every man who holds a slave; so that I might have dignified my different masters by the names of Sidi Ganus, Sidi Meaarah, Sidi Harriet. and Sidi Bel Cossim. This term, by the Moors and Arabs, is also applied to their Saints. When it is bestowed upon a native, having the power of Sidi Hesham, I do not know how extensive its meaning becomes. This Sidi Hesham resided about fifty miles N. E. from Wadinoon, and was often there during my residence in that place. He always was accompanied by a numerous body-guard of well armed Arabs, sometimes amounting to thirty, mounted upon elegant, fleet, well trained horses. He was always received by the natives of Wadinoon, with the most distinguished respect. The most splendid dinner, which the place could provide, was spread before him. His guard was also treated with that kind of attention, which even great folks bestow upon those who follow in the train of a great character.

While I was a resident there, he was scouring the country with six hundred mounted Arabs, spreading terror and exciting consternation wherever he went. He often robbed the caravans, bound from Soudan to Fez and Morocco, securing his plunder in the fastnesses of the Atlas mountains, which, as has been mentioned, bound the long valley in which Wadinoon is situated at the northeast. But a short time before I arrived there, the Moorish troops belonging to the Emperor of Morocco, Moolay Solimaan. drove Sidi Hesham from his holds, to the south of Wadinoon; but could not pursue him through the desert, where he and his clan were *at home*. The Moors encamped upon a small hill upon the east of the town, planted their cannon there, and alarmed the place for a number of days. Great numbers of slaves fled from their Arab masters, and joined the Moorish army. They however decamped without destroying the place, which might easily have been effected by a twelve pounder; there being no cannon in the town. Indeed, had it been lined with a park of artillery, the total ignorance of the Arabs in enginery, would have rendered them useless.

I shall have occasion to mention the country inhabited by this powerful chief, in my tour from Wadinoon to Mogadore.

Sidi Hesham, in his person, is six feet high. He is an old man, with a very full white beard hanging low on the breast. His *haick* and turban were of the finest texture of that country. His fine blue broadcloth cloak was trimmed quite round with red silk. His morocco boot-legs reached from his knees, and were made fast to his Moorish slippers, over which were buckled large silver spurs. His belts were broad, and of red Morocco, crossing at the breast and at the back. From one was suspended his immense powder-horn, almost covered with broad bands of shining brass; from the other hung his long burnished cutlass. Around his waist was wound his broad scarlet sash, confining his belts to his body. His long Moorish musket was decorated with silver bands from the lock to the muzzle. The breech was of ivory, and that part of the stock composed of black wood, was filled with ivory stars curiously inlaid.

His horse was an Arabian courser, of the highest blood, and a beautiful milk-white. His flowing mane separated in the middle, covering his neck upon each side. His fore-top was confined by a broad forehead piece hanging down over his eyes, and almost concealing them. His long thick tail fell to the ground. He was caparisoned with a Moorish saddle, covered with red broadcloth. The stirrups covered half of the bottom of Hesham's feet. His portmanteau was striped with black, yellow, and red, and richly tasselled at each end. When mounted upon this courser, Sidi Hesham would excite admiration, mingled with terror. The appearance of the principal *Sidis* is similar to that of Hesham. Their horses and muskets differ but little; and take them and their clans together, perhaps the world hardly affords a more desperate band.

The Jews formerly resorted to Wadinoon in considerable numbers for the purposes of traffic; but a *Jew* is esteemed but little higher than a Christian, although they are never enslaved. At the time I came to this place, I often saw them there; but during my residence, a Jew was guilty of some deception or fraud in regard to a letter sent by the *Sheick*, or governor, to Sidi Hesham, and a *decree* was passed, that no Jew should enter the town; and I never saw an *Israelite* there after that time. An intelligent Jew informed me that by the law, none of his race were permitted to purchase or hold Christian slaves upon pain of death; and that a Jew was slain but a short time before, for violating it, by having one in his possession. They stand in awe of both Moors and Arabs. It is a subject of wonder, that the *Jews*, the once favoured people of Heaven, should, even down to the nineteenth century, humble themselves before the descendants of Ishmael, the most despised and degraded of all the ancient children of Abraham.

The season had now advanced to the month of September. The tobacco was sufficiently ripened, to cut and cure. It is not so large as that produced in North-America, but very similar in its appearance. The method of curing it is, by cutting off the stock, just above each leaf, beginning at the bottom one. A bunch is then tied together at the union of the leaf with the stock. It is then laid upon the flat roofs of the rooms within the main walls of the houses, and remains there until sufficiently dried and cured to smoke at home, or send off to the desert. Snuff is made by pulverizing dried tobacco between stones. and mixing with it a weed of strong and delicious flavour. With this they frequently rub their teeth, which are almost invariably white.

Merchants are constantly arriving at Wadinoon from the Zahara desert, belonging to different wandering tribes. Among them, I often saw my kind master Hasmet Webber, of whom, and from everyone who arrived here from the desert, I inquired concerning the situation of the Christian slaves among the wandering Arabs; and learned that two Americans, one white and one black were dead. From the accounts I received, I suspect the white slave must have been *Antonio*, and the black one *Dick*. Hamet always seemed rejoiced to see me, and frequently told me he saved my life. This I believed without his assertion. I always acknowledged my gratitude, and told him I would amply reward him if he would come to my country. He would ask me. what I would give? He asked me if there was a God in my country? wondered why Christians did not *Sulle*; and be circumcised; and would devoutly exclaim "*Sheda Mahommed, Rahsool Allah.*"

CHAPTER 20

Ransom of Porter

While at Wadinoon, I took every opportunity in my power to ascertain the nature of the government in operation. My advantages to obtain correct information upon this important subject were of necessity limited; but I will communicate what little I do know.

The *Sheick*, or governor, has a council consisting of all the principal natives of Wadinoon. They frequently assemble at the governor's house, both to make laws and judge upon the violations of them. The government of Wadinoon extends through most of the tribes inhabiting the northern parts of the Desert of Zahara. From all the observations I made, and from all the information I could obtain, I feel confident that the tribes have a distinct government among themselves, exercised by their several *Sheicks*; and that the government of Wadinoon exercised a sort of supreme control over the whole. This conclusion is drawn from the fact, that minor offences are tried and punished upon the desert; and that those of greater enormity are tried and punished by the authority of that place; sometimes by a council holden at the *Sheick's* house in Wadinoon; and sometimes by the *Sheick* and council holding a session, or court, in the interior, upon the desert.

During my residence, a controversy arose between a part of the tribe of the *Wiled Aboussebah*, and a part of the *Wiled Adrialla*, at the *B'led Mouessa Ali*. The first mentioned tribe demanded a number of *Izhmaels*, or camels of burthen, of the last. The Adrialla refused, and a contest ensued. Expresses were immediately despatched to Wadinoon for the *Sheick* and council to repair to the scene of controversy. The express arrived at 12 o'clock at night, and in less than thirty minutes, the *Sheick* and council were armed, mounted, and upon the march. Bel Cossim's son, Hamada, went in his stead.

Before they arrived at the *B'led Mouessa Ali*, a battle had commenced. It was fought by armed Arabs mounted upon horses. While the battle was raging, the *Sheick* and council arrived, and a cessation of hostilities immediately took place. A number of the Aboussebah were slain and five of their horses. The Adrialla lost no men, and but a single horse. The *Sheick* and council decided the controversy in favour of the Adrialla; and the Aboussebahs were compelled to forfeit to them a number of camels, as a compensation for the injury. The particulars of this contest, and the manner of its settlement, I had from the Spanish slave who has before been mentioned, and who was himself in the action, upon the side of the Adrialla. The *Sheick* and council were absent from Wadinoon seven days upon this business.

I never knew the public authority interfere to enforce the collection of debts; leaving it to creditors to obtain satisfaction in their own way; which is generally done by taking off the blanket, &c. from the back of a debtor without ceremony, if he refuses payment. Difficulties but rarely occur from this source, and I never saw any character, in any part of Africa, that exercised the functions of a lawyer.

The punishment for offences and breaches of the peace is, by imposing a fine. I never saw any corporal punishment inflicted for any offence. A part of the fine is paid to the witnesses, upon the conviction of the offender.

Marriage is effected by the parents of the parties intending to join in wedlock. Private interviews are never permitted between the parties, until after the marriage rites are solemnized. The parents of the bride furnish the necessary household furniture, and the groom must furnish a house to put that and his bride in. A feast of *keskoosoo, el-ham*, and fruits, is always given at a marriage, and it is always concluded with a dance. The Mahommedan priest who marries them, receives a reward proportion ate to the wealth of the groom.

At the birth of a child, a feast is also given to the connections of the parents of it; and if it belongs to the *Sheick*, or to a principal Arab, the feast is splendid, and numerously attended. The different sexes upon these, as well as upon all other occasions, feast in different apartments, and often upon different days.

The interment of the dead is also attended with a feast. There being but a little over six hundred inhabitants of all kinds at Wadinoon. but three or four deaths happened while I was there. One was that of Braham Badullah's (the *Sheick's*) mother. A great quantity of *keskoosoo* was made upon this occasion, in which all the female slaves assisted; and the feast was wholly confined to the female sex. In the graveyard, is a building of two apartments for the different sexes to perform religious ceremonies in. There are a number of burying grounds in the vicinity of Wadinoon, and great numbers of monuments of rough stones standing in the ground, without any inscriptions upon them. This would induce a foreigner to conclude, that this place was formerly much larger than it was in 1816.

At about a mile distant from the town, is a natural, circular mound of a quarter of a mile diameter, and very regular. It rises as many as seventy-five feet above the surface of the valley. Near the top of it, is a circular brush fence, within which was formerly interred a saint, whom the natives called Sidi Timah. He was esteemed a prophet, and was supposed to possess the power of healing diseases. His memory is cherished with the most solemn veneration. The natives never pass this mound without performing religious ceremonies, facing inwards. They annually celebrate the day of his death, cooking all kinds of food within the fence, and pouring it upon the ground, or leaving it in the pots. Within the fence, is an immense number of them, some having the appearance of great antiquity.

Whatever is deposited within this fence, is always entirely secure. The natives continue to pray to this saint, and believe that he still heals their diseases by his divine power. I have often seen the natives, when sick, proceed with the most solemn devotion, to this mound, and pray to Sidi Timah. At the base of it are three vaults, in which some great characters have been interred. The natives say, that the ghost of an aged female, buried at a little distance, rises often in the night season and walks around the ashes of Sidi Timah. Single graves are often seen with large heaps of brush and stones placed upon the top. Between the town and this mound, I saw the ruins of an ancient wall, enclosing a considerable piece of ground, now covered with bushes, which the natives told me was in past ages occupied by the *en-sahrau*. Similar places are seen in other parts of the country near Wadinoon. Modesty requires that I should leave the privilege of conjecturing to the reader.

There are at Wadinoon no professors of medicine; but all the inhabitants have a mode of relieving their own pains and those that are sick, peculiar to themselves. They administer a bitter weed for internal complaints. For rheumatism, cramps, &c. the patient lies down upon the belly, and a man jumps up and down upon his back. This is the *modus operandi*, and whether it produces relief *secundum artem*, I know not; but cures are effected in this way. Tar and grease are applied to flesh wounds. The headache is cured by pinching the forehead and temples with the fingers, or biting them with the teeth.

The amusements of the men at Wadinoon consist in training and riding horses, which they do with the greatest skill and elegance. Shooting at a mark is an amusement common to everyone, and some fire with admirable accuracy. Casting a single stone at a number of small ones, standing loosely upon the ground, is often practised. They often throw in a *murzoon* each, a silver piece of two cents value, and the most skilful ones get the whole.—Dancing is the only amusement in which the sexes unite. The music is made upon a *tambarine*, not unlike those often seen in N. England. The natives are passionately fond of music; and however wretched it is, it almost captivates them. A Moor, from Fez, arrived while I was at Wadinoon, with a rude fiddle, which, so far from "*discoursing most eloquent music*" would make a hearer recollect Burns' description of a "*Scotch scraper, whose tones imitated the dying agonies of a sow under the hands of the butcher.*" He however received many presents, and went off well loaded. By the use of the musket, as an amusement, the Arabs acquire all the knowledge of the manual exercise they possess; there being no such thing as instruction in this, or in military manoeuvring.

About the middle of October 1816, Porter received a letter from Mr. Willshire dated the 8th of that month, which I read. It informed him that the terms of his ransom were agreed upon between him, and his (Porters) master, who sent to his wife, by a messenger, to send Porter immediately to Mogadore. Bel Cossim discovered that Porter had been ransomed, and felt anxious to obtain a large ransom for me. I went with him to the house of Porter's master, having written a hasty line to Mr. Willshire, in relation to my own situation, which I gave to Porter. Porter left Wadinoon with the messenger, and I returned to my slavery with little hopes of being ransomed, as Bel Cossim was determined to hold me, until he could obtain an exorbitant sum for my liberation.

This letter to Mr. Willshire was never answered; nor did I ever receive any answer to those I before had written, nor to those I afterwards wrote. I feel the utmost assurance, that that excellent man had the best reasons for his silence, as he afterwards deeply interested himself in my discharge. My master Bel Cossim had been the owner of many Christian slaves, and purchasing them at a low rate, and demanding a great sum for their ransom, was one of the great sources of his great wealth, I was now the only Christian slave in Wadinoon, except Davis, who has been mentioned as one of the crew of the prize ship that was wrecked in May 1816.

During the whole of the month of November, and a port of December, I was constantly employed in building a mud wall around the extensive gardens of Bel Cossim. It was nearly completed, when the rainy season commenced; and the hard labour of six weeks was demolished in a day.

In the month of December a serious quarrel commenced between the town of Wadinoon and *Akkadia*, a town occupied by the *Shilluh*, about fifteen miles to the north, in the same valley in which Wadinoon is situated. The quarrel was occasioned by some injury a *Shilluh* woman had sustained from my master Bel Cossim, Brahim Abdallah his brother, or Hamada his son. The two towns espoused the cause of their own people. Wadinoon was in perpetual alarm from this time, until I left it, in the February afterwards. The *Shilluh* were determined, if possible, to have the blood of Bel Cossim or Hamada. No regular warfare was carried on between the parties; but constant depredations were committed by each. The ordinary business of farming could not be prosecuted by individuals singly, but they went out in large parties to cultivate the land, each one being armed with a musket. Night alarms were incessant. My master kept an armed man in his battlement, and was in constant fear of his life. He acted as if guilt preyed upon him; and shewed by his conduct that *"the wicked flee when no man pursueth."* He was universally detested, even by his own neighbours; and nothing but the security which wealth often affords to a villainous wretch, preserved him from assassination in his own house.

From the 15th of December the rainy season continued for five days and nights, and there could hardly be said to have been for that time a cessation. From the north, and the south, the water poured down in torrents from the two ranges of mountains before described, into the valley which, as mentioned, is six miles in width, diminishing as it stretches toward the Atlas mountains. From these mountains, for a great distance, and from an immense height, the rivers of water, suddenly created by the rain, all bent their course to the eastern boundary of this great valley. The smaller valleys all discharged their watery contents into it. In a short time, the great valley began to present a river of shallow water six miles in width, excepting where the adjoining mountains projected into it. Upon these projections, which might *now* be called promontories, the numerous villages or towns were situated.

The water continued to rise for six days, until the whole valley, from the Atlas mountains to Wadinoon, and from thence southwest to the sea, a distance probably of one hundred and fifty miles, was covered with water from five to eight feet in depth. Wadinoon was entirely surrounded with the flood, and upon the south side of the valley, this immense body of water passed with a considerable current. In three days after the rain ceased, the valley was nearly emptied of water. For a number of days, accounts were constantly received of disasters. Numerous camels, and great quantities of goods and grain were destroyed; and many lives were lost. Wadinoon suffered but a little, from its elevated situation, although some gardens situated low in the valley were injured, and many walls of the houses and the gardens sustained injury from the long continuance of the rain. From appearances in the neighbourhood of Wadinoon, it must formerly have suffered severely, either from floods or enemies, as there are great numbers of walls in ruins.

During the rain, I was almost constantly exposed to it, in securing tobacco, digging drains to carry off water, and in other services. Some of the small rooms were partially demolished; and, during the rain, an ancient wall, standing within the main walls of Bel Cossim's house, fell with a tremendous crash into the inner yard. Fortunately, no man or beast was situated within its destructive reach.

As soon as the waters had subsided from the face of the earth, the ploughing commenced. The ground in this valley is never ploughed in the *dry season;* as it would be useless to put seed into it during the continuance of it. It is impossible to imagine a scene of greater activity and animation than this valley presented. From the *Sheick* to the black slave—from the camel of twenty-five hands in height, to the most diminutive mule—Moors, Arabs, Arrabbere Shilluhs, Christian and African slaves, were all in motion. Zahara poured in her hordes of famished Ishmaelites, and the long valley disgorged her contents of surfeited merchants. At the dawn of day, Mahomet was worshipped; and the *keskoosoo* was swallowed with despatch. The beasts were geared to the plough, and, followed by men. were hastily driven to the adjoining fields.

From the rising to the setting sun, they both travelled as steadily as that scorching luminary and never ceased labour, until darkness rendered it impracticable. The *keskoosoo* was again eaten, and the exhausted, fatigued, and despairing slave was permitted, for a season, to repose. This service I was compelled, incessantly, to perform for forty days. An unusual quantity of ground was ploughed this season, as many fields were cleared of bushes which must have been of six year's growth. Some of the oldest people told me they never knew so much ploughed.

The soil, within this valley, when a sufficient quantity of rain falls, is astonishingly fertile. It is of a dark rich colour; has but few stones and is easily cultivated. The grain is sowed before it is ploughed, and one ploughing serves for the whole. The plough is of the most simple construction. It consists of a small, crooked piece of hard wood, forming a knee. The perpendicular part of it makes the handle; the horizontal part, the bottom of the plough; the forward end of that is shod, or pointed with iron; the beam is mortised into the handle, in such a manner, as to give the bottom a proper pitch, depending upon the angle the knee makes. It is very light, and may be carried, without difficulty, in one hand. The people plough with every species of animals in their possession—camels, horses, asses, mules, and cows. Each one drives his own beast, and holds his own plough. The camel is guided by a single rein, fastened by a ring into one of its nostrils. A man and beast will generally plough an acre in a day. While the last fields were ploughing, those first ploughed, had barley twenty inches high.

As the grain came up, the flights of locusts began to infest the country. They came from the southeast Without a view of one of these flights. a man can have no idea of the horror excited upon their approach. When they are above the spectator, in the atmosphere, they almost obscure the sun—-when they light upon the vegetables on the earth, they completely cover them, and, in a very few minutes, devour them. I have before described the manner of gathering and cooking these insects upon the desert. They are sometimes boiled at Wadinoon for food for men and beasts. Early in the morning, before they begin to fly, I have known a bushel and a half gathered from a bush six feet high. They cover them as completely as a swarm of bees do the bough upon which they light. The locust of Africa more nearly resembles the large grasshopper of N. England than any other insect. The body is of a reddish brown colour, about two inches in length, and a quarter of an inch through. From the head to the end of the wings is nearly three inches. When devouring vegetation, they make a noise similar to small pigs eating grain. Bel Cossim had five acres of guinea corn totally destroyed, while some fields near were untouched.

Upon the 5th of February, 1817, the great *Moloode* was holden at Akka about an hundred miles east of Wadinoon. These, as I learned, are annually held in different parts of the country. It is a sort of *wholesale fair*, and the natives, by wholesale, attend them. Wadinoon was almost divested of male inhabitants, leaving the female Ishmaelites to manage affairs at home. I urged Bel Cossim. to carry me there and sell me; but he declined. He however took a letter from me directed to Mr. Wiltshire, which I afterwards found at a Jew's house among the Shilluh.

After the ploughing was through, the people were employed in digging into the earth *muttomorahs*, to contain the grain when harvested, They are dug into stone, or earth and shelving rocks united as hard as stone. A circular hole, of four feet diameter, is dug until it comes to a greyish slate stone. Another round hole is then begun, of one foot and a half diameter at the top. and as it is dug into the stone, is constantly widened. By these means, the hole becomes large enough to let the body into it, and there to continue to peck up the stone, and pass the fragments out of the hole at the top. Some of these are dug large enough to contain from three to five hundred bushels.

When the grain is put in the small hole is covered with a flat stone, and the large one filled even with the surface of the ground, securing the grain from the weather, and concealing it from thieves. These vaults are made to preserve grain for a time of famine. Bel Cossim had numbers of these vaults, and shewed me grain taken from them which had remained in them three years, in the soundest possible state. I was employed in digging one of these *muttomorahs*, in the lowest state of dejection, expecting to be taken from it, only to be compelled to assist in securing the immense fields of Bel Cossim's grain, when a cheering prospect of redemption burst upon me, like the light of the sun, after the cheerless gloom of a Lapland winter.

CHAPTER 21

Author Purchased by a Shilluh

Upon the 16th day of February, 1817, as I was at the market in Wadinoon, where I saw Davis, and also Brown, who had arrived in December, a Shilluh presented to me a piece of manuscript, asking me if the language was *Inglesis?* I immediately saw that it was, and read it. It was headed "Mogadore" but was not dated. The substance of it was in very nearly this language.

> To any Christian Slave—
> You are requested to sign this paper at the bottom, with your name; and mention the name of the vessel in which you were wrecked—the place where, and the time when, and of what nation you are; and return it to the one who offers it to you.

The paper had no signature, and was written in an elegant hand. My master was eyeing me with real Arab sagacity. I pressed the *Shilluh* to explain—he looked at Bel Cossim, remained mute a minute, and discovered the arch cunning of his tribe. He then loudly said, in Arab, "*I shall go in the morning to Mogadore, and will carry a letter for you*" and immediately walked hastily off to the fair. Bel Cossim also went off, and left me to reflect upon this strange interview. Hope and despair alternately prevailed in my mind. I had before concluded that my fate was fixed for life; and my Mahommedan acquaintance at Wadinoon, which embraced almost every male Arab and Moor in the place, had often urged me to espouse the faith of a good Mussulman—relieve myself from slavery—take an Ishmaelitish wife, and become great. I cannot tell what increasing misery might have driven me to; but I was determined to resist this apostasy to the last.

Upon the next morning, (17th) the Shilluh with two companions, all mounted upon mules, called early at the house of Bel Cossim. He asked me if my letter was ready, and appeared to be in the greatest possible haste. I ran in to entreat my master for a piece of paper and a reed to write with. He immediately came out and spoke with the Shilluh. They began an earnest conversation in the Shilluh tongue, which I did not fully understand; but soon learned from some Arabic words used, that Bel Cossim demanded two hundred dollars for my ransom, and that the Shilluh offered one hundred and fifty. My master declared that the money was sent from the Consul at Mogadore for my ransom—the Shilluh denied it: said he wanted me for his own slave, and was about departing.

Bel Cossim came down to one hundred and seventy-five dollars, and the Shilluh hastily rode off. The pains of death itself could not exceed my distress. My master noticed my agony, and very coolly said, "*never mind it. He will soon be back—he has got the money.*" I did not allow myself to hope it; but very soon saw the Shilluh returning. The money was paid—I took the last mess of *keskoosoo* under the walls of Bel Cossim Abdallah's house, and left it forever. We had not proceeded more than a mile, before the Shilluh hastily returned back—made a bargain with the master of the Spaniard frequently mentioned, and sent off an Arab with a mule after him to the Bl'ed Mouessa Ali. At night the Spaniard arrived at Wadinoon. As to Brown and Davis the Shilluh declared them to be *uzmuntoots* (pirates) and would not buy them. They joined in writing a letter to Mr. Wiilshire which the Shilluh took.

During the absence of the Arab who went after the Spaniard, I went about the town with Davis and Brown, joining with them in lamentations that they were still to remain in slavery. I felt by no means certain concerning myself. I was still the property of an Ishmaelite, and still subject to the capricious whims of that indescribable race of creatures; I however had animating hopes. During the day, I never entered the walls of Bel Cossim's house, although urged to go in and eat. I kept in view of my Shilluh master. About 8 o'clock in the evening, the Shilluh. with three companions, the Spaniard and myself set off from the *great* town of Wadinoon, which I have minutely and faithfully described, on our way toward the B'led Sidi Hesham. At about ten miles distance, which we travelled rapidly in the dark, over stones and bushes, we arrived at a *Douar* of tents—refreshed ourselves with *laisk* and *zate*—took a little rest and again started.

The Shilluh presented me and the Spaniard, a new pair of Moorish slippers each. The natives were mounted and we were on foot, running all night. As we were passing the town of Akkadia, with which

Wadinoon was still at war, and in the country of Sidi Hesham the great bandit, we were in constant apprehension of being murdered and robbed. In the night, we passed a narrow defile leading through the Atlas mountains, which of course, I cannot describe. We heard the distant hooting of the natives and the trampling of horses. We travelled with the utmost caution. Frequently we were passed by mounted Arabs, and carefully concealed ourselves. I knew it to be the object of Sidi Hesham to get into his possession all the Christian slaves he possibly could, in order to extort an enormous ransom from the Christian powers. I learned from Mr. Wiltshire, that the ransom of the crew of the British brig *Surprise*, which I have before mentioned as being in his possession, only seventeen in number, amounted to five thousand dollars, besides expenses and presents to a large amount.

Upon the next morning, (18th) the Shilluh barely stopped to *sulle*. Our course from Wadinoon thus far had been about E. N. E. During this day we bore a little more to the northward; and at about 10 a. m., stopped at the house of one of the Shilluh, and were comfortably refreshed. We were now in the country of the Shilluh, a race included among the Berrebbers. This country, from the best accounts I could obtain, extends from Mogadore. south-westward to the borders of Sidi Hesham's dominions, and from the western coast of Africa to the eastern limits of the western termination of the Atlas mountains. We continued to travel gradually until 2 p. m. when we came to a market; stopped a short time; ate a few dates, and proceeded on our journey, still passing branches of the Atlas mountains.

At nearly sunset we came into view of an extensive level country. It was one of the grandest views imaginable. Before we descended, we could extend the eye across this immense and truly delightful country, and catch a distant glimpse of the range of mountains running from Santa Cruz, eastward, to the Atlas mountains. My Shilluh master exclaimed, "*Ria. Robbinis! shufe Santa Cruz*"—There, Robbins! see Santa Cruz. I should degrade my feelings if I attempted to describe them. As we passed along we often saw clusters of well built mud and stone houses, and single ones scattered along through the whole country. Extensive barley fields were constantly in sight, some of which shewed a gloomy track of desolation left through them by the recent passage of a flight of locusts. Date trees, fig trees, *argan* and olive trees: prickly pears, &c. were almost constantly in sight, although the date tree is not so common here as to the eastward of the Atlas mountains. At about nine in the evening, we put up at the house of an acquaintance of the

Shilluh. I found the worship precisely the same as I had noticed it, in every part of Africa I had seen.

The next morning, (19th) by 2 o'clock, we were again upon our journey. The Shilluh appeared extremely anxious to expedite the journey. My slippers were worn through, and I was most excessively fatigued. But the thoughts of travelling toward the desired regions of civilization made me forget that fatigue, which would otherwise have been insupportable. Before sunrise, after *sulle* was performed, the companions of the Shilluh left him. The Spaniard and I now became the objects of his particular attention. We passed a great number of monuments, the surfaces of which were composed of clay, whitewashed, having, at a little distance, the appearance of marble. Some were in the shape of an obelisk, and others were carried up square. We travelled so hastily, that I could not give them a particular examination.

The Shilluh pointed out one that was erected in honour of Sidi Hamet a Mouesa, whom he mentioned with great veneration. When passing near them the Shilluh would face them, and repeat over some of the ritual, as I concluded, not having yet sufficiently learned the Shilluh language to understand him. At about sunrise we came to a town nearly as large as Wadinoon. We passed through it, and near the gardens which were constructed like those in that place. I did not learn the name of the town, as we made no stop. Upon the east of the town, and near to it, we passed a very considerable stream of pure water, running from the S. E. and to the N. W. and N. The gardens were near its banks, which were thickly lined with date trees; but it was past their bearing season at this place. The water was let into the gardens, from a pond, formed by a dam across the stream above the town. This stream the natives called *El-wad Schlem*.

It was about six rods in width, and. where we passed it, so shallow that we forded it on foot. After passing the stream, we continued in a N. E. direction, and soon ascended and descended a considerable hill, and came again into the level country which was still fertile, but was suffering from drought. At nine o'clock, we came to a small village, called by the natives *Widnah*, and stopped for a short time. From this village, might be seen many others, all of which appeared to be in a flourishing condition. This level country extended far to the N. W. being bounded upon the S. E. by the Atlas mountains, branches of which frequently stretched some distance into it, leaving valleys between them. After breakfast, we joined a number of the inhabitants, and went to a market, which is called *soag*.

The markets from Wadinoon to Santa Cruz are so arranged, being holden upon different days in the week, that travellers can every day be accommodated with an open market. The description of the markets and fairs at Wadinoon will, with little variation, apply to all that are established through this range of country. One article, however, which is a principal one at that place, is never seen among the Shiliuh—*tobacco*; this being considered among them as a detestable weed, and the use of it as a transgression. At these markets, or *soags*, I saw great numbers of Jews, being the first I had seen since they were prohibited from trading at Wadinoon. We crossed a stream, more rapid in its current, and greater in its depth, than the one last mentioned, and continued our course to the eastward. Before sunset we reached a very beautiful level country, with scattered houses covering a great extent of it. It was covered with extensive barley fields, and the usual fruit trees common to the Shilluh country.

This was the residence of my Shilluh master. He conducted me, and my Spanish companion, to the mansion of El'ajjah Mahomet. who was called by the natives, *Sharif*. Every object around us had the appearance of wealth and comfort. We were shewed into a very good apartment, and a repast of dried figs was spread before us. El'ajjah Mahomet informed us, that he had sent the ransom money to Wadinoon for us, that he would, in the morning, furnish us with paper to write on to *Sweahrah* (Mogadore) to the *Contz*, (consul;) and, as soon as we received an answer, we should immediately start for that place: and, that if we wished, he would furnish us with mules to ride upon. For supper, we had boiled eggs, *khobs*, and, for the first time in Africa, a cup of tea.

The distance from Wadinoon to this place, to which the natives gave no particular name that I can remember, is about one hundred and thirty miles, in the course we travelled; the general course being just about N. E. We travelled with great rapidity for footmen, the Spaniard and I having travelled it without mules, in forty-five hours.

The next morning, the 20th of February, 1817. before we arose, we were served with tea, *el ham*, and *keskoosoo*, in our apartment. We soon walked out with El'ajjah Mahomet to the house of a Jew, where we were treated with *carmoose*, brandy. I there wrote a letter for myself to Mr. Willshire, and another for the Spaniard to the Spanish Consul at Mogadore. Our protector immediately despatched an express, on foot, with the letters. Astonishing to relate, he returned at the end of seven days. The Jews had here a small manufactory for making knives, scimitars, scabbards, breast-plates, ear-rings, and all the variety of trinkets in demand among the natives. There were many of these children of Israel in this place, and, as in all others, despised and abused; although they were the largest dealers in the place.

We remained at this place until the 16th of March, and were uniformly treated by the good El'ajjah Mahomet with the utmost kindness. In his house, was an apartment set apart for worship, and used for no other purpose. Whenever a stranger arrived he inquired for the *zham*, or place of worship, and water to prepare for the performance of religious rites This was immediately furnished, and they retired to their devotions. Every scattering house has such a closet for prayer, but in villages there is a sham common to all. El'ajjah Mahomet uniformly expressed the utmost indignation against the Wiled D'leim, and spoke in wrath of Bel Cossim.

I found the Jews in this part of the country, in making their bills and accounts, make use of the ten digits precisely like those in use here. Out bill was made in this manner; but I never, at Wadinoon, nor in any other place, saw them used by the natives. They write their numbers from right to left, their left hand figure being always the unit.

I was sensibly struck with the great superiority of the Shilluh, over all the other races of Mahometans in Africa. They were mild and friendly in their dispositions, and seemed to want nothing but the benign influence of Christianity, to render them a most estimable race of men. They are lighter in their complexion than the Arabs, and speak a language so different, that they cannot understand each other.

The country of the Shilluh is under the dominion of the Emperor of Morocco. Two tax-gatherers from Fez, which also belongs to the Emperor, were here, and spent a day at El'ajjah Mahomet's house with me, and I conversed with perfect ease with them. They exercised great authority, and if the least hesitation was shewn in paying the required tribute, the Moorish musket and cutlass would soon enforce it. I saw a blanket forced from a native who was either unable or unwilling to pay his quota. They told me, upon inquiry, that the money was going to the *Sooltaun*, and that it was gathered yearly.

The productions of this delightful country are, horned cattle, some sheep, and goats, horses, asses, mules, and a few male camels for burthen. Grain and fruits are produced in abundance. Almonds, honey, peach-meats, and wax are articles of trade. *Noose*, a moss taken from trees, is in great demand for colouring morocco leather, and great quantities of it are transported to Mogadore. *Argan* trees abound everywhere in this part of the continent.

I had not opportunity to learn particularly concerning the mines of different ores in the Atlas mountains, which make the southern boundary of the Shilluh country; but at the Jews' manufactory, I saw a mountaineer offer to a Jew a lump of ore which he pronounced copper. The native who brought it said he got it out of a hole so deep that the end could not be discovered; and that water was constantly running down in it. I was requested to examine it, as the natives suppose every *ensahrau* acquainted with the precious metals. As I am ignorant of mineralogy, my opinion would settle nothing upon the question; but I took it to be copper. The mountaineer declared it to be gold. From hearing it frequently mentioned at Wadinoon. and being urged by Bel Cossim to go to work upon ore, which he would shew me, no doubt remains upon my mind but that ore abounds in this part of Africa.

During my stay in the Shilluh country, I increased my acquaintance with the Spaniard, and had from him, in the Arabic language, a history of his slavery with the Arabs. He told me he had been upon the desert eight years: that he belonged to a Spanish privateer, and was upon a cruise for French vessels in 1809, off the western coast of Africa; that the water of the vessel was nearly expended, and that he, and three others of the crew, were sent ashore, in the boat, for water, and that they were all captivated by the Arabs. He said he was among the blacks in the southern part of the continent, and was there for some time, upon the banks of a river, with fertile and cultivated land, having horned cattle upon it. He said he knew not the fate of two of his companions; but one of them we found upon our arrival at Mogadore. Upon being presented to the Spanish Consul, he could not speak his native tongue, and to me he always appeared as a native of Africa, and was often, by the Arabs, mistaken for such. His brief story, related to me, induced a belief in my mind of its accuracy.

While we remained at El'ajjah Mahomet's, he went to the governor at Terudant to obtain a passport for us to Mogadore, as without it we could not pass the town of Santa Cruz. He also carried a letter from the governor to Sidi Hesham. and obtained authority of some kind from him He informed us, that all this was indispensably necessary, to secure a safe passage to Mogadore. The messenger sent to Mogadore brought back a letter in Arabic, to our protector, and a present of a loaf of sugar. He informed us that all necessary arrangements were made, and that in a short time the preparations of food, &c. for our journey would be completed.

Chapter 22

Cheering American Flag

Upon the 7th, the food, consisting of *khobs*. butter, and barley meal, was packed ready for transportation; and, at one o'clock, a. m. upon the 8th, the Spaniard and I, mounted upon one mule, and El'ajjah Mahomet and a boy upon another, started upon our journey. Our hearts were dilated with gratitude towards El'ajjah Mahomet, and Mr. Willshire, and thankfulness to heaven, and we directed our course N. N.W. toward Santa Cruz. At about 8 a. m. we forded the largest stream I had yet seen in Africa, being, I judged, fifteen rods in width. The natives called this river *El-wad Sta*. We took a winding course, to avoid the immense sand-hills which lay between us and the sea. These lay in great drifts, like snow banks. I saw the uppermost boughs of numerous fig-trees, just above the sand drifts. This was about twenty miles from the sea. How long these sand hills have been forming, must be left to conjecture; but from the circumstance of seeing the tops of trees, a traveller would be led to suppose that they are rapidly extending into the country.

After passing these, we changed our course to the N.W. being in sight of Santa Cruz, and, what was to me the most animating sight, the ocean. My Spanish companion was frantic with joy. He leaped up; threw out his hands; exclaiming, "*Ioga! ioga! ria el Bahar, ria el Bahar*". This was the first time I had seen the ocean since December, 1815. From this point the Atlas mountains, lying upon our right, appeared in all their grandeur. Their tops, rising in succession one after another, were covered with snow. The rays of the sun, striking upon them, gave them the most brilliant appearance. We reached Santa Cruz at 3 p. m. The passport was offered at the fort—a present of *henneh* was made to the commander, and after this we were permitted to enter the lower town. It is a town compactly built of stone, and walled. The main street runs through the town from one gate to the other. Being built upon the side of a hill, one street rises above another, and the houses, being low, the roofs in the next street below the spectator may be seen.

There is another settlement called the upper town, surrounded by a very high wall. The land upon which the place stands is very elevated, rising, I should judge, as many as twelve hundred feet above the level of the sea. This wall has the appearance of a fortress, being filled with port-holes. The dwelling-houses are all built within it. I was informed by the Moors that there was a mine within the walls of this place, but that nobody but an *en-sahrau* dare descend it. From the lower town, the passage to the upper one is by a winding road around the hill, which is difficult of ascent. The prospect from this place is extensive and grand. Situated high upon the commencement of the range of mountains, extending from this place east to the Atlas mountains, the spectator has a view of the whole range and also of the Atlas. This is a place of the greatest importance, it being the key to the dominions of the emperor of Morocco, and the only passage from the western coast of Africa into that empire, excepting Terudant, which is situated about ninety miles to the east of Santa Cruz, which is called by the natives *Agadeer*.

This place was formerly holden by the Portuguese. The Moors informed me that the *en-sahrau* (Christians) settled it, built the fortress, and cultivated the adjoining country; that the Moors, taking advantage of a long drought and distressing famine, besieged the place, and compelled them to abandon it; and that the emperor of Morocco has ever since held possession of it himself. A few cannon still remain, and a few are sufficient to defend it against the encroachments of the Arabs, who, notwithstanding their power upon the desert, are, from their mode of warfare, weakness itself, compared with the power arising from modern tactics. The bay before the town is very open, and furnishes but a poor harbour for the protection of shipping. There were fifteen or twenty open fishing boats in the bay, and I saw two from which the Moors were landing fish; but had no opportunity to give them an examination.

Upon the 9th, we passed the north gate of the town at sunrise, upon our journey toward Mogadore. The country through which we travelled was made up of one rocky hill succeeding another. But little land was susceptible of cultivation, and this was chiefly in the valleys. A few houses were scattered along in them, and occasionally a cottage was seen at a great height upon the mountains on our right. We continued upon the sea coast, and passed one considerable stream, and a number of streamlets. The passage through the country, for it can hardly be called a road, was almost constantly thronged with loaded camels and mules from Mogadore, transporting iron, grain, *haicks* and other articles. At about 2 p. m. we came to a place which offered to the traveller two different passages; the one near the sea, the other over the mountains; the latter being, as I was told, the shortest course. I saw numerous loaded camels coming from the passage next to the sea.

This passage was described by El'ajjah Mahomet as the best, although the longest. This was the passage through which Capt. Riley and my shipmates travelled in their passage to Mogadore soon after we were captured, and they were purchased by Sidi Hamet. Capt. Riley mentions a place in this passage by the name of the *Jew's Leap*; but as I was conducted through the passage over the mountains, I did not see, and cannot describe it. Our passage over the mountains was such as to excite the fearful apprehensions of those who were about to attempt it; and almost beyond the power of description from those who had effected it. It was a zigzag course up a mountain, forming an angle of ascent of at least forty-five degrees.

This extraordinary passage was made over an artificial path constructed by cutting and wearing a narrow track into the rocks of the mountain, about twenty feet, and the same distance to its outer edge, each ascending a little. These tracks were made in and out of the mountain, until we ascended nearly to its summit, which, from the place where we began to rise, was at least one thousand feet. We made this passage on foot; driving the loaded mules before us. Before we reached the summit, we came to one of these tracks, worn into the rocks by travelling, of about forty rods in length. This track was only of sufficient width to permit the mules and their followers to pass singly. Had either fallen from this contracted path, over the shelving rocks composing the side of the mountain, immediate death must have been the inevitable consequence. We then came to a long, dark, natural passage between two mountains of as much as two miles in length, ascending but a very little.

At the end of this passage, upon the top of the mountain, is a level country of about five miles in length, and three in width; in a pretty high state of cultivation, with houses situated thinly upon every part of it. The contrast it furnished to the rocky and almost inaccessible mountains that lead to it, is as great as nature can afford. Here we rested awhile, and travelled leisurely over this piece of ground; the inhabitants all showing to El'ajjah Mahomet the most distinguished respect. We then began to descend the mountain upon the northeast side, which was also very steep in places, but much less so than where we ascended. We then came to a valley through which a stream runs of considerable size, and passes off upon the left to the sea. After passing it the country became more sandy, and as we were gradually rising we again had a full view of the Atlantic ocean. At about sunset we put up at the house of an acquaintance of El'ajjah Mahomet.

Upon the 10th we continued through a country that was sandy, until towards noon, when we entered a valley lying between two mountains, losing sight of the sea, where we saw many beautiful gardens constructed similarly to those at Wadinoon, and watered by a small stream issuing out of the mountains. Our passage, for seven or eight miles, was level, leading between mountains in a zigzag course, frequently so narrow that but one could pass at a time. It was the most romantic scene that the mind can conceive. Our good protector kept generally upon his mule, while the Spaniard and I alternately rode and walked, in company with the boy.

We now travelled through a country of hills and valleys, almost everywhere covered with the *Argan* tree, and loaded with fruit, which resembles the damson in shape, and of a yellow colour. From the meats of these, oil in great abundance is manufactured. About sunset we passed the dry bed of a large river, and came into a wilderness composed of the *Argan* tree. Darkness came on, and we gathered a quantity of wood, to spend the night, there being no house in sight. At length we heard the barking of dogs, and descried the light of a fire. We approached, and found it completely surrounded with a wall composed of thorn bushes twenty feet high. We requested water, but could procure none; and with great difficulty obtained a little fire. We attempted to repose around the fire, but enjoyed but little rest.

The dogs within the wall, with the highest ferocity, were constantly gnashing their teeth, and attempting to force a passage through the picket of thorns to assail us. This species of dogs is common in every part of Africa that I had seen, and are the most ferocious of the whole canine race. I have often seen them tear and lacerate the blacks in the most terrible manner. Almost every native has more or less of them with him, whether travelling or at rest.

The next morning, at an early hour, we started upon the last day's journey to Mogadore. We passed in the fore part of the day through a forest of *Argan* trees. For the whole distance from Santa Cruz to

Mogadore, the traveller is accommodated with water secured in cisterns. These are built with great care and much labour. Some of them are thirty feet in length, and eight or ten in width. They are sunk into the earth from five to eight feet, and stoned and plaistered within; over them, rising about five feet above the surface, is built a flat roof, made of poles, reeds, and mud, and smoothly plaistered. The entrance is at one end down a flight of stairs leading to the water. Upon the roofs are often seen travellers refreshing themselves with food, and partaking of the fine water contained within. The water is conducted into them by little channels cut into the surface of the earth. After refreshing ourselves at one of these fine reservoirs, we came into a plane sandy country.

Upon rising a small sand hill we again had a view of the Atlantic—of an island which forms the harbour of Mogadore, and of a ship and a brig. This was the first shipping I had beheld since we left the wreck of the Commerce at Cape Bajador, nearly nineteen months before. The joy of my Spanish companion almost produced delirium. We soon came in sight of Sweahrah, the longed-for Mogadore, situated very low upon the borders of the ocean, and, it being high tide, appearing to be almost surrounded with water. We continued to travel near the beach, and having upon our left a block of buildings enclosed within a wall of stone, plaistered, presenting a front of at least two hundred feet in length. Above this wall, I discovered four distinct roofs covered with green tile, coming to a point in the centre. El'ajjah Mahomet informed me that it belonged to Moolay Solimaan, emperor of Morocco.

Near to this was situated a small fort. The town is nearly three miles distance from this place. Continuing on, we passed a rapid river, by fording. Our protector now dressed himself in elegant Moorish stile; and as we followed him, we passed a number of buildings or monuments, erected in honour of some Mahommedan saints as I concluded, for we were directed to dismount our mules, dismiss our slippers, and walk by barefooted. We approached the walls of the town to within half a mile of the south gate, and stopped. El'ajjah Mahomet left us and entered the town. I very soon saw a gentleman of elegant appearance approaching rapidly toward us. He came directly up to me, and with the benignity of benevolence illuminating his countenance, called me familiarly by name, shook me cordially by the hand, and requested me to mount the mule and ride into town.

Upon saying I could as well walk, he said, "*You must be fatigued—I insist upon your riding;*"—I entered the town with him, and my Spanish companion, whom he conducted to the Spanish Consul's, taking me with him to his own house, where I was immediately supplied with the best refreshments. It will be recollected that the Shilluh declined to purchase Brown and Davis at Wadinoon, but to my surprise and to my joy, I found them at Mi. Willshire's house, having arrived there tour days before.

The American flag was immediately hoisted upon the top of the house, and I, together with Brown and Davis, were directed to give three cheers. When I arrived, I was clad in an old woollen frock shirt, as my whole apparel; my hair had grown at random in every direction; and my beard presented one evidence of a *Mahometan*. A *Jewish* barber was immediately ordered, and gave to my hair and beard a more *Christian* appearance. Clothing was as soon as possible furnished by Mr. Willshire, and I began to think I should in time regain my native tongue, my American habits, and my native country. For nearly two years I had spoken the Arabic tongue, and felt myself excessively mortified to find I conversed so imperfectly in the English language.

Chapter 23

Description of Mogadore

Mr. Willshire, under whose protection I was now placed, and to whom I shall, till death, feel under the deepest obligations that gratitude can dictate, is a native of the city of London; of about twenty-five years of age, of the most elegant person, and of the most accomplished manners. He has resided at Mogadore a number of years, and has at that place a large mercantile establishment. He has had for a considerable time, vessels under the American and English colours. I supposed him to be very wealthy, from the number of stewards, clerks, and assistants, in his employ. He invariably had religious service performed at his splendid mansion upon the Sabbath, at which English gentlemen and ladies, sea-captains, and oilier foreigners attended. He performed service himself in the Episcopalian mode, with the most solemn devotion, and his house appeared to me to, be a real Bethel; and so far as art imperfect man can judge of the heart, I should think *his* a fit abode for the Holy Spirit.

It must be left for the future biographer to erect a monument to his virtues; but I must not, I cannot omit to inform my renders that to this modern Howard, this divine philanthropist, our unfortunate countrymen are indebted for their redemption from the most miserable bondage that the miserable sons of Adam ever endured. To know the manner in which he expends much of his immense income, would be to learn, that with him wealth is devoted to the noblest of all purposes, diminishing human woe, and augmenting human happiness. He has, by his munificence, secured the favour, even of Mahommedans, with all their antipathy against Christians. Scarcely is there a Moor or an Arab through the whole of Suse and the Great Western Desert, who is of any consequence, but he has engaged to assist him in his benevolence. No sooner does he learn of a Christian slave of any country, than he despatches a Moor, a Shilluh, or an Arab to bring the wretched creature to taste the fruits of his ransoming benevolence. The paper I mentioned at Wadinoon was written by this ministering angel of mercy.

The town of Mogadore is situated upon the Western coast of Africa, and, from the most approved charts, in 31° 15' N. Latitude, and 9° W. Longitude. It is, in every point of view, the most important place in the empire of Morocco. It stands upon a peninsula, projecting into the Atlantic ocean, and its waters wash its north and west sides; and, at high tide, nearly make it an island. A high wall, composed of stone and mortar, is built near the borders of the peninsula, and within it is situated the town in three distinct sections, separated from each other by inner walls. The *Moors* occupy the main section upon the east; and the few *Christian* merchants the western one, containing the fortress, together with some natives; and the Jews the north section exclusively. It is strongly fortified, having double walls upon the south and east sides, from which points it is approached from the country. It is in shape a parallelogram, and strongly fortified at each corner, especially at the northeast and southeast, by heavy mounted brass and iron cannon.

Upon the water port, at the west side, is a battery of cannon containing between forty and fifty heavy brass pieces. There is but one entry into that section of the town occupied by the Jews, and this gate is constantly guarded by an armed Moor. At night it is always locked, cutting off the despised sons of Jacob from intercourse with any part of mankind. Even in the daytime, intercourse with them is almost prohibited. During my residence, I went into this part of the town with an English seaman, formerly of the wrecked brig *Surprise*, and was immediately taken before an *alcayd*, or officer, and compelled to apologize for this intrusion. Upon learning that I was from Wadinoon, I was afterwards permitted to visit the Jews. They have a number of synagogues, as places of worship. Upon Friday afternoon, at six o'clock, their Sabbath commences, and ends at the same time upon Saturday afternoon. During this time, they neither light a candle or lamp, make a fire, cook, nor touch their hands to any laborious service. Their food is previously cooked. I never saw them worship in their synagogues, which I exceedingly regret.

The Jews are permitted to have open shops in every part of the town, until eight o'clock, p. m. after which time every Jew, excepting those at Mr. Wiltshire's and a few others, were enclosed within the walls of their town, until daylight the next morning. They are compelled to wear black slippers and caps, and not allowed to dress their heads in red, or feet in yellow.

The general market is situated in the main town. It is well supplied with beef, mutton, fowls, bread, and almost every variety of vegetables. The grain market is inclosed on a square through which a narrow street passes. Upon the borders of this square, are great numbers of very small shops owned by Moors and Jews, supplied with every article which fancy would admire, convenience desire, or necessity crave.

There are a number of manufactories for *haicks* or blankets. The loom and shuttle appeared to be similar to our domestic ones. By a decree, the blankets here manufactured are prohibited from exportation, and are reserved for transportation into the deserts. These are made wholly of wool. There are also manufactories for iron tools, of every necessary kind; and although they do not look like those of Sheffield and Birmingham ware, many of them are well made. The Jews manufacture snuff by pulverizing tobacco in large mortars. The grain is manufactured into flour by horses. A sweep is attached to the main wheel of the mill. Which being connected with a number of cog-wheels, gives the stone a velocity nearly equal to some of our mill-stones carried by water.

The streets of this town are straight, although short, intersecting each other, generally, at right angles. In the main town, are streets running through the whole of it. They are narrow, and over some of them in the fortress section, an arch extends from one side of the street to the other. The houses are built of stone and lime, generally of one, although some are two and three stories high. The roofs are mostly flat. The streets have a handsome appearance in passing them, the houses being generally plaistered or whitewashed.

The public buildings are those devoted to pious uses, having a steeple, or tower running to a considerable height, and built square to the top. From the top, projects a crane, upon which it hung a white flag to summon the people together. In addition to this notice, a Moor ascends to the top, and with a loud voice, exhorts the inhabitants to come and worship, by exclaiming—"*Allah Hu!*"[1] Upon this notice, many of the people are seen to leave their temporal concerns, and repair to their temple to attend to devotional exercises. This is repeated four times a day at regular seasons. It is singular, that the mode of worship, where I witnessed it here, was precisely the same as I had. thousands of times, noticed it upon the Zahara desert, at Wadinoon.

---
1. See Lord Byron's *Giaour*—line 734.

and in various other parts of Africa. If the Mahommedans can claim no other merit, they an at least entitled to the character of consistency and uniformity in their religious ceremonies.

The people of Mogadore appeared to be mild, peaceable, and affable in their manners. Being a Christian, it was not safe for me to venture to go often abroad, around the town, for fear of insults or injury; and I kept generally at Mr. Willshire's; although, in the daytime, I frequently walked about the place. I never saw nor heard the least disturbance; witnessed no mobs or riots, and the town appeared to be a place where the operation of a good police was known and obeyed.

This town, in its greatest length, must be three quarters of a mile, and in breadth, over half a mile. It is very compactly built, and from the best accounts I could obtain, has within it, of different nations, thirty thousand inhabitants. Of this population, the principal part are Moors; the Jews are estimated at about six thousand, and the Christians, while I was there, could not have exceeded fifty. The town is supplied with water from the river running two miles to the southward of it. It is transported in kegs loaded upon asses; and the beach from the town to the river is constantly lined with these animals passing from and to the town. An island is situated about two miles from the shore, and forms the harbour. Upon it is a strong fortification; and foreigners are not permitted to land upon it.

The entry into the harbour is upon the north of this island through a narrow rocky channel. In the winter, the harbour is rendered insecure from the strong southwest wind blowing directly into it, and the bottom being sandy, the anchorage is bad. From information derived from Mr. Willshire, I learned that many shipwrecks have here happened. The wreck of an English brig was lying there while I was in the place. Capt. Wm. Rogers of Cape Ann, with whom I returned to America, gave me a most interesting account of the loss of a part of his crew in this harbour, I think in the winter of 1815. The limits of this work preclude the insertion of the melancholy narrative, any farther than to say, that his schooner parted one of her cables—that he and two of his crew went on board an English vessel to replace it; and while absent, the remaining crew abandoned the schooner, entered the boat, and were dashed into eternity upon the shore. The schooner was saved, and the captain obtained a crew of Moors and Jews to navigate her to Boston.

I afterwards saw and conversed with a Jew who was one of the crew, at Mogadore. Mr. Willshire informed me that a few years since, a Spanish vessel entered this harbour with a large crew. without a cargo; and not being permitted to trade from that circumstance, having nothing but specie, she sailed down the coast to fish, between Cape Non and Santa Cruz, was taken by surprise by the natives, and her whole crew massacred.

I might enrich this journal with many more interesting communications from this intelligent gentleman, but they must be omitted. I resided with him from the 11th to the 22nd March, and shall for ever reckon the days spent under his hospitable roof, as the most pleasing of my life. Everything within the compass of human exertion was done to render my stay delightful. He had snatched me and my companions from the most forlorn and miserable slavery, placed me in a temporal paradise, and pointed the way to my country and my friends. I cannot imagine a situation upon earth, all things considered, more enviable than the one he fills. I forgot the splendour of his mansion, and the magnificence that surrounded him, in the more brilliant traits of his mind.

A good description of his dwelling would be the history of architecture. Upon the 15th, he informed me that he had received a letter from the Hon. James Simpson, American Consul General at Tangier, relative to our passage home, requesting him, as soon as we were sufficiently recruited for the journey, to send us to Tangier, if no passage to America could be found at Mogadore. He assured us that in a few days everything should be in readiness for the journey, that he would despatch an *alcayd*, or an Emperor's soldier, to guard us on the way, and that he had obtained a passport from the Emperor for this purpose.

CHAPTER 24

Escape by Night

Upon the 22nd, the *alcayd* and two muleteers presented themselves to Mr. Wiltshire, with three large mules; one each, for Brown, Davis, and myself. The *alcayd* was elegantly armed and mounted upon a horse, and the muleteers were to go on foot. We were well supplied with provisions for five days, which would carry us to the town of Azamor. We also had a sufficient supply of money for our expenses. We now took an affectionate leave of Mr. Willshire, received his blessing and good wishes, and started upon our journey. We passed the south gate at 8 a. m., passed the east battery, and directed our course toward Tangier. We kept the coast for some distance, and were joined by another *alcayd*, with a servant bound to Fez. He continued with us for ten days, and added much to the pleasure of our journey. We travelled moderately, and the muleteers kept up on foot. The country through which we passed upon the first day was rather barren and thinly inhabited.

We stopped tor the night at sun an hour high, and lodged under bushes: the cattle being fettered. There were a few inhabitants near us, who brought us fowls, eggs, and *keskoosoo*, and refused any compensation for them. Before daylight, upon the 23rd, we were again mounted and on our journey. The *alcayd* who conducted me was the same one, he told me, who was the guide of Capt. Riley, and pointed to a path which he then travelled; but now chose one that went farther into the country. We travelled over land very level, highly cultivated, loaded with grain, and often presenting *douars* of pitched tents. Through the 24th, the country had the same appearance, and at night we lodged in the centre of a large collection of tents. Wherever a *douar* of tents is met with, one is found devoted to pious uses, called a *zham* facing to the east.

The traveller always goes there to worship and to lodge; and is always there treated with kindness and respect. The *alcayd* who guided and guarded us, and the one who joined us, would be regarded, in every portion of the globe, as first rate men. They were dignified in their manners, affable in their deportment, and affectionate in their treatment. No pains were spared to make us comfortable, and our journey pleasant. We were not, however, permitted to lodge in the tents, devoted to the worship of Mahomet, being nothing but Christians ourselves. The next day (25th) we came in sight of the Atlantic, and stopped to feed the cattle near a walled town, which the *alcayd* entered. After resting a short time, we prosecuted our journey, passing stone buildings standing singly, some villages, a considerable river, the country abounding with *Argan* trees, and at 10 p. m. put up near a walled town, the gates of which were closed.

The inhabitants came out and sold us fowls and eggs, and we slept without the mud walls, in the blankets furnished us by Mr. Willshire. Upon the 26th, we passed a country more hilly, and, at 2 p. m. reached the town of Azamor, having passed a great number of saint-houses. We always had to dismount and pass them on foot, while our devotional guard offered up worship to that prophet, whose followers never seem to forget his supposed divinity, or omit to adore him. The town is situated upon the west side of the River Ommirabih, upon elevated ground. The town in shape nearly resembles a right angled triangle. The river forms the base, the ocean the side, and the country the hypotenuse. It is chiefly built of stone, and completely walled with a very high plaistered stone wall. Around its southeast corner or fortress, it is ditched; and from the ditch to the battery, is thrown up a body of earth and stone, ascending as steep as the roof of a house. The battery, rising thirty feet above the top of this ascent, would seem to render it impregnable. Upon the battery are mounted forty or fifty iron and brass pieces of cannon. The town has the appearance of antiquity. In its suburbs, which we passed, are various manufactories of leather, pottery, &c.

We here replenished our stock of provisions, and upon the morning of the 27th, as soon as the gates were opened, we again started upon our journey, and passed the River Ommirabih in a ferry boat. We saw great numbers of fishing boats, and upon examining the fish taken, I found them to be shad; precisely like those caught in Connecticut River, and they made me think of that beautiful stream, upon the banks of which I was born. This river must be thirty-five rods in width. It is a clear, handsome stream, and the largest I had passed in Africa, although upon the desert of Zahara I had passed many dry beds of rivers much wider. The country here was not very fertile, but in the course of the day we passed many *douars* of tents, and at night put up at a large one situated two miles out of our regular course. A *douar* of tents consists of different numbers and arranged in different manners—some in a square, some in a triangle, and the one we reached this night was in a perfect circle, pitched within ten feet of each other.

As I approached with Brown and Davis on foot, we were assailed by hundreds of dogs, and it was with the greatest difficulty we could defend ourselves from them with heavy clubs. We entered the *douar* before night, and a small tent was pitched for the two *alcayds*, for us, two Moors who had joined us at Azamor and the muleteers, in the centre of the circle. The two *alcayds* were in the tent, the muleteers had gone to water the mules, and the rest of us were reposing around the tent. It was immediately surrounded by natives led by curiosity to see Christians, who inquired of the *alcayds* where we were from and where bound. Upon being informed that we were from the Desert, and bound to the Sidi or Emperor, and discovering us to be Americans or Englishmen, they immediately entered into conversation among themselves, which the *alcayd* from Fez learned to be a menace toward us. They remembered the lesson not long before taught the Algerines by Commodore Decatur and Lord Exmouth, and undoubtedly would seek revenge in any way.

The *alcayd* from Fez, with fury mingled with dignity, said that the Emperor had sent for us, and demanded of them what they meant by their plots? They explained by denying any plottings, and soon retired. I never saw the authority of an individual so suddenly operate upon a multitude. Very soon we saw twenty or thirty armed horsemen approaching us with great speed. They halted near our tent. I expected my journey to Tangier and for life was now to be ended. Each Moor had a musket, and they were but a rod or two from the tent. The *alcayds* remained perfectly composed, and my fears were dismissed, when I saw these inimitable horsemen begin their Moorish sports. They exclaim, *hah! hah! hah!*—drop the rein upon the horses' neck—incline the body far forward—put the horse into full speed, and aiming at some distant object, fire their muskets, and with one hand give it a sudden turn around the head. The horse, being perfectly trained, comes to a halt as soon as the gun is fired. It was in my view the most elegant display of the equestrian art I ever witnessed. The feats of the circus are but puerile triflings in comparison with it. For an hour I witnessed this amusement. It called to mind the tournaments in the age of chivalry.

After they retired, we were refreshed; and when silence reigned through the whole circle of tents, at least a mile in circumference, and darkness had shrouded the earth with her sable mantle, we cautiously began to leave a place where destruction might, in the twinkling of an eye, have awaited us; and where the *alcayds*, ourselves, and the muleteers, might have sunk into the grave, leaving the Emperor in ignorance of the fate of his officers, and our friends of our destiny. For five hours we sought in vain for the path we took that lead us to this *douar*. and upon finding it, we travelled with as great speed as possible, taking the muleteers behind us. This was the dictate of compassion, but as often as we did it, our *alcayd* would remonstrate against it; and I had occasion myself to regret it; for the old muleteer belonging to me, while I was relieving him from the fatigue of running, came very nigh relieving my pockets of all the money belonging to Brown, Davis, and myself.

Through the 28th, we travelled at no great distance from the ocean, and at 10 a. m. passed the town of Darlbeda situated upon it. It appeared of considerable size, and was walled; but we did not enter it. At meridian, we passed the town of Afidallah. Toward night, we passed a well built stone bridge, arched, and railed with stone. Continuing on, we forded a small stream, and came to a forest of *Argan* trees. We lodged upon the outside of the walls of a town of some size. It was dark when we reached, and dark when we left it; and unless we possessed those *"optics keen, to see what is not to be seen"* we could not describe it.

Upon the 29th, continuing near the ocean, we had a distant view of the town of Rabat; the country being remarkably level, fertile, and well cultivated. The inhabitants all lived in tents here, and the fields abounded with immense droves of horned cattle. Large numbers of fattened oxen were driving toward Rabat. It was a most delightful day's journey, and the animal and vegetable productions of the country indicated the highest enjoyment. We reached the aqueduct, which conducts water into the town, at about a mile's distance from the walls of it. This aqueduct is so constructed that, for the most of the way, the water is carried above the ground, in a kind of flume. The fountain that supplies it is eight miles from the town; and at that place is an high tower.

When we came to the aqueduct, we stopped, and the *alcayds* entered the town, having with them a letter from Mr. Willshire to Mr. Abouderham, English Vice Consul at Rabat. The mules, having fed upon grass, we mounted them, and entered the town ourselves, and were immediately introduced to the consul by our *alcayd*. He informed us, that Mr. Wiltshire had requested him to furnish us with everything that we wanted to prosecute our journey. I informed him that we were sufficiently supplied with money, but wished, in that town, to replenish our stock of provisions, which were now nearly exhausted. Brown, Davis, and I dined at his house, but he said, as it was the Jewish Sabbath, no business could that day be transacted. I understood he was a Jew himself, but he was dressed in Christian habit.

After partaking of refreshments we were conducted by our *alcayd*. to a public house, where a room was provided for our accommodation. This was the first building that might be called a public house, that I had seen in Africa. This being a place of great business, the house having many apartments, was resorted to by travellers from Fez, Morocco, and all the adjoining country.

CHAPTER 25

Passage to Gibraltar

After securing our baggage in our apartment, I went out to examine the town. It has one principal street running parallel with the shore of the River Beregreb, which bounds it upon the north. Upon the west, it is bounded by the Atlantic, and upon the south and east it is bounded by an outer wall which is built about half a mile from the inner wall, upon which cannon are mounted. Between these two walls are very fine gardens, laid out with much taste, abounding with fig, orange, lemon, and many other fruit trees. Each garden had a well near it, from which water was drawn by horses, and wheel machinery; but as I could not examine them, I will not attempt a particular description It is strongly fortified next to the sea.

In this town, were a number of *zhams*, or mosques for religious worship. The buildings are compactly and well built of stone; and, as is almost universally the case through the whole country. plaistered or whitewashed, having a neat and handsome appearance. There are a great number of narrow streets or alleys leading into the principal street upon the river, some of which are long and handsomely built. The street upon the river, in which is the great market, was thronged by people of almost every description, I there saw Jews, Turks, Europeans, Greeks. Arabs, Shilluhs, and people from all the Barbary states; each using his native tongue, each dressed in the mode of his country, and each showing their peculiar manners.

The Jews in this place, as at Mogadore, have a section of the town exclusively occupied by them. The Moors constitute the principal population; but the number of inhabitants I did not learn, and cannot estimate any otherwise than by saying, that the town is more compactly built than Mogadore, and covers, I should judge. nearly double the quantity of ground.

The river admits vessels of burthen, and I there saw a Spanish, a French, and a Portuguese vessel, and a small Moorish frigate lying at anchor. From its appearance to me, it was a place of the greatest trade upon the western coast of Africa, and altogether the best and safest harbour. It is entered through a narrow channel, at the mouth of the river, which then widens into a large bay. A sand bar lies off the mouth of the river, which may be passed with vessels drawing eight feet of water, as such were loading when I was there; and as the tide rises eight or ten feet, vessels of much larger burthen may then pass in and out. I continued rambling about the place until the hour of refreshment and rest.

Upon the 30th we remained in this town, and I was constantly upon the foot, examining every natural and artificial curiosity that fell within my observation. There were various manufactories of blankets, cottons, silks, woollen cloths, leather, earthenware and some few of hardware, especially of muskets, scimitars, and cutlasses.

I saw immense quantities of shad caught in the same manner as they are taken in the rivers of New England. They were of excellent flavour, and of the same size and appearance of those here caught.

Mr. Abouderham paid for our apartments, and supplied us gratuitously with a quantity of excellent bread. Having ourselves procured the other necessary provisions for four or five days, we left this place upon the morning of the 31st, having been treated with the greatest politeness and hospitality by the Consul, of whom we now took leave, and passed the river in a ferry boat, to the town of Sallee, lying upon the opposite side of the river, and about a mile from its banks. I had learned at Rabat, that a Jewish feast was to be holden this day in that place, and in this. Great numbers of bullocks were slain the last day I remained in Rabat, and almost the first striking object that attracted my attention in this place, was a great number of Jews, richly dressed, marching in procession, barefooted, each having the Old Testament before him, and each reading aloud.

We remained spectators, until the whole passed, and saw the street strewed with flowers. We then passed directly through the town; which is a place of considerable size, having a number of mosques, and is strongly walled and fortified by numerous pieces of cannon. In the vicinity were beautiful gardens filled with the fruits and vegetables common to this part of the country. It also produced cotton, and I saw numbers engaged in manufacturing that article. The people, judging of them from their deportment toward us, retain the ferocious manners of the ancient inhabitants, who were a swarm of pirates. They menaced us as we passed, denouncing us as Christian dogs; and had it not been for the presence and authority of our *alcayd*, the other having left us at Rabat, bound to Fez, Ave should undoubtedly have found our passage impracticable, and have been in danger of our lives.

We passed out through the north gate, and at a mile's distance, came to a broad high wall, having three arched gateways as passages through it This wall extends as much as three miles; upon the top of which is an aqueduct, from which the water descends into an artificial watering place, near the arches, and supplies the town of Sallee. It has the appearance of great strength and antiquity. The country, as we proceeded on, was generally level and very fertile Toward noon we passed near the borders of a lake of fresh water, about two miles in length, and an half mile in breadth; and by the middle of the afternoon, we were ferried over a river of a mile in width. I learned the name of this river to be Midiah, and saw near its mouth the ruins of an ancient fortified town, with fortifications built in the Portuguese manner. This town is called Mamora; but we did not enter it. The ferryman stole my only pair of shoes, which were supplied by another pair obtained from the *alcayd*. We soon cane to a *douar*, and tarried there through the night.

Upon the first of April, we continued to travel through a country somewhat hilly, having *douars* of tents, droves of cattle, and numerous inhabitants. At 9 a. m. we reached the end of a large lake, having a number of small islands, upon which I discovered saint-houses erected. It abounded with ducks, and a great number of small boats, or rather rafts, filled with the natives, were hunting them. Through the whole day we travelled upon the western borders of this lake, and at night put up within a few rods of its shore. We were refreshed with fowls and eggs procured for a trifling sum; indeed, for the whole passage, provisions were obtained at the cheapest rate, and of excellent quality. The next morning we crossed the north end of this lake, and had a distant view of the town of Laraiche, leaving it upon our left, and bearing to the eastward toward a large town, situated upon the banks of the River Saboo.

We reached this river at night, having passed by many villages with thatched roof cottages. We lodged upon the south banks of the river, upon which were many of the finest gardens that can be imagined. They abounded with every tree, shrub, and vegetable calculated to charm the eye, and gratify the appetite. I never before, nor since, beheld a scene so perfectly enchanting. It reminded the traveller of the finest descriptions of romance, and made him think of the Elysian Fields.

Early in the morning of the 3rd, we reached the high banks of the Saboo, which was a narrow stream, and forded it. The passage from the river to the town had that kind of beauty which renders the power of description feeble. The town was almost concealed from the eye of the traveller by labyrinths composed of almost every species of the most beautiful fruit trees. The town was, to appearance, of very great extent. The houses which I saw were low; very thickly built, and thatched with coarse grass. I was struck with the great number of mosques. The one I passed was about ten feet square at the base, diminishing but very little to the top, and was at least sixty feet in height. In passing the whole town, I counted twenty-eight of these mosques.

I regretted exceedingly that I could not have entered the town, which, from its extent, and every appearance, induced me to conclude that it contained the greatest population of any town I had seen in the country. I noticed three funeral processions in the suburbs. The name of this place, as I learned, is Dar-el Hamara. We stopped upon the borders of the place, until provisions were obtained, and then proceeded upon our journey some distance from the sea, through a clay country of hills and valleys, abounding with small streams of water, and at night lodged at a *douar*.

Upon the fourth, we passed over a very high mountain, covered with wood and abounding with wild boars, which the natives called *helloof*. From this place I had a view of the Rock of Gibraltar to the northward, and of Mount Atlas to the eastward. There were vast numbers of cork-wood trees, with rough bark three or four inches thick, from which the cork is manufactured. Many of them were entirely stripped of their bark. They resemble the oak of our country. Upon descending the mountain, we reached an extensive level country filled with tents and thatched huts as far as the eye could reach. We lodged at a small stone church devoted to the use of travellers and religious worship.

Upon the 5th day of April, at about 10 a. m. we reached the town of Tangier, and were conducted to the house of the Hon. James Simpson. American consul general at that place. He received us with dignified affability, welcomed us to his house, and rejoiced at the prospect we now had of a speedy return to our country. Brown, Davis, and I were conducted to a boarding house, and were requested to visit him as often as possible during our stay. The town of Tangier is too well known to need from me a description, indeed I little thought of noticing any surrounding object, I was so completely engrossed with the delightful and exhilarating thought of leaving a country in which I had gone through almost *"all the variety of untried being."* Upon the 6th, being Sunday, we remained at our quarters most of the day; we however saw many Spaniards resorting to the Roman Catholic churches to attend divine service.

For almost two years I had dragged out a miserable existence among the followers of Mahomet, and this was the first time, for that period, excepting at Mr. Wiltshire's, that I had observed men offering adoration to the Saviour of the World. A flood, of ideas rushed into my mind. I was in sight of the bay of Gibraltar, from which we sailed in the Commerce. The scenes through which my shipmates and I had passed since that time hurried through my memory. I cast my eye toward my beloved country, and reflected, with delight, that some of them were enjoying its blessings. I also, in imagination, retraced the desert of Zahara, and the coast of Africa, and remembered with excruciating anguish, that Mr. Williams, Barrett, Hogan, Antonio, and Dick, were either enduring the sufferings from which I had escaped, or were relieved from them by a miserable death. The only consolation I found from this distressing consideration was, that the same Merciful Being, who had snatched me from the accumulated horrors that had long surrounded *me*, might also save *them*.

Upon Monday morning, (7th,) Mr. Simpson sent a messenger, requesting us to visit his splendid gardens two miles from town. We immediately repaired thither. They were situated upon the top of an elevated hill which he, in veneration for the imperishable honour of his great compatriot in the revolutionary war, has dignified with the name of Mount Washington. Mr. Simpson is a venerable old man, of seventy years; and, from his treatment to us, and other Americans, shews that he has not forgotten his attachment to his unfortunate countrymen in the exalted station he fills, and the splendour that surrounds him.

From these delightful gardens Tangier presents a handsome appearance. The houses are low in general, but the Consular residences are very magnificent. In this place are Consuls from America, France, Great Britain, Sweden, Denmark, Holland, Spain, and Portugal.

Mr. Simpson addressed a letter to Mr. B. Henry, American Consul at Gibraltar, and delivered it to a Spanish captain upon the 8th. Upon that day, at 4 p. m. we entered on board a small Spanish vessel, and left the continent of Africa. We arrived at Gibraltar early the next morning, the passage being about thirty miles. Upon the 9th of April, 1817, the health officer came on board, and immediately gave us liberty to land at the port. We were immediately conducted to the residence Mr Henry. Upon reading the letter of Mr. Simpson, he gave us a small sum of money to refresh ourselves with, for which he required a receipt. He ordered us to appear before him at 4 p. m. which we did.

He then told us that it was too expensive for us to live on shore, and that we must go on board the U. S. brig *Spark*, then lying at Gibraltar, until we could get a passage to America, adding, that she was in want of hands, and that by entering on board, we might obtain clothing from our advance pay. As much as we needed clothing, our weakness was such as totally incapacitated us from doing duty on board a public vessel, and in that way to procure them. We little expected to be received by an *American* consul, and treated in this manner, after the tender treatment we had met with from an *alcayd* of Morocco, Mr. Wiltshire, and Mr. Simpson.

By good fortune, without the aid of Mr. Henry, we fell in with Capt. Stanwood, of the ship *Hero*, bound to Boston, on board of which Brown and I entered. We went ashore frequently, and applied to Mr. Henry for clothing. He told us he thought we had clothing sufficient, and shewed the most perfect indifference to our applications. Knowing that we were in an unfit situation to commence a voyage to America, and being totally destitute of resources ourselves, I ventured to write to Consul Simpson, at Tangier, entreating his assistance. As soon as a return could be had, I received from that benevolent gentleman the following answer:

Tangier, 17th April, 1817.

Sir—Yesterday I received your letter of the 14th inst. and hope you may, with your two companions, be at last accommodated with a passage in the ship *Hero*; that you may all speedily be restored to your country and families.—Let Davis inform the relations of George Hall, that the Spanish consul here has promised me, the Spaniard, who is the cause of his not having obtained his freedom with them (Brown and Davis) shall be forthwith redeemed.

They may rely on Hall being freed at some time, should Mr. Wiltshire not be able to effect it before, by reason of the Arab persisting in his determination not to release the one without the other. I have written Mr. Henry on the subject of your being provided (the three) with such clothing as may be requested; and I have no doubt but that gentleman will do whatever may be found necessary on the occasion.

I wish you well, and am,
Sir, your obedient servant,
James Simpson

P. S. 1st—We have not had any intelligence from Mogadore since you left it.

Mr. Archibald Robbins.

P. S. 2nd—18th April. Advice has been received of Hall's redemption being agreed, and the ransom sent down.

J. S.

The above letter I found at Mr. Henry's office. The letter of the American Consul general to him had an effect, which the entreaties of forlorn and destitute Americans, just escaped from Ishmaelitish slavery, could not produce; and he immediately furnished necessary clothing to Brown and myself, Davis having previously left the *Hero*.

Upon the 30th April, Captain Stanwood sailed from Gibraltar, and, after a pleasant passage, we arrived in Boston upon the 30th day of May, 1817.

When I landed at Boston, I entirely forgot the destitute situation I was in, from the reflection that I was in the American Republic. My health and strength were restored, and I was enabled to work my passage on board the schooner *Pearl*, Capt. Ingraham, to Saybrook. From thence to Wethersfield I travelled on foot, where I was received by my connections and former companions with a cordiality which convinced me that I was still esteemed: and that the scenes of degradation, slavery, and misery through which I had passed, instead of diminishing, had augmented their attachment.

ALSO FROM LEONAUR
AVAILABLE IN SOFTCOVER OR HARDCOVER WITH DUST JACKET

BOOTS AND SADDLES by *Elizabeth B. Custer*—The experiences of General Custer's Wife on the Western Plains.

FANNIE BEERS' CIVIL WAR by *Fannie A. Beers*—A Confederate Lady's Experiences of Nursing During the Campaigns & Battles of the American Civil War.

LADY SALE'S AFGHANISTAN by *Florentia Sale*—An Indomitable Victorian Lady's Account of the Retreat from Kabul During the First Afghan War.

THE TWO WARS OF MRS DUBERLY by *Frances Isabella Duberly*—An Intrepid Victorian Lady's Experience of the Crimea and Indian Mutiny.

LADIES OF WATERLOO by *Charlotte A. Eaton, Magdalene de Lancey & Juana Smith*—The Experiences of Three Women During the Campaign of 1815: Waterloo Days by Charlotte A. Eaton, A Week at Waterloo by Magdalene de Lancey & Juana's Story by Juana Smith.

DESPATCH RIDER by *W. H. L. Watson*—The Experiences of a British Army Motorcycle Despatch Rider During the Opening Battles of the Great War in Europe.

TWO YEARS BEFORE THE MAST by *Richard Henry Dana. Jr.*—The account of one young man's experiences serving on board a sailing brig—the Penelope—bound for California, between the years 1834-36.

A SAILOR OF KING GEORGE by *Frederick Hoffman*—From Midshipman to Captain—Recollections of War at Sea in the Napoleonic Age 1793-1815.

LORDS OF THE SEA by *A. T. Mahan*—Great Captains of the Royal Navy During the Age of Sail.

COGGESHALL'S VOYAGES: VOLUME 1 by *George Coggeshall*—The Recollections of an American Schooner Captain.

COGGESHALL'S VOYAGES: VOLUME 2 by *George Coggeshall*—The Recollections of an American Schooner Captain.

TWILIGHT OF EMPIRE by *Sir Thomas Ussher & Sir George Cockburn*—Two accounts of Napoleon's Journeys in Exile to Elba and St. Helena: Narrative of Events by Sir Thomas Ussher & Napoleon's Last Voyage: Extract of a diary by Sir George Cockburn.

KIEL AND JUTLAND by *Georg Von Hase*—The Famous Naval Battle of the First World War from the German Perspective.

AVAILABLE ONLINE AT **www.leonaur.com**
AND FROM ALL GOOD BOOK STORES

ALSO FROM LEONAUR
AVAILABLE IN SOFTCOVER OR HARDCOVER WITH DUST JACKET

ESCAPE FROM THE FRENCH *by Edward Boys*—A Young Royal Navy Midshipman's Adventures During the Napoleonic War.

THE VOYAGE OF H.M.S. PANDORA *by Edward Edwards R. N. & George Hamilton, edited by Basil Thomson*—In Pursuit of the Mutineers of the Bounty in the South Seas—1790-1791.

MEDUSA *by J. B. Henry Savigny and Alexander Correard and Charlotte-Adélaïde Dard* —Narrative of a Voyage to Senegal in 1816 & The Sufferings of the Picard Family After the Shipwreck of the Medusa.

THE SEA WAR OF 1812 VOLUME 1 *by A. T. Mahan*—A History of the Maritime Conflict.

THE SEA WAR OF 1812 VOLUME 2 *by A. T. Mahan*—A History of the Maritime Conflict.

WETHERELL OF H. M. S. HUSSAR *by John Wetherell*—The Recollections of an Ordinary Seaman of the Royal Navy During the Napoleonic Wars.

THE NAVAL BRIGADE IN NATAL *by C. R. N. Burne*—With the Guns of H. M. S. Terrible & H. M. S. Tartar during the Boer War 1899-1900.

THE VOYAGE OF H. M. S. BOUNTY *by William Bligh*—The True Story of an 18th Century Voyage of Exploration and Mutiny.

SHIPWRECK! *by William Gilly*—The Royal Navy's Disasters at Sea 1793-1849.

KING'S CUTTERS AND SMUGGLERS: 1700-1855 *by E. Keble Chatterton*—A unique period of maritime history-from the beginning of the eighteenth to the middle of the nineteenth century when British seamen risked all to smuggle valuable goods from wool to tea and spirits from and to the Continent.

CONFEDERATE BLOCKADE RUNNER *by John Wilkinson*—The Personal Recollections of an Officer of the Confederate Navy.

NAVAL BATTLES OF THE NAPOLEONIC WARS *by W. H. Fitchett*—Cape St. Vincent, the Nile, Cadiz, Copenhagen, Trafalgar & Others.

PRISONERS OF THE RED DESERT *by R. S. Gwatkin-Williams*—The Adventures of the Crew of the Tara During the First World War.

U-BOAT WAR 1914-1918 *by James B. Connolly/Karl von Schenk*—Two Contrasting Accounts from Both Sides of the Conflict at Sea During the Great War.

AVAILABLE ONLINE AT **www.leonaur.com**
AND FROM ALL GOOD BOOK STORES